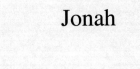

Jonah

CONCORDIA COMMENTARY

A Theological Exposition of Sacred Scripture

JONAH

Silvia — יְשׁוּעָ֫תָה לַֽיהוָ֔ה

"Salvation belongs to Yahweh."

(Jon. 2:10b, HT)

Love it! Live it!

R. Reed Lessing

R. Reed Lessing.

1.30.08

THE SCRIPTURES

TESTIFY TO ME

Concordia Publishing House

Saint Louis

Library of Congress Cataloging-in-Publication Data

Lessing, R. Reed (Robert Reed), 1959–
    Jonah / R. Reed Lessing.
        p.   cm. — (Concordia commentary)
    Includes bibliographical references and indexes.
    ISBN-13: 978-0-7586-0273-2
    ISBN-10: 0-7586-0273-1
    1. Bible. O.T. Jonah—Commentaries. I. Title. II. Series.

    BS1605.53.L47   2007
    224'.92077—dc22

                2006038915

1 2 3 4 5 6 7 8 9 10   16 15 14 13 12 11 10 09 08 07

To my wife, Lisa, and our children, Abi, Jonathan, and Lori.
God has made us a family (Ps 68:6),
and nothing will ever separate us from his love
in Christ Jesus our Lord (Rom 8:39).

Contents

Editors' Preface

What may a reader expect from the Concordia Commentary: A Theological Exposition of Sacred Scripture?

The purpose of this series, simply put, is to assist pastors, missionaries, and teachers of the Scriptures to convey God's Word with greater clarity, understanding, and faithfulness to the divine intent of the text.

Since every interpreter approaches the exegetical task from a certain perspective, honesty calls for an outline of the presuppositions held by those who have shaped this commentary series. This also serves, then, as a description of the characteristics of the commentaries.

First in importance is the conviction that the content of the scriptural testimony is Jesus Christ. The Lord himself enunciated this when he said, "The Scriptures … testify to me" (Jn 5:39), words that have been incorporated into the logo of this series. The message of the Scriptures is the Good News of God's work to reconcile the world to himself through the life, death, resurrection, ascension, and everlasting session of Jesus Christ at the right hand of God the Father. Under the guidance of the same Spirit who inspired the writing of the Scriptures, these commentaries seek to find in every passage of every canonical book "that which promotes Christ" (as Luther's hermeneutic is often described). They are Christ-centered, *Christological* commentaries.

As they unfold the scriptural testimony to Jesus Christ, these commentaries expound Law and Gospel. This approach arises from a second conviction—that Law and Gospel are the overarching doctrines of the Bible itself and that to understand them in their proper distinction and relationship to one another is a key for understanding the self-revelation of God and his plan of salvation in Jesus Christ.

Now, Law and Gospel do not always appear in Scripture labeled as such. The palette of language in Scripture is multicolored, with many and rich hues. The dialectic of a pericope may be fallen creation and new creation, darkness and light, death and life, wandering and promised land, exile and return, ignorance and wisdom, demon possession and the kingdom of God, sickness and healing, lost and found, guilt and righteousness, flesh and Spirit, fear and joy, hunger and feast, or Babylon and the new Jerusalem. But the common element is God's gracious work of restoring fallen humanity through the Gospel of his Son. Since the predominant characteristic of these commentaries is the proclamation of that Gospel, they are, in the proper sense of the term, *evangelical.*

A third, related conviction is that the Scriptures are God's vehicle for communicating the Gospel. The editors and authors accept without reservation that the canonical books of the Old and New Testaments are, in their entirety, the inspired and inerrant Word of God. The triune God is the ultimate author of the Bible; every word is inspired by the Holy Spirit, who did also, at the same time, make use of the knowledge, particular interests, and styles of the human writers. Thus, while individual books surely are marked by distinctive features, the canon of Scripture has its own inner unity, and each passage must be understood in harmony with the larger context of the whole. This commentary series pays heed to the smallest of details because of its acceptance of *plenary and verbal inspiration* and interprets in accord with the analogy of faith following the principle that *Scripture interprets Scripture.* Both are necessary because the entirety of the Bible is God's Word, *sacred* Scripture, calling for *theological* exposition.

A fourth conviction is that, even as the God of the Gospel came into this world in Jesus Christ (the Word incarnate), the scriptural Gospel has been given to and through the people of God, for the benefit of all humanity. God did not intend his Scriptures to have a life separated from the church. He gave them through servants of his choosing: prophets, sages, evangelists, and apostles. He gave them to the church and through the church, to be cherished in the church for admonition and comfort and to be used by the church for proclamation and catechesis. The living context of Scripture is ever the church, where the Lord's ministry of preaching, baptizing, forgiving sins, teaching, and celebrating the Lord's Supper continues. Aware of the way in which the incarnation of the Son of God has as a consequence the close union of Scripture and church, of Word and Sacraments, this commentary series features expositions that are *incarnational* and *sacramental.*

This Gospel Word of God, moreover, creates a unity among all those in whom it works the obedience of faith and who confess the truth of God revealed in it. This is the unity of the one holy Christian and apostolic church, which extends through world history. The church is to be found wherever the marks of the church are present: the Gospel in the Word and the Sacraments. These have been proclaimed, confessed, and celebrated in many different cultures and are in no way limited nor especially attached to any single culture or people. As this commentary series seeks to articulate the universal truth of the Gospel, it acknowledges and affirms the confession of the scriptural truth in all the many times and places where the one true church has been found. Aiming to promote *concord* in the confession of the one scriptural Gospel, these commentaries seek to be, in the best sense of the terms, *confessional, ecumenical,* and *catholic.*

All of those convictions and characteristics describe the theological heritage of Martin Luther and of the confessors who subscribe to the *Book of Concord* (1580)—those who have come to be known as Lutherans. The editors and authors forthrightly confess their subscription to the doctrinal exposition of Scripture in the *Book of Concord.* As the publishing arm of The Lutheran Church—Missouri Synod, Concordia Publishing House is bound to doctrinal agreement with the Scriptures and the Lutheran Confessions and seeks to herald the true Christian doctrine to the ends of the earth. To that end, the series has enlisted confessional Lutheran authors from other church bodies around the world who share the evangelical mission of promoting theological concord.

The authors and editors acknowledge their debt to Martin Luther as an exegete, particularly the example of his hermeneutical method. Luther's method (practiced by many others as well) included (1) interpreting Scripture with Scripture according to the analogy of faith (that is, in harmony with the whole of Christian doctrine revealed in the Word); (2) following the contours of the grammar of the original languages; (3) seeking the intended meaning of the text, the "plain" or "literal" sense, aware that the language of Scripture ranges from narrative to discourse, from formal prose to creative poetry, from archaic to acrostic to apocalyptic, and it uses metaphor, type, parable, and other figures; (4) drawing on philology, linguistics, literature, philosophy, history, and other fields in the quest for a better understanding of the text; (5) considering the history of the church's interpretation; (6) applying the text as authoritative also in the present milieu of the interpreter; and (7) above all, seeing the present application and fulfillment of the text in terms of Jesus Christ and his corporate church; upholding the Word, Baptism, and the Supper as the means through which Christ imparts salvation today; and affirming the inauguration, already now, of the eternal benefits of that salvation that is yet to come.

To be sure, the authors and editors do not feel bound always to agree with every detail of Luther's exegesis. Nor do they imagine that the interpretations presented here are the final word about every crux and enigmatic passage. But the work has been done in the spirit of Luther and in harmony with the confession of the church: grace alone, faith alone, Scripture alone, Christ alone.

The editors wish to acknowledge their debt of gratitude for all who have helped make possible this series. It was conceived at CPH in 1990, and a couple of years of planning and prayer to the Lord of the church preceded its formal launch on July 2, 1992. During that time, Dr. J. A. O. Preus II volunteered his enthusiasm for the project because, in his view, it would nurture and advance the proclamation of the Christian faith as understood by confessors of the Lutheran church. The financial support that has underwritten the series was provided by a gracious donor who wished to remain anonymous. Those two faithful servants of God were called to heavenly rest a few short years later.

During the early years, former CPH presidents Dr. John W. Gerber and Dr. Stephen J. Carter had the foresight to recognize the potential benefit of such a landmark work for the church at large. CPH allowed Dr. Christopher W. Mitchell to devote his time and energy to the conception and initial development of the project. Dr. Mitchell has remained the CPH editor and is also the Old Testament editor. Dr. Dean O. Wenthe has served on the project since its official start in 1992 and is the general editor, as well as a commentary author. Mrs. Julene Gernant Dumit (M.A.R.) has been the CPH production editor for the entire series. In 1999 Dr. Jeffrey A. Gibbs, already a commentary author, joined the editorial board as the New Testament editor.

CPH thanks Concordia Theological Seminary, Fort Wayne, Indiana, for kindly allowing its president, Dr. Dean O. Wenthe, to serve as the general editor of the series and to dedicate a substantial portion of his time to it for many years. CPH also thanks Concordia Seminary, St. Louis, Missouri, for permitting Dr. Jeffrey A. Gibbs to devote a significant share of his time to his capacity as the New Testament editor. Those two seminaries have thereby extended their ministries in selfless service for the benefit of the church.

The editors pray that the beneficence of their institutions may be reflected in this series by an evangelical orientation, a steadfast Christological perspective, an eschatological view toward the ultimate good of Christ's bride, and a concern that the wedding feast of the King's Son may be filled with all manner of guests (Mt 22:1–14).

> Now to him who is able to establish you by my Gospel and the preaching of Jesus Christ, by the revelation of the mystery kept secret for ages past but now revealed also through the prophetic Scriptures, made known to all the nations by order of the eternal God unto the obedience of faith—to the only wise God, through Jesus Christ, be the glory forever. Amen! (Rom 16:25–27)

Author's Preface

In University City, Missouri, close to where I live, there is a sidewalk called the St. Louis Walk of Fame. The sidewalks on both sides of the Delmar Loop are filled with brass stars and bronze plaques honoring people from the St. Louis area who have made major contributions to the cultural heritage of the United States of America. Musician Chuck Berry and baseball greats Bob Gibson, Lou Brock, and Ozzie Smith have a place in the stars. Had the prophet Jonah not been from Gath Hepher but from St. Louis, I'm sure that he would join the likes of Ulysses S. Grant and Joseph Pulitzer because Jonah in the biblical firmament is a star of the first magnitude.

The book's influence can be seen in such diverse literature from *Pinocchio* to *Moby Dick*. The inspired author of Jonah did his work so well that his book continues to delight and challenge the simple soul as much as the sophisticated scholar. Children commonly love Jonah and many adults are fascinated with it. Outsiders who have minimal knowledge or interest in the Bible know enough about Jonah to laugh at a joke based on the story. This makes the book of Jonah a strong contender for the best-known story in the OT, and it is undoubtedly one of the great literary masterpieces in the Bible. Jesus compares himself to Jonah when speaking of his resurrection (Mt 12:40–41), and probably for that reason, Jonah appears more often than any other OT figure in the Christian art in the Roman catacombs.

By means of only 689 words in the original Hebrew text, in the narrative of Jonah we meet a huge storm on the Mediterranean Sea, take a tour of Sheol, discover the insides of a great fish, watch a plant come and go in a day, suffer from a hot east wind over distant lands, and even meet repentant sailors and Ninevites. Yet most surprising of all is that we meet "Yahweh, the God of the heavens, … who made the sea and the dry land" (Jonah 1:9). This God surprises us again and again with his out-of-this-world love that pursues reluctant and stubborn sinners, like Jonah, like us.

In Jonah the name Yahweh (יהוה, usually translated "the LORD") is mentioned twenty-two times, Elohim (אֱלֹהִים, "God") twelve times, El (אֵל, "God") once (4:2), and the combination Yahweh Elohim four times (1:9; 2:2, 7 [ET 2:1, 6]; 4:6), for a total of thirty-nine references to the deity in four chapters. In contrast, the name "Jonah" occurs only eighteen times. Clearly this is a story about the God of Abraham, Isaac, and Jacob, and his accepting grace for all people, even their animals (4:11)!

A narrator committed to happy endings would have tied his work up into a well-crafted knot in chapter 4, but instead we are left with a frayed rope that can't be so neatly tied together. Jonah is not an easily packaged narrative, effortless to unwrap, read, and set aside. Rather, from the first until the last, it is a narrative packed with surprises. Jonah is like a can that contains a coiled spring. Opening it innocently, we are shocked as the spring leaps out! Most of us are fine with Jonah as a Sunday school lesson, but it is a life-changing call to repentance and mission disguised as a "bedtime story" that simply takes our breath away!

In the elementary Hebrew classes at Concordia Seminary in St. Louis, Missouri, after the basics of the Hebrew language are mastered, it is customary to read through the book of Jonah. Having been privileged to teach these classes at the seminary since 1999, I have become captivated by this small book that packs such a powerful punch. Due to these readings with my students through Jonah, I now consider myself to be a member of that informal society of baptized believers who, down through the ages, have discovered a narrative that is endlessly fascinating and theologically stimulating. I thank all of my students at Concordia Seminary, especially those who in elementary Hebrew have enriched my study of Jonah.

In light of the fact that students at institutions of higher learning, including Concordia Seminary, often use the book of Jonah as their first entrée into the Hebrew Scriptures, this commentary seeks to assist such learners. It does so chiefly by means of its detailed analysis of every phrase in the book.

Prior to my ministry as professor of exegetical theology, it was my privilege to serve as pastor of Christ the Servant Lutheran Church in West Monroe, Louisiana, and Trinity Lutheran Church in Broken Arrow, Oklahoma. These parishes tolerated me as one who in so many ways exhibited the lackluster characteristics of Jonah. I am forever thankful for the ties that bind our hearts in Christian love.

My deepest appreciation goes to my colleagues in the Department of Exegetical Theology at Concordia Seminary; it is from these brother scholars that my mind has been broadened and my spirit renewed, time after time. I thank two colleagues in the seminary's Department of Systematic Theology—Drs. Kent Burreson and Joel Okamoto. The former contributed to the excursus on Luther's theology of Baptism; the latter's insights on open theism added much to the excursus entitled "When Yahweh Changes a Prior Verdict." I also thank the administration of the seminary that graciously supported this project by providing me time to complete it. Jeremiah Johnson, my graduate research assistant for the 2004–2005 academic year, has done a stellar job in assisting the project along the way. Rev. Kevin Golden's doctoral work on the connections between Jonah and Noah are hereby acknowledged and appreciated. Debbie Roediger is unfailing in her support of the seminary's faculty. I am most grateful for her help in bringing the bibliographic information together. I am also indebted to Dr. Christopher Mitchell of Concordia Publishing House, who is the editor of this volume. I am amazed by his tireless energy, meticulous care and attention to detail, and his gracious gifts of time and encouragement. His scholarly gifts are a tremendous blessing to this entire commentary series. Mrs. Julene Dumit, the production editor for the series, also deserves my highest praise for her countless suggestions that have been incorporated into this book.

But it is to my dear wife, Lisa, and our three children, Abi, Jonathan, and Lori, that I owe the greatest debt of gratitude. They are truly the loves of my life.

It is said that travel broadens the mind. The narrative of Jonah takes the unwilling prophet southwest to Joppa, northwest toward Tarshish, down into the belly of the fish, farther down into Sheol, eastward toward the great city of Nineveh, and then finally east of the city under a miraculous plant. This is a gasp-and-gulp journey, and joining him all the way is Yahweh, who uses the trip to confront the uneven roads, unwanted rocks, and winding valleys of Jonah's heart. The extent to which Jonah is changed by his travel remains uncertain—indeed, the narrative itself subtly ends with the notion that the journey is not yet over, for Jonah or for us! The adventure still awaits readers who recognize in Jonah a large part of themselves.

This is a story about the great God Yahweh who is still calling us out of settled places into the unknown world of compassion, forgiveness, and mission. My hope, dear reader, is that the trip will broaden your world, enrich your heart, and motivate you to stay on the path that leads to the one greater than Jonah, Jesus our Lord. To him be glory in the church throughout all generations, forever and ever. Amen! Let the journey begin!

September 22, 2006
Commemoration of Jonah, Prophet of Yahweh

Principal Abbreviations

Books of the Bible

Gen	2 Ki	Is	Nah	Rom	Titus
Ex	1 Chr	Jer	Hab	1 Cor	Philemon
Lev	2 Chr	Lam	Zeph	2 Cor	Heb
Num	Ezra	Ezek	Hag	Gal	James
Deut	Neh	Dan	Zech	Eph	1 Pet
Josh	Esth	Hos	Mal	Phil	2 Pet
Judg	Job	Joel	Mt	Col	1 Jn
Ruth	Ps (pl. Pss)	Amos	Mk	1 Thess	2 Jn
1 Sam	Prov	Obad	Lk	2 Thess	3 Jn
2 Sam	Eccl	Jonah	Jn	1 Tim	Jude
1 Ki	Song	Micah	Acts	2 Tim	Rev

Books of the Apocrypha and Other Noncanonical Books of the Septuagint

1–2 Esdras	1–2 Esdras
Tobit	Tobit
Judith	Judith
Add Esth	Additions to Esther
Wis Sol	Wisdom of Solomon
Sirach	Sirach/Ecclesiasticus
Baruch	Baruch
Ep Jer	Epistle of Jeremiah
Azariah	Prayer of Azariah
Song of the Three	Song of the Three Young Men
Susanna	Susanna
Bel	Bel and the Dragon
Manasseh	Prayer of Manasseh
1–2 Macc	1–2 Maccabees
3–4 Macc	3–4 Maccabees
Ps 151	Psalm 151
Odes	Odes
Ps(s) Sol	Psalm(s) of Solomon

Reference Works and Scripture Versions

ABD	*The Anchor Bible Dictionary.* Edited by D. N. Freedman. 6 vols. New York: Doubleday, 1992
AC	Augsburg Confession
ACCS	Ancient Christian Commentary on Scripture
AE	American Edition of *Luther's Works.* 55 vols. St. Louis: Concordia; Philadelphia: Fortress, 1955–1986
ANEP	*The Ancient Near East in Pictures Relating to the Old Testament.* Edited by J. B. Pritchard. 2d ed. Princeton: Princeton University Press, 1969
ANET	*Ancient Near Eastern Texts Relating to the Old Testament.* Edited by J. B. Pritchard. 3d ed. Princeton: Princeton University Press, 1969
ANF	*The Ante-Nicene Fathers.* Edited by A. Roberts and J. Donaldson. 10 vols. Repr. Peabody, Mass.: Hendrickson, 1994
Ap	Apology of the Augsburg Confession
BDAG	Bauer, W., F. W. Danker, W. F. Arndt, F. W. Gingrich. *A Greek-English Lexicon of the New Testament and Other Early Christian Literature.* 3d ed. Chicago: University of Chicago Press, 2000
BDB	Brown, F., S. R. Driver, and C. A. Briggs. *A Hebrew and English Lexicon of the Old Testament.* Oxford: Clarendon, 1979
BDF	Blass, F., A. Debrunner, and R. W. Funk. *A Greek Grammar of the New Testament and Other Early Christian Literature.* Chicago: University of Chicago Press, 1961
BHS	*Biblia Hebraica Stuttgartensia.* Edited by K. Elliger and W. Rudolph. Stuttgart: Deutsche Bibelgesellschaft, 1967/1977
CCSL	Corpus Christianorum: Series latina. Turnhout: Brepols, 1953–
CSEL	Corpus scriptorum ecclesiasticorum latinorum
DCH	*The Dictionary of Classical Hebrew.* Edited by D. J. A. Clines. Sheffield: Sheffield Academic Press, 1993–
Ep	Epitome of the Formula of Concord
ESV	English Standard Version of the Bible
ET	English translation
FC	Formula of Concord
GKC	*Gesenius' Hebrew Grammar.* Edited by E. Kautzsch. Translated by A. E. Cowley. 2d ed. Oxford: Clarendon, 1910

HALOT	Koehler, L., W. Baumgartner, and J. J. Stamm. *The Hebrew and Aramaic Lexicon of the Old Testament.* Translated and edited under the supervision of M. E. J. Richardson. 5 vols. Leiden: Brill, 1994–2000
IDB	*The Interpreter's Dictionary of the Bible.* Edited by G. A. Buttrick. 5 vols. Nashville: Abingdon, 1962, 1976
Jastrow	Jastrow, M., comp. *A Dictionary of the Targumim, the Talmud Babli and Yerushalmi, and the Midrashic Literature.* 2 vols. Brooklyn: P. Shalom, 1967
JB	Jerusalem Bible
Joüon	Joüon, P. *A Grammar of Biblical Hebrew.* Translated and revised by T. Muraoka. 2 vols. Subsidia biblica 14/1–2. Rome: Editrice Pontificio Istituto Biblico, 1991
KJV	King James Version of the Bible
LC	Large Catechism of Martin Luther
LCL	Loeb Classical Library
LEH	Lust, J., E. Eynikel, and K. Hauspie. *A Greek-English Lexicon of the Septuagint.* 2 vols. Stuttgart: Deutsche Bibelgesellschaft, 1992–1996
LSB	*Lutheran Service Book.* St. Louis: Concordia, 2006
LXX	Septuagint
MT	Masoretic Text of the Hebrew Bible
NASB	New American Standard Bible
NEB	New English Bible
NIV	New International Version of the Bible
NKJV	New King James Version of the Bible
NPNF[1]	*The Nicene and Post-Nicene Fathers.* Series 1. Edited by P. Schaff. 14 vols. Repr. Peabody, Mass.: Hendrickson, 1994
NPNF[2]	*The Nicene and Post-Nicene Fathers.* Series 2. Edited by P. Schaff and H. Wace. 14 vols. Repr. Peabody, Mass.: Hendrickson, 1994
NRSV	New Revised Standard Version of the Bible
NT	New Testament
OT	Old Testament
Payne Smith	Payne Smith, R. *A Compendious Syriac Dictionary.* Oxford: Clarendon, 1903
PG	Patrologia graeca. Edited by J.-P. Migne. 162 vols. Paris, 1857–1886
PL	Patrologia latina. Edited by J.-P. Migne. 217 vols. Paris, 1844–1864
RSV	Revised Standard Version of the Bible and Apocrypha

SC	Small Catechism of Martin Luther
SD	Solid Declaration of the Formula of Concord
Str-B	Strack, H. L., and P. Billerbeck. *Kommentar zum Neuen Testament aus Talmud und Midrasch.* 6 vols. in 7. Munich: Beck, 1922–1961
TDNT	*Theological Dictionary of the New Testament.* Edited by G. Kittel and G. Friedrich. Translated by G. W. Bromiley. 10 vols. Grand Rapids: Eerdmans, 1964–1976
TDOT	*Theological Dictionary of the Old Testament.* Edited by G. J. Botterweck, H. Ringgren, and H.-J. Fabry. Translated by J. T. Willis et al. 15 vols. at present. Grand Rapids: Eerdmans, 1974–
TLH	*The Lutheran Hymnal.* St. Louis: Concordia, 1941
TLOT	*Theological Lexicon of the Old Testament.* Edited by E. Jenni and C. Westermann. Translated by M. E. Biddle. 3 vols. Peabody, Mass.: Hendrickson, 1997
WA	Weimar Ausgabe ("Edition") of Martin Luther's Works. *Luthers Werke: Kritische Gesamtausgabe.* 65 vols. Weimar: Hermann Böhlau, 1883–1993
WA Br	Weimar Ausgabe Briefwechsel ("Correspondence"). *Luthers Werke: Kritische Gesamtausgabe. Briefwechsel.* 18 vols. Weimar: Hermann Böhlau, 1930–1985
WA TR	Weimar Ausgabe Tischreden ("Table Talk"). *Luthers Werke: Kritische Gesamtausgabe. Tischreden.* 6 vols. Weimar: Hermann Böhlau, 1912–1921
Waltke-O'Connor	Waltke, B. K., and M. O'Connor. *An Introduction to Biblical Hebrew Syntax.* Winona Lake, Ind.: Eisenbrauns, 1990

Icons

These icons are used in the margins of this commentary to highlight the following themes:

Trinity

Temple, Tabernacle

Incarnation

Passion, Atonement

Death and Resurrection,
Theology of the Cross,
the Great Reversal

Christus Victor,
Christology

Baptism

Catechesis,
Instruction, Revelation

Lord's Supper

Ministry of Word and Sacrament,
Office of the Keys

The Church

Worship

Sin, Law, Death

Hope of Heaven,
Eschatology

Justification

Bibliography

Aalders, Gerhard Charles. Genesis. Translated by William Heynen. Vol. 1. Grand Rapids: Zondervan, 1981.

Abraham, William J. *Divine Revelation and the Limits of Historical Criticism*. Oxford: Oxford University Press, 1982.

Abramson, Glenda. "The Book of Jonah as a Literary and Dramatic Work." *Semitics* 5 (1977): 36–47.

Ackerman, James S. "Satire and Symbolism in the Song of Jonah." Pages 213–46 in *Traditions in Transformation: Turning Points in Biblical Faith*. Edited by Baruch Halpern and Jon D. Levenson. Winona Lake, Ind.: Eisenbrauns, 1981.

Aejmelaeus, Anneli. "Function and Interpretation of כי in Biblical Hebrew." *Journal of Biblical Literature* 105 (1986): 193–209.

Aichele, George, and Gary A. Phillips. "Introduction: Exegesis, Eisegesis, Intergesis." *Semeia* 69/70 (1995): 7–18.

Albright, W. F. "New Light on the Early History of Phoenician Colonization." *Bulletin of the American Schools of Oriental Research* 83 (1941): 14–22.

———. "The Oracles of Balaam." *Journal of Biblical Literature* 63 (1944): 207–33.

Alexander, T. Desmond. "Jonah and Genre." *Tyndale Bulletin* 36 (1985): 35–59.

———. *Jonah: An Introduction and Commentary*. Bound with *Obadiah: An Introduction and Commentary* by David W. Baker and *Micah: An Introduction and Commentary* by Bruce K. Waltke. Tyndale Old Testament Commentaries. Downers Grove, Ill.: InterVarsity, 1988.

Allen, Leslie C. *The Books of Joel, Obadiah, Jonah and Micah*. Grand Rapids: Eerdmans, 1976.

Almbladh, Karin. *Studies in the Book of Jonah*. Acta Universitatis Upsaliensis: Studia Semitica Upsaliensis 7: Stockholm: Almqvist & Wiksell, 1986.

Alonso Schökel, Luis. *A Manual of Hebrew Poetics*. Rome: Pontifical Biblical Institute, 1988.

Alt, Albrecht. "The God of the Fathers." Pages 44–55 in *Essays on Old Testament History and Religion*. Translated by R. A. Wilson. Garden City, N.Y.: Archer Books, 1968.

Alter, Robert. *The Art of Biblical Narrative*. New York: Basic, 1981.

———. "Introduction to the Old Testament." Pages 11–35 in *The Literary Guide to the Bible*. Edited by Robert Alter and Frank Kermode. Cambridge, Mass.: Belknap Press of Harvard University Press, 1987.

Andersen, Francis I., and A. Dean Forbes. " 'Prose Particle' Counts of the Hebrew Bible." Pages 165–83 in *The Word of the Lord Shall Go Forth: Essays in Honor of David Noel Freedman in Celebration of His Sixtieth Birthday*. Edited by Carol L. Meyers and M. O'Connor. Winona Lake, Ind.: Eisenbrauns, 1983.

Andersen, Francis I., and David Noel Freedman. *Amos*. Anchor Bible 24A. New York: Doubleday, 1989.

———. *Hosea*. Anchor Bible 24. New York: Doubleday, 1980.

Archer, Gleason L. *A Survey of Old Testament Introduction*. Chicago: Moody, 1964.

Arthur, David. *A Smooth Stone: Biblical Prophecy in Historical Perspective*. Lanham, Md.: University Press of America, 2001.

Balentine, Samuel E. *The Hidden God: The Hiding of the Face of God in the Old Testament*. Oxford: Oxford University Press, 1983.

———. *The Torah's Vision of Worship*. Minneapolis: Fortress, 1999.

Band, Arnold J. "Swallowing Jonah: The Eclipse of Parody." *Prooftexts* 10 (1990): 177–95.

Bar-Efrat, Shimeon. *Narrative Art in the Bible*. Sheffield: Almond, 1989.

Barr, James. *The Concept of Biblical Theology: An Old Testament Perspective*. Minneapolis: Fortress, 1999.

———. "Revelation through History in the Old Testament and in Modern Theology." *Interpretation* 17 (1963): 193–205.

———. *The Semantics of Biblical Language*. London: Oxford University Press, 1961.

Barré, Michael L. "Jonah 2,9 and the Structure of Jonah's Prayer." *Biblica* 72 (1991): 237–48.

Bartelt, Andrew H. *The Book around Immanuel: Style and Structure in Isaiah 2–12*. Winona Lake, Ind.: Eisenbrauns, 1996.

———. "Dialectical Negation: An Exegetical Both/And." Pages 57–66 in *"Hear the Word of Yahweh": Essays on Scripture and Archaeology in Honor of Horace D. Hummel*. Edited by Dean O. Wenthe, Paul L. Schrieber, and Lee A. Maxwell. Saint Louis: Concordia, 2002.

Barton, John. *Understanding Old Testament Ethics: Approaches and Explorations*. Louisville, Ky.: Westminster John Knox, 2003.

Bauer, Johannes Baptist. "Drei Tage." *Biblica* 39 (1958): 354–58.

Ben Zvi, Ehud. *Signs of Jonah: Reading and Rereading in Ancient Yehud*. Sheffield: Sheffield Academic Press, 2003.

Bendor, Shunya. *The Social Structure of Ancient Israel: The Institution of the Family (Beit 'Ab) from the Settlement to the End of the Monarchy*. Jerusalem: Simor, 1996.

Benoit, P., J. T. Milik, and R. de Vaux, eds. *Les Grottes de Murabbaʿat*. 2 vols. Discoveries in the Judaean Desert 2. Oxford: Clarendon, 1961.

Berlin, Adele. *The Dynamics of Biblical Parallelism*. Bloomington: Indiana University Press, 1985.

Bewer, Julius A. *A Critical and Exegetical Commentary on Jonah*. In *A Critical and Exegetical Commentary on Haggai, Zechariah, Malachi and Jonah* by Hinckley

G. Mitchell et al. International Critical Commentary 25. Edinburgh: T&T Clark, 1912.

Bickerman, Elias Joseph. "Les deux erreurs du prophète Jonas." *Revue d'histoire et de philosophie religieuses* 45 (1965): 232–64.

———. *Four Strange Books of the Bible: Jonah, Daniel, Koheleth, Esther.* New York: Schocken, 1967.

Bolin, Thomas M. *Freedom beyond Forgiveness: The Book of Jonah Re-examined.* Sheffield: Sheffield Academic Press, 1997.

Booth, Wayne C. "Metaphor as Rhetoric: The Problem of Evaluation." Pages 47–70 in *On Metaphor.* Edited by Sheldon Sacks. Chicago: University of Chicago Press, 1979.

Bottéro, Jean. *Religion in Ancient Mesopotamia.* Translated by Teresa Lavender Fagan. Chicago: University of Chicago Press, 2001.

Bowers, R. H. *The Legend of Jonah.* The Hague: Nijhoff, 1971.

Boyd, Gregory A. *God of the Possible: A Biblical Introduction to the Open View of God.* Grand Rapids: Baker, 2000.

Brenner, A. "The Language of Jonah as an Index of Its Date." [In Hebrew.] *Beth Mikra* 24 (1979): 396–405.

Brichto, Herbert Chanan. *Toward a Grammar of Biblical Poetics: Tales of the Prophets.* New York: Oxford University Press, 1992.

Brinkman, J. A. *A Political History of Post-Kassite Babylonia 1158–722 BC.* Analecta Orientalia 43. Rome: Pontifical Biblical Institute, 1968.

Brongers, H. A. "Bemerkungen zum Gebrauch des adverbialen $w^{e\varsigma}att\bar{a}h$ im Alten Testament." *Vetus Testamentum* 15 (1965): 289–99.

Broshi, Magen. "The Expansion of Jerusalem in the Reigns of Hezekiah and Manasseh." *Israel Exploration Journal* 24 (1974): 21–26.

Brown, William P. *The Ethos of the Cosmos: The Genesis of Moral Imagination in the Bible.* Grand Rapids: Eerdmans, 1999.

Brueggemann, Walter. *The Book That Breathes New Life: Scriptural Authority and Biblical Theology.* Minneapolis: Fortress, 2005.

———. *Genesis.* Interpretation: A Bible Commentary for Teaching and Preaching. Atlanta: John Knox, 1982.

Burrows, Millar. "The Literary Category of the Book of Jonah." Pages 80–107 in *Translating and Understanding the Old Testament: Essays in Honor of Herbert Gordon May.* Edited by Harry Thomas Frank and William L. Reed. Nashville: Abingdon, 1970.

Cahill, Thomas. *The Gifts of the Jews: How a Tribe of Desert Nomads Changed the Way Everyone Thinks and Feels.* New York: Doubleday, 1998.

Calvin, John. *Commentaries on the Twelve Minor Prophets.* Vol. 3. Translated by John Owen. Grand Rapids: Eerdmans, 1950.

————. *Institutes of the Christian Religion.* Edited by John T. McNeill. Translated by Ford Lewis Battles. 2 vols. Philadelphia: Westminster, 1960.

Canary, Robert H., and Henry Kozicki, eds. *The Writing of History: Literary Form and Historical Understanding.* Madison: University of Wisconsin Press, 1978.

Carrithers, Michael, Steven Collins, and Steven Lukes, eds. *The Category of the Person: Anthropology, Philosophy, History.* Cambridge: Cambridge University Press, 1985.

Carroll, Robert P. *Jeremiah.* Philadelphia: Westminster, 1986.

Cassuto, Umberto. "The Beginning of Historiography among the Israelites." 1951. Pages 7–16 in *Biblical and Oriental Studies.* Vol. 1: *Bible.* Translated by Israel Abrahams. Jerusalem: Magnes, 1973.

Childs, Brevard S. "The Canonical Shape of the Book of Jonah." Pages 122–28 in *Biblical and Near Eastern Studies: Essays in Honor of William Sanford LaSor.* Edited by Gary A. Tuttle. Grand Rapids: Eerdmans, 1978.

————. *Introduction to the Old Testament as Scripture.* London: SCM Press, 1979.

————. "Jonah: A Study in Old Testament Hermeneutics." *Scottish Journal of Theology* 11 (1958): 53–61.

Christensen, Duane L. *Transformations of the War Oracle in Old Testament Prophecy: Studies in the Oracles against the Nations.* Harvard Dissertations in Religion 3. Missoula, Mont.: Scholars, 1975.

Clements, Ronald E. *Prophecy and Tradition.* Growing Points in Theology. Atlanta: John Knox, 1974.

————. "The Purpose of the Book of Jonah." Pages 16–28 in *Congress Volume: Edinburgh, 1974.* Supplements to Vetus Testamentum 28. Leiden: Brill, 1975.

Clifford, Richard J. *The Cosmic Mountain in Canaan and the Old Testament.* Cambridge, Mass.: Harvard University Press, 1972.

————. *Fair Spoken and Persuading: An Interpretation of Second Isaiah.* New York: Paulist, 1984.

Craig, Kenneth M. *A Poetics of Jonah: Art in the Service of Ideology.* Columbia: University of South Carolina Press, 1993.

Crenshaw, James L. "The Expression *Mî Yôdēaʿ* in the Hebrew Bible." *Vetus Testamentum* 36 (1986): 274–88.

Crouch, Walter B. "To Question an End, to End a Question: Opening the Closure of the Book of Jonah." *Journal for the Study of the Old Testament* 62 (June 1994): 101–12.

Dahood, Mitchell. *Psalms I, 1–50.* Anchor Bible 16. Garden City, N.Y.: Doubleday, 1966.

Danby, Herbert, trans. *The Mishnah.* Repr., London: Oxford University Press, 1972.

Daube, David. "Death as a Release in the Bible." *Novum Testamentum* 5 (1962): 82–104.

Davidson, Richard. *Typology in Scripture: A Study of Hermeneutical* τύπος *Structures*. Berrien Springs, Mich.: Andrews University Press, 1981.

Davies, Graham I. "The Uses of *R" Qal* and the Meaning of Jonah IV 1." *Vetus Testamentum* 27 (1977): 105–11.

Davis, Charles. "Our Modern Identity: The Formation of Self." *Modern Theology* 6 (1990): 159–71.

Day, John. "Problems in the Interpretation of the Book of Jonah." Pages 32–47 in *In Quest of the Past: Studies on Israelite Religion, Literature and Prophetism*. Edited by A. S. van der Woude. Brill: Leiden, 1990.

———. *Yahweh and the Gods and Goddesses of Canaan*. Sheffield: Sheffield Academic Press, 2000.

De Beaugrande, Robert-Alain, and Wolfgang Ulrich Dressler. *Introduction to Text Linguistics*. New York: Longman, 1981.

DeHaan, Martin R. *Jonah, Fact or Fiction?* Grand Rapids: Zondervan, 1957.

Delitzsch, Franz. *A New Commentary on Genesis*. Vol. 1. Translated by Sophia Taylor. Edinburgh: T&T Clark, 1899.

Dentan, Robert C. "The Literary Affinities of Exodus XXXIV 6f." *Vetus Testamentum* 13 (1963): 34–51.

DeWette, Wilhelm M. L. *Lehrbuch der historisch-kritischen Einleitung in kanonischen und apokryphischen Bücher des Alten Testamentes*. Berlin: Reimer, 1817.

Dillenberger, John. *God Hidden and Revealed: The Interpretation of Luther's* Deus Absconditus *and Its Significance for Religious Thought*. Philadelphia: Muhlenberg, 1953.

Dozeman, Thomas B. "Inner-Biblical Interpretation of Yahweh's Gracious and Compassionate Character." *Journal of Biblical Literature* 108 (1989): 207–23.

Dreyfus, Hubert L., and Paul Rabinow, *Michel Foucault: Beyond Structuralism and Hermeneutics*. 2d ed. Chicago: University of Chicago Press, 1983.

Driver, S. R. *An Introduction to the Literature of the Old Testament*. New York: Scribner, 1899.

Duval, Yves Marie. *Le livre de Jonas dans la littérature chrétienne grecque et latine: Sources et influence du Commentaire sur Jonas de saint Jérôme*. 2 vols. Paris: Études augustiniennes, 1973.

Ebeling, Gerhard. *Word and Faith*. Translated by James W. Leitch. London: SCM Press, 1963.

Edwards, Richard Alan. *The Sign of Jonah in the Theology of the Evangelists and Q*. London: SCM Press, 1971.

Eichrodt, Walther. *Theology of the Old Testament*. Translated by J. A. Baker. 2 vols. London: SCM Press, 1961, 1967.

Elat, Moshe. "Phoenician Overland Trade within the Mesopotamian Empires." Pages 21–35 in *Ah, Assyria … : Studies in Assyrian History and Ancient Near Eastern*

Historiography Presented to Hayim Tadmor. Edited by Mordechai Cogan and Israel *Eph'al*. Jerusalem: Magnes, 1991.

Elert, Werner. *The Structure of Lutheranism*. Translated by Walter A. Hansen. St. Louis: Concordia, 1962.

Eliade, Mircea. *The Myth of the Eternal Return*. [In some editions titled *Cosmos and History*.] Translated by Willard R. Trask. Princeton: Princeton University Press, 1954.

Ellison, H. L. "Jonah." Pages 359–91 in vol. 7 of *The Expositor's Bible Commentary*. Grand Rapids: Zondervan, 1985.

Ellul, Jacques. *The Judgment of Jonah*. Translated by Geoffrey W. Bromiley. Grand Rapids: Eerdmans, 1971.

Emerton, John A. "The Problem of Psalm LXXXVII." *Vetus Testamentum* 50 (2000): 183–99.

Erickson, Millard J. *What Does God Know and When Does He Know It? The Current Controversy over Divine Foreknowledge*. Grand Rapids: Zondervan, 2003.

Eybers, I. H. "The Purpose of the Book of Jonah." *Theologica evangelica* 4 (1971): 216–19.

Feinberg, Leonard. *Introduction to Satire*. Ames: Iowa State University Press, 1967.

Ferreiro, Alberto. *The Twelve Prophets*. Ancient Christian Commentary on Scripture, Old Testament 14. Downers Grove, Ill.: InterVarsity, 2003.

Feuillet, André. "Les sources du livre de Jonas." *Revue biblique* 54 (1947): 161–86.

Filbeck, David. *Yes, God of the Gentiles, Too: The Missionary Message of the Old Testament*. Wheaton, Ill.: Wheaton College, 1994.

Fishbane, Michael A. *Biblical Interpretation in Ancient Israel*. Oxford: Clarendon, 1985.

———. *Text and Texture: Close Readings of Selected Biblical Texts*. New York: Schocken, 1979.

Fishelov, David. "The Prophet as Satirist." *Prooftexts* 9 (1989): 195–211.

Frankfort, Henri, et al. *Before Philosophy: The Intellectual Adventure of Ancient Man*. New York: Penguin, 1989.

Freedman, David Noel. "Did God Play a Dirty Trick on Jonah at the End?" *Bible Review* 6/4 (August 1990): 26–31.

———. "Prose Particles in the Poetry of the Primary History." Pages 49–62 in *Biblical and Related Studies Presented to Samuel Iwry*. Edited by Ann Kort and Scott Morschauser. Winona Lake, Ind.: Eisenbrauns, 1985.

Fretheim, Terence E. "Jonah and Theodicy." *Zeitschrift für die alttestamentliche Wissenschaft* 90 (1978): 227–37.

———. *God and World in the Old Testament: A Relational Theology of Creation*. Nashville: Abingdon, 2005.

———. *The Message of Jonah: A Theological Commentary*. Minneapolis: Augsburg, 1977.

———. "The Repentance of God: A Key to Evaluating Old Testament God-Talk." *Horizons in Biblical Theology* 10/1 (June 1988): 47–70.

Frye, Norbert. *Anatomy of Criticism: Four Essays.* Princeton: Princeton University Press, 1957.

Fuller, Russell E. "The Minor Prophets Manuscripts from Qumran, Cave IV." Ph.D. diss., Harvard University. Ann Arbor: University Microfilms, 1988.

Gerhard, Johann. *Loci Theologici.* Edited by Eduard Preuss. 10 vols. in 4. Berlin: Gustav Schlawitz, 1863–1885.

Gibbs, Jeffrey A. *Matthew 1:1–11:1.* Concordia Commentary. St. Louis: Concordia, 2006.

———. "Regaining Biblical Hope: Restoring the Prominence of the Parousia." *Concordia Journal* 27 (2001): 310–22.

Glasson, T. Francis. "The Final Question—In Nahum and Jonah." *Expository Times* 81 (1969/1970): 54–55.

Goitein, S. D. "The Song of Songs: A Female Composition." Page 58–66 in *A Feminist Companion to the Song of Songs.* Edited by Athalya Brenner. Feminist Companion to the Bible 1. Sheffield: Sheffield Academic Press, 1993.

Goitein, S. D. F. "Some Observations on Jonah." *Journal of the Palestine Oriental Society* 17 (1937): 63–77.

Good, Edwin M. *Irony in the Old Testament.* 2d ed. Sheffield: Almond, 1981.

Goppelt, Leonhard. *Typos: The Typological Interpretation of the Old Testament in the New.* Translated by Donald H. Madvig. Grand Rapids: Eerdmans, 1982.

Gordon, Cyrus H. *Ugaritic Textbook.* Rome: Pontifical Biblical Institute, 1965.

———. "The Wine-Dark Sea." *Journal of Near Eastern Studies* 37 (1978): 51–52.

Gottwald, Norman K. *All the Kingdoms of the Earth: Israelite Prophecy and International Relations in the Ancient Near East.* New York: Harper & Row, 1964.

Gray, John. *I and II Kings.* 2d ed. London: SCM Press, 1970.

Green, Barbara. *Jonah's Journeys.* Collegeville, Minn.: Liturgical Press, 2005.

Greenberg, Moshe. *Biblical Prose Prayer as a Window to the Popular Religion of Ancient Israel.* Berkeley: University of California Press, 1983.

Grether, Oskar. *Name und Wort Gottes im Alten Testament.* Giessen: Töpelmann, 1934.

Gruber, Mayer I. *Aspects of Nonverbal Communication in the Ancient Near East.* 2 vols. Studia Pohl 12. Rome: Pontifical Biblical Institute, 1980.

Guilhamet, Leon. *Satire and the Transformation of Genre.* Philadelphia: University of Pennsylvania Press, 1987.

Gunkel, Hermann. *The Legends of Genesis: The Biblical Saga and History.* Translated by W. H. Carruth. Repr., New York: Schocken, 1964.

———. *Schöpfung und Chaos in Urzeit und Endzeit.* Göttingen: Vandenhoeck & Ruprecht, 1885.

Gunn, David M. "New Directions in the Study of Biblical Hebrew Narrative." *Journal for the Study of the Old Testament* 39 (1987): 65–75.

Hackett, Jo Ann. *The Balaam Text from Deir 'Alla*. Chico, Calif.: Scholars, 1980.

Hallo, William W. (writing on Mesopotamia), and William Kelly Simpson (writing on Egypt). *The Ancient Near East: A History*. New York: Harcourt Brace Jovanovich, 1971.

Halpern, Baruch. "Jerusalem and the Lineages in the Seventh Century BCE: Kinship and the Rise of Individual Moral Liability." Pages 11–107 in *Law and Ideology in Monarchic Israel*. Edited by Baruch Halpern and Deborah W. Hobson. Journal for the Study of the Old Testament: Supplement Series 124. Sheffield: JSOT Press, 1991.

Hamilton, Victor P. *The Book of Genesis: Chapters 1–17*. New International Commentary on the Old Testament. Eerdmans: Grand Rapids, 1990.

Hampl, Patricia. "In the Belly of the Whale." Pages 289–301 in *Out of the Garden: Women Writers on the Bible*. Edited by Christina Büchmann and Celina Spiegel. New York: Ballantine, 1995.

Hanson, Anthony Tyrrell. "The Scriptural Background to the Doctrine of the '*Descensus ad Inferos*' in the New Testament." Pages 122–56 in *The New Testament Interpretation of Scripture*. London: SPCK, 1980.

Harden, Donald B. *The Phoenicians*. London: Thames & Hudson, 1962.

Harstad, Adolph L. *Joshua*. Concordia Commentary. St. Louis: Concordia, 2004.

Hart-Davies, D. E. "The Book of Jonah in the Light of Assyrian Archaeology." *Journal of the Transactions of the Victoria Institute* 69 (1937): 230–47.

Haupt, P. "Jonah's Whale." *Proceedings of the American Philosophical Society* 46 (1907): 151–64.

Hegel, Georg Wilhelm Friedrich. *Lectures on the Philosophy of Religion*. Translated by E. B. Speirs and J. Burdon Sanderson. 3 vols. London: Routledge & Kegan Paul, 1962.

Heller, Thomas C., Morton Sosna, and David E. Wellbery. *Reconstructing Individualism: Autonomy, Individuality, and the Self in Western Thought*. Stanford: Stanford University Press, 1986.

Hempel, Johannes. *Das Ethos des Alten Testaments*. Berlin: Töpelmann, 1938.

Henderson, David W. *Culture Shift: Communicating God's Truth to Our Changing World*. Grand Rapids: Baker, 1998.

Hengel, Martin. *Crucifixion*. Translated by John Bowden. Philadelphia: Fortress, 1977.

Hengstenberg, Ernst W. *Christology of the Old Testament*. 4 vols. Repr., Edinburgh: T&T Clark, 1925.

Herrmann, S. A. "Die Tartessosfrage und Weissafrike." *Petermanns geographische Mitteilungen* 99 (1942): 353–66.

Hesse, Eric W., and Isaac M. Kikawada. "Jonah and Genesis 11–1." *Annual of the Japanese Biblical Institute* 10 (1984): 3–19.

Hill, David. *The Gospel of Matthew*. London: Oliphants, 1972.

Holbert, John C. "Deliverance Belongs to Yahweh! Satire in the Book of Jonah." *Journal for the Study of the Old Testament* 21 (1981): 59–81.

Holladay, William L. *Jeremiah 1: A Commentary on the Book of the Prophet Jeremiah, Chapters 1–25*. Hermeneia. Philadelphia: Fortress, 1986.

Horne, Milton P. *Proverbs–Ecclesiastes*. Macon, Ga.: Smyth & Helwys, 2003.

Hummel, Horace D. "Enclitic *Mem* in Early Northwest Semitic, Especially Hebrew." *Journal of Biblical Literature* 76 (1957): 85–107.

———. *Ezekiel 1–20*. Concordia Commentary. St. Louis: Concordia, 2005.

———. *The Word Becoming Flesh: An Introduction to the Origin, Purpose, and Meaning of the Old Testament*. St. Louis: Concordia, 1979.

Hunter, W. Bingham. *The God Who Hears*. Downers Grove, Ill.: InterVarsity, 1986.

Hurvitz, Avi. "The Chronological Significance of 'Aramaisms' in Biblical Hebrew." *Israel Exploration Journal* 18 (1968): 234–40.

———. "The History of a Legal Formula: *kōl ʾ ᵃšer-ḥāpēṣ ʿāśāh* (Psalms cxv 3, cxxxv 6)." *Vetus Testamentum* 32 (1982): 257–67.

Isserlin, B. S. J. *The Israelites*. Minneapolis: Augsburg Fortress, 2001.

Jacob, Edmond. *Theology of the Old Testament*. Translated by Arthur W. Heathcote and Philip J. Allcock. New York: Harper, 1958.

Jemielity, Thomas. *Satire and the Hebrew Prophets*. Louisville, Ky.: Westminster/John Knox, 1992.

Jensen, H. James, and Malvin R. Zirker, Jr., eds. *The Satirist's Art*. Bloomington: Indiana University Press, 1972.

Jepsen, Alfred. "Anmerkungen zum Buche Jona." Pages 297–305 in *Wort-Gebot-Glaube: Beiträge zur Theologie des Alten Testaments*. Edited by Hans Joachim Stoebe. Abhandlungen zur Theologie des Alten und Neuen Testaments 59. Zurich: Zwingli, 1970.

Jeremias, Jörg. *Die Reue Gottes: Aspekte alttestamentlicher Gottesvorstellung*. Neukirchen-Vluyn: Neukirchener, 1975.

Johnston, Philip. *Shades of Sheol: Death and Afterlife in the Old Testament*. Downers Grove, Ill.: InterVarsity, 2002.

Jones, F. "The Topography of Nineveh." *Journal of the Royal Asiatic Society* 15 (1855): 324–45.

Joyce, P. M. "Individual Responsibility in Ezekiel 18?" Pages 185–96 in *Studia Biblica* (Sixth International Congress on Biblical Studies). Vol. 1. Edited by E. A. Livingstone. Sheffield: Sheffield Academic Press, 1979.

Joyner, Charles W. *Down by the Riverside: A South Carolina Slave Community*. Urbana: University of Illinois Press, 1984.

Just, Arthur A., Jr. *Luke 1:1–9:50.* Concordia Commentary. St. Louis: Concordia, 1996.

Kaiser, Otto. *Isaiah 13–39.* Translated by R. A. Wilson. Philadelphia: Westminster, 1974.

Kaiser, Walter C., Jr. "The Blessing of David: A Charter for Humanity." Pages 298–318 in *The Law and the Prophets: Old Testament Studies Prepared in Honor of Oswald Thompson Allis.* Edited by John H. Skilton, Milton C. Fisher, and Leslie W. Sloat. Nutley, N.J.: Presbyterian and Reformed, 1974.

———. *Toward Old Testament Ethics.* Grand Rapids: Zondervan, 1983.

Kaltner, John, and Steven L. McKenzie, eds. *Beyond Babel: A Handbook for Biblical Hebrew and Related Languages.* Leiden: Brill, 2002.

Kamp, Albert H. *Inner Worlds: A Cognitive Linguistic Approach to the Book of Jonah.* Translated by David Orton. Boston: Brill Academic Publishers, 2004.

Katzenstein, H. Jacob. *The History of Tyre: From the Beginning of the Second Millennium B.C.E. until the Fall of the Neo-Babylonian Empire in 539 B.C.E.* 2d ed. Jerusalem: Goldberg's, 1997.

Kaufmann, Yehezkel. *The Religion of Israel: From Its Beginnings to the Babylonian Exile.* Translated and abridged by Moshe Greenberg. Chicago: University of Chicago Press, 1960.

Kautzsch, Emil. *Biblische Theologie des Alten Testaments.* Tübingen: Mohr (Siebeck), 1911.

Keil, Carl Friedrich. *The First Book of Moses.* Translated by James Martin. In vol. 1 (3 vols. in 1) of Commentary on the Old Testament in Ten Volumes by C. F. Keil and Franz Delitzsch. Repr., Grand Rapids: Eerdmans, 1978.

———. *The Twelve Minor Prophets.* Translated by James Martin. 2 vols. Vol. 10 (2 vols. in 1) of Commentary on the Old Testament in Ten Volumes by C. F. Keil and Franz Delitzsch. Repr., Grand Rapids: Eerdmans, 1978.

Keller, Carl A. "Jonas: Le portrait d'un prophète." *Theologische Zeitschrift* 21 (1965): 329–40.

Kennedy, James Hardee. *Studies in the Book of Jonah.* Nashville: Broadman, 1956.

Kidner, F. Derek. "The Distribution of Divine Names in Jonah." *Tyndale Bulletin* 21 (1970): 126–28.

Klopfenstein, Martin A. *Scham und Schande nach dem Alten Testament.* Zurich: Theologischer, 1972.

Koch, Klaus. "Gibt es ein Vergeltungsdogma im Alten Testament?" *Zeitschrift für Theologie und Kirche* 52 (1955): 1–42. Abridged translation published as "Is There a Doctrine of Retribution in the Old Testament?" Pages 57–87 in *Theodicy in the Old Testament.* Edited by James L. Crenshaw. Philadelphia: Fortress, 1983.

———. *The Prophets.* 2 vols. Philadelphia: Fortress, 1983.

———. "Der Spruch 'Sein Blut bleibe auf seinem Haupt' und die israelitische Auffassung vom vergossenen Blut." *Vetus Testamentum* 12 (1962): 396–416.

Koch, Timothy R. "The Book of Jonah and a Reframing of Israelite Theology: A Reader-Response Approach." Ph.D. diss., Boston University, 2003.

Koestler, Arthur. *The Art of Creation.* New York: Macmillan, 1964.

Kolb, Robert. " 'What Benefit Does the Soul Receive from a Handful of Water?': Luther's Preaching on Baptism, 1528–1539." *Concordia Journal* 25 (1999): 346–63.

Kooij, Arie van der. *The Oracle of Tyre: The Septuagint of Isaiah XXIII as Version and Vision.* Supplements to Vetus Testamentum 71. Leiden: Brill, 1998.

Kugel, James L. *The Idea of Biblical Poetry: Parallelism and Its History.* New Haven, Conn.: Yale University Press, 1981.

LaCocque, André, and Pierre-Emmanuel Lacocque. *Jonah: A Psycho-Religious Approach to the Prophet.* Columbia: University of South Carolina Press, 1990.

LaCugna, Catherine Mowry. *God for Us: The Trinity and Christian Life.* San Francisco: Harper, 1991.

Laetsch, Theodore. *The Minor Prophets.* St. Louis: Concordia, 1956.

Landes, George M. "Creation and Liberation." Pages 138–41 in *Creation in the Old Testament.* Edited by Bernhard W. Anderson. Issues in Religion and Theology 6. Philadelphia: Fortress, 1984.

———. "The Kerygma of the Book of Jonah: The Contextual Interpretation of the Jonah Psalm." *Interpretation* 21 (1967): 3–31.

———. "Linguistic Criteria and the Date of the Book of Jonah." *Eretz-Israel* 16 (1982; Harry M. Orlinsky Volume): 147–70.

———. "The 'Three Days and Three Nights' Motif in Jonah 2:1." *Journal of Biblical Literature* 86 (1967): 446–50.

Lane, William. *The Gospel according to Mark.* Grand Rapids: Eerdmans, 1974.

Lawrence, Paul J. N. "Assyrian Nobles and the Book of Jonah." *Tyndale Bulletin* 37 (1986): 121–32.

Lemaire, André. "Tarshish-*Tarsisi*: Problème de Topographie Historique Biblique et Assyienne." Pages 44–62 in *Studies in Historical Geography and Biblical Historiography: Presented to Zechariah Kallai.* Edited by Gershon Galil and Moshe Weinfeld. Leiden: Brill, 2000.

Lemanski, Jay. "Jonah's Nineveh." *Concordia Journal* 18 (1992): 40–49.

Lessing, R. Reed. *Interpreting Discontinuity: Isaiah's Tyre Oracle.* Winona Lake, Ind.: Eisenbrauns, 2004.

———. "Just Where Was Jonah Going? The Location of Tarshish in the Old Testament." *Concordia Journal* 28 (2002): 291–93.

———. "Orality in the Prophets." *Concordia Journal* 29 (2003): 152–65.

———. "Pastor, Does God Really Respond to My Prayers?" *Concordia Journal* 32 (2006): 256–73.

————. "Preaching Like the Prophets: Using Rhetorical Criticism in the Appropriation of Old Testament Prophetic Literature." *Concordia Journal* 28 (2002): 391–408.

————. "The Redactional Interpretation of Discontinuity in Prophetic Texts: Isaiah 23 as a Test Case." *Concordia Journal* 30 (2004): 294–315.

————. "Satire in Isaiah's Tyre Oracle." *Journal for the Study of the Old Testament* 28 (2003): 89–112.

————. "What Really Happened at Sinai?" *Concordia Journal* 30 (2004): 288–89.

Levenson, Jon D. *Creation and the Persistence of Evil: The Jewish Drama of Divine Omnipotence*. San Francisco: Harper & Row, 1988.

Levin, David. *In Defense of Historical Literature: Essays on American History, Autobiography, Drama, and Fiction*. New York: Hill & Wang, 1967.

Levin, Samuel R. *The Semantics of Metaphor*. Baltimore: Johns Hopkins University Press, 1977.

Levine, Etan. "Jonah as a Philosophical Book." *Zeitschrift für die alttestamentliche Wissenschaft* 96 (1984): 235–45.

Lewis, C. S. *Fern-Seed and Elephants, and Other Essays on Christianity*. Glasgow: Fontana, 1975.

Limburg, James. *Jonah: A Commentary*. Louisville, Ky.: Westminster/John Knox, 1993.

Lindblom, Johannes. "Lot-Casting in the Old Testament." *Vetus Testamentum* 12 (1962): 164–78.

Lockwood, Gregory J. *1 Corinthians*. Concordia Commentary. St. Louis: Concordia, 2000.

Lods, Adolphe. *La Religion d'Israël*. Paris: Hachette, 1939.

Lohfink, Norbert. "Jona ging zur Stadt hinaus (Jon 4, 5)." *Biblische Zeitschrift* 5 (1961): 185–203.

Long, V. Philips. *The Art of Biblical History*. Grand Rapids: Zondervan, 1994.

Loretz, Oswald. "Herkunft und Sinn der Jona-Erzählung." *Biblische Zeitschrift* 5 (1961): 18–29.

Luckenbill, Daniel David. *Ancient Records of Assyria and Babylonia*. 2 vols. Chicago: University of Chicago Press, 1926–1927.

Madhloum, Tariq. "Excavations at Nineveh: A Preliminary Report (1965–1967)." *Sumer* 23 (1967): 76–79 and plates 1–13.

Magness, J. Lee. *Sense and Absence: Structure and Suspension in the Ending of Mark's Gospel*. Atlanta: Scholar's Press, 1986.

Magonet, Jonathan. *Form and Meaning: Studies in the Literary Techniques in the Book of Jonah*. Sheffield: Almond, 1983.

Maier, Walter A., III. "Does God 'Repent' or Change His Mind?" *Concordia Theological Quarterly* 68 (2004): 127–43.

————. "The Healing of Naaman in Missiological Perspective." *Concordia Theological Quarterly* 61 (1997): 177–96.

Marcus, David. *From Balaam to Jonah: Anti-Prophetic Satire in the Hebrew Bible.* Atlanta: Scholars, 1995.

Marlowe, W. Creighton. "Music of Missions: Themes of Cross-Cultural Outreach in the Psalms." *Missiology* 26 (1998): 445–56.

Mather, Judson. "The Comic Art of the Book of Jonah." *Soundings* 65 (1982): 280–91.

Matties, Gordon H. *Ezekiel 18 and the Rhetoric of Moral Discourse.* Atlanta: Scholars, 1990.

McCurley, Foster R. *Ancient Myths and Biblical Faith: Scriptural Transformations.* Fortress: Philadelphia, 1983.

McDaniel, Ferris L. "Mission in the Old Testament." Pages 7–23 in *Mission in the New Testament: An Evangelical Approach.* Edited by William J. Larkin, Jr., and Joel F. Williams. Maryknoll, N.Y.: Orbis, 1998.

McGrath, Alister. "Whatever Happened to Luther?" In "Has God Been Held Hostage by Philosophy? A Forum on Free-Will Theism, a New Paradigm for Understanding God." *Christianity Today* 39/1 (January 9, 1995): 34.

Mendenhall, George E. "The Relation of the Individual to Political Society in Ancient Israel." Pages 89–108 in *Biblical Studies in Memory of H. C. Alleman.* Edited by J. M. Myers, O. Reimherr, and H. N. Bream. Locus Valley, N.Y.: Augustin, 1960.

Meyers, Carol. "The Family in Early Israel." Pages 1–47 in *Families in Ancient Israel.* Louisville, Ky.: Westminster John Knox, 1997.

Meynet, Roland. *Rhetorical Analysis: An Introduction to Biblical Rhetoric.* Sheffield: Sheffield Academic Press, 1998.

Miall, David S., *Metaphor: Problems and Perspectives.* Atlantic Highlands, N.J.: Humanities, 1982.

Miles, John A. "Laughing at the Bible: Jonah as Parody." *Jewish Quarterly Review* 65 (1975): 168–81. Reprinted as 203–15 in *On Humour and the Comic in the Hebrew Bible.* Edited by Yehuda T. Radday and Athalya Brenner. Journal for the Study of the Old Testament: Supplement Series 92. Sheffield: Almond, 1990.

Milik, J. T. "Textes Hébreux et Araméens." Pages 65–205 in vol. 1 of *Les Grottes de Murabbaʿât.* Edited by P.Benoit, J. T. Milik, and R. de Vaux. 2 vols. Discoveries in the Judaean Desert 2. Oxford: Clarendon, 1961.

Miller, Gregory J. "Fighting Like a Christian: The Ottoman Advance and the Development of Luther's Doctrine of Just War." Pages 41–57 in *Caritas et Reformatio: Essays on Church and Society in Honor of Carter Lindberg.* Edited by David M. Whitford. St. Louis: Concordia, 2002.

Miller, Patrick D. *Sin and Judgment in the Prophets: A Stylistic and Theological Analysis.* Society of Biblical Literature Monograph Series 27. Chico, Calif.: Scholars, 1982.

Mitchell, Christopher W. "Job and the Theology of the Cross." *Concordia Journal* 15 (1989): 156–80.

———. *Our Suffering Savior: Exegetical Studies and Sermons for Ash Wednesday through Easter Based on Isaiah 52:13–53:12*. St. Louis: Concordia, 2003.

———. *The Song of Songs*. Concordia Commentary. Saint Louis: Concordia, 2003.

Moberly, R. W. L. "Theology of the Old Testament." Pages 452–78 in *The Face of Old Testament Studies: A Survey of Contemporary Approaches*. Edited by David W. Baker and Bill T. Arnold. Grand Rapids: Baker, 1999.

Morgan, G. Campbell, *The Minor Prophets: The Men and Their Messages*. Westwood, N.J.: Revell, 1960.

Muecke, D. C. *The Compass of Irony*. London: Methuen, 1969.

Muilenburg, James. "The Linguistic and Rhetorical Usages of the Particle כי in the Old Testament." *Hebrew Union College Annual* 32 (1961): 135–60.

Muraoka, T. *Emphatic Words and Structures in Biblical Hebrew*. Jerusalem: Magnes, 1985.

Murphy, Roland E. *The Tree of Life: An Exploration of Biblical Wisdom Literature*. 3d ed. New York: Doubleday, 2002.

Nissinen, Martti, ed. *Prophecy in Its Ancient Near Eastern Context: Mesopotamian, Biblical, and Arabian Perspectives*. Atlanta: Society of Biblical Literature, 2000.

Nixon, Rosemary A. *The Message of Jonah: Presence in the Storm*. Downers Grove, Ill.: InterVarsity, 2003.

Nogalski, James. *Redactional Processes in the Book of the Twelve*. Beihefte zur Zeitschrift für die alttestamentliche Wissenschaft 218. Berlin: de Gruyter, 1993.

Ogden, G. S. "Time, and the Verb היה in O.T. Prose." *Vetus Testamentum* 21 (1971): 451–69.

Old, Hughes Oliphant. *The Shaping of the Reformed Baptismal Rite in the Sixteenth Century*. Grand Rapids: Eerdmans, 1992.

Olmstead, Albert Ten Eyck. *History of Assyria*. New York: Scribner, 1923.

Orlinsky, Harry M. "Nationalism-Universalism and Internationalism in Ancient Israel." Pages 206–36 in *Translating and Understanding the Old Testament: Essays in Honor of Herbert Gordon May*. Edited by Harry Thomas Frank and William L. Reed. Nashville: Abingdon, 1970.

Orth, Michael. "Genre in Jonah: The Effects of Parody in the Book of Jonah." Pages 257–81 in *The Bible in the Light of Cuneiform Literature: Scripture in Context III*. Edited by William W. Hallo, Bruce William Jones, and Gerald L. Mattingly. Lewiston, N.Y.: Mellen, 1990.

Oswalt, John N. *The Book of Isaiah: Chapters 1–39*. Grand Rapids: Eerdmans, 1986.

Otto, Eckart. *Theologische Ethik des Alten Testaments*. Stuttgart: Kohlhammer, 1994.

Pannenberg, Wolfhart. *Basic Questions in Theology: Collected Essays*. Translated by George H. Kehm. Vol. 1. Philadelphia: Fortress, 1970.

Parrot, André. *The Arts of Assyria*. Translated by Stuart Gilbert and James Emmons. New York: Golden Press, 1961.

———. *Nineveh and the Old Testament*. Translated by B. E. Hooke. Studies in Biblical Archaeology 3. London: SCM Press, 1955.

Peckham, Brian. *History and Prophecy: The Development of Late Judean Literary Traditions*. Garden City, N.Y.: Doubleday, 1993.

Pedersen, Johannes. *Israel: Its Life and Culture*. Vol. 1–2 (first vol. of 4 vols. in 2). London: Oxford University Press, 1926.

Peifer, Claude J. "Jonah and Jesus: The Prophetic as Sign." *The Bible Today* 21 (1983): 377–83.

Perkins, Larry. "The Septuagint of Jonah: Aspects of Literary Analysis Applied to Biblical Translation." *Bulletin of the International Organization for Septuagint and Cognate Studies* 20 (1987): 43–53.

Perowne, T. T. *Obadiah and Jonah*. Cambridge: Cambridge University Press, 1905.

Petersen, David L., and Kent Harold Richards. *Interpreting Hebrew Poetry*. Minneapolis: Fortress, 1992.

Pieper, Francis. *Christian Dogmatics*. 4 vols. St. Louis: Concordia, 1950–1957.

Pinnock, Clark H. *Most Moved Mover: A Theology of God's Openness*. Grand Rapids: Baker, 1991.

Pinnock, Clark H., Richard Rice, John Sanders, William Hasker, and David Basinger. *The Openness of God: A Biblical Challenge to the Traditional Understanding of God*. Downers Grove, Ill.: InterVarsity, 1994.

Piper, John. *Let the Nations Be Glad! The Supremacy of God in Missions*. 2d ed. Grand Rapids: Baker, 2003.

Placher, William C. *The Domestication of Transcendence: How Modern Thinking about God Went Wrong*. Louisville, Ky. Westminster John Knox, 1996.

Polzin, Robert. *Samuel and the Deuteronomist: 1 Samuel*. Part 2 of A Literary Study of the Deuteronomic History. San Francisco: Harper & Row, 1989.

Pope, Marvin H. *El in the Ugaritic Texts*. Leiden: Brill, 1955.

Porter, J. R. "The Legal Aspects of the Concept of 'Corporate Personality' in the Old Testament." *Vetus Testamentum* 15 (1965): 361–80.

Preuss, Horst Dietrich. *Old Testament Theology*. Translated by Leo Perdue. 2 vols. Louisville, Ky.: Westminster John Knox, 1995–1996.

Provan, Iain W. "Ideologies, Literary and Critical: Reflections on Recent Writing on the History of Israel." *Journal of Biblical Literature* 114 (1995): 585–606.

Provan, Iain W., V. Philips Long, and Tremper Longman III. *A Biblical History of Israel*. Louisville, Ky. Westminster John Knox, 2003.

Pusey, E. B. "Jonah." Pages 371–427 in vol. 1 of *The Minor Prophets*. 1860. Repr., Grand Rapids: Baker, 1965.

Raabe, Paul R. "Look to the Holy One of Israel, All You Nations: The Oracles about the Nations Still Speak Today." *Concordia Journal* 30 (2004): 336–49.

————. *Obadiah*. Anchor Bible 24D. New York: Doubleday, 1996.

————. "Why Prophetic Oracles against the Nations?" Pages 236–57 in *Fortunate the Eyes That See: Essays in Honor of David Noel Freedman in Celebration of His Seventieth Birthday*. Edited by Astrid B. Beck, Andrew H. Bartelt, Paul R. Raabe, and Chris A. Franke. Grand Rapids: Eerdmans, 1995.

Rad, Gerhard von. "The Form-Critical Problem of the Hexateuch." Pages 1–78 in *The Problem of the Hexateuch and Other Essays*. Translated by E. W. Trueman Dicken. London: Oliver & Boyd, 1966.

————. *God at Work in Israel*. Translated by John H. Marks. Nashville: Abingdon, 1980.

————. *Old Testament Theology*. Translated by D. M. G. Stalker. San Francisco: Harper & Row, 1962, 1965.

————. *Der Prophet Jona*. Nuremberg: Laetare, 1950.

————. "Some Aspects of the Old Testament World-View." Pages 144–65 in *The Problem of the Hexateuch and Other Essays*. Translated by E. W. Trueman Dicken. London: Oliver & Boyd, 1966.

————. "The Theological Problem of the Old Testament Doctrine of Creation." Pages 131–43 in *The Problem of the Hexateuch and Other Essays*. Translated by E. W. Trueman Dicken. London: Oliver & Boyd, 1966.

Radday, Yehuda T., and Athalya Brenner, eds. *On Humour and the Comic in the Hebrew Bible*. Journal for the Study of the Old Testament: Supplement Series 92. Sheffield: Almond, 1990.

Réau, Louis. *Iconographie de la Bible: Ancien Testament*. Vol. 2, part 1, of *Iconographie de l'art chrétien*. Paris: Presses Universitaires de France, 1956.

Rice, Richard. "Divine Foreknowledge and Free-Will Theism." Pages 121–39 in *The Grace of God, the Will of Man: A Case for Arminianism*. Edited by Clark H. Pinnock. Grand Rapids: Academie, 1989.

Richards, I. A. *The Philosophy of Rhetoric*. Oxford: Oxford University Press, 1936.

Ricoeur, Paul. *Hermeneutics and the Human Sciences: Essays on Language, Action, and Interpretation*. Edited, translated, and introduced by John B. Thompson. Cambridge: Cambridge University Press.

Rigney, Ann. "Narrativity and Historical Representation." *Poetics Today* 12 (1991): 591–605.

Roaf, Michael. *Cultural Atlas of Mesopotamia and the Ancient Near East*. New York: Facts on File, 1990.

Roberts, J. J. M. "A Christian Perspective on Prophetic Prediction." *Interpretation* 33 (1979): 240–53.

Robinson, Bernard P. "Jonah's Qiqayon Plant." *Zeitschrift für die alttestamentliche Wissenschaft* 97 (1985): 390–403.

Robinson, H. Wheeler. "The Hebrew Conception of Corporate Personality." Pages 49–62 in *Werden und Wesen des Alten Testaments: Vorträge gehalten auf der*

Internationalen Tagung Alttestamentlicher Forscher zu Göttigen vom 4.–10. September 1935. Edited by Paul Volz, Friedrich Stummer, and Johannes Hempel. Beihefte zur Zeitschrift für die alttestamentliche Wissenschaft 66. Berlin: Töpelmann, 1936. Reprinted as pages 1–20 in *Corporate Personality in Ancient Israel*. Philadelphia: Fortress, 1964.

Robinson, Theodore H. *Die Zwölf kleinen Propheten: Hosea bis Micha*. Tübingen: Mohr (Siebeck), 1938.

Roehrs, Walter R. "Divine Covenants: Their Structure and Function." *Concordia Journal* 14 (1988): 7–27.

Rofé, Alexander. "Classes in the Prophetical Stories: Didactic Legenda and Parable." Pages 143–64 in *Studies on Prophecy: A Collection of Twelve Papers*. Supplements to Vetus Testamentum 26. Leiden: Brill, 1974.

———. *The Prophetical Stories: The Narratives about the Prophets in the Hebrew Bible, Their Literary Types and History*. Jerusalem: Magnes, 1988.

Roser, Timothy. "Can God Be Persuaded? A Discussion of the Immutability of God in Luther's Catechesis on Prayer." Ph.D. diss., Concordia Seminary, 2005.

Roux, Georges. *Ancient Iraq*. Cleveland: World, 1964.

Rowley, H. H. *The Faith of Israel: Aspects of Old Testament Thought*. London: SCM Press, 1956.

———. *The Missionary Message of the Old Testament*. London: Carey Kingsgate, 1955.

Rowley, H. H., ed. *Studies in Old Testament Prophecy*. Edinburgh: T&T Clark, 1950.

Ryken, Leland. *Words of Delight: A Literary Introduction to the Bible*. Grand Rapids: Baker, 1987.

Saebo, Magne. "Yahweh as *Deus absconditus*: Some Remarks on a Dictum by Gerhard von Rad." Pages 43–55 in *Shall Not the Judge of All the Earth Do What Is Right? Studies on the Nature of God in Tribute to James L. Crenshaw*. Edited by David Penchansky and Paul L. Redditt. Winona Lake, Ind.: Eisenbrauns, 2000.

Sakenfeld, Katharine Doob. *The Meaning of Hesed in the Hebrew Bible: A New Inquiry*. Missoula, Mont.: Scholars, 1978.

Salters, Robert. B. *Jonah and Lamentations*. Old Testament Guides. Sheffield: JSOT Press, 1994.

Sanders, John. *The God Who Risks: A Theology of Providence*. Downers Grove, Ill.: InterVarsity, 1998.

Sarna, Nahum M. *Genesis: The Traditional Hebrew Text with the New JPS Translation/Commentary*. JPS Torah Commentary. Philadelphia: Jewish Publication Society, 1989.

Sasson, Jack M. *Jonah*. Anchor Bible 24B. New York: Doubleday, 1990.

———. "On Jonah's Two Missions." *Henoch* 6 (1984): 23–30.

———. *Ruth: A New Translation with a Philological Commentary and a Formalist-Folklorist Interpretation*. Baltimore: Johns Hopkins University Press, 1979.

Schmid, Hans Heinrich. "Creation, Righteousness, and Salvation: 'Creation Theology' as the Broad Horizon of Biblical Theology." Pages 102–17 in *Creation in the Old Testament*. Edited by Bernhard W. Anderson. Philadelphia: Fortress, 1984.

Schoors, A. "The Particle *Ki*." *Oudtestamentische Studiën* 21 (1981): 240–76.

Schultz, Hermann. *Old Testament Theology*. Vol. 2. Translated by J. A. Paterson. Edinburgh: T&T Clark, 1892.

Schultz, Richard L. "The Ties That Bind: Intertextuality, the Identification of Verbal Parallels, and Reading Strategies in the Book of the Twelve." Pages 27–45 in *Thematic Threads in the Book of the Twelve*. Edited by Paul L. Redditt and Aaron Schart. Beihefte zur Zeitschrift für die alttestamentliche Wissenschaft 325. Berlin: de Gruyter, 2003.

Scott, R. B. Y. "The Sign of Jonah: An Interpretation." *Interpretation* 19 (1965): 16–25.

Sebeok, Thomas A. *Style in Language*. Cambridge, Mass.: Technology Press of Massachusetts Institute of Technology, 1960.

Seitz, Christopher R. *Isaiah 1–39*. Interpretation: A Bible Commentary for Teaching and Preaching. Louisville, Ky. John Knox, 1993.

Sherwood, Yvonne. *A Biblical Text and Its Afterlife: The Survival of Jonah in Western Culture*. Cambridge: Cambridge University Press, 2000.

Simon, Uriel. *Jonah: The Traditional Hebrew Text with the New JPS Translation/Commentary*. JPS Bible Commentary. Philadelphia: Jewish Publication Society, 1999.

Simpson, William Kelly, ed. *The Literature of Ancient Egypt: An Anthology of Stories, Instructions, and Poetry*. New Haven, Conn.: Yale University Press, 1972.

Smith, George Adam. *The Book of the Twelve Prophets*. Rev. ed. Vol. 2. New York: Harper & Brothers, 1928.

Smith, James. "The Destruction of Foreign Nations in Hebrew Prophetic Literature." Ph.D. diss., Hebrew Union College—Jewish Institute of Religion, 1969.

Smothers, Thomas G. "A Lawsuit against the Nations: Reflections on the Oracles against the Nations in Jeremiah." *Review and Expositor* 85 (1988): 545–54.

Snaith, Norman H. *Notes on the Hebrew Text of Jonah*. London: Epworth, 1945.

Snyder, Graydon F. *Ante Pacem: Archaeological Evidence of Church Life before Constantine*. Macon, Ga.: Mercer University Press, 1985.

Soskice, Janet Martin. *Metaphor and Religious Language*. Oxford: Clarendon, 1985.

Sternberg, Meir. *Expositional Modes and Temporal Ordering in Fiction*. Baltimore: Johns Hopkins University Press, 1978.

———. *The Poetics of Biblical Narrative: Ideological Literature and the Drama of Reading*. Bloomington: Indiana University Press, 1985.

Stuart, Douglas. *Hosea–Jonah*. Word Bible Commentary 31. Waco, Tex.: Word, 1987.

Swetnam, James. "No Sign of Jonah." *Biblica* 66 (1985): 126–30.

Thomas, D. Winton. "A Consideration of Some Unusual Ways of Expressing the Superlative in Hebrew." *Vetus Testamentum* 3 (1953): 209–24.

Tomback, Richard S. *A Comparative Semitic Lexicon of the Phoenician and Punic Languages*. Missoula: Scholars, 1978.

Tov, Emmanuel. *The Greek Minor Prophets Scroll from Naḥal Ḥever*. Discoveries in the Judaean Desert 8. Oxford: Clarendon, 1990.

Trépanier, Benoit. "The Story of Jonas." *Catholic Biblical Quarterly* 13 (1951): 8–16.

Trible, Phyllis. "Divine Incongruities in the Book of Jonah." Pages 198–208 in *God in the Fray: A Tribute to Walter Brueggemann*. Edited by Tod Linafelt and Timothy K. Beal. Minneapolis: Fortress, 1998.

———. *Rhetorical Criticism: Context, Method, and the Book of Jonah*. Minneapolis: Fortress, 1994.

———. "Studies in the Book of Jonah." Ph.D. diss., Columbia University, 1962. Ann Arbor: University Microfilms, 1963.

Trigg, Jonathan D. *Baptism in the Theology of Martin Luther*. Leiden: Brill, 1994.

Tromp, Nicholas J. *Primitive Conceptions of Death and the Nether World in the Old Testament*. Rome: Pontifical Biblical Institute, 1969.

Tsirkin, J. "The Hebrew Bible and the Origin of Tartessian Power." *Aula orientalis* (1986): 179–85.

Tucker, W. Dennis. *Jonah: A Handbook on the Hebrew Text*. Waco, Tex.: Baylor University Press, 2006.

Van Dyke Parunak, H. "A Semantic Survey of *NHM*." *Biblica* 56 (1975): 512–32.

Voelz, James W. *What Does This Mean? Principles of Biblical Interpretation in the Post-Modern World*. 2d ed. St. Louis: Concordia, 1997.

Walton, John H. "The Object Lesson of Jonah 4:5–7 and the Purpose of the Book of Jonah." *Bulletin for Biblical Research* 2 (1992): 47–57.

Ware, Bruce A. "An Evangelical Reformulation of the Doctrine of the Immutability of God." *Journal of the Evangelical Theological Society* 29 (1986): 431–46.

———. *God's Lesser Glory: The Diminished God of Open Theism*. Wheaton, Ill.: Crossways, 2000.

Watson, Wilfred G. E. *Classical Hebrew Poetry: A Guide to Its Techniques*. Sheffield: JSOT Press, 1984.

Watts, J. D. W. "This Song: Conspicuous Poetry in Hebrew Prose." Pages 345–58 in *Verse in Ancient Near Eastern Prose*. Edited by Johannes C. de Moor and Wilfred G. E. Watson. Alter Orient und Altes Testament 42. Neukirchen-Vluyn: Neukirchener, 1993.

Weisman, Ze'ev. *Political Satire in the Bible*. Atlanta: Scholars, 1998.

Wellhausen, Julius. *Prolegomena to the History of Ancient Israel*. 1878. Repr., New York: Meridian, 1957.

Wendland, Ernst R. *The Discourse Analysis of Hebrew Prophetic Literature: Determining the Larger Textual Units of Hosea and Joel.* Lewiston, N.Y.: Mellen, 1995.

Wenham, Gordon J. *Genesis 1–15.* Word Biblical Commentary 1. Waco, Tex.: Word, 1987.

———. *Story as Torah: Reading the Old Testament Ethically.* Edinburgh: T&T Clark, 2000.

West, Mona. "Irony in the Book of Jonah: Audience Identification with the Hero." *Perspectives in Religious Studies* 11 (1984): 233–42.

Westermann, Claus. "Creation and History in the Old Testament." Pages 11–38 in *The Gospel and Human Destiny.* Edited by Vilmos Vajta. Minneapolis: Augsburg, 1971.

———. *The Praise of God in the Psalms.* Translated by Keith R. Crim. Richmond: John Knox, 1965.

Whiston, William, trans. *The Works of Josephus.* Complete and unabridged in 1 vol. New updated ed. Peabody, Mass.: Hendrickson Publishers, 1987.

Wilch, John R. *Ruth.* Concordia Commentary. Saint Louis: Concordia, 2006.

Wildberger, Hans. *Isaiah 1–12.* Translated by Thomas H. Trapp. Continental Commentaries. Minneapolis: Augsburg Fortress, 1991.

Williamson, H. G. M. "The Origins of Israel: Can We Safely Ignore the Bible?" Pages 141–51 in *The Origin of Early Israel—Current Debate: Biblical, Historical and Archaeological Perspectives.* Edited by Shmuel Ahituv and Eliezer D. Oren. Beer-Sheva 12. Beer-Sheva: Ben-Gurion University of the Negev Press, 1998.

Wilson, Robert Dick. "The Authenticity of Jonah." *Princeton Theological Review* 16 (1918): 280–98, 430–56.

———. "מנה, 'To Appoint,' in the Old Testament." *Princeton Theological Review* 16 (1918): 645–54.

Wiseman, Donald J. "Jonah's Nineveh." *Tyndale Bulletin* 30 (1979): 29–51.

———. "Law and Order in Old Testament Times." *Vox evangelica* 8 (1973): 5–21.

Witherington, Ben. *Jesus the Seer: The Progress of Prophecy.* Peabody, Mass.: Hendrickson, 1999.

Wolde, Ellen J. van. "Texts in Dialogue with Texts: Intertextuality in the Ruth and Tamar Narratives." *Biblical Interpretation* 5 (1997): 1–28.

———. "Trendy Intertextuality?" Pages 43–49 in *Intertextuality in Biblical Writings: Essays in Honour of Bas van Iersel.* Edited by Sipke Draisma. Kampen, The Netherlands: Uitgeversmaatschappij J. H. Kok, 1989.

Wolff, Hans Walter. *Joel and Amos.* Translated by Waldemar Janzen, S. Dean McBride, Jr., and Charles A. Muenchow. Hermeneia. Philadelphia: Fortress, 1977.

———. *Obadiah and Jonah.* Translated by Margaret Kohl. Minneapolis: Augsburg, 1986.

———. *Studien zum Jonabuch*. Biblische Studien 47. Neukirchen-Vluyn: Nuekirchener, 1965.

Woodard, Branson L. "Death in Life: The Book of Jonah and Biblical Tragedy." *Grace Theological Journal* 11 (1990): 3–16.

Woodhouse, John W. "Jesus and Jonah." *Reformed Theological Review* 43 (1984): 33–41.

Wright, Christopher J. H. *An Eye for an Eye: The Place of Old Testament Ethics Today*. Downers Grove, Ill.: InterVarsity, 1983.

Wright, G. Ernest. *God Who Acts: Biblical Theology as Recital*. London: SCM Press, 1952.

Young, Edward J. *My Servants the Prophets*. Grand Rapids: Eerdmans, 1952.

Zimmerli, Walter. *Ezekiel*. Translated by Ronald E. Clements. 2 vols. Philadelphia: Fortress, 1979–1983.

Zlotowitz, Meir. *Yonah/Jonah: A New Translation with a Commentary Anthologized from Talmudic, Midrashic and Rabbinic Sources*. Brooklyn, N.Y.: Mesorah, 1980.

Introduction

Jonah is the best known among the twelve Minor Prophets. Perhaps the chief reason for the narrative's familiarity lies not only with the great fish, but also because it offers a totally different kind of story from that of the other prophetic books. Through the millennia Jonah has captivated its readers—from Jewish midrash to Herman Melville.

Jonah is a book that is so famous that echoes of it abound in literature and the arts, and so people seem to "know" it even if they have never consciously read the Bible.[1] People think of it a double act: Jonah and the whale, Moses and Pharaoh, David and Goliath. Yet a story as familiar as Jonah and the whale is bound to suffer. Some aspects get amplified, others are forgotten, and the narrative gets flattened into a two-dimensional flannel graph. In this way its radical call to repentance, faith, and mission is lost.

Jonah is radical (from the Latin *radix*, "root") for at least two reasons. First, the book deals with core issues such as forgiveness, death, resurrection, mission, and grace. Phyllis Trible describes the presentation of Yahweh in Jonah "as chilling as it is comforting" and suggests that the "sovereignty, freedom, retribution, vindictiveness, violence, repentance, mercy and pity [of God in Jonah] sound the disjunctions … at the core of Israel's God."[2]

Second, the narrative is radical because it shakes so many preconceived ideas about how God operates in our world. Isn't he only interested in the elect? Doesn't he remain in heaven, above all of the toil and turmoil of this world? And aren't there times when he simply gives up on prodigals? These assumptions, and more, are shown to be misguided, if not flat-out wrong.

The book is hardly a theological lightweight. Until recently it played a part in the major liturgical festivals of three religious traditions. Up to the Second Vatican Council, Jonah was read in the Holy Saturday liturgy of the Roman Catholic Church. It still retains this place in the liturgical calendar of the Greek Orthodox Church. In Judaism, Jonah is the haftarah (reading from the Prophets) for Yom Kippur, the Day of Atonement. In forty-eight verses there are thirty-nine references to God. This high frequency of references to the Deity underlines the theological character of the narrative in contrast with some other biblical texts, which make little or no reference to Yahweh.[3]

---

[1] This seems to account for Patricia Hampl's suggestion that Jonah, "unlike its slender prophetic neighbors in the canon, is the story known in the bones, the story you can't remember not knowing, a memory so old it's like an ounce of yourself" ("In the Belly of the Whale," 291).

[2] Trible, "Divine Incongruities in the Book of Jonah," 206, 208.

[3] The Song of Songs has only one reference to Yah(weh) by way of saying that love is the "flame of Yah" (Song 8:6). The book of Esther has no direct references to God, though an allusion may be in Esth 4:14.

The book of Jonah is not what it is popularly thought to be. The narrative is not a fish story. How can the great fish, which is mentioned only in 2:1, 2, 11 (ET 1:17; 2:1, 10), occupy center stage? Neither is Jonah the same kind of prophetic book as Isaiah, Jeremiah, or Ezekiel. It is also obvious that the book of Jonah is quite different from the rest of the Minor Prophets. Instead of a collection of a prophet's pronouncements on various occasions, with perhaps a biographical note now and then, Jonah is an extended narrative about a prophet who delivers only one concise prophecy on one occasion. Aside from the brief prophecy that Nineveh would be changed (3:4), the only other words of Jonah reported are his confession of faith (1:9) and instructions to the sailors (1:12), his psalm in chapter 2, and his peevish complaints to Yahweh in chapter 4.

We can imagine the book of Jonah as perhaps being in the third section of the Hebrew canon, the Writings. As a short narrative about a memorable figure from Israel's history as it concerns other nations, Jonah would have fit well there, next to the books of Ruth and Esther. The other prophetic books contain such phrases as נְאֻם־יהוה ("the utterance of Yahweh") and כֹּה אָמַר יהוה ("thus said Yahweh"), but Jonah lacks these and other standard prophetic vocabulary. In fact, נָבִיא ("prophet") and נָבָא ("to prophesy") are not even used in the book.

Further distance between Jonah and his contemporaries, the eighth-century classical (writing) prophets, is that prophetic stories in the OT often glorify the prophet in the sense that he is revealed as a faithful mediator of Yahweh's Word. But Jonah is no hero; he is portrayed throughout most of the book in a very poor light. Gerhard von Rad puts it this way: "God is here glorified not through his ambassador, but in spite of his ambassador's complete refusal."[4]

The prophet's journey to Nineveh to deliver his message is another extraordinary phenomenon. Prophetic oracles against the nations are common in the OT, but they were normally delivered on the prophet's native soil for the benefit of fellow Israelites.[5] The political missions of Elijah and Elisha to Damascus (1 Ki 19:13–15; 2 Ki 8:7–13) are the nearest parallels, but Jonah's journey still remains of a different nature. Still another contrast with normal prophetic experience is that whereas Moses (e.g., Ex 3:11; 4:1, 10), Elijah (e.g., 1 Ki 19:4), and Jeremiah (e.g., Jer 1:6) shrank from their assignments, Jonah's blunt refusal (Jonah 1:3) goes far beyond their hesitation.

So what kind of a narrative is this? Jonah doesn't seem to have a lot in common with any prophet, much less any other book in the OT. Terence Fretheim writes of Jonah: "It has no exact counterpart in the Old Testament or in known literature from the ancient Near East."[6] The classification of the book

---

[4] Von Rad, *Old Testament Theology*, 2:291.

[5] See, for example, Isaiah 13–23 and Jeremiah 46–51. However, Ezekiel was in Babylon when he delivered his oracles against the nations (Ezekiel 25–32). The message of judgment upon Israel's enemies would comfort Israel. At the same time, it is reasonable to expect that the surrounding nations would hear of the prophecies and would be called to repentance.

[6] Fretheim, *Jonah*, 72.

is elusive. Augustine's response to an inquiry made by a potential Christian convert perhaps gets at this best:

> What he asks about the resurrection of the dead could be settled. ... But, if he thinks to solve all such questions as ... those about Jonas ... he little knows the limitations of human life or of his own.[7]

Adding to Augustine's comments is Father Mapple in Herman Melville's *Moby Dick* who states this about Jonah: "This book, containing only four chapters ... is one of the smallest strands in the mighty cable of the Scriptures. Yet what depths of the soul does Jonah's deep sea-line sound! What a pregnant lesson to us is this prophet!"[8]

In spite of all these differences between Jonah and the other books in the prophetic corpus, he, like other prophets, was sent by Yahweh to speak a divine message. Hence his book is included in the prophetic canon. He is the same "Jonah" mentioned in 2 Ki 14:25, where he is called a "prophet" (נָבִיא).

Jonah is presumably one of "the twelve prophets" mentioned by ben Sirach: "May the bones of the twelve prophets send forth new life from where they lie, for they comforted the people of Jacob and delivered them with the faith of hope" (Sirach 49:10). All the Hebrew and Greek manuscripts of Jonah include it among the Minor Prophets.[9]

Still, numerous questions abound. Were the sailors and Ninevites actually converted to faith in Yahweh, the God of Israel? How does the psalm in chapter 2 fit into the narrative? How could a man stay alive in a large fish for three days and three nights? What kind of plant would grow and wither in a single day (4:6–10)? And why does the book end with a question (4:11)? The answers to these questions, and more, begin with a discussion of the book's genre.

The Genre of Jonah

While it is clear that Jonah, like other prophets, was sent by Yahweh, the God of Israel, to preach a message of repentance, the book of Jonah differs from other prophetic books, so it is not clear how its genre should be classified.[10] That the classification of any book's genre is thoroughly bound up in its interpretation is a given; one simply cannot be separated from the other. Because Jonah has received a great variety of genre labels, there has been tremendous debate concerning the intended meaning and message of the book.[11]

---

[7] Augustine, letter 102 (*St. Augustine: Letters* [trans. Wilfrid Parsons; Fathers of the Church; Washington, D.C.: Catholic University of America Press, 1953], 176).

[8] Herman Melville, *Moby Dick* (1851; repr., Chicago: Encyclopedia Britannica, 1952), 31 (chapter 9).

[9] The order of the twelve Minor Prophets in Hebrew manuscripts is the same as in English Bibles (Obadiah, Jonah, Micah). In the Greek manuscripts of the LXX, Obadiah precedes Jonah and Nahum follows it.

[10] Genre is a series of common literary conventions, encoded into a text by an author, that limits and focuses the author's intended meaning. Strictly speaking, a genre is a choice by the author of the best set of literary conventions by which to convey meaning and intent.

[11] For an overview of the discussion, see Salters, *Jonah and Lamentations*, 41–48.

OT genres include historical narratives, genealogies, legal documents, prophecies, laments, songs, parables, and more. But what kind of genre is Jonah?[12] Numerous generic names have been used to define the book.[13] Among recent writers there has been a strong move away from referring to Jonah as either allegory or midrash. Now the preference is to classify Jonah as didactic fiction.[14] Other scholars label Jonah as a story about a prophet,[15] a parable,[16] a legend,[17] a didactic history,[18] a philosophical treatise,[19] a tragedy,[20] an ironic short story,[21] a novella,[22] a comedy,[23] and a parody.[24] More recently Ehud Ben Zvi states that the book's genre is that of a " 'meta-prophetic' book."[25] But it is uncertain whether those genres were known in the ancient Near East. Those who describe the genre of Jonah with terms like "saga," "fiction," "folklore," and the like are not so much telling us about the actual genre of the narrative as they are expressing their own lack of confidence in the historical reliability of the book. These scholars are making what they consider to be an assessment of the text's historicity and are not seriously dealing with the question of genre.

This commentary will proceed with the understanding that the genre of Jonah is narrative history. Other prophetic books of the OT contain the genre of narrative histories (e.g. Is 7:1–17; chapters 36–39; Amos 7:10–15), yet the book of Jonah, with the exception of its psalm (2:3–10 [ET 2:2–9]) is completely composed in this genre.

The beginning of Jonah gives generic signals that indicate that it is intended to be treated as factual narrative. The first word of the text, וַיְהִי (literally, "And it came to pass," Jonah 1:1), is a genre marker that often is the OT's way of

---

[12] Compare the thorough discussion by Millar Burrows in "The Literary Category of the Book of Jonah."

[13] See Bowers, *The Legend of Jonah.*

[14] For a fuller discussion, see Alexander, "Jonah and Genre."

[15] For example, von Rad calls it "the last and strangest flowering of this old and almost extinct literary form" (*Old Testament Theology*, 2:291).

[16] The most detailed elaboration of Jonah as a parable is that of Rofé, "Classes in the Prophetical Stories: Didactic Legenda and Parable," 153–64.

[17] Jepsen, "Anmerkungen zum Buche Jona," 299.

[18] Alexander, "Jonah and Genre."

[19] Levine, "Jonah as a Philosophical Book," 236.

[20] Woodard, "Death in Life: The Book of Jonah and Biblical Tragedy."

[21] West, "Irony in the Book of Jonah: Audience Identification with the Hero."

[22] Wolff, *Obadiah and Jonah*, 85.

[23] For example, Mather, "The Comic Art of the Book of Jonah." Mather calls Jonah "a rich comic invention" (p. 280) consisting of "the devices of burlesque and parody" (p. 281).

[24] Band, "Swallowing Jonah: The Eclipse of Parody"; Brian Peckham, *History and Prophecy*, 690, and Miles, "Laughing at the Bible: Jonah as Parody."

[25] Ben Zvi, *Signs of Jonah*, 85. Ben Zvi defines a meta-prophetic book as a prophetic book that deals with or is devoted to issues that are of "relevance for the understanding of the messages of other prophetic books." His study discusses how the literati in Judah during the Persian period read the book of Jonah against the background of other writing prophets.

signaling the beginning of a historical account (e.g., Josh 1:1; Judg 1:1; 1 Sam 1:1; Ruth 1:1). The whole phrase that begins Jonah 1:1, וַיְהִי֙ דְּבַר־יְהֹוָ֔ה אֶל־, "And the Word of Yahweh came to ..." begins sections of other historical narratives involving prophets.[26] This suggests that Jonah also begins as a historical narrative involving a prophet, and perhaps as if it is to be connected to the historical narrative of Jonah in 2 Ki 14:25–28. The Hebrew vocabulary for parable, the noun מָשָׁל or the verb מָשַׁל, is not used anywhere in the book.

It has been fashionable in the philosophy of history to argue that narratives involve art, not science, and literature, not facts. Some drive a wedge between literary and historical study, then treat all biblical narratives like Jonah as nothing more than elaborate novels.[27] The general presumption among these scholars is that where the degree of artistic narration is high, the chance is less plausible that the text is an accurate reflection of historical reality. This methodology may be summarized as follows: causal analysis is given priority over description and narration, the general is given priority over the unique.[28] Given this state of affairs, is a divorce between Jonah's narrative style and history inevitable, or is a happy marriage possible, even necessary?

The answer is that narrative history is making a strong comeback in the field of historical studies.[29] After a period of decline during which more statistical, quantifying histories were preferred, narrative history is again considered to be a valid way of conveying the past. Scholars of history are calling into question the idea that narrative literature and history are unrelated or mutually exclusive categories.[30] Modern interpreters of history may dream of escaping from the ordinary or natural language in the biblical text to the highly formal language of the sciences, but the fact of the matter, as Hayden White remarks, is that the modern interpretation of history "as a discipline is in bad shape today because it has lost sight of its origins in the literary imagination."[31]

In an essay published in 1951, Umberto Cassuto put forth the argument that "both Israelite and Greek historiography developed from earlier epic-

---

[26] For example, 1 Ki 16:1; 17:8; Is 38:4; Jer 1:4; Ezek 3:16; cf. Hag 1:3. Commenting on "And the Word of Yahweh came to ..." in Ezek 3:16, Zimmerli, *Ezekiel,* 1:145, states: "There lies in the mention of the coming of Yahweh's word a reference to its eminently historical character and its relation to events." Hummel, *Ezekiel 1–20,* 99, adds: "The advent of the divine Word causes events to take place, as is supremely true in the advent of Jesus Christ, the Word made flesh [Jn 1:14]."

[27] See, for example, Gunn, "New Directions in the Study of Biblical Hebrew Narrative."

[28] Provan, Long, and Longman, *A Biblical History of Israel,* 20, summarize this belief in the words of G. E. Lessing: "Accidental truths of history can never become the proof of necessary truths of reason." See "On the Proof of the Spirit and of Power," *Lessing's Theological Writings* (trans. Henry Chadwick; London: Adam and Charles Black, 1956), 53.

[29] This discussion is dependent upon Provan, Long, and Longman, *A Biblical History of Israel,* 76–97.

[30] As to how this impacts biblical studies, see Provan, "Ideologies, Literary and Critical."

[31] White, "The Historical Text as Literary Artifact," in Canary and Kozicki, *The Writing of History,* 62.

lyrical poems." He further stated his belief that the Israelites, even before the Greeks, were the first historians.[32] Provan, Long, and Longman are hesitant to embrace the specifics of Cassuto's proposal, yet they do believe that the connection he makes between narrative historiography and literature is correct.[33] This calls into question the tendency of some biblical scholars to discount the historical value of biblical narratives, including Jonah, simply because they are story-like in form.[34]

The resurgence of interest in narrative history raises anew the questions of the relationship between history and literature. In fact, literary understanding— far from being tangential to the historical question—is a necessary condition of historical understanding, and both literary and historical understandings are necessary conditions of competent biblical interpretation. Robert Alter's comments are helpful:

> For a reader to attend to these elements of literary art is not merely an exercise in "appreciation" but a discipline of understanding: the literary vehicle is so much the necessary medium through which the Hebrew writers realized their meanings that we will grasp the meanings at best imperfectly if we ignore their fine articulations as literature.[35]

The marriage between literary and historical concerns is desirable and necessary. It is quite possible that a writer faithfully represents the historical data without embellishment while also employing the use of literary conventions. This means that where biblical texts like Jonah make historical truth claims, ahistorical readings are perforce misreadings. To stress the artistic characteristics of Jonah (like its irony, satire, structure, key words, etc.) is not out of step with what historians in general do when interpreting texts that convey real history. Indeed, historical scholars realize that their genre has to include some amount of rhetoric. For example David Levin observes: "One of the first contributions that the critic of history can make is to serve as an intelligent reader who is willing to understand and discuss the rhetoric in which history is written."[36]

Perhaps an analogy of an artistic portrait best summarizes this commentary's understanding of how Jonah fits within the genre of a historical narrative. A portrait is *both* art and history, that is, it is an artistic creation serving a referential end. On the one hand, in appreciating a portrait, we may admire its artistry, the consummate brushwork, the well-conceived composition, the

---

[32] Provan, Long, and Longman, *A Biblical History of Israel*, 81, summarizing Cassuto, "The Beginning of Historiography among the Israelites."

[33] Provan, Long, and Longman, *A Biblical History of Israel*, 81. For a more thorough discussion of the relationship of history and literature, see Long, *The Art of Biblical History*, 149–54.

[34] See, for example, Williamson, "The Origins of Israel: Can We Safely Ignore the Bible?"

[35] Alter, "Introduction to the Old Testament," 21.

[36] Levin, *In Defense of Historical Literature*, 23.

judicious selection of detail. However, we would miss the main point if we would fail to recognize that all of this artistry is marshaled to serve a historical purpose—to capture a true and telling likeness of historical events. This failure is comparable to ahistorical approaches to Jonah that are encountered in biblical studies today.[37] They are in awe of the narrator's gift of literary art, but see it as serving no historical purpose.

We would also miss the point if we were to approach a portrait fully aware of its referential, historical intent but with little understanding of the artistic medium in which it is rendered. The danger is that lack of awareness of *how* the medium communicates may lead to misunderstandings of just *what* the medium communicates. This failure is comparable to some studies on Jonah that seek to mine the text for historical information but don't approach it with sufficient literary sensitivity.

The narrative of Jonah is a portrait of a prophet and events in which he participated. When viewing a portrait painting, we instinctively look for selectivity of detail, simplification, coloration, patterned composition, some freedom in arrangement, and so forth—and we do not assume that these features detract from the historical likeness. Indeed, in the hands of an accomplished artist, the referential intent of the piece is furthered by the artistic techniques. Good portraits focus on basic contours and essential features with just enough suggestive detail to prompt the viewer's mind to fill in the rest.[38]

This, then, is this commentary's approach to the book of Jonah. Just as the best way to "read" a portrait and to grasp its significance is to combine historical interest with competent appreciation of the artistic medium employed, so the best way to read Jonah is to combine historical interest with a competent appreciation of the literary medium employed by the inspired author. In short, the better our understanding is of the artistic workings of Jonah, the better will be our grasp of the historical subjects it depicts.

This commentary will proceed, then, disagreeing, along with David Levin, with the common "assumption that a natural law decrees hostility between good literature and serious history, between literary effects and factual accuracy."[39] While acknowledging, for example, the schematic, patterned behavior of the sailors and the Ninevites, the commentary will not set these literary characteristics in opposition to the historical import of the picture painted. The genre of Jonah, then, is narrative history, but it is history nonetheless. The adjective *narrative* does not undermine the noun *history*.

---

[37] Some advocates of such literary approaches refrain from discussing the historical dimension of the texts they study. Indeed, some are very careful to distinguish their work from that of historical reconstruction (see Sternberg, *The Poetics of Biblical Narrative*, 24–26).

[38] See Long, *The Art of Biblical History*, 71–73.

[39] Levin, *In Defense of Historical Literature*, 3, who goes on to say that "this assumption inhibits many literary critics as well as historians."

Jonah: Fact or Fiction?

To interpret the genre of Jonah as narrative history—with equal emphasis on its narrative art *and* historical accuracy—brings us directly into the eye of the tornado in Jonah studies that can be described in a five-word question. Is Jonah fact or fiction?

The tendency to view Jonah as fictional is a relatively recent development. By way of contrast, the vast majority of early Jewish and Christian writers believed that the events recorded in the narrative actually occurred. Among Jewish writers, Josephus clearly views the book of Jonah as historical and incorporates the story into his history of the Jewish people. He writes: "But, since I have promised to give an exact account of our history, I have thought it necessary to recount what I have found written in the Hebrew books concerning this prophet [i.e., Jonah]."[40] R. H. Bowers writes about how the early church interpreted Jonah:

> The written documents, then, of the first five centuries of Christianity, provide consistent recording of the apologetic use of the Jonah legend [sic] as a proof-text for eschatological assertion, in which Judaic typology based on the concrete reality of historical events, rather than Greek allegory based on abstractions, is most evident.[41]

For over two thousand years, most Christians and Jews have viewed the book of Jonah as a historical narrative—as fact. Such unanimity of tradition cannot be easily dismissed. Yet there has emerged, in more recent centuries, a perspective that views the narrative more like one of Christ's parables. This debate has made the book of Jonah one of the most visible outposts along the liberal-conservative battle line. Theological conservatives defend the historicity of the book, while liberals have aimed much of their arsenal of ridicule toward "fundamentalist literalism" at the traditional position on Jonah.

From the liberal side of the spectrum is this typical comment by John Holbert: "To ask the historical question of Jonah is to ask the wrong question."[42] Indeed, for many the book of Jonah is "just another fish story." Skepticism is not confined to the account of the "great fish" (2:1 [ET 1:17]). Other historical questions are raised with incredulity: Why is the king of Nineveh not given any name? How could a great city—along with its animals—repent so quickly after just a five-word sermon (3:4b)? And why is there no record of such a massive conversion in the Assyrian annals?

Late nineteenth- and early twentieth-century scholars who questioned the authenticity of the book tended to interpret Jonah as an allegorical piece of fiction. One such interpretation holds that Jonah represents Israel, which, after the

---

[40] Josephus, *Antiquities*, 9.208 (9.10.2; trans. R. Marcus; LCL [Cambridge, Mass.: Harvard University Press, 1937], 109, 111); see 9.206–14 (9.10.1–2).

[41] Bowers, *The Legend of Jonah*, 31–32; see his survey of early church treatments of Jonah on pages 20–32.

[42] Holbert, "Deliverance Belongs to Yahweh! Satire in the Book of Jonah," 59.

preexilic storms of international stress, was swallowed by Babylon (the fish), then was released to go reluctantly to the nations with the proclamation of the universal God.[43] On the whole, this effort at allegorical interpretation has been abandoned, for some pieces of the story will not fit into any allegorical mold. More recently, some prefer to call the book a parable,[44] using the word more or less loosely to mean a story with a didactic point.[45]

When some assert that Jonah is fictional—whether they view it as an allegory, a parable, or a fable—they have been influenced by the principle of analogy articulated by Ernst Troeltsch.[46] Troeltsch's argument was that the distinguishing mark of reality is harmony with the normal, customary, or frequently attested events and conditions as people experience them. People are to view the records of the past in terms of their experience of the present and arrive at judgments on what is historical by reflecting on their "normal experience." This principle of analogy has been a central reason why many people reject the historicity of Jonah: it is certainly not a "normal human experience" to be swallowed by a great fish, vomited up onto dry land after spending three days and three nights in the belly of that same fish, witness an instantaneous conversion of a huge pagan city (along with its animals), and see a big plant come and go in a day!

However, even if we are somehow able to ascertain what events are "customary" or "frequently attested," why should we think that a claim is untrue simply because it does not conform to our "common human experience"? For example, using this criterion, we would not believe as "real history" that Hannibal crossed the Alps with his elephants or that a man landed on the moon! These events have no analogy in our common human experience. Obviously, if Troeltsch's argument is consistently applied to the study of the past, it would lead to absurdities, for we would be required by his tenets to reject otherwise compelling testimony about unusual or unique events.

---

[43] See, for example, Smith, *The Book of the Twelve Prophets*, 2:523–28.

[44] See, for example, Allen who attributes the genre of parable to the entire book (*Joel, Obadiah, Jonah and Micah*, 177).

[45] For example, Childs, "Jonah: A Study in Old Testament Hermeneutics," 54. Among the arguments given by Childs are the following: The historical references within the book not only are without verification, but according to the analogy of historical science their occurrence is extremely improbable. There is no historical evidence that Nineveh ever repented. Moreover, the references to the size of the city (3:3) and the title of its king (3:6) merely reflect popular folklore. Finally, the story of a man being swallowed by a fish, living three days in its belly, and being spewed out safely on dry land sounds like an adaptation of a popular myth found in Greek literature. (The Greek myth of someone almost being swallowed by a big fish is that of Perseus and Andromeda.)

[46] Ernst Troeltsch, "Über historische und dogmatische Methode in der Theologie," in *Gesammelte Schriften* (Tübingen: Mohr, 1913), 2:729–53.

This discussion of Troeltsch's analogy follows, to a large extent, the summary and analysis put forth in, Provan, Long, and Longman, *A Biblical History of Israel*, 70–73. See their discussion for how this analogy relates to the history of Israel. For a trenchant critique of Troeltsch, see Pannenberg, *Basic Questions in Theology*, 1:39–50.

The fact of the matter is that it is impossible to define what "common human experience" is, and even if we could define it, why should it be accepted as the touchstone of historical reality? Appeal to "common human experience" is in truth nothing other that a rhetorical device of great use to those who favor a "scientific" (naturalistic) view of the universe, in which God never intervenes—a device whose deployment is intended to obscure that it is the evaluator's interpretation of his own *individual* experience (an interpretation perhaps shared by other people who have the same worldview as the historian). C. S. Lewis writes:

> The canon, "If miraculous, unhistorical," is one they [historical-critical scholars] bring to their study of the texts. … But if one is speaking of authority, the united authority of all the Biblical critics in the world counts here for nothing. On this they speak simply as men; men obviously influenced by, and perhaps insufficiently critical of, the spirit of the age they grew up in.[47]

The principle of analogy in fact never operates in a vacuum. It relies on the critic's subjective interpretation of his own historical context. There is always "an intimate relation between analogy and its context or network of background beliefs."[48] Therefore, no good reason exists to believe that just because one testimony does not violate our sense of what is normal and possible, it is more likely to be true than another. Neither is there any reason to believe that an account that describes the unusual or the unique is for that reason to be suspected of unreliability. And so history—and in this case, the historicity of Jonah—cannot be based on predictability. It is better to base it upon testimony.[49]

Three representative testimonies provide a sampling of how we can interpret the historical claims in the Jonah narrative. The first ancient testimony witnessing to the validity of the events recorded in Jonah, particularly the mass conversion of the Ninevites, is the fact that from 772 to 745 BC, the reigns of the Assyrian kings Assur-dan III and Assur-nirari V were times of great political instability brought about by natural or political crises or both. This means that general anarchy prevailed in the empire and that Nineveh was a city with its own autonomy. As a semi-independent city-state there could be a "decree of the king and his nobles" (Jonah 3:7).[50] Moreover, a natural[51] or political

---

[47] Lewis, *Fern-Seed and Elephants*, 113.

[48] Abraham, *Divine Revelation and the Limits of Historical Criticism*, 105.

[49] For a full discussion on the role testimony plays in relating the events of the past, see Provan, Long, and Longman, *A Biblical History of Israel*, 36–50.

[50] Lawrence, "Assyrian Nobles and the Book of Jonah," builds an argument for a mid-eighth-century framework for Jonah by demonstrating that during that time Assyria was dominated by three named regional governors. That explains both the weakness of the Assyrian monarchy and the mention of nobles in Jonah 3:7.

[51] Wiseman, "Jonah's Nineveh," 47–50, offers a choice of natural disasters (eclipse, earthquake, or famine) that may have coincided with Jonah's visit to Nineveh and precipitated widespread religious fervor. Wiseman adduces an Assyrian rite of royal substitution after an eclipse (the *sar puhi* ritual) to explain why the king of Nineveh remains unnamed in Jonah.

crisis may have served as the circumstance that rendered the Ninevites open to Jonah's pronouncement that "in forty days" the city "would be changed" (3:4). Jay Lemanski uses the Assyrian Eponym Chronicle to demonstrate that the mid-eighth century BC was one of Assyrian weakness and therefore vulnerability and openness to repentance.[52] As Theodore Laetsch writes: "Nineveh's conversion at Jonah's preaching in a time of threatening national ruin is therefore—aside from God's grace—quite reasonable also from a purely psychological point of view."[53]

A second testimony supports the size of the city as described in Jonah 3:3: "Nineveh was a great city belonging to God, a walk of three days."[54] Some have criticized that description, especially its implication that it took three days to traverse the city, as inaccurate for Nineveh in the eighth century BC. Again, ancient testimonies confirm that the narrator of Jonah is correct in his description of Nineveh (see "A Walk of Three Days" in the commentary on 3:3b). For example, one way of discussing the three-day journey of Jonah 3:3 is by understanding this description to be a reference to the so-called "Greater Nineveh" or "Assyrian Triangle." This interpretation posits that "Nineveh" in the narrative of Jonah is meant to include the area surrounding the city, including the places listed in Gen 10:11–12.[55] An area this large would warrant a three-day journey. In this way "Nineveh, the great city" (1:2; 3:2; 4:11) may mean something like "the Nineveh district."[56] A different way to interpret the three-day journey, while also relying on ancient testimony, is to follow work of Wiseman, who interprets the three days to denote a diplomatic process: a day for arrival, a day for the visit, and a day for departure.[57]

The third and most definitive testimony to the historical accuracy of Jonah rests upon the witness in the NT of our Lord and Savior. Jesus declares that he is "one greater than Jonah" (Mt 12:41; Lk 11:32). Jesus prefaces his connection to Jonah with this comparison: "Just as Jonah was three days and three nights in the belly of the great fish, so will the Son of Man be three days and three nights in the heart of the earth" (Mt 12:40). The comparison assumes that Jonah's experience was actual history and that Christ's own resurrection on the third day is just as certainly a historical fact; it is "the sign of Jonah" (Mt 12:39).

---

[52] Lemanski, "Jonah's Nineveh."

[53] Laetsch, *The Minor Prophets*, 215–16.

[54] There is no doubt that the first part of the clause (וְנִינְוֵה הָיְתָה עִיר־גְּדוֹלָה לֵאלֹהִים) states that "Nineveh" was "large" or "great." However, there are at least four different ways to understand לֵאלֹהִים (literally, "to God"). First, this commentary takes the לְ as denoting possession, meaning "a great city *belonging to God*." Second, לֵאלֹהִים could function as a superlative, meaning that Nineveh was the most important city. Third, the phrase could indicate Nineveh's importance to God. Fourth, if the noun אֱלֹהִים is taken as a true plural ("gods"), the phrase could mean that many "gods" were worshiped in the city. See further the textual note and commentary on 3:3.

[55] Proponents of this interpretation are listed in Bewer, *Jonah*, 52.

[56] Helpful is Hart-Davies, "The Book of Jonah in the Light of Assyrian Archaeology."

[57] Wiseman, "Jonah's Nineveh," 38.

Moreover, Jesus warns, "The men of Nineveh will rise at the judgment with this generation and they will condemn it, for they repented at the preaching of Jonah" (Mt 12:41; Lk 11:32). In this saying too, Jesus assumes that the characters and events in the book of Jonah are real and historical. He contrasts the Ninevites' repentance with the unbelief of the present generation. Moreover, "this generation" of unbelievers shall be condemned on the Last Day by the converted Ninevites, who shall participate in the resurrection to eternal life.

The interpretive hermeneutic used by Jesus in Mt 12:39–41 and Lk 11:29–32 is typological. Biblical typology always presupposes the historicity of the type. Typology is never mere analogy or illustration, but involves an inner historical and salvific continuity between the promise and the fulfillment.[58] Horace Hummel explains this about the witness of Jesus:

> For those who demur that Jesus was only arguing analogically (for which any parable or other tale would serve as well as historical fact), the clinching refutation would appear to be Jesus' reference to the "men of Nineveh." He obviously regards them not only as historical figures, but as still available to "arise at the judgment with this generation and condemn it" [Mt 12:41; Lk 11:32].[59]

Laetsch's arguments for the historicity of Jonah also build upon the testimony of Jesus. Based upon Mt 12:39–42, he makes the following points:

1. There is no indication that Jesus is referring to a parable or quoting from a legend or that the Pharisees regarded the story of Jonah as an allegory or a myth.
2. There is no indication that Jesus or his opponents regarded Jonah or the repenting of the Ninevites as less historical than Solomon or the queen of the south.
3. If Jonah's sojourn in the belly of the fish was non-historical, then according to Christ's own logic his authenticating sign would be based upon a non-factual event.[60]

Laetsch continues:

> As Jesus lay in the grave three days, as Jesus rose again, as these are historical facts, so is the three-day captivity of Jonah in the fish's belly and his deliverance not a legendary story, a mere parable, but irrefutable fact, historical truth. Else Christ would never have regarded it as a sign and prophecy of His own burial and resurrection after three days.[61]

Luther is just as robust in defending the historicity of Jonah as a pure miracle:

> But this story of the prophet Jonah is so great that it is almost unbelievable, yes it even sounds like a lie, and more full of nonsense than any poet's fable. If it were not in the Bible, I'd consider it a silly lie. Because if one thinks about it, Jonah was three days in the huge belly of the whale, where he could

58 See Davidson, *Typology in Scripture*, 416–24.

59 Hummel, *The Word Becoming Flesh*, 325.

60 Laetsch, *The Minor Prophets*, 218.

61 Laetsch, *The Minor Prophets*, 218.

have been digested in three hours and changed into the flesh and blood of the whale. He could have died there a hundred times, under the earth, in the sea, inside the whale. Isn't that living in the midst of death? In comparison with this miracle, the wonder at the Red Sea was nothing.[62]

There are no valid reasons to reject the inspired testimony of the OT and NT, nor the corroborating support of Assyrian history and the ancient traditional Jewish and Christian interpretation, all of which support the historical framework in the Jonah narrative. Tradition has identified the Jonah of the narrative with "Jonah the son of Amittai, the prophet who was from Gath-hepher" (2 Ki 14:25), who foretold to Jeroboam II the reestablishment of Israel's ancient boundaries.[63] The narrative of Jonah is not some kind of "biblical Pinocchio" that should be classified as a legend, a tale, or a fable. It is a historical narrative couched with satire and irony.[64] It is not fiction, but fact.[65]

The Date of Writing

The time of the events in the narrative can be readily dated to the middle of the eighth century BC. The time of the narrative's composition is fraught with more questions. However, the dating of the narrative of Jonah is not a driving factor in the interpretation of its historicity. It is an unrealistic and unproductive enterprise to argue for a specific time that Jonah was written. Sasson writes:

> Because, however, Jonah is not a writing prophet but rather one about whom narratives are recorded, the dating of his book is not a test for religious or theological orthodoxy in the same way as is his survival in the fish's belly. Therefore, traditionalists can be free to decide whether Jonah himself or a later admirer wrote the book bearing his name, even when they do not question the historical accuracy of the activities reported in that book.[66]

The limit for the earliest date of the book is set by the identity of "Jonah ben Amittai" (Jonah 1:1) with the prophet of the same name from Gath-hepher, who according to 2 Ki 14:25 prophesied to Jeroboam II (ca. 786–746 BC) that his kingdom would be extended to Davidic size. Jonah cannot have been written any later than the third century BC, as it is mentioned in Ben Sirach (49:10) and possibly cited in Tobit (14:4, 8).

Given the great variety of linguistic interpretations of the Hebrew used in Jonah, it is not surprising that estimated dates for the narrative's writing range

---

[62] WA TR 3.551 (§ 3705), translated by and quoted in Limburg, *Jonah*, 120–21.

[63] "The threefold identity, that of the prophet's name, that of the father's name, that of office, make the identity of the Jonah who fled before the Lord and later went to Nineveh and the Jonah of 2 Kings 14:25 practically certain" (Laetsch, *The Minor Prophets*, 215). This is also the view taken by Luther (AE 19:3–4).

[64] Cf. Alexander, "Jonah and Genre."

[65] The following also argue for the historicity of the book: Stuart, *Hosea–Jonah*, 440–42; Alexander, *Jonah*, 74–77; Trépanier, "The Story of Jonas."

[66] Sasson, *Jonah*, 20.

over a span of six centuries.[67] Most date the writing of the narrative in the late fifth or early fourth century BC based on the book's implication that Yahweh, the God of Israel, is the universal God over all peoples. These scholars claim that this universal implication "best accords with a postexilic date and may be understood as a protest against a xenophobic mood in the somewhat self-righteous reforming zeal of those years."[68] This view understands postexilic Israel as being nationalistic and particularistic, while also experiencing crisis over unfulfilled prophecies.[69]

Several criticisms have been raised against this view. The primary observation is that there is no substantial historical evidence (apart from a highly irregular reading of Ezra-Nehemiah, which overemphasizes putative ethnic conflicts) to substantiate any Israelite particularism in the postexilic era.[70] Second, the reference to Jonah in 2 Ki 14:25 does not portray him as a zealous Israelite nationalist, contrary to the claim of commentators who consider the book to be an anti-exclusivist protest. Third, this picture of Jonah/Israel as bitter, narrow, and petty after the events of 587 BC has resulted from an overemphasis on and misinterpretation of Jonah's anger in chapter 4. Even though more recent works eschew this interpretation, the view of Jonah as a corrective against a hypothetical Israelite provincialism is still put forward, albeit in more abstract terms.[71]

When trying to adduce a date for the narrative, many nineteenth- and early-twentieth-century scholars judged certain words and terminology to be typical of Late Biblical Hebrew and/or due to Aramaic influence.[72] In many respects this linguistic debate about so-called late Hebrew features and Aramaisms in Jonah is indicative of the problems that beset OT exegesis as a whole when faced with the issue of the history of the Hebrew language. The OT itself comprises almost the entire corpus of Classical Hebrew; there are few other ancient

---

[67] Stuart has the oldest date at about 760 (*Hosea–Jonah*, xliii), while Haupt, "Jonah's Whale," 159, gives the latest date of about 100 BC. Sasson opts not to assign a firm date, although he leans toward its final composition in the postexilic period (*Jonah*, 26–28).

[68] So Good, *Irony in the Old Testament*, 39.

[69] Typical is Good, who speaks of the "arrogant isolationism" of Israel which would have permeated this period (*Irony in the Old Testament*, 53–54). Similar is Fretheim, *Jonah*, 29–38. Wolff places Jonah in the early Hellenistic period (*Obadiah and Jonah*, 76–78), as does Nogalski (*Redactional Processes in the Book of the Twelve*, 272). For a useful survey of older interpretations of the book, see Bickerman, "Les deux erreurs du prophète Jonas," or Bickerman, *Four Strange Books of the Bible*, 14–19.

[70] So von Rad, *Old Testament Theology*, 2:292, and Sasson, *Jonah*, 26, including n. 25.

[71] Evidence that this interpretation is enduring is Allen's commentary, which sees Jonah's target as a nameless "community embittered by its legacy of national suffering and foreign opposition" (*Joel, Obadiah, Jonah and Micah*, 188–91; the quote is on p. 191).

[72] An early example is Driver, who lists seven Aramaisms (*An Introduction to the Literature of the Old Testament*, 322). More recent articulations of this argument are Rofé (*The Prophetical Stories*, 152–57) and Brenner, who sees in the language of Jonah indications of the transition from Classical to Late Biblical Hebrew, a transition that occurred during the exile ("The Language of Jonah as an Index of Its Date").

texts written in the OT era in Hebrew or closely related languages (e.g., Moabite, Phoenician, Aramaic). Therefore, there are few external criteria by which to date biblical texts, and it becomes almost impossible to date changes in the language or to determine why given changes occurred, for example, whether or not they were caused by Aramaic influence. Often a Hebrew feature that is for one scholar a certain indication of a later linguistic phenomenon is for another scholar proof of great antiquity.

Words in Jonah that allegedly fall into the category of Late Biblical Hebrew or so-called Aramaisms include the following.[73] The nouns are מַלָּח, "sailor" (1:5); סְפִינָה, "ship" (1:5); קְרִיאָה, "message" (3:2); טַעַם, "decree" (3:7); and רִבּוֹ, "ten thousand, myriad" (4:11). The verbs are עָשַׁת, (in Hithpael) "to think" (1:6); שָׁתַק, "to calm down" (1:11); מָנָה, (in Piel) "to appoint, provide" (2:1; 4:6, 7, 8); קָדַם, (in Piel) "to plan, anticipate" (4:2); and עָמַל, "to labor over, raise" (4:10). The following Classical Hebrew vocabulary is used with unusual (allegedly late or Aramaic) syntax or meaning: חָשַׁב, (in Piel) "to consider, think" (1:4), with an inanimate subject, in this case, the ship; the verb חָתַר ("to dig") when applied to rowing (1:13); מִזַּעְפּוֹ (1:15) meaning "rage, anger," whether it is the noun זַעַף or the Qal infinitive construct of זָעַף; the phrase וַיֵּרַע אֶל ("was evil to," 4:1); and חוּס עַל, "to have pity upon" with an inanimate object, the qiqayon plant (4:10). One expression is אֱלֹהֵי הַשָּׁמַיִם ("the God of the heavens," 1:9). Particles include the relative pronoun שֶׁ in 1:7, 12; 4:10 and the compound prepositions in which it is embedded (בְּשֶׁלְּמִי, 1:7, and בְּשֶׁלִּי, 1:12). Finally, the book frequently uses אֶל ("to") and עַל ("upon") with no discernable difference.

This cumulative evidence has led many to conclude Jonah is a postexilic document. However, the noun מַלָּח ("sailor," 1:5) is not Aramaic at all, but more probably Phoenician. Ezek 27:9 uses מַלָּח in his oracle against the Phoenician island fortress of Tyre. Most now believe that the relative pronoun שֶׁ did not necessarily replace אֲשֶׁר at a late date; rather, it emanates from the Northern Kingdom.[74] That רִבּוֹ, "ten thousand, myriad" (4:11), is Aramaic and allegedly therefore late is ruled out in light of its use in Ps 68:18 (ET 68:17) and Hos 8:12, both considered to be preexilic texts.

Even if all or most of the above forms are Aramaic (a position few would hold today), they do not prove the postexilic authorship of the book. As early as Hezekiah's reign in the eighth century BC, Aramaic was the language of diplomats, and even the political and military rulers of Judah understood Aramaic (2 Ki 18:26; Is 36:11). In the Northern Kingdom, the native land of Jonah, the early presence of Aramaic forms and expressions is readily explained by the close proximity of Syria and Phoenicia, and particularly by the thirty years

---

[73] See Allen, *Joel, Obadiah, Jonah and Micah*, 187, and Laetsch, *The Minor Prophets*, 219–20. Laetsch provides an initial rationale for understanding these features as compatible with an early, eighth-century-BC date for the book.

[74] Cf. Goitein, "The Song of Songs," 64.

of Syrian domination before the rule of Jeroboam II (2 Kings 13). This oppression, along with the years of warfare for the deliverance of Israel (2 Ki 13:25; 14:23–28), influenced not only the political, military, and business language with Aramaisms, but affected also the literary and religious language of the Northern Kingdom. It is Oswald Loretz who pioneered this idea that the Aramaisms in Jonah may in fact reflect Canaanite-Phoenician influence and therefore do not indicate a postexilic date.[75]

Therefore, the argument about the presence of Aramaisms may be turned on its head: some words actually make a strong argument for identifying the narrator of the book with the Jonah of 2 Ki 14:25 and dating it early, during the reign of Jeroboam II. Other recent evidence from the Ugaritic language demonstrates that many such "Aramaisms" were even older than Israel; indeed, they are increasingly understood as "Northwest Semitisms." Leslie Allen confirms that comparative material demonstrates that many of the alleged Aramaisms in Jonah, on which earlier critical conclusions were based, are in fact common to Northwest Semitic.[76] Likewise, Karin Almbladh deems foreign elements poor indicators of date and instead analyzes Jonah on the basis of its Hebrew constructions alone.[77]

George Landes evaluates the linguistic debate in Jonah and concludes that linguistics does not offer a sure guide for deciding when the narrative was composed. In fact, he demonstrates that in many cases the narrator writes good preexilic Hebrew.[78] Sasson seconds this analysis and says: "Hebrew and Aramaic had the potential to influence each other's *vocabulary* at practically all periods of the Hebrew kingdoms (tenth to sixth centuries B.C.E.)."[79] Elsewhere Sasson declares: "Thus, it is our opinion that, despite an enormous literature on the subject, dating a Hebrew text on literary and linguistic bases will continue to be a most unreliable approach as long as our extrabiblical corpus of Hebrew vocabulary remains as sparse as it is presently."[80] Indeed, the complete lack of Persian or Greek loan words in Jonah, together with the paucity of character-

---

[75] Loretz, "Herkunft und Sinn der Jona-Erzählung." According to Loretz, the so-called "Aramaisms" in Jonah found their way into the book via Phoenician rather than through Aramaic.

[76] Allen, *Joel, Obadiah, Jonah and Micah*, 186, quoting A. M. Honeyman, "Semitic Epigraphy and Hebrew Philology," in *The Old Testament and Modern Study: A Generation of Discovery and Research* (ed. H. H. Rowley; Oxford: Clarendon, 1951), 278. Allen notes that "A. Hurvitz has laid down careful guidelines for assessing linguistic peculiarities that have often been regarded as late Aramaisms" (see Hurvitz, "The Chronological Significance of 'Aramaisms' in Biblical Hebrew").

[77] Almbladh, *Studies in the Book of Jonah*, 44–46.

[78] Landes, "Linguistic Criteria and the Date of the Book of Jonah." This is by far the fullest and most detailed study on the dating of the language of Jonah. Landes considers not only the supposed Aramaisms, but also other dateable linguistic features. He concludes that with the possible exception of יִתְעַשֵּׁת in 1:6, not one word belongs exclusively to the postexilic age.

[79] Sasson, *Jonah*, 204.

[80] Sasson, *Ruth*, 244.

istics distinctive of Late Biblical Hebrew, suggests that the critical dating of Jonah at the time of Ezra and Nehemiah or later is in error. It is quite unlikely that the narrator wrote in the postexilic period and deliberately archaized the language of his story to bring it into conformity with its obvious preexilic setting.

To conclude, the analysis of the linguistic evidence indicates that there are few reasons for maintaining a late date for the narrative's composition. It is conceivable that Jonah could have been composed in the eighth century BC, especially if a narrator from the Northern Kingdom is envisaged, perhaps even Jonah himself from Gath-hepher.[81]

Another issue in the dating of the narrative is the perfect verb הָיְתָה ("Nineveh *was* a great city") in 3:3. Some take this to imply that the narrator of Jonah had to be someone living after 612 BC, *after* Nineveh fell to the Babylonians. G. S. Ogden attempts to prove that the use of הָיָה in the Qal perfect always carries a strict sense of past or completed action. He holds that a stative or continuing sense in the Qal (which could mean "Nineveh has been and still is a great city") is observable only in its use in direct speech.[82]

However, Ogden's understanding is not correct because the verb הָיָה may indicate a state that still continues in the speaker's time (cf. Ex 2:22).[83] Moreover, if prior time is an essential component in a circumstantial clause, Hebrew frequently adds a word or phrase such as לְפָנִים, "previously," or בָּעֵת הַהִיא, "at that time," but there is no such indication of prior time in Jonah 3:3. Therefore, הָיְתָה in 3:3 cannot be used to imply that Nineveh was no longer in existence when the narrative was written. Rather, in this verse the narrator states that when Jonah arrived in Nineveh, it had been—and in Jonah's day still was—a great city. Also, given the fact that the entire report of Jonah's mission to Nineveh is recorded with perfect verbs (translated in the past tense in English), there is no reason why the comment about Nineveh should be couched differently.

In conclusion, Jonah's mission to Nineveh can be dated within the historical context of the eighth century BC, but the text does not contain any specific details regarding the book's author or date of writing. As it stands, the narrative of Jonah is an anonymous and undated work. Hence, although the events

---

[81] If the book of Jonah originated in the north, it would seem necessary to assume that it was composed prior to the capture and destruction of Samaria in 722/721 BC, since after that time much of the northern population was deported to Assyria and replaced by people from elsewhere (see 2 Ki 17:23–24).

[82] Ogden, "Time, and the Verb היה in O.T. Prose," 451–53. Among those who argue for a stative sense of the verb in Jonah 3:3 are Perowne, *Obadiah and Jonah*, 74, and Wilson, "The Authenticity of Jonah," 454–55.

[83] GKC, § 106 g, states that the perfect can be used to express "facts which were accomplished long before, or conditions and attributes which were acquired long before, but of which the effects still remain in the present." See also Stuart, *Hosea–Jonah*, 432. Compare Gen 3:1: "Now the serpent *was* [הָיָה] more crafty than any of the wild animals." That description was true at the time when Adam was still in Eden, and as a reference to Satan, it remained true at the later time when Genesis was composed by Moses.

described pertain to the eighth century BC, it is possible that the book itself may have been composed later. However, the evidence points to a preexilic and not a postexilic date of writing, and it is not impossible that the narrator was Jonah himself (cf. 2 Ki 14:25).

Stated another way, the testimony of the OT canon links Jonah with the other eighth-century prophets Hosea, Amos, and Micah in the Book of the Twelve. This means the book is intended to be understood as a true narrative about a person from the eighth century BC. Jonah's link with that time is also evident from his identification as "the son of Amittai" (Jonah 1:1 and 2 Ki 14:25). This canonical context in the Minor Prophets and the reference to Jonah in 2 Kings both suggest that no matter when the story may have been written, it needs to be understood in the context of the ancient Near Eastern world of the eighth century BC, when Assyria was the rising world power and Nineveh was a great city.

Jonah as Satire with Irony

By now we are beginning to realize that the book of Jonah is unlike any other prophetic book in the OT. The list of reasons has steadily been growing. Jonah is a prophetic book whose genre is historical narrative except for the psalm in chapter 2.[84] It is a narrative that makes unusual—yet factual—historical claims.[85] Its language appears to reflect an eighth-century-BC Northern Kingdom dialect of Hebrew.[86] These three characteristics together in one prophetic book are singular to Jonah. In this section we add another unique feature to this list, namely, the author's use of satire and irony. This section, therefore, will argue that if the narrative's genre is historical narrative, then its literary tone is satire with irony for a specific purpose.

Satire

Defining "satire" in any comprehensive manner is difficult.[87] There are various definitions of the term that sometimes contradict each other. For example, some literary critics are doubtful whether or not a generic definition of satire can be achieved. Neither is there an easy definition of irony, which is the chief component of satire. According to D. C. Muecke there is "no brief and simple definition that will include all kinds of irony while excluding all that is not irony."[88]

---

[84] See "The Genre of Jonah" above.

[85] See "Jonah: Fact or Fiction?" above.

[86] See "The Date of Writing" above.

[87] Jensen (introduction to *The Satirist's Art*, ix–x, referring to the play *Peer Gynt* by Henrik Ibsen) writes: "Satire's essence is as illusive as the center of Peer Gynt's onion. It is unlike other important kinds of literature because it lacks a definable cathartic effect, or at least so far, no one has isolated a general effect closely enough for generic definition."

[88] Muecke, *The Compass of Irony*, 14.

Still, certain elements do seem essential for satire, and by coming to terms with them, we can reach something at least resembling a definition. Arthur Koestler's insights are helpful:

> It [satire] focuses attention on abuses and deformities in society of which, blunted by habit, we were no longer aware; it makes us suddenly discover the absurdity of the familiar and the familiarity of the absurd.[89]

The principle means of being satirical is by using irony, which is the most sophisticated linguistic device for imparting double entendre and even paradoxical meaning to ordinary words. It is Muecke who gives what some judge to be the best list of formal criteria for irony. He notes that all irony (1) "is a double-layered or two-storey phenomenon," (2) presents some kind of opposition between the two levels, and (3) contains elements of "innocence" or unawareness.[90] By using irony, the satirist stimulates the audience to share his or her sharp criticism.[91] Irony as a verbal and literary means (with a variety of artistic devices, such as puns and wordplays) is also employed in other genres besides satire, especially comedy. But whereas irony in comedy arouses laughter and promotes fun, irony in satire evokes disdain and contempt.

Authors use satire to ridicule in indirect ways. Though subtle, satire is pointed and powerful. It has the following general characteristics:[92]

1. It has a definite target.
2. It is characterized by indirect attack and subtlety. The charge comes from the flanks rather than head-on.
3. It attacks inferior excesses; hypocrisy is one classic and familiar example.
4. It is usually external in viewpoint. That is, the actions of the character being satirized are emphasized rather than his or her inner thoughts.

Satire became a literary term to depict the mode initiated by Lucilius in the second century BC. He designed it as a new genre, different from the others that prevailed in classical literature, such as elegy, tragedy, and comedy. Many who study the beginnings of satire tend to see in Lucilius and his followers Horace (63–8 BC) and Juvenal (ca. AD 60–130) the forerunners of this literary strategy, which developed later, mainly during the period of the Renaissance, as an influential literary genre.

But what, as Ze'ev Weisman asks, is the relevance of applying the literary term "satire," "whose origin lies in classical Roman literature," to the OT? He writes:

---

[89] Koestler, *The Art of Creation*, 73.

[90] Muecke, *The Compass of Irony*, 19–20.

[91] Alter observes: "The process of literary creation … is an unceasing dialectic between the necessity to use established forms in order to be able to communicate coherently and the necessity to break and remake those forms because they are arbitrary restrictions and because what is merely repeated automatically no longer conveys a message" (*The Art of Biblical Narrative*, 62).

[92] For an overview of OT satire, especially as it relates to the prophets, see Lessing, "Isaiah's Use of Satire in His Tyre Oracle," 91–95.

The use of later and even modern terms for the study of ancient literature, and of the Hebrew Bible in particular, is permissible as long as the scholar is aware of the risk involved. These arise from the fact that the borrowed term was initiated and coined in an alien cultural milieu, remote in time and place.[93]

Cautiously the term "satire" may be uprooted from its cultural homeland and transferred to the different OT environment. Analysis of the characteristics of political satire in each of the OT's main divisions (the Torah, the Prophets, and the Writings) and in most of its literary types (e.g., narrative, prophetic dirge, parable, prophetic lawsuit, elegy, and fable) leads to the conclusion that it should be recognized as a widespread literary phenomenon in the OT. In fact, Hebrew literature is capable of highly sophisticated satire.[94] The supposition, therefore, is that the features characterizing satire as a literary phenomenon did exist in OT times, hundreds of years before satire was articulated as a literary strategy in the classical world.

Two studies that address prophetic satire in detail are David Fishelov, "The Prophet as Satirist," and Thomas Jemielity, *Satire and the Hebrew Prophets*. Jemielity's book deserves close attention, both because it is the most thorough work of the topic to date and because it makes several points that have a direct relevance for understanding the book of Jonah. Two of Jemielity's arguments pertain to this discussion. First, he notes the pervasive use of shame in both prophetic literature and satire.[95] Both prophetic literature and satire function "in a society where ridicule looms large as a humiliation to be avoided or as an especially satisfying form of punishment for one's enemies."[96] Second, he demonstrates that both satire and prophecy borrow, mix, and ironically invert genres.[97] He writes:

> Critical analyses of satire and prophecy recurrently point to the mixture of speech forms as a major feature of both, a fertile field for the appearance of all sorts of forms, each a form of forms using and subverting the shape of language familiar from other discourse and from other walks of life.[98]

---

[93] Weisman, *Political Satire in the Bible*, 1; see his discussion on pages 1–8.

[94] See, for example, Marcus, *From Balaam to Jonah: Anti-Prophetic Satire in the Hebrew Bible*. Marcus identifies "at least 14 satires in biblical narratives" (p. 6), narratives that target both foreigners and Israelites. Foreigners are satirized in the story of the tower of Babel (Gen 11:1–9), in the story of Ehud (Judg 3:12–30), and in the book of Esther. Examples of satires against Israelites include the story of Jephthah and the Ephraimites (Judg 12:1–10), the story of Micah and the Danites (Judges 17–18), and the stories of the Levite and his concubine and the civil war (Judges 19–21). Elsewhere in the OT, the prophets use satire as a literary device in characterizing rebellious or stubborn people or in their attacks against foreign nations. Also helpful is Ackerman, "Satire and Symbolism in the Song of Jonah," 220.

[95] Jemielity, *Satire and the Hebrew Prophets*, 21–49. For an in-depth study on shame, see Klopfenstein, *Scham und Schande nach dem Alten Testament*.

[96] Jemielity, *Satire and the Hebrew Prophets*, 15.

[97] Jemielity, *Satire and the Hebrew Prophets*, 50–83.

[98] Jemielity, *Satire and the Hebrew Prophets*, 58.

This use and subversion of familiar language is a major characteristic in the book of Jonah.[99] For example, Elijah's experiences, familiar from the account in 1 Kings, are turned upside down in Jonah's life. Elijah's tremendous victory on Mount Carmel in 1 Kings 18 was followed by Jezebel's ensuing death threat (1 Ki 19:2), after which Elijah expressed a desire to die (1 Ki 19:4). After God displayed his grace toward the Ninevites, Jonah expressed a desire to die (Jonah 4:3, 8) even though his life was in no danger.

If a lexicon of the OT does not include a term for "satire," it certainly includes innumerable instances of many words associated with the idea. The verb לָעַג, "to mock," and the noun לַעַג, "mocking," not only depict a kind of satirical attitude toward individuals or people, but also reflect the way this attitude was expressed. They match "satire," which in its very nature is a verbal expression of taunt and mockery.[100] Additionally, the verbs בָּזָה and בּוּז mean "to despise, disdain, hold contempt" for someone. In the same semantic field are the Hiphil of כָּלַם, "to disgrace," and the noun כְּלִמָּה, "disgrace"; the Piel of חָרַף, "to reproach," and the noun חֶרְפָּה, "reproach, scorn"; the Piel of תָּעַב, "to abhor," and the noun תּוֹעֵבָה, "abomination"; the Piel of קָלַל, "to curse," and the noun קְלָלָה, "curse"; the Piel of שָׁקַץ, "to detest," and the noun שֶׁקֶץ, "detestable thing"; the Hiphil of בּוֹשׁ, "to shame," and the noun בֹּשֶׁת, "shame"; קָלַס, "to deride," and the noun קֶלֶס, "derision"; מָשָׁל, "byword"; and מַנְגִּינָה, "mocking song." Ps 44:14–16 (ET 44:13–15) uses six of these words (חֶרְפָּה, בֹּשֶׁת, כְּלִמָּה, מָשָׁל, קֶלֶס, לַעַג). Words with senses that are antithetical include יָרֵא, "to fear, respect"; the Piel of כָּבַד, "to honor"; and the Piel of הָלַל, "to commend, praise." Jemielity's words provide a fitting conclusion of the discussion at this point:

> To look, then, in the Hebrew Scriptures for the ridicule that feeds on a sense of shame and enjoys the power of humiliation—for what literary criticism later calls satire—is no anachronism. A thorn by any other name would pierce as sharply.[101]

Ryken notes that "there are two main techniques in satire, and literary critics name them after two Roman satirists who practiced them. Horatian satire (named after Horace) is light, urbane, and subtle. ... Juvenalian satire (named after Juvenal) is biting, bitter, and angry. ... Biblical satire tends to have a serious and angry tone."[102] Radday and Brenner cite with approval John Miles'

---

[99] On the mixing of forms in satire, see Guilhamet, *Satire and the Transformation of Genre.* He writes: "This appropriation of other forms is unique to satire and is one of its chief identifying characteristics" (p. 13; see also pp. 16, 165).

[100] See Jer 20:7–8, where Jeremiah laments that he has become a "laughingstock" (שְׂחוֹק) and the object of mocking (the verb לָעַג). Because he is ridiculed for his prophetic ministry, the Word of Yahweh, which he proclaims, has become for him "a reproach and a byword" (לְחֶרְפָּה וּלְקֶלֶס). These terms express the suffering and distress of an individual (or of the nation in Pss 44:14 [ET 44:13]; 79:4) experiencing ridicule.

[101] Jemielity, *Satire and the Hebrew Prophets,* 31.

[102] Ryken, *Words of Delight,* 330.

insistence that "ancient humour was typically a laughing at rather than a laughing with."[103]

The presence of satire in a text is not easily proven.[104] On the other hand, face-to-face verbal satire is usually not difficult to decipher. The satirical speaker may wink or smile, exaggerate the tone, or subtly modify his or her manner in countless ways in order to signal that the words themselves do not speak the whole truth. However, the strictures on writing do not permit such immediate indicators, so it may often seem a "safer" choice to take a writer's words at face value without risking the kind of reading between the lines that is necessary for a satiric interpretation. Signals of satire are often difficult to detect because the essence of satire is to be indirect. A straightforward satirical statement would be a contradiction in terms.

It is an accurate assumption that authors provide certain signals to indicate satirical intention. These verbal markers are usually very subtle and indirect because that is the essence of satire. Such semantic conflict may appear in the relationship between a given text and its situational context. For example, in 4:1 the statement "It was evil to Jonah" takes on a different meaning in the context of the Ninevites' conversion in 3:5–9. When these types of discrepancies between text and context converge, it is safe to ask if the author is employing satire.[105]

How can satire be distinguished from the straightforward statements with which it is often mixed in the same text? The key is to be alert to the text's context.[106]

In paying attention to the context and narrative of Jonah, studies in the last thirty years have demonstrated that the book is filled with satiric irony. Though the term is anachronistic if applied to Jonah, Menippean satire is a type of satire that Michael Orth uses to describe the book of Jonah.[107] This is satire "in which the characters speak for themselves and are made to look ridiculous through their actions."[108]

---

[103] Radday and Brenner, "Between Intentionality and Reception" in *On Humour and the Comic in the Hebrew Bible*, 18, citing Miles, "Laughing at the Bible: Jonah as Parody," in *On Humour and the Comic in the Hebrew Bible*, 214.

[104] W. F. Stinespring, "Irony and Satire," *IDB* 2:727, comments: "The terrific impact of this satire is often avoided or evaded by readers or exegetes who wish to see the Bible as a book entirely of sweetness and light. ... In general, the extent of satire in the Bible is probably unknown to many."

[105] To view these principles in an exegetical study, see Wendland, *The Discourse Analysis of Hebrew Prophetic Literature*.

[106] Regarding the importance of context, De Beaugrande and Dressler state: "Knowledge and meaning are extremely sensitive to the **contexts** where they are utilized" (*Introduction to Text Linguistics*, 94).

[107] Menippean satire is named after the third-century-BC Greek satirist Menippus. Orth, "Genre in Jonah." Orth describes Menippean satire as "a combination of prose and verse, focused on a philosophical theme but dealing with it comically and parodying earlier works" (p. 259).

[108] Ackerman, "Satire and Symbolism in the Song of Jonah," 228.

Irony

Irony, as noted briefly above, is the means by which satire is communicated.[109] In the most basic sense, irony is a figure of speech in which (1) the intended meaning is the opposite of that which is stated, for example, referring to a jalopy as a priceless car, or (2) an event or statement occurs or is used in a way that is just the opposite of what would be expected, for example, a pastor has nothing to say in a sermon.[110] The basis of irony is a perception of incongruity, and irony is normally used in literature as a vehicle for criticism. Irony serves to point out inconsistencies in a situation between what is and what ought to be. In this sense, it is closely related to satire, which uses irony.

An example of irony that is used to satirize comes from the annunciation of Samuel in 1 Samuel 1–3. Eli the priest, who at first grossly misconstrues what Hannah is doing, prays for, or perhaps promises, the fulfillment of her prayer (1 Sam 1:17). Whatever his intent was, his words appear to be sufficient to make Hannah feel reconciled with her initial situation (1 Sam 1:18). As Eli's statement is meant as a consoling prediction, later in the narrative he is shown to be an ignorant conduit of divine intervention. Hannah up to this point has not even told Eli what she is praying for, only that she is pleading to Yahweh in great anguish (1 Sam 1:15–16). This—albeit in a very subtle manner—begins the subversion of Eli's role as a priestly intercessor. Later in the narrative, Eli will be cut off, and his wicked sons will be replaced in the sanctuary by Hannah's child Samuel (1 Sam 4:17–18). It will be Samuel, and not Eli, who hears the Word of Yahweh (1 Samuel 3). As the historian introduces Samuel, it is paramount to state at the outset that his authority will derive neither from cultic function, like the priests before him, nor from military power, like the judges before him and the kings after him, but from prophetic experience— from the Word of Yahweh. So Hannah's silent, private prayer and the obtuseness of the well-meaning priest who superfluously offers himself as the intercessor for the mother of the child who will be Yahweh's replacement of his leadership (1 Sam 3:11–14) provide an ironic and a satirical critique of the house of Eli.

Most commentators on Jonah either ignore the irony of the book or mention it in a tone of apology, apparently assuming that everything in the Bible is

---

[109] Frye describes the relationship between satire and irony in *Anatomy of Criticism*. He observes that "satire is militant irony" (p. 223). He goes on to say: "Irony is consistent both with complete realism of content and with the suppression of attitude on the part of the author. Satire demands at least a token fantasy, a content which the reader recognizes as grotesque, and at least an implicit moral standard, the latter being essential in a militant attitude to experience" (p. 224).

[110] Alonso Schökel, *A Manual of Hebrew Poetics*, 157, writes:

The Greek and Latin classics left us two basic forms of irony: rhetorical irony, which consists in saying the opposite of what one intends, but allowing this to be understood; and dramatic irony ... , which consists in making a character say something which he does not understand or the implications of which he has not grasped.

Watson terms these two types "verbal" and "situational" irony, respectively (*Classical Hebrew Poetry*, 308). Both are present in the book of Jonah.

23

intended to be read with earnest solemnity. But similar irony is evident in some of the teachings of Jesus, for example, when he spoke of covering a lamp after lighting it (Mt 5:15) or of carefully straining a gnat out of one's beverage and calmly swallowing a whole camel (Mt 23:24) or of a camel vainly trying to squeeze through the eye of a needle (Mt 19:24). The book of Jonah is full of exactly this kind of irony. Luther comments on the use of irony in Jonah when he reflects on the faith of the Ninevites in comparison with the faith of Jonah and writes: "God's Word bears fruit mainly where this is least expected and, conversely, produces least where most is expected."[111]

The work of Edwin Good demonstrates how irony is used in the book of Jonah to satirize him.[112] Put together, the following ironies make Jonah more difficult to swallow than the fish found Jonah to be!

The first group of ironies relates to what one would expect of an Israelite prophet.

1. Jonah abandons the task Yahweh calls him to do (1:3).
2. Jonah sleeps during the storm while the heathen pray (1:5).
3. The unbelieving captain has to urge a believing Israelite—Jonah—to pray (1:6).
4. Jonah appears to remain unrepentant until the end of chapter 4, but the unbelieving sailors (1:16) and Ninevites (3:5–9) repent, believe, and are saved.
5. Jonah's anger over the salvation of the Ninevites (4:1) occurs precisely when Yahweh turns his anger away from them (3:10).
6. The sailors and the Ninevites perform classic acts of Israelite piety (making vows, sacrificing, clothing themselves with sackcloth, fasting, and repenting [1:16; 3:6–8]), while Jonah does none of them even though he promised to offer sacrifice with thanksgiving and fulfill his vow (2:10 [ET 2:9]).

Another set of ironies relates to the incongruities in Jonah's actions in their relationship to each other, as well as in relationship to the results we would expect from his actions.

1. Jonah flees from Yahweh (1:3), yet confesses that he worships Yahweh (1:9).
2. Jonah recognizes that Yahweh sent the storm due to his disobedient behavior (1:12), yet he does not repent.
3. Jonah's preaching met with overwhelming success (3:5–10) despite the great wickedness of the city and the meagerness of his reluctant efforts (3:3–4).
4. Jonah expresses joy over the gift of extra shade (4:6) at the same time he twice expresses his desire to die (4:3, 8).
5. Jonah expresses joy over his own salvation (2:10 [ET 2:9]) but anger over Nineveh's salvation (3:10–4:1).
6. Jonah wishes for death (4:3, 8) upon his success as a prophet.
7. Jonah is angry to the point of death over the destruction of an unimportant plant (4:8).

---

[111] AE 19:96.

[112] Good, *Irony in the Old Testament*, 41–55. See also Miles, "Laughing at the Bible: Jonah as Parody."

8. Jonah, seeking to avoid the task of a missionary, ends up being Yahweh's vessel in converting both the sailors and the Ninevites (1:9, 16; 3:5–9).

9. The psalm (2:3–10 [ET 2:2–9]) with its emphasis on thanksgiving is unexpected because it is surrounded by a narrative that shows Jonah as angry and rebellious.

Other miscellaneous ironies include the following:

1. Yahweh delivers Jonah by means of the great fish (2:1 [ET 1:17]) in spite of his lack of proper fear and worship (shown by the sailors in 1:5, 10, 16) or faith and repentance (shown by the Ninevites in 3:5–9).

2. Jonah receives salvation (2:10 [ET 2:9]) and then begrudges the same salvation when Yahweh grants it to the Ninevites (3:10–4:11).

3. Jonah's confession that "salvation belongs to Yahweh" (2:10) contrasts starkly with his actions, which would indicate that his attitude was that "salvation belongs to me; I get to decide who gets saved and who gets damned!"

4. Jonah first offers to give his life (1:12, 15), but throughout the psalm (2:3–10 [ET 2:2–9]), he thanks Yahweh for saving his life.

A number of the ironies described above support this statement by Terence Fretheim: "It is thus striking the degree to which the psalm [2:3–10 (ET 2:2–9)] participates in the irony of the rest of the book, and may in fact heighten that irony in significant ways."[113]

Put in narrative form, the ironies stack up like this. Commanded to go (1:2), Jonah flees (1:3). With everyone else scurrying and praying to save the swamping ship, Jonah sleeps (1:5). Commanded to pray by the captain, Jonah rolls over and snores on (1:6). Asked by the sailors his land and occupation, the prophet who had sought to escape God's domain on the high seas chants a confession of faith in Yahweh, "who made the sea and the dry land" (1:9). Jonah hits the water, and the sea calms instantly (1:15). Jonah hits Nineveh, mounts the first available street-corner soap box, and proclaims the city's impending doom—not even introducing the oracle with a "thus says Yahweh" (see 3:4; cf. Is 7:7). In saying "Nineveh will be changed" (3:4), Jonah thought it would be "destroyed" (as many translations render 3:4), but instead the city was "changed" through repentance and was saved. Jonah's lone voice (3:4) in the huge city becomes a booming command rattling the rafters of Nineveh, making the king come down from his throne, plunging the city into the most comprehensive sackcloth-and-ashes conversion ever heard of in the ancient Near East, including even the animals (3:5–9). The king commands, "No food, no water—everyone cry out to God with gusto" (cf. 3:7–8). Think of the racket that would be made by unwatered and unfed animals—and kids! Yahweh's anger cools down (3:10)—and then Jonah's anger heats up (4:1). As he had lectured the sailors about fear of the Creator God (1:9), he now proceeds to lecture Yahweh and complain that God is simply too full of mercy and love (4:2). Jonah implies that sparing the city makes God look wishy-washy, like a capricious Oriental monarch; when a city deserves zapping, he should zap it! Yah-

[113] Fretheim, *Jonah*, 55.

weh asks whether it is proper for Jonah to be so hot and angry (4:4), then proceeds to heat things up further by bringing on the worm, the sirocco, and the sun (4:6–8). Now Jonah is hot over the loss of his qiqayon plant—hot enough to die (4:8). "Look here," says God, "you pity plants, but I pity people, even their animals" (4:10–11).

The Purpose of Satire in This True and Didactic Story

Because of this pervasive use of irony intended to satirize, current biblical scholars identify Jonah with satire.[114] However, many also suppose that it exaggerates or distorts the actual events it narrates. Milton Burrows is one of the most ardent adherents of this view. He writes: "In purpose and method it [Jonah] belongs to the same general type of literature as Don Quixote or Gulliver's Travels," and he defines the satire in Jonah as "roughly … a caricature in words."[115] Others also locate unhistorical elements of satire in Jonah. For example, Terence Fretheim believes the narrative uses "ridicule, absurdity, burlesque, exaggeration, humor, or other ways of intensifying incongruities."[116]

But against depictions of Jonah as ahistorical due to its irony and satire, the use of these literary techniques should not lead us to jettison the text's historical accuracy. It is a doubtful methodology to classify Jonah as satirical with no historical moorings because no distinct class of satirical literature existed in ancient Israel.[117] Jonah, "a satirical, didactic … short story,"[118] is at the same time a historically true narrative.[119]

The narrator combines irony and satire in his factual account of history for a purpose. This purpose is, first, to expose that not only Jonah but also the audience for which the narrative was written have deviated in some ways from Yahweh, the God of Israel; second, to restore the audience to repentance and true faith in Israel's God; and third, to strengthen the missionary outreach of God's people. The narrative is didactic because it instructs the audience through

---

[114] For example, Good, *Irony in the Old Testament*, 40–41; Allen, *Joel, Obadiah, Jonah and Micah*, 178; Ackerman, "Satire and Symbolism in the Song of Jonah," 216–17, 227–29; Holbert, "Deliverance Belongs to Yahweh! Satire in the Book of Jonah"; Miles, "Laughing at the Bible: Jonah as Parody." Indeed, because of the numerous studies of the satirical nature of Jonah, Jemielity omits the book completely in his discussion of satire in the prophets (*Satire and the Hebrew Prophets*, 15–16). Older studies too noted satirical elements in Jonah. For a comprehensive list that surveys the issue beginning with Thomas Paine in *Age of Reason* (1793), see Holbert, "Deliverance Belongs to Yahweh!" 76–77, n. 7.

[115] Burrows, "The Literary Category of the Book of Jonah," 95–96.

[116] Fretheim, *Jonah*, 51–52.

[117] Cf. Day, "Problems in the Interpretation of the Book of Jonah," 39.

[118] Fretheim, *Jonah*, 72.

[119] If a definition of narrative is "a representation of a sequence of non-randomly connected events" (Rigney, "Narrativity and Historical Representation," 591), then a definition of narrative history would be "a representation of a sequence of non-randomly connected, actual events of the past" (Provan, Long, and Longman, *A Biblical History of Israel*, 84, who also cite this quote from Rigney).

indirect and constructive criticism via satire. That is to say, the narrator does not oppose his audience directly in the manner typical of prophetic judgment speech, in which the prophet declares certain death for the king and people and destruction for the temple and cult (e.g., Is 5:1–7; Amos 5:18–27; Jeremiah 7 and 26; Ezekiel 7 and 21). Instead, the narrative's satire of Jonah is intended to lead the audience to recognize its own similar hypocrisy, repent of it, and return to Yahweh in renewed and sincere faith that confesses the enormity of his grace toward all people. This same purpose is evident in Jesus' preaching (e.g., Mt 6:1–18; 18:21–35).

Who was the original audience for whom the narrator wrote Jonah? It is clear that the author of Jonah opposes Israelites who, like Jonah, tried to limit the grace of Yahweh to themselves. These people are those who, after the prophetic word is grudgingly proclaimed and repentance and salvation are accomplished, claim that this is a "great evil" (4:1). They claim to affirm Yahweh's power to save (2:10 [ET 2:9]), having witnessed it in their own life, but they are disobedient and hypocritical Hebrews, angered by Yahweh's will to save even Gentiles. They would rather die than live if such gracious events can occur (4:3, 8). The narrative attacks this kind of narrow-mindedness that limits the grace of God as if it were the sole possession of deserving Israelites and as if it were not freely available to all people through faith alone (see Lk 18:9–14).

Which group or groups the narrator had in mind cannot be identified specifically. However, throughout Israel's history there were hypocritical Israelites who wished to believe that God's grace was only for them. Such hypocritical attitudes and behaviors are not limited to any time or people. Yea, their number is legion! Jonah's intended audience may have included false prophets in Israel, who claimed great insight and divine callings, but who ultimately were devoid of substance and who directed their anger at the faithful servants of Yahweh. For example, false prophets opposed Micaiah ben Imlah (1 Kings 22), and the false prophet Hananiah opposed Jeremiah (Jeremiah 28). See also Ezekiel 13.

The historical person and actions of Jonah are meant to point to a group of people much like the pompous, prideful, and pretentious prophet. In the same way, the figure of the elder brother in Lk 15:11–32 points to the Pharisees and scribes (Lk 15:1–2), and the parable of the Good Samaritan (Lk 10:30–37) is an indictment against the expert in the Law (Lk 10:25–29)—and both also condemn the hypocrite in us all should we begrudge the forgiveness and welcome shown to all penitent sinners by God in Christ.

The original group addressed via Jonah may have been some definite group in Jonah's own day. In 2 Ki 14:25 Jonah appears as a prophet of national conquest and glory; he would have been appealing to the four hundred false prophets of Ahab's court (1 Ki 22:6). Jonah may represent the nationalistic, optimistic prophets of his day who supposed that God's judgment was exclusively for foreigners and his mercy was exclusively for Israel. However we conceive of the original group under critique, Brevard Childs is correct that the book

"serves as a critical prophetic judgment on Israel in line with the rest of the prophetic witness of the Old Testament."[120]

Regardless of the original audience, Jonah has wide applications both to ancient Israel and the modern church. Sinful human nature has not changed in the millennia since Jonah lived. People today share his propensity to arrogate God's favor to themselves and to exclude others from his grace. The message that God, the ultimate author of all Scripture, conveys through Jonah is timeless. The book calls us to repentance from selfishness and to renewed faith in the one true God, who freely forgives all who call upon his name, manifested supremely in the life, death, and resurrection of Jesus, the "one greater than Jonah" (Mt 12:41). The same God who converted and saved the Gentile sailors and Ninevites welcomes all peoples into his kingdom through faith in Christ.

The truth that the narrative brings home is twofold: (1) compassion is supreme in Yahweh's "gracious and merciful" (4:2) ways of dealing with his creatures; and (2) it is a universal compassion, extending not just to Israelites, but to all peoples equally, even to their animals (4:11).[121] What is satirized by the narrative of Jonah's behavior is a self-centered and arrogant religious attitude that denies or ignores these two truths about the one true and triune God.

The satirical tone of the narrative is therefore not accidental or incidental. Rather, it is the very essence of the narrator's intention. The function of Yahweh's final question in the book (4:10–11), then, is to challenge the attitude of this group among the author's contemporaries, as well as of those people of all times and all places who exhibit the characteristics of Jonah.

This prophetic capacity in Israel to have a "religion against itself" sets her theological perspective into an uncommon mode in the history of the world's religions. The tendency on the part of religious institutions is to be protective of the "insiders" and to be suspicious of, and rail against, the "outsiders." But our suspicions should be raised if a leader or group seldom speaks or acts in ways that indict its own insiders. We should be skeptical if the critical evaluative work of a community is always directed against others. We should have our doubts if the God of whom such persons speak never convicts his spokesmen or their supporters, because then sharp questions need to be raised about the adequacy of their portrayal of God. We need to address how best to be God's spokesmen both for and against our own Christian church. Our fundamental calling is to proclaim God's searing condemnation of all sins—including our own—as well as the Gospel of God's plenary forgiveness in Christ.

The book of Jonah is a model for such critical work in the church. God's spokesmen need to discern those areas in the body of Christ that need divine condemnation and to speak boldly and compassionately about them, even if it means speaking into the teeth of a storm. This is what St. Paul means when he

---

[120] Childs, *Introduction to the Old Testament as Scripture*, 426.

[121] See further "Jonah and Noah" below in the introduction.

states: "What business is it of mine to judge those outside [the church]? Are you not to judge those inside?" (1 Cor 5:12). His use of οὐχί ("not") in the last clause demands an affirmative answer. This is also what it means to say that the church continually needs reforming based on the Word of God. The church always needs corrective critique and evangelical reformation, after the manner of the book of Jonah.

Luther understood this self-critical role of leaders in the church. For example, in *The Babylonian Captivity of the Church* (1520)[122] and *Against the Heavenly Prophets* (1525),[123] Luther's cry was *Ecclesia semper reformanda est*, "The church always needs to undergo reformation." One example is a statement he made in 1518, in response to calls for Germany to participate in a crusade against the Ottoman Empire, which was a threat to Europe. "It is meaningless, he said, to fight an external war when one is overcome at home by a spiritual war." The first action against the Turks, Luther counseled, is for Christians genuinely to repent.[124]

The Narrative and Its Structure

Although on the surface the narrative of Jonah appears to be simple and straightforward, underlying it is a complex use of language. Herbert Brichto comments on the narrative's literary genius:

> The Book of Jonah is from beginning to end, in form and content, in diction, phraseology, and style, a masterpiece of rhetoric. It is the work of a single artist, free from editorial comment or gloss; every word is in place, and every sentence.[125]

The narrative of Jonah is a model of literary artistry, marked by symmetry and balance.[126] It is an ornate tapestry of rhetorical beauty. Its symmetry produces rhythm, contrast, emphasis, and continuity. The narrative is exquisitely designed and not only discloses a profound theology, but communicates it in subtle ways. This should not surprise us because subtlety characterizes the essence of satire and irony.

Whether OT narratives employ satire and irony or not, they "are generally reticent to make their points directly, preferring to do so more subtly."[127] In a

---

[122] AE 36:3–126.

[123] AE 40:73–223.

[124] Miller, "Fighting Like a Christian," 43 (see also p. 53, nn. 12–13), citing a letter from Luther to Georg Spalatin, December 21, 1518 (WA Br 1.282), and also *Grund und Ursach aller Artikel D. Martin Luthers* (1521; WA 7.443; the 1520 Latin version is on 7.140–41), where Luther expressed similar thoughts.

[125] Brichto, *Toward a Grammar of Biblical Poetics*, 68.

[126] See, for example, Magonet, *Form and Meaning: Studies in the Literary Techniques in the Book of Jonah*, and Trible, *Rhetorical Criticism: Context, Method, and the Book of Jonah*.

[127] Provan, Long, and Longman, *A Biblical History of Ancient Israel*, 91; see their discussion on pages 91–93.

close-knit culture like ancient Israel, there was a much higher degree of agreement between its members about religion and ethics than there is in post-modern secularized and pluralistic societies. There was correspondingly less need for the author to spell out norms and values, because the readers or hearers were likely to share them.

The more closely we look at Hebrew narratives, the more we are compelled to recognize the complexity and subtlety with which they are organized. To this end, they employ a wide array of more indirect means in developing characterizations. Mention of physical details, for instance, is seldom if ever random. When we read that Jacob is born grasping Esau's heel (Gen 25:26), Ehud is left-handed (Judg 3:15), David is "ruddy, with a fine appearance and handsome looks" (1 Sam 16:12), and Goliath is over nine feet tall (1 Sam 17:4), we should anticipate (though not insist) that such details in some way serve the characterization or the action of the narrative. In the case of Jonah, that his name in Hebrew means "dove" is a subtle suggestion already in 1:1 that we are reading about someone who lacks the courage necessary to carry out his calling faithfully; compare Hos 7:11, where Ephraim (the Northern Kingdom) is "like a dove, silly and lacking a heart," who fails to trust in Yahweh and instead calls on Egypt and Assyria for protection.

Interpretation, then, involves close attention to the subtle details. One detail that we dare not miss in the narrative of Jonah is repetition. Key words and word stems (*Leitworte*), motifs, similar situations (sometimes called "type-scenes" or "stock situations"), and the like are used by the narrator in a masterful way. For those who have eyes to see, Jonah maximizes all of these classical features of Hebrew narrative. The narrator is a master craftsman of language, literary conventions, imagery, and syntax. This literary genius has crafted one of the most symmetrical books of the Bible. The parallel structures often produce a kind of crescendo in development, where certain images or motifs are produced in the first part of the story and then brought to a climax in a subsequent scene.[128]

That Jonah falls into two parts (chapters 1–2 and chapters 3–4) is obvious from the parallelism between 1:1–3 and 3:1–3. This parallelism, however, extends beyond the openings of the two parts. Of the seven scenes comprising the four chapters, the second scene (1:4–16) and the fifth scene (3:3b–10) correspond to each other, as also do the third scene (2:1–11 [ET 1:17–2:10]) and scenes 6 and 7 (4:1–3; 4:4–11). These connections go further still, as there is a narrative continuum, a coherent unfolding story in which the meanings of earlier events are progressively, even systematically, revealed or enriched by the addition of subsequent data. This technique of placing parallel accounts in

---

[128] This literary strategy is used in other ancient Near Eastern writings. For example, in the Gilgamesh Epic, multiple dream reports play important functions in the development of the plot (*ANET*, 76, 77, 82, 83, 88, and 95).

dynamically complementary sequence is evident at the very beginning of the OT: Genesis 1 and 2 are complementary rather than overlapping accounts of creation. An example of this complementary feature in Jonah is in chapters 1 and 3: both describe Jonah in a social situation in which a pagan group under its leader appeals to God for help. Another example is in chapters 2 and 4: in both Jonah is devoid of human company and speaks with God.[129]

The narrative's remarkable, almost mathematical and technical precision is often used in the narrative to convey irony, which is then the vehicle to satirize Jonah. For example, scene 2 (1:4–16) creates perfect symmetry between the number of words before and after Jonah's confession in 1:9. The confession itself is ironic as we ask, How can Jonah state that Yahweh is the God of the heavens and the sea and the dry ground, even as he is fleeing from this God? Where can he go to escape such a universal God? This and other facets that we shall see lead Jonathan Magonet to apply to Jonah a phrase that has been applied both to drama and to ritual: "strategic mystification."[130]

To ensure that we do not miss this symmetry used in the service of irony, the narrator uses identical or nearly identical terms in corresponding parallel scenes. Often in Hebrew narrative, when elements relating to the plot are arranged similarly, it is the author's intent to communicate through a host of literary devices. These devices include repetition, the use of key words or concepts, point of view, characterization, reticence, omission, and dialogue.[131] One of the most common literary devices in Hebrew narrative is the use of a key word (*Leitwort*), which is "a word or a word-root that recurs significantly in a text, a continuum of texts, or in a configuration of texts."[132] By following these repetitions, we see that the meaning of scenes becomes more striking—and in Jonah's case, more ironic.

An example where a repeated word in a single episode serves as the chief means of thematic exposition is the confrontation between Samuel and Saul over the king's failure to destroy all of the Amalekites and all of their possessions (1 Samuel 15).[133] This text contains a series of variations on the repeated terms "listen" (שָׁמַע), "voice, sound" (קֹל), and "word" (דָּבָר). Samuel exhorts Saul to "*listen* to the *sound* of the *words* of Yahweh" (1 Sam 15:1). When Saul returns as a victor in battle, Samuel becomes troubled by the "sound" of sheep

---

[129] This view is against Sasson, who remarks that any attempts to find symmetry between chapters 2 and 4 are "farfetched and much too dependent on a highly accommodating analytic language" (*Jonah*, 204).

[130] Magonet, *Form and Meaning*, 112.

[131] A classic example is that of the relationship between Genesis 38 (Judah's relationship with Tamar) and the surrounding narrative of Joseph (Genesis 37, 39–50). See Alter, *The Art of Biblical Narrative*, 3–22.

[132] Martin Buber, *Schriften zur Bibel*, vol. 2 of *Werker* (Munich: Kösel, 1964), 1131, translated and quoted by Alter, *The Art of Biblical Narrative*, 93.

[133] This example comes from Alter, *The Art of Biblical Narrative*, 93–94.

and cattle, which he is "hearing" (1 Sam 15:14). Samuel then condemns Saul (1 Sam 15:22):

הִנֵּה שְׁמֹעַ מִזֶּבַח טוֹב
לְהַקְשִׁיב מֵחֵלֶב אֵילִים:

Behold, to listen is better than sacrifice,
to heed [is better] than the fat of rams.

Broken, Saul apologizes that he has not heeded the "words" of Yahweh through Samuel and instead "listened" to the "voice" of the people (1 Sam 15:24), which here is the exact opposite of "the voice of Yahweh" (1 Sam 15:19, 20, 22).

What we find very often in Hebrew narrative, then, is an integrated use of repetition through words, phrases, images, and/or ideas.[134] The repetition of an identical word or phrase after an interval enables an examination of the earlier events in a new way and gives the author a way to drive his point home. Key words mark the connections between thematically parallel narrative units and enable the reader to see the central theme of the events. Unfortunately, the repetitions of these words are often lost in translations for it is considered poor English style to repeat the same word in a single context. But these lead words are often the key to grasping the narrator's point of emphasis and/or the theme of the text.

The narrator of Jonah uses a variety of key words to communicate his important points. The high frequency of the same words in the book functions in a dynamic fashion and might be compared to the motif of a symphony. For example, the verb קָרָא, "call," occurs eight times (1:2, 6, 14; 2:3 [ET 2:2]; 3:2, 4, 5, 8) and the verb קוּם, "arise," six times (1:2, 3, 6; 3:2, 3, 6). This allows the narrator to achieve a sense of depth in characterization through mere repetition (what appears—by modern standards—to be a meager and rudimentary use of language).

Repetition also has the effect of communicating the meaning that a word may have carried in earlier contexts into a later context, where it provides depth and insight. For example, in 1:2 Yahweh proclaims that the "evil" (רָעָה) of the people of Nineveh has come before him. Later the Ninevites turn from their

---

[134] Additional examples of the literary device of repetition are as follows: In Genesis 1 the clause "And God saw that it was good" (Gen 1:10, 12, 18, 21, 25; see also Gen 1:4) builds up to "God saw all that he had made, and behold, it was *very good*" in Gen 1:31. In the book of Judges, the clause "But [insert an Israelite tribe] did not drive out [the inhabitants of Canaan]" (Judg 1:21, 27, 29, 30, 31, 33; see also Judg 1:19, 28, 32) accents that Israel's problem throughout the book will be that if Israel does not destroy the enemy, the enemy will destroy her. The barrenness of Israel's three matriarchs Sarah (Gen 11:30), Rebekah (Gen 25:21), and Rachel (Gen 29:31) highlights the fact that "God chose the foolish things of the world to shame the wise, and God chose the weak things of the world to shame the strong, and God chose the lowly things of the world and the despised things—and the things that are not" (1 Cor 1:27–28). Michael Fishbane, *Text and Texture*, 40–62, argues that the entire Jacob narrative is structured by means of two words, blessing and birthright—in Hebrew a pun: בְּרָכָה (*berakah*) and בְּכֹרָה (*bekorah*).

"evil" (רָעָה), and Yahweh relents of the "evil" (רָעָה) he had threatened to bring upon the city (3:10). Then in the next verse, Jonah considers the salvation of the repentant city to be a "great evil" (רָעָה גְדוֹלָה, 4:1), ironically a worse "evil" than the original sinfulness of Nineveh! In this way the narrator accomplishes with one word what might take another one paragraph. The use of רָעָה throughout the narrative conveys, without need for explicit commentary, a hypocritical aspect of Jonah's character.[135]

The repetition of words in written material can quickly become monotonous, but in oral discourse—and Jonah was originally designed to be communicated through oral reading—the speaker can play upon the repeated word or words, varying pitch, volume, and tempo for dramatic effect. The careful design of the narrative is intended to communicate through the ear rather than just the eye.[136]

More examples of how key words are repeated in the narrative of Jonah are as follows: The first chapter ends with the sailors offering sacrifices to Yahweh and making vows (1:16), and in 2:10 (ET 2:9) Jonah pledges to offer sacrifice and repay his vow to Yahweh, so the prophet is brought to the same situation as the formerly unbelieving sailors—the last place in the world he would ever want to be! Chapters 1 and 2 both include the themes of crisis, prayer, deliverance, and worship. It is clear that the events in chapter 3 closely correspond with those in chapter 1; for example, 3:9 corresponds with 1:6 in its tentative expression of hope and its identical final clause. Moreover, the demonstration of divine grace in 3:10 is the intended parallel to that in 2:1, 11: Jonah's deliverance from deserved destruction has a sequel in the sparing of Nineveh.

The prophet's complaint in 4:1–3 is in stark contrast to his song of praise in 2:3–10 (ET 2:2–9), but it is significant that they each have a similar introduction using the Hithpael of the verb פָּלַל, "to pray" (2:2; 4:2). The key word in the psalm, חֶסֶד, "loyal love" (2:9 [ET 2:8]), recurs in 4:2. The salvation themes that drew forth Jonah's praise in the psalm are ironically the very ones that cause him grief in his second prayer. Occurring in 1:6, 14; 3:9; and 4:10 is אָבַד, "to perish." The penultimate verse of the book (4:10) artistically reuses אָבַד, "to perish," in a surprising way,[137] and then the final verse (4:11) includes the key phrase "Nineveh, the great city" (נִינְוֵה הָעִיר הַגְּדוֹלָה), which opened both parts of the book (1:2, opening chapters 1–2, and 3:2, opening chapters 3–4).

---

[135] See the noun רָעָה, "evil," in Jonah 1:2, 7, 8; 3:8, 10; 4:1, 2, 6. See also the verb רָעַע, "to be evil," in 4:1.

[136] For a full discussion of the issues that relate to orality in the OT, see Lessing, "Orality in the Prophets."

[137] The first three instances of אָבַד, "to perish," are all negated first person plural forms with human subjects: "We will not perish" (1:6; 3:9) or "Do not let us perish" (1:14). But in 4:10 Yahweh speaks of the qiqayon plant, which "perished."

All these threads draw the book into a neatly woven fabric that demonstrates a carefully structured composition intended to use irony in a way to satirize Jonah and maximize the grace of God.

The overall structure of Jonah can be allocated to two contrasting parallels: at sea (chapters 1 and 2) and at Nineveh (chapters 3 and 4). Schematically, this structure of the book appears as follows:[138]

Chapters 1–2	*Chapters 3–4*
Word of Yahweh comes to Jonah (1:1)	Word of Yahweh comes to Jonah (3:1)
Content of the Word (1:2)	Content of the Word (3:2)
Response of Jonah (1:3)	Response of Jonah (3:3–4)
Gentile response (1:5)	Gentile response (3:5)
Action of the captain (1:6)	Action of the king (3:6–9)
Sailors and Jonah (1:7–15b)	Ninevites and God (3:10b)
Disaster averted (1:15c)	Disaster averted (3:10c)
Response of sailors (1:16)	Response of Jonah (4:1)
Yahweh and Jonah (2:1–10 [ET 1:17–2:9])	Yahweh and Jonah (4:2–3)
Yahweh's response (2:11)	Yahweh's response (4:6–11)

From this perspective, the function of Jonah 1 and 2 is largely preparatory in that it is designed to set the scene and to prepare us for Jonah 3 and 4, in which the primary encounter between Yahweh and Jonah takes place. Chapters 1 and 2 parallel chapters 3 and 4 in several respects. Both chapters 1 and 2 and chapters 3 and 4 begin with a notice that the Word of Yahweh comes to Jonah and that the prophet is commissioned to speak out against Nineveh. As a result of these attempts to commission Jonah to speak, something entirely unexpected happens: in chapters 1 and 2, Jonah attempts to flee from Yahweh rather than to carry out his instructions; in chapters 3 and 4, Nineveh, a city with one of the worst reputations for evil in the entire OT, actually repents and seeks Yahweh's forgiveness. In both sections, the unexpected event sets the scene for an encounter between Jonah and Yahweh: in chapters 1 and 2, a great fish swallows Jonah, and he thanks Yahweh for extending mercy; in chapters 3 and 4, Jonah sulks about Yahweh's decision to show mercy to Nineveh.

This two-part structure also highlights a parallel between the sea and Nineveh. In chapters 1 and 2, the events at sea display Yahweh's power extending beyond the land of Israel; he governs events upon and within the sea. Chapters 3 and 4 again display Yahweh's power beyond Israel's territory, this time in Nineveh.

The above two-part structure and the seven-scene structure are compatible, like looking at two sides of the same coin. The seven scenes, then, are as follows: Scene 1 is the account of Jonah's call and his reaction (1:1–3). Scene 2 takes place on board a ship in the midst of a storm at sea (1:4–16). The setting for scene 3 is inside the great fish (2:1–11 [ET 1:17–2:10]). In scene 4 Yahweh gives Jonah his assignment a second time (3:1–3a). Scene 5 takes place

---

[138] This follows, to a large extent, Nixon, *Jonah*, 24.

in Nineveh (3:3b–10), and scene 6 consists of Jonah's prayer in Nineveh (4:1–3). The final scene takes place outside the city, beginning and ending with Yahweh questioning the prophet (4:4–11).[139] The first, fourth, and seventh scenes are set in motion with the words of Yahweh (1:1; 3:1; 4:4). The second and third scenes are introduced with the acts of Yahweh (1:4; 2:1 [ET 1:17]). The sixth scene is introduced by Jonah's reaction to Yahweh's action (4:1). The first two scenes end with Yahweh as the object of the action (1:3, 16), the third and fifth scenes conclude with Yahweh/God as the subject of the action (2:11 [ET 2:10]; 3:10), and the entire book concludes with the words of Yahweh (4:10–11).

The seven-scene structure leads to the major themes of the narrative:

- Yahweh is the Alpha and Omega of the book of Jonah (cf. Rev 1:8).
- Yahweh is in control of the heavens, the sea, and the dry land (Jonah 1:9).
- He may do whatever he pleases (1:14).
- His pleasure is to extend grace and mercy, even to Gentiles, such as the Ninevites (4:10–11).

Although the narrator of Jonah makes use of irony and satire, literary structures and verbal devices, these do not imply that his work is fictional.[140] A distinction needs to be drawn between form of presentation and content. The fact that the narrator employs particular literary conventions and strategies attests to his skill as an author and does not call into question the historicity of his account. There is no reason why he cannot use his skills to present an accurate account of what actually took place. The narrative of Jonah is a finely written literary masterpiece that has a high degree of irony to satirize those in the writer's community who were exhibiting the characteristics of Jonah, namely, the desire to limit God's grace.[141] Just as the author wrote for an actual audience of real people, so the events he narrates are not fiction, but fact.[142]

The History of Interpretation

Like all biblical books, Jonah is part of the continuum of Scripture, with connections to earlier and later books. Since echoes of Genesis 6–10 reverberate in Jonah, this commentary devotes an introductory section to that

---

[139] The Masoretic Text places a פ for פְּתוּחָה (a major paragraph marker; literally "open," meaning the rest of the line is blank) after 2:11 (ET 2:10), indicated that the major break in the story comes at the end of chapter 2. It places a ס for סְתוּמָה (a minor paragraph marker; literally, "closed," meaning that after a blank space, text resumes later on the same line) after 2:10 (ET 2:9) and 4:3, indicating lesser breaks at those points.

[140] Hence the claim of Fretheim, *Jonah*, 66, is unjustified: "The carefully worked out structures in the book … suggest a non-historical intention of the author's part. Such a concern for structure and symmetry is not as characteristic of straightforward historical writing and is more suggestive of an imaginative product."

[141] See further "The Purpose of Satire in This True and Didactic Story" in "Jonah as Satire with Irony" above.

[142] See further "Jonah: Fact or Fiction?" above.

topic.[143] The location assigned to Jonah in the OT canon is itself a statement about the early interpretation of the book.[144] Jesus' own interpretation of Jonah in Mt 12:39–42 and Lk 11:32 is discussed in the excursus "The Sign of Jonah" after the commentary on chapter 2.

After Jesus' interpretation in the NT itself, one of the earliest Christian interpretations of the narrative is that Jonah, knowing with prophetic insight that Nineveh would repent and be delivered, was reluctant to carry out his mission since the end result, the salvation of Gentiles, would bring great shame upon his own unrepentant people, Israel.[145] This interpretation drew a parallel between that shame for impenitent OT Israel and the shame ascribed to Jews who rejected Jesus as the Messiah. This interpretation picks up on Mt 12:41, where Jesus states, "The men of Nineveh will arise at the judgment with this generation and condemn it, for they repented at the preaching of Jonah, and now one greater than Jonah is here." Gentile Christians saw themselves represented by Nineveh in the story: former pagans who repented and were accepted by God. Jonah represented the narrow-minded Israelites who took offense at the salvation of Gentiles, just as did many Jews in the early church era.

But not all early Christians were of this opinion. Jerome, for example, believed that the purpose of the narrative was to encourage Israelites to repent, and so he held that in the early church era the book served to invite Jews to repent and believe in Jesus. The fact that Jonah's three days and three nights in the fish prefigured the period between the crucifixion and resurrection of Jesus (Mt 12:40) suggested to Jerome that Jonah was a type of Christ, and so the association of Jonah with narrow-mindedness was played down.[146]

For Augustine, Jonah is both a sign of Jesus and the embodiment of carnal Israel. Fleshly Israel was a staunch opponent of the divine campaign to save all peoples and thus was opposed to the spirit of the Christian Gospel. Schizophrenically, for Augustine Jonah remains a Christ-figure, overwhelmed by the "Jewish waves" that crash over him, frothing "Crucify him, crucify him"—and yet Jonah himself is also the embodiment of the Jew.[147]

Luther explains that Jonah's name (יוֹנָה) means "dove," and he is "a prototype of the Holy Spirit and of His office, namely, of the Gospel."[148] At the same time, Luther, like Augustine, sees Jonah as an embodiment of the begrudging spirit of Israelites who thought God's grace should be limited only to themselves, as summed up in Ps 79:6: "Pour out Thy anger on the nations that

---

[143] See "Jonah and Noah" below in the introduction.

[144] See "Jonah's Place in the Book of the Twelve" below in the introduction.

[145] For a useful survey of older interpretations of the book and its parts, see Bickerman, "Les deux erreurs du prophète Jonas," or Bickerman, *Four Strange Books of the Bible*, 14–19.

[146] Bolin, *Freedom beyond Forgiveness*, 28–29; Bickerman, *Four Strange Books of the Bible*, 18–19. See Jerome, *Commentariorum in Ionam* (CCSL 76:376–419).

[147] Augustine's reading of Jonah, found in various of his writings, is discussed by Duval, *Le livre de Jonas*, 511–23.

[148] AE 19:97.

do not know Thee and on the kingdoms that do not call on Thy name."[149] In Luther's reading, Jonah no longer orbits the realm of Christological superlatives but is emphatically grounded in the prophet's salvation from Sheol. The Reformer had no patience with some of the church fathers' "silly deference" to the prophets, which he snaps, takes "such extremes that they [the fathers] even preferred to violate Holy Scripture, to force it and stretch it, before they would admit that the saints were sinners."[150]

In the twentieth century, it became popular to see the book of Jonah as a postexilic reaction to the exclusivist, xenophobic type of Yahwism assumed to be typified by Ezra and Nehemiah.[151] This follows Julius Wellhausen's scenario in which a struggle between two opposing forces resulted in a great synthesis. One side was a religious tradition characterized by individuality, variety, and high ethical criteria (early Israelite religion, the classical prophets—especially Amos), while the other was a rigid, legalistic, centripetal force that sought a stifling homogeneity (the Deuteronomic school and the Priestly writer). In the struggle between these two forces, it was those who espoused centralization and codification who emerged victorious.[152]

Wellhausen's vision was heavily informed by a nineteenth-century Romanticism, which extolled individuality and the primitive. Proponents of his view grouped Jonah together with Ruth and Isaiah 40–66 as part of a pure, progressive golden core addressed to xenophobes clutching their copies of Ezra and Nehemiah. Jonah is then a testament to how the OT was writhing internally, purging itself of its oldness, trying frantically, like Lady Macbeth, to wash its hands of "damned [trouble] spot[s]."[153]

Yet this caricature of postexilic Israelites (who for Wellhausen were no longer Israelites, but Jews) as legalistic owes more to the misreading of the polemical views of Paul and the Gospels than to any realistic historical observations of the sixth–fourth centuries BC. Ronald Clements critiques the Wellhausen view as follows:

> The entire story [of Jonah] fails to raise any single example of those issues which we know deeply affected the relationships of Jews with non-Jews in the post-exilic period. The questions of mixed language, mixed marriages and of the complexities raised by considerations of cultic holiness and pagan uncleanness are not mentioned. … The so-called separatism of Nehemiah

---

[149] AE 19:93.

[150] AE 19:44–45.

[151] For example, Rowley, *The Missionary Message of the Old Testament*, 68–69. Jonah is then coupled with Ruth as two appeals against postexilic exclusivism. A broader overview of the development of this view of Jonah and the underlying presuppositions and biases that inform it is in Bickerman, *Four Strange Books of the Bible*, 19–27.

[152] This model is the guiding structure for each of Wellhausen's chapters analyzing the various elements of Israel's religion (*Prolegomena to the History of Ancient Israel*, 17–170, 402–8, 411–18).

[153] William Shakespeare, *Macbeth*, act 5, scene 1.

and Ezra was not so much concerned with making a distinction between Jew and Gentile, … but with a division between Jews and those who laid claim to being Jews. The issues which reveal themselves in the Chronicler's history are primarily those of a growing separation between communities living in the territories of Judah and Samaria regarding the status and obligations of those who claimed to be heirs of the promises given to Israel.[154]

The book of Jonah doesn't address any of these issues. This cumulative evidence—both internal and external—undercuts the critical understanding of the purpose of Jonah, which rests very heavily on assumptions and identifications that have to be supplied from outside the narrative itself.

Following Clements' critique of the Wellhausenian view, current interpretation of Jonah has jettisoned any attempt to historically reconstruct the book's place in Israel's history. Instead, it has focused upon Jonah's rhetorical and literary features. Clearly it was Phyllis Trible's unpublished doctoral dissertation in 1962 that inaugurated this new approach to Jonah.[155] Noteworthy among those who follow Trible's literary approach to Jonah are Jonathan Magonet[156] and Jack Sasson.[157]

Jonah and Noah

A summary of the discussion up to this point is as follows: Jonah is a highly sophisticated literary masterpiece that fits the genre of historical narrative.[158] The structure and use of key words convey numerous ironies that are intended to satirize Jonah, and those like him, who seek to limit the grace of God to themselves and who resent the God of Israel extending salvation to all—even Gentiles—through faith.[159]

Adding to these characteristics of the narrative are the literary patterns it shares with the story of Noah in Genesis 6–10.[160]

There is a paucity of work explicating the intertextual bond between the narratives of Jonah and Noah. An examination of Jonah commentaries will find the two narratives connected only by brief notes about idiomatic expressions employed in both texts.[161] However, several scholars have argued for a more full-fledged intertextual relationship between them.

---

[154] Clements, "The Purpose of the Book of Jonah," 19.

[155] Trible, "Studies in the Book of Jonah." The gist of Trible's doctoral work is in her book *Rhetorical Criticism: Context, Method, and the Book of Jonah.*

[156] Magonet, *Form and Meaning: Studies in the Literary Techniques in the Book of Jonah.*

[157] Sasson, *Jonah* (Anchor Bible).

[158] See "The Genre of Jonah" above.

[159] See "Jonah as Satire with Irony" above.

[160] The case for intertextuality in the book of Jonah (though not in that idiom) was first make by Feuillet in "Les sources du livre de Jonas."

[161] For example, Sasson, *Jonah*, notes the use of נִחַם in Jonah (3:9–10; 4:2) and Gen 6:6–7 (p. 262), the use of חָמָס in Jonah 3:8 and Gen 6:11, 13 (p. 259), and the word בַּעֲדִי in Jonah 2:7 as an abbreviated form of וַיִּסְגֹּר יְהוָה בַּעֲדוֹ in Gen 7:16 (p. 190). Yet in each of these cases,

One of the few pieces of biblical scholarship that seeks to establish an intertextual link between Jonah and Noah is the dissertation of Timothy Koch.[162] Koch's insights are helpful, but on their own they are unable to substantiate an intertextual connection between Jonah and Noah.

What is lacking in Koch's analysis is found in Albert Kamp's study of Jonah, in which he states: "With the *same lexemes* the flood story presents topics of wickedness, wrong paths and violence, to which YHWH reacts with change."[163] Kamp does not offer an extensive methodology for the identification and analysis of the intertextual relationships.[164] As the subtitle of his work indicates, the overall focus of Kamp's work is the cognitive linguistic study of Jonah. Within that study, Kamp discusses the Jonah-Noah intertextual relationship in one section of one chapter. It is not a central issue of his work; nevertheless, his attention to grounding intertextual connections on textual evidence is a positive contribution that invites closer investigation of the Jonah-Noah intertextual relationship based on a sound methodology.

Kamp's overall observation is that both Jonah and Noah use the same lexemes in "a dynamic network of reversal and change." Kamp explicates how both texts describe humans as doing "evil" (רָעָה, Gen 6:5; Jonah 1:2, etc.) and "violence" (חָמָס, Gen 6:11, 13; Jonah 3:8). In Genesis, God "sees" (רָאָה, Gen 6:5, 12) this evil and "changes his verdict" (Niphal of נָחַם, Gen 6:6–7) about the people he has "made" (עָשָׂה, Gen 6:6–7) and decides to destroy them. By contrast, in Jonah, God "sees" (רָאָה, Jonah 3:10) the repentance of the Ninevites and "changes his verdict" (Niphal of נָחַם, 3:10; also in 3:9; 4:2), deciding not to "do" (עָשָׂה, 3:10) what he had threatened, that is, deciding not to destroy them. Kamp also notes tension between faithful Noah and unfaithful Jonah as seen in their names: "נחם (Gen 5.29) resonates in [Noah's] name and he finds grace in YHWH's eyes (חֵן in Gen 6.8),"[165] while Jonah's actions make "his introduction as the son of Amittai, 'son of a faithful one' [Jonah 1:1], rather ironic. For unlike Noah, Jonah does not live up to his name."[166]

Sasson offers citations of the use of the parallel term or phrase also in other texts. He does not argue for any deliberate Jonah-Noah intertextual links.

[162] Koch, "The Book of Jonah and a Reframing of Israelite Theology: A Reader-Response Approach," 286–91.

[163] Kamp, *Inner Worlds: A Cognitive Linguistic Approach to the Book of Jonah*, 209 (emphasis added).

[164] Kamp (*Inner Worlds*, 86, n. 41) cites Wolde, "Texts in Dialogue with Texts," and on that basis argues that in order to identify intertextual references the reader is to pay attention to "1. the repetition of words and semantic fields, 2. the repetition of large text-units or structures, 3. agreements in theme or genre, 4. analogy in character descriptions, 5. agreements in plot, and 6. agreeing narratological representations."

[165] The verb נָחַם, whose Niphal refers to God "changing his mind," is used in the Piel to say that Noah will "comfort" people (Gen 5:29). The first two Hebrew letters of that verb also form Noah's name (נֹחַ), and those two letters in reverse order form the word "grace" (חֵן).

[166] Kamp, *Inner Worlds*, 209–10.

Kamp explores further intertextual connections revolving around the role of water.[167] In the Noah narrative, water destroys life, except for that in the ark, which is preserved. Jonah too is preserved in the midst of the water. The Ninevites are spared despite their evil and violence, but Noah's contemporaries are destroyed. Thus, parallel issues arise, but the "unfolding or denouement takes place in quite a different way."[168]

Ben Zvi is a third scholar who notes significant parallels between Noah and Jonah. These parallels include the following: Gen 6:7 is an example of divine repentance alongside Jonah 3:10.[169] The presence of חָמָס, "violence," among Noah's contemporaries (Gen 6:11, 13) and the Ninevites (Jonah 3:8) is a key element of their sinfulness.[170] Jonah's name means "dove," and that is reminiscent of the dove used by Noah (Gen 8:10–12). In Genesis the dove is associated with "good tidings followed by the disappearance of the messenger"; like that dove, Jonah, God's messenger, "attempts to fly away (cf. Jon. 1:3)."[171] And there is a distinction between Jonah and Noah with regard to their offering of sacrifices to Yahweh following deliverance from the waters.[172]

Eric Hesse and Isaac Kikawada also note the close ties between these narratives in their article "Jonah and Genesis 11–1." As the title of their article suggests, they argue "that the underlying narrative progression of Jonah is the exact reverse of the topical progression of the Primeval History."[173] When discussing the reason for the many allusions from Genesis 1–11 in Jonah, these authors arrive at the following conclusion about the book of Jonah:

> This is a radical reinterpretation of the Mosaic covenant. The framework of the people to whom the covenant applies has been expanded to cover the Israelites and the Ninevites alike. This implies that the covenant binds all of humanity and, for that matter, even the cattle.[174]

Hesse and Kikawada are essentially correct, though the focus of their work does not allow them to specifically undertake a detailed analysis of Genesis 6–10 in relation to the book of Jonah. What follows is an attempt to build upon Koch, Kamp, ben Zvi, and Hesse and Kikawada.

Recognizing the connections between Jonah and Noah is essential to understanding how Jonah's missional theology unfolds. To postulate connections

---

[167] Many scholars have identified this connection involving the prominent role of water, including drowning or near drowning. For example, in a recent work Barbara Green sees Jonah as "cousin … to many biblical water motifs" (*Jonah's Journeys*, 133).

[168] Kamp, *Inner Worlds*, 214–15.

[169] Ben Zvi, *Signs of Jonah*, 36.

[170] Ben Zvi, *Signs of Jonah*, 53, including n. 44.

[171] Ben Zvi, *Signs of Jonah*, 41.

[172] Ben Zvi, *Signs of Jonah*, 122. Ben Zvi states: "Unlike the story of Noah (see Gen 8.20), Jonah does not and cannot offer sacrifices once he reaches dry land. Instead, he hopes to fulfill his vows at the temple of YHWH (2.10)."

[173] Hesse and Kikawada, "Jonah and Genesis 11–1," 3.

[174] Hesse and Kikawada, "Jonah and Genesis 11–1," 16.

between Noah and Jonah we need a responsible methodology. If such connections can be established, Genesis 6–10 will facilitate the proper interpretation of the narrative of Jonah.[175] These comments by Richard Schultz are helpful:

> In seeking significant verbal parallels, one should look for *verbal and syntactical correspondence* that goes beyond one key or uncommon term or even a series of commonly occurring terms, also evaluating whether the expression is simply formulaic or idiomatic. Thus one also should look for indications of *contextual awareness*, including *interpretive re-use*, which indicates verbal *dependence* which is conscious and purposeful, even though one may not be able to determine the direction of borrowing with any certainty. If such dependence can be posited, one's knowledge of the *quoted* text will facilitate the proper interpretation of the *quoting* text.[176]

Schultz argues for a reasoned, critical assessment of legitimate intertexts. His focus on the interpretive reuse is of great import as it takes us beyond simply noting the appearance of an intertext to the issue of elucidating how the borrowed material is transformed and so also affects the interpretation of the new context into which it is placed.

The most striking verbal parallel between the Pentateuch and Jonah is the reuse of the formula from Ex 34:6–7 in Jonah 4:2: "a gracious and merciful God, slow to anger and abounding in loyal love, and changing your verdict about evil."[177] In these and other cases, the narrator of Jonah uses older OT themes and ideas not because of his deficiency in narrative skill, still less as an act of plagiarism, but in order to create connections and contrasts between the past and the current setting of Jonah. This literary device is a sort of déjà vu technique that invites us to note the similarity, make comparisons and/or contrasts, and draw thematic and theological correlations between biblical episodes.

Since the time of Moses (fifteenth century BC), the ancient Israelites who read or heard the Scriptures were, for all intents and purposes, informed by the view of history as put forward by the Pentateuch. That history is framed by genealogies and progressive covenants that led the God who created the heavens and the earth ultimately to concern himself with Israel—and with Israel alone. This history can be conceived of as a series of covenants. First, Yahweh makes a covenant with all of creation (Gen 9:8–17). Then, from among the descendants of those who survive the flood, he chooses Abra(ha)m and his descendants (Gen 12:1–3) and makes a covenant with him (Gen 15:9–21; 17:1–14). Later, he confirms the covenant he made with Abraham and his offspring (Ex

---

[175] This reading strategy is defined in Schultz, "The Ties That Bind: Intertextuality, the Identification of Verbal Parallels, and Reading Strategies in the Book of the Twelve," who discusses these issues of biblical intertextuality. Perhaps the single most important contribution to the study is Fishbane, *Biblical Interpretation in Ancient Israel*.

[176] Schultz, "The Ties That Bind: Intertextuality, the Identification of Verbal Parallels, and Reading Strategies in the Book of the Twelve," 32.

[177] The same or a similar formula is in Num 14:18; Deut 4:31; Joel 2:13; Nah 1:3; Pss 78:38; 86:5, 15; 103:8; 111:4; 112:4; 116:5; 145:8; Neh 9:17, 31; 2 Chr 30:9.

24:1–11) and then leads these descendants of Abraham to take possession of the land of Canaan.

In this sequence of covenants, each one becomes more definitive, restrictive, and specific than preceding one(s). By identifying the God of creation with the God who chooses Israel, the Pentateuchal history affirms that Yahweh is not merely a tribal god among others, but is in fact the one and only God, the God who is supreme over all creation, all events, all places, and all times—and he has elected Israel as his own. Just as it is one and the same God who makes all the covenants, so each of the progressively more specific covenants can be seen as part of one overarching covenant of grace that extends throughout the OT and is fulfilled by the new covenant in Christ.[178]

What is discovered through the narrative of Jonah is the same identification of God as the God of the covenants—but with the current running *in the opposite direction*! When we read Jonah we are pushed back in time, all the way back to Noah. The Pentateuch declares that the God of all creation is also the God of Noah, and he becomes the God of Abraham, Isaac, and Jacob, and then the God of Israel at Mount Sinai. Yet here in Jonah—for the first time in the OT—this assertion is offered in its reverse form: the God of Israel, who appeared at Sinai and who previously appeared as the God of Abraham, Isaac, and Jacob *has always been* the God of Noah, and indeed, the God of all creation! That is to say, the starting point for Israel's history is not the covenant at Sinai or the prior covenant with Abraham and his offspring. The first covenant is the one God made with Noah, which encompassed *all* subsequent humanity—plus many animals besides (cf. Jonah 4:11). And the God who made that covenant with Noah is the same God who created the heavens and the earth and all that is in them, including the first people and animals (Genesis 1; cf. Jonah 1:9).

In Jonah, the very God who seems to have winnowed out entire peoples and nations and tribes and families in choosing Israel is presented as the God who has always and all along been the compassionate, merciful God of Israel, to be sure, but *also* the God who created and sustains the Edomites, Ishmaelites, Canaanites, and Amalekites—in short, the God who is the author of all life, who made a covenant with all humanity through Noah, and who reigns over everything and everyone, including, of course, the Ninevites!

Nowhere in the narrative of Jonah is this connection with Noah made explicit. Yet, from the moment that Jonah says to the mariners in Jonah 1:9, "A Hebrew I am, and Yahweh, the God of the heavens, I worship, who made the sea and dry land," we enter a current that takes us back to the God of Abraham, Isaac, and Jacob and then farther back in the direction of Noah's God and finally back to the Creator. The one who made the sea and the dry land is the one

---

[178] See Roehrs, "Divine Covenants: Their Structure and Function," and the excursus "Covenant" in Harstad, *Joshua,* 744–56.

who cares for all peoples and all animals. God demonstrated this care by saving eight people to continue the human race and by saving the animals in the ark. He established his first covenant with the promise that he would continue to care for all creation (Gen 8:21–22; 9:8–17).

What constitutes this current that takes us on a ride toward the life and times of Noah and even back to creation itself? One answer is found in the presence throughout the narrative of Jonah of what is termed a "Noahic milieu." There are numerous and, it would seem, intentional connections between the narratives of Noah and Jonah. Jonah's statement "A Hebrew I am" (1:9) is an oblique reference to Abraham, who was the first known "Hebrew" (עִבְרִי first occurs in Gen 14:13). That statement and Jonah's recitation from Ex 34:6–7 in Jonah 4:2 convey that a steady stream runs back to God as he had revealed himself at Mount Sinai, to his dealings with the first Hebrews, to his covenant with Noah, and finally to him as Creator of the entire cosmos. With this understanding—and no other—can we build enough consistency in our understanding of the narrative to comprehend Jonah's intense misery in chapter 4, where he complains that he knew it was consistent with God's character to care for those formerly violent but repentant Ninevites (4:2); it was "just like God" to have compassion on them and their animals.

A good but admittedly non-technical way of describing this intertextuality is a technique that has garnered notoriety in the world of popular music. "Sampling" involves taking snippets of other artists' songs and weaving them into a new song. Such "samples" act as accents to the song itself. They also bring in the musical and affective associations that the listeners have with those songs being sampled. Samplings represent a kind of "musical intertextuality." Although a new song can be enjoyed on its own merits without listener knowledge of any other tunes, samples provide the aware audience with additional, potentially meaningful dimensions to their musical experience.[179]

Just so, Jonah can be said to "sample" the narrative of Noah in order to re-contextualize and revivify Yahweh's covenant with all people and animals.[180]

---

[179] The technique is, in fact, nothing new. Consider the lyrics of the well-known patriotic song "You're a Grand Old Flag" (George M. Cohan, lyricist, 1906), which "samples" the much older song "Auld Lang Syne" (published in the later part of the eighteenth century but based on even older ballads); the sampled line from "Auld Lang Syne" is in italics:

> You're a grand old flag.
> You're a high flying flag
> And forever in peace may you wave. …
> *Should auld acquaintance be forgot,*
> Keep your eye on the grand old flag.

The use of "Should auld acquaintance be forgot" brings to "You're a Grand Old Flag," which is a musical affirmation of patriotism, the feeling of community by evoking a song traditionally sung by close friends and family seeing in the new year together.

[180] This discussion of sampling extends, of course, to all intertextual citations, references, and allusions in the book of Jonah. For a more comprehensive treatment of other intertextual ties, see Magonet, *Form and Meaning*, 65–84, and Simon, *Jonah*, xxxvi–xxxix.

More technically, Gerhard von Rad calls this aspect of the OT *Vergegenwärti-gung*, translated as "the fresh presentation," "updating," or "reactualization."[181] Although the narrative of Jonah can be appreciated without any awareness of these reactualizations, recognition of the Noahic connections sprinkled throughout the book take us in the direction of Yahweh's care for his entire creation.

What follows, then, is a list of phrases, characters, and images from Genesis 6–10 that find resonance within the narrative of Jonah. The narrator's reuse of Noahic words, phrases, and motifs is intended to take us to the universal promises God made in Gen 9:8–17, which would include the Ninevites, and indeed all people.

1. "Forty days and forty nights" (Gen 7:4) was the period of time that the rains lasted, producing the universal deluge that destroyed all human and animal life that was not with Noah in the ark. Similarly, "forty days" is the amount of time from the moment of Jonah's prophecy until Nineveh is to be destroyed (3:4). This association of "forty days" as a period of impending destruction, but with a new beginning by God's grace, is a link between these two stories.[182]

2. "One hundred twenty" (Gen 6:3) was the number of years allotted by Yahweh to human life. It is also how many thousands of people are in Nineveh at the end of the story of Jonah (4:11).

3. In general terms, "the evil of mankind" (רָעַת הָאָדָם, Gen 6:5) was what Yahweh observed on the face of the earth, prompting the flood. Regarding the Ninevites, Yahweh declares, "Their evil has arisen before me" (עָלְתָה רָעָתָם לְפָנָי, Jonah 1:2). "Evil" (רָעָה) is one of the key words in the book of Jonah, used nine times (1:2, 7, 8; 3:8, 10 [twice]; 4:1, 2, 6).

4. More specifically, "violence" (חָמָס, Gen 6:11, 13) was the reason for God's decision to destroy the earth and its inhabitants by means of the flood. "Violence" (חָמָס, Jonah 3:8) is also the specific sin that the Ninevites recognize as part of their own "evil" way of life (רָעָה, 3:8), and from it they repent.[183]

5. God's creation originally had been "very good" (Gen 1:31), but became corrupted because of mankind's "evil" (Gen 6:5). Therefore, Yahweh changed his disposition toward mankind. This is expressed in Gen 6:6–7 with the Niphal of נָחַם, which usually is translated as "was sorry": "Yahweh was sorry that he

---

[181] The approach and terminology is exemplified throughout both volumes of von Rad's *Old Testament Theology*.

[182] A period of "forty days" occurs in other texts; for example, it is the time it takes to embalm Joseph (Gen 50:3); the amount of time Moses spent on top of Sinai with God (Ex 24:18); how long the scouts spy out the promised land (Num 13:25); the number of days that Goliath taunts Israel (1 Sam 17:16); and the period of time that Ezekiel is instructed to lie on his right side, signaling the number of years that Judah is to be punished (Ezek 4:6). Of all these references, "forty days" is connected with punishment or destruction only in the flood narrative, Jonah, and Ezek 4:6.

[183] Orlinsky, makes the connections between the words "evil" (רָעָה) and "violence" (חָמָס) in both the Noah narrative and the book of Jonah ("Nationalism-Universalism and Internationalism in Ancient Israel," 231).

had created mankind" (וַיִּנָּחֶם יְהוָה כִּי־עָשָׂה אֶת־הָאָדָם, Gen 6:6). The implication is that Yahweh "changed the verdict" of "very good" that he had previously decreed about the creation. Thus he decided to destroy mankind (Gen 6:7). The Ninevites use the same verb, the Niphal of נָחַם, to express their hope that Yahweh might turn from his earlier decree that he would destroy them: "Who knows whether God may turn and change his verdict?" (מִי־יוֹדֵעַ יָשׁוּב וְנִחַם הָאֱלֹהִים, Jonah 3:9). This is exactly what God does in 3:10, and in 4:2 Jonah states that it was characteristic of Yahweh to do this. Both 3:10 and 4:2 also use the Niphal of נָחַם.

6. In the Noah narrative, God decides to wipe out both "mankind" (אָדָם) and "animals" (בְּהֵמָה), and those two nouns occur together in Gen 6:7; 7:21, 23. Yet God saved both Noah's family and the animals in the ark. The book of Jonah is remarkable for its deliberate inclusion of animals along with people: both the Ninevites and their animals repent (3:7–9), and in his final question God refers to his compassion for both the Ninevites and their animals (4:10–11).[184] "Mankind" (אָדָם) and "animals" (בְּהֵמָה) occur together in Jonah 3:7–8 and 4:11.

7. The ark (תֵּבָה, Genesis 6–9) is the means that God provided to protect Noah, his family, and the animals from the flood. The ark may be compared to the ship that Jonah boards (1:3), and even more to the great fish (2:1 [ET 1:17]), which turns out to be the "vessel" that Yahweh provides to protect Jonah from the overwhelming flood waters and Sheol.

8. "The deep" bursts forth to begin the flood (תְּהוֹם, Gen 7:11; the same word is also used in Gen 1:2; 8:2). Jonah in his psalmic prayer uses this same term, "the deep," to refer to the waters that surrounded him (תְּהוֹם, Jonah 2:6).

9. As Yahweh destroyed life by means of the flood, the "waters" (מַיִם, frequent in Genesis 7–8) covered the "dry land" (חָרָבָה, Gen 7:22). The distinction between the two is crucial, for the difference was between life and death. Even though Jonah uses a different Hebrew term for "dry land," יַבָּשָׁה (1:9, 11; 2:11; used also in Gen 1:9–10), the prophet identifies Yahweh as the one who made "the sea and the dry land" (Jonah 1:9). The distinction between the two is crucial: the sailors, fearing death at sea, sought to return the ship to "dry land" (1:13), and Yahweh had the great fish vomit Jonah onto "dry land" (2:11 [ET 2:10]) so that he did not perish in the "waters" (מַיִם, 2:6 [ET 2:5]).

---

[184] Nixon, *Jonah*, 167–68, writes:

> In the story of Noah's ark, all species of animals shared with humanity in both the calamity of the flood and the eventual deliverance. The story tells how, in the ark, they were miraculously preserved together and together shared a new beginning. While significant differences [between people and animals] are indicated in Genesis 1:24–31, these verses speak of the animals sharing the same day of creation with humankind. We may suppose from this an intended and close relationship between these two orders of creation. It is this mutual interdependence between human beings and animals that underlies the inclusion of animals at Nineveh.

The humans and the animals are both included in repentance (Jonah 3) and as objects of God's compassion (Jonah 4).

10. After the flood, Yahweh decreed capital punishment for murder as a statute to be observed for all humanity: "I will require a reckoning for human life. Whoever sheds the blood of a human, by a human shall that person's blood be shed" (Gen 9:5–6). This standard of justice is also part of the natural law written upon the hearts of all people (cf. Rom 2:14). The sailors demonstrate an awareness of this when they plead with Yahweh not to kill them as a punishment for throwing Jonah overboard into the sea (1:14).

11. In the flood narrative, God caused a "wind" (רוּחַ, Gen 8:1) to blow for the purpose of causing the flood waters to subside. (רוּחַ referring to Yahweh's "Spirit" occurs in Gen 6:3, and רוּחַ means "breath" in the phrase "breath of life" in Gen 6:17; 7:15, 22.) In Jonah, Yahweh hurls a "wind" (רוּחַ) upon the sea to create a storm (1:4) and later sends a searing "wind" (רוּחַ) from the east that adds to Jonah's misery (4:8).

12. In Genesis, Noah sent out a "dove" (יוֹנָה) three times. The first time, "the dove found no place to set its foot, and it returned to him" (Gen 8:8–9). The second time, Noah "sent out the dove," and it found dry land (Gen 8:10–11; the third time, it did not return [Gen 8:12]). The name "Jonah" (יוֹנָה) is Hebrew for "dove." Yahweh sent Jonah twice. The first time, in Jonah 1–2, the prophet does not alight on dry ground, but ends up in the water! Yahweh then sends Jonah a second time (3:1–2), and he remains on the dry land.

13. After the flood, Noah, back on dry land, "offered burnt offerings on an altar" (וַיַּעַל עֹלֹת בַּמִּזְבֵּחַ, Gen 8:20). After the mariners were delivered from the great storm, they "sacrificed a sacrifice [וַיִּזְבְּחוּ־זֶבַח] to Yahweh" (1:16). Once Jonah recognizes that Yahweh has delivered him from Sheol, he pledges to Yahweh, "I will indeed sacrifice to you" (אֶזְבְּחָה־לָּךְ, 2:10 [ET 2:9]). The verb זָבַח, "sacrifice," in Jonah 1:16 and 2:10 is the root of the noun "altar" (מִזְבֵּחַ) in Gen 8:20. In all three cases—Noah, the mariners, and Jonah—their offerings to Yahweh are a thanksgiving for their deliverance from death by drowning.

14. Yahweh pledges to Noah, his family, and to all living creatures after the flood, "Never again will I destroy every living creature as I have done" (Gen 8:21). This pledge is, to a great extent, the motivation behind Jonah's reluctance to be Yahweh's prophet to Nineveh. He knows that this God, who is "gracious and merciful" (4:2), has voluntarily given up total destruction—at least by flood—as a means for dealing with humanity's evil and violence.

15. In the covenant Yahweh established after the flood, he specifically included not only mankind, but also animals, domestic and wild: "Behold, I am establishing my covenant with you and your descendants after you and with every living creature. … And I will remember my covenant that is between me and you and every living creature of all flesh" (Gen 9:9–10, 15). The umbrella of this covenant is extended to non-Israelite humans (Gentiles, like the Ninevites) as well as their animals, whose donning of sackcloth and bleating perhaps serve to remind Yahweh of this promise (Jonah 3:7–9; see also Yahweh's compassion for their animals in 4:11).

16. The phrase הָעִיר הַגְּדֹלָה is used in Gen 10:12 and Jonah 1:2; 3:2; 4:11 (the phrase without the articles is in 3:3). In Jonah the phrase describes Nineveh as "the great city." In Gen 10:12 it might refer to Calah (about eighteen miles south of Nineveh and sometimes considered part of Greater Nineveh) or to Nineveh or to the area encompassing both.

17. Shem, Ham, and Japheth were the sons of Noah (Gen 6:10), and from these the whole earth was populated after the flood (Gen 9:18–19). The descendants of Ham included Nimrod, who went into Assyria and built Nineveh, the great city (Gen 10:6–12). Hence God's covenant with Noah and his descendants extends to Assyria, to Nineveh, and to its residents. The narrative of Jonah takes it as a given that this covenant is operative and that the Ninevites (and Assyrians), despite their evil and violence, are included in it.

Some critics might describe these connections between Noah and Jonah as "trendy intertextuality"[185] or " 'banal' source-hunting"[186] rather than an intentional reuse of the Noah narrative by the author of Jonah. One response may borrow from Raymond Brown. In *An Introduction to the Gospel of John*, Brown addresses the issue of whether there exist sacramental references in the Gospel of John and why such references should occur by way of symbolism, which the later Christian church would not recognize, leading to a loss of recognition of the sacramental content of this Gospel. Drawing on the work of Oscar Cullman, Raymond Brown argues that "baptism and the eucharist were familiar to the early Christian communities, and … therefore symbolic references to them would be easily recognized" in the early church.[187] In much the same way, references to foundational texts such as that of Noah would have been so engrained in the life and thought of Israel that Jonah's audience would readily recognize allusions to it. Sadly, the passage of time has led to the loss of recognition of such connections.

This comparison of the narratives of Noah and Jonah allows Scripture to interpret Scripture, and it leads to the question posed by St. Paul: "Is he only the God of the Jews? Is he not also (the God) of the Gentiles? Yes, also of the Gentiles!" (Rom 3:29). The Greek negative particle οὐχί, "Is he not … ?" expects yes for an answer. The God of Israel never ceases to be the God of all creation. As Childs states, this means that Jonah is "a genuine Old Testament witness directed against a misunderstanding of the election of Israel."[188] That is to say, Jonah's reactions in chapter 4 to Nineveh's conversion reflect a ten-

---

[185] "Trendy Intertextuality?" is the title of an article by Ellen van Wolde, which does not, however, discuss the specific example of the use of the Noah narrative in Jonah.

[186] This phrase is used by Aichele and Phillips, "Introduction: Exegesis, Eisegesis, Intergesis," 9, to describe the view of Julia Kristeva about what intertextuality, properly defined, is not. The use of the Noah account by the author of Jonah is not under discussion.

[187] Raymond E. Brown, *An Introduction to the Gospel of John* (updated ed.; New York: Doubleday, 2003), 230.

[188] Childs, "The Canonical Shape of the Book of Jonah," 127.

sion in Israel between a universal and a parochial view of Yahweh. It is through the Noahic milieu within Jonah that Yahweh's universal compassion is stated, making the narrative an evangelistic and missionary document of the first rank.

The reaction to Yahweh's universal concern for all peoples, and even their animals, is represented in the narrative by Jonah himself—a member of the "establishment" in Israel that embraced the parochial view that Yahweh was only concerned with Israel. This narrow view is satirized in that Jonah is disobedient, reluctant, and angry even after a completely successful mission to Nineveh. Jonah is critiqued by the many allusions to the Noahic covenant, which Yahweh in compassion promised to "all flesh on the earth" (Gen 9:17) and guaranteed with a rainbow (Gen 9:12–17).

In contrast to the narrative's critique of Jonah, it treats the pagans positively, since eventually they turn to Yahweh in faith. The sailors are depicted as sincere. They pray to their gods as best as they know how (1:5a). They try their best to save the ship (1:5b), even when they suspect that Jonah has brought trouble on them. When Jonah advises them to cast him overboard (1:12), they are reluctant to sacrifice his life and do so only as a last resort, after they have prayed to Yahweh (1:13–14). Later they sacrifice to Yahweh and make vows (1:16).

Like the sailors, the Ninevites are also given a positive treatment. To be sure, Yahweh knows of their "evil" (1:2). But immediately on hearing Jonah's preaching, they believe in God and repent en masse, and everyone puts on sackcloth and fasts—even their animals (3:5–9). They turn from their "evil" and "violence" (3:8).

Although some counter that neither the word "Israel" nor the word "Gentile" is used in the book of Jonah, we may compare it to the parable of the Good Samaritan (Lk 10:30–37). That parable does not explicitly refer to the conflict between Jews and Samaritans, but it would be a bold and erroneous commentator on Luke's Gospel who would ignore that conflict in his interpretation of the passage. Just so, it will be the purpose of this commentary to highlight the missional thrust of Jonah. "God so loved the world …" (Jn 3:16a), and that world includes even the Ninevites and their animals.

Jonah and Elijah

We have already witnessed, by means of the discussion of Jonah and Noah, that the narrator of Jonah is willing and able to use prior texts and rework them for his purposes.[189] In Jonah 2:3–10 (ET 2:2–9), the narrator also records Jonah's use of the Psalter. He cites the prophet's reuse of Ex 34:6–7 in Jonah 4:2.[190] Another set of intertextual links exists between Jonah and Elijah. Most

---

[189] See "Jonah and Noah" above.

[190] See further the commentary on 4:2.

interpreters mention these links, but only David Marcus fully develops the relationship between these two prophets.[191]

When the narrator of Jonah records these earlier texts, he indicates his ability—and even propensity—to rework earlier OT themes and ideas. He does this in order to contrast the past with the current setting of Jonah. This literary device is a sort of déjà vu technique that invites readers to note similarities and compare differences between Jonah and earlier OT texts. It follows, therefore, that to postulate and explore the connections between Elijah and Jonah is to enter into the rhetorical strategy and literary artistry of the book of Jonah.

The way the narrator begins Jonah 1:1 and his naming of the prophet as "Jonah the son of Amittai" link him with the brief account of this same Jonah in 2 Ki 14:25–28.[192] That passage describes Jonah as ministering during the reign of Jeroboam II (ca. 786–746 BC). Thus Jonah stands in the sequence of prophets from the Northern Kingdom that includes Elijah (1 Kings 17–2 Kings 2), Elisha, Hosea, and Amos; the latter two were likely contemporaries of Jonah. Because Jonah comes in the sequence after Elijah and Elisha, many phrases in the book of Jonah find their closest biblical parallels in the narratives about those two great prophets from the Northern Kingdom. An account involving a great fish (2:1 [ET 1:17]) as well as a small worm (4:7) would not have been out of place in the narratives about Elijah and Elisha. The book of Kings recounts numerous encounters between those prophets and Yahweh's miraculous use of creation.[193]

The book of Jonah could have been placed after the reference to Jonah the son of Amittai in 2 Ki 14:25 and not interrupt the narrative flow of 2 Kings to any great degree. Jonah and Elijah are both from the Northern Kingdom, and their ministries involve Yahweh's miraculous use of creation. The clause that begins Jonah 1:1, וַיְהִי דְּבַר־יְהוָה אֶל־, "Now the Word of Yahweh came to ... ," is used in connection with Elijah in 1 Ki 17:2, 8; 21:17, 28. These affinities subtly lead to this conclusion: the author of the Jonah narrative intends that we compare Jonah with Elijah. This comparison contributes to the overall message of the book, accomplished through satire with irony.[194]

More specific—and indeed more satirical—connections between Jonah and Elijah begin in Jonah 1:2, where Yahweh calls Jonah to "arise, go"

---

[191] Marcus, *From Balaam to Jonah*, 131–33. Some of the other scholars who have connected Jonah to Elijah are Magonet, *Form and Meaning*, 102; Wolff, *Studien zum Jonabuch*, 80–81, 168; and Stuart, *Hosea–Jonah*, 435.

[192] See the textual notes and commentary on Jonah 1:1.

[193] In the Hebrew canon 1–2 Kings is a single book. Even a representative list of its miracles involving creation is impressive: ravens bring food (1 Ki 17:1–8), fire and rain appear (1 Kings 18), a lion kills a man (1 Ki 20:35–36), the Jordan is parted and a whirlwind carries Elijah to heaven (2 Ki 2:1–14), and an ax head floats (2 Ki 6:1–7). See the excursus "Yahweh, the Creator God" in the commentary on Jonah 1.

[194] See "Jonah as Satire with Irony" above.

(קוּם לֵךְ) to Nineveh. This call for a prophet to go to a foreign land is paralleled only in 1 Ki 17:9, where Yahweh commands Elijah also to "arise, go [קוּם לֵךְ] to Zarephath, which is in Sidon." Immediately after that command, Elijah "arose and went to Zarephath" (1 Ki 17:10). Following that normal biblical pattern of divine command followed by prophetic obedience, we expect the Jonah narrative to continue, "So Jonah got up and went to Nineveh." But instead, "Jonah arose to flee to Tarshish" (1:3). He does not proclaim the "Word of Yahweh" (1:1) that had come to him. Jonah is certainly no Elijah!

Jonah flees "away from the presence of Yahweh" (מִלִּפְנֵי יְהוָה, Jonah 1:3). Using a similar expression, but with a starkly different force, both Elijah (1 Ki 17:1; 18:15) and Elisha (2 Ki 3:14; 5:16) invoke Yahweh as God, saying, "As Yahweh lives … in whose presence I stand" (חַי־יְהוָה … אֲשֶׁר עָמַדְתִּי לְפָנָיו). This expression identifies these prophets as Yahweh's servants who hear his Word and faithfully execute his commands. It suggests that the prophet stands in Yahweh's heavenly council to perceive the divine Word and obey (cf. 1 Ki 22:19; Jer 23:18, 22). Whereas Elijah faithfully stands in the presence of Yahweh and is obedient to his bidding, Jonah seeks to escape his presence—so earnestly that for emphasis the phrase "away from the presence of Yahweh" occurs twice in Jonah 1:3.

Jonah again appears as an "anti-Elijah" when we consider that Jonah flees because he begrudges Yahweh's gracious characteristics (see Jonah 4:2), whereas Elijah flees because Jezebel seeks to kill him (1 Kings 19). At the point when Elijah feels defeated, Yahweh asks him, "What are you doing here?" (מַה־לְּךָ פֹה, 1 Ki 19:9). The first two Hebrew words are identical to the captain's anxious cry in Jonah 1:6, "What are you doing in a deep sleep?" (מַה־לְּךָ נִרְדָּם). Jonah's "deep sleep" goes far beyond the exhausted sleep of Elijah when he is on the run from Jezebel (1 Ki 19:5).[195]

Yahweh takes special care of Elijah through animals and plants: ravens feed him (1 Ki 17:4–6) and a plant shades him (1 Ki 19:4). Elijah's death wish (1 Ki 19:4) comes after the death threat by Jezebel (1 Ki 19:2) prompted by his success on Mount Carmel (1 Kings 18), but God sends an angel to feed and encourage him (1 Ki 19:5–6) on his way to Mount Sinai, where he seeks Yahweh's presence. The animals and plants have parallels in Jonah in more explicitly miraculous forms: Yahweh commands a fish to safeguard Jonah through the ocean's depths (chapter 2 [ET 1:17–2:10)]), causes a qiqayon plant to grow in a single day to shade him (4:6), but then sends a worm to destroy the plant on the following morning (4:7). Ironically, Jonah's death wishes (4:3, 8–9) come after fleeing from the presence of Yahweh (1:3)—the very presence Elijah is running toward (1 Ki 19:8)! The shared elements magnify the contrasts between these two prophets and further diminish the stature of Jonah as compared to Elijah.

[195] See the textual notes and commentary on the Niphal of רָדַם ("fall into a deep sleep") in Jonah 1:5.

A closer look at Elijah's death wish demonstrates further satire when it is compared to Jonah 4:3, where the pouting prophet asks Yahweh to take his life. In 1 Kings 19, in his flight from Jezebel, Elijah begs Yahweh to take his life (1 Ki 19:4). Elijah's motivation appears to be twofold: he believes he is a failure as a prophet because he is the only true follower of Yahweh left (1 Ki 19:10), and he believes he is going to die anyway at the hands of the wicked queen. Thus Elijah overlooks Obadiah and the hundred Yahwistic prophets still in hiding (1 Ki 18:3–4) and also God's power to preserve him despite the rage of foes. Yahweh commissions Elijah to anoint Elisha as his successor (1 Ki 19:16) and promises to preserve seven thousand people in Israel who do not worship Baal (1 Ki 19:18).

In Jonah 4:3 the prophet laments, "Yahweh, take my life from me" (יְהוָה קַח־נָא אֶת־נַפְשִׁי מִמֶּנִּי). Here Jonah strikes a noble pose by echoing the prayer of Elijah in 1 Ki 19:4: "Yahweh, take my life" (יְהוָה קַח נַפְשִׁי). Elijah continued, "For I am no better than my fathers" (כִּי־לֹא־טוֹב אָנֹכִי מֵאֲבֹתָי, 1 Ki 19:4). Jonah uses the same adjective and preposition (טוֹב מִן, "better than"), but adapts the words to say, "For my death would be better than my life" (כִּי טוֹב מוֹתִי מֵחַיָּי, Jonah 4:3). Later in chapter 4, Jonah again prays for death, this time under his qiqayon plant (4:7–8), like Elijah before him, who sat under a broom tree and prayed for death at a time of crisis (1 Ki 19:4). Elijah, wearied by his endless struggle with Baalism, was convinced that he would not succeed where his fathers had failed. He believed that it was time to join them in death. Shockingly, Jonah is disappointed with the very success of his mission: Nineveh repented and was spared by Yahweh! Jonah has Elijah's depression without Elijah's excuse.

As Elijah experienced a revelation of Yahweh on Mount Horeb, Jonah also receives divine revelation in 4:10–11. Besides some of the patriarchs, Moses, and Jonah in 4:10–11,[196] only two other OT prophets explicitly receive Yahweh's Word outside the boundaries of the promised land: Elijah at Mount Horeb (1 Ki 19:8–18) and Ezekiel in Babylon (e.g., Ezek 1:3; 3:16; 6:1). Elijah travels to Horeb and has a dramatic encounter with Yahweh, who speaks to him in the "soft murmuring sound" (or "still, small voice," קוֹל דְּמָמָה דַקָּה, 1 Ki 19:12). Elijah and Ezekiel both respond by faithfully preaching and acting upon the divine Word. In striking contrast, Jonah petulantly bickered with God about his personal discomfort outside of the promised land (4:8), and the book ends without indicating whether Jonah responded in faith to the "extraterrestrial" revelation of Yahweh's Word.

In both 1 Kings 19 and Jonah 4, Yahweh deals with his prophet by means of his creation and then edifies him through his Word. In Elijah's case, the prophet finally understands that Yahweh's work will not be accomplished by

---

[196] Presumably Jonah was in Israel when the Word of Yahweh first came to him (1:1), and also when the Word came to him a second time (3:1) after the fish had vomited him upon the shore of Israel.

the wind, earthquake, or fire (1 Ki 19:11–12). Rather, Yahweh will accomplish his great purposes through a "gentle whisper" (1 Ki 19:12), that is to say, by the power of his Gospel Word and through the ministries of Elijah and his successor, Elisha (1 Ki 19:15–18). In Jonah's case, Yahweh deals with the prophet by means of the storm, the great fish, his second chance (3:1), and the qiqayon plant, and accomplishes his purpose through the Word he gives Jonah to preach (3:4). After all that, Jonah's lack of responsiveness is shocking.

These comparisons and contrasts between the Elijah and Jonah lead us to a conclusion. If Elijah is the most daring, courageous, victorious Yahwistic prophet in Israel's history,[a] and indeed one of the major fulfillments of Yahweh's promise to raise up a prophet like Moses (Deut 18:15), then Jonah is the antithesis of this mighty hero of old.

In the process of his narration of true history,[197] the author of Jonah uses in his new literary creation established forms from the account of Elijah's life. By mixing the old with the new, he is able to communicate coherently as he employs elements from the older narrative for new purposes. This use of familiar language is a major characteristic in the narrative of Jonah. As we have seen, it includes allusions to Elijah that satirize Jonah. The goal of this satire is to show Jonah's need for repentance, and likewise to drive the reading audience of the book to repentance from narrow nationalism, and to instill renewed faith that includes zeal for evangelism to all peoples and nations. By this means, the narrator challenges his audience to aspire not to the likes of Jonah, but to Elijah, that most eminent OT prophet, whose ministry was marked by compassion and concern for others beyond the borders of Israel (1 Ki 17:7–24).

In the fullness of time, God the Son would come to minister, suffer, die, and rise on the third day, furnishing "the sign of Jonah" (Mt 12:39; 16:4; Lk 11:29).[198] The Prophet from Galilee, as one greater than Jonah (Mt 12:41), would recall the ministry of Elijah (Lk 4:24–26) and send his disciples to extend God's salvation to the ends of the earth.

(a) See Mal 3:23 (ET 4:5); Mt 11:13–14; 17:3–4, 10–12; Lk 1:17; Jn 1:21, 25

Jonah's Place in the Book of the Twelve

Jonah is the fifth book in the section of the OT known as the Minor Prophets.[199] There are, of course, differences between Jonah and the other books that comprise the twelve Minor Prophets.[200] For the most part, these other

---

[197] See "Jonah: Fact or Fiction?" above.

[198] See the excursus "The Sign of Jonah" in the commentary on Jonah 2.

[199] The order of the twelve Minor Prophets in English Bibles follows that of Hebrew manuscripts, with Obadiah preceding Jonah and Micah following it. The Greek manuscripts of the LXX order the Minor Prophets differently: Hosea, Amos, Micah, Joel, Obadiah, Jonah, Nahum, Habakkuk, Zephaniah, Haggai, Zechariah, Malachi.

[200] Apparently the first description of the Minor Prophets as "the twelve prophets" is in the apocryphal book of Ecclesiasticus (49:10), written in the early second century BC. The twelve are Hosea through Malachi. While Daniel precedes Hosea in English Bibles, in the Hebrew canon Daniel is considered a Wisdom book and so is among the Writings.

prophetic books are collections of oracles, with an occasional narrative about a particular prophet (e.g., Amos 7:10–15). In stark contrast, Jonah is a narrative about a prophet with only one true prophetic oracle, and a brief one at that (3:4, five words in Hebrew; see also his confession in 1:9, by which he first carries out his prophetic office). In comparison with the other eleven Minor Prophets, who generally were faithful even under persecution, Jonah's disobedience comes as a shock. Likewise, the miraculous incident in which Jonah is swallowed by the great fish has no parallels in the other Minor Prophets.[201] Not quite so different are the Jonah passages that refer to Yahweh speaking to the great fish and appointing the qiqayon plant, a worm, and a wind, but these do tend to distance the narrative of Jonah from the other books in this section of the OT.

In spite of these differences from the other Minor Prophets, Jonah is placed in this corpus in a position that contributes to the overall message of the OT canon. Jonah follows Obadiah to temper that prophet's diatribes against the Gentile nation of Edom: Jonah demonstrates Yahweh's mercy toward the Gentile sailors and the people of Nineveh. Jonah precedes the book of Micah, but it is not clear what specifically connects these two books. It might simply be that Jonah precedes Micah in a chronological manner, that is, the events recounted in Jonah took place earlier in the eighth century BC, and Micah prophesied in the second half of that century and possibly into the next.

Following Micah is Nahum, which celebrates Yahweh's destruction of Nineveh for its crimes against Israel and other ancient Near Eastern peoples. This indicates that while Yahweh shows mercy to the Ninevites when they repented in the eighth century BC, he will punish the subsequent generations in the seventh century when the city goes back to its former ways. This shows that God treats the Gentile Ninevites in the same way that he treats his people Israel, whose infidelity eventually led to their fall.

Moreover, although at first glance Jonah and Nahum appear to be very different, similarities do in fact exist. In both books Nineveh is the enemy that inspires dread in the hearts and minds of people. Both books refer to the same theological themes of judgment and grace. Both draw on the same text, Ex 34:6–7: "You are a gracious and merciful God, slow to anger and abounding in loyal love, and changing your verdict about evil" (Jonah 4:2), and "Yahweh is slow to anger and of great might, and Yahweh will by no means acquit [the guilty]" (Nah 1:3). Both books conclude with a question (Jonah 4:11; Nah 3:19), and they are the only two books in the Bible to do so.

Another possible reason for Jonah's place in the order of the Minor Prophets is that the compilers of the canon believed they were placing these twelve books in roughly chronological sequence, just as Isaiah, Jeremiah, and Ezekiel are in historical order. The twelve are largely in chronological order,

[201] Dramatic miracles are more common in the ministries of the prophets Elijah and Elisha, and the early national leaders Moses and Joshua, than in the ministries of the writing prophets, such as the twelve. Jonah's "resurrection" from the fish might be compared to the resurrections performed through Elijah and Elisha (1 Ki 17:17–24; 2 Ki 4:18–37; 13:21).

since a number of the earlier books are from the eighth century (Hosea, Amos, Jonah, Micah, whose ministry possibly extended into the seventh century, and perhaps Joel), some of the middle books are from the seventh century (Nahum, Zephaniah, and probably Habakkuk), and the three concluding books are from the late sixth and the fifth centuries (Haggai, Zechariah, and Malachi). Jonah the son of Amittai (Jonah 1:1) is also named in 2 Ki 14:25, which places the prophet during the reign of Jeroboam II (2 Ki 14:23; ca. 786–746 BC). Thus it is fitting that Jonah follows other eighth-century minor prophets, Hosea and Amos, who were likely his contemporaries. Immediately preceding Jonah is Obadiah, whose date is uncertain, but it is possible that the compilers of the canon dated it to the eighth century.[202] Jonah is slightly older than the next book, Micah, who ministered later in the eighth century and possibly into the seventh.

Themes in Jonah

Some reduce Jonah to a single theme such as the universal scope of Yahweh's judgment and salvation, versus the nationalistic view that the God of Israel is concerned with that people alone. Other proposed themes are true versus false prophecy, divine justice versus divine mercy, the commanding presence and power of Yahweh, deliverance by Yahweh, or repentance—human and divine. But biblical narratives, even those with scarcity of detail, are able to convey a multiplicity of themes. Good literature—which certainly describes Jonah—is often evocative, using character and plot to stimulate our imagination, rather than to communicate in a comprehensive and systematic manner. Like many OT narratives, the author's strategy in Jonah is to avoid explicit praise or condemnation of any of the people in the book. Instead, the narrator conveys criticism of recalcitrant Jonah and praise of the repentant Gentiles (the sailors and the Ninevites) in other, more subtle ways.[203]

The way that the narrator of Jonah recounts history with minimal overt commentary is similar to portions of the historical books, especially Samuel and Kings. Robert Polzin's point about 1 Samuel applies to Jonah as well: "The narrator's overall style is to point rather than say, reflect rather than project."[204] It is therefore a hubristic assumption that for a work of such high literary art we can say with confidence, "The theme of Jonah is X," and fill in the X with twenty-five words or less. Jonah is too complex a narrative to postulate one theme. The view of a multiplicity of themes is preferred.

So what are the dominant ideas in the book? By a word association, "Jonah" would undoubtedly prompt the reaction of "whale," but a subject that takes up

---

[202] The book of Obadiah itself contains no information that enables a certain identification of its date. Proposals range from the ninth through the fifth centuries. Some of these proposals appeal to other OT passages containing the name Obadiah. For a survey, see Raabe, *Obadiah*, 47–56. Raabe argues for a date in the early exilic era, between 587 and 553 BC.

[203] See "Jonah as Satire with Irony" above in the introduction.

[204] Polzin, *Samuel and the Deuteronomist*, 149.

only three verses (2:1–2, 11 [ET 1:17–2:1, 10]) out of a total of forty-eight cannot be regarded as the narrative's main concern. Campbell Morgan penned these wise words: "Men have been looking so hard at the great fish that they have failed to see the great God."[205] The greatness of Yahweh is certainly one of the major themes in Jonah. Yahweh is the Creator of the land and the sea (1:9), who controls the world and uses the natural world to achieve his purposes. The storm, sea, fish, plant, worm, sun, east wind, and everything else are all under his control. Yahweh does what he pleases (1:14).

Yet Yahweh does not act capriciously. The cosmic Creator Yahweh is the God who works through Law (judgment) and Gospel (salvation), and in the end, the repentant sinners receive mercy and salvation. Therefore, instead of stressing the greatness of Yahweh's raw power, it would be more accurate to say that a major theme of the book is the greatness of Yahweh's grace. As "the Judge of all the earth" (Gen 18:25), Yahweh condemns a foreign city for its evil (Jonah 1:2) and proclaims judgment upon all its inhabitants as sinners (3:4). Yahweh is God over all the nations, and he has placed upon them all the obligation of obedience to natural law and morality, which are evident in creation and the conscience, but all people fail to live up to his standards of righteousness (cf. Rom 1:18–20; 2:14–15). Yahweh would have been justified if he had simply destroyed Nineveh without warning. Instead, he sent his prophet Jonah to preach that in forty days the city would be changed (3:4). His ultimate purpose is to drive sinners to repentance and faith (3:5) and show mercy to them (3:10; 4:2). In doing so, we learn that he takes "no delight in the death of the wicked" (Ezek 18:32) but wants "all people to be saved and come to the knowledge of the truth" (1 Tim 2:4).

Throughout the narrative, Yahweh is the God who delivers. The sailors are saved from the raging storm (Jonah 1:15). Jonah is saved from drowning in the sea as well as from Sheol (2:1 [ET 1:17]). The Ninevites are saved from destruction (3:10). Even though Jonah was angry about Yahweh saving the Ninevites, "Yahweh God provided a qiqayon plant ... to be shade over his [Jonah's] head and to save him from his evil" (4:6).

In summary, although strict justice would demand that the idolatrous sailors, the evil Ninevites, and even the prodigal Jonah should perish, over and over Yahweh's mercy prevails and grants new life. "Salvation belongs to Yahweh" (יְשׁוּעָתָה לַיהוָה, 2:10 [ET 2:9]). Indeed, "Mercy and forgiveness belong to the Lord our God" (Dan 9:9), and not to Jonah or anyone else to dispense or to withhold according to their whim and will.

The narrative of Jonah also carefully guards against the presumption that human repentance, sacrifice, prayer, fasting, vows, sackcloth (1:14–16; 2:3, 10 [ET 2:2, 9]; 3:5–9), or other works of penitence somehow merit or elicit divine mercy. Yahweh cannot be manipulated by humans, who would then become

---

[205] Morgan, *The Minor Prophets*, 69.

the arbiters of their own future. The sovereignty of Yahweh is highlighted in the "perhaps" of the captain in 1:6 and the "who knows" of the king of Nineveh in 3:9. People cannot take Yahweh's grace for granted. Yet without fail in the narrative, Yahweh shows mercy to the penitent, and even to their animals.

We may arrange the themes in Jonah into three categories:[206]

1. Jonah teaches that all people need repentance (contrition and faith). See the sailors in 1:14; Jonah in chapter 2; and the Ninevites in 3:5–9. This encourages Israel to repent. It shows the possibility of even the most sinful unbelievers repenting and being saved through faith. And it identifies repentance as the correct response to prophecy.

2. Jonah teaches that even Gentile unbelievers may be converted. See the sailors in 1:16 and the Ninevites in 3:5–9. This encourages a missionary concern. It condemns Israelite exclusivism. And it condemns Israel's reaction against God forgiving the Gentiles.

3. Considering Jonah in its canonical context invites this question: Why does Yahweh save Nineveh in this book and then later allow the Assyrians to destroy the Northern Kingdom of Israel?[207] Two answers can be given: First, it affirms God's freedom to act graciously by saving Gentiles, as well as his justice in executing deserved judgment for those members of his people who become apostate (cf. Romans 9–11; 2 Pet 2:17–22). And second, it balances the relationship between God's mercy and his justice.[208]

Category 2 has been, by far, the most popular option among interpreters of the narrative. It depends on equating Jonah with Israel; that is, Jonah is a representative of the values and opinions of skewed Israelite theology. One of the book's major themes, then, is to urge Israel not to act like Jonah.

Category 3 focuses more on understanding Yahweh's methods and his attributes through the agency of Jonah's situation. Category 1 urges Israel to identify with Nineveh; that is, instead of urging Israel to not act like Jonah, the book is urging that Israel should respond as Nineveh responded. The narrative nowhere drives home that point explicitly, but it may be implicit. Alexander rightly observes that this approach ignores the inclusion of chapter 4.[209] If the lesson were only that Israel should be as willing to repent as Nineveh was, the narrative could have ended after chapter 3.[210]

---

[206] Cf. Alexander, *Jonah*, 81–91, who presents four major categories. The following analysis is a modification of his.

[207] However, we must note that eventually Assyria itself was destroyed and thus did not escape divine judgment, as prophesied by Nahum.

[208] Fretheim has one of the more developed approaches of this type. He sees Jonah in light of the debate concerning the question of Yahweh's compassionate acts toward those who are evil: "Are God's *compassionate* actions just?" (Fretheim, "Jonah and Theodicy"; the quote is on p. 227; see also Fretheim, *Jonah*, 23–24).

[209] Jonah 4 contains the object lesson about the growth and demise of the qiqayon plant.

[210] Alexander, *Jonah*, 83.

While not discounting these themes, the viewpoint taken in this commentary is that narrative's main theme is the triune God's use of Law and Gospel to judge and forgive the sailors, the Ninevites, and Jonah himself. Yahweh is fully justified in condemning all people as sinners who deserve both temporal punishment and eternal death. Yahweh hurls the storm that threatens the lives of the sailors and disobedient Jonah (1:4–15), and through his prophet he pronounces judgment upon pagan Nineveh (3:4). All these people deserved to perish. Yet Yahweh proves himself to be a gracious God (Jonah 4:2), just as he proves time and again throughout the Scriptures, culminating in Christ's redemptive work for the sake of all people. It is Yahweh himself who turns from his wrath to show mercy toward the undeserving because of his own gracious character. Thus Yahweh calms the storm that he himself had sent, sparing the lives of the mariners, who turn to him in true faith (1:16). He sends the fish to rescue Jonah from a watery grave (2:1 [ET 1:17]), and after three days Yahweh "raises" Jonah to new life (2:11 [ET 2:10]) as a type of Christ's resurrection. Yahweh moves even the fierce unbelieving Ninevites to repentance and saving faith (3:5–10). The book concludes with Yahweh's question that coaxes resentful Jonah to acknowledge Yahweh's propriety in having pity on those he has made (4:11).

The Text of Jonah

Jonah is a remarkably well-preserved text.[211] Its reliability is virtually unquestioned. Even the Targum, which is significantly expansionistic in other books of the Minor Prophets, contains a relatively small number of explanatory glosses in Jonah.[212] Of the seven scrolls of the Minor Prophets found in Qumran cave 4, two preserve fragments of Jonah.[213] These fragments, along with a Hebrew copy from Wadi Murabba'at, dating to the early second century AD, and a Greek text from Naḥal Ḥever from the late first century BC, demonstrate the text's remarkable stability.[214] A comparison between the Masoretic Text and the Wadi Murabba'at document proves that the differences are minimal, thus attesting to the faithful transmission of Jonah.[215] In the few cases where the text may need emendation there are several good textual studies available.[216]

---

[211] The most recent and comprehensive comparative study of the Masoretic Text and the ancient versions is that of Trible, "Studies in the Book of Jonah," 1–57. Apart from this unpublished work, Bewer's contributions in *A Critical and Exegetical Commentary on Jonah* in the International Critical Commentary series are noteworthy.

[212] Stuart, *Hosea–Jonah*, 443.

[213] Fuller, "The Minor Prophets Manuscripts from Qumran, Cave IV," 5–38, 141–50.

[214] Milik, "Textes Hébreux et Araméens," 181–84, 205; Tov, *The Greek Minor Prophets Scroll from Naḥal Ḥever*, especially 28–33, 84–85, 102–58.

[215] Milik, "Textes Hébreux et Araméens," 183–84, 205.

[216] Sasson's commentary (*Jonah*; Anchor Bible) is foremost in this respect. Trible, "Studies in the Book of Jonah," 1–65, and Landes, "Linguistic Criteria and the Date of the Book of Jonah," are also outstanding.

The critical edition of the Masoretic Text in *BHS*[217] is used in this commentary. The assumption in this commentary is that the Masoretic Text is not a clumsy redaction, but faithfully preserves the text of the artful narrative of Jonah.

---

[217] This edition is based on the Hebrew manuscript Leningradensis, datable to AD 1008/1009, named after the city where it has long been kept, formerly called Leningrad, now St. Petersburg, Russia.

Jonah 1:1–16

Yahweh's First Call to Jonah and the Sailors' Conversion

Introduction to Jonah 1

The literary structure of Jonah 1 is comprised of two basic subunits or scenes, each of which begins with action by Yahweh that provides the basis for action on the part of the other major protagonists in the narrative. The first scene, 1:1–3, presents Yahweh's initial commission to Jonah to speak to the city of Nineveh, as well as Jonah's attempt to flee from Yahweh by sea. The second scene, 1:4–16, describes Yahweh's creation of a storm at sea and how this threatens the ship on which Jonah travels. This scene narrates the interaction between Jonah and the ship's sailors. The mariners do everything possible to save both themselves and Jonah, but are eventually compelled to throw Jonah overboard.

Jonah 1 is parallel with Jonah 3. Robert Alter labels relationships like this "type scenes," where elements in the first scene are repeated, developed, and expanded in the second scene.[1] The similarities and differences between the different scenes of the same theme invite comparison and contrast as well as drive home certain ideas by means of repetition. In the book of Jonah, chapters 1 and 3 display the characteristics of type scenes and must accordingly be interpreted together.

In both 1:1–3 and 3:1–3 Yahweh commissions his prophet in this way: "the Word of Yahweh" comes to Jonah, telling him to "arise, go to Nineveh, the great city," and proclaim Yahweh's message of judgment against it. Chapters 1 and 3 both testify to the power of Yahweh's Word. Jonah's confession of faith (1:9) and his proclamation of Yahweh's Word (3:4) are brief but each brings about the conversion of pagan non-Israelites to true, saving faith in Yahweh. These conversions of Gentiles foreshadow the ingrafting of great numbers of Gentiles into the church of Jesus Christ by the power of the Gospel of justification through faith alone.

As we read in chapter 1 about the sailors on the ship, who fearfully pray and eventually turn to Yahweh, we are being prepared for reading in chapter 3 about the Ninevites in the great city, who likewise repent and call upon Yahweh. The captain of the ship takes on the same role as the king of Nineveh in

---

[1] Alter, *The Art of Biblical Narrative*, 47–62. Genesis contains familiar examples of how Hebrew narrative uses type scenes. Three different times a patriarch moves to a southern region (twice driven by famine), where he pretends that his wife is his sister. He narrowly avoids a violation of the conjugal bond by the local ruler and is then sent away, once with gifts (Gen 12:10–20; chapter 20; 26:1–12). Another type scene is when Hagar flees or is driven into the wilderness because of Sarah's hostility and discovers a miraculous well (Genesis 16; 21:9–21). The Hagar narratives are a variation of the recurrent story of bitter rivalry between a barren, favored wife and a fertile co-wife or concubine. This situation, in turn, suggests another common type scene in the OT: a woman who long was barren gives birth to a hero (e.g., 1 Sam 1:1–20; cf. also Lk 1:5–25). This commentary considers such type scenes not to be mere literary creations, but recurring patterns in factual history.

leading those under his authority to turn to Yahweh. Both Gentile leaders are concerned about dying. The captain of the ship (1:6) and the king of Nineveh (3:9) each seek Yahweh's mercy for the express purpose "so we will not perish" (וְלֹא נֹאבֵד).

Both chapters contain powerful irony: while pagan non-Israelites (Gentiles) are converted to rudimentary, yet genuine faith in the God of Israel, the Israelite Jonah, who already believed in the one true God (1:9), increasingly turns away from Yahweh and toward himself in self-centered anger. The narrative satirizes Jonah's narrow selfishness as he begrudges the mercy Yahweh shows to the foreigners. In that way the narrative teaches us, the reading audience, that just as the one true God welcomes all sinners who repent and turn to him in faith, we too should welcome all repentant believers in Jesus, the "one greater than Jonah" (Mt 12:41). Baptized believers in Christ from all peoples and nations are members of the household of God (see Ephesians 2) and children of the heavenly Father (see Ephesians 3).

The second scene, Jonah 1:4–16, is built according to a concentric or chiastic pattern with a conclusion:[2]

A   Yahweh hurls the storm (1:4)
   B   The sailors pray and act (1:5a–b)
      C   Jonah acts (lies down and sleeps, 1:5c)
         D   The captain and the sailors question Jonah (1:6–8)
            E   Jonah confesses his faith in Yahweh (1:9)
         D'   The sailors question Jonah (1:10–11)
      C'   Jonah speaks (1:12)
   B'   The sailors act and pray (1:13–14)
A'   The sailors hurl Jonah into the sea, and the storm ends (1:15)
Conclusion (1:16)

In the Hebrew text, there are ninety-four words from 1:4, the beginning of the scene, to the beginning of the speech in 1:9. There are also ninety-four words in 1:10–15. The conclusion in Jonah 1:16 stands outside the pattern. Both the chiastic structure and the exact balance of number of words (ninety-four) both before and after the speech in 1:9 serve to place the focus of scene 2 on Jonah's confession of faith in 1:9, which stands at the midpoint of this chiastic structure.

In speaking of Hebrew rhetoric, Roland Meynet writes:

Instead of developing its argumentation in a linear way, in the Graeco-Roman fashion, to a conclusion which is the point of resolution of the discourse, it is organized most of the time in an involutive manner around a centre which is the focal point, the keystone, through which the rest finds cohesion. The centre of a concentric construction most of the time presents certain specific

---

2   This analysis for the most part follows Limburg, *Jonah*, 47–48. Lohfink was the first to suggest that the account of Jonah's sea voyage (1:4–16) formed a concentric structure ("Jona ging zur Stadt hinaus (Jon 4, 5)," 201.

characteristics: it is often of a different shape and genre than the rest of the text, it is very often a question, or at least something which is problematic, which in all cases is enigmatic.[3]

Not only are Jonah's words in 1:9 numerically at the center of scene 2, this is also the first time in the narrative where Jonah speaks. Both of these characteristics lead to the conclusion that Jonah's confession of Yahweh in 1:9 is crucial for understanding the entire chapter, and indeed, the entire book. See further the excursus "Yahweh, the Creator God."

Jonah's confession (1:9) in the second scene of chapter 1 is analogous to his brief sermon (3:4) in the second scene of chapter 3. Though both are quite brief, both accomplish the salvation of formerly unbelieving Gentiles by prompting them to repentance and faith in the one true God. Thus both chapters highlight the efficacious power of the spoken Word of God in a way that is relevant for the pastor's prophetic and apostolic office of preaching (see Rom 10:1–17).[4]

---

[3] Meynet, *Rhetorical Analysis*, 175. Similarly, Bartelt argues in *The Book around Immanuel* that Isaiah's prophecy that a virgin shall conceive and bear a son to be named Immanuel (Is 7:14) is at the center of Isaiah 2–12. By his count of all the syllables in those chapters, the exact middle falls in the break between וְקָרֵאת שְׁמוֹ, "and she shall call his name," and עִמָּנוּ אֵל, Immanuel" (p. 256). Another example of this rhetorical strategy is in Moses' Song by the Sea (Exodus 15), where the center of the song becomes the focal point by means of a question: "Who is like you, O Yahweh, among the gods? Who is like you, majestic in holiness, terrible in glorious deeds, doing wonders?" (Ex 15:11). Yet another example is that the assertion "for you are with me" in Ps 23:4 is in the numerical middle of the psalm; in the Hebrew text there are twenty-six words both before and after that clause.

[4] See also "Preaching as 'The Highest Office in Christendom' " in Lockwood, *1 Corinthians*, 52–53, commenting on 1 Cor 1:10–17.

Jonah 1:1–3

Scene 1: Jonah's First Call

Translation

1 **¹Now the Word of Yahweh came to Jonah the son of Amittai, saying, ²"Arise, go to Nineveh, the great city, and call out against it, for their evil has arisen before me." ³But Jonah arose to flee to Tarshish away from the presence of Yahweh. He went down to Joppa and found a ship going to Tarshish. He paid its price and boarded it to go with them to Tarshish away from the presence of Yahweh.**

Textual Notes

1:1 וַיְהִי דְּבַר־יְהוָה אֶל־יוֹנָה—The first word in the book is וַיְהִי, the third singular Qal imperfect of הָיָה with *waw* consecutive. Hebrew historical narratives typically are introduced by this verb form without a grammatical subject, which then can be translated as "and it happened" or "and it came to pass." It functions much like the English clauses "once there was" or "and so it happened that." וַיְהִי begins the historical books of Joshua, Judges, 1 and 2 Samuel, Ruth, and Esther (see also Neh 1:1b). It also begins the prophet Ezekiel, which opens with a narrative section. In all those cases except for 1 Sam 1:1, it lacks a subject.

Here וַיְהִי has a subject (דְּבַר־יְהוָה) and takes a prepositional phrase (אֶל־יוֹנָה): "Now the Word of Yahweh *came* to Jonah." The formula וַיְהִי דְּבַר־יְהוָה אֶל־ ("Now the Word of Yahweh came to …") is frequent in the OT, especially in Jeremiah and Ezekiel, where it describes divine messages coming to the respective prophet (e.g., Jer 1:4, 11, 13; 16:1; Ezek 3:16; 6:1; 7:1). Generally it is used "only when contexts and circumstances regarding the prophet and his mission are already established in previous statements."[1] Thus Elijah is introduced in 1 Ki 17:1, and then וַיְהִי דְּבַר־יְהוָה אֶל־ introduces subsequent messages from Yahweh (1 Ki 17:2, 8; 21:17, 28; see also the similar expressions in 1 Ki 18:1, 31; 19:9). The way this formula generally is used elsewhere in the OT, together with the close affinities between Jonah and Elijah,[2] gives the impression that Jonah is in the first place a narrative that begins prior to Jonah 1:1, making the brief description of Jonah in 2 Ki 14:25 the starting point. Thus by the way the narrator begins the book of Jonah, he assumes that his audience has previous knowledge of the prophet from 2 Kings 14.

---

[1] Sasson, *Jonah*, 67. See Sasson's full discussion on pages 66–68. An exception is 1 Ki 16:1, where the Word of Yahweh comes to Jehu, who had not been introduced previously. Most of the time וַיְהִי refers to individuals who have already been mentioned in the narrative.

[2] See "Jonah and Elijah" in the introduction. In the Hebrew canon 1 Kings and 2 Kings comprise a single Hebrew book. Therefore, even though Elijah exits that book in 2 Kings 2, the affinities between him and Jonah link that book's brief account of Jonah to the book of Jonah.

Narratives are introduced by וַיְהִי *within* other prophetic books (e.g., Isaiah 36–39; Jeremiah 28; 36–44). However, the use of וַיְהִי to *begin* Jonah differs because it introduces an entire narrative about a prophet.[3]

At the beginning of Jonah, then, conventional language is used in an unconventional way. This literary move is a subtle hint that in Jonah there will be many more inversions of earlier OT narratives.

The construct phrase דְּבַר־יְהוָה ("the Word of Yahweh") occurs around two hundred fifty times in the OT. With few exceptions it refers to a Word spoken by Yahweh to a prophet. Almost universally it is "a technical term for the prophetic word of revelation,"[4] and it is the formula that gives the prophetic books their distinctiveness. Approximately one hundred fifteen of its occurrences are as subject of the verb הָיָה, "to be," which in these instances is usually translated "came," as here in Jonah 1:1. The expression "the Word of Yahweh came to …" is often called the "word-event formula" because "the advent of the divine Word causes events to take place, as is supremely true in the advent of Jesus Christ, the Word made flesh."[5] Other prophets like Isaiah (e.g., 40:8 and 55:10–11) and Jeremiah (e.g., 1:9; 15:16; 23:28) speak of the power of this divine Word and its ability to direct and control history. Much of the time we have no idea how the prophets received the divine Word. In many cases it comes through a vision (e.g., Is 1:1) as a result of the prophet being in Yahweh's council (cf. 1 Ki 22:19; Jer 23:18, 21–22; Amos 3:7). But just how exactly Jonah received this Word is not known.

בֶּן־אֲמִתַּי—Both here and in 2 Ki 14:25 Jonah is called "the son of Amittai." His father's name is based on the verb אָמַן, which in the Hiphil means "to believe," as in Jonah 3:5 (in the Niphal it means "be certain; faithful"). But אֲמִתַּי is closer in form to the noun אֱמֶת, "truth" or "faithfulness," which is derived from that verb (see Joüon, § 97B e). The *yod* at the end of אֲמִתַּי may be regarded as a hypocoristicon (shortened form of יָהּ or יהוה), allowing "Amittai" to mean something like "Yahweh is true/faithful."

The Hebrew phrase "son of" frequently expresses a category: a "son of valor" (1 Sam 14:52) is a "valiant man." Conversely, a "son of iniquity" (Ps 89:23 [ET 89:22]) is an "iniquitous man." Jonah's lineage may be a wordplay on that kind of usage of "son." If so, Jonah's lineage, by analogy, may imply that he should be a "son of faithfulness/truth." Quite often in Hebrew narrative when a relational epithet is attached to a character, the narrator is telling us something substantial without recourse to explicit commentary. For example, Michal oscillates between being the wife of David and the daughter of Saul (1 Sam 25:44; 2 Sam 6:16). Tamar, most painfully, is identified as the sister of Ammon when he rapes her (2 Sam 13:10–11). So here, the

---

3   The book of Ezekiel (1:1) too begins with וַיְהִי. Ezekiel 1 is first person narrative, so it differs from Jonah 1, which is third person narrative. Most of the book of Ezekiel consists of prophetic oracles uttered by the prophet, whereas in Jonah, his only prophetic utterance is in 3:4 (see also his confession in 1:9).

4   Grether, *Name und Wort Gottes im Alten Testament*, 76, quoted by W. H. Schmidt, "דָּבָר," *TDOT* 3:111.

5   Hummel, *Ezekiel 1–20*, 99.

irony of Jonah's relationship with his father is that the prophet will abandon "faithfulness" at the first opportunity and will speak the "truth" in chapter 3 only under duress, and even then not fully understanding the character of Yahweh, whose Word he proclaims. (His lack of understanding and resentment at the enormity of Yahweh's grace become obvious in chapter 4.) The first of many ironies is now before us. These ironies contribute to the book's satire of Jonah and those who, like him, would restrict Yahweh's grace only to their own people.[6]

The call of Jonah only gives us his father's name. By comparison, some prophetic calls in the OT provide more precise settings by offering the names of reigning kings (e.g., Is 6:1; Hos 1:1; Micah 1:1) or other chronological determinants, for example, "two years before the earthquake" (Amos 1:1). Jonah is like Joel, Obadiah, Nahum, Habakkuk, and Malachi in that the book contains no precise indication as to when the events recorded actually occurred. The narrator assumes we will know (or find out) the time frame of the prophet by going to the narrative's true beginning, 2 Ki 14:25.

לֵאמֹר:—Hebrew narrative commonly uses this Qal infinitive construct of אָמַר, "to say," with preposition לְ to introduce direct discourse. It is translated as "saying," but it could be omitted, with the quotation marks indicating the beginning of the speech.

1:2 קוּם לֵךְ—From out of the blue, like a sudden bolt of lightning, a strange word is heard. Yahweh's double command with the imperatives קוּם and לֵךְ (from הָלַךְ), "arise, go," will be repeated in 3:2. Yahweh addresses other prophets with this same double command (Balaam in Num 22:20; Moses in Deut 10:11; Jeremiah in Jer 13:4, 6), notably Elijah (1 Ki 17:9).[7] This connection and comparison of Jonah to Elijah will return in chapter 4 of Jonah. It is worth noting here, however, that among the prophets, only Elijah and Jonah are sent on missions to foreign lands, and both with this same double imperative: Elijah to Zarephath ("Arise, go [קוּם לֵךְ] to Zarephath, which is in Sidon," 1 Ki 17:9) and Jonah to Nineveh (Jonah 1:2; 3:2).

The imperatives "arise" (קוּם) and "go" (לֵךְ, from הָלַךְ) are not joined by a conjunction; the combination illustrates the rhetorical device of asyndeton (literally, "unconnected"). It produces a hurried rhythm that here elicits a prompt response by Jonah. The verb קוּם, "to rise, arise," is often used in an auxiliary manner when the main activity is denoted by the following verb (here, לֵךְ, "go"; Waltke-O'Connor, § 34.5.1a). Yahweh's command for Jonah to "arise" contrasts with Jonah's subsequent, opposite behavior: he "descends" (the literal translation of יָרַד) in 1:3, 5; 2:7, and in 2:3 he is all the way down in Sheol. Ironically, Jonah's entire intent in chapter 1 will be opposed to following Yahweh's call and command, "Arise, go to Nineveh"!

אֶל־נִינְוֵה הָעִיר הַגְּדוֹלָה—"Nineveh" (נִינְוֵה) is called "the great city" (הָעִיר הַגְּדוֹלָה) here and in 3:2 and 4:11. Both the noun עִיר, which is in apposition to נִינְוֵה, and the adjective גְּדוֹלָה, which modifies עִיר, have the article because Nineveh, as a proper name,

---

[6] See "Jonah as Satire with Irony" in the introduction.

[7] The double command is spoken by one person to another in Gen 28:2; 1 Sam 9:3; 2 Sam 13:15; 1 Ki 14:12; 2 Ki 8:1; Song 2:10, 13; by Pharaoh to Moses and Aaron in Ex 12:31; and by Yahweh to sinful people in Micah 2:10.

is definite (Joüon, § 138 a). Normally an adjective does not directly modify a proper noun, so this phrase with הָעִיר is used instead of just נִינְוֵה הַגְּדוֹלָה, "Nineveh the great" (Joüon, § 141 c; Waltke-O'Connor, § 14.2e). Jonah is called to no backwater village, but a great metropolis in Assyria. The designation "great" for a city is rare in the OT. Jerusalem is named "the great city" in the prediction of its destruction in Jer 22:8 and Gibeon is so named in Josh 10:2.

The adjective גָּדוֹל, "great," is the most frequent word in Jonah, used fourteen times.[a] In the other eleven Minor Prophets this adjective occurs a total of only thirty-one times. Everything that is "great" in Jonah is produced by Yahweh or by Yahweh's deeds.[8] For example, in chapter 1 גָּדוֹל refers to the means Yahweh uses to carry out his purposes: a "great wind" and a "great storm" (1:4a, 4b, 12). Throughout Jonah גָּדוֹל is used six times to describe Nineveh or the Ninevites (1:2; 3:2, 3, 5, 7; 4:11). The implication is that Nineveh's grandeur stems from Yahweh as well, a point made directly in 4:10–11.

Thus it is ironic when the adjective גָּדוֹל describes Jonah's response to Yahweh saving Nineveh: the prophet considered the city's salvation to be "a great evil" (רָעָה גְדוֹלָה, 4:1). The only time Jonah expresses "great joy" is when he is comfortably couched under the qiqayon plant provided by Yahweh (שִׂמְחָה גְדוֹלָה, 4:6). Yahweh's goal then becomes for Jonah to broaden his "great joy" to include the deliverance of the great city—but this appears to be a great challenge!

וּקְרָא עָלֶיהָ—The pairing together of the verb קָרָא, "call, proclaim" (here the Qal masculine singular imperative), and the preposition עַל, "upon, against," often has negative overtones (see BDB, s.v. קָרָא, 3 d). For example, in 1 Ki 13:2 the man of God calls out by the Word of Yahweh against the syncretistic altar at Bethel. For similar uses of the verb קָרָא and the preposition עַל, see Jer 49:29; Lam 1:15; Ps 105:16.

כִּי־עָלְתָה רָעָתָם לְפָנָי:—Sometimes כִּי introduces speech (see BDB, 1 b), and the Jerusalem Bible takes this clause as stating the content of what Jonah is to proclaim: "Inform them that their wickedness has become known to me." However, that understanding of כִּי should be rejected here. The actual wording of the proclamation Jonah is to address to Nineveh is not revealed here, nor when Yahweh issues his second call to Jonah in 3:2. The content of the proclamation is only revealed when Jonah preaches it in 3:4.

Of the many meanings and nuances of כִּי, its causal and asseverative forces interlock here. As a causal conjunction, it introduces the motivation or reason why Yahweh is sending Jonah to preach against the city: "for/because their evil has arisen before me." At the same time, it can have asseverative force here and signal emphasis: "truly/indeed their evil has arisen before me." Though one word must finally be selected in the translation, "for" should not be taken to exclude the other possible meanings.[9]

(a) Jonah 1:2, 4 (twice), 10, 12, 16; 2:1; 3:2, 3, 5, 7; 4:1, 6, 11

---

[8] A possible exception is in the merismus of 3:5, "the men of Nineveh—from the least of them to the *greatest* of them," but see Rom 13:1.

[9] Studies on כִּי include Aejmelaeus, "Function and Interpretation of כִּי in Biblical Hebrew"; Muilenburg, "The Linguistic and Rhetorical Usages of the Particle כִּי in the Old Testament";

The form of עֳלָה is third feminine singular Qal perfect (עָלְתָה) because its subject is the feminine noun רָעָה with third masculine plural suffix (רָעָתָם). As a noun רָעָה recurs in 1:7, 8; 3:10b; 4:1, 2, 6, and it occurs as an adjective in 3:8, 10c.[10] That רָעָה can refer to moral "evil" is well illustrated in Ezek 6:11: "Thus says the Lord Yahweh: Clap your hands, and stamp your foot, and say, 'Alas!' because of all the evil abominations [כָּל־תּוֹעֲבוֹת רָעוֹת] of the house of Israel; for they shall fall by the sword, by famine, and by pestilence." Yet other possible nuances of the noun may be present here. It may denote fierceness or wildness, as in Gen 37:20, 33 (Joseph's brothers claim that "a wild beast" [חַיָּה רָעָה] devoured him), and those qualities aptly pertained to the Assyrians, notorious for their cruelty in war. The related adjective רַע may refer to something of poor or inferior quality, as in Jer 24:2. רַע may mean "bad" or "unpleasant" in the sense of something that causes pain or grief, as in Prov 15:10, where it is best translated "severe": "There is severe [רַע] discipline for him who forsakes the way; he who hates reproof will die." That nuance is relevant for רָעָה later in Jonah when it refers to the storm that imperiled the ship and its crew (1:7–8) and when it refers to Yahweh's threatened destruction of Nineveh (3:10c). In Is 45:7 Yahweh describes his actions poetically using opposites: "I form light and create darkness; I make weal and create evil/woe [וּבוֹרֵא רָע]; I am Yahweh, who does all these things."

Of course, Yahweh, speaking through Isaiah, does not mean that he creates evil in the theological sense. Rather, he affirms that he is the author of judgment against sin. Sinful people perceive this judgment as injurious and evil. Hence the storm sent by Yahweh is called an "evil" (רָעָה) by the sailors in 1:7–8, and the threatened destruction of Nineveh is called an averted "evil" in 3:10 (see the commentary on 3:10). In Is 28:21 God's righteous judgment in accord with divine Law is referred to as Yahweh's "alien work," and that terminology is used in Lutheran theology to distinguish God's "alien work" (*opus alienum*) of condemning the sinner by his Law from his "proper work" (*opus proprium*) of justifying the sinner for Christ's sake by his Gospel.

In Jonah the noun or adjective רָעָה is used in connection with all the main characters: Yahweh (3:10b; 4:2), Jonah (4:1, 6), the sailors (1:7–8), and the Ninevites (1:2; 3:8, 10b). Throughout Jonah רָעָה has a number of different meanings, depending on which character causes the "evil" (or threatens "judgment") and which character is the victim of or is affected by someone else's "evil." The narrator could have chosen a different word each time to express different shades of meaning, but by reusing this one word he allows each usage to recall and anticipate the other usages, multiplying the levels of correspondence and contrast between the respective subjects or contexts related to the word.

This complexity and ambiguity is already present in this first appearance of רָעָה in the book. Does רָעָתָם ("their evil") refer to the evil deeds perpetuated by the Ninevites (as most translations suggest), or does "their evil" refer to "their judgment," which Yahweh is about to bring down upon them? (רָעָה clearly refers to their prophesied "judgment" in 3:10c.) The ambivalence points to the problem of the "localiza-

---

Schoors, "The Particle *Ki*"; Muraoka, *Emphatic Words and Structures in Biblical Hebrew*, 158–64.

[10] Moreover, the related verb רָעַע, "be evil," occurs in 4:1.

tion" of evil that recurs throughout the book. Where is it? Who caused it? Who's got it? How can they rid themselves of it?

In the first eight verses of chapter 1 there are three occurrences of רָעָה (1:2, 7, 8). In 1:2 it is normally translated so as to convey a sense of moral evil deserving God's judgment. Thus the RSV, NIV, and NRSV translate it "wickedness," which merits punishment (cf. 2 Sam 12:7–15; 1 Ki 21:17–24; Is 31:1–3; Micah 2:1–5). However, when רָעָה reappears in Jonah 1:7–8, it refers to the storm that threatened the lives of the sailors even though Yahweh sent it on account of Jonah. There the NRSV translates it "calamity" (NIV has "calamity" in 1:7 and "trouble" in 1:8), while the RSV and ESV use "evil." The biblical depiction of Nineveh (also confirmed by extrabiblical sources) requires that there be a moral and culpable quality to רָעָה in 1:2. But that is not so in 1:7–8, where the speakers who use the noun are not the main target of God's punitive action.

1:3 וַיָּקָם יוֹנָה לִבְרֹחַ תַּרְשִׁישָׁה—The verb קוּם (here Qal third masculine singular imperfect with *waw* consecutive) at first projects continuity between Jonah's action here and Yahweh's command to him in 1:2, קוּם, "arise." The repetition of the same verb here would encourage the translation, "*And so* Jonah arose …" However, in light of the rest of the clause, by the end of which we know *why* Jonah "arose" ("to flee to Tarshish away from the presence of Yahweh"), the *waw* signals discontinuity and so is translated disjunctively, "*But* Jonah arose …"

The Qal infinitive construct of בָּרַח, "to flee," with the preposition לְ (and a furtive patach under the final guttural ח, hence לִבְרֹחַ) signals Jonah's purpose or intent. The verb בָּרַח rarely refers to flight from a threatening battle or an acute danger. Usually it refers to evasion or escape from continuing, unpleasant situations, for example, tensions and tragedies within the tribe (e.g., Gen 16:6, 8).

In Jonah *every human action described by an infinitive construct verb form fails to accomplish the intention of its human subject*, while *every divine action described by the infinitive construct verb form comes to fruition*—with the sole exception of לַעֲשׂוֹת ("the evil he promised *to do* to them") in 3:10, which thus highlights Yahweh's grace in deciding *not* to bring judgment upon Nineveh ("and he did not do it," 3:10). This grammatical usage of infinitives underscores two of the central ideas of the narrative. First, *Yahweh's will is done, and it is chiefly done in showing mercy to people like the Ninevites*. Second, *the plans of people are contingent upon Yahweh*.[11]

The following verses illustrate how infinitive constructs, when they refer to *human* actions, always denote *action in vain*. In 1:3 Jonah goes down into the ship "to go" (לָבוֹא) with the sailors to Tarshish—but he never arrives there. In 1:5 the sailors try "to lighten" (לְהָקֵל) the boat and thus save themselves from the storm and Yahweh's wrath—but that method does not avail. In 1:13 the sailors try "to return" (לְהָשִׁיב) the ship to the dry land—but they are unable to do so. In 2:5 Jonah expresses confident faith that he will once again "gaze" (לְהַבִּיט) upon Yahweh's temple in Jerusalem, but the book never states whether Jonah returned to Jerusalem, and chapter 4 ends with Jonah outside Nineveh. In 3:4 "Jonah began to enter [וַיָּחֶל יוֹנָה לָבוֹא]

---

[11] As noted by Good, *Irony in the Old Testament*, 47.

the city a walk of one day," but the city required a walk of three days (3:3), so he apparently did not finish his journey throughout the city before the inhabitants repented. In 4:2 Jonah recalls his failed attempt "to flee" (לִבְרֹחַ) from Yahweh in chapter 1.

In contrast, when Yahweh ordains events using infinitive constructs, he always succeeds (with the exception of 3:10). In 2:1 Yahweh appoints a great fish "to swallow" (לִבְלֹעַ) Jonah. In 4:6 the qiqayon plant grows over Jonah's head "to be" (לִהְיוֹת) shade for him. Also in 4:6 Yahweh seeks "to save" (לְהַצִּיל) Jonah from his evil disposition (4:1). At the end of the narrative, Yahweh's question (4:10–11) leaves us unsure whether or not Yahweh had changed Jonah's evil disposition, but previous usages of the infinitive construct with Yahweh as the subject invite the interpretation that Jonah was finally delivered; probably Jonah was persuaded to accept—and perhaps even to give thanks—that Yahweh had acted graciously toward the repentant Ninevites. The one case where an infinitive with Yahweh as the actor "fails" in is 3:10: "God changed his verdict about the evil he promised *to do* [לַעֲשׂוֹת] to them." The theology expressed by the grammar is that only God has the power to avert judgment and break the rules by which events (and, so to speak, the language that describes these events) are governed. Yahweh's judgment is overridden by his own compassion (cf. Jonah 4:10–11).

We may conclude, then, that by means of these infinitive constructs throughout Jonah the narrator subtly demonstrates the impotence of people (especially Jonah) in contrast to Yahweh's ability to do whatever pleases him (1:14), especially to act graciously.

The direction in which Jonah seeks "to flee," and the destination he vainly tries to reach, is denoted by תַּרְשִׁישָׁה. This is תַּרְשִׁישׁ (transliterated as "Tarshish") with the locative or directional ending (ה-), which is always unaccented. Hence the disjunctive *zaqeph* accent on תַּרְשִׁישָׁה is on the penultimate syllable (-שִׁ-).

Tarshish

"Tarshish" is mentioned three times in 1:3 and once more in 4:2. Just where is Tarshish?[12] This question has plagued OT scholars for generations. Some have attempted to equate the city with Tunis in North Africa;[13] still others believe it is some "distant paradise"[14] or simply understand Tarshish to mean "the sea."[15]

In the ancient sources there are at least three problems that frustrate any attempt to definitively locate Tarshish. The first is similar spellings of words that in some cases refer to different places:

---

[12] For an overview of the issues involved, see Lessing, "Just Where Was Jonah Going? The Location of Tarshish in the Old Testament."

[13] So Herrmann, "Die Tartessosfrage und Weissafrike."

[14] C. H. Gordon, "Tarshish," *IDB* 4:518.

[15] Gordon, "The Wine-Dark Sea," states that in some contexts the Targumim translate תַּרְשִׁישׁ by "the sea." He also references a statement by Jerome in his commentary on Is 2:16 indicating that the Hebrew scholars of his day maintained that תַּרְשִׁישׁ is a Hebrew word for "sea" (cf. LXX Is 2:16; *Commentariorum in Esaiam* [CCSL 73:37]). Gordon uses this to argue that תַּרְשִׁישׁ is actually a color of the sea, dark wine to be exact.

1. Tarzi or Tarzu in Neo-Assyrian texts
2. TRZ in Aramaic legends on coins
3. Tarsha in Hittite documents
4. Ταρτησσός, referring to Tartessus in Spain, in, for example, Herodotus, Strabo, and Appian[16]
5. Ταρσοί, referring to Tarsus in Cilicia, in Xenophon[17]
6. Ταρσεύς, referring to Tarsus in Cilicia, in Plutarch and Strabo[18]
7. Ταρσός, referring to Tarsus in Cilicia, in, for example, Strabo, Diodorus Siculus, and the NT (Acts 9:30; 11:25; 22:3)[19]
8. Ταρσός or Θάρσος in Josephus, who, in his discussion of Gen 10:4 and Jonah, equates Tarshish with Tarsus in Cilicia[20]
9. Ταρσεῖς in 2 Macc 4:30
10. טרסוס in later Jewish sources, for example, Targum Neofiti Gen 10:4[21]

The second dilemma is that in the OT, תַּרְשִׁישׁ can have at least four different meanings. Depending upon context, it may denote the following:

1. A personal name, for example, "Tarshish," the descendant of Javan (Gen 10:4; 1 Chr 1:7)
2. A type of vessel (e.g., 1 Ki 10:22; 22:49 [ET 22:48]; Is 2:16; 60:9; Ps 48:8 [ET 48:7])
3. A seaport (Is 23:6, 10)
4. A precious stone, possibly a gem such as jasper (e.g., Ex 28:20; Ezek 28:13)

Third, often the word is simply transliterated in the Septuagint (Θάρσις) and Vulgate (*Tharsis*), and a transliteration does not provide much help in identification. In some verses, the LXX identifies Tarshish with the most famous of the Phoenician colonies, the city of Carthage, located on the north coast of Africa. For example, תַּרְשִׁישׁ in Ezek 27:12 is rendered by the LXX as Καρχηδόνιοι. That LXX reading is supported by the Vulgate only in Ezek 27:12, which reads *Carthaginenses*.

Much current scholarship equates Tarshish with the Phoenician colony of Tartessus at the mouth of the Baetis River, known today as the Guadalquivir River, in southwestern Spain.[22] Representative is this comment by Victor Hamilton: "Most scholars have identified Tarshish with Tartessus, a mining village in southwestern Spain."[23]

---

[16] Herodotus, *Histories*, 1.163.1; 4.152.1; Strabo, *Geography*, 3.2.11–12, 14; Appian, *The Foreign Wars*, "The Wars in Spain," 1.2.

[17] Xenophon, *Anabasis*, 1.2.23, 25, 26.

[18] Plutarch, *Moralia*, 469, 605; Strabo, *Geography*, 14.5.8.

[19] Strabo, *Geography*, 14.3.1; 14.5.9–12, 15; Diodorus Siculus, *Library*, 14.20.2, 4.

[20] Josephus, *Antiquities*, 1.127 (1.6.1) and 9.208 (9.10.2).

[21] This list is adapted from the one in van der Kooij, *The Oracle of Tyre*, 44–45. See the discussion on pages 44–46.

[22] Following the lead of Albright, "New Light on the Early History of Phoenician Colonization," representatives of this view are as follows: Tsirkin, "The Hebrew Bible and the Origin of Tartessian Power"; Wildberger, *Isaiah 1–12*, 117; I. Kalimi, "Tarshish," *Eerdmans Dictionary of the Bible* (ed. David Noel Freedman; Grand Rapids: Eerdmans, 2000), 1276; see also D. W. Baker, "Tarshish (Place)," *ABD* 6:333.

[23] Hamilton, *The Book of Genesis: Chapters 1–17*, 333.

The recent work by André Lemaire goes a long way toward clearing up the confusion.[24] Passages that shed particular light on the problem are those in the OT where Tarshish is listed along with other countries. These texts are Gen 10:2–4; Is 66:19; and Ezek 27:12–24.[25] Given the geographical horizon of Gen 10:2–4, the assumption that Tarshish is some place far away (i.e., in Spain or Western Europe) does not seem correct. Specifically, Gen 10:4 states: "The sons of Javan [Greece] are Elishah [Cyprus], Tarshish, Kittim [Kition, a city on the southeast coast of Cyprus], and Dodanim [perhaps the island of Rhodes]." Because all of these places are in the vicinity of Greece, this text suggests that Tarshish is near Greece as well. Is 66:19 and Ezek 27:12–15 confirm that the location of Tarshish is close to Greece (Javan); the island of Rhodes (LXX Ezek 27:15); and Tubal and Meshech, which were in Asia Minor.[26]

The only helpful extrabiblical toponym reference to Tarshish[27] is one of the royal inscriptions of the Assyrian king Esarhaddon.[28] This text contains a description of the campaign of the year 671 BC, when Esarhaddon besieged the island city of Tyre. It reads: "All the kings who live in the area of the sea, from Cyprus and Javan to Tarshish, threw themselves at my feet, and I received heavy tribute."[29] Since the kings from Cyprus, Greece (Javan), and Tarshish submit to Esarhaddon, Tarshish must be in the same vicinity as Cyprus and Greece. Consequently, it is reasonable to understand the Tarshish of the OT as referring not to southern Spain, but rather to *Tarsus* in Cilicia, the hometown of St. Paul (Acts 22:3).

The city of Tarsus is situated about ten kilometers from the Mediterranean coast, on the river Cydnus, which was navigable in antiquity. Tarsus played a strategic role as control of it assured the control of the Cilician Gates. Tarsus lies at the opening of the passage from the central Taurus Mountains to the sea. Moreover, Tarsus was well-known for the metals and minerals that passed through it as they were transported from the Taurus Mountains and by ship to other ports.

> The Taurus Mountains are … an area in which innovative technology in metals took place. Long assumed to be the "silver mountains" of Hittite and Akkadian legends, the range abounds with extensive cedar forests and polymetallic ore deposits. … Silver, lead, copper, gold, iron, and tin are among some of the mineralizations within these mountains.[30]

---

[24] Lemaire, "Tarshish-*Tarsisi*: Problème de Topographie Historique Biblique et Assyienne."

[25] Other texts in the OT where Tarshish occurs as the name of a country are of no help in finding its location, that is, Ps 72:10; Jer 10:9; and here in the book of Jonah.

[26] For how the Old Greek translation of Is 66:19 favors the view that Tarshish is in Asia Minor, see van der Kooij, *The Oracle of Tyre*, 42.

[27] Lemaire discusses extrabiblical references to Tarshish, for example, the Nora Stele ("Tarshish-*Tarsisi*," 50–51). These references only confirm the connection between Tarshish and silver.

[28] On this inscription, see K. Galling, "Tarsis," *Biblisches Reallexikon* (ed. Kurt Galling; 2d ed.; Tübingen: Mohr, 1977), 332. "The idea that Asia Minor is the geographical horizon of the passage in the inscription of Esarhaddon is supported by a description of a similar political situation two years later" (van der Kooij, *The Oracle of Tyre*, 43; for details, see the discussion there).

[29] Cf. Van der Kooij, *The Oracle of Tyre*, 43; *ANET*, 290.

[30] K. A. Yener, "Taurus Mountains," *The Oxford Encyclopedia of Archaeology in the Near East* (ed. Eric M. Meyers; New York: Oxford University Press, 1997), 5:155.

Relating Tarshish with Tarsus of Cilicia clarifies not only the narrative in Jonah, but also the following OT accounts. First, "ships of Tarshish" (e.g., 1 Ki 22:49 [ET 22:48]; Is 2:16; 60:9; Ps 48:8 [ET 48:7]) were ships that originally carried valuable metals from the Taurus Mountains through Tarsus. These ships later became synonymous with power, wealth, and prestige, so much so that Isaiah could include them with "all that is proud and lofty" (Is 2:12). Second, in Isaiah's oracle against Tyre, the prophet gloats over Tyre's imminent downfall by telling the city's inhabitants to "cross over to Tarshish" (Is 23:6), a command that would have been possible for the island's inhabitants as Tarsus was a main Phoenician trading partner at the time. Moreover, the prophecy in Is 23:10 that "Tarshish will no longer have a harbor" for shipping exports and imports came to pass when Tyre fell under Assyrian domination and the merchants in Tarshish had no place to sell their wares. Third, due to the mining activity that took place in the Taurus Mountains, we can understand why in some passages "Tarshish" refers to a precious stone, possibly a gem such as jasper (e.g., Ex 28:20; Ezek 28:13; Song 5:14).

In Jonah it is also possible to understand Tarshish as functioning in a double entendre—as a specific geographical location but also as any place of luxury, desire, and delight. Cyrus Gordon suggests that "whatever the original identification of Tarshish may have been, in literature and popular imagination it became a distant paradise."[31] For Jonah, therefore, *Tarshish may be both a place in Asia Minor and a pleasant place of security.*

Jonah's constant search for security begins here with his desire to go to Tarshish. It continues in 1:5 as he lays down and sleeps deeply in the inner recesses of the ship. Jonah's longing for a safe place appears to be high on his agenda in 4:5 as he makes a booth for himself. In every instance, Yahweh strips Jonah of these places and things so that the prophet must finally meet and depend on Yahweh alone in 4:10–11.

מִלִּפְנֵי יְהוָה—The phrase מִלְּפְנֵי יהוה ("from the presence of Yahweh") occurs twice in 1:3 and again in 1:10. Throughout the OT, the noun פָּנֶה, "face," usually is plural (פָּנִים) and in construct (פְּנֵי־) with the person whose "face" is in view. In combination with the preposition לְ (לִפְנֵי), it means "in the presence of, before" (BDB, s.v. פָּנֶה, II 4). Attached to that combination here is the preposition מִן, so מִלְּפְנֵי means "from the presence of" (BDB, s.v. פָּנֶה, II 5 a).

The prophets Elijah (1 Ki 17:1; 18:15) and Elisha (2 Ki 3:14; 5:16) used the expression חַי־יהוה ... אֲשֶׁר עָמַדְתִּי לְפָנָיו, "As Yahweh lives ... in whose presence I stand." The historian uses that phrase to identify Elijah and Elisha as Yahweh's servants who hear his word and execute his commands.

Closely linked with this is the idea of the prophet standing in Yahweh's heavenly council to perceive the divine Word. Though passages that express that idea do not explicitly refer to Yahweh's "presence" (פָּנִים), it would certainly seem to be implicit (see Jer 23:18, 22; 1 Ki 22:19; Job 1:6; 2:1).

---

[31] C. H. Gordon, "Tarshish," *IDB* 4:517–18.

The phrase "the presence of Yahweh" first appears in the OT in Genesis 3–4. The first instance refers to Adam and Eve while in Eden: "The man hid himself, and [so did] his wife, from the presence of Yahweh God" (וַיִּתְחַבֵּא הָאָדָם וְאִשְׁתּוֹ מִפְּנֵי יְהוָה אֱלֹהִים, Gen 3:8). The second is in Gen 4:16: "Cain went away from the presence of Yahweh and lived in the land of Nod" (וַיֵּצֵא קַיִן מִלִּפְנֵי יְהוָה וַיֵּשֶׁב בְּאֶרֶץ־נוֹד). The "land of Nod" is literally "the land of wandering," a place where people live apart from Yahweh's presence. Those who cut themselves off from Yahweh's presence are homeless exiles with no salvation, blessing, or joy. But just as Yahweh protected Adam and Eve with coverings and Cain with a mark, so he will protect Jonah with a ship, and later, a great fish (2:1 [ET 1:17]) and a qiqayon plant (4:6).

To be in the presence of Yahweh was something the psalmist David longed after (Ps 16:11). David associated exclusion from Yahweh's presence with being deprived of salvation, joy, and Yahweh's Holy Spirit (Ps 51:13–14 [ET 51:11–12]). David cherishes Yahweh's presence by yearning "to walk back and forth before God in the light of life" (לְהִתְהַלֵּךְ לִפְנֵי אֱלֹהִים בְּאוֹר הַחַיִּים, Ps 56:14 [ET 56:13]). The OT specifically localizes Yahweh's earthly presence at the tabernacle (Ex 40:34) and then the temple (1 Ki 8:10). The divine presence finally was incarnated in Jesus (Jn 1:14; Col 1:19; 2:9). Those who live outside of this presence will inhabit "outer darkest," where there is "weeping and gnashing of teeth" (Mt 8:12).

וַיֵּרֶד יָפוֹ—The verb is the Qal third masculine singular imperfect with *waw* consecutive of יָרַד, "to go down," which occurs twice in 1:3 and also once in 1:5 and once in 2:7 (ET 2:6; "to the roots of the mountains I went down"). In chapter 2 other vocabulary is used to say that Jonah descends into the belly of the fish (2:1 [ET 1:17]) and ultimately to Sheol (2:3 [ET 2:2]).

The narrator uses vocabulary for Jonah "arising" (קוּם in 1:2, 3, 6; 3:2, 3) and "descending" in a subtle manner. When Jonah is at his lowest point geographically (2:3, 7 [ET 2:2, 6]), he is "brought up" by Yahweh (וַתַּעַל, 2:7 [ET 2:6]), and when he is at his highest point geographically, he appears to abandon all hope of life (4:5–9). Jesus states the theology of the cross this way: "For everyone who exalts himself will be humbled, and he who humbles himself will be exalted" (Lk 14:11; 18:14).

The use of יָרַד in 1:3 (twice); 1:5; 2:7 (ET 2:6) contrasts with the verb עָלָה, "to go up" (whose Hiphil is in 2:7 [ET 2:6]), which is normally employed for travel up to Jerusalem and the temple so that Israelites may encounter the presence of Yahweh (see עָלָה in, e.g., Is 2:3 ‖ Micah 4:2; Jer 31:6; Ezra 1:3; 7:7; and the Psalms of Ascent, Psalms 120–134). Hence in Jonah 1:3 יָרַד strengthens the idea that Jonah is going in the opposite direction: not "up" to Yahweh but "down" and away from Yahweh.

Here the verb is followed by יָפוֹ ("Joppa"), an accusative of place denoting the destination of travel (Joüon, § 125 n). Since Joppa is a seaport, the verb יָרַד probably has a physical meaning in terms of elevation: "to go down (to the sea shore)."[32]

Voting with his feet, Jonah hotfoots it to Joppa. Archaeological excavations reveal that the east Mediterranean port of Joppa (modern Jaffa, located at the southern boundary of modern Tel Aviv) was settled perhaps as early as the seventeenth cen-

---

[32] Cf. *HALOT*, s.v. ירד, Qal, 2. Cf. also Kennedy, *Studies in the Book of Jonah*, 18.

tury BC. There are several references to Joppa in Egyptian records of the fifteenth and fourteenth centuries BC.[33] It was probably controlled for most of the early part of the first millennium BC by the Philistines who settled in the coastal region to the south of Joppa. As the only natural harbor on the coast of Palestine south of the Bay of Acco, it was an important seaport for the surrounding region, especially Jerusalem.

Joppa is first mentioned in the OT as being in the territory of Dan in the early fourteenth century BC, but Dan soon lost control of its allotted territory (Josh 19:40, 46–47). Subsequently, Joppa remained outside Israelite control. Therefore the point in Jonah (eighth century BC) might be that even before he boards his ship, Jonah is seeking to escape Yahweh's presence by going there.

Joppa comes into particular prominence as the port where cedar wood from Lebanon was delivered for the building of Solomon's temple in the tenth century BC (2 Chr 2:15 [ET 2:16]) and the rebuilding of the temple in the late sixth century BC (Ezra 3:7). In the NT Peter is called to Joppa, where Luke writes about how "a disciple named Tabitha" is raised from the dead (Acts 9:36–42). It is then recorded that Peter "stayed in Joppa for many days with a certain Simon, a tanner" (Acts 9:43).

וַיִּמְצָא אֳנִיָּה ׀ בָּאָה תַרְשִׁישׁ—The verb מָצָא (here Qal third masculine singular imperfect with *waw* consecutive) can mean "to find" something after seeking or searching for it (see BDB, Qal, 1 a). Its indefinite direct object is אֳנִיָּה, a feminine noun that is a general Hebrew term for a "ship." The masculine singular אֳנִי can refer to "a fleet of ships," but the feminine refers to a single "ship" (GKC, § 122 t). Modifying it is בָּאָה, which is the Qal feminine singular participle of בּוֹא. The Masoretic accent (-אָ) on its last syllable indicates that it is the participle rather than the Qal third feminine singular perfect (which would be accented on the penultimate syllable: בָּאָה). While בּוֹא usually means "come," it can, as here, mean "to go" (away) to a place (see BDB, Qal, 4). The noun תַרְשִׁישׁ is another accusative of place referring to a destination of travel (Joüon, § 125 n), like יָפוֹ ("Joppa") in the preceding clause. Hence the ship either is going to sail to Tarshish (in which case the participle has a future force, GKC, § 116 d) or is a ship that regularly plies the Tarshish route.

There were two main types of seagoing vessels used in the ancient Mediterranean: the round ship and the long ship. The Nineveh relief depicting Luli's flight from the island of Tyre shows both.[34] The "ships of Tarshish"[b] were the long ships, possibly oar boats. This type of vessel is to be expected for bulk trade in metal. Jacob Katzenstein writes:

> Just as the Egyptians called certain of their vessels by geographical names, apparently to designate their destinations, e.g. ship-of-Byblos (*kpnt*) or ship-of-Crete (*kftj*[*w*]), the Tyrians apparently called the large ship in which they travelled great distances ship-of-Tarshish.[35]

(b) 1 Ki 22:49 (ET 22:48); Is 2:16; 23:1, 14; 60:9; Ezek 27:25; Ps 48:8 (ET 48:7); 2 Chr 9:21

---

[33] J. Kaplan and H. R. Kaplan, "Joppa," *ABD* 3:946–47.

[34] Harden, *The Phoenicians*, 169. Note Pliny's statement that a Tyrian invented the cargo ship (*Natural History*, 7.57).

[35] Katzenstein, *The History of Tyre*, 112. Both Kaiser (*Isaiah 13–39*, 163) and Oswalt (*The Book of Isaiah: Chapters 1–39*, 429) also believe Tarshish ships were a class of merchant

Ezekiel's oracle against Tyre (Ezekiel 27) gives some idea of the sort of vessel sailing the Mediterranean, with fir planks, a mast of cedar, a pine deck (27:5–6), and powered both by oars made of oak (27:6) and by linen sails (27:7).[36] Although Ezekiel is a sixth-century prophet, it is believed that chapter 27 accurately reflects Phoenician commerce in earlier centuries, including the time of Jonah.[37]

Ships going to Tarshish are well-known in the OT. 1 Ki 22:48 reports how Jehoshaphat made "ships of Tarshish to go to Ophir for gold, but they did not go, for the ships were wrecked at Ezion-geber" (cf. 2 Chr 20:35–37). Psalm 48 praises the God who "by the east wind did shatter the ships of Tarshish" (48:8 [ET 48:7]), indicating that the tradition about these ships was well-known. In Is 23:14 the ships of Tarshish are exhorted to "howl because your stronghold has been devastated" (see also Is 23:1). Finally, in Ezek 27:25–26 Tarshish ships break apart "in the heart of the sea." Taking these texts together, "a 'ship going to Tarshish' [Jonah 1:3] roughly culturally translates as 'the Titanic going out on her maiden voyage.' "[38] The analogy is almost exact, for Tarshish ships are proud, noble structures (Is 2:16), a symbol of everything that is "proud and lifted up" against Yahweh (Is 2:12), carrying precious cargoes, and they are destined to be shattered "by the east wind" (Ps 48:8 [ET 48:7]) and to promptly break apart "in the heart of the sea" (Ezek 27:25–26). This means that at the outset of his scheming to flee from Yahweh, Jonah is doomed to fail!

וַיִּתֵּן שְׂכָרָהּ—The verb is the Qal third masculine singular imperfect of נָתַן ("to give") with *waw* consecutive. The noun שָׂכָר can mean "wages" for work done or "expense" or "payment" (*HALOT*, 1, 3 b, 3 a, respectively). It has a third singular feminine pronominal suffix (הָ-), referring to the feminine noun אֳנִיָּה, "ship." Hence this clause is, literally, "He gave her/its payment," that is, he paid for the ship. Translations usually say that Jonah paid "the fare" (RSV, NIV, NASB) or "his fare" (NRSV, NEB, JB). However, according to Sasson, it wasn't until Roman times that the ancient world had a specific word for "fare"—"a charge for the purchase of space in an expedition, seagoing or otherwise."[39]

The idea expressed here is not that Jonah pays a fare, but rather that he hires or makes a payment for the services of the ship and its crew. The nuance underscores the magnitude of Jonah's action; he has financed an entire ship for his disobedience!

---

ships capable of traveling the open sea and that these ships took their name from the city of the same name.

[36] Ezek 27:26, "Into great waters your rowers have brought you; the east wind has broken you in the heart of the seas," has three elements common to Jonah, expressed by the same Hebrew vocabulary: (1) a destructive east wind (רוּחַ קָדִים) sent by God occurs also in Jonah 4:8; (2) the ship is almost broken (the verb שָׁבַר) in Jonah 1:4; and (3) "the heart of the seas" (לְבַב יַמִּים) is where Jonah ends up in 2:4 (ET 2:3).

[37] Some interpreters even go so far as to speculate that Ezekiel drew on a Phoenician text that predated him. See Katzenstein, *The History of Tyre*, 154. Elat writes: "This prophecy [Ezekiel 27] originated from a Phoenician poem that glorified Tyre during her golden age from the beginning of the 10th until the second half of the 8th century B.C.E." ("Phoenician Overland Trade within the Mesopotamian Empires," 24).

[38] Sherwood, *A Biblical Text and Its Afterlife*, 250.

[39] Sasson, *Jonah*, 84.

Chapter 1 supports this. That Jonah has access to the ship's "innermost recesses" (1:5) makes sense if he has hired the entire boat. That also explains why the sailors hesitate to throw Jonah overboard (1:13–14) even after they discern that he has endangered the entire ship. Even the captain does not order Jonah off the ship, but merely asks him to pray (1:6).

וַיֵּרֶד בָּהּ—The verb form וַיֵּרֶד is repeated from earlier in the verse. Here יָרַד takes the preposition בְּ with third feminine singular suffix (בָּהּ) referring to the feminine noun אֳנִיָּה, "ship." The verb and prepositional phrase together mean "to go on board" the ship or "to embark." Conversely, יָרַד with the preposition מִן in Ezek 27:29 means "to disembark."

לָבוֹא עִמָּהֶם תַּרְשִׁישָׁה—The Qal infinitive construct of בּוֹא with the preposition לְ indicates purpose: "to go with them to Tarshish." However, as with other infinitives that have human subjects, this purpose shall not succeed. See the first textual note on 1:3. Previously the verse referred to אֳנִיָּה (the "ship"), so the masculine plural suffix on עִמָּהֶם ("with *them*") must refer to the sailors associated with the ship (GKC, § 135 p) even though they are not explicitly mentioned until 1:5.

מִלִּפְנֵי יְהוָה:—This identical phrase concluded the first half of the verse (see the second textual note on 1:3). Now "away from the presence of Yahweh" also concludes the second half of the verse. The repetition emphasizes its importance. It denotes not merely the direction of Jonah's attempted escape. It also includes the one who is being abandoned (cf. Is 45:20–25; Job 20–21; 24). Jonah is leaving behind no one less than Yahweh, his God. Yet ironically Jonah can still confess Yahweh as his God in 1:9!

Commentary

1:1 In this verse the two major characters are named: Yahweh and Jonah. They contend throughout the narrative as protagonist and antagonist. With the exception of "Amittai," Jonah's father, all other human characters in the narrative remain unnamed. The rest of the characters are used as a foil to highlight the relationship between the prophet and his God. In this way, Yahweh and Jonah take center stage with the spotlight fixed on them.

One of the best ways to gain a sense of what a particular Hebrew narrative is about is to pay close attention to how it begins and ends, as well as to how it is structured as a whole. For example, the book of Joshua begins (1:2, 3, 6, 11, 13, 15 [twice]) and ends (24:8, 11, 13) with an emphasis on Yahweh's fulfillment of his promise to give Israel the land as well as on the nation's consequent responsibility to serve him faithfully (24:14–27). Attention to structure, therefore, provides general parameters for the interpretation of Joshua as a whole and provides insights into its main message. In the case of Jonah, the narrative begins with the Word of Yahweh (1:1), and it ends with Yahweh's words (4:10–11). We may safely say, therefore, that the narrative is concerned with the effects and consequences of the divine Word.

The noun "word" (דָּבָר) and the cognate verb דָּבַר, "speak, promise," figure prominently within the narrative of Jonah and actually gain momentum as

the events unfold.[40] Here in 1:1, the narrator informs us that "the Word of Yahweh [דְּבַר־יְהֹוָה] came to Jonah." In parallel fashion, the message is repeated in 3:1: "And the Word of Yahweh [דְבַר־יְהוָה] came to Jonah," and this time the next verse gives the word greater emphasis: "Proclaim … the message which I am speaking to you" (וּקְרָא אֵלֶיהָ אֶת־הַקְּרִיאָה אֲשֶׁר אָנֹכִי דֹּבֵר אֵלֶיךָ). In 3:3 Jonah arises and goes to Nineveh according to Yahweh's Word (כִּדְבַר יְהוָה). It is this word the prophet delivers in 3:4. Yahweh's word reaches the king in 3:6: "This word [הַדָּבָר] reached the king of Nineveh." Then in 3:10 God changes his verdict when he sees their deeds, and the word he spoke against Nineveh is changed: "God changed his verdict about the evil he promised [דִּבֶּר] to do to them, and he did not do it." After Yahweh fulfilled his Word (in the way he saw fit) in chapter 3, Jonah expresses his own word in his prayer in 4:2: "Ah, Yahweh! Was not this my word [דְבָרִי] … ?" These statements throughout the narrative about the "word" and "speaking" highlight the contrast between divine and human words, and Yahweh's word of Gospel for the Ninevites finally overrides all other words (cf. Rom 5:20).

When Hebrew narrative starts an account of a new character not previously introduced, it can begin with a noun followed by a verb (e.g., Gen 3:1; 2 Ki 5:1). The use of the prophetic formula "Now the Word of Yahweh came to Jonah" signals that the narrative of Jonah actually begins in another place (see the first textual note on 1:1). This place is 2 Ki 14:23–28. The account in 2 Kings 14 anchors Jonah in the eighth century BC as a prophet who preached to the Israelite king Jeroboam II (ca. 786–746 BC). 2 Ki 14:25 states: "He [Jeroboam II] restored the border of Israel from Lebo-hamath [in Aram/Syria] as far as the Sea of the Arabah [i.e., the Dead Sea], according to the Word of Yahweh, the God of Israel, which he spoke by the hand of his servant Jonah the son of Amittai, the prophet who was from Gath-hepher."

Jeroboam II—or Jeroboam the son of Joash—changes the map of Israel as he extends the country's northern border to Lebo-hamath (the Entrance to Hamath, south of Kadesh) and the southern border to the Dead Sea. The large extent of Jeroboam's kingdom, including both northern Israel and southern Judah, ruled by Jeroboam's ally or vassal Uzziah, rivals that of the combined kingdom of David and Solomon. Jeroboam II is economically successful but spiritually bankrupt. Yet, in spite of his wickedness, through Jonah, Yahweh brings about good in the midst of evil (cf. Gen 45:8–11; 50:20; Rom 8:28). This turn of events is as follows:

> For Yahweh saw the affliction of Israel—that it was very bitter; there was none left, neither slave nor free; there was no helper for Israel. But Yahweh had not said he would blot out the name of Israel from under heaven, so he saved them by the hand of Jeroboam the son of Joash.

---

[40] The noun refers to Yahweh's "Word" in Jonah 1:1; 3:1, 3 and possibly also in 3:6 (see the textual note on 3:6). The verb refers to Yahweh "speaking" in 3:2, 10. Only in 4:2 does either refer to a human utterance: while praying to Yahweh, Jonah refers to his prior "word" before he fled.

And the rest of the events of Jeroboam, and all that he did, and his might, how he fought and how he recovered Damascus and Hamath for Judah in Israel, are they not written in the book of the events of the days of the kings of Israel? (2 Ki 14:26–28)[41]

It is ironic that when Yahweh calls Jonah to extend his same grace to Nineveh, the prophet flees.

On one level the narrative of Jonah is an exploration of the significant theological themes of 2 Ki 14:25–28. In both texts Jonah is associated with Yahweh's grace in the face of evil. While 2 Kings speaks of Yahweh's compassion toward Israel despite the wickedness of her king, Jeroboam II, so likewise the narrative of Jonah speaks of Yahweh's mercy towards Nineveh in spite of her wickedness.

Yahweh's grace towards the Northern Kingdom is then intimately connected with Jonah's proclamation of Yahweh's Word in 2 Kings ("the Word of Yahweh, the God of Israel, which he spoke," כִּדְבַר יְהוָה אֱלֹהֵי יִשְׂרָאֵל אֲשֶׁר דִּבֶּר, 2 Ki 14:25). Despite the habitual wickedness of the king, Yahweh's desire to help and save Israel is unquenchable. He does not override the wicked king, but rather uses the king's personal ambition to bring deliverance for his people. When referring to the same situation, Amos 6:14 points to the ultimate ineffectiveness of Jeroboam's strategy. Israel did not need expanded borders, but an expanded heart for Yahweh.

Jonah was a contemporary of Amos and Hosea and may even have been one of the "sons of the prophets" (2 Ki 2:3–7) who was a protégé of Elisha. According to rabbinic tradition, Jonah was the son of the widow of Zarephath whom Elijah restored to life in 1 Kings 17, and the rabbis unanimously identify Jonah with the prophet Jonah mentioned in 2 Ki 14:25.[42] Jonah is also the last in the sequence of prophets in the Northern Kingdom mentioned in the book of Kings (Ahijah, 1 Ki 11:29–39; 14:1–18; Jehu, 1 Ki 16:7–13; the prophets mentioned in 1 Ki 20:13–22, 28; Micaiah, 1 Kings 22; Elijah and Elisha, 1 Kings 17–2 Kings 13).

In this line of the prophets in 1 and 2 Kings, Jonah comes after Elijah and Elisha. Many phrases from the narrative of Jonah find their closest biblical parallels in the stories about Elijah and Elisha (1 Kings 17–2 Kings 13). An account involving a great fish (as well as a small worm) would not have been out of place among the narratives about Elijah and Elisha. Narratives in Kings recount encounters involving prophets and lions (1 Ki 13:20–32; 20:35–36), bears (2 Ki 2:23–25), ravens (1 Ki 17:4–6), and a donkey (1 Ki 13:20–32). The

---

[41] Josephus comments on Jonah and Jeroboam's campaign, concluding: "So Jeroboam made an expedition against the Syrians, and overran all their country, as Jonah had foretold" (*Antiquities*, 9.205 [9.10.1]; trans. Whiston, *The Works of Josephus*, 259).

[42] Bolin, *Freedom beyond Forgiveness*, 17, citing *Pirqe Rabbi Eliezer*, 33, for the tradition about Jonah being the boy raised by Elijah. That tradition is also found in *Midrash Psalms*, on Ps 26:9. For a discussion of Jonah in Jewish tradition, see Bolin, *Freedom beyond Forgiveness*, 14–18.

narrative of Jonah could have easily been placed after the reference to Jonah the son of Amittai in 2 Ki 14:25 and have not interrupted the narrative flow of 2 Kings to any great degree.

Jonah appears to function much like other prophets in 1 and 2 Kings. The account recorded in 1 Ki 22:6–28 shows that court prophets and true prophets were often at odds with each other. Court prophets, who prophesied in Yahweh's name what the king wanted to hear, acted to uphold the existing social order. It was their task to secure the prerogatives of the king and to defend the realm against outside enemies by instilling confidence that God was on the side of the incumbent king. The true prophets, on the other hand, were typically allied with a secondary cultural group, a small band of believers (cf. 1 Ki 19:10–18; 2 Kings 2). The true prophets generally saw themselves as defenders of Israel's older social and religious values, resting on the Torah of Moses, which had been supplanted by the very different religion and value system of Israel's syncretistic society. True prophets were, as a result, adversaries of the existing regime. Where the institutional prophets predicted glory and loot for the unfaithful leaders, the "outsiders" predicted their defeat and failure. The ministries of Elijah and Micaiah ben Imlah (1 Kings 22) manifest these basic dichotomies: Yahweh versus Baal; the disenfranchised and persecuted faithful versus the incumbent king with all his royal power; and individuals calling for reformation versus those trying to enforce communal solidarity by maintaining the status quo.

That Yahweh's Word came to Jonah (Jonah 1:1, as in 2 Ki 14:25–28) distinguishes him as a true prophet. Yet because of the advent of the divine Word, Jonah is now caught in this schism. Shall he function as a court prophet for the evil king Jeroboam II, who no doubt would want him to continue to prophesy about Israel's expansion and superiority?[43] Or should he obey the call to serve as a spokesman to Nineveh on behalf of Yahweh, the God he knows to be "gracious and merciful … changing [his] verdict about evil" (Jonah 4:2)?

We should not be surprised that *Jonah* initially evades Yahweh's call. "Jonah" (יוֹנָה) is the Hebrew noun for "dove" (e.g., Gen 8:8–12; Song 1:15; 4:1), and in Hos 7:11 "dove" is synonymous for "double-minded." Hosea writes: "Ephraim became like a dove [כְיוֹנָה], silly and brainless. They called to Egypt; they went to Assyria." The participle פוֹתָה, translated "silly," connotes spiritual foolishness and gullibility; the Aramaic Targum renders it שְׁרִיחֲתָא, "vapid, senseless" (Jastrow). The phrase translated "brainless" (אֵין לֵב, literally, "without a heart or mind") connotes infidelity and lack of discernment. So Ephraim is not like a dove in its innocence (cf. Mt 10:16), but rather like a dove in its aimless activity, flying from one place to another—first to Egypt, then to Assyria—as a frightened and gullible people who trusts not in Yahweh.

---

[43] Jonah's prophecy of salvation for Israel in 2 Ki 14:25–28 stands in stark contrast with his somewhat later contemporary Amos (cf. Amos 5:18–27; 6:13–14, 7:11).

Nonetheless, something more reprehensible than timidity is present. Hosea constantly emphasizes Israel's culpable ignorance; the people had abandoned covenant knowledge of Yahweh (cf. Hos 4:6). Enmeshed in theological error, they misjudge the political situation and have no self-knowledge. Israel demonstrates blindness at its worst in the people's incomprehensible refusal to return to Yahweh or to seek him "in all this" (Hos 7:10), in spite of the severity of all the disasters that had overwhelmed them since they deserted Yahweh (cf. Amos 4:6–11; Jeremiah 44). Israel failed to return even in spite of the gracious warmth and openness of Yahweh's constant invitation (Hos 14:3).

In many respects, this dovish demeanor depicted in Hosea matches the person called "dove," Jonah. To some extent, then, the equation is Jonah = dove = Israel. This may be a not-so-subtle way to make the point that Jonah is not only a historical individual, he also represents Israel. However, against any allegorical interpretation, this does not mean the narrative depicts a merely figurative account of Israel's historical experiences.

In other texts the dove is easily put to flight, seeking a secure refuge in the mountains (Ezek 7:16; Ps 55:7–9 [ET 55:6–8]), and it moans and laments when in distress (Is 38:14, 59:11; Nahum 2:8 [ET 2:7]). When in deep trouble, the psalmist longs for wings like a dove so that he can escape to find shelter elsewhere (Ps 55:5–9 [ET 55:4–8]).

With everything that "dove" means in these OT texts, that Jonah is named—well, *Jonah*—is characteristic of other OT names that predict subsequent narrative action. For example, Eglon's name (עֶגְלוֹן, Judg 3:12) suggests the Hebrew word for "calf" (עֵגֶל). This ruler of the occupying Moabite power turns out to be a "fatted calf" readied for slaughter through the wiles of one Ehud (Judg 3:15–22). Ahab's wife from the kingdom of Tyre and Sidon—the infamous Jezebel (אִיזֶבֶל, 1 Ki 16:31)—has a name that means "no nobility." On the more positive side, the name Moses most likely means "to draw out" (Ex 2:10). He was drawn out of the waters of the Nile as an infant. Then as an eighty-year-old man, Moses miraculously leads Israel through the Red Sea and in so doing draws them out of Egypt, out of the house of bondage. Moses also miraculously draws water out of a rock, twice (Ex 17:6; Num 20:11). Indeed, often in the shadowy foreimage of a Hebrew name we are able to anticipate what the future holds.

Jonah's hometown is Gath-hepher about fifteen miles west of the Sea of Galilee in the territory of Zebulun (Josh 19:13; see also Josh 19:10). It is identified with the modern Arab village of Meshed, located between Nazareth and Kefar Kana (Cana), approximately four kilometers east of Sepphoris in Galilee.[44] Meshed, in fact, takes its name from the memory of Jonah. The Arabic *el meshed* means "martyr's grave," and a grave of Jonah can be found there.

---

[44] R. Greenberg, "Gath-hepher," *ABD* 2:909. "In the fourth century AD Jerome said the prophet's tomb was not far from Sepphoris" (Nixon, *The Message of Jonah*, 32). See Jerome, *Commentariorum in Ionam*, prologue (CCSL 76:378).

1:2 From the snapshot of Jonah in 2 Ki 14:23–28 we see a prophet who, to some extent, comes to be associated with Israel's national boundaries. Yahweh's call for him to go beyond Israel's borders recalls other similar calls in the OT. Abram is called to leave his homeland in Mesopotamia in order to find a new land of blessing (Gen 12:1–3), while Moses is called to lead Israel out of Egypt to the promised land (Ex 3:1–14). Balaam is sent to Moab from where, greatly to the chagrin of Balak, the king of Moab, he blesses Israel (Numbers 22–24). Elijah is called to the Gentile town of Zarephath in Sidon to take refuge with a widow (1 Ki 17:9). Noah, Joshua, Ruth, David, Amos, and Jeremiah all turn their back on the established norms and enter into new ways of living.

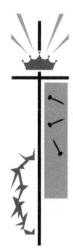

To the profound dismay of official Judaism, Jesus also frequently breaks through conventional social, geographical, and moral boundaries of his day. He travels not only through Samaria (e.g., John 4) but also to the coastal Canaanite stronghold (Mt 15:21). He speaks publicly with women (e.g., Jn 4:27; 8:10), socializes with sinners (Mk 2:15), touches lepers (Lk 5:12–13), heals the Samaritan leper (Lk 17:11–19), and challenges the law of the Sabbath in the interests of human well-being (Lk 6:6–11). Even more significantly, in his incarnation Jesus breaks through the boundary of heaven to dwell among us, "full of grace and truth" (Jn 1:14). In his atoning death he crosses over from righteousness to sin (2 Cor 5:21), and in his resurrection he breaks down the boundary between death and life (Rom 6:9). At the heart of the Gospel, then, is this breaking down of conventional boundaries, extending the grace of God to the furthest place.

Jonah as Sinner and Saint

So just who is this Jonah, who refuses to extend God's kingdom all the way to encompass Nineveh, and instead flees from Yahweh? Scholars' answers to this question are many and varied. He is "self-centered, lazy, hypocritical and altogether inferior to the wonderful pagans who surround him."[45] Jonah is *revêche et têtu* ("cantankerous and bad-tempered"),[46] "good-for-nothing."[47] Jonah is a mutant dove, more like a hawk,[48] who is "self-centered, self-righteous, and self-willed."[49] He is a "religious monster."[50]

The best description of Jonah is that he, like every believer in the one true God, is *simul iustus et peccator*, "simultaneously sinner and saint."[51] He is ac-

---

[45] Holbert, "Deliverance Belongs to Yahweh!" 70.

[46] Lods, *La Religion d'Israël*, 196, cited in Keller, "Jonas," 329.

[47] Wolff, *Obadiah and Jonah*, 109.

[48] LaCocque and Lacocque, *Jonah*, 31.

[49] Burrows, "The Literary Character of the Book of Jonah," 97.

[50] Allen, *Joel, Obadiah, Jonah and Micah*, 229.

[51] Likewise, Job appears in this same light as simultaneously a sinner and a saint. Like Jonah in 2:3–10 (ET 2:2–9), Job can utter great confessions of faith (e.g., Job 13:15–16; 19:23–27). Like Jonah in 4:2, Job can attack God (e.g., 7:20–21; 9:22–24; 16:7–17). And also like Jonah in 4:3, 8–9, Job can despair of life itself (3:1–26; cf. 9:16–18; 14:18–22). See Mitchell, "Job

counted righteous through faith (Gen 15:6), and sometimes he displays this righteousness by his saintly conduct and words, but at other times his old sinful nature prevails, and he behaves unfaithfully (as with St. Paul in Romans 7) and thus needs to repent. This is the view of Jonah taken by Luther. He compares Jonah to Elijah, whom James describes this way: "Elijah was a man with the same nature as us" (James 5:17). Luther understands Jonah to be like Elijah, indeed like every Christian.[52] He writes of Jonah in the beginning of his comments on Jonah 4:

> Here again we see an example of what I said at the beginning of this prophet and have said often in other places and Scripture everywhere expresses: There still remain in the saints remnants of the flesh, and the saints do not get rid of them until that old Adam is completely destroyed.[53]

Luther's insights mean that as we read the narrative, we are forced to switch back and forth between identifying with Jonah in his faith—especially in his psalm in chapter 2 and his faithful obedience in 3:3—while also rejecting his disobedience, half-truths, arrogance, pride, and anger. Terence Fretheim discusses Jonah's status as *simul iustus et peccator*:

> To recognize this has important implications for the interpretation of the book. This means, for example, that God's actions in the book are not directed toward re-integrating Jonah into the community of believers. He is not even *fundamentally* concerned with getting Jonah to be obedient to his commands. For even after Jonah is obedient (3:3) the issue remains. This was a matter secondary to the larger issue, and would be placed in proper perspective once the theological problem was settled.[54]

Jonah is a sinner-saint whose chief problem is the application of the Gospel. This is more specifically detailed as follows. He is a Hebrew who worships Yahweh and confesses him as the "the God of the heavens, … who made the sea and the dry land" (1:9), and yet he attempts to flee from Yahweh's presence (1:3). Jonah knows, as he prays from the deep, that "salvation belongs to Yahweh" (2:10 [ET 2:9]); he confesses that Yahweh is "a gracious and merciful God, slow to anger and abounding in loyal love," a God who changes "his verdict about evil" (4:2). But he would rather die than see Yahweh's grace and mercy be extended to Gentiles in free and full operation (4:3, 8).

Jonah is put to shame by the behavior of the pagans to whom he begrudges Yahweh's forgiveness. A pagan ship captain summons the sleeping prophet to

---

and the Theology of the Cross," especially p. 176.

Luther discusses this aspect of the lives of OT saints in his Genesis lectures (e.g., AE 2:166, 168–69, 171–72, 204–5, 240; 3:355), and he uses the phrase in the two versions of his Galatians commentary (AE 26:232; 27:231). The specific language does not appear in the Lutheran Confessions, but the doctrine is prominent, especially in AC IV, VI, and XX; Ap IV and XX; and FC III.

[52] AE 19:6.

[53] AE 19:26–27.

[54] Fretheim, *The Message of Jonah*, 20.

prayer (1:6), and pagan sailors row hard to save his life (1:13) and finally with reluctance obey his command to throw him overboard (1:14–15). Their hearts are more tender than his. These pagans are converted to true faith: they worship "Yahweh with great worship" and sacrifice "a sacrifice to Yahweh" (1:16), whose Word and will Jonah disregards. Later, the men of Nineveh repent and sit in sackcloth and ashes. They believe God when Jonah preaches (3:5–9) and find Yahweh to be a gracious God who changes his verdict concerning evil (3:10). Jonah responds with suicidal rage, protesting the undeserved compassion of Yahweh (4:1–3), the very compassion to which he owes his life (2:7 [ET 2:6]).

This means that as sinner and saint at the same time, Jonah is a divided man. He exhibits signs of faith (2:10 [ET 2:9]; 3:3–4) as well as signs of unbelief (4:1). Jonah can pray (2:3–10 [ET 2:2–9]) and express the faith of Israel (4:2) and yet flee from Yahweh (1:3), quarrel with Yahweh (chapter 4), and even seek his own death (4:3, 8). Yet even if his true confession in 4:2 is in a begrudging context, Jonah approaches Yahweh with the kind of honesty that is typical of Israelite piety. In chapter 4 he sounds a lot like the psalmist in Ps 44:10–18 (ET 44:9–17):

> But now you have rejected and humbled us; you no longer go out with our armies. You made us retreat before the enemy, and our adversaries have plundered us. You gave us up to be devoured like sheep and have scattered us among the nations. You sold your people for a pittance, gaining nothing from their sale. You have made us a reproach to our neighbors, the scorn and derision of those around us. You have made us a byword among the nations; the peoples shake their heads at us. My disgrace is before me all day long, and my face is covered with shame at the taunts of those who reproach and revile me, because of the enemy, who is bent on revenge. All this happened to us, though we had not forgotten you or been false to your covenant. (NIV)

So Jonah, like the psalmist, opens his heart to Yahweh just as it is. His psalm of chapter 2 uses traditional vocabulary from the Psalter and even concludes with vows and sacrifices typical of Israelite piety (2:10 [ET 2:9]). Jonah is disobedient, but he never loses faith in Yahweh, and God does not reject him. The list of Jonah's sins is extensive: flight, complaint, frustration, stubbornness, self-pity, mercurial anger, repeated and strenuous wishes for death. Yet despite all these, even to the end, he continues to trust that Yahweh, who is "gracious and merciful" (4:2), will be that way toward him, and indeed Yahweh remains so.

The only other instance when Yahweh sent a prophet to a foreign king was when he commissioned Elisha to anoint Hazael king over Syria (2 Ki 8:7–15; see also 1 Ki 19:15–16). That journey too was explicitly self-destructive: Elisha carries out Yahweh's command while weeping as he tells Hazael, "I know the evil that you will do to the people of Israel: you will set fire to their fortresses; you will slay their young men with the sword, and you will dash in pieces their little ones, and you will rip open their women with child" (2 Ki

8:12). Aware of that narrative, we are prepared to expect that a similar experience is in store for Jonah. So, from the very beginning, Jonah is on a kamikaze course, a plot where he and his nation are moving toward self-annihilation. In sparing Nineveh (3:10), Yahweh allows the Assyrians to become the agents of his judgment against the Northern Kingdom of Israel several decades later, in 722/721 BC (2 Ki 17:6).

Not only does Jonah stand with Elisha, but also in the long line of prophets who are called upon to speak about the nations. Oracles about the nations constitute almost one-fourth of the material in the Latter Prophets.^c Why does Yahweh send prophets to speak about the nations? Because as "the Judge of all the earth" (Gen 18:25), he has claims on the Moabites, Edomites, Amalekites, and—in Jonah's case—especially the Ninevites.

(c) Isaiah 7:3–16; 8:1–4; 10:5–34; 13–23; 34; 37:21–29; Jeremiah 25:15–38; 27:1–11; 46–51; Ezekiel 25–32; 35; 38–39; Joel 4:1–17 (ET 3:1–17); Amos 1:3–2:3; Obadiah; Jonah 3:4; Micah 4:11–13; 5:4–5 (ET 5:5–6); 7:11–17; Nahum; Habakkuk 2; Zeph 2:4–15; Hag 2:21–22; Zech 9:1–8; Mal 1:2–5

"Nineveh, the Great City"

Jonah contains more references to Nineveh than any other OT book (nine of the seventeen OT references). The city is also mentioned in an aetiology concerning the origin of several Mesopotamian cities in Gen 10:8–12; in 2 Ki 19:36 ‖ Is 37:37; and in Nahum and Zephaniah. Both of those prophetic books emphasize Nineveh's role as the symbol of the Assyrian Empire, the mortal enemy of Israel, renowned for brutal conquest and butchery.

Nineveh was some five hundred miles from Jonah's home of Gath-hepher in Israel. Its ruins now lie across the Tigris River from the modern Iraqi town of Mosul, two hundred and twenty miles north-northwest of Baghdad.[55] A series of archeological digs from the first in 1842 through 1990 has uncovered a wealth of information.[56] Excavations reveal a walled city with a perimeter of approximately seven and three-quarters miles during the city's height in the seventh century. Twenty-five thousand tablets containing the library collection of Ashurbanipal (668–627 BC) were also discovered. Two mounds remain at the site: one is named Kuyunjik, and the other, known as Nebi Yunus, meaning "the prophet Jonah," stands by a mosque marking the place where the prophet is supposedly buried, near an arsenal built by Esarhaddon (680–669 BC).

Archaeological excavations and cuneiform texts indicate that Nineveh endured for thousands of years. It was Sennacherib (704–681 BC) who made Nineveh the capital of the Assyrian Empire.[57] He enlarged its circumference from

---

[55] A brief overview of the city and its history can be found in Roaf, *Cultural Atlas of Mesopotamia and the Ancient Near East*, 186–87.

[56] For a review of the work up to 1967, see Madhloum, "Excavations at Nineveh: A Preliminary Report (1965–1967)." Many of the early modern excavators made much of the fact that the cuneiform sign for Nineveh is the compound of a fish in a house (Parrot, *Nineveh and the Old Testament*, 24).

[57] This means that Nineveh would not have been the capital of Assyria until over forty years after the death of Jeroboam II (ca. 746 BC), the Israelite king at the time Jonah ministered (2 Ki 14:23–28). Some state the erroneous idea that Nineveh was the capital of Assyria dur-

9,300 cubits (approximately three miles) to 21,815 cubits (approximately seven miles).[58] Sasson writes that during Sennacherib's reign, "the town achieved massive constructions, with trapezoidal-shaped fortifications running eight miles around the perimeters."[59] Modern archaeological surveys confirm the basic accuracy of ancient documents that discuss the city's dimensions.[60] Albert Olmstead writes in 1923 in his *History of Assyria*: "Nineveh owes to Sennacherib its position as the capital par excellence of the Assyrian empire."[61]

The following kings of Assyria were contemporaries of Jonah and Jeroboam II (ca. 786–746 BC):

1. Adad-nirari III (810–783)
2. Shalmaneser IV (782–773)
3. Assur-dan III (772–755)
4. Assur-nirari V (754–745)[62]

More specifically, the years 772–745 BC, during the reigns of Assur-dan III and Assur-nirari V, were a time of great political instability in Assyria.[63] "This was a period of local autonomy in Assyrian regions as well as in Babylonia."[64] For example, an important Assyria official—Shamshi-ilu—seems to have enjoyed a long and successful career (ca. 792–752 BC), for during the reign of Shalmaneser IV (782–773 BC), this Shamshi-ilu records on two stone lions at the Syrian city of Til Barship his victory over Argishtish, king of Urartu, without making any mention of the Assyrian king. According to Georges Roux, this is "unprecedented in Assyrian records."[65] Nor is Shamshi-ilu an exception. It is possible to identify a number of other important officials who, although paying nominal allegiance to the Assyrian king, appear to have exercised considerable independence during the first half of the eighth century.[66]

It is possible, therefore, to surmise that at the time of Jonah's ministry, Nineveh, while not yet the capital of Assyria, was an independent or semi-independent city-state with its own ruler. With the Assyrian administrative system

---

ing the time of Jonah, for example, Walter R. Roehrs, *Concordia Self-Study Commentary* (St. Louis: Concordia, 1979), OT, 619; Laetsch, *The Minor Prophets*, 234.

[58] In comparison, Babylon, the largest Mesopotamian city, covered 2,500 acres. Jerusalem grew from 10 acres when David made it his capital to 40 acres by the eighth century. After the fall of Samaria in 722/721 BC, Jerusalem almost quadrupled in size to about 150 acres (as noted in Broshi, "The Expansion of Jerusalem in the Reigns of Hezekiah and Manasseh," 23–24).

[59] Sasson, *Jonah*, 71.

[60] Jones, "The Topography of Nineveh," 324; see also Madhloum, "Excavations at Nineveh," 77.

[61] Olmstead, *History of Assyria*, 318.

[62] These dates are based on relative dating; see Lemanski, "Jonah's Nineveh," 42.

[63] As noted by Lemanski, "Jonah's Nineveh," 44–46.

[64] Brinkman, *A Political History of Post-Kassite Babylonia 1158–722 BC*, 218.

[65] Roux, *Ancient Iraq*, 251.

[66] Lawrence, "Assyrian Nobles and the Book of Jonah," 125–26.

in a state of disarray, it would have been natural for local rulers to take control over the affairs of their city.[67]

In addition to political instability during the lifetime of Jonah, Nineveh also experienced great economic hardship as well as various other catastrophes.[68] These calamities may in part explain why Nineveh felt the wrath of God and repented. As Laetsch has written: "Nineveh's conversion at Jonah's preaching in a time of threatening national ruin is therefore—aside from God's grace—quite reasonable also from a purely psychological point of view."[69]

Nineveh's independence from the greater Assyrian government at this time explains why no trace of the city's repentance survives in Assyrian records. Before long, Nineveh was brought back under the immediate control of Assyria by Tiglath-pileser III (745–727 BC), at which time any religious reforms accomplished by native rulers would have been completely overturned.

Nineveh's glory was not long lived, as the Medes and Babylonians combined forces and besieged the city in August of 612 BC, utterly destroying it, just as Nahum predicts.[70] The entire prophecy of Nahum, delivered by this prophet from Elkosh (1:1) sometime before Nineveh's downfall in 612 BC, gives a picture of this "city of bloodshed" (Nah 3:1). Nineveh is full of lies, booty, and dead bodies without end, a city that is likened to a shapely harlot out to seduce all nations (Nah 3:1–4; cf. Zeph 2:13–15). "What has become of that lions' den?" Nahum asks sarcastically (2:12), "a city of bloodshed, all of it a deceit and full of plunder—the prey never stops" (3:1). The book ends with these ominous words: "All who hear the news about you clap their hands over you. For upon whom has not come your unceasing evil?" (Nahum 3:19 ESV). Among Israel's enemies at the time of Jonah Nineveh was truly the "chief of sinners" (cf. 1 Tim 1:15). Xenophon passed by in 401 BC with his retreating Greek army and described what once was Nineveh as "a great stronghold, deserted and lying in ruins."[71]

When comparing the portrayal of Nineveh in Nahum and Zephaniah with that in Jonah, there is some common ground on the linguistic level. For example, in Jonah 1:2 Nineveh is accused of evil (רָעָה), which rises up before Yahweh, while רָעָה is used to describe the king of Nineveh in Nah 1:11 and 3:19. In Jonah 3:7–9 the king of Nineveh and his nobles command each person to turn away "from his evil way" (מִדַּרְכּוֹ הָרָעָה) and practice of "violence" (חָמָס).

---

[67] Tiglath-pileser III brought this state of affairs to an end. Hallo writes: "The semiautonomous Assyrian proconsulships were broken up into smaller administrative units and their governors thereby deprived of the virtually sovereign power that the interval of royal weakness had allowed them to assume" (*The Ancient Near East: A History*, 133).

[68] For the details, see Lemanski, "Jonah's Nineveh," 47.

[69] Laetsch, *Minor Prophets*, 215–16.

[70] The partially reconstructed text of Nabopolassar, the conquering Babylonian king, states that "the city was seized and a great defeat he [Nabopolassar] inflicted upon the entire population. … The city they turned into ruin-hills and heaps of debris" (*ANET*, 304–5).

[71] Xenophon, *Anabasis*, 3.4.10 (trans. C. L. Brownson; LCL [Cambridge, Mass.: Harvard University Press, 1921], 469); see 3.4.10–12.

In 3:10 God sees that the people of Nineveh have turned "from their evil way" (מִדַּרְכָּם הָרָעָה).

Nineveh is described in Nah 3:1 as bloody (דָּמִים) and full of "deceit" (כַּחַשׁ) and "plunder" (פֶּרֶק). In Zeph 2:13–15 Nineveh is described as an exultant city (הָעִיר הָעַלִּיזָה).[72] But those terms in Nahum and Zephaniah are absent from Jonah with the exception of דָּם used in a different context in Jonah 1:14. Thus there is little support for the view that Jonah was dependent on either Nahum or Zephaniah.

In other sections of the OT, Assyria is described as idolatrous and full of pride. Isaiah's vivid imagery of an advancing army describes a coming day of darkness and destruction (Is 5:25–30). Later in the book, it becomes clear that the military might is Assyria (e.g., Is 8:7; chapters 36–37). Assyria is featured as the force that devours the surrounding countryside, leaving Jerusalem tottering like a pathetic hut (Is 1:8); a swarm of killer bees from across the river for which Yahweh whistles (Is 7:18); the razor that he uses to shave the nations' genitalia and expose them to shame (Is 7:20); the rod of Yahweh's anger and the staff of his fury (Is 10:5). Assyria taunts the king of Judah, "I will give you two thousand horses, if you are able, for your part, to put riders on them" (Is 36:8), and proclaims to the inhabitants of Jerusalem—even in the Hebrew language—that they are destined to "eat their own dung and drink their own urine" (Is 36:12).

The Assyrians invented the idea of deporting entire populations to distant lands (2 Ki 15:29; 17:6; Is 36:16–17), but are remembered most for their inhumane warfare as depicted in these two examples of the battle rhetoric of Ashurnasirpal II (883–859 BC):

> I stormed the mountain peaks and took them. In the midst of the mighty mountain I slaughtered them; with their blood I dyed the mountain red like wool. With the rest of them I darkened the gullies and precipices of the mountains. I carried off their spoil and their possessions. The heads of their warriors I cut off, and I formed them into a pillar over against their city; their young men and their maidens I burned in the fire.[73]

> I built a pillar over against his city gate, and I flayed all the chief men who had revolted, and I covered the pillar with their skins; some I walled up within the pillar, some I impaled upon the pillar on stakes, and others I bound to stakes round about the pillar.[74]

This battle cry, together with the depictions in Isaiah (eighth century BC), Nahum (seventh century BC), and Zephaniah (seventh century BC), means that the very word "Nineveh" would raise a note of high anxiety in any prophet's mind. The city is the very symbol of utter moral degradation. In a sense, Nin-

---

[72] Isaiah and Zephaniah use the adjective עַלִּיז to characterize "exultant" cities (Is 22:2; 23:7; 32:13; Zeph 2:15) and people (Is 24:8; Zeph 3:11) that will be destroyed. The verb עָלַז is often used of the wicked and of Israel's enemies (2 Sam 1:20; Jer 11:15; 50:11; Ps 94:3).

[73] Luckenbill, *Ancient Records of Assyria and Babylonia*, vol. 1, § 447.

[74] Luckenbill, *Ancient Records of Assyria and Babylonia*, vol. 1, § 443.

eveh corresponds to that cipher for Rome that throbs through the book of Revelation, "Babylon the great" (e.g., Rev 17:5). Nineveh connotes what is big and bad, an intolerable affront to Yahweh (compare Jonah 1:2 to Gen 4:10; 6:11, 12; 18:20, 21; Rev 16:19). The command to Jonah, "Arise, go to Nineveh" (1:2) should be heard against the background of this picture of Nineveh painted by these texts.

But what right does Yahweh have to hold Nineveh accountable for its "crimes against humanity"? Nineveh's wickedness is the violation of the moral Law of Yahweh, which even foreign nations are obliged to keep (cf. Amos 1–2) and which they disregard at their own peril.[75] This idea is expressed in Isaiah's famous comparison: "The ox knows its owner, and the ass its master's crib, but Israel does not know, my people do not understand" (Is 1:3). While certainly implying the covenant relationship between Yahweh and Israel based upon the covenant Yahweh made with Abram (Gen 15:9–21), Isaiah lays his primary emphasis on the unnaturalness of Israel's rebellion, which stands in sharp contrast to the purely instinctive natural reactions of animals (cf. Jer 8:7). In stressing this idea of "natural law," John Barton does not mean that Israelite culture knew about the Western natural law tradition with all its refinements. Rather, he holds that the term reflects the ethical ideas of the OT that are known by all people, including in this case, the Ninevites.

Amos' oracles in chapters 1 and 2 lay at the heart of this understanding of natural law. Amos—like the book of Jonah—appeals to a kind of natural law about international conduct that is self-evidently right. If the validity of moral rules governing the conduct of the nations is, in fact, presupposed by Yahweh, then it is only right that he is their Judge.

This is sometimes called "international law" in the sense not of an internationally agreed-upon code of ethics, but of the divine Law, visible in creation and attested by the conscience, and obligatory for all humankind, whether or not they accept it. In Amos 1–2 the nations are not denounced for sins they could not have been expected to recognize as such (e.g., violations of the Torah), but rather for "crimes against humanity." Amos preaches against the nations not simply because of their disobedience to Yahweh, but more so for failing to follow the dictates of their own moral sense. This idea of natural law undergirds Jonah 1:2 and Yahweh's judgment of Nineveh.

The monumental influence of Karl Barth's radical distinction between natural revelation and biblical revelation (to the degree that he looked unfavor-

---

[75] The discussion of OT ethics that follows relies on Barton, *Understanding Old Testament Ethics*. Among others, Barton interacts with these studies of ethical issues in the OT: Johannes Hempel's *Das Ethos des Alten Testaments* (1938), the second volume of Walther Eichrodt's *Theology of the Old Testament* (1967), and Eckart Otto's *Theologische Ethik des Alten Testaments* (1994). In his collection of essays that appeared in a variety of other publications and are now gathered into one volume, Barton holds that studies of OT ethics are often hampered by at least two weaknesses. First, they focus on Pentateuchal laws to the exclusion of other sections in the OT, specifically prophecy. Second, they emphasize the theonomy model of ethics to the exclusion of natural law.

ably upon texts like Romans 1 and 2; Acts 17:24–31; and OT Wisdom literature) has caused many to neglect this doctrine of natural revelation.[76] Yet Paul's speech on the Areopagus (Acts 17:22–31) starts from the doctrine of creation. Paul does not mention the people of Israel, the patriarchs or the prophets, or Moses and David. No OT text is cited. The only text Paul explicitly quotes is from a Greek poet. Paul's argument concludes with resurrection, about which he had been preaching earlier (Acts 17:18). Judgment and resurrection are themes of special revelation, but the way in which Paul presents his argument proceeds from natural theology.

In Romans 1 and 2 Paul lists a series of arguments that contain natural theology. In Rom 1:18–32 he explains the wrath of God against human wickedness on the grounds that "what can be known of God is plain to them, because God has revealed it to them" (Rom 1:19). Ever since the creation of the world, his invisible nature has been clearly perceived in the things that have been made. Therefore, all peoples—including the Ninevites—are without excuse. Paul goes on to say that because pagan peoples disregard natural revelation, they ironically worship natural things and indulge in unnatural desires, with the result that they fall under God's judgment. In Rom 2:12–16 Paul states that although Gentiles do not have the revealed Law of God—as given by Moses— they may nevertheless by nature (φύσις, Rom 2:14) do things that come under the function of that Law. They "show the work of the Law written in their hearts, their conscience [συνείδησις] witnessing together with it, and their thoughts among themselves accusing or even defending [them]" (Rom 2:15). Both the words "nature" (φύσις) and "conscience" (συνείδησις) indicate that all human beings have some valid knowledge of God, gained from "nature" (the creation) and their "conscience." Even after humanity's fall into sin, which has corrupted both nature and the human conscience, that natural knowledge of God includes a sense of moral right and wrong, in harmony with the Second Table of the Ten Commandments (Ex 20:12–17; Deut 5:16–21).

The Lutheran Confessions affirm this biblical witness as they teach that God's Law is written upon the hearts of all people, beginning with Adam and Eve: "For our first parents did not live without the law even before the fall. This law of God was written into the heart, for they were created in the image of God."[77] So when Yahweh sends his prophet Jonah to Nineveh in 1:2, this shows that God is the city's Overlord who "commands all people everywhere to repent" (Acts 17:30).

1:3 This verse is very repetitive; Tarshish is mentioned three times and "away from the presence of Yahweh" twice. But the repetition is necessary in order to build the following chiasm:

---

[76] This is discussed in Barton, *Understanding Old Testament Ethics*, 49, who cites the discussion of Barth by James Barr in *Biblical Faith and Natural Theology* (Oxford: Clarendon, 1993).

[77] FC Ep VI 2. See also the discussion in Pieper, *Christian Dogmatics*, 1:531–33.

A   But Jonah arose to flee to *Tarshish* away from *the presence of Yahweh.*
B   He went down to Joppa
C   and found a ship
D   going to *Tarshish.*
C'   He paid its price
B'   and boarded it
A'   to go with them to *Tarshish* away from *the presence of Yahweh.*[78]

What the words proclaim the structure subverts. Jonah is trapped! The irony is that "the presence of Yahweh" surrounds Jonah, even in his flight to Tarshish. Ps 139:7–10 indicates the impossibility of fleeing from Yahweh:

> Where shall I go from your Spirit?
> *Where shall I flee from your presence?*
> If I go up to the heavens, you are there;
> if I make my bed in Sheol, behold, you [are there].
> If I rise up on the wings of the dawn,
> if I dwell at the end of the sea,
> even there your hand will lead me,
> your right hand will hold me.

Furthering the literary artistry of Jonah 1:3 are four finite verbs ("he went down," "he found," "he paid," "he went down/boarded") framed by two infinitive constructs with the preposition לְ ("to flee" and "to go"), each joined to the same accusative destination, "to Tarshish away from the presence of Yahweh." Exquisite and balanced Hebrew indeed!

Usually Yahweh's Word is the perfect performative:[79] for him to speak is for him to create and accomplish what his Word says. The God who says, "Let there be light," and "There was light" (Gen 1:3), commands Elijah, "Arise, go to Zarephath" (1 Ki 17:9), and Elijah "arose and went to Zarephath" (1 Ki 17:10). Yahweh tells Jeremiah, "Arise, go to the Euphrates" (Jer 13:6), and Jeremiah arises and goes there (Jer 13:7). According to this normal biblical pattern, after Yahweh's command, "Arise, go to Nineveh" (Jonah 1:2), we expect the Jonah narrative to continue, "So Jonah arose and went to Nineveh." Instead, Jonah arises to flee. It's as though outside his door Jonah hangs a large sign with these words: Do Not Disturb!

In this way the biblical pattern of prophetic responsiveness is broken and a strong sense of shock is created. To compare Jonah with Moses, we would have to envision Moses throwing water on the burning bush or pawning the miraculous staff to Aaron to escape confrontation with Pharaoh! Normally prophets protest their inability to speak. Moses protests that he is not a "man of words" (Ex 4:10). Jeremiah fears that he does not "know how to speak" (Jer 1:6). Isaiah insists that his lips are unclean (Is 6:5). But Jonah goes the opposite direction—without saying a word! He appears to have some kind of spiritual lockjaw, making it impossible to converse with Yahweh. The last thing

---

[78] As noted by Trible, *Rhetorical Criticism*, 129, citing Lohfink, "Jona ging zur Stadt hinaus (Jon 4, 5)," 200–201.

[79] Sherwood, *A Biblical Text and Its Afterlife*, 244. The following biblical comparisons come from Sherwood.

Jonah would say at this point is, "Here am I, send me" (Is 6:8). He arises and flees and makes the journey from Gath-hepher to Joppa, about sixty miles. In ignoring Yahweh's Word, Jonah appears to be a poor and pitiable excuse for a prophet. The satire is just getting started![80]

These words from a slave song from All Saints Parish, South Carolina, demonstrate just how bad Jonah looks when we compare him with other OT prophets.

> God sent Jonah to Ninevy land.
> Jonah disobey my God command
> Paid his fare and he got on board.
> Children, don't you do that!
>
> Don't you do that!
> Don't you do that!
> God got His eye on you!
> Don't you do that!
> Don't you do that!
> Don't you idle your time away![81]

The prophetic response to Yahweh is stated classically in these words: "The lion has roared; who does not fear? The Lord Yahweh has spoken; who will not prophesy?" (Amos 3:8). Based upon this principle, Jonah is a deserter in Yahweh's army. The Word comes to the prophet who should be a faithful dove,[82] and he flies away! Jonah not only ignores Yahweh, he will also ignore the storm (1:5) and Yahweh again in 4:5. He says nothing to Yahweh. This evoked from Luther the comment that one of the consequences of sin is that "it renders people mute." Luther continues:

> Oh, it hurts to uncover your own shame and to turn your glory into disgrace. But in the end this will have to be done, or man will find no rest and peace of mind. As Ps. 32:3 says: "When I declared not my sin, my body wasted away through my groaning all day long."[83]

Jonah's silence is striking. It mimics that of Adam in Gen 2:15–25. After Yahweh warns Adam under the penalty of death not to eat from the tree of knowledge, his response is not recorded. Instead, the narrative moves on and in doing so makes his silence a prelude to his outright rebellion in Genesis 3.

Told to go to the northeast of his hometown of Gath-hepher, Jonah heads off in the opposite direction, toward the port of Joppa to the southwest. Here is another reminiscence of Elijah, who runs away to Beersheba because of a threat from Jezebel (1 Ki 19:2–3). However, unlike Elijah, Jonah ironically runs away before he delivers his message!

---

[80] See "Jonah as Satire with Irony" in the introduction.

[81] Quoted from Joyner, *Down by the Riverside*, 163–64.

[82] "Jonah the son of Amittai" (יוֹנָה בֶן־אֲמִתַּי) means " 'dove' the son of 'Yahweh is faithful.' " See the first and second textual notes on 1:1.

[83] AE 19:59.

Jonah not only is silent and on the run, but he also "went *down* [וַיֵּרֶד] to Joppa," then "he went down/boarded [וַיֵּרֶד]" the ship. This is the exact opposite of what he was told to do, namely, "Arise!" (קוּם, 1:2). This leads to the following downhill slide. He goes down into the innermost parts of the ship (1:5), is thrown overboard (1:15), and finally descends to the realm of death, "Sheol" (2:3), at "the roots of the mountains" (2:7). In the OT, "going down" usually represents movement toward death (see, e.g., Ps 88:5–7 [ET 88:4–6]; Prov 5:5). Down, down, down, down is our inevitable path when we move in disobedient directions away from the Word of Yahweh. So the narrative indicates how Jonah is completely separating himself from Yahweh: horizontally toward Tarshish and vertically toward the bottom of the sea.

Yahweh's Gracious Presence

"The presence of Yahweh" (לִפְנֵי יְהוָה twice in 1:3) does not refer to God's omnipresence; Jonah knows he can't escape from that (1:9). Rather, Jonah is fleeing from Yahweh's gracious, incarnational, sacramental presence, which in the OT era was centered in the tabernacle and then the Jerusalem temple. There Yahweh in his glory dwelt above the cherubim. To escape from that presence, Jonah must leave the land of Israel and the temple in Jerusalem. Supporting this interpretation is the fact that Jonah experiences no Word of Yahweh when he is on the ship, in the sea, or within the great fish (1:3–2:11 [ET 2:10]). It is only after he is deposited again on the dry land, that is, presumably somewhere along the coast of Israel, that the Word of Yahweh comes to him a second time (3:1).

This means there were at least two modes of Yahweh's presence in the OT: his gracious, localized presence, which was the focus of Israel's life of worship, and his powerful omnipresence throughout the world. His gracious presence is in view in texts like Ex 33:14–16, where Moses speaks of Yahweh's presence accompanying his people, in this case by means of the pillar of fire and the pillar of cloud. Yahweh dwelt in the sanctuary and later the Jerusalem temple, where believers could encounter him, receive his forgiveness for their sins, and rejoice in his gift of everlasting life (see "your holy temple" in Jonah 2:5, 8). Yahweh's omnipresence is affirmed in texts like 1 Ki 8:27, where Solomon confesses that Yahweh transcends all boundaries, for "the heavens, even the highest heavens, cannot contain you" (see also Jer 23:24; Prov 15:3).

Also today God continues to be present in at least these two ways. God became incarnate in Jesus Christ, in whom resides the fullness of divine grace and truth (Jn 1:14–17). God promises that his grace in Christ is now present through his Word and the Sacraments, Baptism and the Lord's Supper.[84] Indeed, since Christ is God, he can promise to remain with his disciples through-

---

[84] See, for example, Acts 2:38–39; Col 2:11–14; 1 Pet 3:21; Mt 26:26–28; AC V, which confesses that the Gospel and the Sacraments are the sole means through which the Holy Spirit acts to create faith; LC IV 41–46; V 20–27.

out the world and throughout earthly history as they teach and baptize (Mt 28:19–20), and in his Supper he gives his true body and blood, given and shed for the forgiveness of sins (1 Cor 10:16–17; 11:23–29).[85] At the same time, God is also present everywhere, so that we can call upon him "at all times and in all places."[86] Luther's comments are helpful:

> It is therefore possible to flee from God in the sense that we may run off to a place where there is neither Word, faith, and Spirit nor the knowledge of God. In that way Jonah fled from the presence of the Lord, that is, he ran away from the people and the land of Judah, in which God's Word and Spirit and faith and knowledge were present; he fled to the sea among the Gentiles, where there was no faith, Word, and Spirit of God.[87]

Thus when Jonah resolves to flee from the presence of Yahweh, he is not intending to cut himself off completely from his God. Rather, Jonah decides to sever his connections with that place where and the people to whom God's Word and will were made known, namely, the land and people of Israel. Viewed from this perspective, Jonah's flight is not from Yahweh, but from the Word of Yahweh—from his Word of Gospel for Nineveh (cf. 4:2). Jonah seeks a spot where he will no longer need to listen to such words of grace, especially for the evil, pagan Ninevites!

The sign of prophetic receptivity is to stand in the presence of Yahweh (1 Ki 17:1; 18:15; 2 Ki 3:14; 5:16; Jer 15:19). To stand in the presence of someone also connotes readiness to serve another (1 Ki 10:8). Understood this way, Jonah's flight is not only from Yahweh's means of grace, but also from being in the prophetic service of his God.

The Israelite View of the Sea

For Israelites the sea was a fearful and threatening realm, the habitation of the primordial serpent of chaos (Is 27:1; Ps 74:13–14), and so inimical to God that he set explicit boundaries for it (Jer 5:22; Job 38:8–11). One reason for Israel's fear of the sea is that the country was landlocked. During the conquest (ca. 1400 BC), the people of Israel did not succeed in conquering the coastal districts. Although the blessings of Jacob and Moses speak of Zebulun as dwelling beside the sea (Gen 49:13; Deut 33:18–19; see also Josh 19:10–16),

---

[85] Christian dogmaticians traditionally speak of at least three modes of Christ's presence: (1) his ordinary bodily presence as a man, visible during his earthly ministry; (2) his spiritual mode of presence by which the risen Christ left the closed sepulcher, passed through closed doors to appear to his disciples, and is physically present in every celebration of the Lord's Supper; and (3) his divine mode of omnipresence since he is one person of the triune God. See FC SD VII 98–103, quoting Luther, *Confession concerning Christ's Supper* (AE 37:222–24). Also relevant is the personal union of the divine and human natures of Christ (FC SD VIII). See also Pieper, *Christian Dogmatics*, 2:166–279.

[86] These words come from the Proper Preface, spoken or chanted at the beginning of the Service of the Sacrament (e.g., *Lutheran Service Book Altar Book* [St. Louis: Concordia, 2006], 145).

[87] AE 19:45.

this tribe could never completely establish itself there, so it was confined to living in central Galilee (Judg 1:30; 3:1–3). Asher was also allotted a portion reaching the Mediterranean (Josh 19:24–31), but like Zebulun it lived among the Canaanites, its allotted portion belonging to the country that yet remained to be captured by Israel (Judg 1:31–32). Later, in the twelfth century BC, the Sea Peoples—or Philistines—became entrenched along the coast.

With no access to the sea and no experience of it, for most Israelites the sea was "the great unknown." During the monarchy, the coastal districts were at times under Israelite control, but not permanently, nor did this bring acquaintance with the sea. Any ships used by Israelites were staffed by Phoenicians (1 Ki 9:26–28; 10:11; 2 Chr 8:17–18). Only once in the OT is there a reference to seafaring occupations by worshipers of Yahweh (Ps 107:23–32). In the psalms, the sea's roaring suggests Yahweh's enemies (cf. Pss 46:3–4 [ET 46:2–3]; 65:6–8 [ET 65:5–7]; 93:4). In Daniel's vision the four monstrous beasts, symbolic of Yahweh's national foes, come up out of the tumult of the "great sea" (Dan 7:2–3). The evil associations of the tempestuous sea are continued in the NT (see, e.g., Mt 8:24–27, 31–32; Rev 12:17–13:1; 21:1).

Given the general Israelite fear of the sea, it is remarkable that Jonah is *so* desperate that he will embark on such a dangerous journey—into the sea! This, coupled with Jonah apparently chartering the entire ship for himself,[88] portrays a man who will do anything to escape from Yahweh's word and call. Leslie Allen writes: "The Hebrews were landsmen with little experience of the sea. That Jonah was prepared to entrust himself to an ocean-going boat rather than face up to God's call must have struck the hearers as proof positive of his mad determination."[89]

Why does Jonah risk it all by going on a ship? Josephus suggests that fear motivates Jonah to run away: "But he went not [to Nineveh], out of fear; nay, he ran away from God to the city of Joppa."[90] But Josephus is wrong. The text never states that Jonah is afraid (contrast Elijah in 1 Ki 19:3). Nor does it indicate that the prophet views his task as too difficult or beneath his dignity. Unlike Moses, Gideon, Isaiah, or Jeremiah (Ex 4:10; Judg 6:15; Is 6:5; Jer 1:6), he does not express feelings of inadequacy. He does not object that the message is too difficult for the people to hear (cf. Is 6:11; Jer 20:9). Thus while other prophets draw back at times from the call of Yahweh, and some run out of fear, no others seek to flee from "the presence of Yahweh" (Jonah 1:3) simply because God is too merciful (see 4:2)!

This reason for Jonah's flight is delayed in the narrative; it is not revealed until 4:2. Terence Fretheim writes: "The author thus holds back on the real reason until his audience is fully identified with Jonah and is brought along to the

---

[88] See the fifth textual note on 1:3.

[89] Allen, *Joel, Obadiah, Jonah and Micah*, 205.

[90] Josephus, *Antiquities*, 9.208 (9.10.2; trans. Whiston, *The Works of Josephus*, 259).

point where the truth of the matter can have its sharpest impact."[91] The delay causes us to pause to consider why we are running from Yahweh. Most of us will not admit to the reason given in 4:2—at least not initially. Most Christians do not object outright to the fact that God is merciful, yet they may in effect deny the scope of God's mercy by withholding forgiveness from certain fellow sinners who are penitent (cf. Mt 18:21–35; 2 Cor 2:5–11).

It appears that Jonah would have quickly gone to Nineveh if he could have been certain Nineveh would be destroyed. When the cup of wrath is full, as it was in Nineveh's case, Yahweh should give it to them to drink (see Is 10:12–19; Jer 25:15–38; Joel 4:13 [ET 3:13]), not drink it down himself (cf. Mt 20:22; 26:39; Jn 18:11). Jonah is disobedient because his understanding of the Gospel has run amuck. He thinks that the Gospel is for himself and other Israelites, not for pagan foreigners! The issue between Jonah and Yahweh is a theological one that pertains to the Gospel and its application to sinners. "Thus, in the interpretation of the book, we need to remember that it is not Jonah's faith which needs reviving so much as his theology which needs changing."[92] Luther's words summarize this point:

> We must gladly and willingly become fools for God's sake, accord Him the honor, and concede that He is wise and just in all His words and works, as Abraham did when he sacrificed his son Isaac (Gen. 22:2 ff.). He did not first ask how this would agree with God's prior statement (Gen. 21:12): "Through Isaac shall your descendants be named." For if he had reflected long on this and debated, he would have become confused and in the end have fallen into disobedience, just as Jonah does here when he compares Nineveh with Israel. He ponders this question for a long time and finally falls into disobedience.[93]

Summary of Scene 1

Going to fierce, pagan Nineveh to preach is not a coveted assignment for a Hebrew prophet who likely enjoyed favor under the king of Israel, Jeroboam II. It appears that Jonah's ministry was quite comfortable until Yahweh's Word came, directing him to arise and go to address the most violent people in the ancient Near East. This prophet refuses to obey the divine Word. Instead, Jonah buys a ship, hires its crew, and takes off for Tarshish.

Jonah's reaction is the opposite of the response of Moses, who repeatedly deflected Yahweh's wrath against Israel by seeking grace and mercy for the people, even at the risk of his own life (Ex 32:11–14; Num 11:1–3; 14:10–28; 21:4–9). Samuel also interceded when the Philistines marched against Israel (1 Sam 7:7–9). In 2 Ki 19:14–19 repentant Hezekiah's prayer directed to Yahweh in the Holy of Holies leads to the retreat of the Assyrians (cf. also 2 Chronicles 29–30). Jonah does no such thing on behalf of Nineveh. Instead

---

[91] Fretheim, *The Message of Jonah*, 77.

[92] Fretheim, *The Message of Jonah*, 79.

[93] AE 19:52.

of arising as Yahweh commands, he decides to go down to Joppa and into the ship. This movement downward is a movement toward death. As Rosemary Nixon states: "Although taken from a different context, the words of Democritus are an apt description of Jonah's choice: 'This is not really living poorly, it is dying slowly.' "[94]

With Jonah fleeing to Tarshish, the tension that will drive the narrative is now set. This raises two questions:[95]

1. What will happen to a prophet who disobeys his God's command and tries to "flee … away from the presence of Yahweh" (1:3)?
2. What will happen to Nineveh, the great, but wicked, city?

    The answers are provided as follows:

*   Scenes 2 (1:4–16) and 3 (2:1–11 [ET 1:17–2:10]) deal with the first question.
*   Scenes 4 (3:1–3a) and 5 (3:3b–10) deal with the second question.
*   Scenes 6 (4:1–3) and 7 (4:4–11) are concerned with both questions.

---

[94] Nixon, *The Message of Jonah*, 75, quoting the Greek philosopher Democritus (460–370 BC).

[95] These questions and answers are from Limburg, *Jonah*, 44.

Jonah 1:4–16

Scene 2: The Storm at Sea

Translation

1 ⁴Then Yahweh hurled a great wind upon the sea, and there was a great storm at sea. As a result, the ship thought itself to be broken. ⁵So the sailors became afraid, and they called out, each man to his god(s). They hurled the gear that was in the ship into the sea in order to lighten from upon them. But Jonah went down to the innermost recesses of the ship, lay down, and fell into a deep sleep. ⁶So the captain approached him and said to him, "What are you doing in a deep sleep? Arise, call to your God; perhaps that God of yours will show compassion toward us so we will not perish."

⁷Then the men began talking to each other, "Come, let us cast lots so that we might know on whose account this evil has come to us." So they cast lots, and the lot fell to Jonah.

⁸They said to him, "Tell us, please, on whose account this evil has come to us! What is your occupation? And from where have you come? What is your land? And from what people are you?"

⁹So he said to them, "A Hebrew I am, and Yahweh, the God of the heavens, I worship, who made the sea and the dry land."

¹⁰Then the men feared a great fear and said to him, "What is this you have done?" For the men knew that away from the presence of Yahweh he was fleeing, because he had told them.

¹¹So they said to him, "What shall we do to you so that the sea may calm down from [raging] against us, for the sea is growing more stormy?"

¹²Then he said to them, "Lift me up and hurl me into the sea so that the sea may calm down from [raging] against you; for I know that it is on my account that this great storm is against you."

¹³The men rowed hard to return [the ship] to the dry land, but they were not able, because the sea continued to storm against them. ¹⁴Then they called out to Yahweh and said, "We pray, O Yahweh, do not let us perish on account of the life of this man, and do not place against us innocent blood. For you are Yahweh; just as you please, you do." ¹⁵So they lifted up Jonah and hurled him into the sea. Then the sea ceased from its anger. ¹⁶So the men worshiped Yahweh with great worship, sacrificed a sacrifice to Yahweh, and vowed vows.

Textual Notes

1:4 וַיהוָה הֵטִיל רוּחַ־גְּדוֹלָה֙—The placement of the subject (יהוה) before the verb (הֵטִיל, Hiphil third masculine singular perfect of טוּל) can indicate emphasis and contrast (Joüon, § 155 nb). The contrast is between Yahweh's action and Jonah's action (1:3; see also the fifth textual note on 1:5). The narrator emphasizes that the storm comes from Yahweh: "Then *Yahweh* hurled a great wind upon the sea." This fact is

98

further developed as it becomes clear that, in spite of the best efforts of the sailors, only the appeasement of this particular God can save their lives.

Sentences in Hebrew syntax within continuous narratives state special emphasis on the subject of a verb by modifying the usual Hebrew word order, which is verb-subject-object. This modification shifts the focus from the activity to the actor. This syntax, with the subject in an emphatic position before the verb, is located in narrative contexts in the following verses: 1:4a ("then Yahweh hurled"); 1:4c ("as a result, the ship"); 1:5 ("but Jonah"); 1:14 ("for you are Yahweh"); 3:3b ("now Nineveh"); 3:7b ("people … must not"); 4:10 ("you yourself had pity"); and 4:11 ("shall I myself not have pity"). This syntax occurs in poetic contexts in 2:4 (ET 2:3; "and an ocean current … all your breakers and your waves"); 2:5 (ET 2:4; "then I myself said"); 2:6 (ET 2:5; "the deep"); 2:11 (ET 2:10; "but I").

Due to the narrator's skillful art of repetition—which allows a word to have several different shades of meaning—the words and images used in Jonah take on greater depth. The verb טוּל usually occurs in the Hiphil, meaning "to hurl, throw, cast." It is always in the Hiphil in Jonah (1:4, 5, 12, 15). It can refer to throwing a javelin (Hiphil in 1 Sam 18:11; 20:33). When Yahweh is the subject or implied agent, it generally has a punitive sense, for example, Yahweh warns that he will hurl Judah into exile (Hiphil in Jer 16:13; 22:26) and throw Pharaoh to the ground (Hiphil in Ezek 32:4), and Jehoiachin will be hurled into exile (Hophal in Jer 22:28).

Yet throughout chapter 1 טוּל is used in a salvific manner. The sailors will "hurl" the ship's cargo overboard (1:5) in the attempt to save themselves. Then they will "hurl" Jonah overboard (1:15), as he instructed (1:12), in order to be saved. Viewed in this light, Yahweh "hurls" the storm upon the sea not to destroy Jonah, but to save Jonah from his own attempt to flee away from Yahweh's presence (cf. 4:1 and "to save him from his evil," 4:6), and ultimately also to save the sailors through Jonah's confession (1:9) and the Ninevites through his preaching (3:4).

The direct object of the verb is רוּחַ־גְּדוֹלָה, "a great wind." In the only other OT passages with this phrase, it refers to an extraordinary phenomenon (1 Ki 19:11; Job 1:19). In some contexts, רוּחַ may mean "breath," "spirit," or "Spirit" (cf. πνεῦμα in Jn 3:5–8). In Gen 1:2 God's רוּחַ is "hovering over the face of the waters." In Ezek 37:5 Yahweh says to the dry bones in the valley, "Behold, I will cause רוּחַ to enter you." In Is 11:1–4 the longed-for Shoot from the stump of Jesse is endowed with Yahweh's רוּחַ and sevenfold gifts (cf. Rev 1:4; 3:1; 4:5; 5:6). In all these texts, the רוּחַ of God manifests his power to bring order out of chaos, life out of death, and justice (justification) in place of wickedness. Pss 104:4 and 135:7 also speak of the רוּחַ of God as his agent in creation. Understood in this way, the "great wind" is Yahweh's means to bring order out of the chaos caused by Jonah. In Jonah 4:8 Yahweh will again use a wind, רוּחַ קָדִים חֲרִישִׁית ("a scorching east wind"), in still another attempt to confront Jonah with his small heart and renew him in faith.

אֶל־הַיָּם—Here אֶל is used with a meaning more common for עַל, namely, that Yahweh hurled the storm "*upon* the sea" (see BDB, s.v. אֶל, *Note* 2). Compare the Hiphil of טוּל with עַל meaning "hurl to a distant land" in Jer 16:13; 22:26 and "throw to/upon the ground" in Ezek 32:4.

וַיְהִי סַעַר־גָּדוֹל בַּיָּם—The noun סַעַר ("storm") recurs in Jonah 1:12, while the verb סָעַר, "be stormy," is in 1:11, 13. Both words possess the characteristics of ono- matopoeia, hinting at the sound of the wind as it comes forth from the lips. Ps 107:25 uses the feminine noun סְעָרָה to state that a windstorm is under Yahweh's control: "For he spoke and raised the storm wind that lifted up its [the sea's] waves" (וַיֹּאמֶר וַיַּעֲמֵד רוּחַ סְעָרָה וַתְּרוֹמֵם גַּלָּיו). And it is Yahweh who curbs and controls the sea.^a Jonah admits as much in 1:9 and is finding it out—firsthand—already in 1:4.

(a) Psalms 29; 77:17–20 (ET 77:16–19); 89:10 (ET 89:9); 107:23–30; 148:7–8

וְהָאֳנִיָּה חִשְּׁבָה לְהִשָּׁבֵר:—Literally, this is "The ship considered itself to be bro- ken." The noun אֳנִיָּה, "ship," is emphasized in two ways. First, its strong disjunctive accent, a *zaqeph qaton* (-ָ֔-), marks a pause after "ship." Second, contrary to normal word order, it is placed in front of the verb חִשְּׁבָה, the Piel third feminine singular per- fect of חָשַׁב, "to think, plan, consider." Only here in the OT does this verb have an inan- imate subject. We expect Jonah to "consider" his actions and their consequences, but he does not. It is left to the ship to "think" about what will happen next. The inanimate, manmade object is more responsive to Yahweh than the animate man he created, who is his very own prophet. How ironic! This description of the ship demonstrates the He- brew custom of attributing human characteristics to inanimate objects. For example, the land sins (Ezek 14:13) and vomits out its inhabitants (Lev 18:25). In Is 23:1 Yah- weh commands "ships of Tarshish" to "howl" (הֵילִילוּ ׀ אֳנִיּוֹת תַּרְשִׁישׁ).¹

The verb לְהִשָּׁבֵר is the Niphal infinitive construct of שָׁבַר with the preposition לְ. Some argue for the Niphal to have an intransitive, middle meaning, "to break" (Waltke-O'Connor, § 23.2.1a, including example 3b), but because of the agents in the context (the "storm" sent by "Yahweh"), the passive meaning is more appropriate ("be broken" by them).

1:5 וַיִּירְאוּ הַמַּלָּחִים—The verb is the third masculine plural Qal imperfect with *waw* consecutive of יָרֵא, which appears in Jonah four times, all in chapter 1 (1:5, 9, 10, 16). In Jonah the cognate noun יִרְאָה occurs twice (1:10, 16). Usually the verb means "to fear," but when God is the object, it can have the meaning "show reverence to" (*DCH*, Qal, 2c; cf. BDB, Qal, 3) or "worship," as in 1:9 (see the second textual note on 1:9). "The content of the verb [יָרֵא] is varied by context-sensitive classificators in such a way as to cover the entire semantic range in all its variety, from alarm in the face of everyday threats through fear of numinous powers to fear of God."² As in any language, Hebrew word meanings and nuances depend on the context. It is therefore not always sufficient to cite lexicons and grammars when trying to pinpoint the im- port of a particular word or construction, nor is it enough to parallel phraseology with a comparable statement in the OT.

Once the storm hits them, the sailors react with fear (וַיִּירְאוּ הַמַּלָּחִים, 1:5). In re- sponse to their inquiries, Jonah indicates that he is a worshiper of Yahweh, the God

---

¹ That this personification of a ship is an idea shared throughout the ancient Near East is seen in the early Middle Kingdom Egyptian "Tale of the Shipwrecked Sailor." The sailor's ship, caught in a storm, is said to have "died" (Simpson, *The Literature of Ancient Egypt*, 52).

² H. F. Fuhs, "יָרֵא," *TDOT* 6:295.

of the heavens (וְאֶת־יְהוָה אֱלֹהֵי הַשָּׁמַיִם אֲנִי יָרֵא, 1:9). The sailors are then overwhelmed with great fear (וַיִּירְאוּ הָאֲנָשִׁים יִרְאָה גְדוֹלָה, 1:10). Finally, after the sailors recognize the calming of the sea as a miracle, they worship Yahweh, who stilled the storm, with great worship (וַיִּירְאוּ הָאֲנָשִׁים יִרְאָה גְדוֹלָה אֶת־יְהוָה, 1:16). In both 1:10 and 1:16 the noun is used with the verb for added emphasis, and in each verse the noun and verb have the same meaning ("fear" in 1:10; "worship" in 1:16).

Thus the narrator uses יָרֵא in different ways to indicate that the events in chapter 1 transform the sailors from sheer terror to an awe at the awareness of being in Yahweh's presence and finally to trust, belief, and worship of this great God. Or to state it more literally following the Hebrew, the sailors move from fear, to great fear, to great fear/worship of Yahweh. Their conversion from fear to faith takes place through Jonah's confession that he is a Hebrew who fears/worships Yahweh, the God of the heavens, who created the sea and the dry land (1:9).

The subject of the verb in 1:5 is the plural of מַלָּח, "sailor," which in the OT occurs only here and in Ezek 27:9, 27, 29. Since מַלָּח in Ezekiel 27 refers to Phoenicians, known for their travel and trade by sea, and it is attested in Phoenician, the term likely is borrowed from that Semitic language, which is closely related to Hebrew.[3] The Phoenician and Syriac cognates suggest a connection between מַלָּח, "sailor," and מֶלַח, "salt," probably by way of the salt-water sea.

וַיִּזְעֲקוּ אִישׁ אֶל־אֱלֹהָיו—The use of the plural verb (Qal third masculine plural imperfect of זָעַק with waw consecutive, "*they* called out") with a singular noun (אִישׁ in a distributive sense, "each man") is a common phenomenon in Hebrew. It is logical because the preceding context refers to a plurality of people (הַמַּלָּחִים, "the sailors") who are performing the action. Similar constructions occur in 1:7 and 3:8.

In reference to pagan deities, the plural noun אֱלֹהִים can refer to either "gods" (BDB, 1 d) or a "god or goddess" (BDB, 2 a). Therefore, the best translation of אֱלֹהָיו here is "his god(s)" because it is impossible to decide if each sailor was praying to the same national (Phoenician?) god (of the sea?), if different sailors were invoking different deities, or if each sailor was praying to the same pantheon of deities, perhaps invoking as many gods as possible.

וַיָּטִלוּ אֶת־הַכֵּלִים אֲשֶׁר בָּאֳנִיָּה אֶל־הַיָּם—The Hiphil (third masculine plural imperfect with waw consecutive) of the verb טוּל, "to hurl," is employed once again, as in 1:4 (see the first textual note on 1:4). Here and in 1:12, 15, the verb takes the prepositional phrase אֶל־הַיָּם, hurl "into the sea" (see BDB, s.v. אֶל, 2). בָּאֳנִיָּה repeats the term אֳנִיָּה, "ship," from 1:3–4, with the definite article[4] and the preposition בְּ. Thus the sailors "hurled the gear that was in the ship into the sea." For a similar procedure during another Mediterranean storm, see Acts 27:18–19, 38.

---

[3] See Tomback, *A Comparative Semitic Lexicon of the Phoenician and Punic Languages*, 179; Almbladh, *Studies in the Book of Jonah*, 19.

[4] The *metheg* beside the *qamets* (-בָּ) indicates that the *qamets* is long, representing the definite article. Without the *metheg*, the vowel would be short (*qamets chatuph*), corresponding to the composite *shewa* with *qamets chatuph* (-אֳ-), thus, בָּאֳנִיָּה, "in *a* ship."

According to Ezek 27:12–25, a ship on the Mediterranean might carry such cargo as precious metals, horses and mules, ivory, and various other products.[5] The direct object here is הַכֵּלִים, the plural of כְּלִי with the definite article. The same term also appears in Ezek 27:13 in a construct phrase usually translated "*vessels* of bronze." Yet it is not clear specifically what the sailors jettisoned. כְּלִי is a very general term that can denote "any kind of vessel, made of any kind of material for any purpose."[6] It may refer to cooking vessels (2 Sam 17:28), containers (Gen 42:25), furnishings (Lev 11:32), tools (1 Ki 19:21), weapons (Judg 18:11), jewels (Is 61:10), clothing (Deut 22:5), cult paraphernalia (Ex 25:9), musical instruments (1 Chr 16:42), or baggage (1 Sam 9:7). Here הַכֵּלִים undoubtedly refers to the ship's cargo, but may include other kinds of objects as well, such as the ship's equipment (cf. Acts 27:19). Hence it is translated by the general term "gear."

לְהָקֵל מֵעֲלֵיהֶם—The Hiphil infinitive construct of קָלַל, "to be light," with the preposition לְ forms a purpose clause, literally, "to make light/lighten from upon them." The sailors' action may be designed to lighten the ship and so help it ride out the storm. The cargo may also be intended as a sacrifice to appease the angry sea or another offended god. But their efforts are completely futile in accomplishing either purpose.

Translations usually add the pronoun "lighten *it*," implying that they seek to lighten the ship. However, nothing in this phrase refers directly to the (feminine singular) ship, and the nearest antecedent is not the "ship," but the preceding noun, "the sea" (הַיָּם). In other passages, the Hiphil of קָלַל is used with the combination of the prepositions מִן and עַל ("from upon") with a pronoun referring to the person whose burden or weight is lightened (e.g., Ex 18:22). The prepositional phrase here, מֵעֲלֵיהֶם ("from upon them"), does not refer to the ship. The construction here resembles that in 1 Sam 6:5, where the Philistines offer objects to appease the wrath of Yahweh against them: אוּלַי יָקֵל אֶת־יָדוֹ מֵעֲלֵיכֶם, "Perhaps he [Israel's God] will lighten his hand from upon you." See also Jonah 1:12, which uses the same combination of prepositions as here: "The sea may calm down *from* [raging] *against you*" (מֵעֲלֵיכֶם). The parallels in 1 Sam 6:5 and Jonah 1:12 support the interpretation that by jettisoning their cargo the sailors hope to appease the angry sea, which manifested divine wrath that the sailors believed was "upon" or "against" them. Thus the syntax implies that the pagan sailors are trying to appease the sea deity יָם ("Yamm," the Canaanite sea god named often in the Ugaritic texts) by sacrificing their wares.[7] This interpretation resonates with the statement earlier in 1:5 that "they called out, each man to his god(s)."[8]

---

[5] Ezekiel wrote in the sixth century BC, but his description of Tyre's commerce by sea likely is accurate also for the eighth century BC, the time of Jonah.

[6] K.-M. Beyse, "כְּלִי," *TDOT* 7:170.

[7] Sasson, *Jonah*, 94, says that the use of טוּל with אֶל rather than עַל "suggests that the sailors did not cast their load overboard to lighten the ship only, but that they sought to appease the sea with offerings."

[8] As noted by Trible, *Rhetorical Criticism*, 136.

וְיוֹנָה יָרַד אֶל־יַרְכְּתֵי הַסְּפִינָה—The unusual syntax in which the subject "Jonah" precedes the verb "went down" recalls the same arrangement when the subject "Yahweh" preceded the verb "hurled" in 1:4 (see the first textual note on 1:4). The parallel suggests increasing opposition between Jonah and Yahweh; indeed, they have entered into a power struggle. Yahweh speaks (1:1–2); Jonah flees (1:3); Yahweh throws (1:4); Jonah goes down (1:5).

This is now the third time in the narrative that the verb יָרַד appears (it occurred twice in 1:3). Throughout the OT, and especially in the Psalms (e.g., 22:30 [ET 22:29]; 30:4, 10 [ET 30:3, 9]; 55:16 [ET 55:15]), יָרַד can describe a descent into Sheol, the dust, or the pit. As George Landes points out, the motif of descent is continued in chapter 2, where Jonah descends to "the belly of Sheol" (2:3 [ET 2:2]) and "the underworld" (2:7 [ET 2:6]).[9]

The subject-verb syntax also indicates a contrast between Jonah's behavior and that of the sailors. While Yahweh and Jonah as subjects precede their respective verbs in 1:4 and 1:5, "the sailors" as the subject follows the verb (וַיִּירְאוּ הַמַּלָּחִים, 1:5; see also 1:7a). The sailors are in a tizzy, shouting prayers and throwing their cargo overboard. The noise and tumult of sea and sailors is deafening. Yet Jonah goes down to sleep deeply, like a baby. As at the start of 1:4, the narrator emphasizes the subject of a sentence by pulling it around in front of the verb; the translation tries to catch this emphasis with "But Jonah …"

To translate this phrase as a pluperfect, "Jonah *had gone* down into the inner part of the ship" (so RSV), is misleading. Hebrew has no distinct grammatical indicators to signal a pluperfect, and none is required by the context here; the context favors the simple past.[10] To translate יָרַד in the pluperfect implies that the statements in the verse are not episodic, when in fact they are. That is to say, when the sailors were crying to their god(s) and throwing cargo overboard, Jonah went down. This understanding throws the actions of Jonah into greater suspense. What kind of person would go down to the bottom of a ship to sleep deeply during such a storm at the same time others are scrambling for their very lives?

The noun סְפִינָה is a hapax legomenon, but Akkadian, Arabic, and Aramaic cognates support the meaning "ship." Allen suggests that it comes from סָפַן, "to cover," and denotes a ship covered with a deck,[11] but this is speculative. The Akkadian cognate is found in a seventh-century Assyrian document,[12] so any attempt to regard Jonah as a postexilic writing cannot use סְפִינָה as evidence.

The phrase אֶל־יַרְכְּתֵי הַסְּפִינָה ("to the innermost recesses of the ship") is difficult to understand due to our lack of knowledge about the inner construction of ancient ships. יַרְכְּתֵי is the plural construct of יְרֵכָה, which can refer to the "furthest recesses"

---

[9] Landes, "The Kerygma of the Book of Jonah," 25.

[10] In contrast to the clause here, the context will require the pluperfect "he had told them" at the end of 1:10. Others see Jonah's action as his response to the storm (e.g., Snaith, *Notes on the Hebrew Text of Jonah*, 13).

[11] Allen, *Joel, Obadiah, Jonah and Micah*, 207, n. 24.

[12] As noted by Sasson, *Jonah*, 101.

and "depths" (see BDB) or "innermost part" (*HALOT*, 2 b). Examples of its use in other parts of the OT add to this understanding. David and his men hid themselves from Saul "in the innermost parts of the cave" (בְּיַרְכְּתֵי הַמְּעָרָה, 1 Sam 24:4). The king of Babylon, who had set himself high among the nations, is humiliated and brought down "to Sheol, to the depths of the pit" (אֶל־שְׁאוֹל תּוּרָד אֶל־יַרְכְּתֵי־בוֹר, Is 14:15). For Jeremiah the image of a great tempest, stirring "from the farthest parts of the earth" (מִיַּרְכְּתֵי־אָרֶץ, Jer 25:32), is a token of Yahweh's judgment upon international evil. The image is extended in Jer 31:8, where Yahweh comes to gather his people "from the farthest parts of the earth" (מִיַּרְכְּתֵי־אָרֶץ) to restore them to their homeland.

The use of יְרֵכָה indicates that Jonah goes as far as possible from the surface of the ship; he is as low as he can go. This action again epitomizes his flight from Yahweh as "going down" (יָרַד, 1:3 [twice], 5) in contrast to Yahweh's call to "arise" (1:2).

וַיִּשְׁכַּב וַיֵּרָדַם:—Jonah goes even farther down! He "lay down" (Qal third masculine singular imperfect of שָׁכַב with *waw* consecutive) then "fell into a deep sleep." וַיֵּרָדַם is the Niphal third masculine singular imperfect of רָדַם with *waw* consecutive; the final syllable has *patach* (דָם- instead of דֵ-) because it is in pause (GKC, § 51 m). The latter verb occurs only seven times in the OT, always in the Niphal.[b] It generally describes a trancelike state[13] or deep sleep, such as experienced by Daniel when he had his visions of the end time interpreted to him by angelic figures (Dan 8:18; 10:9).

(b) Judg 4:21; Jonah 1:5–6; Ps 76:7 (ET 76:6); Prov 10:5; Dan 8:18, 10:9

More specifically, the narrative contexts in which רָדַם or the cognate noun תַּרְדֵּמָה[14] occur suggest a cluster of several ideas. תַּרְדֵּמָה is the "sleep" that Yahweh causes to fall upon Adam so he can create Eve from his side (Gen 2:21), so it is a sleep that lies beyond the pain threshold and is associated with creation. תַּרְדֵּמָה is also the "sleep" that falls upon Abram (Gen 15:12) when Yahweh gives his promise about the future. And it is in the phrase "sleep of Yahweh," which falls upon Saul and his encampment so that David can steal his spear and jug of water (1 Sam 26:12). The verb refers to Sisera's stage of "sleeping" just prior to his death at the hands of Jael (Judg 4:21). The Hebrew verb and noun can refer to a sleep that takes place when a revelation from Yahweh is given (Job 4:13; 33:15; Dan 8:18; 10:9).

Do any of those associations apply to Jonah here? At this stage of the narrative no revelations come to Jonah; in fact, he is fleeing from the revelation of Yahweh's Word, which came to him in 1:1–2. So Jonah's deep sleep indicates that he is separated from the action on deck. And Jonah is not detached in a general way. By going down to the bottom of the ship and by falling into a deep sleep, he is completely disconnected. He has cut himself off from Yahweh and also from the needy people in the boat and in Nineveh.

Since throughout Jonah the narrator assumes that his audience is fully conversant with Israel's earlier textual traditions and has an ear finely attuned to detecting

---

[13] Sasson, *Jonah*, 103, understands it as a "trance."

[14] תַּרְדֵּמָה also occurs just seven times in the OT: Gen 2:21; 15:12; 1 Sam 26:12; Is 29:10; Job 4:13; 33:15; Prov 19:15.

similarities and differences in phraseology,[15] a look at the Elijah narrative yields several interpretive insights. Elijah fled from Jezebel, the pagan queen who sought to kill him and other prophets of Yahweh. He went into the desert near Beersheba and asked Yahweh to take his life so that he would die (1 Ki 19:4), then "he lay down and slept" (וַיִּשְׁכַּב וַיִּישָׁן, 1 Ki 19:5). Additional similarities between these two prophets emerge in Jonah 4:6–8, where Jonah sits under a qiqayon plant and prays for death. Just so, Elijah had sat under a broom tree when he expressed his wish to die (1 Ki 19:4). We may conclude that here in Jonah 1:5, one of the narrator's goals is to compare Jonah with Israel's mightiest prophet of old: Elijah. However, compared to the mighty prophet from Tishbe in Gilead, who had courageously proclaimed the Word of Yahweh (1 Kings 17–18) and faced death because of it (1 Ki 19:1–2), Jonah, who sleeps while fleeing from the presence and Word of Yahweh, appears small, petty, and almost an "anti-prophet."[16]

1:6 וַיִּקְרַב אֵלָיו רַב הַחֹבֵל—The Qal of קָרַב is intransitive in meaning ("to approach, come near"), but the form of its imperfect (יִקְרַב) is that of a stative verb (see Joüon, § 41 b; the stative meaning "to be near" is advocated by Joüon, § 41 f). Not much is known about the hierarchy aboard Phoenician ships, but רַב can be used as a noun meaning "chief," so the construct phrase רַב הַחֹבֵל likely means *chief of the sailors,* i.e. captain" (BDB, s.v. רַב II). The singular חֹבֵל here must be used as a collective ("chief of the *sailors*" rather than "… sailor"). The noun חֹבֵל appears in the OT only in Jonah 1:6 and Ezek 27:8, 27–29. Both narratives are concerned with ships going to or associated with Tarshish (Ezek 27:25–26; Jonah 1:3). חֹבֵל appears to be a Phoenician loanword that is a synonym of the Phoenician loanword מַלָּח, "sailor" (Ezek 27:9, 27, 29; Jonah 1:5). חֹבֵל probably is derived from חֶבֶל, "rope," which can be used in the tackle of a ship (Is 33:23), and so it literally means "rope-puller" (BDB, s.v. חֹבֵל).

וַיֹּאמֶר לוֹ מַה־לְּךָ נִרְדָּם—The captain's words are, literally, "what to you—sleeping?" נִרְדָּם is the Niphal participle of the same Niphal verb (רָדַם) that referred to Jonah falling asleep; see the last textual note on 1:5. The participle is an attributive accusative of state (Joüon, §§ 127 a, 161 i; cf. GKC, § 120 b). In the OT the formulation מַה־לְּ is always an accusing question spoken by a superior to an inferior party.[c] It is used with a participle only here and in Ezek 18:2 (see Joüon, § 161 i). It may indicate inappropriate behavior also in Ezek 18:2.

קוּם קְרָא אֶל־אֱלֹהֶיךָ—The two verbs are Qal masculine singular imperatives. The context of this verse allows understanding אֱלֹהֶיךָ (and הָאֱלֹהִים in the following clause) as the usual plural of majesty used to refer to the one true "God" of Israel (see BDB, s.v. אֱלֹהִים, 3; GKC, §§ 124 g, 145 h–i) rather than "gods."

אוּלַי יִתְעַשֵּׁת הָאֱלֹהִים לָנוּ—The adverb אוּלַי, "perhaps," usually introduces a hope (BDB, 1). In the OT this verb עָשַׁת occurs only here (Hithpael third masculine singular imperfect). The Qal of עָשַׁת in Jer 5:28 probably is a homograph meaning "grow fat" (so BDB; *HALOT* is similar). Although the Aramaic cognate עֲשַׁת is attested in

(c) E.g., 1 Ki 19:9; Is 3:15; 22:1; Ezek 18:2; cf. Jn 2:4

---

[15] See "Jonah and Noah" in the introduction for remarks on such intertextuality.

[16] See further "Jonah and Elijah" in the introduction.

Dan 6:4 and often in early Aramaic, it is difficult to render a precise translation of the Hebrew. For the clause here, BDB offers "perhaps God will give a thought to us," and *HALOT* proposes "to recollect, bear in mind" as the meaning of the verb. However, because Jonah 1:6 is closely related to 3:9, the best way to proceed is to translate יִתְעַשֵּׁת as a close semantic equivalent to the Niphal of נָחַם in 3:9. It likely has the meaning "have pity, compassion, good intention."[17] לָנוּ then means "toward us." In light of אֱלֹהֶיךָ ("your God") in the previous clause, the article on הָאֱלֹהִים can be understood as a demonstrative: "that God of yours" (see GKC, § 126 a–b).

וְלֹא נֹאבֵד:—The negated imperfect (Qal first common plural of אָבַד) forms a result clause: if God has compassion, "we will not perish."

1:7 וַיֹּאמְרוּ אִישׁ אֶל־רֵעֵהוּ—As in 1:5 (אִישׁ וַיִּזְעֲקוּ), a plural verb is used with the singular noun אִישׁ in a distributive sense ("each man"), which here, as often in the OT, is followed by רֵעֵהוּ (the noun רֵעַ with third masculine singular suffix), "his neighbor, fellow." Literally, "They said, each man to his neighbor," this is rendered "The men began talking to each other."

לְכוּ וְנַפִּילָה גוֹרָלוֹת—The Qal imperative of הָלַךְ (here masculine plural), "Come," often is used simply as a prelude to further action (BDB, s.v. הָלַךְ, Qal, I 5 f (2)). The Hiphil of נָפַל ("make fall down") is often used with גּוֹרָל, "lot," meaning "to cast lots" (see BDB, s.v. נָפַל, Hiphil, 3). Here the first common plural Hiphil clearly has the cohortative form (ending in unaccented הָ-) and meaning, serving as an indirect imperative: *let us* cast lots. Later in the verse, the idiom will be repeated with the Hiphil imperfect of נָפַל and *waw* consecutive (גּוֹרָלוֹת וַיַּפִּלוּ). Then the lot's verdict will be stated with the Qal imperfect of נָפַל and *waw* consecutive: וַיִּפֹּל הַגּוֹרָל עַל־יוֹנָה, "the lot fell to Jonah."

וְנֵדְעָה בְּשֶׁלְּמִי הָרָעָה הַזֹּאת לָנוּ—The cohortative נֵדְעָה (Qal of יָדַע) forms a purpose clause: "so that we might know." The compound בְּשֶׁלְּמִי is composed of the preposition בְּ, the relative particle שֶׁ (also in 1:12; 4:10), the preposition לְ denoting possession, and the interrogative pronoun מִי. It likely means "on whose account" (cf. GKC, § 150 k). The construction is modeled on a similar Aramaic term.[18] The relative particle שֶׁ is thought to indicate a northern dialect of Hebrew; it is common in Phoenician and the Solomonic books of Ecclesiastes and Song of Songs.

For the noun רָעָה, see the last textual note on 1:2. English requires supplying a verb in the last clause: "this evil *has come* to us."

1:8 וַיֹּאמְרוּ אֵלָיו הַגִּידָה־נָּא לָנוּ—The sailors address Jonah respectfully with the emphatic (הָ-) masculine singular Hiphil imperative of נָגַד and particle of entreaty, נָא: "They said to him, 'Tell us, please …' "

בַּאֲשֶׁר לְמִי־הָרָעָה הַזֹּאת לָנוּ—The first two words have the same elements (בְּ, אֲשֶׁר, לְ, and מִי) as בְּשֶׁלְּמִי in 1:7, except here the relative is the usual, longer form (אֲשֶׁר). The meaning is also the same: *on whose account* this evil [has come] to us." Rather than a separate question ("On whose account has this evil come to us?"), this is best taken as an object clause (the object of the imperative הַגִּידָה). The sailors implore

---

17 Cf. Almbladh, *Studies in the Book of Jonah*, 20.

18 Almbladh, *Studies in the Book of Jonah*, 20–21.

Jonah to tell them who is responsible ("tell us on whose account … "). Since the sailors already suspect that Jonah is the culprit, this clause initiates the following four questions they ask of Jonah. Some want to delete this clause, alleging that it is superfluous because the lot has already answered (1:7).[19] However, we should retain it because the MT is sound, and the sailors are requesting confirmation of the lot's verdict. Such caution on their part accords well with their piety 1:5, their politeness in 1:8a, and their reluctance to take the irrevocable step in 1:13. The redundancy between 1:7 and 1:8 matches the repetition later, when the mariners ask, "What is this you have done?" (מַה־זֹּאת עָשִׂיתָ, 1:10), and then, "What shall we do to you?" (מַה־נַּעֲשֶׂה לָּךְ, 1:11).

The following four questions concern Jonah's vocation, origin, homeland, and people. These separate questions contain a great deal of redundancy, so it comes as no surprise that Jonah gives a single response to them in 1:9, although he does not answer all four of them (see the commentary on 1:9).

מַה־מְּלַאכְתְּךָ—The noun מְלָאכָה, "work," usually denotes "work entailing skill" as opposed to brute physical labor.[20] Therefore, it is translated here as "occupation."

וּמֵאַיִן תָּבוֹא—The interrogative adverb אַיִן ("where?") is always prefixed with the preposition מִן, and the combination thus asks "from where, whence?" It is not uncommon for Hebrew to use an imperfect verb (here Qal second masculine singular of בּוֹא) to refer to past action whose force continues in the present time; it is best rendered with an English perfect ("have you come").

מָה אַרְצֶךָ—The noun אֶרֶץ can have cosmological ("earth"), physical ("ground"), political ("country"), geographical ("district, province"), or theological (the place of burial after death; Sheol) connotations. Here the sailors probably have only the third and fourth ideas in mind.

וְאֵי־מִזֶּה עַם אָתָּה:—The interrogative adverb אֵי often occurs in construct with the demonstrative זֶה or, as here, מִן plus זֶה (BDB, s.v. אֵי, 2 b). This clause is, literally, "where from this people are you?" (cf. Waltke-O'Connor, § 18.4b, example 10). עַם usually refers to a "people" in terms of their ethnicity. Jonah answers this last question first in 1:9 by declaring that he is a "Hebrew." In Western Semitic languages like Phoenician and Punic, עַם often "serves to designate the populace of a city or town." This more localized, "municipal" meaning of the word "is attested as early as the 8th century in the Karatepe inscriptions, where it designates the inhabitants of the city without any institutional or familial connotations."[21] Especially if the sailors are Phoenician, and here perhaps are speaking that language that was so similar to classical Hebrew, it is possible that they are referring to the populace of a city.

1:9 וַיֹּאמֶר אֲלֵיהֶם עִבְרִי אָנֹכִי—The adjective and substantive עִבְרִי is nearly transliterated by its meaning in English, "Hebrew." It is formed by adding the gentilic ending (י-) to the name "Eber" (עֵבֶר). It refers to people descended from Eber (Gen 10:24), who was a progenitor of Abraham (Gen 11:15–26). Thus "Hebrew" distinguishes that people from whom the Israelites would come from other Semites in Syria-

---

[19] A full discussion of the proposed emendation is in Allen, *Joel, Obadiah, Jonah and Micah*, 209, n. 31.

[20] J. Milgrom and D. P. Wright, "מְלָאכָה," *TDOT* 8:326.

[21] E. Lipinski, "עַם," *TDOT* 11:167.

Palestine. It occurs thirty-four times in the OT, first in Gen 14:13, which describes Abram as a "Hebrew." While all descendents of Eber logically would be eligible to be called "Hebrews," the OT uses the term only for those who belong to the seed of Abraham.[22]

From the patriarchal era into the early monarchy, "Hebrew" (עִבְרִי) is the customary term when Israelites identify themselves to foreigners (as here) or when foreigners identify Israelites (see GKC, § 2 b, for a full listing of relevant passages). Joseph and his brothers were called "Hebrews" while in Egypt (Gen 39:14; 43:32), and the Israelite slaves in Egypt likewise were called "Hebrews" (e.g., Ex 1:16, 19; 3:18). This usage continues until they free themselves from Philistine control (e.g., 1 Sam 4:6, 9; 13:19; 14:21; 29:3). An Israelite who is forced into debt slavery is also referred to as a "Hebrew" (Deut 15:12; Jer 34:9).

The term is frequently identified as a cognate of the Akkadian ḫabiru/ʿapiru,[23] which refers to landless persons who stand outside of settled civilization and law. This identification is disputed,[24] yet most interpret עִבְרִי to denote someone who resides outside of his own land.

This expresses Jonah's status exactly. He is fleeing from his own land and his own God.

וְאֶת־יְהוָה אֱלֹהֵי הַשָּׁמַיִם אֲנִי יָרֵא—The direct object is placed first for emphasis, as reflected in the translation ("Yahweh … I worship"). יָרֵא is the Qal masculine singular participle, with the pronoun אֲנִי as subject. The participle is not limited to present time; here the clause could be rendered "I have always and still do worship …" The verb can have a wide range of meanings, from "fear" (see the first textual note on 1:5; see also 1:16), to "reverence," to "worship," depending on the context. When יָרֵא has יהוה ("Yahweh") as its direct object, as here and in 1:16, the verb means "to worship"[25] and includes both fear of Yahweh's wrath and faith that Yahweh has averted his wrath and is gracious (see 4:2; cf. Joüon, § 121 l). Its use with Yahweh expresses a central concept in OT theology.[26] Luther simply but eloquently conveys that faith involves both Law (fear) and Gospel (love and trust) when he explains the First Commandment: "We should fear, love, and trust in God above all things."[27]

The Tetragrammaton (יהוה) is inextricably linked to Ex 3:13–15, and specifically the clause אֶהְיֶה אֲשֶׁר אֶהְיֶה, "I am who I am" (Ex 3:14). The passage implies that "Yahweh" derives from the verb used three times in Ex 3:14, הָיָה, "to be." The

---

[22] For a discussion on the term, see D. N. Freedman and B. E. Willoughby, "עִבְרִי," *TDOT* 10:430–45.

[23] The Amarna Letters include the first extrabiblical references to ʿapiru. For a discussion of their relevance for this issue, see Provan, Long, and Longman, *A Biblical History of Israel*, 170–72.

[24] See N. P. Lemche, "Ḫabiru, Ḫapiru," *ABD* 3:6–10, and N. P. Lemche, "Hebrew," *ABD* 3:95, for overviews.

[25] Cf. Sasson, *Jonah*, 97: "The verb acquires a theological significance and fear is replaced by reverence."

[26] Cf. H. F. Fuhs, "יָרֵא," *TDOT* 6:297.

[27] SC I 2 (*Luther's Small Catechism with Explanation* [St. Louis: Concordia, 1986, 1991], 9).

vocalization of the initial *yod* as "Yah-" (if that is correct) may denote a causative, Hiphil form. If so, Yahweh may mean "the One who causes to be" or "the Creator." The form could also be Qal, in which case the name may mean "the One who is, exists." The emphasis of the name may be "I am present to create" and to re-create, that is, to redeem and save. The narrative in Exodus 3 identifies Yahweh as the God of the patriarchs in Genesis (Ex 3:15–16) who is now present to redeem the people of Israel from slavery and bring them into a new land (Ex 3:17). A further exposition of the significance of this name is in Ex 34:6–7, which focus particularly on the merciful, compassionate, and redemptive attributes of Yahweh. The OT covenant name of God finds its fulfillment in Jesus, whose name means "Yahweh saves" (cf. Mt 1:21).[28]

The phrase אֱלֹהֵי הַשָּׁמַיִם ("the God of the heavens") occurs also in Gen 24:3, 7; Ezra 1:2; Neh 1:4, 5; 2:4, 20; 2 Chr 36:23; see also Ps 136:26. See also the Aramaic phrase אֱלָהּ שְׁמַיָּא in Dan 2:18, 19, 37, 44; Ezra 5:11, 12; 6:9, 10; 7:12, 21, 23. The Greek equivalent describes the one true God in Rev 11:13; 16:11. The phrase identifies Yahweh as the supreme Deity, the ultimate source of all power and authority. By this title Yahweh is presented as no mere local god, but one to whom all peoples may look for help. "The God of the heavens" is the God who called Abraham and issued his gracious promises to him (Gen 24:7).

אֲשֶׁר־עָשָׂה אֶת־הַיָּם וְאֶת־הַיַּבָּשָׁה׃—The verb עָשָׂה usually means "do," but with God as subject, it can have the nuance "create" (see BDB, s.v. עָשָׂה, II 1 b). We might expect the object here to be הָאָרֶץ, "the (whole) earth/world," but instead Jonah names "the God of the heavens" as the one "who made" the two regions of the earth, "the sea [הַיָּם] and the dry land [הַיַּבָּשָׁה]." יַבָּשָׁה is one of several OT terms for "dry land." It is rather uncommon (fourteen times in the OT) and occurs especially in the narratives of creation and redemption. Redemption can be described as a new creation (e.g., Is 65:17; 2 Cor 5:17; Gal 6:15; Rev 21:1–2). "The sea" (הַיָּם) and "the dry land" (הַיַּבָּשָׁה) occur together in the creation (Gen 1:9–10) and in references to the exodus redemption (Ex 14:16, 22, 29; 15:19; Ps 66:6; Neh 9:11) as well as in Jonah 1:9, 13 (cf. 2:11 [ET 2:10]).[29] This suggests that Jonah confesses Yahweh not only as Creator but also as the one who provided "the dry land" that the Israelites stepped on when crossing the Red Sea (Exodus 14–15) and the Jordan River (Joshua 3–4). In Ex 14:22 Yahweh makes dry ground for Israel to pass safely through the Red Sea waters. A similar miracle is repeated at the Jordan River in Joshua 3–4 (יַבָּשָׁה is in Josh 4:22), which later will be the site of Jesus' Baptism (Mt 3:13–17).[30] The new creation speech of Is 44:3 compares pouring water on dry land to Yahweh pouring out his Spirit upon his people, which is fulfilled in the NT on Pentecost and by the Sacrament of Baptism (e.g., Acts 1:5; 2:38–39; 11:16; 1 Cor 12:13).

---

[28] "Jesus" is a Greek form of "Joshua" (see Harstad, *Joshua*, 12–13). For the Tetragrammaton, one may see further the excursus "The LORD (יהוה)" in Harstad, *Joshua*, 47–51.

[29] Jonah 2:11 (ET 2:10) has הַיַּבָּשָׁה and not הַיָּם. However, the fish that vomits Jonah onto "the dry land" was in the sea, so "the sea" is implicit from the context.

[30] Harstad, *Joshua*, 166, connects Israel's crossing of the Jordan with the Baptism of Jesus. For Jesus' Baptism, one may see "Jesus Appeared at the Jordan to Be Baptized by John (3:13–14)" in Gibbs, *Matthew 1:1–11:1*, 177–78.

Yahweh is the Creator, and his gift of "the dry land" accomplished the salvation of his OT people. This salvation is part of Jonah's confession of Yahweh in 1:9. Moreover, Yahweh will deliver Jonah when the great fish vomits him onto "the dry land" in 2:11 (ET 2:10). Thus when the prophet is given a new chance to respond to God's Word, he experiences a "new creation" through a "new exodus deliverance." In light of Paul's sacramental portrayal of Israel's exodus through the sea in 1 Cor 10:1–2, Jonah in chapter 2 experiences a type of "baptism" and gives indication of his new life of faith by following Yahweh's command to go to Nineveh (3:3). "The sea" and "the dry land" (1:9), then, entail Yahweh's gift of deliverance, which results in his new creation.

Ironically, Jonah in chapter 2 praises Yahweh for his salvation (2:10 [ET 2:9]), but then begrudges Yahweh in chapter 4 (4:1–2) for providing the same gift of salvation for the Ninevites.

1:10   וַיִּירְא֤וּ הָאֲנָשִׁים֙ יִרְאָ֣ה גְדוֹלָ֔ה—Hebrew often uses cognate accusative constructions with a verb and an object from the same root to strengthen and emphasize the idea denoted by the verb (GKC, § 117 q). The narrator of Jonah shows a predilection for cognate accusative constructions: one here in 1:10; three in 1:16; and one each in 4:1 and 4:6.

Here the verb יָרֵא (Qal third masculine plural imperfect with *waw* consecutive), "to fear," has as its object the noun יִרְאָה, "fear." The same cognate accusative construction ("they feared a great fear") occurs in 1:16, though there it has the nuance "the men worshiped Yahweh with great worship." The repetition brackets the events in between. For the verb יָרֵא, see the first textual note on 1:5, where the sailors "became afraid," and also the second textual note on 1:9, where Jonah uses it for himself ("I worship").

וַיֹּאמְר֤וּ אֵלָיו֙ מַה־זֹּ֣את עָשִׂ֔יתָ—The interrogative מָה ("what?") can have a variety of nuances. Usually the feminine form (זֹּאת) of the demonstrative pronoun זֶה is used to refer to an action or event (see BDB, s.v. זֶה, 1 a; Joüon §§ 143 g, 152 a). The verb עָשָׂה (here Qal second masculine singular perfect) refers to the action Jonah "has done." Commentators are almost unanimous in understanding the mariners' question, "What is this you have done?" more as an exclamation of shock than a request for new information, because 1:10 goes on to state that Jonah had already told them what he had done. Yahweh uses the identical question (but with the appropriately feminine form of the same verb) in Gen 3:13 to communicate his anguish to Eve and call her to repentance: "And Yahweh God said to the woman, 'What is this you have done?' " (מַה־זֹּ֣את עָשִׂ֔ית).

Thus Jonah is portrayed here as being like the very first sinner. A more powerful and shocking correspondence could not have been used. In both narratives the culprits seek to hide from Yahweh, and both times their disobedience has serious repercussions on the lives of others.

כִּי־יָדְע֣וּ הָאֲנָשִׁ֗ים כִּי־מִלִּפְנֵ֤י יְהוָה֙ ה֣וּא בֹרֵ֔חַ—The first כִּי is causal (see BDB, 3 b), since it introduces the reason for the mariners' preceding exclamation: "*for/because* the men knew …" The second כִּי introduces an accusative object clause (see BDB, 1 a) stating *what* "the men knew": "*that* away from the presence of Yahweh he was fleeing." The prepositional phrase מִלִּפְנֵי יְהוָה ("away from the presence of Yahweh") occurred twice in 1:3, and the verb בָּרַח (here Qal masculine singular participle: בֹּרֵחַ, "fleeing") was also used in that verse (see the first and second textual notes on 1:3).

In both 1:10 and 1:12 a causal כִּי ("for") is followed by the verb "know" (יָדַע) and a second כִּי clause that states what is known in order to accent vital information and to account for motivation. The second כִּי clause introduces the reason for the men's exclamation in 1:10 and the reason for Jonah's imperatives in 1:12. In 1:10 the first כִּי is followed by regular syntax (verb preceding subject: כִּי־יָדְעוּ הָאֲנָשִׁים). In 1:12 כִּי is followed by alternate syntax (participle preceding pronoun: כִּי יוֹדֵעַ אָנִי, literally, "for knowing (am) I."[31]

כִּי הִגִּיד לָהֶם:—Another clause beginning with a causal כִּי explains how and why "the men knew" Jonah was fleeing. In this context, the perfect verb (Hiphil third masculine singular of נָגַד) must be translated as a pluperfect (cf. Joüon, § 118 d): literally, "because he *had revealed* to them," presumably before Yahweh had hurled the storm (1:4). The Hiphil of נָגַד can mean "to declare, make known, reveal" (see BDB, 2). The use of this verb (rather than one of the more generic verbs אָמַר or דִּבֶּר, "say, speak") implies that Jonah had fully disclosed the preceding events recounted in 1:1–3.

1:11 וַיֹּאמְרוּ אֵלָיו מַה־נַּעֲשֶׂה לָּךְ וְיִשְׁתֹּק הַיָּם מֵעָלֵינוּ—The imperfect (first common plural) of עָשָׂה has a modal nuance: "What *should/must* we do to you?" (see Joüon, § 113 m). לָּךְ is the preposition לְ with second *masculine* singular suffix. Normally this combination is לְךָ (as in 1:6), but in pause (indicated by the *zaqeph* accent, -לֹ) the vowels are reversed.

The Qal imperfect of שָׁתַק with conjunctive *waw* (וְיִשְׁתֹּק) has a telic force, forming a purpose clause: "What should we do to you *so that* the sea *may calm down*?" (see Joüon, §§ 116 e, 161 m, 169 i; GKC, § 165 a 1 (γ)). The verb שָׁתַק occurs also in 1:12. It means to "grow silent" (*HALOT*) or "be quiet" (BDB). The only other occurrences of שָׁתַק in the OT are in Prov 26:20, which refers to the cessation of human strife, and Ps 107:30, where sailors pray and then rejoice when God stills the storm, making the waters to "be calm," and enables their voyage to be successful.

The prepositional phrase מֵעָלֵינוּ (מִן plus עַל with first common plural suffix) is pregnant, since it implies a verb that must be supplied in brackets in translation, such as "from [raging] against us?"

כִּי הַיָּם הוֹלֵךְ וְסֹעֵר:—This כִּי too is causal ("for ..."). The clause explains the reason for the sailors' preceding urgent question. But does this clause belong inside or outside of the quotation? It could be the narrator's explanation: "For the sea was growing more stormy." But because the reference to the "storm" in 1:12 is within Jonah's speech, it is best to place this reference to the sea storming within the speech of the sailors in 1:11 ("... for the sea is growing more stormy").

The Qal participle of הָלַךְ can be used idiomatically with another participle in a kind of hendiadys (BDB, Qal, I 4 d; GKC, § 113 u). Here it is joined by *waw* with the

---

[31] Trible, *Rhetorical Criticism*, 143, argues that the repeated use of כִּי in 1:10–13 creates structure in this section. She believes its occurrences alternate between (a) the causal use ("for") and (b) the emphatic or asseverative use ("indeed") in the pattern abab: "for the men knew" (1:10); "indeed the sea" (1:11); "for knowing I ..." (1:12); "indeed the sea" (1:13).

Qal masculine singular participle of סָעַר, "to storm." The idiom here expresses both duration and increasing intensity: "was growing more and more stormy" (see Joüon, § 123 s). The same idiom (הוֹלֵךְ וְסֹעֵר) recurs at end of 1:13, but there it probably indicates only duration: "continued to storm." The verb סָעַר, "to storm," is cognate to the noun סַעַר, "a storm," in 1:4, 12. Both belong to the semantic field of words that describe meteorological phenomena.[32] Because almost all of the words in this semantic field are used in descriptions of Yahweh's theophanies, and because the "storm" is his doing (1:4), the implication here is that Yahweh is manifesting his power and his presence "in, with, and under" the storm.[33]

1:12 וַיֹּאמֶר אֲלֵיהֶם שָׂאוּנִי וַהֲטִילֻנִי אֶל־הַיָּם—Jonah replies to the sailors using two imperatives. The first is the Qal masculine plural imperative of נָשָׂא, "to lift up," with first common singular suffix (שָׂאוּנִי), hence "lift me up." The second is the Hiphil masculine plural imperative of טוּל, "to hurl," also with first common singular suffix (וַהֲטִילֻנִי), "hurl me." The Hiphil of טוּל was also used to describe how Yahweh first "hurled" the storm (1:4) and how the sailors jettisoned their cargo (1:5). The solution corresponds to the original problem.

וְיִשְׁתֹּק הַיָּם מֵעֲלֵיכֶם—The Qal imperfect of שָׁתַק and the combination of prepositions "from against" (מִן plus עַל, here with second masculine plural suffix) are both repeated from 1:11 (see the first textual note on that verse). Here too the imperfect verb has a telic force: *so that* the sea *may calm down* from [raging] against you."

כִּי יוֹדֵעַ אָנִי כִּי בְשֶׁלִּי הַסַּעַר הַגָּדוֹל הַזֶּה עֲלֵיכֶם:—As in 1:10, a causal כִּי is followed by the verb יָדַע ("to know") and a second כִּי clause stating what is known (see the third textual note on 1:10). Jonah confesses that he is the one who has incurred the divine wrath: literally, "for knowing (am) I that on my account this great storm is against you." Usually perfect forms of יָדַע are used to express present knowledge (see BDB, 1 a). The use here of the masculine singular participle יוֹדֵעַ with the pronoun אֲנִי (in pause, אָנִי) as subject is more forceful: "I certainly know," "I know full well." בְשֶׁלִּי is the combination of the preposition בְּ, the relative pronoun שֶׁ, the preposition לְ, and the first common singular pronominal suffix (יֿ-). It means "on my account, because of me." It corresponds to בְּשֶׁלְּמִי, "on whose account," in 1:7 (see the third textual note on 1:7).

1:13 וַיַּחְתְּרוּ הָאֲנָשִׁים—The Qal of the verb חָתַר (here third common plural imperfect with *waw* consecutive), "to dig, burrow, hollow out," can be used for tunneling through the stone wall of the temple (in a vision in Ezek 8:8) or, literally, digging through the mud-brick wall of a house (Ezek 12:5, 7, 12; Job 24:16). It can be used metaphorically, as for example, in Amos 9:2, where Yahweh speaks of people who "burrow" into Sheol, seeking to escape his wrath: "If they dig [יַחְתְּרוּ] to Sheol, from

---

[32] H.-J. Fabry, "סָעַר," *TDOT* 10:293.

[33] "Because meteorological phenomena are nowhere portrayed merely for the sake of scientific aims, even the completely realistic description of the mighty sea storm in Jonah 1 is already referring metaphorically to Yahweh's theophany" (Fabry, *TDOT* 10:294). See, for example, סַעַר in Jer 23:19; 25:32 and סְעָרָה in 2 Ki 2:1, 11; Is 29:6; Jer 23:19; Ezek 1:4; Job 38:1; 40:1.

there my hand will seize them." Here the sailors "dug" into the water with their oars. Some translations have "rowed hard" (KJV, ESV).

לְהָשִׁיב אֶל־הַיַּבָּשָׁה וְלֹא יָכֹלוּ—The Hiphil infinitive construct of שׁוּב with the preposition לְ forms a purpose clause: "to return to the dry land." However, that English is deceptive because the Hiphil of שׁוּב is transitive: "to return *something*, bring something back." The translation must supply the implied direct object: "to return [the ship] to the dry land." The *waw* on וְלֹא is adversative: "*but* they were not able." The Qal perfect of יָכֹל, "be able, succeed," would be יָכְלוּ, but it is in pause here, as indicated by the *athnach* (-כָֽ-), so the stem vowel reappears (יָכֹֽלוּ).

כִּי הַיָּם הוֹלֵךְ וְסֹעֵר עֲלֵיהֶם:—See the second textual note on 1:11, which had the same idiom (הוֹלֵךְ וְסֹעֵר). Here it probably means that the sea "was going on and being stormy" (BDB, s.v. הָלַךְ, Qal I 3), that is, "continued to storm," without necessarily getting worse.

1:14 וַיִּקְרְאוּ אֶל־יְהוָה וַיֹּאמְרוּ—The sailors specifically "called out to Yahweh." After a phrase with the verb קָרָא, the verb אָמַר often introduces a direct quote.

אָנָּה יְהוָה—Jonah will use this same invocation in his prayer in 4:2. אָנָּה is a "strong part[icle] of entreaty" (BDB) that can be rendered "beseech" or "pray," with "I" or "we" supplied, depending on the speaker(s). The Tetragrammaton here is vocative, hence, "We pray, O Yahweh." This represents a strong supplication to Yahweh. The same invocation as here (יהוה with either אָנָּה or אָנָּא) is used in 2 Ki 20:3 ‖ Is 38:3; Pss 116:4, 16; 118:25; Neh 1:5 (cf. Dan 9:4). In some of these situations the prayer is a matter of life or death.

אַל־נָא נֹאבְדָה בְּנֶפֶשׁ הָאִישׁ הַזֶּה—The negative particle אַל with the cohortative Qal form (נֹאבְדָה) of אָבַד forms a negative petition: "May we not perish" (Joüon, § 114 f). The Qal imperfect of the same verb, אָבַד, was used in 1:6, where the sailors attempted to placate their gods, hoping, "we will not perish" (וְלֹא נֹאבֵד). The particle of entreaty נָא is often used with a cohortative and usually is rendered "I/we pray" (see BDB, 3 a). However, Sasson opines: "Despite the opinion of many grammarians, we cannot really sense much difference between the forms in which it occurs and those in which it is absent."[34] Therefore נָא is treated as a discourse marker with the volitive verb form (the cohortative נֹאבְדָה) and is left untranslated.

The noun נֶפֶשׁ is versatile. Frequently, as here, it means "life." Occasionally it denotes a person's "soul" or "inner life." At least twice in the OT it means "neck" (Jonah 2:6 [ET 2:5]; Ps 69:2 [ET 69:1]). Its specific meanings are deduced from context and association with other words. The preposition בְּ on it (בְּנֶפֶשׁ) has a causal force, "*on account of* the life of this man."[35]

וְאַל־תִּתֵּן עָלֵינוּ דָּם נָקִיא—The negative אַל with the second masculine singular Qal imperfect of נָתַן forms a negative petition: literally, "May you not place upon/against us innocent blood" (cf. *HALOT*, s.v. נתן, Qal, 12; BDB, s.v. נָתַן, Qal, 2 b). The OT speaks of "blood" being "upon" someone (דָּם with בְּ or עַל) who is guilty of a sin worthy of death (see BDB, s.v. דָּם, 2 i). The adjective "innocent, blameless"

---

34 Sasson, *Jonah*, 132.

35 See BDB, s.v. בְּ, III 5, and Wolff, *Obadiah and Jonah*, 119.

is usually spelled נָקִי. As the marginal Masoretic note indicates, twice in the OT it is spelled with a final א, hence נָקִיא. In both of those passages (Joel 4:19; Jonah 1:14), נָקִיא modifies דָּם, "blood." Similarly, נָקִי frequently modifies דָּם (e.g., Deut 19:13; 2 Ki 24:4; Ps 94:21; see BDB, s.v. דָּם, 2 d). "Innocent blood" means "the blood of an innocent person" who is put to death without justifiable cause. Jonah has committed no crime (e.g., murder) against the sailors that would justify their imposition of capital punishment upon him.

The verb נָתַן with "innocent blood" (דָּם נָקִי) in the sense of "to place innocent blood," and thus to be guilty and held accountable to God, occurs in only two other places in the OT, Deut 21:8 and Jer 26:15.

Deuteronomy 21 prescribes a rite for atonement when a person has been killed and the murderer is unknown.[36] The rite is based on the presupposition of communal guilt and responsibility. Since the guilty person cannot be found, all Israel is under the threat of punishment—the innocent along with the guilty. The elders of the nearest city are to sacrifice a heifer and wash their hands over its corpse, then pray: "Atone for your people Israel, whom you redeemed, O Yahweh, and may you not place innocent blood in the midst of your people Israel" (Deut 21:8).

Because of the numerous echoes of earlier OT texts throughout Jonah, it is possible that the sailors are quoting וְאַל־תִּתֵּן דָּם נָקִי ("may you not place innocent blood") from Deut 21:8, although in that verse it is followed by the prepositional phrase בְּקֶרֶב עַמְּךָ יִשְׂרָאֵל ("in the midst of your people, Israel"), whereas Jonah 1:14 uses עָלֵינוּ ("against us").

Throughout the narrative of Jonah, the author quotes and alludes to earlier texts, often in ironic ways. The irony here is that a clause spoken by Yahweh to Moses as part of Israel's foundational Torah is now spoken by non-Israelites. In fact, the sailors are more concerned about life than is Jonah.

Thomas Bolin notes that "Robert Ratner adduces the strict penalties enjoined upon those who harbor runaway slaves in several ancient Near Eastern legal corpora, treaties and contracts from the first and second millennia as the background for Jonah 1." Based upon his analysis, Ratner believes Jonah is a runaway servant of Yahweh, and by association with Jonah, the sailors are accomplices in his crime. That is why their final plea to Yahweh in 1:14 has legal overtones and evokes the atonement rite in Deut 21:1–9.[37]

In Jer 26:15 Jeremiah warns the Israelites that if they listen to the priests and the prophets who call for his death because of his faithful preaching of Yahweh's Word, "You will be placing innocent blood [דָּם נָקִי אַתֶּם נֹתְנִים] upon yourselves and upon this city and upon her inhabitants." Jeremiah is innocent, and the people are guilty of apostasy; they are the ones who deserve death. In Jonah 1:14 the situation is the re-

---

[36] The context in Deut 21:8–9 makes clear that נָתַן is being used in a technical phrase for legal responsibility for blood that is shed. See Koch, "Der Spruch 'Sein Blut bleibe auf seinem Haupt,'" 406–8. More frequent and generalized terminology with "innocent blood" uses שָׁפַךְ, "to shed, pour out" (e.g., Deut 19:10; Is 59:7).

[37] Bolin, *Freedom beyond Forgiveness*, 87, citing Robert Ratner, "Jonah, the Runaway Servant," *Marrar* 5–6 (1990): 281–305.

verse: the sailors are innocent, but the prophet is disobedient. The sailors' words are charged with irony because they declare that Jonah's blood is "innocent," when in fact he is guilty of not obeying Yahweh's Word to "arise, go to Nineveh" (1:2). Nevertheless, what their words put forth correctly is that Yahweh does not want Jonah to die, but to live and to undertake his mission to Nineveh.[38]

כִּי־אַתָּה יְהוָה כַּאֲשֶׁר חָפַצְתָּ עָשִׂיתָ—The mariners confess faith in Yahweh and his omnipotence: literally, "for you, Yahweh, just as you please, you do." The two Qal perfect verbs (both second masculine singular) have a timeless (gnomic) force and so are translated as English present tense. Often God is the subject of חָפֵץ, meaning to "delight in, have pleasure in" or to be *pleased* to do a thing (BDB, 2 a–b). Similar confessions of God's omnipotence using חָפֵץ and עָשָׂה are in Pss 115:3; 135:6.

1:15 וַיִּשְׂאוּ אֶת־יוֹנָה וַיְטִלֻהוּ אֶל־הַיָּם—The sailors "lifted up Jonah and hurled him into the sea," just as Jonah had instructed in 1:12. The third masculine plural imperfect verbs with *waw* consecutive (וַיִּשְׂאוּ is the Qal of נָשָׂא and וַיְטִלֻהוּ is the Hiphil of טוּל) correspond to the imperatives in 1:12 (שָׂאוּנִי וַהֲטִילֻנִי).

וַיַּעֲמֹד הַיָּם מִזַּעְפּוֹ—The verb עָמַד usually means "to stand," but it can also mean "*stop, cease* doing a thing" (BDB, Qal, 2 d). מִזַּעְפּוֹ is either the noun זַעַף or the Qal infinitive construct (so GKC, § 61 c) of the verb זָעַף with the preposition מִן and third masculine singular pronominal suffix (וֹ-) referring to the "sea" (הַיָּם). The noun זַעַף occurs only five other places in the OT, all referring to the "rage, anger" of a person or of Yahweh.[39] Likewise, the verb זָעַף occurs only five other places in the OT, all referring to people who are either "dejected" or "enraged" (though the Aramaic זָעַף means "to storm"). Thus just as the ship was personified in 1:4, the term here personifies the sea as expressing Yahweh's anger. Everything and everyone appears to be filled with some kind of emotion—that is, except Jonah.

1:16 וַיִּירְאוּ הָאֲנָשִׁים יִרְאָה גְדוֹלָה אֶת־יְהוָה—The first four words are identical to the first clause of 1:10 ("Then the men feared a great fear"). Here, however, the context indicates that the "fear" is directed toward God in faith. Therefore, the verb יָרֵא, "to fear, dread; respect, worship," here means "to worship," as it did also in 1:9 (see the second textual note on 1:9). For the same reason, the cognate noun יִרְאָה here has the corresponding meaning, "worship." The verb וַיִּירְאוּ here takes two direct objects (see Joüon, § 125 u, footnote 1), יִרְאָה גְדוֹלָה ("great fear/worship") and אֶת־יְהוָה ("Yahweh"). The first accusative (יִרְאָה גְדוֹלָה) is called an "accusative of the internal object" because the noun (יִרְאָה) is from the same root as the verb (וַיִּירְאוּ). See Joüon, § 125 q–r, and GKC, § 117 p–q. This is the only time in the OT where the Qal of יָרֵא has two direct objects. Because Hebrew normally places the cognate accusative as close as possible to the verb of the same root, יִרְאָה גְדוֹלָה is the first direct object, and אֶת־יְהוָה is placed asyndetically at the end of the clause. (The syntax of the next clause is similar: וַיִּזְבְּחוּ־זֶבַח לַיהוָה.) English requires placing the second direct object ("Yahweh") first and rendering the first direct object ("great worship") adverbially: "The men worshiped Yahweh with great worship."

---

[38] Cf. Craig, *A Poetics of Jonah*, 71.

[39] H. Ringgren, "זַעַף; זָעֵף," *TDOT* 4:111.

This verse is part of the escalating expression of fear and faith aboard the ship in chapter 1:

- "The sailors became afraid" (וַיִּירְאוּ הַמַּלָּחִים, 1:5).
- Jonah confesses, "Yahweh … I worship" (וְאֶת־יְהוָה … אֲנִי יָרֵא,1:9).
- "The men feared a great fear" (וַיִּירְאוּ הָאֲנָשִׁים יִרְאָה גְדוֹלָה, 1:10).
- "The men worshiped Yahweh with great worship"
  (וַיִּירְאוּ הָאֲנָשִׁים יִרְאָה גְדוֹלָה אֶת־יְהוָה, 1:16).

The construction of the verb here with its second direct object, אֶת־יְהוָה, parallels the construction in Jonah's confession in 1:9, where the participle takes the direct object וְאֶת־יְהוָה. The similar syntax leads to the conclusion that Jonah in 1:9 and the sailors in 1:16 *make the same confession of faith and direct the same worship to Yahweh.* And through the same faith and worship, *both Jonah, the Israelite, and the Gentiles have equal standing in the eyes of Yahweh.* This fact Jonah cannot tolerate. Just as he asks to be hurled overboard in 1:12–15, the salvation of other Gentiles (the Ninevites) will be so "evil" to him that he will ask for death (4:3, 8–9).

וַיִּזְבְּחוּ־זֶבַח לַיהוָה—This is the second of the three cognate accusative constructions in 1:16. The verb זָבַח (Qal third masculine plural imperfect with *waw* consecutive), "to sacrifice," takes as its direct object the cognate noun זֶבַח, "a sacrifice." When the verb has its literal meaning, as here, an animal is slaughtered and eaten by the worshipers (as also in, e.g., Deut 12:15, 21; 1 Ki 19:21).[40]

Jonah in 2:10 (ET 2:9) will use the same two verbs (זָבַח, "to sacrifice," and נָדַר, "to vow") that describe the sailors in 1:16, reinforcing that they and Jonah share the same faith in Yahweh.

וַיִּדְּרוּ נְדָרִים:—The verb נָדַר (Qal imperfect third masculine plural with *waw* consecutive), "to vow," here takes as its direct object the plural of the cognate noun נֶדֶר, "a vow."

1:17 In the MT and the ancient translations, chapter 1 ends with 1:16, and chapter 2 has eleven verses. English translations consider the first verse of chapter 2 to be 1:17. In other words, MT 2:1 is English 1:17. As a result, English translations have seventeen verses in chapter 1 and only ten verses in chapter 2. Throughout this commentary, the MT numbering comes first, with the English numbering given in parentheses or brackets.

Commentary

1:4 The first scene of Jonah (1:1–3) ended with the repeated statement that Jonah fled "away from the presence of Yahweh" (1:3). The second scene begins by emphasizing Yahweh's reaction; unusually, the Hebrew subject, "Yahweh," precedes the verb "hurled" in 1:4. This verse introduces the key ideas that frame the chapter: "hurl" (טוּל, four times in the chapter), "the sea" (הַיָּם, eleven times), and "fear/worship" (the verb יָרֵא four times and the noun יִרְאָה twice).

---

[40] See J. Bergman, "זָבַח," *TDOT* 4:11.

Up to this point in the narrative Yahweh has spoken, Jonah has not. When other prophets are confronted with a sign of theophany, they express awe in faith. For example, when fire consumes Gideon's offering, he cries, "Ah, Lord Yahweh! For now I have seen the angel of Yahweh face to face" (Judg 6:22). When Isaiah sees a vision of Yahweh in his temple, he cries out, "Woe to me! For I am ruined! For I am a man of unclean lips, and among a people of unclean lips I live. For my eyes have seen the King, Yahweh of hosts!" (Is 6:5). See also Jeremiah 1 and the storm theophanies in Ezekiel 1–3 and Job 38–40. But as in Jonah 1:3, so also in 1:4, Jonah's response to Yahweh is complete silence.

Called to "arise" (1:2), Jonah "went down" (1:3, 5). Called to go northeast on land to Nineveh, Jonah goes southwest to Joppa and then attempts to go northwest by sea to Tarshish. These tensions in the first three verses now begin to play out. Yahweh hurls the storm, but not to inflict wanton destruction. He is no arbitrary Herod who slays all in order to slay one (Mt 2:13–18). Yahweh derives no pleasure from the death of anyone (cf. Ezek 18:32). His target is Jonah, but his goal is to save this Israelite and also the pagan Gentile sailors.

As Jonah flees, Yahweh goes with him by means of this storm. The prophet cannot get rid of Yahweh! He cannot hide, travel, sleep, or put himself in such a situation that Yahweh will ever give up on him.

Yahweh does not dialogue with Jonah here; that will ensue in chapter 4. Rather, he sends wind and storm, maneuvers the lots cast by the sailors, then commands a great fish to swallow and spit him out. All of this lays the groundwork for the discussion in chapter 4. Through it all, Yahweh's love never lets go of Jonah. As the "Hound of Heaven,"[41] Yahweh will not quit. He persists in seeking out his prophet in the hope that Jonah will come to embrace the Gospel, which is for everyone. Indeed, through the witness (1:9) and preaching (3:4) of his reluctant prophet, the Gospel will convert Gentiles (the sailors and Ninevites).

Because Jonah flees from the presence of his God, Yahweh sends a storm. The sea kicks up, the sailors fearfully pray, and their captain seeks out the prophet. Even the ship, fearing a wreck, becomes a nervous wreck: "The ship thought itself to be broken" (1:4).[42] The only impassive person—or thing—is Jonah.

Jonah's sin of fleeing from the presence of Yahweh has adverse effects on creation—in this case, the sea, the ship, and the sailors. George Landes writes: "To the biblical writers, the forces of nature were not morally neutral."[43] The

---

[41] This is the title of a poem by Francis Thompson (1859–1907).

[42] Three rhetorical devices place attention upon the ship: prosopopoeia, onomatopoeia, and alliteration. These devices underscore the terror of the storm hurled by Yahweh. Prosopopoeia attributes a human category to an inanimate object: "the ship thought." Onomatopoeia uses words that sound like their meaning, namely, boards cracking from the force of water: חִשְּׁבָה לְהִשָּׁבֵר, ḥisseba lehissaber, "thought to be broken." Alliteration is the repetition of consonants and vowels in proximate words (ḥisseba lehissaber).

[43] Landes, "Creation and Liberation," 141.

sea storms not only because of Yahweh's anger, but also because it is reacting to Jonah's sin. God has woven into his creation a moral fabric that results in a reciprocal relationship between human morality and natural consequence (cf. Rom 1:18–32).[44] The sin of Adam and Eve brought death and corruption into the formerly "very good" creation (Genesis 1–3). The sins of the Canaanites defiled the land, so that it vomited them out, as it also would the Israelites when they would commit the same sins (Leviticus 18 and 20; Ezekiel 16 and 23). Thus human actions can have environmental consequences. William Brown argues for the notion of the ethos of creation that arises from the interplay of human moral actions and the environment.[45] That "Yahweh hurled a great wind upon the sea" (Jonah 1:4) provides a vivid picture of Yahweh on the "pitcher's mound of heaven," throwing a mighty wind at the sea, which results, upon impact, in the "great storm" (1:4). Scripture teaches that Yahweh is in control of the wind and the sea.[d] Thus after Jesus stills the storm, the disciples ask in astonishment, "Who is this, that even the wind and the sea obey him?" (Mk 4:41; see Mk 4:37–41 and parallels).

(d) E.g., Ex 10:13–19; Num 11:31; Job 26:12; Pss 107:25, 29; 135:7; Is 50:2; Jer 49:32–36; Amos 4:13; Nah 1:4

In some OT texts, a storm is the setting for a theophany that answers the inner storm in a believer's life of faith. For example, after Job's prolonged experience of suffering and inner turmoil, "Yahweh answered Job out of the stormwind [הַסְּעָרָה]" (Job 38:1). Yahweh instructs Elijah to "stand on the mount before Yahweh" (1 Ki 19:11) as the vantage point from which the prophet witnesses a storm that corresponds to his own vocational crisis of faith. As if to underline Jeremiah's stormy anxiety in his prophetic vocation, he speaks of "the storm of Yahweh" (Jer 23:19) breaking on the heads of the false prophets. In all of these instances the outside storm correlates with an inner struggle of faith, and from the storm Yahweh speaks to his chosen person (see also, e.g., Ezek 1:4; Zech 9:14).

Throughout Jonah 1 the storm continues to grow. In 1:11 the mariners cry out, "The sea is growing more stormy," and in 1:13 the narrator reports that "the sea continued to storm against them." This is the first of at least three "growing" themes in the narrative. The others are the growing fear/worship of the sailors (1:5, 10, 16), the designations of Nineveh that grow longer (1:2; 3:2, 3; 4:11), and the qiqayon plant that grows in one day (4:6, 10). It is ironic that as the storm, the fear/worship, the descriptions of Nineveh, and the qiqayon increase, Jonah decreases in his prophetic stature until finally he wants to die (4:3, 8–9).

---

[44] Koch, "Is There a Doctrine of Retribution in the Old Testament?" 66, argues that the Hebrew Bible portrays a connection between actions and what he calls "built-in consequences." Koch broadens his study of the "deed-consequence connection" (*Tat-Ergehen Zuzammenhang*) in his study of the Hebrew motif "way" (דֶּרֶךְ) as both a way chosen and a resulting way of life (K. Koch, "דָּרַךְ," *TDOT* 3:270–73, 275–93, and Koch, *The Prophets*. For an evaluation see Miller, *Sin and Judgment in the Prophets*, 111–36 and passim.

[45] Brown, *The Ethos of the Cosmos*, 10–33.

To summarize the narrative up to this point, previously Jonah had been in control, or at least believed that he had control over his life. As a prophet, he had made sure and certain predictions of Israelite expansion to Jeroboam II (2 Ki 14:25). Then in this book Jonah had decided on his Tarshish destination and paid a considerable sum of money to hire the ship and its crew. Jonah must have been a man of means, able to finance his flight from Yahweh's presence. But once this storm hits, Jonah loses control. His assertive move to take charge of his own destiny and his considerable financial wherewithal to bring it about become irrelevant. Now Yahweh dominates the narrative. Jonah's position, prestige, plans, and purchasing power are of no effect!

1:5 This verse is definitely a case of "All lost! To prayers, to prayers! All lost!"[46] Throwing articles overboard in order to lighten the ship is a common practice in storms. For example, Herodotus reports a tale of Xerxes I being caught in a storm off Greece. The king was told by the helmsman that lightening the ship was the only way to save it. So Xerxes asked for volunteers to jump into the sea. The ship thus lightened was then able to weather the storm.[47]

Based on the Hebrew syntax (see the textual notes), Trible opines that the sailors are attempting "to lighten" (that is, "to appease") the sea by using their cargo as an offering.[48] Sasson argues for a similar meaning: the sailors throw their things *for* the sea, in order to appease it.[49] They jettison their cargo for both practical and religious reasons. The cargo is a sacrifice to the gods, specifically to the Canaanite sea god, Yamm, whose name (יָם) means "sea."[50] In Canaanite mythology Yamm annually battles the fertility god Baal for the rule of the land. The struggle has its setting in the late fall, during the early part of the rainy period in Canaan. At this time Yamm becomes so rough that the ancients feared to sail. With waves beating against the shore and threatening to flood the lower areas, Yamm was understood to be waging war as a chaotic power. Yamm's other name, Nahar ("river"), probably refers to the chaos that results from violent rainstorms or melting snow that turn riverbeds into destructive torrents. Together Yamm and Nahar seem to represent all water that threatens—rather than contributes to—vegetation and human survival. Baal is also called Hadad, the storm god who brings the rains that result in the growth of vegetation (at least until the summer drought) upon which people and animals depend. The battle of the natural forces lasts for some time. Yamm is strong but always eventually loses out to Baal. It is this god of the sea that the sailors attempt to placate in the midst of this violent storm.

---

[46] Shakespeare, *The Tempest*, act 1, scene 1.

[47] Herodotus, *Histories*, 8.118–19.

[48] Trible, "Studies in the Book of Jonah," 210–11.

[49] Sasson, *Jonah*, 94.

[50] For a discussion about this god, see McCurley, *Ancient Myths and Biblical Faith*, 19–21. See also Day, *Yahweh and the Gods and Goddesses of Canaan*, 68–90.

That the seamen "hurled the gear" (1:5) establishes a parallel between their action and that of Yahweh, who earlier "hurled a great wind upon the sea" (1:4). First, the sailors respond to Yahweh's throw with a counter throw. Second, the sailors demonstrate concern for their lives, just as Yahweh is concerned for the lives of those in Nineveh (cf. 4:11). Contrast these similarities between Yahweh and the pagan mariners with the Israelite Jonah, who goes down into the innermost recesses of the ship, where he falls fast asleep. On Jonah's closed door is a sign that reads, "I don't care!" Like Peter, James, and John (Mt 26:40, 43), the divinely chosen prophet Jonah is sound asleep at the crucial time when he should have been praying even more than the others were.

On deck the sailors move from inner emotion to outward cry to vigorous action; below deck Jonah moves from action to inaction to total withdrawal. As they increase, he decreases. The antithesis between the sailors and Jonah could not be any sharper than this. But there's more. Jonah is in "a deep sleep" during the storm (1:5–6). The personified ship is alert and thinks itself about to be broken (1:4). So both the animate sailors and the inanimate ship diminish Jonah again. By going into a deep sleep in the innards of the vessel, Jonah in effect reduces himself to an object. He is replacing the indifferent wares that the sailors hurled into the sea! This contrast between the pagan and inanimate outsiders who respond better than the Israelite insider is a prominent theme that acts as a unifying thread that knits together all four chapters of the narrative.

On another level, 1:5 may also indicate that resisting God is the harder route (cf. Acts 26:14). Jonah is so exhausted by trying to evade his unwelcome duty of going to Nineveh, precipitating his flight to Joppa, that as soon as he is on board he goes down into the hold and falls fast asleep.

In the OT the motif of lying down and sleeping is sometimes a description of death and burial. In Psalm 88 the psalmist laments, "I am reckoned with those who descend to the pit" (Ps 88:5 [ET 88:4]). In fact, he claims that Yahweh has placed him "in the lowest pit" (88:7 [ET 88:6]). Using language and imagery similar to that in Jonah's psalm in chapter 2 (see "the depth" and "breakers" in Jonah 2:4), the psalmist mourns that like the slain who lie in the grave (Ps 88:6), he has gone down to "the dark regions of the depths" (Ps 88:7 [ET 88:6]), where he is crushed by "all your breakers" (Ps 88:8 [ET 88:7]). Job expresses the "sleep of death" theme in 14:12: "Man lies down and does not rise; till the heavens are no more, they will not awake or be roused from their sleep." This prompts Luther to call Jonah's sleep a "sleep of death," saying, "There he lies and snores in his sin."[51]

Ps 107:23–32 contains several ideas parallel to this verse in Jonah. Travelers on the ocean see Yahweh's wonders (107:23–24). When a storm is sent by Yahweh, the skills of the crew are inadequate to save them (107:25–27). Prayers are offered to Yahweh in distress (107:28), and Yahweh calms the storm

---

[51] AE 19:57–58. Luther also states of Jonah: "It is like saying that he is blinded, obdurate, and submerged in sin, yes, dead, lying in the pit of his unrepentant heart."

to the joy of the travelers (107:29–32). Here in Jonah 1:5, the sailors' gods are false, so their prayers and offering are in vain, but within their misguided belief system, their actions are thoroughly logical.

Luther notes that the truth of Rom 1:19 is enacted here. When these sailors realize that their own gods will not avail, they urge Jonah, "Call to your God" (Jonah 1:6). In that way, they give evidence of the universal, natural knowledge of God. "Although they do not have true faith in God, they at least hold that God is a being able to help on the sea and in every need."[52] Luther goes on to contrast this natural knowledge of God with true faith: "So there is a vast difference between knowing that there is a God and knowing who or what God is. Nature knows the former—it is inscribed in everybody's heart; the latter is taught only by the Holy Spirit."[53]

The verbs "to become afraid" (יָרֵא) and "to call out" (זָעַק or צָעַק) are used together only in Jonah 1:5 and Ex 14:10, which has an almost identical expression: "They became very afraid, and they called out" (וַיִּירְאוּ מְאֹד וַיִּצְעֲקוּ). This is one of the many echoes of Exodus 14 in Jonah. Other parallels include "sea" and "dry land" (Jonah 1:9, 13 and Ex 14:16, 22, 29); "worshiped Yahweh" (Jonah 1:16 and Ex 14:31); and "they believed in God/Yahweh" (Jonah 3:5 and Ex 14:31); and "was this not my word?" (only in Jonah 4:2 and Ex 14:12).

By the end of 1:5 Jonah is as far away from Nineveh as possible. He is lying down in the bottom of a ship bound for Tarshish, wrapped in a deep sleep. But it is not merely that Jonah is unwilling to go to Nineveh. More to the point, Jonah is unwilling to let God be God. As a result he is unable to be the person God intends and unable to see others as God sees them. The mariners and the Ninevites are pagans who follow other gods; they are outside the covenant mercies of Yahweh. In Jonah's eyes, that makes them not worth calling to repentance and faith. Preferring the shadow to the light, the comfort to the struggle, his own destination rather than the one to which God called him, Jonah remains cocooned in a belief system that protects him from expending himself, ministering, and preaching the saving Word to others.

Still the storm rages. The sailors have not called on the right god yet. Yamm does not answer. Since their false religion is no solution and their "works" of prayer and hurling sacrifices bring no salvation, they rightly conclude that the answer must lie in someone else.

1:6 How can it be that a man overtaken by such a violent storm can sleep so deeply? The usual Hebrew verb for "to sleep" is יָשֵׁן, but the verb here in 1:5–6 is רָדַם, which indicates more than ordinary sleep (see the textual notes). With this verb we are told that Jonah is sleeping so soundly that he is not aware of the storm or of the activity on board the ship or of the approach of the captain. Is 42:19 is an apt description of the prodigal prophet at this point in his

---

[52] AE 19:53.

[53] AE 19:55.

ministry: "Who is blind but my servant, or deaf as my messenger whom I send?" Jonah is so blind and so deaf that a pagan shipmaster admonishes him to pray. The captain is more aware of the power of prayer than the fleeing prophet! The heathen captain seeks divine deliverance while Jonah seeks oblivion. The irony, coupled with satire, could not be any more biting!

The captain attempts to awaken Jonah so that the prophet might intercede for the mariners. When in a raging storm, the more gods that are invoked, the better! Prophets are often expected to intercede in a time of crisis; see Moses at Israel's golden calf apostasy in Ex 32:11–14 and Amos in the locust and fire disasters (Amos 7:1–6). But Jonah does not respond to the captain. His silence is deafening! Jonah is a prophet, but he does not speak!

It is not unusual for people in profound states of denial to seek out extreme ways of dealing with their situation. Sleep, alcohol, sex, and drugs offer escape and release from the implications of reality. Seen in this light, Jonah's sleep is a way of escaping the implications of Yahweh's call uon his life. This prophet's sleep is not a sign of faith and serenity, in contrast to when Jesus is asleep in the boat during the storm (Mt 8:23–27; Mk 4:35–41; Lk 8:22–25). Unlike Jesus, Jonah's sleeping in the storm suggests paralysis rather than faith. And of course, Jesus, as God incarnate, had the power to still the storm, whereas Jonah is powerless to do so. (See further the excursus "The Sign of Jonah.")

The captain recognizes Jonah for the deep sleeper that he is. The captain asks, "What are you doing in a deep sleep?" using the participle of the same verb (Niphal of רָדַם) that described the prophet in 1:5 ("Jonah … fell into a deep sleep"). Clearly the sailors have exhausted their resources, and the aid of Jonah's God might tip the balance. The captain then uses the same imperatives as in 1:2, when Yahweh commanded Jonah to "arise" (קוּם) and "call" (קְרָא) to Nineveh. This repetition of key words, a common feature throughout the book,[54] communicates at least four important ideas.

First, the use of "arise" (קוּם) and "call" (קְרָא) in both 1:2 and 1:6 reiterates the huge gulf between the active, praying sailors and the sleeping, disobedient "prophet" of Yahweh, who refused to "arise" and "call" to Nineveh. Second, this repetition indicates that Jonah has not escaped the presence of Yahweh; God's call to "arise" and "call" comes even through the mouth of a pagan captain! Third, by the time the narrative gets to 1:7, all three of Yahweh's imperatives in 1:2 have been reissued, either by the captain ("arise" and "call" in 1:6) or by the sailors: לְכוּ, "Come," in 1:7 is the masculine plural imperative of הָלַךְ, whose masculine singular imperative (לֵךְ) Yahweh had used in 1:2, "*Go* to Nineveh."

This means that Yahweh is still speaking to Jonah, now through the captain and the sailors. Yahweh will communicate with Jonah through other means throughout the narrative, including a great fish, a qiqayon plant, a worm, and

---

[54] On this aspect, see Magonet, *Form and Meaning*, 13–28; Wolff, *Studien zum Jonabuch*, 36–40; Fretheim, *The Message of Jonah*, 39–50.

a hot east wind. Elsewhere in the OT are examples of Yahweh speaking through animals (Balaam's ass in Num 22:28) and pagan foreign leaders (the Babylonian general Nebuzaradan in Jer 40:1–5), so these means of communication in Jonah are not unique. Indeed, God can use Assyria (Is 10:5), Babylon (Jer 1:15), and climactically, the Herods and Pilate to accomplish his redemptive purposes for the world in his Son (Mt 2:13–15; Lk 23:8–12, 24–25; Jn 19:19–22; Acts 4:27–28).

Throughout Jonah, subtle hints in the text compare and contrast this prophet with Elijah.[55] The tragic question to the defeated Elijah, "What are you doing here?" (1 Ki 19:9), begins with the same two Hebrew words as the captain's anxious cry in Jonah 1:6, "What are you doing in a deep sleep?" Jonah's "deep sleep" goes far beyond the exhausted sleep of Elijah when he is on the run from Jezebel. Jonah's exhaustion comes after fleeing from the presence of Yahweh—the very presence Elijah was running toward (1 Ki 19:8)! These common and contrasting elements magnify the differences between these two prophets and satirize the infidelity of Jonah. The purpose of this satire is to drive the reading audience of the book to repent of such Jonah-like disobedience, and to be faithful evangelists of Yahweh's salvation, even as Elijah was (1 Kings 18; 2 Kings 2; Mt 17:3–4, 10–12; Rom 11:2; James 5:17).

As the text unfolds, the captain fills the same narrative role as the king of Nineveh. Both leaders are concerned not just about their own life (as is Jonah), but about the lives of others, and they look to Yahweh for that life. Both turn to the one true God for deliverance. The captain and the king both express humility before this God, who is their only hope so that they and their people do not "perish." The captain says, "*Perhaps* [אוּלַי] that God of yours will show compassion toward us so we will not perish" (1:6), and similarly the king says, "Who knows [מִי־יוֹדֵעַ] whether God may turn and change his verdict and turn away from the fierceness of his anger so we will not perish" (3:9). Yahweh will act as it pleases him, which may or may not conform to human patterns or expectations. The sailors will express this in 1:14: "For you are Yahweh; just as you please, you do."

Many of the human reactions throughout the narrative deal with the question of life and death. This issue is particularly focused in the use of the verb "perish" (אָבַד), which occurs four times in the book, first in 1:6, then in 1:14; 3:9; 4:10. The first three times אָבַד occurs with the adverb "not" (לֹא or אַל) to express a hope or make a plea. The fourth time it occurs in the affirmative to report the demise of the qiqayon plant. The strategic use of אָבַד in design and dialogue pinpoints a pervasive motif. The captain (1:6), the sailors (1:14), and the king of Nineveh (3:9) all pray for life in the face of death, so that they will not "perish." These people, along with Yahweh (4:10), use אָבַד.

However, Jonah never uses אָבַד, "perish." Instead, in Jonah's speech he employs the noun מָוֶת, "death," three times (4:3, 8–9). In those verses Jonah

---

[55] See "Jonah and Elijah" in the introduction.

twice utters an identical prayer to Yahweh: "My death would be better than my life!" (4:3, 8). The verb מוּת, "die," occurs once, literally saying of Jonah, "he asked his life to die" (4:8). The noun "death" and the verb "die" occur only in 4:3, 8–9. No other characters in Jonah ever use מָוֶת, "death," or the verb מוּת, "die." This discrete use of vocabulary indicates that Jonah lacks hope. Instead of praying that he and others "not perish," he is immersed in a depression so deep that he even prays for death.

The verb "call, proclaim" (קָרָא) is another key word in the narrative, used eight times, and the related noun קְרִיאָה, "call," occurs once (3:2). The verb is in the prophetic introductions (1:2; 3:2, 4) and the ensuing scenes that report the reactions of the pagans (1:6, 14; 3:5, 8). It has two different senses. Three times it refers to the proclamation of Yahweh's Word to Nineveh (1:2; 3:2, 4; this is also the sense of the noun "call" in 3:2). Once it refers to the proclamation of a fast in 3:5 as an act of repentance in response to the proclamation of Yahweh's message. Four times it refers to people who "call"—or who tell others to "call"—to Yahweh in distress: the captain (1:6); the sailors (1:14); Jonah (2:2 [ET 2:1]); and the Ninevites (3:8). Taken together, these uses of קָרָא demonstrate that all of the participants—Jonah as well as the unbelievers—are placed on the same level. "There is no difference among them in their need for deliverance from the hand of God."[56] All need to hear the proclamation of Yahweh's Word, whose purpose is to drive them to repentance and instill saving faith. Moreover, Yahweh hears all those who "call" to him, regardless of whether they are Israelites (the prophet Jonah) or they are former pagan polytheists who have been converted to faith in him. This is exactly what Peter finds out through his vision and ensuing visit to the household of Cornelius:

> Peter opened his mouth and said, "Truly I now realize that God does not show favoritism, but in every people one who fears him and does righteousness is acceptable to him." (Acts 10:34–35)

Jonah 1:6 introduces the first of twelve questions asked throughout the narrative. In 1:6 the captain questions Jonah. The sailors will interrogate him with six questions in 1:8, 10–11. The king of Nineveh asks a rhetorical question in 3:9. In the final chapter, Jonah puts an angry question to Yahweh (4:2), who addresses three questions to Jonah (4:4, 9, 11). The use of questions is especially characteristic of Wisdom literature.[57] The aim of such questions is to teach the readers. Since ten of the twelve questions are directed toward Jonah, the narrator is subtly placing us, the readers, in Jonah's position. We will watch the narrator do this in a not-so-subtle way in 4:10–11. Thus the questions put

---

[56] Fretheim, *The Message of Jonah*, 47.

[57] Questions occur in Proverbs in, for example, 1:22; 5:16, 20; 6:9, 27, 28; in Ecclesiastes in, for example, 1:10; 2:2, 15, 19, 22, 25; 3:9, 21; in Job in, for example, 2:9, 10; 3:11, 12, 16, 20–23.

to Jonah are also asked of us. They are designed to lead us to the same repentance and renewed faith that Jonah needs.

1:7 It is safe to assume that the mariners would not have set sail on such a voyage had there been a hint of bad weather. They assume the unexpected storm has a supernatural cause and investigate who must have offended the divine. Someone's sin has to be responsible for this calamity! To the ancient mind, storms were not the products of impersonal meteorological forces but were directed to specific ends by specific wills. If the person at fault is found and dealt with, the danger may pass.

The sailors are sure that among their number is a guilty person who, like a magnet, has attracted to the ship a demonstration of divine anger. To find the culprit they cast lots. In casting lots,[58] the mariners make two theological assumptions. First, the storm is a divine punishment for the misdeed of someone on board the ship. Second, a deity will communicate through the casting of lots.

The casting of lots—the throwing of some inanimate object in order to learn the divine will—is well-known in ancient Israelite and Near Eastern cultures. Among the many uses of lot casting in the OT, the technique is used to discover a wrongdoer (Josh 7:10–21; 1 Sam 14:36–43), choose a king (1 Sam 10:20–21), assign a tribe its inheritance (Josh 14:2), distribute booty (Nah 3:10), and settle disputes (Prov 18:18). The theological basis is this:

> The lot is cast into the lap,
> > but from Yahweh is its every verdict. (Prov 16:33)

The practice continued into the NT. The Roman soldiers cast lots for the clothing of the crucified Christ in fulfillment of Scripture (Jn 19:23–24, citing Ps 22:19 [ET 22:18]). The Eleven prayed and cast lots to select an apostle to succeed Judas Iscariot (Acts 1:26).

In Jonah 1:7 the sailors may have inscribed shards of pottery with the names of those on board the ship; then from among the shards they grabbed the one with Jonah's name. That the sailors had to resort to this activity shows that Jonah's desire to remain unknown and escape responsibility was greater than his willingness to alleviate the suffering and even prevent the deaths of others.

Word repetition is again important as the sailors decide to "cast lots so that we might know on whose account this evil [הָרָעָה] has come to us." The "evil" (רָעָה) of Nineveh that arose before Yahweh (1:2) had triggered the entire episode. But instead of responding to the call of Yahweh to deal with that "evil," Jonah has engendered further "evil" upon bystanders—the sailors. Ironically, Jonah, by his flight and inaction, has precipitated doom for the pagans—but the wrong pagans! So when Yahweh directs the lot to fall to Jonah, the "evil" is rightly ascribed to him—instead of to Nineveh. Could the satire be more pointed? Jonah, by refusing to announce Nineveh's "evil," which would lead

---

[58] Cf. Lindblom, "Lot-Casting in the Old Testament."

to repentance, has instead brought "evil" upon the less guilty. In response to Yahweh's call for him to preach, Jonah kept quiet. It is the pagans who, by means of casting lots, finally compel the Israelite prophet to speak—for the first time in the book (1:9). But when he does speak, Jonah will make no confession of his evil.

At the end of 1:7 the motif of "descending" continues. It began when Jonah "went down to Joppa" and then down into the ship, that is, "boarded it" (יָרַד twice in 1:3). It continues when "Jonah went down to the innermost recesses of the ship" to lie down and sleep (1:5). The sailors literally "throw down" (Hiphil of נָפַל) lots, and the lot "fell" (נָפַל) to Jonah (1:7). This action prefigures the sailors' later action of hurling Jonah into the sea (1:15).

So Jonah wins the lottery—or rather, he loses it! And so the question that began this verse, in essence, "Who rocked the boat?" is answered at the end of the verse: Jonah!

1:8 Once the lot falls to him, Jonah is immediately placed on trial, but this is no ordinary courtroom interrogation. The questions are not formulated by a ruminating attorney absorbed in the finer details of the case, but by terrified sailors clinging to their lives in the midst of a howling gale! A salvo of short questions is fired at Jonah. Their brevity is in keeping with the dire circumstances on the boat.

Jonah is "stormed" in staccato-like fashion with four questions. Each of the first three consists of only two Hebrew words. The tone on board the ship has changed from the captain's pleas for help (1:6) to the urgent demands of the sailors in 1:8. The sailors' questions constitute the third time Jonah is addressed. First, the command from Yahweh led to his flight (1:2). Second, the command of the captain met with his silence (1:6). But this third time Jonah is trapped, and the interrogatives accomplish what the earlier imperatives did not. This effect of the interrogatives upon Jonah foreshadows developments in chapter 4, where instead of issuing commands, Yahweh asks questions.

The sailors' interrogation in 1:8 and Jonah's answers in 1:9 are inversely related. The sailors first make a request of the culprit: "Tell us, please, on whose account this evil has come to us." Second, they question Jonah about his identity: "What is your occupation? And from where have you come? What is your land? And from what people are you?" (1:8). Jonah only responds to their questions about his identity: "A Hebrew I am, and Yahweh, the God of the heavens, I worship, who made the sea and the dry land" (1:9). He admits no culpability in his speech here, though later the narrator will inform us that earlier Jonah had divulged it to them: "For the men knew that away from the presence of Yahweh he was fleeing, because he had told them" (1:10).

The sailors already know the answer to their first request of Jonah because the lot answered it (and according to 1:10, Jonah himself previously had admitted as much). Therefore, some scholars advocate deleting "on whose account this evil has come to us!" Yet people may request information or ask a question when they already know the answer for the purpose of soliciting confession. This was Yahweh's strategy in Gen 3:11 when he asked Adam, "Have you eaten from the tree of which I commanded you not to eat?" Yahweh wants Adam to confess, "Yes, I have. Please forgive me." But Adam's response was hardly that; he blamed Eve and Yahweh for creating her as his companion (Gen 3:12). In like manner, the sailors want Jonah to say, "It is my fault. I have brought you to the brink of death." But guilty Jonah doesn't fully confess his sin. The key word "evil" (רָעָה) is missing from his confession in 1:12: "For I know that it is on my account that this great storm is against you."

1:9 At long last, Jonah breaks his silence and finally speaks. In any Hebrew narrative, the point at which the main character first speaks is worthy of special attention. In most instances the initial words are a key revelation of the person's character. That Jonah answers the sailors, but incompletely, offers a key insight into who he is. Jonah confesses Yahweh, but he does not confess his sin. He declares that he is a worshiper of Yahweh, but he is on the lam from Yahweh—at the same time! Could hypocrisy be stated any more clearly? Jonah is fleeing from Yahweh, whom he confesses as omnipotent, on the very sea that he confesses that Yahweh has made. The creed is true doctrine, but in Jonah's mouth, we have to wonder whether it is confessed in true faith.

Jonah does not call what he has done "evil"—the term that the sailors use in their request in 1:8. He had already demonstrated this same character flaw in 1:3, when he shirked his responsibility to address (and rectify) Nineveh's "evil" (1:2) through his ministry, but instead fled toward Tarshish. Again Jonah shrugs off "this evil" (1:7–8) with a more neutral phrase, accepting responsibility only for "this great storm" (1:12). His avoidance of responsibility for "evil" climaxes in 4:1, where the salvation of repentant Nineveh is to him a "great evil." Rather than confess the salvation of these Gentile sinners by grace alone, he would rather die (4:3, 8–9). In fact, when Yahweh seeks "to save him from his evil" (4:6), the prophet again misses his opportunity to confess and receive forgiveness. By the end of the book, "evil" no longer belongs to the Ninevites, who have been converted; it belongs to the resentful Israelite prophet!

Throughout the book Jonah never completely confesses his evil. It festers and grows until it becomes a "great evil" (4:1) and threatens to overcome him. Jonah spurns the counsel of King David in Ps 4:5 (ET 4:4), which St. Paul quotes:

> "Be angry, but do not sin." Do not let the sun go down upon your anger, and
> do not give room for the devil. (Eph 4:26–27)

Jonah's evil anger builds, and by chapter 4, he therefore becomes a sitting duck for the devil's attacks (cf. Gen 4:7).

The sailors—not to mention the Ninevites—have their own gods (Jonah 1:5), who surely will help them; right? "No," says Yahweh, the Creator of the heavens and the earth, the sea and the dry land. Jonah speaks and finally carries out his prophetic office. The general revelation of God in his creation, and the religious instincts that God has put in the hearts of all people, even the pagan unbelievers, are not sufficient to make a person "wise unto salvation"; only the revealed Word of God can do that (2 Tim 3:15). Yahweh's special revelation comes only through his Word. This Word, spoken by his reluctant prophet, is the appointed means by which all can be saved—even the mariners, and later, the Ninevites (see Jonah 3:4–10)!

Hebrew writers sometimes place their main thrust in the center of a narrative.[59] Following this rhetorical strategy, Jonah's confession (1:9) is exactly in the middle of scene 2, understanding this scene as 1:4–15, with 1:16 as its conclusion. Jonah's words in 1:9 are carefully placed at the midpoint of a chiastic structure.[60] There are ninety-four Hebrew words from the beginning of the scene in 1:4 to the beginning of Jonah's speech in 1:9, and there are ninety-four Hebrew words in 1:10–15. Both the chiastic structure and the exact balance of the number of words place the focus on Jonah's confession in 1:9, which is Yahweh's means for saving the sailors.[61]

It is difficult to correlate all four of the precise questions asked in 1:8 with the answer of Jonah in 1:9. Often in Hebrew narrative technique, the last in a series of questions is answered first. Following this style, Jonah's עִבְרִי אָנֹכִי ("A Hebrew I am") answers the mariner's last question ("From what people are you?") first.

"Yahweh, the God of the heavens, I worship, who made the sea and the dry land" is a creedal statement about the triune God that echoes other texts (see the textual notes and Gen 1:9–10, where Yahweh makes "the dry land" appear out of the "seas," and Pss 95:5; 136:26). See also the excursus "Yahweh, the Creator God." It is probable that Jonah's confession is a sincere expression of his true faith, albeit in a context sullied by disobedient actions. Jonah believes in Yahweh as Creator, while at the same time he flees from the context where Yahweh makes himself known in specific, salvific ways. Whatever Jonah's intention is, this confession functions as the means of grace whereby the sailors are brought to saving faith. Such is the power of Yahweh's Word, which is efficacious, accomplishing his redemptive purposes (Is 55:10–11).

Jonah's confession implies that Yahweh is the providential controller who holds the world in his hand and manifests his powerful presence through the natural world in order to achieve his purposes of salvation. Yahweh's power over his creation is displayed throughout the narrative: in the hurricane-like wind (1:4), the tempestuous sea (1:11), the obedient great fish (2:1 [ET 1:17]), the qiqayon plant (4:6), the worm (4:7), and the scorching east wind (4:8). Jonah himself dramatically portrays the futility of opposing Yahweh's will. Try

---

[59] Numerical balance also occurs in Jonah 4. See "Introduction to Jonah 4." There are other biblical examples of a central assertion being placed in the numerical middle. For example, the clause "for you are with me" (Ps 23:4) is in the numerical middle of Psalm 23; in the Hebrew text there are twenty-six words both before and after it. See further "Introduction to Jonah 1."

[60] See "Introduction to Jonah 1."

[61] This structural analysis comes from Limburg, *Jonah*, 47–48.

as he might to take charge of his own life and destiny, Yahweh is in control throughout the four chapters, just as the sailors confess in 1:14: "You are Yahweh; just as you please, you do." Yahweh controls the heavens, the earth, and the dry ground. His desire is to save all people throughout his creation (1 Tim 2:4). The book of Jonah shows that this includes heathen Gentiles: the mariners and especially the Ninevites!

That Jonah uses "the God of the heavens" (אֱלֹהֵי הַשָּׁמַיִם) does not necessitate assigning a postexilic date to the narrative. Jonah may be confessing that it is Yahweh who is "the God of the heavens" as opposed to Baal, whose title in the Ugaritic texts is sometimes "Baal in heaven" (Baal Shamen).[62] Since in 1:5 the sailors may have sacrificed their cargo in worshiping another Ugaritic god, Yamm ("sea"), Jonah is confessing that Yahweh, not Baal, is the one who subdues the sea's chaos. Order and life come from Yahweh, and not the storm deity Baal (see the commentary on 1:5). In Is 50:2 Yahweh says: "Behold, by my rebuke I dry up the sea [יָם], I make the rivers [נְהָרוֹת] a desert" (ESV).

"The sea" and "the dry land" in Jonah's confession constitute a merism (literally, "division"), a rhetorical device whereby the whole (the earth) is divided into two opposite constituent parts.[63] Understood this way, "the sea" and "the dry land" identify Yahweh as the God over everyone and everything. Sasson writes: "With this clause, therefore, Jonah is telling the sailors that God is not solely the Lord of heaven, but also the creator of all that is found beneath the firmament; in effect, the ruler over the whole universe."[64]

It is often easier to stand by creedal statements than to walk by them. Jonah's theology here is correct but—like other believers, ancient and modern—his right theology has not yet led to right actions. There is an incongruity between the prophet's confession of Yahweh as Creator of the universe and his attempt to escape from Yahweh by sea. In this context, the verb "to worship" (יָרֵא) is perhaps best understood as denoting a true faith that has been too weak to overcome Jonah's arrogance and nationalistic pride.

Jonah's confession, translated literally according to the Hebrew word order, splits the phrase "Yahweh, the God of the heavens ... who made the sea

---

[62] Baal is the Canaanite storm and fertility god. He is the most significant pagan deity mentioned in the OT. In some extrabiblical texts Baal is called Hadad. In Canaanite mythology, attested in the Ugaritic texts, Baal is the warrior par excellence, and his defeat of the forces of chaos, represented by the god Yamm ("sea"), provided order in the world. A number of elements of the Baal cult are attested in the OT. Elijah battled four hundred ecstatic prophets of Baal on Mount Carmel (1 Kings 18). The cutting mentioned in the ritual (1 Ki 18:28) was probably related to the cult of the dead, as the death of Baal is equated with drought, and Israel had experienced drought for three previous years in fulfillment of Elijah's prophecy. The biblical prohibition against cutting the body in mourning (Lev 19:28; Deut 14:1) may be aimed in part against the Baal cult. McCurley, *Ancient Myths and Biblical Faith*, 46–49, discusses Baal's role in Ugaritic texts and how they are polemicized in the OT.

[63] Merism is the naming of the two extremes to refer to the entire class, including the members in between those extremes. Other examples of this device in Jonah are "days" and "nights" (2:1 [ET 1:17]); "least" and "greatest" (3:5); and "people" and "animals" (3:7–8; 4:11).

[64] Sasson, *Jonah*, 119.

and the dry land" with "I worship." This awkward Hebrew syntax illustrates the rhetorical device called hyperbaton (literally, "transposed"): Jonah separates words that belong together.[65] Ironically, by this wording Jonah has surrounded himself ("I") with the God he is seeking to flee from ("Yahweh … I … who made the sea and the dry land")! This recalls how the narrator surrounded Jonah's flight from Yahweh with "the presence of Yahweh," used in both in the first clause of 1:3 and at the end of 1:3. The irony is stronger in 1:9 because here Jonah's own words undercut him!

1:10 The sailors "feared a great fear." This is the third appearance of the verb יָרֵא ("fear, worship") in the narrative thus far (previously 1:5, 9). Its force has been intensified by Jonah's use of it in his confession ("I worship," 1:9). The sailors' reaction indicates that these pagans recognize the precariousness of Jonah's flight more clearly than he does. They see a human being challenging his God! "Away from the presence of Yahweh" is repeated here for the third time in the chapter (the first two were in 1:3).

"What is this you have done?" is the sixth question addressed to Jonah since his flight. The sailors will ask one more question in 1:11: "What shall we do to you?" Each of these questions in 1:8–11 concerns Jonah's identity and responsibility. Their building intensity parallels the heightening intensity of the storm. Jonah's failure to conform his life to his professed faith in Yahweh caused this external threat, both for himself and for those around him. As the English poet John Donne put it, "No man is an island, entire of itself."[66]

The sailors react in a way more indicative of faith than does the Israelite Jonah. He is reacting in a manner we would expect from an unbeliever. The sailors cannot imagine anyone treating his deity in such a fashion. They have a fear and respect for the divine that Jonah does not. This is an ongoing theme in the narrative: the Gentile outsiders display greater reverence and understanding than the Israelite insider, Jonah, who remains mostly clueless.

1:11 With the sailors reeling from the howling storm, their sense of urgency escalates. They press Jonah for a solution, realizing that he alone knows how to respond to his own God in such a catastrophic situation.

1:12 A certain ambivalence hovers over this verse. Why does Jonah ask to be thrown overboard? Is his primary motivation to perish? He will pray for death in 4:3, 8 (see also 4:9). Or is it to save the lives of the sailors? Or is it to appease Yahweh's wrath? Or is it a mixture of all three? In opting for the "assisted suicide" interpretation H. W. Wolff states:

> We hear only one thing: [Jonah] wants to die. … [He is] seeking refuge from [Yahweh] in death. Only the actual circumstances differ here from the circumstances in 4:3, 8; but we should not assume that there is any essential difference between the plea in 1:12 and the plea in 4:3, 8.[67]

---

[65] As noted by Trible, *Rhetorical Criticism*, 141.

[66] John Donne, *Devotions upon Emergent Occasions*, meditation 17.

[67] Wolff, *Obadiah and Jonah*, 118.

Jonah's proposal appears to be a noble gesture of self-sacrifice by one who recognizes his own role in bringing calamity upon others. But if Wolff's way of reading the text is correct, there is a straight line between Jonah's "deep sleep," in 1:5–6, his request to be cast into the sea in 1:12, and his prayers for death in 4:3, 8. Thus upon closer examination, 1:12 reveals Jonah's continuing refusal to take responsibility—not only for his prophetic role, but even for his own life.

If we adopt this interpretation, it follows that Yahweh's creation of the storm was not intended to kill anyone, although it certainly threatened to do so. Rather, it was intended to prompt Jonah to carry out his prophetic assignment. Yahweh doesn't want Jonah to die; he wants Jonah to preach! Seeing the storm, Jonah shows contempt for his own life. He would rather die than carry out Yahweh's commission to go to Nineveh. Put another way, Jonah does not want to die to his theological worldview and be transformed into a missionary to Nineveh (as will happen in chapter 2 and 3:1–4); instead, Jonah opts for death by drowning. He reckons that it is better for him to die than endure the consequences of the Gospel (as he says outright in 4:3, 8). Edwin Good confirms this understanding when he writes: "Perhaps we must see Jonah's offer not as a sudden burst of generosity but as his perception that death might yet be a way out of his frightful mission."[68]

The sailors do everything they can to preserve life. The captain and the king of Nineveh do not want to perish (1:6; 3:9). Yahweh changes his verdict concerning the disaster that would have killed the Ninevites (3:10). Jonah is the only person in the narrative who has such a cheap view of life that he seeks death. He does not value his own life, nor does he value the Ninevites, whose lives would be preserved when they would repent and believe in God because of Jonah's preaching. Thus Jonah does the opposite of what St. Paul counsels Pastor Timothy: "Closely watch your life and the doctrine; remain in them. For doing this you will save both yourself and those who hear you" (1 Tim 4:16).

Another line of interpretation is advocated by Jerome, who sees Jonah as a prototype of Jesus.[69] According to this interpretation, by offering himself as a sacrifice, Jonah is indicating his desire to save the sailors. This seems to be a valid understanding in light of his purpose clause, "so that the sea may calm down from [raging] against you," and his admission of blame, "for I know that it is on my account that this great storm is against you" (1:12).[70] Seen in this light, Jonah's deliverance by means of the great fish (2:1 [ET 1:17]) is a vin-

---

[68] Good, *Irony in the Old Testament*, 45.

[69] Jerome, *Commentariorum in Ionam*, on 1:12–15 (CCSL 76:390–92). Jerome's comments on 1:15 are translated in Ferreiro, *The Twelve Prophets*, ACCS 14:134.

[70] Cf. Allen, *Joel, Obadiah, Jonah and Micah*, 211, who understands the verse this way: "By now he [Jonah] has realized how terrible is the sin that has provoked this terrible storm. The only way to appease the tempest of Yahweh's wrath is to abandon himself to it as just deserts for his sin. His willingness to die is an indication that he realizes his guilt before God."

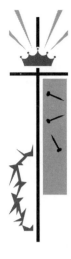

dication of his sacrifice. Thus Jonah's actions and rescue after three days would be analogous to Paul's argument about Jesus the Christ:

> He emptied himself, taking the form of a slave. And being in the likeness of men, and being found in form as a man, he humbled himself and became obedient until death—death of a cross! Therefore God highly exalted him. (Phil 2:7–9)

The vindication of Jonah's sacrifice will be his "exaltation" from the depths of the sea to the dry land of safety and new life (Jonah 2:11 [ET 2:10]).

Adding credence to this view of 1:12 are the two verbs that Jonah uses. (Both are used again when the sailors carry out his instructions in 1:15.) First, Jonah commands the sailors, "Lift me up." This use of the verb נָשָׂא is odd because Jonah should not need to instruct the sailors how to toss him overboard; they knew how to do this (see 1:5). Since נָשָׂא seldom refers to lifting up a person, but often occurs with the nouns "sin" and "iniquity," in which case it can mean "to forgive,"[71] Sasson sees Jonah using נָשָׂא to connote that his evil and sin will be lifted up and taken away from the ship when he is hurled into the sea.[72] The second verb, "hurl" (טוּל), was first used in 1:4 when "Yahweh hurled a great wind upon the sea." It was used again when the sailors "hurled the gear that was in the ship into the sea" (1:5). Jonah may reason that Yahweh's will is to hurl not only the storm, but also his prophet into the sea, and that is why the storm was not stilled by the sailors hurling their cargo overboard (1:5). Thus Jonah thinks that Yahweh's desire will be satisfied if they hurl him overboard, much as an efficacious sacrifice appeases Yahweh's wrath.

Confirming this interpretation further is the end of 1:12, where Jonah admits, "For I know that it is *on my account that this great storm* is against you." His admission is parallel to 1:7, where the sailors say, "Come, let us cast lots so that we might know *on whose account this evil* has come to us." The parallelism connects Jonah's confession of responsibility for the "storm" (1:12) to the "evil" befalling the sailors (1:7) due to Jonah's flight from Yahweh (1:3). Jonah knows, then, that he stands under Yahweh's judgment and that his death would be the just penalty that he deserves.

That Jonah sacrifices himself for the sake of the sailors to satisfy Yahweh's justice is indicated by further close parallels between 1:5 and 1:12:

> They *hurled the gear* that was in the ship into the sea in order to lighten *from upon them* [מֵעֲלֵיהֶם].

> *Hurl me* into the sea so that the sea may calm down *from against you* [מֵעֲלֵיכֶם].

This parallelism suggests that as Jonah sleeps in the cargo hold of the vessel, he becomes, in effect, a substitute for the wares removed from the innards of the ship and hurled overboard. Now Jonah insists that one last ware, namely

---

[71] See, for example, נָשָׂא with עָוֹן in Ex 34:7; Lev 16:22; Ps 85:3 (ET 85:2); נָשָׂא with חֵטְא in Is 53:12; נָשָׂא with חַטָּאת in Ex 32:32; Ps 25:18; and נָשָׂא with both עָוֹן and חַטָּאת in Ps 32:5.

[72] Sasson, *Jonah*, 124–25.

himself, be hurled to the sea so that it may cease from its raging. As a human offering, Jonah can accomplish what the inanimate sacrifices have not.

In a much greater way, the sinless Jesus, true God and true man, assumed the sins of the world and died to make satisfaction for God's righteous wrath (cf. 2 Cor 5:21). His sacrifice accomplished what animal and even human sacrifices never could; his atoning death has infinite value because he is the Son of God.

A final reason for the "Jonah as appeasing sacrifice" interpretation is that there are several examples in ancient literature of a belief that a storm at sea could be caused by a guilty traveler. In 411 BC the orator Antiphon wrote a defense for a man accused of murdering a companion. As proof of the man's innocence, he cites the fact that the accused had subsequently traveled by ship and no harm had come to him or his traveling companions. He writes:

> I hardly think I need remind you that many a person with unclean hands or some other form of defilement who has embarked on shipboard with the righteous has involved them in his own destruction. Others, while they have escaped death, have had their lives imperiled owing to such polluted wretches.[73]

On Paul's voyage to Rome, a storm overtakes the ship, and it is wrecked on the island of Malta. As Paul gathers brushwood for a fire on the beach, a viper clings to his hand. Some who see this say to each another, "Fully this man must be a murderer; though saved from the sea, justice has not allowed him to live" (Acts 28:4). Their words imply that the shipwreck was aimed at or caused by Paul, who somehow escaped from it, but not from justice. Clearly this belief, which informs the attitudes of the sailors in Jonah 1, was prevalent in the ancient world.

A third possible interpretation of 1:12 involves a variation of the second. Perhaps Jonah admits that he is guilty but is unwilling to repent. Therefore, he plans to satisfy Yahweh's justice by taking upon himself the punishment he deserves, but he has no real regard for those on board the ship. Jonah decides to take matters into his own hands and have the sailors kill him in order to show Yahweh how to act justly! As it turns out, Yahweh is in charge (1:14), and he chooses not to take Jonah's life as payment for his evil. Instead, Yahweh breaks through the scheme that says that all sinners must suffer the full punishment for their actions. His appointment of the great fish (2:1 [ET 1:17]) to save Jonah is Yahweh's demonstration of the Gospel, by which he forgives sinners. This is his preferred way of dealing with all people—including the Ninevites!

All three explanations for Jonah's behavior have merit. These multiple interpretations are possible because of a common technique in Jonah known as a "gap" in information.[74] Gaps invite us to ponder Yahweh's purposes and the

---

[73] Antiphon, *Herodes*, 82, quoted in Bolin, *Freedom beyond Forgiveness*, 82.

[74] This idea of a "gap" in Israelite narrative literature has been analyzed by M. Perry and M. Sternberg, "The King through Ironic Eyes: The Narrator's Devices in the Biblical Story of

prophet's motivation. As we do so, we are brought closer to answering the questions "What would *I* have done if I were Jonah?" and "How does God regard *me*?" The narrator will bring us to this same point of close identification with Jonah in 4:10–11 with his use of the biggest gap in the story.

However we fill in the gap in 1:12, one thing is certain: the behavior of the sailors toward Jonah (1:13–14) is exemplary. They fear killing a man even when he requests it and it likely would save their own lives. The ethical standards of these Gentiles is far higher than that of the Israelite. The satire is intended to be sharp, sharp enough to pierce the hardest heart.[75]

1:13 The plot of the narrative would go much more "swimmingly" (pun intended) if the sailors simply would "go with the flow" and utter something like this: "You are indeed a disobedient prophet who has brought evil upon us. You deserve to be thrown overboard! Heave ho; let's throw and go!" But instead the sailors refuse to carry out his request that they take his life—revealing their higher ethics—and instead dig[76] into the water with their oars to take him back to shore. Yet the futility of their digging represents the puny muscles of people up against the impressive biceps of Yahweh, the God who created and controls the massive sea and storm.[77]

Caught between the devil and the deep blue sea—between Jonah's death and their own—the sailors are indeed in a catch-22. Normally it is the prophet's role to attempt to save people from some divinely inspired disaster or punishment (e.g., Amos 7:1–6). But here it is the pagan sailors who attempt to save a prophet of Yahweh who refused to preach—ironic indeed!

These positive actions of the mariners stand in stark contrast with the behavior of Jonah. They have been thrown into a life-threatening storm through no fault of their own. They have lost their cargo. Yet they still seek to save the life of the man responsible for all the chaos. The sailors are models of true for-

---

David and Bathsheba and Two Excurses on the Theory of the Narrative Text," *Hasifrut* 1 (Tel Aviv, 1968): 263–92 (Hebrew; English summary, pp. 449–52). The argument in this study is that "the narrator evades an explicit rendering or formulation of thoughts, but directs the reader to infer them from what is rendered explicitly" (p. 450). That is, the narrator exploits the fact that if the reader wishes to make sense of the story, he must infer or supply what is not explicitly communicated. In the narrative of David and Bathsheba, which Perry and Sternberg analyze, one of the main gaps is whether or not Uriah was aware of his wife's adultery. Perry and Sternberg proceed to show how the text provides no definite answer; the reader could construct either thesis.

[75] The high ethics of the sailors in contrast to Jonah bring to mind contemporary issues regarding the sanctity of all human life, from the moment of conception to the natural end of life. For example, their reluctance to take Jonah's life even though it might save their own could be applied to the issue of human cloning: Christians cannot justify the destruction of human embryos even if cells harvested from them could be used to cure diseases and prolong the lives of others. Another application could be to the end of life: Christians cannot justify "mercy killings," that is, taking the lives of innocent people by any means, even if a person requests death.

[76] See the first textual note on 1:13.

[77] See the excursus "Yahweh, the Creator God."

giveness. Their actions demonstrate the Pauline diction in Eph 4:32: "Be kind unto one another, compassionate, forgiving each other, just as God in Christ forgave you."

Navigational experience spanning the centuries teaches mariners to remain in open sea during a storm since rocks threaten and waves rise higher in shallower water. Against that wisdom, these sailors attempt to return to "the dry land" (הַיַּבָּשָׁה, 1:13). The futility of the sailors is underscored by the use of this term. Jonah used the identical term when he told them in his confession of faith in 1:9 that it is Yahweh who created and controls "the dry land" as well as "the sea" in which their boat now founders. Israelite prophecy and liturgy both had taught for centuries that people cannot escape Yahweh's presence. How could the sailors hope to escape one part of Yahweh's realm and reach a destination beyond his control? Both Jonah and the sailors are doomed.

The narrator uses repetition as a literary device to heighten the tension until it reaches its climax. First he writes: "There was a great storm at sea" (1:4). Then he says: "The sea is growing more stormy" (1:11). Here in 1:13, he notes: "The sea continued to storm against them." The sea's turmoil increases along with the frantic state of those on board. It is almost time to abandon ship!

1:14 The sailors are in a double jeopardy, in a no-win situation. They are suffering because of Jonah's evil, yet placing themselves in a position to cry, "Man overboard!" may bring Yahweh's further wrath upon them for their own evil. The mariners will perish if Jonah stays on board; but they rightly may perish if they throw a man overboard! Their only recourse is to plead for acquittal from Yahweh. So unlike Jonah, the sailors do not flee from Yahweh (1:3), nor do they remain silent (throughout chapter 1 Jonah never speaks to Yahweh). Instead, they pray to the one true God.

Yahweh's command for Jonah to "call" (קְרָא, 1:2) was met by his silence. So it is ironic that the Gentile sailors here carry out Yahweh's command: "And they called" (וַיִּקְרְאוּ). In 1:5 they had "called out, each man to his god(s)." Their words in 1:11 could mean that they sought deliverance from Yamm ("sea"), the Canaanite storm god. Now their prayer in 1:14 marks the first time in the narrative that the sailors invoke the name of Yahweh. They have come to believe that Israel's God is the one and only God over the universe, and the only God who can save them. Jonah's confession (1:9) has led them to saving faith.

Their prayer is in the pattern of the most common Hebrew prose prayers:

1. Invocation ("O Yahweh")
2. Petition ("Do not let us perish on account of the life of this man, and do not place against us innocent blood")
3. Motivation for the petition ("For you are Yahweh; just as you please, you do")

The invocation in the sailors' prayer is a standard form in a time of distress: "O Yahweh" (אָנָּה יְהוָה; see the second textual note on 1:14). This demonstrates their commendable faith and respect for Yahweh. Clearly they have taken to heart a great deal of truth about Yahweh since offering their vain prayers to other deities (1:5; cf. 1:11). Ironically, they themselves now offer an

135

efficacious prayer to Yahweh in place of Jonah's failure to pray to his God, even at the captain's bidding (1:6).

The petition of the sailors is twofold. First, "Do not let us perish on account of the life of this man." They want to remind Yahweh that throwing Jonah overboard is Jonah's solution, not theirs. They acknowledge that murder is a capital crime for which they could perish if Yahweh held them responsible. The sailors state their case that they are not a properly constituted court that can sift through all the evidence and at length arrive at a proper, God-pleasing decision. Rather, the mariners remind Yahweh that he was responsible for singling out Jonah through the casting of lots (1:7). So they are driven to plead their innocence for dropping Jonah to certain death, and ask that it not be the cause of their own death.

Laetsch writes: "These Gentiles had the Fifth Commandment [Ex 20:13; Deut 5:17] written in their hearts [Rom 2:14–15] and revolted from slaying a man who had, as far as they knew, done nothing worthy of death."[78] The Fifth Commandment's prohibition of murder had been spelled out for the first time in Yahweh's words to Noah after the flood:[79] "Whoever sheds the blood of man, by man shall his blood be shed, for in the image of God he made man" (Gen 9:6). Human beings were created by God as inherently sacrosanct. To take an innocent human life is to sin against the God who created and preserves all life, and who would save each life.

The sailors' second request is: "Do not place against us innocent blood" (Jonah 1:14). The phrase "innocent blood" does not mean that the sailors believe Jonah is innocent; the lots (1:7) and Jonah himself (1:10) have told them otherwise. Rather, if he has misled them so that they are making the wrong move, they are not to be held responsible (cf. Deut 21:8–9). The sailors want to be sure that they are doing the will of Yahweh. A greater contrast with Jonah cannot be made.

Finally, the sailors append the motivation for their petition in a way we would expect from Jonah: "For you are Yahweh; just as you please, you do." This expression, writes Sasson, "looks very much as if it could be used at any time that a Hebrew wanted to compare God's limitless freedom of action to the pagan gods' more restricted movements."[80]

Jonah's confession in 1:9 used the verb עָשָׂה, "to do, act, make," in "who *made* the sea and the dry land." It is used here by the sailors ("you *do*") as a prelude to their full worship of Yahweh in 1:16. Sandwiched in between these two uses of עָשָׂה are two others, in 1:10 and 1:11: "What is this you have *done*?" (מַה־זֹּאת עָשִׂיתָ, 1:10) and "What shall we *do* to you?" (מַה־נַּעֲשֶׂה לָּךְ, 1:11). The two uses of עָשָׂה in 1:10–11 compared to the two uses in 1:9, 14 are a contrast

---

[78] Laetsch, *The Minor Prophets*, 227.

[79] Cf. "Jonah and Noah" in the introduction.

[80] Sasson, *Jonah*, 136.

between the impotence of people and Yahweh's omnipotence. Later, 4:5 will use the same verb to say that Jonah "made" (וַיַּעַשׂ) a booth to shelter him from the sun. As could be predicted by that point, Jonah's effort is in vain, for throughout the narrative it becomes increasingly clear that "man proposes, but Yahweh disposes!" The only other verse in Jonah with עָשָׂה is 3:10: after the Ninevites repented, "God changed his verdict about the evil that he threatened *to do* to them, and he did *not do* [it]." There it is evident that God alone has the power to change his wrath into mercy, and his mercy rests on those who believe in him. That will become evident in 1:15–16 too.

The exact expression "just as you please, you do" (כַּאֲשֶׁר חָפַצְתָּ עָשִׂיתָ) is unique in the OT, but similar expressions occur four other places (Is 46:10; Pss 115:3; 135:6; Eccl 8:3).[81] Four of these instances (Is 46:10; Jonah 1:14; Pss 115:3; 135:6) refer to Yahweh, while Eccl 8:3 refers to an earthly king. But all five denote the limitless power of a supreme authority, who can "do whatever he pleases." This is not merely a rhetorical expression; it likely is a legal formula from the domain of jurisprudence that recognizes the broad power of the sovereign.[82] More specifically, in Is 46:10; Pss 115:3; 135:6, the context of this expression lauds Yahweh as supreme and condemns idolatry. In Is 46:6–7 Yahweh mocks those who pay to have idols made and then worship them. This exhortation follows in Is 46:9–10:

Remember the former things of long ago,
for I am God, and there is no other;
[I am] God, and there is none like me.
I make known the end from the beginning,
from ancient times, what is not yet done,
saying, "My counsel will stand,
and all my desire I will do [וְכָל־חֶפְצִי אֶעֱשֶׂה]."

Similarly, Ps 115:3–4 states:

Our God is in the heavens;
all that he pleases, he does [כֹּל אֲשֶׁר־חָפֵץ עָשָׂה].
Their idols are silver and gold,
the work of the hands of man.

And finally Ps 135:5–6, 15 declares:

For I myself know that Yahweh is great,
and our Lord above all gods.
All that Yahweh pleases, he does [כֹּל אֲשֶׁר־חָפֵץ יְהוָה עָשָׂה],
in the heavens and on the earth,
in the seas and all the deeps. …
The idols of the nations are silver and gold,
the work of the hands of man.

---

[81] Pss 115:3; 135:6; and Eccl 8:3 all have כֹּל אֲשֶׁר ("all that"), rather than כַּאֲשֶׁר ("just as"): "All that he pleases, he does." Is 46:10 uses כֹּל and the noun חֵפֶץ, rather than the verb חָפֵץ: "All my desire I will do."

[82] Hurvitz, "The History of a Legal Formula."

In this group of texts at least two ideas are present. The first is that Yahweh is the only true God. Therefore, he alone can do whatever he wishes; no other "gods" can carry out their plans or desires. The second is that Yahweh's power extends from heaven over all creation, including the sea and the chaotic waters. Every other ruler or authority is under him. He alone is worthy of worship.

This means that when the sailors confess Yahweh's omnipotence in 1:14, it functions as a polemic against the worship of anyone but Yahweh. They have come to know more than the fact that Yahweh is a mighty storm God, more powerful than Yamm; Yahweh is their only hope of salvation, both from the storm now and for eternity. The mariners have come to believe in Yahweh as the only God. The manmade idols of the nations are but nothing.

The sailors confess that Yahweh does as he pleases (cf. Ps 115:3; 135:6), while Jonah expresses his frustration because Yahweh does precisely that! The words of the sailors constitute total submission and worship, not unlike the words of Jesus in the garden of Gethsemane (Mt 26:39; Mk 14:36; Lk 22:42). Irony abounds: the sailors' saving faith is now vividly etched against the background of Jonah's disobedience.

1:15 After their prayer of faith and worship, the sailors carry out the instructions Jonah gave in 1:12. The verbs "lift up" (נָשָׂא) and "hurl" (טוּל) in 1:15 are repeated from 1:12. There is a causal relationship between all four uses of טוּל, "hurl," in chapter 1. Yahweh "hurled" the great wind (1:4), so the sailors were forced to "hurl" their cargo overboard (1:5), but to no avail, so Jonah asks the sailors to "hurl" him overboard (1:12), and finally the sailors have no other choice but to do just that (1:15). "The act of God in sending the storm has consequences which are revealed not merely on the level of the narrative itself, but also on the 'subliminal' level of the word that repeats and repeats itself through the episode."[83] Expressed theologically, when Yahweh acts, whether by word or action (he "hurled" the storm [1:4]), his will eventually will be done (the sailors "hurled" Jonah [1:15]). Yahweh's efficacious power is what the sailors confessed in the preceding verse (1:14).

To recap, in 1:1–3 the Ninevites were the wicked ones whom Jonah deemed unworthy of life; he refused even to try to save them through preaching Yahweh's Word to them. Yet, ironically, now he is the wicked one, unworthy of life, and doomed to die as a consequence of his sin. Jonah is now in the same place as Nineveh was!

The sailors throw Jonah overboard, thus making him the sacrifice. The sea becomes quiet (1:15), indicating that it is Yahweh, the God of Jonah (1:9) and now the God of the mariners (1:14), who controls the waves.

1:16 "They feared a great fear [or perhaps 'worshiped a great worship'] and said to each other, 'Therefore, who is this that even the wind and the sea

---

[83] Magonet, *Form and Meaning*, 16–17.

obey him?' " (Mk 4:41). So exclaim the disciples when Jesus calms the tempest on the Sea of Galilee. Under different circumstances, the sailors appear to make the same confession of faith and worship in Jonah 1:16. Indeed, the crisis is finally resolved and the response is "Yahweh, he is God!"

In Aristotelian terms, change comes through reversal and recognition. Reversal is the change to the opposite state of affairs.[84] The storm ceases (1:15). Recognition "is a change from ignorance to knowledge."[85] The sailors have come to know and believe in Yahweh as their God (1:16). In this case, reversal effects recognition as the sailors turn from their own gods (1:5) and from Yamm, the deity of the sea (1:11) to the worship of Yahweh (1:14, 16). As Luther stated, the sailors "are also delivered from death, also from unbelief and from sin, and they are brought to a knowledge of God so that they now become pious and true servants of God, such humble and timid servants."[86] Indeed, Yahweh is "found by those who did not seek" him (Is 65:1). Another relevant verse from Isaiah—especially in light of the sailors' sacrifices and vows—is about the conversion of another Gentile people: "The Egyptians will know Yahweh on that day. They will serve [him] with animal sacrifice [זֶבַח, as in Jonah 1:16] and grain offering. They will vow vows [נָדַר and נֵדֶר, as in Jonah 1:16] to Yahweh and fulfill [them]" (Is 19:21). Egyptians, yes—but also pagan sailors!

The narrator plays on the verb "fear" (יָרֵא) throughout the chapter. The sailors "became afraid/feared" in 1:5 and 1:10, referring to their terror in the storm. Now the same verb, together with its cognate noun, is used for their "worship" of Yahweh in 1:16. The response of the sailors is striking in its simplicity and overpowering in its implications. They can now make the same confession of faith as Jonah did in 1:9, where he used יָרֵא ("Yahweh ... I *worship*"). The identical syntax in both 1:9 and 1:16 (יָרֵא with אֶת־יְהוָה) confirms this interpretation: now both Jonah and the mariners embrace the one true God, Yahweh, the God of the heavens, the sea, and the dry land!

The sailors' actions prompt several interpretive questions. They threw their cargo overboard (1:5), so where do they find livestock to sacrifice? The Qal of זָבַח ("to sacrifice"), used here (וַיִּזְבְּחוּ), almost always refers to sacrificing animals. What animals did they sacrifice? Jerome resolves these difficulties with these insights:

> They offered animal sacrifices that, certainly to take matters literally, they could not do in mid-waters; but it is that the sacrifice to God is a humble spirit. Elsewhere, it is said "Offer God a thanksgiving sacrifice, pay your vows to the Most High" (Ps 50:14). Again, "we shall repay our vows that we have promised" (Hos 14:3). This is how, at sea, they slaughter animals and they

---

[84] Aristotle, *Poetics*, 11.

[85] Aristotle, *Poetics*, 11 (trans. S. Halliwell; LCL [Cambridge, Mass.: Harvard University Press, 1927], 41). As a third element in plot, Aristotle also mentions suffering as the result of "a destructive or painful action." That element fits the earlier plight of the sailors.

[86] AE 19:69. Luther goes on to write: "What pure, God-fearing, and Christian consciences these people now have!"

spontaneously offer thereby others, vowing never to distance themselves from him whom they have begun to worship.[87]

It is improbable that the sailors made burnt offerings on board a wooden vessel that earlier was emptied of most, if not all, of its cargo, and "thought itself to be broken" (1:4). They offered worship and made vows immediately while at sea, and those vows likely included promises to offer sacrifice. Then once on land, they offered their sacrifices and again worshiped Yahweh.

Vows are a commonly employed means to repay Yahweh for divine help in a time of crisis, such as Jacob's vow for Yahweh's protection while journeying (Gen 28:20–22; 31:13) or Hannah's vow for the birth of her son Samuel (1 Sam 1:11). The verb נָדַר, "to vow," and its cognate accusative, נֶדֶר, "a vow" occur together, making an emphatic statement of devotion, in other verses, including Gen 28:20; 31:13; Num 6:2; 2 Sam 15:7–8; Is 19:21.

Ex 14:31 uses some of the same language in Jonah 1:16 when it states: "Israel saw the great hand [deed] that Yahweh did against the Egyptians, and the people feared/worshiped Yahweh [וַיִּירְאוּ הָעָם אֶת־יְהוָה], and they believed in Yahweh [וַיַּאֲמִינוּ בַּיהוָה] and in Moses, his servant." The faith and fear/worship of Yahweh on the shores of the Red Sea is equivalent to what Jonah 1:16 describes. The clause "they believed in Yahweh" is echoed in Jonah 3:5, when the "men of Nineveh believed in God" (וַיַּאֲמִינוּ אַנְשֵׁי נִינְוֵה בֵּאלֹהִים).[88] Ironically, words used to describe Israel's faith in Yahweh at one of the nation's most defining moments—the deliverance from Egypt—are used in the narrative of Jonah to describe pagans who were converted into believers! Ironic also is that the loss of life initiated by the sailors—Jonah's quick exit—gives them unpredicted life—a life through faith that shall endure for eternity!

Jonah 1:16 has three clauses:

So the men worshiped Yahweh with great worship,
sacrificed a sacrifice to Yahweh,
and vowed vows.

The clauses shrink in Hebrew from six to three to two words. The syntax mirrors the narrative as the sailors also shrink from the scene.[89] Important as a foil to Jonah throughout chapter 1, they are no longer needed. They disappear from the narrative as Jonah disappears into the sea. But given Jonah's failure

---

[87] Jerome, *Commentariorum in Ionam* (CCSL 76:392–93).

[88] The two reactions of Israel, "the people feared/worshiped Yahweh" and "they believed in Yahweh," are divided into two different sections in Jonah: in chapter 1 the sailors "feared/worshiped Yahweh" (1:16), and in chapter 3 the Ninevites "believed in God" (3:5). The author of Jonah also divides the events of 1 Kings 19: the prophet lies down and sleeps in 1 Ki 19:5 and Jonah 1:5, while other elements in 1 Kings 19 do not occur in Jonah until chapter 4, for example, the plant beneath which the prophet takes refuge and his request to die. See Magonet, *Form and Meaning*, 73–74.

[89] Compare a similar literary style in 1:5. First, fifteen Hebrew words describe the sailors (וַיִּירְאוּ ... מֵעֲלֵיהֶם). Then five Hebrew words describe Jonah's attempt to disappear in the innards of the vessel (וְיוֹנָה יָרַד אֶל־יַרְכְּתֵי הַסְּפִינָה). Finally, two terse Hebrew words describe him escaping into sleep (וַיִּשְׁכַּב וַיֵּרָדַם).

thus far to flee from the presence of Yahweh, we have every reason to think Jonah might fail again in this endeavor. Yahweh remains with him!

Summary of Scene 2

Moshe Greenberg's words aptly summarize this scene:

> Their [the sailors'] prayer climaxes their service to the story as a spiritually sensitive foil to the unresponsive, finally lethargic, prophet. While he slept in the teeth of the storm, they prayed each to his [g]od; while he refused to warn Nineveh away from disaster, these heathen sailors risked their lives to save his; whereas he was in rebellion against his God, they acknowledged his sovereignty in their prayer to him.[90]

In contrast to Jonah, the sailors—these "paid extras" (hired in 1:3)—demonstrate remarkable self-restraint, concern for the safety and welfare of Jonah, and reverence toward Jonah's God (cf. 1:6, 14) culminating in faith and worship of Yahweh (1:16). On the other hand, Jonah seems to be little concerned with the fate of those around him, his own responsibility as a prophet of Yahweh, or even his own well-being. Jonah sinks (!) in our estimation while the sailors rise, both figuratively and literally!

So there is a pattern of countermovement in chapter 1. Told to "arise" (1:2) instead Jonah flees from Yahweh and continues his inexorable descent, first below deck in his prone position in the ship's hold, then, by the end of the chapter, dropping like a stone into the depths of the sea. The sailors rise in faith and draw near to Yahweh with worship, sacrifices, and vows. The satire is directed at Jonah who, by the end of this chapter, appears self-centered, lazy, hypocritical, and altogether inferior to the wonderful sailors now above him (literally too, in the boat on the surface). Jonah's behavior is particularly outrageous in the light of other narratives about Israelite prophets, such as Isaiah, who dares to go barefoot and naked for three years just to get his message out (Isaiah 20); Jeremiah, who courageously faces his enemies (e.g., Jeremiah 36); and Ezekiel, who when reviled refuses to stop preaching (Ezek 33:30–33).

Jonah certainly is not (yet) in the great company of these prophets.[91] Yet he is unable to escape the mercy of Yahweh—not by flight (1:3), not by "deep sleep" (1:5–6), and, as the next chapter will demonstrate, not by drowning (2:1 [ET 1:17]). The love of Yahweh that seeks out even evil Nineveh will not be thwarted, and neither will he let go of his prophet.

The second scene in the narrative (1:4–16) also suggests a pattern in the usage of terms for God. "Yahweh" is the covenant name of God, revealed to his redeemed people. It is "Yahweh" who calls his prophet (1:1–3). Elohim (translated "God," "god," or "gods," depending on the context) is used for the gods of the non-Israelite sailors (1:5) and is the term used by their captain for Jonah's "God" (twice in 1:6). The sailors hear about "Yahweh" from Jonah

---

[90] Greenberg, *Biblical Prose Prayer*, 16.

[91] Compare "the goodly fellowship of the prophets" in the Te Deum (*LSB* 223).

(1:9) and by 1:14–16 they are praying to and worshiping "Yahweh." Jonah's confession (1:9) connects the two terms when he identifies "Yahweh" as the Elohim ("God") who made the sea and the dry land. These important changes in terms for the divine prepare us for the nuances in the rest of the book, especially with the Piel of the verb מָנָה, "to provide, appoint," which has as its subject "Yahweh" in 2:1; "Yahweh God" in 4:6; "(the) God" in 4:7; and "God" in 4:8.

There are Jonah-like people in the NT who exhibit a kind of spiritual myopia. They have trouble seeing that the grace of God the Father in his Son, Jesus, is for all peoples. Admission into God's kingdom is free for anyone by grace alone, regardless of one's past sins or ethnicity. God's welcome goes out to all, "both the bad and the good" (Mt 22:10). One example of the Jonah mindset is a leader of the synagogue who wants to keep the letter of the Law instead of rejoicing in a woman made whole by Jesus' word and touch (Lk 13:10–17). To mention just one more example, Paul confronts Peter when he refuses to eat with Gentile Christians (Gal 2:11–14). "As so often," writes Allen, "the effect of this OT book [Jonah] is to lay a foundation upon which the NT can build."[92]

---

[92] Allen, *Joel, Obadiah, Jonah and Micah*, 194.

Excursus

Yahweh, the Creator God

The narrative of Jonah—from beginning to end—asserts that Yahweh has created, governs, and cares for all of creation. The opening formula of 1:1 (וַיְהִי, sometimes translated "and it came to pass") and the reference to Jonah in 2 Ki 14:25–28 link the narrative of Jonah with similar events involving the creation in 1–2 Kings, a single Hebrew book that contains a high concentration of miracle stories connected with prophets.[1] The list is impressive. In Elijah's ministry, ravens bring him food (1 Ki 17:1–7); bread and oil multiply (1 Ki 17:8–16); fire and rain appear (1 Kings 18); and wind, an earthquake, and fire are manifest (1 Ki 19:11–12). In Elisha's ministry, fire comes down from heaven (2 Ki 1:10, 12); the Jordan is parted, and he witnesses a whirlwind carrying Elijah to heaven (2 Ki 2:1–14); water is purified (2 Ki 2:19–22); bears kill young boys (2 Ki 2:23–24); oil is multiplied (2 Ki 4:1–7); stew is purified (2 Ki 4:38–41); bread is multiplied (2 Ki 4:42–44); and an ax head floats (2 Ki 6:1–7).

The Jonah narrative includes miraculous events involving a storm, a great fish, a qiqayon plant, a worm, and a scorching east wind. Thus it fits well with the numerous narratives in 1–2 Kings that describe Yahweh as one who, through his prophets, is intimately involved in his creation. Jonah's confession of "Yahweh, the God of the heavens … who made the sea and the dry land" at the midpoint of the storm scene illustrates this point (Jonah 1:9).[2] This verse places Jonah in the mainstream of the OT's confession about Yahweh as the Creator.[3] The content of Jonah's confession is essentially the same as that in the First Article of the Apostles' Creed ("I believe in God, the Father Almighty, maker of heaven and earth") and the Nicene Creed ("I believe in one God, the Father Almighty, maker of heaven and earth and of all things visible and invisible").

Perhaps the most obvious tenet of the doctrine of Yahweh in Jonah is that after creating the heavens and the earth, Yahweh has not retired from the world. He controls all creatures, both the largest (a great fish, 2:1 [ET 1:17]) and the smallest (a worm, 4:7). The action begins with Yahweh hurling a great wind upon the vast sea (1:4) and ends as he again sends a wind, this time directed at Jonah (4:8). His care for creation is poignantly expressed in the last words of the book: "a great number of animals" (4:11).

Unfortunately, the practice of regarding history as the chief point of orientation for the OT—while marginalizing Yahweh's actions in, with, and for his creation—has governed its interpretation for the last one hundred years, if

---

[1] See the first textual note and the commentary on 1:1.

[2] See "Introduction to Jonah 1."

[3] For example, Genesis 1–2; 14:19; Deut 32:6; 2 Ki 19:15; Is 42:5; 45:12, 18; Mal 2:10; Pss 121:2; 146:5–6.

not longer. The rise of Darwin's theory of evolution no doubt contributed to the skeptical marginalization of creation by scholars in the last century. The emphasis on history at the expense of creation has made its way into almost all modern literature about OT Israel. This has been the case inside the guild of biblical scholarship, where commentaries and theologies alike have been based on this premise. But it has also been embraced and promoted by ancient Near Eastern and comparative scholars outside the OT field, whose broader perspective, one might have thought, would have provided a vantage point to question the traditional, but artificial, split between history and creation. In the early 1960s James Barr observed:

> No single principle is more powerful in the handling of the Bible today than the belief that history is the channel of divine revelation. ...

> Historians of theology in a future age will look back on the mid-twentieth century and call it the revelation-in-history period.[4]

The scholarship of Gerhard von Rad (1901–1971) is one of the main reasons why the historical paradigm governed the study of the OT, while the larger realm of creation was relegated to the background and assigned a marginal status. In 1936 von Rad published "The Theological Problem of the Old Testament Doctrine of Creation."[5] In this essay, he demonstrates his great debt to Karl Barth, while Barth, for his part, postulated a dialectical theology that grew out of his antagonism between revelation and natural theology.[6]

Influenced by Barth, von Rad believed that creation "performs only an ancillary function. ... It is but a magnificent foil for the message of salvation."[7] The OT's focus is upon what Yahweh does in *history*, as distinct from what he may do in *nature*. As such, von Rad excluded nature as a central arena of Yahweh's concern and care. He identified as Israel's earliest creeds passages like Deut 6:20–24; 26:5–10; and Josh 24:1–13 that supposedly were the nation's core confession.[8] These texts say nothing about creation.

Von Rad's work became the foundation for the slogan "God's mighty deeds in history," which was taken up in the United States chiefly by George Ernest Wright. For Wright too, the natural world played a decidedly peripheral role in biblical thought; he called it "a handmaiden, a servant of history."[9] Wright's

---

[4] Barr, "Revelation through History in the Old Testament and in Modern Theology," 193–94.

[5] Von Rad, "The Theological Problem of the Old Testament Doctrine of Creation," in *The Problem of the Hexateuch and Other Essays*.

[6] Brueggemann discusses the relationship between Barth and von Rad in *The Book That Breathes New Life*, 83–84.

[7] Von Rad, "The Theological Problem of the Old Testament Doctrine of Creation," 134. In his last book before his death, *Wisdom in Israel* (Nashville: Abingdon, 1972), von Rad gives a more prominent place to creation theology.

[8] Von Rad, "The Form-Critical Problem of the Hexateuch."

[9] Wright, *God Who Acts*, 43. Wright's work is continuous with Karl Barth's rejection of "religion."

main thesis was that Yahweh is sui generis and has nothing in common with the gods and goddesses of Canaan. He wrote: "God is known and addressed primarily in the terms which relate him to society and to history. The language of nature is distinctly secondary."[10] More recently, Horst Dietrich Preuss affirmed that emphasis: "Yahwistic faith is primarily election faith on which is based faith in salvation." He supposed that creation theology, like the religious festivals, "belonged to the elements of the piety of a sedentary civilization which were later assigned to Yahwistic faith."[11] He saw creation as an add-on and therefore not central to Israel's kerygma.

The view of creation as peripheral has spread beyond the borders of OT scholarship. It is found, for example, in the writings of the great comparative scholar Mircea Eliade.[12] He believed that when Israel first began writing her history, she transcended or left behind the world of nature. In this transcendence, Israel's society emerged, as Eliade put it, "from the paradise of animality (i.e., from nature)."[13]

This historical paradigm for interpreting OT texts and understanding Israel's faith rests on four claims: (1) that history is a category distinct from creation and nature; (2) that OT religion is grounded in history rather than the creation; (3) that Israel's religion in this regard was different from other ancient religions, which were grounded in creation; and (4) that the OT's unique historical consciousness was an advance in the evolution of human thought. But these assumptions contain a fatal flaw: they all are based on the cultural worldview of modern OT interpreters rather than the worldview of ancient Israel.[14]

The assumption that history and the creation are distinct categories of thought appears to depend most directly on the idealistic philosophical tradition as it was articulated by G. W. F. Hegel. As did the great idealists before him, Hegel divided the world into two metaphysically distinct orders, the spiritual and the material, and he used these dualistic categories to explain the history of religion. The oldest religions of the ancient Near East, according to Hegel, could be assigned to the material side of this ledger in that they identified God directly with the creation. The religion of Israel, by contrast, could be assigned to the spiritual side, since it separated Yahweh from the creation and connected him instead with humanity, spiritual individuality, and freedom, that is, with historical existence. In Israelite religion, according to Hegel, "Man is

---

[10] Wright, *God Who Acts*, 49.

[11] Preuss, *Old Testament Theology*, 1:237.

[12] This section follows a paper delivered at the annual meeting of the Society of Biblical Literature in Atlanta, Ga., on November 23, 2003, by Theodore Huebert entitled "Beyond *Heilsgeschichte*."

[13] Eliade, *The Myth of the Eternal Return*, 155.

[14] Brueggemann discusses the *zeitgeist* of Barth and von Rad in which they developed their theology in *The Book That Breathes New Life*, 62–63.

exalted above all else in the whole creation,"[15] while "Nature is represented as thus entirely negated, in subjection, transitory."[16]

Another assumption that frequently functioned to reinforce this distinction between history and nature arose from Albrecht Alt in his essays in the 1920s and 1930s. Alt linked the distinctive characteristics of Israel's life and thought with Israel's desert beginnings. In his analysis "The God of the Fathers," Alt claimed that the link between Yahweh and the creation was broken in Israel's early desert experience. He wrote:

> The seeds of a completely different development from that of local and nature gods were implanted at the very inception of the cult: the god was not tied to a greater or lesser piece of earth, but to human lives, first that of an individual, and then through him to those of a whole group. ... The gods of this type of religion show a concern with social and historical events.[17]

Because of this marginalization of creation, the creation account in Genesis has customarily been identified as a prologue to what follows. Von Rad thought that the "pre-patriarchal history" in Genesis 1–11 was added last and derived "from a totally different sphere of culture and religion" than the indigenous Israelite sagas of the patriarchs and Moses, which followed.[18] Nahum Sarna's comments in the introduction to his Genesis commentary are representative: "The theme of Creation, important as it is, serves merely as an introduction to the book's central motif: God's role in history. The opening chapters are a prologue to the historical drama that begins in chapter 12."[19] Each of these interpreters clearly had a history-centered paradigm: creation is alien to—and the mere prologue for—the real historical religion of the patriarchs and Moses.

However, this dichotomy between spirit and matter is not part of the conceptual framework of the OT. God created people as whole living beings with a physical body and soul or spirit. Moreover, God remains active in history as he preserves and redeems his people. Toward the end of his life, von Rad recognized this problem: "The Old Testament draws no such distinction between Nature and history."[20]

The formulations of von Rad, Wright, and others began to unravel in the 1970s. One reason for this dismantling was the work of James Barr, who wrote a book that sent seismic shocks throughout the *Heilsgeschichte* movement.[21] In it, he suggests that the etymological word studies upon which much of this

---

[15] Hegel, *Lectures on the Philosophy of Religion*, 2:198.

[16] Hegel, *Lectures on the Philosophy of Religion*, 2:189.

[17] Alt, "The God of the Fathers," 54–55.

[18] Von Rad, "The Form-Critical Problem of the Hexateuch," 63–65.

[19] Sarna, *Genesis*, xiv.

[20] Von Rad, "Some Aspects of the Old Testament World-View," 155.

[21] Barr, *The Semantics of Biblical Language*.

interpretation had been based were methodologically weak. Brevard Childs also assisted in this deconstruction. In a series of studies, he made the case that reliance on history alone is an untenable approach to the OT.[22] And in 1971 Claus Westermann composed a seminal essay that argued for a more balanced view of creation in OT theology.[23] He wrote: "The acting of God in creation and his acting in history stand in relation to one another in the Old Testament; the one is not without the other. … Creation and history arise out of the same origin and move toward the same goal."[24]

Another voice in this growing chorus was that of Frank Moore Cross. In his influential book *Canaanite Myth and Hebrew Epic*,[25] Cross argued that Israel's faith is a combination of creational and redemptive ideas. Rather than posit an "either/or" between these two modes of expression, Cross offered a "both/and" approach. Yahweh is not just the enactor of historical deeds in Israel. He is also the one who ordered and commanded all of reality. Redemptive acts have creational ends.

More recently, Terence Fretheim in *God and World in the Old Testament: A Relational Theology of Creation* has argued for not putting asunder what Yahweh has joined together—his concern for his creation and his actions in history. According to Fretheim, the fact "that the Bible begins with Genesis, not Exodus, with creation, not redemption, is of immeasurable importance in understanding all that follows."[26] Key to Fretheim's view of creation is that Yahweh is a relational Creator who has made a relational world: "The world could be imaged as a giant spiderweb. Every creature is in relationship with every other, such that any act reverberates out and affects the whole, shaking the entire web in varying degrees of intensity." Fretheim points out that humans are so deeply interconnected with the rest of the creation that human sin has a devastating effect upon the whole world.[27] Some examples of this interconnectedness include the ground bringing forth thorns and thistles after Adam and Eve fell into sin (Gen 3:17–18); the world being inundated by a flood as a result of rampant sin (Genesis 6–8); Sodom and Gomorrah becoming an ecological disaster because of wickedness (Gen 13:10–13; 19:24–28); the plagues on Egypt as a result of Pharaoh's genocidal policies (Exodus 7–11); and the prophetic linking of human sin with cosmic deterioration (e.g., Jer 4:22–26; Hos 4:1–3).

---

[22] For example, Brevard S. Childs, *Biblical Theology in Crisis* (Philadelphia: Westminster, 1970), and *Biblical Theology of the Old and New Testaments: Theological Reflection on the Christian Bible* (Minneapolis; Fortress, 1992).

[23] Westermann, "Creation and History in the Old Testament." Westermann's other discussions on this theme include *Creation* (trans. John J. Scullion; Philadelphia: Fortress, 1974) and *Elements of Old Testament Theology* (trans. Douglas W. Scott; Atlanta: John Knox, 1982).

[24] Westermann, "Creation and History in the Old Testament," 24, 34.

[25] Cross, *Canaanite Myth and Hebrew Epic: Essays in the History of the Religion of Israel* (Cambridge, Mass.: Harvard University Press, 1973).

[26] Fretheim, *God and World in the Old Testament*, xiv.

[27] Fretheim, *God and World in the Old Testament*, 173.

Fretheim maintains that the Hebrew noun צְדָקָה ("righteousness") refers to a harmonious world order built by Yahweh into the infrastructure of creation. He builds upon the work of Hans Heinrich Schmid, who argued that צְדָקָה is centered on the idea of order (*Weltordnung*). Schmid understands this as the right ordering of the world, which brings about *shalom* and well-being for the entire created order. This means that wherever righteousness is practiced by human beings in the sociopolitical sphere, that act is in tune with creation and therefore fosters the proper integration of social and cosmic orders. Conversely, when righteousness is not practiced, creation is impacted in negative ways (cf. e.g., Amos 4:6–11; 5:7). Justice, righteousness, politics, and creation are therefore interrelated as aspects of one comprehensive divine order.[28]

Fretheim points out that what Yahweh does in redemption is in the service of his endangered creation. For example, the deliverance of Israel is for the sake of all creation (Ex 9:16). What is at stake is Yahweh's mission for the world (Ex 9:29; 19:5). This means that Yahweh's redemptive activity on behalf of Israel is not an end in itself; it stands in the service of the entire creation.[29]

In many ways, creation provides the point of orientation for Israel's existence, and thus also for the church's faith and life. It is not peripheral, but foundational. For example, as Fretheim notes, creation theology is built into the structure of Exodus. This reality can be seen in the parallels between Exodus and Genesis 1–9:[30]

1. A creational setting (compare Ex 1:7 to Gen 1:28)
2. Anticreational activity (compare Exodus 1–2 to Genesis 3–6)
3. Noah (Gen 6:9–9:17) and Moses (Ex 2:1–10; 25:1; 33:12)
4. The flood (Genesis 7) and the plagues (Exodus 7–11) as ecological disasters
5. Death and deliverance in and through water, with cosmic implications (compare Genesis 6–9 to Exodus 14–15; cf. 1 Pet 3:18–22)
6. The covenant with Noah (Gen 9:8–17) and Abraham (Gen 15:9–21; 17:1–27) and the Sinai covenant with divine promises and signs (Exodus 19–24) and the restatement of the covenant (Ex 34:10)

The tabernacle (Exodus 25–40) also mirrors the days of creation, and thus creation plays a major role in Israel's construction of the tabernacle.[31] The express reason Yahweh gives in Ex 20:11 and 31:17 for Israel's observance of the Sabbath is the six-day creation of the world. This means that the worship of Yahweh at the tabernacle, especially on the Sabbath, is a God-given way for the community to participate in Yahweh's ongoing re-creation of the world. This means of worship anticipated Christ's all-availing, once-for-all atone-

---

[28] Fretheim, *God and World in the Old Testament*, xiii, citing Schmid, "Creation, Righteousness, and Salvation."

[29] Fretheim, *God and World in the Old Testament*, 110.

[30] Fretheim, *God and World in the Old Testament*, 111–12. The following parallels come, in large part, from Fretheim. Cf. Balentine, *The Torah's Vision of Worship*, 63–77, 136–41.

[31] See Fretheim, *God and World in the Old Testament*, 128–31.

ment, which provides an eternal Sabbath rest for all believers (Hebrews 3–10). As Fretheim notes, Israel's tabernacle was "a microcosm of creation" redeemed and restored (cf., e.g., Is 66:1–2; Pss 11:4; 78:69). "It is the world order as God intended, writ small in Israel."[32]

All of this means that disregard for Yahweh's creation, so heavily dependent on the Hegelian dualism of spirit and matter, is antithetical to the faith of the OT. Speaking about Yahweh in the language of "history" as opposed to "creation" is not being faithful to the biblical text. Rather, we must understand Yahweh's redemptive acts in history as his way to restore his creatures and bring about his new creation, which ultimately is in Christ (2 Cor 5:17; Gal 6:15; Revelation 21–22). His work in creating the universe provides the foundation for his work in redemption. And what he does in redemption is to serve his eschatological goal for his corrupted, dying creation. The God of creation and the God of the Gospel are not two gods, but one. All three articles of the Creed confess one and the same God: Father, Son, and Holy Spirit. The God who created the world also redeemed his fallen creatures in the person of his Son, Jesus Christ, who brings the forgiveness of sins and life everlasting.

Yahweh is the Hebrew name of the God who made the heavens and the sea and the dry land (Jonah 1:9). The entire creation is at Yahweh's bidding throughout the narrative of Jonah. He employs creatures (a great fish and qiqayon plant) as his means to deliver his grace and mercy to Jonah. He has compassion upon people as well as upon animals (4:11). Even the pagan mariners and Ninevites are spared after they repent and believe in him.

In the incarnation of Jesus Christ, Yahweh joins creation to history in his most profound way. In the hypostatic union, the two natures in Christ continue in their integrity—his divine nature from eternity and his human nature, which he assumed when he was conceived by the Holy Spirit of the Virgin Mary.[33] From the moment of his conception on, Jesus is and will be forever both fully and true God and fully and true man. The eternal Word has taken on flesh (Jn 1:1, 14), and he alone, "the only-begotten God," has revealed the unseen Father (Jn 1:18).

In 1524 Andreas Karlstadt, one of Luther's companions, opposed the reformer by teaching that Christians must detach themselves from earthly, created things. In the framework of such a theology, Karlstadt taught that the Eucharist did not give an objective assurance of the forgiveness of sins because,

---

[32] Fretheim, *God and World in the Old Testament*, 128. In *Creation and the Persistence of Evil*, Levenson states (p. 86):

> The function of these correspondences [between Genesis 1–2 and Exodus 25–40] is to underscore the depiction of the sanctuary as a world, that is, an ordered, supportive, and obedient environment, and the depiction of the world as a sanctuary, that is, a place in which the reign of God is visible and unchallenged, and his holiness is palpable, unthreatened, and pervasive.

[33] The Athanasian Creed is especially concerned to explain the relationship between the divine and human natures in the one person of Jesus Christ, the second person of the Trinity. One may also see Martin Chemnitz, *The Two Natures in Christ* (trans. J. A. O. Preus; St. Louis: Concordia, 1971; originally published in 1578).

as a part of this creation, it is unable to touch the depth of the soul. Luther refuted this divorce between creation and redemption in his writing *Wider die himmlischen Propheten von den Bildern und Sakrament*.[34] In this treatise, the reformer teaches that the Father works through the flesh of his Son to give us the Spirit and new life. This is the fundamental means of his activity. In another context, Luther writes: "The Spirit cannot be with us in any other way than by physical things, such as the Word, the water [Baptism], the body of Christ [the Supper], and his saints on earth."[35] This is because "the body and flesh of Christ accord well with the Spirit; they even constitute the physical home of the Spirit, and by them the Spirit comes to others."[36]

At his second coming, the risen Lord Jesus will usher in the consummation of this world and its history. All unbelievers will perish eternally in hell. All believers in Christ will enter the new creation in which righteousness dwells, the paradise we shall inhabit forever.[a] Thus "the creation itself will be freed from its bondage to decay into the freedom of the glory of the children of God" (Rom 8:21). How could we hope for anything less from the One whose comprehensive concern in the narrative of Jonah concludes with "a great number of animals" (4:11)? Christ's incarnation, in which he assumed our human nature and took on our flesh and blood, holds the promise of our full redemption, which he secured by his atonement on the cross and guaranteed by his bodily resurrection. Paul writes: "For in this hope we were saved" (Rom 8:24). This hope acknowledges the triune God as Creator and Savior, who will in Jesus Christ restore his creatures and make all things new (Rev 21:1–7).

Creation and redemption must be distinguished from each other, but never divorced. Throughout the narrative of Jonah, Yahweh displays his concern for his creatures. He repeatedly employs parts of his creation as "means of grace."[37] To his prophet Jonah, he brings deliverance through the great fish (2:1 [ET 1:17]) and relief through the qiqayon plant (4:6), and through his prophet's confession (1:9) and preaching (3:4), he brings salvation for the sailors and Ninevites. Even so, through the book of Jonah, he continues to call for repentance and faith and to save all who repent and believe in the one true God.

(a) See, e.g., 1 Thess 4:13–5:11; 2 Thess 1:5–12; 2 Pet 3:1–13; Rev 20:11–22:5

---

[34] *Against the Heavenly Prophets in the Matter of Images and Sacraments* (1525; WA 18.37–214; AE 40:73–223).

[35] Luther, *That These Words of Christ, "This Is My Body," Etc., Still Stand Firm against the Fanatics* (1527; WA 23.193.31–33; cf. AE 37:95).

[36] WA 23.195.3–5 (cf. AE 37:95).

[37] "Means of grace" refers to means through which God works repentance, creates faith, and bestows the forgiveness of sins and eternal life. In the NT God promises to accomplish these as he works through his Word and the Sacraments, Baptism and the Lord's Supper. One may see, for example, 1 Pet 3:18–22, where St. Peter uses a sacramental hermeneutic to connect the salvation of Noah and his family in the ark with the salvation in the risen Christ bestowed in Christian Baptism. Since there are many parallels between the narratives of Noah and Jonah, perhaps the apostle could have cited Jonah in the fish instead of Noah in the ark. See further "Jonah and Noah" in the introduction.

Excursus

Mission in the Old Testament

The worldwide focus in Jonah is evident already in 1:2. The narrative begins with a declaration of Yahweh's concern for far-off "Nineveh, the great city," indicating that he is a God who cares about the great cities and nations of the world. This missional thrust in Jonah is not unique in its context in the Book of the Twelve Minor Prophets. For example, Amos declares Yahweh's claim upon the nations of the world (Amos 1–2), and Obadiah delivers a prophetic oracle about Edom. This same international horizon is also evident in Micah (1:2; 4:1–5; 5:4; 7:16–17) and Nahum, where the spotlight is once again on Nineveh.

Yet generally speaking, most Christians believe that God's concern for all peoples and the Great Commission to all nations began only at the end of the Gospels (Mt 28:18–20; Mk 16:15; Lk 24:44–49; Jn 20:21). But Yahweh's concern for the nations did not begin in the NT, nor does it start in the Book of the Twelve. Rather, his gracious love toward all humanity extends all the way back to Genesis, beginning with the first Gospel promise (Gen 3:15), and forward through Malachi, then through Revelation. By taking a closer look at pivotal OT missional texts, this discussion will show that Jonah is not a soloist trying to be heard above the clatter and noise of discordant non-missional voices. Rather, he is a member of a great choir of missionary voices.

From Creation to the Patriarchs

The first selection of mission texts begins with creation and extends through Yahweh's call to Abram, Isaac, and Jacob.

The first issue of the Great Commission is usually considered to be the promise recorded in Gen 12:1–3:[1]

> Yahweh said to Abram, "Go from your land, from your kin, and from your father's household, to the land that I will show you. I will make you into a great nation, and I will bless you; I will make your name great, and you, be a blessing! I will bless those who bless you, and whoever curses you I will curse; and all families[2] of the earth will be blessed[3] through you."

---

[1] See the discussion of Gen 12:1–3 by Piper, *Let the Nations Be Glad! The Supremacy of God in Missions*, 167–70.

[2] This Great Commission has a family focus that eschews individualism. See the definition of מִשְׁפָּחָה in Meyers, "The Family in Early Israel," 13. For a complete study on מִשְׁפָּחָה, see Bendor, *The Social Structure of Ancient Israel*.

[3] For a discussion of the translation of the Niphal verb וְנִבְרְכוּ as a passive ("be blessed") rather than a reflexive ("bless themselves"), see Filbeck, *Yes, God of the Gentiles, Too*, 62–63. God's promise that all the families of the earth will be blessed through Abram and his Seed is stated in five passages in Genesis (12:3; 18:18; 22:18; 26:4; 28:14). Three of the passages

These verses contain a threefold promise. First, there is the promise of land for Abram and his descendants. Second, his descendants will form a great nation. Third, Abram will be the source of blessing for all the families of the earth. Essential parts of this threefold promise will be repeated later in Gen 18:18; 22:18; 26:4; 28:14. Thus Abram and his children are to be a leaven among the nations, a wellspring of living water, a constant invitation for the Gentiles to learn of the saving deeds of Yahweh. *The seed of Abram is Yahweh's missionary to the world.*

Building on the earlier excursus "Yahweh, the Creator God," we note here that Gen 12:1–3 comes after the creation and subsequent narratives of Genesis 1–11. Creation is the rightful foundation for the subsequent history of Israel. The promises to Abram are linked to creation by means of the land referred to in 12:1. Yahweh's blessing is going to come to the nations through physical, creational means, in the land Abram is promised. Gen 12:1–3 is also closely tied to the breakup of the human race into many nations in Genesis 10–11. Sinful human hubris (the tower of Babel) fractured humanity, but Yahweh's blessing will reunite humanity.[4] Gen 12:1–3 repeats two key words from those chapters that were used to describe the breakup: גּוֹי, often translated "nation" (Gen 10:5, 20, 31, 32; 12:2), and מִשְׁפָּחָה, usually translated "family" or "clan" (Gen 10:5, 18, 20, 31, 32; 12:3). In Gen 22:18, when Yahweh repeats the promise "all families of the earth will be blessed through you" (Gen 12:3) to Abraham, he uses גּוֹי, "nation," instead of מִשְׁפָּחָה, "family": "In your seed all the nations of the earth will be blessed."[5] When he passes on the promise to Isaac (Gen 26:4) he again uses גּוֹי, "nation." But when he reiterates the promise to Jacob he uses מִשְׁפָּחָה, "clan" (Gen 28:14). These various wordings of the promise, using both terms, indicate that Yahweh's blessing through Abraham is for every size of group, from family to clan to nation. No group, no matter how small or large, is to be overlooked or excluded from being blessed through Abraham and his seed.

The verb "to bless" (בָּרַךְ) in Gen 12:2–3 offers still another link between Abram and earlier creation texts in Genesis. "Bless" is the antonym of the verb

---

(12:3; 18:18; 28:14) use the Niphal of בָּרַךְ, "to bless," and two (22:18; 26:4) have the Hithpael, which likely has the same passive meaning or a closely related meaning (e.g., "acquire blessing"). It is significant that in all five of those passages, the promise is rendered as a passive in the Samaritan Pentateuch, the Babylonian (Onkelos) Targum, and the Jerusalem (Pseudo-Jonathan) Targum. All citations of these verses in intertestamental literature as well as in the NT are in the passive. The LXX translates the verb as a future passive (ἐνευλογηθήσονται), and this, in turn, is how it is understood in the NT. See, for example, Acts 3:25: καὶ ἐν τῷ σπέρματί σου [ἐν]ευλογηθήσονται πᾶσαι αἱ πατριαὶ τῆς γῆς. (The promise is also quoted in Gal 3:8.) The promise expressed by the passive verb is therefore totally a gift—not something people perform, but receive from God.

[4] A traditional reading for Pentecost is Gen 11:1–9. There humanity was separated into many nations and languages, but on Pentecost, humanity is reunited by the one Gospel of Jesus Christ that is proclaimed in many languages (Acts 2).

[5] God's restatement of the promise in Gen 18:18 uses גּוֹי as well.

"curse" (אָרַר) used in the curse universally placed on creation because of the first sin (Gen 3:14–19). This blessing through Abram and his seed is the solution to the curse brought upon humanity by Adam and Eve. Just as the curse is universal in its effects, bringing death upon the whole creation, so is the blessing to be the universal cure, bringing justification and eternal life for all in Christ (Rom 5:12–21).

The nations are to be blessed in Abram's seed,[6] the same seed of the woman (Gen 3:15) and the seed of Shem, in whose tents Yahweh dwells (Gen 9:27). This one seed is realized through a succession of representatives who are down payments until Christ himself comes in that same line as the consummation (Rom 9:4–5; Gal 3:5–16). The curse affects the human race universally, but no less extensive in its healing potential is the promised antidote offered by God in Christ. All baptized believers in Christ are sons of Abraham and heirs of all God's gracious promises (Gal 3:26–29).

The connections between Genesis 1–11 and 12:1–3 indicate that it is incorrect to say that Abram was the first to receive the message that God targets all peoples to receive the Gospel. Genesis 1–11 is far from having a nationalistic, Israelite focus. It is one of the most universal sections of the Bible, ending with a list in Genesis 10 of seventy nations—the very "families" (Gen 12:3) and "all the nations of the earth" (Gen 22:18) that will receive the blessing from Yahweh through Abram and his seed according to the promise.

Yet the call of Abram and the promises of the Abrahamic covenant present a different missionary strategy from the one we see in the NT. Rather than send his evangelists and witnesses out to the far-flung corners of the earth (as the risen Christ does in, e.g., Acts 1:8), in the patriarchal narratives, God sets a mission station in the midst of the nations for all to see. If the model in the NT is centrifugal, with God sending his missionaries out from the center at Jerusalem, then the model presented in Gen 12:1–3 is centripetal, with God drawing all peoples in toward the center—the land where Abraham and his seed dwell.

Beginning in Genesis 12, Israel is to live between the extremes of syncretism and isolationism. She is not to become like the nations, nor is she to withdraw from being an active witness to the nations. In 1 Sam 8:19–20 Israel seeks a king so that they might "be like all the other nations." Notorious kings like Solomon, Jeroboam son of Nebat, Ahab, and Ahaz led Israel into a syncretistic lifestyle. To the extent that Israel accommodated and adopted elements of the nations' pagan religions, she ceased to be an evangelistic witness to them. In Jonah, however, it is not syncretism, but Israel's nationalistic isolationism that threatens to quench her evangelistic flame. From the beginning to the end of the book, Jonah seeks to isolate himself from everyone else—even from Yahweh (1:3, 5, 12; 4:1–3, 5, 8–9)!

---

6   The term זֶרַע, "seed," occurs in the divine promises referring to Eve's "seed" in Gen 3:15 and the "seed" of Abraham in, for example, Gen 13:15–16; 15:5, 18; 17:7–10; 22:17–18; the "seed" of Isaac in Gen 26:3–4; and the "seed" of Jacob in Gen 28:4, 13–14.

From Moses to David

The next selection of texts traces how the missional promises in Genesis subsequently impact Israel at Mount Sinai and the Davidic dynasty proclaimed by the prophet Nathan. Moving to the book of Exodus and the events in Egypt and on Mount Sinai, we meet Moses, who is repeatedly described as one whom Yahweh "sent" (שָׁלַח, Ex 3:10–15; Deut 34:11; 1 Sam 12:8; Ps 105:26). Just as Yahweh sends his Word, which accomplishes that purpose for which it is sent (Is 55:10–11), so he sends a whole line of prophets after Moses (Deut 18:15–18) who preach his Word and accomplish what he intends (e.g., Is 6:8; Jer 1:7; Ezek 3:5–6). In fact, what distinguishes the true prophets from the false ones is that Yahweh has not "sent" the false prophets (Jer 14:14–15; 23:21; 28:15; Ezek 13:6), nor has his Word come to them (Deut 18:20; Ezek 13:7), for they "prophesy from their own hearts" (Ezek 13:17) or have been deceived by a "lying spirit" (see 1 Ki 22:19–23).

The verb "to send" (שָׁלַח), used for Yahweh sending prophets, beginning with Moses, lexically links the OT mission with that of the NT. It occurs over eight hundred times in the OT, and over two hundred times Yahweh is the subject. In the LXX, the verb ἀποστέλλω (the root of "apostle") translates three-fourths of these passages where Yahweh is the subject of שָׁלַח.[7] So Yahweh "sends" Moses to deliver his people out of Egypt, out of the house of slaves. This salvation is not for Israel's sake alone, but also for the nations. In Ex 9:14–16 Moses relates these words of Yahweh to Pharaoh:

> For this time I am sending all my plagues into your heart and against your servants and against your people, that you may know that there is no one like me in all the earth [בַּעֲבוּר תֵּדַע כִּי אֵין כָּמֹנִי בְּכָל־הָאָרֶץ]. For by now I could have stretched out my hand and struck you and your people with a plague so that you would have been wiped off from the earth. But for this purpose I have made you stand: that I might show you my power and in order to *proclaim my name in all the earth* [וּלְמַעַן סַפֵּר שְׁמִי בְּכָל־הָאָרֶץ].

Through Moses, Yahweh is here expressing the desire that the Egyptians might come to "know" (יָדַע)—here in its fullest covenantal sense of faith—that he is the only true God "in all the earth." Moreover, Yahweh's purpose is that his saving name be proclaimed "in all the earth," that all peoples might know his saving truth.

The plagues are effective demonstrations of power that bring at least some Egyptians to faith. When Israel leaves Egypt, "a great mixture" of people goes out with them (Ex 12:38). Given the background of the Egyptian religion with all of the gods symbolized by the very elements that were hit by the plagues, they announced Yahweh's victory over the deities and powers of Egyptian religion. In this way, Yahweh's name came to be proclaimed "in all the earth" (see also, e.g., Josh 2:9–11; Pss 76:8–9 [ET 76:7–8]; 106:7–45). The idols of

---

[7] See McDaniel, "Mission in the Old Testament," 12–13.

Egypt, as in every other nation, cult, or religion, are no match for the one and only living God.

The book of Exodus proclaims that God's election of Israel is his very means to bring salvation to all the nations. Ex 19:5–6 states: "Now if you truly listen to me and keep my covenant, then out of all nations you will be my treasured possession, for all the earth is mine. And you will be for me a kingdom of priests and a holy nation." Priests are mediators who not only receive God's gracious forgiveness themselves but also bring it to others through the divinely instituted worship they conduct. That is what Israel was to do for the other nations.

It is a common assumption that while Yahweh had already established his grace-based covenant with Abraham in Genesis 15, Yahweh's covenant with Israel on Sinai was Law-based and conditional.[8] In catechesis and proclamation we often hear something like this:[9] "The covenants Yahweh makes with Abraham (Gen 15:9–21) and David (2 Sam 7:4–17) are unconditional—no strings attached! On the other hand, the covenant made with Israel at Sinai (Ex 19:5–6) is just the opposite: it is conditional." The discussion continues: "And since Israel becomes the people of God at Sinai, her charter as a nation is based upon this conditional covenant; if they obey, then their status remains." The logic concludes with something like this: "Unable to keep the Sinaitic covenant, the Northern Kingdom is exiled in 722/721 and the Southern Kingdom in 587 BC." Then the lesson ends with this: "This is why we need the new covenant in Christ."

Advocates of that view may cite as proof the second Hebrew word of Ex 19:5–6: "Now *if* [אִם] you truly listen to me and keep my covenant, then ... you will be ..." If there is an "if" and "then," the relationship is based on Israel's ability to obey and keep Yahweh's covenant. Only "*if*" they do so, "then out of all the nations" they "will be my treasured possession" (Ex 19:5). This line of thinking means that the people of Israel *become* the people of God at Sinai and remain in this status of "treasured possession" only as long as they respond with obedience. In this way, what happens at Mount Sinai, along with its ad-

---

8   "Conditional" means that God would not fulfill his covenant promises unless the people fully obeyed the covenant's requirements; their disobedience would render the covenant null and void. Since people in this fallen state are sinful, it is not possible for any people not to sin, and any covenant that depended upon complete obedience could not be fulfilled. "Unconditional" means that God would fulfill his promises regardless of the extent to which the people responded with faith and obedience. By saying that God's covenants with Abraham, Israel at Sinai, and David were unconditional, this commentary means that God always remains true to his promises, all of which he fulfills in Christ (e.g., 2 Cor 1:18–20; 2 Tim 2:13). However, that these OT covenants were unconditional does not mean that all of the people received the promised benefits. Those individuals who responded to the covenant with disobedience and unbelief thereby excluded themselves from it. The same is true of the new covenant in Christ (e.g., 2 Tim 2:12).

9   The following discussion of the Sinai covenant is adapted from Reed Lessing, "What Really Happened at Sinai?" *Concordia Journal* 30 (2004): 288–89. Used by permission of *Concordia Journal*.

ditional features of the Ten Commandments (Ex 20:1–17), "smoke" and "fire," "lightnings" and "thunders" (Ex 19:16–19; 20:18), is understood as the OT covenant based on works, not grace—Law, not Gospel. That's why we need Jesus.

However, a closer reading of the Exodus narrative indicates that a relationship between Yahweh and Israel is already in place *before* Sinai, as witnessed by the recurring reference to "my people" (e.g., Ex 3:7, 10; 5:1). The people in Egypt are the inheritors of the promises given to their ancestors (Ex 3:15–17; 6:3–8), the covenant made not only with Abraham, but also with his descendants (Gen 17:7). "My covenant" in Ex 19:5 is a reference to Yahweh's covenant with the patriarchs, which is called "his/my covenant" in Ex 2:24; 6:4–5 and is the only covenant mentioned earlier in the Exodus narrative. This means the Sinai covenant is under the umbrella of the ancestral covenant.

Therefore, far from being a distinctly separate covenant that is conditional and Law-based, a far less comprehensive creative act occurs at Sinai—and this within an already existing covenant, that one made with Abraham. That is to say, Sinai is a closer specification of what was already entailed in Yahweh's unconditional promises made to the patriarchs in the book of Genesis. This understanding is made clear by Moses in Ex 32:13, where he appeals to the Abrahamic covenant in the wake of the breaking of the Sinai covenant (see also Lev 26:40–45; Deut 4:31; 9:27–28). In the Sinai covenant, Yahweh not only gives laws but also gives his sinful people the tabernacle, the priesthood, and the sacrifices that offer abundant provisions for the forgiveness of sins, that the people may receive his bountiful grace.

Since the covenant at Sinai reiterates the grace-based covenant with the patriarchs and does not establish, but reinforces Israel's existing relationship with Yahweh, which is created and sustained by grace alone, it too focuses upon Israel's calling to be Yahweh's missionary to the world. At Sinai the Israelites are distinctly marked and empowered to be evangelists. Put another way, Sinai is a matter of the people's *status* before God by grace, and also of their *vocation*. The flow of thought in Ex 19:5–6 therefore runs like this: "Listen to my voice and do what I command, and in so doing, you shall show yourselves to be the people I have chosen by grace to be mine. I will be your God and fulfill the promises I swore to your ancestors. The nations will see this relationship, and through your mediation some will become a part of my chosen people through faith."

This mandate reiterates the missional strategy already given to Abram in Gen 12:1–3. The clause "You will be for me a kingdom of priests" in Ex 19:6 is understood, then, as Yahweh's (re)commissioning of Israel to be the "go between" between him and the nations. This is already hinted at in Ex 4:22: "Then you will say to Pharaoh, 'This is what Yahweh says: Israel is my firstborn son." For Israel to be Yahweh's *first*born son implies that more children are on the way. These family members are the nations that will be blessed through Abraham and his seed (cf. Gal 3:16). In the OT era, foreigners received this blessing through faith and the OT covenantal means (chiefly circumcision and sacrificial worship at the sanctuary), while in the NT era incorporation takes place through Baptism into Christ and faith in him (e.g., Mt 28:19–20; Gal 3:26–29; Col 2:11–15).

So at Sinai, Israel's status and vocation are not constituted, but are repeated and renewed. In confirming the call to Abram in Gen 12:1–3, Israel at Sinai is once again called to be the channel through which the grace of Yahweh will come to all the nations. A vivid example of this mediating role is in Genesis 18, where Abraham intercedes before Yahweh on behalf of the cities of Sodom and Gomorrah (see also Gen 20:7). From this narrative Christopher Wright concludes:

> We are to intercede even for those we know are facing God's judgment. We are also to proclaim that judgment, but in the hope of the repentance and reprieve, in the spirit of Abraham and not Jonah.[10]

Another example of such priestly service on behalf of the nations is the letter of Jeremiah to the exiles in Babylon: "Seek the peace of the city [וְדִרְשׁוּ אֶת־שְׁלוֹם הָעִיר] to which I [Yahweh] have exiled you. Pray on its behalf to Yahweh" (Jer 29:7). There is more to this command than Yahweh giving the exiles a prudent, pragmatic policy for survival. Rather, it rings true to the authentic mission of the priestly people of God: to be the vehicle of Yahweh's שָׁלוֹם ("peace, wholeness") so that those outside the covenant, even the enemies of Israel, may be brought within. In Jeremiah's case, the enemy is Babylon; in Jonah's case, it is Nineveh.

This strategy finds one of its fulfillments in NT injunctions that Christians fulfill their priestly duty by praying for others, even their enemies (e.g., Mt 5:44; Lk 6:27, 35). The grounds are the same, namely, the redemptive desire and purposes of God in Jesus Christ, whose death reconciled us to God even when we were his enemies (Rom 5:10). As a "royal priesthood" (1 Pet 2:9), we are to pray "for all people," for God "wants all people to be saved and come to the knowledge of the truth" (1 Tim 2:1–4).

Paul himself engages in this intercessory ministry on behalf of the nations. He indicates that as did Abraham and OT Israel, he has a priestly calling to show forth to all the nations the steadfast love of the one true God. He states:

> I have written you boldly on some points, as if to remind you again, because of the grace given to me by God so that I am a minister of Christ Jesus to the Gentiles, *mediating as priest the Gospel of God*, so that the offering of the Gentiles might become acceptable [to God], sanctified by the Holy Spirit. (Rom 15:15–16; cf. Rev 1:6; 5:10)

Even though Israel denied her vocation as restated in the Sinaitic covenant and was a miserable missionary, the ancestral covenant persists throughout the OT era. Yahweh's promises continued even in the midst of the nation's lack of

---

[10] Wright, *An Eye for an Eye*, 126. Along these same lines, see Jer 29:7 and 1 Tim 2:1–4.

evangelistic zeal. Their status remained the same: "my people" (e.g., Hos 11:7–9). And so the Sinaitic covenant was not the covenant that constituted Israel as the people of Yahweh. Rather, the charter was with Abraham, and in this way, grace and mission remain grace and mission—even in the OT!

Building upon the Abrahamic and Sinaitic covenants is Yahweh's covenant with David. His promises to Abraham included eventual kings. This was stated in Gen 17:6, where Yahweh says to the patriarch, "And kings from you will go forth." Following the promise to David of the everlasting dynasty (2 Sam 7:4–17; see also 1 Chr 17:3–15), 2 Sam 7:18–19 states:

> Then King David went in and sat before Yahweh, and he said, "Who am I, O Lord Yahweh, and who is my house, that you have brought me this far? And as if this were too little in your sight, O Lord Yahweh, you have also spoken about the house of your servant in the distant future. Is this a law for the man, O Lord Yahweh?"

The phrase translated "a law for the man" (ESV: "instruction for mankind") is תּוֹרַת הָאָדָם.[11] Here it is best understood as referring to the decree about the Davidic dynasty Yahweh has established for the benefit of all people. This dynasty will culminate in the incarnate Son of God, who will suffer the punishment for the iniquity of all (cf. 2 Sam 7:14). "Lord Yahweh" (אֲדֹנָי יהוה, usually translated "Lord GOD") occurs seven times in 2 Sam 7:18–20, 22, 28–29. This compound of the divine name is used in the pivotal covenant Yahweh made with Abram in Gen 15:2, 8. It occurs in the historical books only seven other times,[a] but never again in 1 or 2 Samuel. Its repeated use in both the promise to Abram in Genesis 15 and in the Davidic covenant of promise in 2 Samuel 7 is too striking to be accidental and without special reason: the two covenants are thereby drawn into a closer relationship. Indeed, the Davidic covenant, just like the Sinaitic covenant, is founded upon the grace-based, missional covenant Yahweh first made with Abraham. The repeated use of "Lord Yahweh" plus the words תּוֹרַת הָאָדָם, "a law for the man," the charter for humanity in Christ, means that Yahweh's plan to bless all nations through Abraham and his seed continues with David and his dynasty. This plan would come to fruition in the "Son of David," the Savior of all humanity (Mt 1:1; cf. Lk 1:32, 69).

(a) Deut 3:24; 9:26; Josh 7:7; Judg 6:22; 16:28; 1 Ki 2:26; 8:53

Abraham, Moses, and David—the three pillars of the OT—are called to be involved in Yahweh's mission to the world. It is therefore not surprising that another high-water mark in the OT includes Yahweh's plan to bring the nations into a saving relationship with himself. In his dedicatory prayer for the temple, Solomon prays:

> As for the foreigner who is not from your people Israel but has come from a distant land on account of your name—for they will hear of your great name and your mighty hand and your outstretched arm—when he comes and prays toward this temple, then may you hear from heaven, your dwelling place, and

---

[11] For a full discussion of this phrase, see Kaiser, "The Blessing of David: A Charter for Humanity."

do all that the foreigner asks of you, so all the peoples of the earth may know your name and fear you, as do your people Israel, and know that your name is called over this house that I built. (1 Ki 8:41–43)

In this prayer, the son of David anticipates that Gentiles will come and worship Yahweh because of his name, power, and saving actions. Solomon expects that Yahweh will hear and respond to their prayers, just as he listens to and answers the prayers of the Israelites, and that these foreigners will fear and believe in the one true God.

Prophecies Both *against* and *for* the Nations

In the prophetic "oracles against the nations," these universal themes continue as Yahweh places his claim upon all the peoples of the earth. But the common designation "oracles *against* the nations" is somewhat of a misnomer, for these oracles are not simply "against" the nations, even if this is predominately the case. Several of these texts speak of Yahweh as one who "restores the fortunes" of some of these nations (e.g., Is 19:23–25; 23:17–19; Jer 46:26; 49:39). Therefore, it is more accurate to understand them (and their abbreviation, OAN) as "oracles *about* the nations." They speak of Yahweh's universal judgment, but also of how his grace is available to all.

The oracles about the nations comprise a major portion of the prophetic writings, so they must be considered to be a foundational genre for the prophetic office.[12] Despite the general neglect of these oracles, they are "a central form of prophetic speech which is so common that we must assume it to be a basic and integral part of the prophetic message and outlook."[13] An important part of being an OT prophet is to announce how the God of Israel is about to exercise his rule over all the nations.

As we have already seen, beginning with the patriarchs, the God who is "Creator of heaven and earth" (Gen 14:19) elects Abraham and his descendants to be his people, and so he makes himself the God of Israel. The oracles about the nations stress the first as well as the second part of that. The God of Israel is also the Creator of all. Yahweh is the living God who made everything, and he intends that all the nations stop looking toward their idols and instead look to him (e.g., Is 17:7–8).

Since oracles about the nations are in every prophetic book except Hosea,[14] we can easily choose any number of them for analysis. However Isaiah's

---

[12] Clements believes these oracles indicate the importance attached to the prophetic task of being "Yahweh's spokesman on international affairs" (*Prophecy and Tradition*, 64).

[13] Christianson, *Transformations of the War Oracle in Old Testament Prophecy*, 1. In the field of OT study, perhaps no material has been so neglected as these oracles (Smothers, "A Lawsuit against the Nations").

[14] Jonah contains one brief oracle against Nineveh (Jonah 3:4). The oracles about the nations constitute a much larger portion of most other prophetic books. They constitute almost one-fourth of the material in the Latter Prophets: Isaiah 7:3–16; 8:1–4; 10:5–34; 13–23; 34; 37:21–29; Jeremiah 25:15–38; 27:1–11; 46–51; Ezekiel 25–32; 35; 38–39; Joel 4:1–17 (ET 3:1–17); Amos 1:3–2:3; Obadiah; Micah 4:11–13; 5:4–5 (ET 5:5–6); 7:11–17; Nahum;

oracles about the nations may provide the best example of how prophets address the nations.[15] Isaiah 13–23 proclaims Yahweh's international authority. These chapters contain ten sections, each of which is labeled a מַשָּׂא, "burden" or "oracle," about a nation or a people:

- Isaiah 13:1–14:27: Babylon (and Assyria, 14:25)
- Isaiah 14:28–32: Philistia
- Isaiah 15–16: Moab
- Isaiah 17–18: Damascus (and Ephraim)
- Isaiah 19–20: Egypt (and Cush)
- Isaiah 21:1–10: "The Desert by the Sea"
- Isaiah 21:11–12: Dumah (Edom?)
- Isaiah 21:13–17: Arabia
- Isaiah 22: Jerusalem
- Isaiah 23: Tyre (and Sidon)

These ten sections proclaim the disasters Yahweh is about to inflict on different parts of the ancient Near East. Isaiah includes Jerusalem in the list and pairs it with a pagan city, Tyre. Jerusalem has acted like a pagan nation (גּוֹי) and therefore stands under God's judgment like the other nations.[16]

The narrative of Jonah in effect makes the same claim: at the start of the book, it is the Ninevites who have "evil" (1:2), but they repent and believe in God (3:5), whereas at the end of the book it is the Israelite Jonah who has "great evil" (4:1).

What is the God of Israel up to in Isaiah 13–23? Why devastate nation after nation? What are his divine purposes? Answers to these questions may be summarized in five ways. Yahweh purposes to

1. execute his wrath in order to eliminate sinners from the earth (Is 13:9; 14:21–23);
2. put an end to human pride and glory (Is 13:11; 14:11–17; 16:6–14; 21:16–17; 23:7–9);
3. defeat his enemies, thereby giving rest to his oppressed people and enabling the return of the exiles (Is 14:1–8, 25; 17:12–14);
4. draw the nations with their homage and tribute to Zion and Zion's messianic King (Is 16:1–5; 18:7; 23:17–18);
5. redirect all people away from their idols and toward himself (Is 17:7–8; 19:1, 16–25).

We see in the list above both Yahweh's alien work (*opus alienum*, condemnation by his Law) and his proper work (*opus proprium*, justification by his Gospel). His "alien" or "strange work," so named in Is 28:21, is to destroy

---

Habakkuk 2; Zeph 2:4–15; Hag 2:21–22; Zech 9:1–8; Mal 1:2–5. For a further discussion, see Raabe, "Why Prophetic Oracles against the Nations?"

[15] These comments on Isaiah 13–23 follow Raabe, "Look to the Holy One of Israel, All You Nations," 338–40, 349.

[16] Isaiah judges Israel and Jerusalem by including them in his list of foreign nations just as in Amos 1–2 and Zephaniah 2–3.

the wicked, debase the proud, and defeat tyranny. His proper work includes restoring Israel to Zion, while also reaching beyond Israel to encompass the nations. They too will look to Yahweh and come to Zion (e.g., Is 2:1–4). They too will be protected by Israel's Messiah (Is 16:3–5; cf. Is 7:14; 9:5–6 [ET 9:6–7]; 11:10). In fact, in Is 19:25 Yahweh calls Egypt "my people" and Assyria "the work of my hands," along with Israel as "my inheritance." Yahweh's ultimate goal is to bring all nations into fellowship with himself, and this fellowship will end the conflicts between nations. Even traditional enemies like Egypt and Assyria will become friends (Is 19:23; cf. Is 2:4).

The vision of all nations streaming to Zion in Isaiah 2 forms the backdrop for all of Isaiah, including chapters 13–23. Yahweh's ultimate purpose is to make Zion a centripetal force that draws all people to him. "No longer bringing the threat of destruction, foreign nations are here described as coming … to listen and to learn."[17]

This ultimate goal will reach its consummation at the parousia of Christ. Then Christ will gather his own from the four corners of the earth (Mk 13:27), and believers in him will come from all directions to the eschatological banquet (Lk 13:29). A great multitude from every nation will sing praise before the throne and the Lamb in Zion (Revelation 7 and 21). Heb 12:22–24 sets forth the fulfillment of Isaiah's Zion theology for the nations:

> But you have come to Mount Zion and to the city of the living God, the heavenly Jerusalem, and to innumerable angels in festal gathering, and to the assembly of the firstborn who are enrolled in heaven, and to God, the judge of all, and to the spirits of the righteous made perfect, and to Jesus, the mediator of a new covenant, and to the sprinkled blood that speaks a better word than the blood of Abel. (ESV)

Within Isaiah, his oracles about the nations reach their clearest definition in his Servant Songs (Is 42:1–7; 49:1–6; 50:4–9; 52:13–53:12). Is 42:1, 6 states:

> Here is my servant, whom I uphold, my chosen one, in whom I delight. I will put my Spirit on him, and he will bring forth justice to the nations [מִשְׁפָּט לַגּוֹיִם יוֹצִיא]. …

> I, Yahweh, have called you in righteousness. I will take hold of your hand. I will keep you, and I will make you to be a covenant for the people and a light for the nations [וְאֶתֶּנְךָ לִבְרִית עָם לְאוֹר גּוֹיִם].

In the second Servant Song, Is 49:6 states:

> He says: "It is too small a thing for you to be my servant to restore the tribes of Jacob and bring back the preserved ones of Israel. I will make you a light for the nations, that my salvation may be to the ends of the earth [וּנְתַתִּיךָ לְאוֹר גּוֹיִם לִהְיוֹת יְשׁוּעָתִי עַד־קְצֵה הָאָרֶץ].

The term "servant" (עֶבֶד) is used twenty times in Isaiah 40–53, exclusively in the singular, and eleven times in Isaiah 54–66, exclusively in the plural. This leads to the conclusion that the "servant" of Yahweh is a term that embodies at

---

17 Bartelt, *The Book around Immanuel*, 236.

one and the same time a reference to the Servant, Jesus Christ, who is the representative of the whole body of OT and NT believers, and the corporate whole that belongs to this single One.[18] In eleven of the twenty singular references, the servant is the whole nation of Israel.[b]

(b) Is 41:8–9; 42:19; 43:10; 44:1–2, 21; 45:4; 48:20

In the four Servant Songs, the Servant is an individual who ministers to Israel and also to the nations, and who sacrifices his life to atone for the sins of all, but emerges as the Victor (Is 42:1–7; 49:1–6; 50:4–9; and especially 52:13–53:12).

That the "servant" of Yahweh is both collective and individual is analogous to the "seed" of Abraham (e.g., Gen 22:17–18), which, in like manner, represents the whole by a singular collective term. This connection is made in Is 41:8, where Israel is called "my [Yahweh's] servant" who is at the same time "the seed of Abraham." In like manner, Moses uses the term "servant" for Abraham, Isaac, and Jacob in Ex 32:13; Deut 9:27, and all Israelites are Yahweh's "servants" in Lev 25:42, 55.

As further evidence of this individual/corporate nature of the servant, many of the titles or descriptions of the individual Servant in Isaiah 40–53 are matched by an identical or very similar ascription for Israel in Isaiah. For example:

Title or Description	Used of Individual	Used of All Israel
"My chosen"	42:1	41:8–9
"My servant"	49:3	44:21
"A light to the nations/peoples"	42:6; 49:6	51:4
"Called me from the womb"	49:1	44:2, 24

One of these descriptions for both the Servant and all Israel is "a light to the nations/peoples." Paul and Barnabas understand this as a reference to the One, who is the representative of the whole. In Acts 13:47 (quoting LXX Is 49:6), Paul declares: "For this is what the Lord has commanded us: 'I have made you [σε, singular] a light to the nations, that you [σε, singular] may be for salvation to the ends of the earth.' " Later in his ministry, Paul testifies before King Agrippa and affirms: "[I am] saying nothing outside of what the prophets and Moses said was going to happen" (Acts 26:22). Paul does not see himself as an innovator or as one who introduces meanings that were not already in the text. Therefore, his application of the words about the singular servant ("you") in Is 49:6 to himself and Barnabas ("us," plural) are in line with the plain assertion of the original OT meaning. Simeon's focus on the same phrase is not on the whole, but rather on the One. He takes the baby Jesus in his arms and declares that this child is "a light for revelation to the nations" (Lk 2:32). The corporate nature of the Servant is simultaneously the One and the many who believe in him.

---

[18] The same conclusion is reached in "The Identity of the Servant" in Mitchell, *Our Suffering Savior*, 24–40, which also draws on NT passages, particularly those in mission contexts.

Acts 1:8 builds upon three Servant allusions from Isaiah. First, the expression "to the end of the earth" is verbally identical to the Greek rendering of the same phrase in Is 49:6. Second, Jesus' instruction for the disciples to wait in Jerusalem until the coming of the Holy Spirit is closest to the wording of Is 32:15, where the destruction of Jerusalem is predicted "until the Spirit is poured upon us from on high and the desert becomes a fertile field." Yahweh echoes Is 32:15 in Is 44:3–4, where he promises to pour out his Spirit and blessing like rain upon a dry and thirsty land. And third, in Isaiah, Yahweh summons his servant Israel to be his witness (Is 43:8–12; 44:8).

Other prophets reiterate Isaiah's universal themes. Representative texts from them are as follows. In echoing Gen 12:3 and Yahweh's promise to Abram, Jeremiah in 4:1–2 indicates that Israel is Yahweh's instrument in and through which blessing will come to the nations. Jer 4:2 states: "And if you swear, 'As Yahweh lives,' in truth, justice, and righteousness, then the nations will be blessed by him [וְהִתְבָּרְכוּ בוֹ גּוֹיִם], and in him they will glory." Robert Carroll puts it well: "Israel's turning means the transformation of the nations."[19] Yahweh designates Jeremiah as "a prophet to the nations" (Jer 1:5; see also 1:10), and the prophet speaks of Yahweh's purposes for all people through Israel in Jer 3:17; 12:14–17; 16:19–21, and also in his oracles about the nations, Jer 25:15–38; 27:1–11; and chapters 46–51. Throughout Jeremiah, Yahweh's plan is to restore not just Israel, but the entire cosmos. The Creator is "God of all flesh" (Jer 32:27; cf. 25:31; 45:5), who works out his divine purposes for creation in and through his plan for Israel.

Like Is 40:5 and Jer 32:27, Joel also refers to "all flesh" (כָּל־בָּשָׂר, Joel 3:1 [ET 2:28]). This expression is used in other contexts to indicate a universal scope (e.g., Gen 6:12–13, 17; Num 18:15; Is 49:26). Yahweh's promise is that "everyone who calls on the name of Yahweh will be saved" (כֹּל אֲשֶׁר־יִקְרָא בְּשֵׁם יְהוָה יִמָּלֵט, Joel 3:5 [ET 2:32]).

In Amos 9:11–12 Yahweh promises to resurrect David's falling booth so that his people "may possess the remnant of Edom and all the nations where my name is called upon them" (וְכָל־הַגּוֹיִם אֲשֶׁר־נִקְרָא שְׁמִי עֲלֵיהֶם). Amos holds out the promise that the future of Israel after 722/721 and 587 BC will once again involve a worldwide mission. This is the point that James brings out to end the dispute at the Jerusalem Council (Acts 15:13–18). He uses Amos 9:11–12 to end the doubts of those who questioned whether God offered to Gentiles the same free grace through faith in Jesus as to Jewish believers in Christ.

Zech 2:15 (ET 2:11) promises: "Many nations will be joined to Yahweh [וְנִלְווּ גוֹיִם רַבִּים אֶל־יְהוָה] in that day and will become my people." The same divine strategy is again stated in Zech 8:20–23. The outcome in Zech 14:16–19

---

[19] Carroll, *Jeremiah*, 156. The language in these verses of Jeremiah is fundamentally drawn from the Abrahamic covenant (Gen 12:3; 22:18; 26:4; Ps 72:17).

envisions the survivors of the nations, who after attacking Israel come to worship Yahweh in Jerusalem.

Mission in the Psalms

From the covenants with Abram in Genesis, Israel in Exodus, and David in 2 Samuel to Isaiah and the prophets, and numerous places in between, Yahweh is proclaimed as Lord over his entire creation and as seeking its restoration through his missionary nation Israel, and ultimately through the One who is his Servant and Son (Mt 1:21; 2:15; 12:18–21). This same global plan of Yahweh is just as evident in the Psalms, which frequently refer to the coming King who is David's Son and Lord (e.g., Psalms 2; 16; 22; 110; 118). Israel's hymnbook also contains over 175 references to the nations of the world.[20]

Yahweh is, for example, the "Most High" (Ps 7:18 [ET 7:17]), whose name is "majestic … in all the earth" (Ps 8:2, 10 [ET 8:1, 9]). The heavens declare his glory to the ends of the earth (Ps 19:2–7 [ET 19:1–6]). He is exalted among the nations and in the earth (Ps 46:11 [ET 46:10]). He is the great King over all the earth (Ps 47:3 [ET 47:2]). Yahweh is to be praised from the rising of the sun to where it sets (Ps 113:3). Being high and exalted above all things, no god is as great as Yahweh (Ps 77:14 [ET 77:13]). He is the "God of gods" (Ps 136:2); he is more awesome than all the angels that surround him (Ps 89:8 [ET 89:7]). Among the gods there is no one like him (Ps 86:8). He is to be feared above all gods, for the other gods are nothing but idols (Ps 96:4–5).

Yahweh rules from "sea to sea, from the River to the ends of the earth" (Ps 72:8). He rules all people justly and guides the nations of the earth (Ps 96:10). He has set his throne in heaven, and his kingdom rules over all (Ps 103:19). Yahweh's universal reign extends throughout eternity. "Yahweh is King for ever and ever" (Ps 10:16). He rules forever by his power (Ps 66:7). He is God "from everlasting to everlasting" (Ps 90:2). His kingdom is eternal, and his dominion endures through all generations (Ps 145:13).

The vastness of Yahweh's creation and the complexities of the operations of nature demonstrate this universal reign of Yahweh. By his Word the heavens and their hosts were made (Ps 33:6). He is the maker of heaven and earth, the seas and everything in them (Ps 146:6). Yahweh does what he pleases in the heavens and on the earth, in the seas and their depths. He makes the clouds rise from the ends of the earth; he sends lightning with the rain and brings out the wind from his storehouses (Ps 135:6–7). He covers the sky with clouds supplying the earth with rain. He makes grass grow on the hills and provides food for the cattle and the young ravens. Yahweh is great and mighty in power; his understanding has no limit (Ps 147:5–9).

Yahweh is the mighty one who speaks and summons the earth from the rising of the sun to where it sets (Ps 50:1). He punishes the nations (Ps 59:6 [ET

---

[20] See Marlowe, "The Music of Missions," 456.

59:5]). He judges the gods of the earth (Ps 82:1, 8). He will crush the rulers of the whole earth (Ps 110:6).

Because Yahweh's dominion is so vast and his deeds are so great, Israel is called upon to "proclaim his deeds among the nations" (Ps 9:12 [ET 9:11]), indeed, to sing of him among the nations (Ps 108:4 [ET 108:3]). Israel is to praise his abundant goodness and joyfully celebrate his righteousness (Ps 145:1–7), with the goal that all people are to extol him (Ps 117:1).

Several psalms accent Israel's centrifugal mission. "I will confess you in the nations, Lord; I will sing about you among the peoples" (Ps 57:10 [ET 57:9]). "Then our mouth was filled with laughter, our tongue with songs of joy. Then they said among the nations, 'Yahweh has done great things with these … so we rejoice' " (Ps 126:2–3). "They will tell of the glory of your kingdom and speak of your might, to make known to the children of men your mighty acts and the glory of the splendor of your kingdom" (Ps 145:11–12). "My mouth will speak the praise of Yahweh; let all flesh praise his holy name for ever and ever" (Ps 145:21).

Over and over again the psalmists call on all people of all lands and nations to praise Yahweh (Pss 47:2 [ET 47:1]; 67:4, 6 [ET 67:3, 5]; 100:1; 117:1). Even more directly, these ancient singers of Israel urge their people to tell, proclaim, and make known the mighty, redemptive deeds of Yahweh (Pss 9:12 [ET 9:11]; 105:1) and to join in singing praises to Yahweh from all the nations (Pss 57:10 [ET 57:9]; 108:4 [ET 108:3]). The expected result is that all the ends of the earth will turn to Yahweh and all the families of the earth will bow down in worship to him (Pss 22:28 [ET 22:27]; 66:4; 86:9).

A specific example of this missional thrust of the Psalter comes from Psalm 87 as it breaks down all borders between Israel and the nations.[21] Ps 87:4 mentions the neighbors of Jerusalem from all four points of the compass: "Rahab" is a symbolic name for Egypt (cf. Is 30:7; Ps 89:11 [ET 89:10]; Job 26:12). "Babylon" appears as Zion's constant adversary in the books of Isaiah and Jeremiah. "Philistia" denotes the southwestern shoreline of Canaan and its inhabitants (cf. Pss 60:10 [ET 60:8]; 83:8 [83:7]). "Tyre" represents the Phoenician nation of merchants to the north (cf. Isaiah 23), while "Cush" may denote the Ethiopian people, living south of Egypt (cf. Ps 68:32 [ET 68:31]). Viewing the geography, we see Zion's place in the center of all these peoples.

It is also at Zion where these nations are born (זֶה יֻלַּד־שָׁם, "this one was born there," Ps 87:4). Some understand that this refers to Israelites dispersed among the nations,[22] but that interpretation overlooks that Yahweh remembers these nations (Ps 87:4) and records their names as each nation is born in Zion

---

[21] The following discussion of Zion as our mother is from a paper entitled "Zion Will Be Called Our Mother," presented by Christl Maier at the annual meeting of the Society of Biblical Literature in San Antonio, Tex., on November 21, 2004.

[22] For example, Emerton, "The Problem of Psalm LXXXVII," 190–98.

(Ps 87:6). In contrast to other Zion Psalms (e.g., Psalms 46; 48), Psalm 87 proclaims not the salvation *of* Zion but the salvation of the nations *through* Zion.

The LXX supports this view since it adds "mother" in its translation of Ps 87:5: "Mother Zion will say this man and that man were born in her, and the Most High himself founded her."[23] Often in the OT Zion is called "daughter" (e.g., Lam 2:10), but rarely is she called "mother." Although only Is 50:1 explicitly uses the Hebrew title "mother" for the city, both Isaiah and Jeremiah characterize the city as a mother bereft of her children (Is 54:1–3; Jer 10:20).

The title of "mother" for Zion or Jerusalem is elaborated by Paul in Gal 4:26, where he follows the LXX of Ps 87:5 (as well as Is 54:1). Paul declares that Gentiles who have been baptized into Christ are sons of Abraham and heirs of the OT promises (Gal 3:26–29); they have equal standing with Jewish Christians in the church and do not need circumcision (cf. Col 2:11–13). In Gal 4:26 he writes: "But the Jerusalem that is above is free, who is our mother" (ἡ δὲ ἄνω Ἰερουσαλὴμ ἐλευθέρα ἐστίν, ἥτις ἐστὶν μήτηρ ἡμῶν). Just as Zion in Psalm 87 is the mother of the nations, so the "Jerusalem that is above"—who is the church—is also the mother of all who believe. Thus Paul says, "There is neither Jew nor Greek" (Gal 3:28), for all who are "born in Zion" are one in Christ.

Mission to Individuals

Up to this point, the discussion has been about how Yahweh—through Israel—seeks to save families and clans, Moabites and Edomites, Canaanites and Hittites, and of course, Ninevites! Yet the OT also indicates that Yahweh calls individuals to embrace the promise of the Seed (Gen 3:15).

A representative list indicates Yahweh's concern not just for the nations in general, but specifically for individuals within these nations. We begin with Melchizedek in Genesis 14. He is described as "king of Salem" and "priest of God Most High" (Gen 14:18). This Canaanite blesses Abram "by God Most High, Creator of heaven and earth" (Gen 14:19), and this is the one to whom Abram gives a tithe of all he took as booty in his rescue of Lot (Gen 14:20). Where, when, and how this Gentile became of believer in the promised Seed, the text doesn't say (cf. Ps 110:4; Heb 7:1–4). But Melchizedek is the "firstfruits" of the Gentile harvest, a believer in the promise that the Savior shall come from the seed of Eve (Gen 3:15) and line of Abram (Gen 12:1–3).

There are others. Jethro is a "priest of Midian" (Ex 3:1; 18:1), but when Moses returns to Midian with news of Yahweh's great deeds of salvation, his father-in-law breaks out into paeans of praise to Yahweh:

> Blessed be Yahweh, who rescued you [plural] from the hand of Egypt and from the hand of Pharaoh, and who rescued the people from being under the hand of Egypt. Now I know that Yahweh is greater than all the gods because

---

23 The LXX (Ps 86:5) reads μήτηρ Σιων, ἐρεῖ ἄνθρωπος, καὶ ἄνθρωπος ἐγενήθη ἐν αὐτῇ, καὶ αὐτὸς ἐθεμελίωσεν αὐτὴν ὁ ὕψιστος.

he did this to those who had acted arrogantly against them [Israel]. (Ex 18:10–11)

Then Jethro brings a burnt offering and other sacrifices to Yahweh. He joins Aaron and all the elders of Israel in breaking bread together and worshiping Yahweh (Ex 18:12).

To Melchizedek and Jethro we might add Balaam, son of Beor, who lived in upper Mesopotamia at Pethor, near the Euphrates River (Num 22:5).[24] His relationship with Yahweh is even more mysterious. He accurately delivers the Word of Yahweh on four different occasions. To be sure, Balaam comes to a grievous end in his apparent effort to placate his Moabite host (Num 31:8), but that does not detract from the fact that here is a Gentile who addresses Yahweh personally in prayer and also gives a direct word from Israel's God. Balaam even foresees the coming Messiah (Num 24:17):

> I see him, but not now; I behold him, but not soon.
> A star will come out of Jacob; a scepter will rise out of Israel.

Consider also Rahab, the prostitute. Israel's entry into the promised land opens with her story as she welcomes and hides the two spies sent out by Joshua. In Josh 2:11 she confesses Yahweh's mighty power, which he displayed in Israel's exodus from Egypt: "When we heard, our heart melted, and a spirit [of courage] no longer held up in any man before you, because Yahweh, your God, is God in heaven above and on the earth below." Two reasons are given for her conversion. The first is the fear instilled in the hearts of her fellow citizens upon hearing of the victories Israel won over nearby pagan peoples and nations on the way out of Egypt. The second reason for Rahab's conversion is that this God, Yahweh, was leading Israel and doing such mighty acts. Why, this God is the Creator of all things! The writer to the Hebrews counts Rahab as one of the faithful heroes of faith. He writes: "By faith, Rahab the prostitute did not perish with those who were disobedient because she received the spies with peace" (Heb 11:31). James declares that she was deemed righteous because of what she did in helping the spies (James 2:25). Rahab is even included in the genealogy of Jesus Christ (Mt 1:5). In many respects, the conversion of Rahab represents a positive evangelistic beginning for Israel in the promised land.[25]

The same could be said of Ruth the Moabite woman. When Boaz, a relative on Naomi's husband's side, finds out who this woman is and the story of her choice to leave her homeland to accompany her mother-in-law, he says:

---

[24] Albright writes: "We may, accordingly, conclude that Balaam was really a North-Syrian diviner from the Euphrates Valley, that he spent some time at the Moabite court, that he became a convert to Yahwism, and that he later abandoned Israel and joined the Midianites in fighting against the Yahwists" ("The Oracles of Balaam," 233). Add to Albright's words the fact that in 1967 an inscription, written by a non-Israelite on plaster from about 700 BC, was found not in Israel but at Tell Deir ʿAlla in the eastern Jordan Valley near Ammon. This extrabiblical evidence is discussed by Hackett in *The Balaam Text from Deir ʿAlla.*

[25] Regarding Rahab's conversion, one may see further Harstad, *Joshua,* 128–36.

"May Yahweh repay your deed. May a full reward be given you by Yahweh, the God of Israel, under whose wings you have come to take refuge" (Ruth 2:12). In fact, the son she later bears for Boaz, named Obed, is the father of Jesse, who is the father of David, in the line of the Messiah (Ruth 4:21–22; Mt 1:5–6).

One of the most stunning Gentile conversions in the OT is that of Naaman.[26] Startlingly, 2 Ki 5:1 indicates that Naaman's victories are given by Yahweh. Through the testimony of a young captive Israelite maiden, Naaman trusts in the word of promise, connected with physical means. His response is recorded in 2 Ki 5:15: "Behold, now I know that there is no God in all the earth except in Israel." Walter Maier III notes:

> The gods of Syria, supposedly superior to Yahweh, could not heal Naaman; thus he sees that what he has been taught, and what he has believed about these gods, is false. They are false gods, they are not really gods at all. They are in fact non-existent, and, if such is the case for Syria's gods, that certainly holds for the gods of other nations. Yahweh cured him; Yahweh exists; indeed Yahweh is the only God in all the earth.[27]

In light of such texts, it should come as no surprise that in the NT Paul ties his mission to the Gentiles to the OT. In Acts 13:46–47, Luke records these bold words of Paul and Barnabas to Jews in the synagogue in Pisidian Antioch: "It was necessary for the Word of God to be spoken first to you. Since you reject it and do not consider yourselves worthy of eternal life, behold, we turn to the Gentiles. For this is what the Lord has commanded us: 'I have made you a light to the nations, that you may be for salvation to the ends of the earth.' "

In Rom 15:8–12 Paul quotes from several OT texts, concluding with Is 11:10 when he writes:

> For I tell you that Christ became a servant of the circumcision [the Jews] for the truth of God, to confirm the promises made to the patriarchs, that the Gentiles may glorify God for his mercy, as it is written: "Therefore, I will confess you among the Gentiles; I will sing hymns to your name." Again, it says: "Rejoice, O Gentiles, with his people." And again: "Praise the Lord, all you Gentiles, and let all the peoples extol him." And again, Isaiah says: "The Root of Jesse will come, even the one who arises to rule the Gentiles; in him the Gentiles will hope."

Paul's words here, especially "to confirm the promises made to the patriarchs, that the Gentiles may glorify God for his mercy," take us back to the beginning, to the first patriarch—Abraham—and the Great Commission in Gen 12:1–3. Paul again restates these promises when he says this in Rom 10:12: "For there is no distinction between Jew and Greek; for the same Lord is Lord of all, richly blessing all who call on him."

---

[26] See Maier, "The Healing of Naaman in Missiological Perspective."

[27] Maier, "The Healing of Naaman in Missiological Perspective," 183.

Even Peter, who at times seems unsure of the extent of Gentile inclusion in the promises to Israel (e.g., Gal 2:11–21), preaches about it in Acts 3:25: "And you are the sons of the prophets and of the covenant God made with your fathers, saying to Abraham, 'And through your offspring all peoples on earth will be blessed.' " After his three visions that confirm God's plan for the nations (Acts 10:10–16), Peter states to the Gentile household of Cornelius in Acts 10:34–35: "Truly I understand that God is not one who shows favoritism, but in every nation the one who fears him and works righteousness is acceptable to him."

Jonah in Biblical Context

Was Jonah's mission to Gentiles unique? Hardly. Israel worships the true God and has the knowledge of his will, but has no monopoly on his concern or his forgiving grace. The sailors and the Ninevites are not condemned on the grounds that they are Gentiles. Nowhere in the narrative of Jonah is there any hint that they should be treated any differently from the people of Israel. They appear simply as human beings in need of repentance and Yahweh's grace and mercy.

Jonah is a prophet to the Gentiles. Just as Gen 12:1–3 is the prequel, so also Mt 28:19–20 is the sequel and continuation of his mission. The narrative of Jonah and its emphasis on Gentile conversions is fulfilled again and again in the ministry of Jesus. One notable example is his praise of the Gentile centurion: "With no one in Israel have I found such faith!" (Mt 8:10 ESV ‖ Lk 7:9). The book of Jonah sings in harmony with the gigantic choir of missional voices in both Testaments. It is a missionary narrative—through and through—that issues an important confirmation of Yahweh's plan for the salvation of all who repent and believe.

Jonah 2:1–11

(ET 1:17–2:10)

Yahweh's Rescue of Jonah and the Prophet's Psalm of Thanksgiving

Introduction to Jonah 2

The Versification of Jonah 1–2

Jonah 2 presents Jonah's prayer to Yahweh from the belly of a great fish. The MT, the LXX, and the Vulgate all end chapter 1 with 1:16, so that chapter 2 begins with Yahweh's appointment of the great fish and ends with Yahweh commanding the great fish to vomit Jonah onto dry land. Thus in the MT, the LXX, and the Vulgate, chapter 2 has eleven verses, and Yahweh's use of the great fish both begins and ends the chapter.

However, English translations consider Yahweh's appointment of the great fish (2:1 [ET 1:17]) to conclude chapter 1, and they begin chapter 2 with Jonah's prayer (2:2 [ET 2:1]). Consequently, in English, chapter 2 has only ten verses, since MT/LXX/Vulgate 2:1–11 corresponds to the English 1:17–2:10. The reason for the English numbering probably is that Jonah 2:1 (ET 1:17) is written in narrative style, as is Jonah 1:1–16, whereas Jonah's prayer (2:3–10 [ET 2:2–9]), excluding the first introductory Hebrew word in 2:3 (ET 2:2), is written in Hebrew poetry. The English numbering may suggest that Yahweh's appointment of a great fish to swallow Jonah (2:1 [ET 1:17]) is God's response to the sailors' prayers, sacrifices, and vows (1:14–16).

In contrast, the numbering of the ancient versions (MT, LXX, Vulgate) suggests that Yahweh appoints the great fish purely out of his own grace. Yahweh saves his rebellious prophet to display his gracious and merciful character (see 4:2) and to enable Jonah to carry out his call to preach to Nineveh (1:1–2), which will save the Ninevites too. The versification in the ancient versions also better reflects the basic structural pattern in both Jonah 1:1–3 and 1:4–16; in both of those scenes Yahweh himself initiates the action, and then the major protagonists of the narrative respond. In chapter 2, then, Yahweh appoints a great fish to swallow Jonah (2:1 [ET 1:17]), Jonah responds with his prayer of faith (2:2–10 [ET 2:1–9]), and then Yahweh again acts graciously when he speaks to the fish that vomits Jonah onto dry land (2:11 [ET 2:10]).

The psalm in chapter 2 (2:2–10 [ET 2:1–9]) is more than a simple continuation of the preceding narrative. As in other sections in the OT, the change from narrative to poetry provides a different genre in which to replay the preceding events in a different key. For example, the Song of Moses (Ex 15:1–18) with the refrain sung by Miriam (Ex 15:20–21) arose out of the events of Exodus 14, sounding fresh depths of praise and joy. In Judges 5, the Song of Deborah celebrates in greater pathos the victory over Sisera detailed in Judges 4. David's poetic lament over the deaths of Saul and Jonathan in 2 Sam 1:17–27 discloses the depths of his grief. In like manner, the psalm of Jonah 2 provides an added dimension to the events in 1:15: "So they lifted up Jonah and hurled him into the sea. Then the sea ceased its anger." That tells us what the sailors saw, but leaves us wondering, What happened to Jonah in the Mediterranean

Sea? Did he repent of his rebellion or perish in his sin? Is all hope lost that he will ever go to Nineveh? These questions and more are answered in chapter 2.

The Place of the Psalm in the Book of Jonah

The relationship between the psalm that comprises most of Jonah 2 and the narrative portion of the book is one of the most vigorously debated exegetical issues concerning the book. Since antiquity, interpreters have perceived incongruence between the poem and the prose text, and this has served as the impetus for the critical study of the book in the last two hundred years.[1] Many critical interpreters have advocated separating the song from the body of the narrative.[2]

Why do so many have difficulty digesting Jonah's song? Why do they want to remove Jonah's poem from its narrative context? Although this list is not exhaustive, what follows are ten of the main reasons.[3] These will be followed by ten corresponding reasons to include the psalm and interpret the book's present canonical form as original.

First, 2:2 states that Jonah "prayed [וַיִּתְפַּלֵּל] to Yahweh his God from the inner parts of the fish." The psalm goes on to show Jonah thanking God for help already rendered. It would seem that the song would fit much better after he is deposited back on dry land (2:11 [ET 2:10]), rather than after his desperate state in 1:12, 15.[4] Josephus overcomes this apparent inconsistency by rearranging the text and placing Jonah's prayer after his ejection from the fish.[5] Another way to handle the apparent lack of logic comes from Ibn Ezra, who interprets the perfect aspect of the verbs in Jonah's song as "prophetic perfects" that predict the future.[6] This strengthens the interpretation that Jonah is looking forward to deliverance when he is in the belly of the great fish.

A second reason adduced for excising the psalm from the narrative is that Jonah's prayer describes the danger of drowning, not his peril in the belly of the fish.[7] Why does he fear the former but say nothing about the danger of being ingested by the latter?

---

[1]   See the discussion in Allen, *Joel, Obadiah, Jonah and Micah*, 181–85. Also helpful is Bolin, *Freedom beyond Forgiveness*, 98–101. Bolin forcefully argues that the psalm is an integral part of the prose text.

[2]   DeWette, *Lehrbuch der historisch-kritischen Einleitung in kanonischen und apokryphischen Bücher des Alten Testamentes*, 298, appears to have been the first to publish the view that the Jonah psalm was an improper insertion borrowed from another source. Typical are these words of Clements: "After we have set aside the psalm of chapter ii as a later addition ..." ("The Purpose of the Book of Jonah," 19).

[3]   The following builds upon Ackerman, "Satire and Symbolism in the Song of Jonah," 213–14.

[4]   Perhaps for this reason the LXX changes several of Jonah's assertions in the song into wishes or questions. See Perkins, "The Septuagint of Jonah," 48–50.

[5]   Josephus, *Antiquities*, 9.213–14 (9.10.2).

[6]   As noted by Allen, *Joel, Obadiah, Jonah and Micah*, 182.

[7]   Kennedy, *Studies in the Book of Jonah*, 38, n. 16, notes the irrelevance of Wellhausen's famous comment that *denn im Bauch des Fisches wächst auch kein Seegras*, "seaweed does

Third, there is dissonance between the faith and character of Jonah in the narrative and the character of Jonah in the prayer. In the prayer, Jonah humbly expresses joyful faith, but in the narratives before and after the psalm he is (except for 3:1–4) entirely resistive and recalcitrant. The song's sincere expression of heartfelt thanks does not correspond to any of Jonah's other prayers or speeches, either in mood or in length. Jonah seems to be seeking death in chapter 1, and in the narrative's last scene he still wants to die (4:3, 8–9).[8] In contrast, Jonah in the prayer knows that his life was in danger and praises God for saving it. He acknowledges Yahweh's power, his separation from his God, and his deliverance from calamity as though it had already taken place. What faith!

Fourth, the Hebrew word for "fish" is masculine in the narrative verses surrounding the prayer (דָּג, 2:1, 11 [ET 1:17; 2:10]), whereas it is feminine at the start of the prayer (דָּגָה, 2:2 [ET 2:1]). Some interpreters suggest that this difference is evidence that the narrative and the psalm come from two separate sources and were joined by a careless editor who did not harmonize the three references in Jonah to a "fish."

Fifth, the psalm is meandering and therefore inappropriate in a story that otherwise has a tight narrative structure.

A sixth reason cited for deleting the psalm from the book is that if it is supposed that the book consists only of two prose sections of narrative (the first section would consist of 1:1–2:1 plus 2:11 [ET 1:1–17 plus 2:10], and the second would consist of chapters 3 and 4), these two sections are carefully balanced in structure and symmetry. This militates against the inclusion of the psalm in the original work, since its presence appears to unbalance the symmetrical arrangement.[9]

Seventh, the language of the psalm departs from that used in the narrative that precedes and follows it. The adjective גָּדוֹל ("great"), which occurs fourteen times in the narrative, appears nowhere in the psalm. Likewise, the noun/adjective רָעָה ("evil") doesn't appear in the psalm. The verb שָׁלַךְ, "throw," which occurs only in 2:4 (ET 2:3), is different from טוּל, "to hurl," which occurs only in 1:4, 5, 12, 15. In the narrative parts of the book, "sea" is always singular (יָם, 1:4, 5, 9, 11, 12, 13, 15), whereas it is plural in its only occurrence in the psalm (יַמִּים, 2:4). "Away from the presence/face of Yahweh" (מִלִּפְנֵי יְהוָה, 1:3, 10) in the narrative becomes in the psalm "from before your eyes" (מִנֶּגֶד עֵינֶיךָ, 2:5 [ET 2:4]). "Perish" (אָבַד) occurs four times in the narrative (1:6, 14; 3:9; 4:10) and easily could have been used in the psalm, but it is not.

---

not grow in the belly of a fish." See Julius Wellhausen, *Die kleinen Propheten* (4th ed.; Berlin: Walter de Gruyter, 1963), 221.

[8] For example, von Rad (*Der Prophet Jona*, 13) contends that the Jonah represented through the psalm is essentially a different person from the Jonah portrayed in the narrative.

[9] The most thorough and detailed analysis of the symmetrical structure of the book (excluding the psalm) is in Trible, *Rhetorical Criticism*.

Eighth, the psalm makes no reference to events in chapter 1, or it describes them differently. For example, from the perspective of the song, it was Yahweh who cast Jonah into the sea ("You cast me toward the depth," 2:4 [ET 2:3]), whereas 1:15 states that it was the sailors, acting at Jonah's request (1:12), who hurled him into the sea.

Ninth, 2:9 (ET 2:8) in the psalm condemns idolaters. In the narrative, however, chapter 1 describes the sailors sympathetically even though they began as idolaters (1:5, before they were converted to faith in Yahweh). Also in the narrative, the condemnations of Nineveh do not mention its idolatry; instead, "evil" and "violence" are the essence of Nineveh's sin (1:2; 3:8, 10).

Tenth, "Aramaisms" (better described as words from a Northern Kingdom dialect) are prevalent in the prose portions of the book, but are absent from the poem.

If these arguments were valid, their cumulative force would seem to deny the validity of interpreting the Jonah psalm as an integral part of the book that otherwise is narrative. What follows, however, is an attempt to demonstrate that most of these arguments are not firmly grounded either in what the text explicitly says or in what it implies. A plausible defense for interpreting the psalm contextually as an original part of the book can be constructed as follows.[10]

First, the narrative of Jonah has many ironies. For example, what other biblical prophet is commanded to arise and go northeastward (1:2), but immediately arises and flees northwestward (1:3)? In fact, the narrative is filled with irony, literally from start to finish.[11] We learn to expect the unexpected from Jonah. His song of thanksgiving when in the belly of a fish makes sense as another major irony in the book. The "inappropriateness" of the psalm disappears when we embrace the ironic nature of the narrative. As sinner and saint simultaneously, Jonah is a divided man. He can confess the faith in Yahweh that is his (1:9), and yet, at the same time, remain adamant in his disobedience (1:12).

Second, upon closer analysis, chapter 2 suggests that Jonah prayed not once, but twice. The psalm is his second prayer, and in it he refers to an earlier prayer: "I called out in my distress to Yahweh" (2:3 [ET 2:2]); "My prayer came to you" (2:8 [ET 2:7]). Jonah does not give the content of his first prayer, but simply refers to it. In Jonah's description of his previous prayer and experience in 2:3–8 (ET 2:2–7), the aspect of the verbal forms is perfect (or imperfect with *waw* consecutive).[12] The descriptions of the circumstances of his first prayer therefore do not correspond to Jonah's present condition in the belly of the fish.

---

[10] Those who provide the most convincing arguments for the inclusive of the Jonah psalm are Landes, "The Kerygma of the Book of Jonah," and Magonet, *Form and Meaning*.

[11] See "Jonah as Satire with Irony" in the introduction.

[12] The one exception is יְסֹבְבֵנִי, translated "surrounded me" in 2:4, 6 (ET 2:3, 5). See the second textual note on 2:4.

Neither does the praise he offers in his second prayer (the psalm) constitute the prayer he spoke in the earlier situation portrayed in the psalm.

Rather, as George Landes points out, Jonah in chapter 2 is recalling an affliction he had already experienced, which evoked from him a cry for help, to which Yahweh graciously responded. In the narrative's logical order of events, Jonah's petition for divine assistance came after he sank into the sea. There he spoke a lament or plea for deliverance; then Yahweh saved him, evoking the psalm of praise (2:3–10 [ET 2:2–9]). Many commentators, failing to discern the order of events the narrator wants us to understand, have claimed that Jonah's psalm belongs properly after 2:11 (ET 2:10).[13] However, as Landes says, "as an expression of grateful praise for a past deliverance, the psalm is not only of an appropriate type but also is correctly positioned in the narrative," that is, after Jonah's ingestion into the fish, rather than after he is regurgitated onto the dry ground. Essentially, 2:11 (ET 2:10) "is a transitional verse describing the prophet's return to the place where the divine commission can be renewed, not his deliverance *per se*."[14]

Consequently, the form and content of the psalm show that its location fits suitably within its present context, and it is in harmony with the succession of events immediately preceding it. A partial outline of the book further clarifies this point. It is arranged to bring out the parallel motifs in the psalm and the relevant portions of chapter 4. Some of the parallels involve opposites (e.g., 2:10 [ET 2:9] versus 4:3) that contribute to the book's satire and irony.[15]

2:1–11	Jonah is delivered.	4:1–11	Nineveh is delivered.
2:2	Jonah prays.	4:2	Jonah prays.
2:3–7b	Jonah refers back to his distress in the deep.	4:2a–c	Jonah refers back to his distress in Israel.
2:7c–8	He asserts God's merciful deliverance.	4:2e	He asserts God's merciful deliverance.
2:9	He draws insight from his deliverance: idolaters forsake the One who loves them.	4:2d	He draws insight from the thought that God may save Nineveh and concludes that he must flee to Tarshish.
2:10	Jonah responds to Yahweh: worship with sacrifices and vows.	4:3	Jonah responds to Yahweh: a plea for death.
2:11	Yahweh responds to Jonah: he speaks to the fish.	4:4–11	Yahweh responds to Jonah: he speaks of judgment and grace.

---

[13] An older school of Jonah scholars had difficulty explaining how the psalm could have become displaced from after 2:11 (ET 2:10). They attributed that displacement to a late redactor's carelessness, lack of sensitivity to the story, or an error in the textual transmission of the book (Landes, "The Kerygma of the Book of Jonah," 15, n. 47).

[14] Landes, "The Kerygma of the Book of Jonah," 15.

[15] The following chart is adapted from the one in Landes, "The Kerygma of the Book of Jonah," 16. The Hebrew versification, which differs from the English versification in Jonah 2, is used in the chart. Jonah 2:1–11 corresponds to 1:17–2:10 in English translations.

Therefore, within the overall structure of chapters 2 and 4, the psalm is almost parallel to the prophet's prayer in 4:2–3. Both the psalm and the prayer in chapter 4 are introduced in the same way with the same verbs, literally, "And he prayed to Yahweh … and he said" (וַיִּתְפַּלֵּל … אֶל־יְהוָה … וַיֹּאמַר, 2:2–3a [ET 2:1–2a]; 4:2 is almost identical). These two prayers differ from each other in form (the psalm is poetry; the prayer in 4:2–3 is prose), type (the psalm is a declarative psalm of praise; the prayer in 4:2–3 is a complaint with a concluding petition), and specific content (the psalm praises Yahweh for having delivered Jonah from destruction in Sheol; the prayer in 4:2–3 complains to Yahweh because he delivered those whom Jonah would have destroyed; this motivates Jonah to ask for his own destruction). Yet they both illustrate the content of that activity described by the verb "to pray" (Hithpael of פָּלַל).

A third reason why the poem should remain is because it is a genuine psalm; both the lament and thanksgiving elements within Jonah's psalm are common features in psalms of individual lament (e.g., Psalms 3–7, 10–14, 16, 17, 22) and in other individual prayers of lament (e.g., Is 38:9–20). James Watts points out that these psalms often violate the chronological order of events that would be followed in a prose account, specifically because the psalmists utter praise or thanks for a promise yet to be fulfilled.[16] That Jonah's full deliverance comes in 2:11 (ET 2:10), after his psalm of praise, is an example of this generic feature. Another example is Hezekiah's prayer, which comes after he is told that God will allow him to live, but before he is healed (Isaiah 38). Daniel praises God for the vision he has received that will save his life, prior to his anxious audience with the king (Daniel 2). In light of this, Jonah's thanksgiving from the innards of the fish is not premature gratitude, even though Jonah will not finally find safety on the dry land until 2:11 (ET 2:10), for Yahweh has already provided a great fish to deliver him from Sheol and has already wrought in him repentance and renewed faith.

The fourth argument for the integrity of the psalm is that in the narrative, the fish plays a positive role as a vehicle of deliverance, which is consistent with Jonah's psalm of praise for deliverance uttered in the belly of the fish. The fish should not be seen as a monster seeking Jonah's death. The narrator uses the neutral term דָּג ("fish," 2:1, 11 [ET 1:17; 2:10]; the feminine is used in 2:2 [ET 2:1]) rather than one of the terms for primordial sea monsters, such as תַּנִּין (e.g., "great sea creature?" in Gen 1:21; "dragon?" in Is 51:9; Ezek 32:2; Ps 74:13) or לִוְיָתָן, "Leviathan" (e.g., Is 27:1; Pss 74:14; 104:26; Job 40:25 [ET 41:1]). The three days and three nights (Jonah 2:1 [ET 1:17]) are the time it takes the fish to bring Jonah back from the underworld of Sheol to the safety of the dry land. The prayer in 2:3–10 (ET 2:2–9) is quite properly a song of thanks because Jonah knows he has already been rescued by the great fish. A straightforward reading of chapter 2 therefore indicates that the psalm is meant as praise for deliverance—not from the fish, but from drowning and from Sheol.

---

[16] Watts, "This Song," 352–55.

The great fish is a means of salvation, not of judgment. This salvific significance of the fish is consistent with the early church's use of the fish as a symbol for Christ, and the Greek word ΙΧΘΥΣ, "fish," as an anagram for "Jesus Christ, of God the Son, Savior." This early church symbolism was based on the interpretation that in certain NT passages, fish represented Christ himself (e.g., Lk 9:13–16).[17]

Fifth, despite some major differences between the language of the psalm and the language of the narrative chapters,[18] there are some strong connections between them. The psalm frequently mentions water and drowning, which relates to the storm on the sea in 1:4–16 and specifically to Jonah being hurled overboard (1:12, 15). Jonah in his psalm alternates between speaking to Yahweh in the second person (e.g., "you" in 2:2e) and speaking about Yahweh in the third person (e.g., "he" in 2:2c); in chapter 1 he speaks about Yahweh in the third person (1:9), and in chapter 4 he speaks to Yahweh in the second person (4:2–3). Even though we expect differences in language, the prose and poetry sections of the book share some key terminology: "to go down" (יָרַד, 1:3 [twice], 5; 2:7 [ET 2:6]), "to sacrifice" (זָבַח, 1:16; 2:10 [ET 2:9]); "to vow" (נָדַר, 1:16; 2:10 [ET 2:9]); "to pass over" (עָבַר, 2:4 [ET 2:3]; 3:6); "to call" (קָרָא, 1:2, 6, 14; 2:3 [ET 2:2]; 3:2, 4, 5, 8); "to come" (בּוֹא, 1:3, 8; 2:8 [ET 2:7]; 3:4); and "to go up" (עָלָה, 1:2; 2:7 [ET 2:6]; 4:6–7).

Further connections between the narrative and the psalm are discussed by Jonathan Magonet, who demonstrates that the psalm is constructed to portray a "consecutive descent" with "almost 'geographical' exactitude."[19] It moves from "ocean current" (2:4b [ET 2:3b]) to "breakers" and "waves" (2:4c [ET 2:3c]) to "the deep" (2:6b [ET 2:6b]) to "the roots of the mountains" (2:7a [ET 2:7a]) and finally to "the underworld—her gate-bars [were] behind me forever" and "destruction" (2:7b–c [ET 2:5b–c]). This provides a strong literary connection between chapters 1 and 2. Jonah's descent from Yahweh begins in 1:3 and is only completed in 2:7c (ET 2:6c). At this point, he is as far away from Yahweh as possible. It is there, most significantly, that a key word is used from chapter 1, "to go down" (יָרַד, used previously in 1:3 [twice] and 1:5).[20]

---

[17] See Just, *Luke 1:1–9:50*, 384, which includes early church art from the Crypt of Lucina.

[18] One difference is that the psalm has instances of archaic language that are absent from the narrative chapters. Another is that the psalm does not refer or allude to many of the events in chapter 1.

[19] Magonet, *Form and Meaning*, 40.

[20] See further the textual notes and commentary on 1:3. Yahweh commanded Jonah to "arise" (1:2), but instead he "went down" (1:3, 5) and away from Yahweh.

More parallel ideas that connect chapter 1 with chapter 2 are as follows:[21]

Chapter 1	Chapter 2
Focus on the sailors	Focus on Jonah
1. Crisis situation: threatened destruction by a storm at sea (1:4)	1. Crisis situation: threatened drowning in the sea (2:4 [ET 2:3])
2. The sailors' response to the crisis: prayer (1:5), ultimately to Yahweh (1:14)	2. Jonah's response to the crisis: prayer to Yahweh (2:3 [ET 2:2])
3. Yahweh's reaction to the sailors' prayer: deliverance from the storm (1:15c)	3. Yahweh's reaction to Jonah's prayer: deliverance from death in Sheol (2:1, 7c [ET 1:17; 2:6c])
4. The sailors' concluding response to Yahweh's salvation: worship of Yahweh with the resolve to perform cultic acts of sacrifice and vows (1:16)	4. Jonah's concluding response to Yahweh's salvation: worship of Yahweh through praise, with the resolve to perform cultic acts of sacrifice and vows (2:10 [ET 2:9])

The connection expressed here is that when faced with similar perils, both at sea, the sailors and Jonah both supplicate Yahweh, then both receive deliverance from him, and finally both perform the same type of response to the source of their salvation. A sincere cry to Yahweh is answered equally, whether it comes from a pagan turned believer (the sailors; see 1:5, 14–16) or from a lifelong believer (Jonah; see 1:9). A similar structure informs chapters 3 and 4, reinforcing this same idea.[22]

As for additional themes that hold all four chapters together, the strong interest in death relates the psalm with the three other chapters. The themes of crisis, crying for help, and deliverance are also common to all chapters. References to worship in the psalm (2:5, 8, 10 [ET 2:4, 7, 9]) are also prevalent in the surrounding narrative (1:5, 6, 14, 16; 3:5, 6, 7, 8). Verbal images, even though expressed with different vocabulary, are also common: throwing, forsaking, the presence of Yahweh, distressful crying, Yahweh hearing and answering.

Sixth, Jonah's joy in his song does not indicate psychological inconsistency, as some would say. Jonah 4:6, describing the prophet's mercurial response when Yahweh ordains the qiqayon plant to shade him, shows that he can be quite exhilarated when he receives favorable treatment, as in chapter 2. Jonah becomes grumpy only when others receive similar grace from God.

Seventh, even though the key word "great," which occurs fourteen times in the prose narrative, is completely absent from the psalm,[23] there is no adjective in the psalm for which the word "great" would have been a fitting synonym. An argument from silence (e.g., the absence of a word) is the weakest form of argument.

---

[21] The following comparison comes, to a large extent, from Landes, "The Kerygma of the Book of Jonah," 26.

[22] See "Introduction to Jonah 3" for the discussion.

[23] As noted by Wolff, *Studien zum Jonabuch*, 61, n. 82.

Eighth, the objection that chapter 1 fails to mention the events presupposed in chapter 2 ignores the significance of a striking narrative device the author uses in constructing his story, namely, his deliberate omission of certain events from their proper chronological sequence, only to introduce them later, where their presence has a much greater force and impact.

George Landes identifies two prayers in the psalm: (1) a prior prayer that was a lament, referred to explicitly in 2:3, 8 (ET 2:2, 7), and (2) a thanksgiving prayer, which includes these references to the prior lament. Landes argues that this flashback feature of the psalm matches the flashback of Jonah's prayer in 4:2, which also refers to a prior utterance of Jonah.[24] Jonah 4:2 indicates that when the prophet first received the divine command to go to Nineveh, he did not immediately proceed to Tarshish (as 1:3 would lead us to understand), but first complained to Yahweh about the unpleasant outcome this whole venture might hold for him, namely, the deliverance of Nineveh. There is no hint in 1:2–3 that Jonah had any words for Yahweh in response to Yahweh's words for him. But that silence of Jonah in 1:2–3 is what the narrator wants;[25] he intentionally delays any account of Jonah's reply until all the events leading up to 4:2 have been narrated. The device of delaying those words enhances their rhetorical effect when they are introduced in 4:2. By saying nothing in 1:2–3 about Jonah's reasons for fleeing to Tarshish, the narrator leaves it to us to guess what the reasons might be. Given the fierce, bellicose reputation of the Assyrians, the most obvious reason would be fear. Another reason, given Jonah's vocation as a prophet to Jeroboam II (see 2 Ki 14:25–28), would be the loss of his positive relationship to that king, along with all of the perks that probably came with it. One of the least obvious reasons is exactly what Jonah states in 4:2: his fear that Yahweh's grace-driven character would result in him saving the Ninevites.

Another example of this same narrative technique of delaying information occurs in 1:10, where the text says the sailors "knew that away from the presence of Yahweh he [Jonah] was fleeing, because he had told them." Here too there is an allusion to a previously unmentioned conversation of Jonah, this time with the ship's crew, which in the chronological sequence of the story belongs somewhere within 1:3. Any description of a conversation between Jonah and the sailors in 1:3 would have interrupted the smooth flow of the narrative at that point, which in terse, rapid strokes paints Jonah's decisive movement to depart quickly from the presence of Yahweh. But in 1:10, reference to Jonah having already informed the crew of what he was doing has its most powerful

---

[24] Landes, "The Kerygma of the Book of Jonah," 15–17. This structural and thematic link between the psalm of chapter 2 and the prayer of 4:2 complements a similar correspondence that has long been noted by scholars between elements in chapters 1 and 3. This yields an overall pattern in Jonah wherein portions of every other chapter are related: chapter 1 is related to chapter 3 (e.g., both begin with commands for Jonah to go to Nineveh), and chapter 2 is related to chapter 4 (both have prayers).

[25] Thus in chapter 1, Jonah remains silent until he speaks his confession in 1:9.

effect because it helps explain the heightening of the sailors' fear, expressed in their question to Jonah, "What is this you have done?" In 1:5 the sailors simply "became afraid," but after they hear Jonah's confession of faith in 1:9, they "feared a great fear" (1:10). In 1:10 the reason for the intensity of their fear is revealed only when we are told that they combined the implications of Jonah's confession with their previous knowledge that he was fleeing from Yahweh's presence.

In light of these examples of this particular feature of the narrator's style, in which he delays revealing information, it is not at all surprising to find yet another example emerging through the contextual interpretation of the psalm.[26] This means that 2:3–9 (ET 2:2–8) exhibits the same flashback style that is in other parts of the book.

A ninth reason for the psalm's integrity within the prose narrative is that there are other examples in the OT where the literary composition entails a poetic piece in the middle of a prose narrative. These are, for example, the Song of the Sea in Ex 15:1–18, the Song of Hannah in 1 Sam 2:1–10, and the Prayer of Hezekiah in Is 38:9–20. Therefore, when the narrative in Jonah is "interrupted" with a poetic psalm, this is in keeping with a literary technique used elsewhere in the OT.

Tenth and finally, much of the debate surrounding a poetic psalm in the midst of an historical narrative is too dependent on the perceived differences between poetry and prose. James Kugel writes:

> If one puts aside the notions of biblical poetry and prose and tries to look afresh at different parts of the Bible to see what it is about them that distinguishes one from another, it will soon be apparent that there are not two modes of utterance, but many different elements which elevate style and provide for formality and strictness of organization.[27]

To use only the two categories of prose versus poetry is like describing sections of the skyline as consisting either of "building" or "no building." This is an oversimplification in the analysis of writing. Hebrew itself has no one word that stands for "poetry" as such over against "prose." There are words for many kinds of poems and songs, but these genre labels do not always help identify the poetic vis-à-vis prose. Rarely do commentators give much attention to the intricate nuances and effects that occur due to the combination and juxtaposition of poetry and prose. Nor do they heed the possible rhetorical effects that such a combination may offer.

The discussion up to this point has sought to evaluate the arguments for and against excising the psalm in chapter 2 and treating it as a later interpolation. The weight of evidence favors the retention of 2:3–10 (ET 2:2–9) as part of the narrator's original draft. It is an essential element in the plot of the nar-

---

[26] For this same stylistic narrative device at one other point in the OT, see Ex 2:11–15, especially 2:12 and 2:14.

[27] Kugel, *The Idea of Biblical Poetry*, 85.

rative, providing a necessary bridge between the events of chapters 1 and 3. Along with the vast majority of recent writers, this commentary regards the book of Jonah as a literary unity that includes the psalm in its present location. This divinely inspired book of Holy Scripture must be interpreted in its extant form.

The Genre of the Psalm

As is often observed, the Jonah psalm is similar in type, purpose, structure, and content to a number of other psalms in the OT that have been classified, particularly since Hermann Gunkel, as thanksgiving songs or hymns, but which, following Claus Westermann, now are perhaps more accurately categorized as "declarative psalms of praise."[28] These psalms thank Yahweh for his acts of deliverance from the kinds of situations described in the psalms of lament, which usually conclude with praise for deliverance (e.g., Psalms 7 and 13).

Some phrases and motifs in the psalm have liturgical connotations, especially "your holy temple" in 2:5, 8 (ET 2:4, 7). Jonah alternatively refers to Yahweh in the third person and addresses him in the second person, and this style is characteristic of some psalms well-suited for use in worship.[29] Jonah's concluding resolve to make a sacrifice and pay a vow are devotional acts that would seem to presuppose a liturgical situation in the temple.

As mentioned above, the psalm has certain features of language, content, and form that are characteristic of Hebrew poetry and that distinguish it from the rest of the book, which is composed in the genre of narrative. Hebrew poetry often preserves archaic language, and the Jonah psalm has at least two archaic linguistic forms or usages.[30] It also has several cosmological motifs similar to those known from the Ugaritic texts, which date to around 1400 BC.[31] All these features would seem to refer the psalm's composition to earlier rather

---

[28] For a full discussion of the greater appropriateness of this title as over against the less-accurate traditional designation "thanksgiving psalms," see Westermann, *The Praise of God in the Psalms*, 102–16. As Landes notes, in light of Westermann's analysis, Jonah 2:3–10 (ET 2:2–9) "is most properly designated a declarative psalm of praise by the individual" ("The Kerygma of the Book of Jonah," 7).

[29] See 2:3b–c, 8a, 9b, 10c for the third person and 2:3e, 4a, 4c, 5, 7c, 8b–c, 10a for the second person. The usual explanation for such style in liturgical psalms is that when the psalmist is recounting, for the benefit of the other worshipers present, what happened to him and the insight he gained from his experience, he employs the divine name in the third person. When he speaks more intimately of how Yahweh has responded to his prayer, he addresses the deity in the second person. This stylistic device is especially characteristic of the declarative psalms of praise (e.g., Psalms 96; 98; 100; 105; 106; 146–150), but is less common in other psalm types.

[30] In both 2:4 (ET 2:3) and 2:6 (ET 2:5) the imperfect (without *waw* consecutive) יְסֹבְבֵנִי ("surrounded me") refers to past time. The imperfect can be used in that same way in Ugaritic (see Gordon, *Ugaritic Textbook*, 68). There is also a possible example of the old Canaanite enclitic *mem*, an emphatic particle: the last *mem* in מְשַׁמְּרִים in 2:9 (ET 2:8). See Hummel, "Enclitic *Mem* in Early Northwest Semitic, Especially Hebrew," 99.

[31] Compare, for example, Pope, *El in the Ugaritic Texts*, 64.

than the later epoch of Israel's psalmodic creativity. Yet none of these features can be used as conclusive criteria for dating either the psalm or its prose context.[32]

The Structure of the Psalm

The structure of the psalm consists of three stanzas: 2:3–5 (ET 2:2–4); 2:6–8 (ET 2:5–7); and 2:9–10 (ET 2:8–9). The first two are marked by their conclusions with the refrain אֶל־הֵיכַל קָדְשֶׁךָ, "toward your holy temple." The theology of the psalm is driven by the refrain of 2:5 and 2:8, which demonstrates vertical typology, the ultimate unity between Yahweh's holy temple on earth with that in heaven. These two stanzas also exhibit parallelism of the following motifs: answered prayer, crisis, banishment, and assurance. The first motif—answered prayer—occurs at the start of the first stanza and at the end of the second, while the other three motifs occur in the same order in both. The progression of the psalm is as follows:

- 2:3 (ET 2:2): a statement of distress, prayer, and answer
- 2:4–5 (ET 2:3–4): a statement of distress, followed by prayer
- 2:6–7b (ET 2:5–6b): a statement of distress
- 2:7c (ET 2:6c): answer to prayer
- 2:8 (ET 2:7): a recapitulation of 2:3 (ET 2:2)
- 2:9–10 (ET 2:8–9): concluding remarks and promises

The four typical elements of the declarative psalm of praise are reproduced: an introductory summary of answered prayer, reports of the personal crisis and divine rescue, and a vow of praise.[33]

The psalm is bound together by an intricate pattern of recurring motifs and phraseology. For example, "Yahweh" is at the beginning and end of the psalm (2:3, 10 [ET 2:2, 9]) and twice in the second stanza (2:7, 8 [ET 2:6, 7]); "voice" (קוֹל) is also used at the beginning and the end (2:3, 10 [ET 2:2, 9]). "Then/but I" (וַאֲנִי) begins the last verse of the first and third stanzas (2:5, 10 [ET 2:4, 9]), and "upon me" (עָלַי) occurs in the first and the second (2:4, 8 [ET 2:3, 7]). "Life" (נֶפֶשׁ) appears twice in the second stanza (2:6, 8 [ET 2:5, 7]). A detailed chart or diagram is not offered because of the lack of consensus and the absence of reasonably plausible results in the understanding of the poetry of the psalm.[34]

Putting the psalm together with the prose introduction and conclusion, the structure of the entire chapter is as follows:[35]

---

[32] Hence Kaufmann's arguments (*The Religion of Israel*, 282–86) for an eighth-century date cannot be refuted on linguistic grounds. See further "The Date of Writing" in the introduction.

[33] See Westermann, *The Praise of God in the Psalms*, 103–4.

[34] For an overview of the numerous attempts to analyze the poetry of the psalm, see Bolin, *Freedom Beyond Forgiveness*, 103–5.

[35] To a large extent, the following chiasm follows Nixon, *The Message of Jonah*, 124.

A   Yahweh appoints a great fish to swallow Jonah (2:1a [ET 1:17a]).

    B   Jonah is in the belly of the fish three days and three nights (2:1b [ET 1:17b]).

    B'   Then Jonah prays from the belly of the fish (2:2–10 [ET 2:1–9]).

A'   Yahweh speaks to the fish, and it vomits Jonah onto dry land (2:11 [ET 2:10]).

By means of this structure, "Yahweh" begins and ends the unit; he is graciously surrounding Jonah to deliver him from Sheol.

Scene 3: Jonah's Deliverance and Prayer

Translation

2 ¹But Yahweh provided a great fish to swallow Jonah, and Jonah was in the inner parts of the fish three days and three nights.

²Then Jonah prayed to Yahweh his God from the inner parts of the fish. ³He said,

"I called out in my distress
to Yahweh, and he answered me.
From the belly of Sheol I cried out;
you heard my voice.
⁴You cast me toward the depth in the heart of the seas,
and an ocean current surrounded me.
All your breakers and your waves crossed over me.
⁵Then I myself said, 'I am driven away from before your eyes.
Surely I will again gaze upon your holy temple.
⁶Waters surrounded me up to my neck.
The deep surrounded me.
Seaweed was bound to my head.
⁷To the roots of the mountains I went down.
The underworld—its gate-bars [were] behind me forever.
Then you brought up my life from destruction, O Yahweh my God.
⁸When my life ebbed away for me, I remembered Yahweh.
My prayer came to you,
to your holy temple,
⁹from (among) those who hold to utterly worthless idols,
who abandon the One who loves them.
¹⁰But I, with a voice of thanksgiving, I will indeed sacrifice to you.
What I have vowed I will indeed repay.
Salvation belongs to Yahweh.'"

¹¹Then Yahweh commanded the fish, and it vomited Jonah onto the dry land.

Textual Notes

2:1 וַיְמַן יְהוָה דָּג גָּדוֹל—The verb is the Piel (third masculine singular imperfect with *waw* consecutive) of מָנָה, which in the Piel means to "appoint, ordain" (BDB), "send" (*HALOT*, 2), or "provide." Its Piel is used four times in the narrative: 2:1 (ET 1:17); 4:6, 7, 8.[1] In the OT, there are ten more occurrences of the Piel of מָנָה (and its Ara-

---

[1] A thorough analysis of this word's use in the OT is Wilson, "מנה, 'To Appoint,' in the Old Testament."

maic cognate, the Pael of מָנָה) with the same sense as in Jonah. Two are in preexilic texts (Ps 61:8 [ET 61:7]; Job 7:3), and eight are in exilic or postexilic texts (1 Chr 9:29; Dan 1:5, 10, 11; Aramaic: Dan 2:24, 49; 3:12; Ezra 7:25).

In each of the statements with this verb in the narrative of Jonah, a different divine epithet is the subject and the object is a different non-human agent. Here "Yahweh [יְהֹוָה] provided a great fish" (2:1 [ET 1:17]). Later, "Yahweh God [יְהֹוָה־אֱלֹהִים] provided a qiqayon plant" (4:6), then, literally, "the God [הָאֱלֹהִים] provided a worm" (4:7), and finally, "God [אֱלֹהִים] provided a scorching east wind" (4:8).[2] These elements of nature are appointed for salvation (the fish and the plant), as well for judgment (the worm and the wind). Each appointed agent is part of a paronomastic construction. The two consonants of the word דָּג (dag, "fish") are also in נָּדוֹל (gadol, "great," 2:1 [ET 1:17]). In 4:6 the appointed plant provides צֵל (tsel), "shade," לְהַצִּיל (lehatsil), "to save" Jonah. In 4:7, the consonants in תּוֹלַעַת (tola'at, "worm") are also in בַּעֲלוֹת (ba'a lot, "when it arose"). In 4:8 the consonants in רוּחַ (ruach, "wind") are also in חֲרִישִׁית (charishit, "scorching").

These texts (2:1 [ET 1:17]; 4:6–8) are brought together by means of the same verb (מָנָה) with a divine name as subject and paronomasia involving the object. This signals that Yahweh is the cosmic Lord over the sea creatures, the land plants, the land animals, and the wind. This points to one of the central motifs of the narrative: *Yahweh, and not Jonah, controls all things for the purposes of salvation.* Ironically, Jonah confessed this very fact in 1:9: "Yahweh, the God of the heavens … who made the sea and the dry land." Fish, plants, animals, and the hot winds obey his call with instant obedience. But does Jonah?

Numerous attempts have been made to identify the species of this "great fish" (2:1 [ET 1:17]). None has met with any success. There are various ocean fish that could accommodate a person in their gullet. Since the narrator uses only the generic word for any kind of "fish" (דָּג), any specific identification is simply a guess.

There are stories of swallowed sailors. One that appears in several commentaries recounts how in 1758 a man fell overboard from a frigate in the Mediterranean and disappeared into a shark's mouth. A gun was discharged at the shark, which promptly spit out the man, shaken but unharmed. The shark was killed and preserved, and the man toured Europe with it on exhibition.[3] Sasson notes that another such experience is related in the *Weekly World News* of June 16, 1987. It reports: "Shark swallows fisherman—then spits him out alive!" Mikado Nakamura, the escapee, then gave an interview from his hospital bed in Kanazaw, Japan.[4]

The fish is large or "great" (נָּדוֹל). This favorite adjective in the narrative also describes Nineveh (1:2; 3:2–3; 4:11), Jonah's evil (4:1), the wind (1:4), the storm (1:12), Jonah's joy (4:6), and the sailors' fear/worship (1:10, 16).

---

[2] This use of the variations of God's name as the subject of מָנָה is noted by Sasson, *Jonah*, 148.

[3] See Keil, *The Twelve Minor Prophets*, 1:398, n. 1; Perowne, *Obadiah and Jonah*, 92–93.

[4] Sasson, *Jonah*, 151, n. 14.

The gender of the Hebrew word for "fish" changes twice in the course of its appearance in this chapter. First, the masculine term דָּג is used in 2:1 (ET 1:17) for the "fish" provided to swallow Jonah. When Jonah prays in the "fish," the feminine form דָּגָה is used in 2:2 (ET 2:1). Finally, when Yahweh commands the "fish" to eject Jonah, the masculine term דָּג reappears (2:11 [ET 2:10]).

What is the reason for this change in gender? All Hebrew nouns are grammatically masculine or feminine, and sometimes the grammatical gender does not correspond to biological gender. Also, Hebrew sometimes is inconsistent in its use of gendered forms. Hebrew can use different genders to distinguish between a true singular and a collective. The masculine singular דָּג refers to a single "fish," whereas the feminine singular דָּגָה is "almost always coll[ective]" (BDB, s.v. דָּגָה), that is, "a shoal of fish" or "schools of fish" (e.g., Gen 1:26, 28; Is 50:2; Ezek 47:9–10). However, the feminine form in Jonah 2:2 (ET 2:1) clearly refers to the same (one) "fish" in 2:1, 11 (ET 1:17; 2:10; cf. GKC, § 122 s–t). The answer as to why the narrator changes genders may lie in the fact that "a story-teller could simply use either gender for an animal—or both at once—when the sex of the animal was of no importance to the tale."[5] Another explanation could be that the feminine form is chosen for 2:2 (ET 2:1) because "from the inner parts of the fish" (מִמְּעֵי הַדָּגָה, 2:2 [ET 2:1]) is parallel to "from the belly of Sheol" (מִבֶּטֶן שְׁאוֹל, 2:3 [ET 2:2]) and Sheol is a feminine noun.[6] Supporting that parallelism is the fact that both הַדָּגָה in 2:2 (ET 2:1) and שְׁאוֹל in 2:3 (ET 2:2) are preceded by a noun for "belly" with a prefixed *mem*.

All those are possibilities, but it is probably best to leave the gender problem unresolved.

Unable to do just that, *Midrash Jonah* expands the masculine and feminine terms for one "fish" into a fabulous story of two fish. First, a male fish swallows Jonah, but when after three days, he has shown no remorse, God concludes that the belly must be "too roomy," since the prophet is not anxious enough to pray. Yahweh then has Jonah swallowed by a pregnant fish with 365,000 small fish in her. Cramped by all of these minnows, Jonah yields his life to God and prays![7]

Conveniently, the Greek term in the LXX used for both the masculine and the feminine Hebrew nouns is a third declension neuter noun (τὸ κῆτος), and thus poses no problem concerning the fish's gender. It may be surmised that the motivation behind the LXX's selection of κῆτος was its ability to translate both Hebrew forms.

This Greek term probably contributed to the association of Jonah with a "whale." κῆτος is the etymological source of cet- and Cetacea, Latin-based terms for the order of aquatic mammals that includes whales. Elsewhere in the LXX, κῆτος translates other great sea creatures or monsters in the OT: לִוְיָתָן ("Leviathan," Job 3:8), רַהַב

---

[5] Sasson, *Jonah*, 156–57, who draws upon two Akkadian letters from Mari dating from about 1765 BC to make this claim.

[6] Sheol clearly is feminine in Ps 86:13, but apparently it is masculine in Job 26:6. See also Ps 27:3, where מַחֲנֶה, which elsewhere always is masculine, is treated as feminine (it is the subject of a feminine verb) because it is parallel to the feminine noun מִלְחָמָה later in the verse (which also is the subject of a feminine verb).

[7] As noted by Sherwood, *A Biblical Text and Its Afterlife*, 116–17.

("Rahab," Job 9:13; 26:12), and תַּנִּין ("dragon," Gen 1:21). In other Greek literature, κῆτος is used by Homer to refer to a "seal,"[8] and the plural is listed by Aristotle alongside the dolphin and the whale as "other Cetacea" (τὰ ἄλλα κήτη).[9] Both Mt 12:40 and Josephus[10] use κῆτος when referring to Jonah in the creature. The Vulgate renders the term with *piscis*, a third declension masculine noun.

E. B. Pusey, writing in 1860, one year after the publication of Darwin's *The Origin of Species*, attempted to classify the fish using "modern works of Zoology."[11] Most contemporary literature connects the fish with either a whale[12] or a shark.[13]

Biblical Hebrew has no technical terminology for these different kinds of aquatic life. The description of marine animals deemed suitable for sacrifice and consumption only stipulates that they must have "fins" and "scales" (Lev 11:9; Deut 14:9), but does not refer to specific species.

Suffice it to say that there are sperm whales in the Mediterranean that would have had a gullet large enough to swallow a human being. The Hebrew terms in Jonah 2 are general enough that they could refer to a whale.

לִבְלֹעַ אֶת־יוֹנָה—This purpose clause is formed with the Qal infinitive construct of בָּלַע with the preposition לְ: Yahweh provided the fish "to swallow Jonah." Both the Qal and Piel forms of the verb mean "gulp, swallow, devour" and almost always have a hostile connotation in the OT.[14] For example, the followers of Korah are swallowed up by the earth (Num 16:30, 32; Ps 106:17), as are Pharaoh and his chariots (Ex 15:12). The psalmist begs Yahweh not to allow the deep to swallow him up (Ps 69:16 [ET 69:15]; cf. Pss 21:10 [ET 21:9]; 35:25; 124:3). Swallowed up is synonymous with being annihilated (Lam 2:2, 5, 8, 16). Samaria was gulped down as a person would eat a ripe fig (Is 28:4). In Is 25:7–8 the Piel still connotes hostility, but that hostility is between Yahweh and humanity's last enemy: Yahweh will "swallow up" the shroud that covers all peoples, and he will "swallow up death forever." See also 1 Cor 15:54.

Richard Clifford points out that Jonah's psalm provides an excellent description of the domain of Mot (the Canaanite god whose name means "death") as described in Ugaritic literature.[15] In these pagan texts, Mot is portrayed as a voracious monster into whose gullet one descends only to go down farther, all the way to the base of the

---

[8] Homer, *Odyssey*, 4.446, 452.

[9] Aristotle, *History of Animals*, 566b (trans. A. L. Peck; LCL [Cambridge, Mass.: Harvard University Press, 1970], 264–65); similar are the references in Aristotle, *Parts of Animals*, 669a, 697a.

[10] Josephus, *Antiquities*, 9.213 (9.10.2).

[11] Pusey, "Jonah," 385–87 (the quote is on p. 386, including note l). Pusey is quoting an Oxford professor, Dr. Rolleston. Pusey reinforces his zoological cataloguing and calculation by citing the report of the shark that swallowed the sailor in the Mediterranean in 1758 (also cited above in this commentary).

[12] Archer, *A Survey of Old Testament Introduction*, 302.

[13] Keil, *The Twelve Minor Prophets*, 1:398, including n. 1.

[14] Cf. Ackerman, "Satire and Symbolism in the Book of Jonah," 220.

[15] Clifford, *The Cosmic Mountain in Canaan and the Old Testament*, 79–86, especially p. 81, n. 55.

mountains.[16] This motif of being swallowed into the netherworld is expressed with different vocabulary in Jonah 2:3, 7 (ET 2:2, 6) and is incorporated into the OT elsewhere (e.g., בָּלַע in Ex 15:12; Num 16:30, 32; Prov 1:12).

וַיְהִי יוֹנָה בִּמְעֵי הַדָּג—The preposition בְּ is attached to the plural construct of מֵעֶה, yielding בִּמְעֵי. In the OT, מֵעֶה always occurs in the plural. Depending on context, it can be translated "internal organs," "inward parts," "intestines, entrails" (2 Sam 20:10), "womb" (Gen 25:23), "breast, chest" (Ps 22:15 [ET 22:14]), or "belly." It is rendered "inner parts" in Jonah 2:1–2 (ET 1:17; 2:1), to distinguish it from בֶּטֶן ("belly") in 2:3 (ET 2:2) and also because this translation resonates with 1:5, where "Jonah went down to the innermost recesses of the ship." In Jonah 2:1–2 (ET 1:17; 2:1), it is normally understood to mean "stomach," since later, at Yahweh's command, the fish "vomited" the prophet out (2:11 [ET 2:10]).

Jonah has sunk to a deeper level. He "went down" to Joppa (1:3) and (literally) "went down" into the ship (1:3), then "went down" into its inner recesses (1:5) and was "hurled" into the sea (1:15). He descends as low as he can go in 2:3 (ET 2:2) and 2:7 (ET 2:6), to the very depths of Sheol. Such is the path of those who forsake the presence of Yahweh (1:3).

שְׁלֹשָׁה יָמִים וּשְׁלֹשָׁה לֵילוֹת:— For numbers three through ten, Hebrew customarily uses the feminine form of the number (here שְׁלֹשָׁה) with the plural of the noun (here the plurals of יוֹם, "day," and לַיְלָה, "night"). The similar phrase שְׁלֹשֶׁת יָמִים occurs in Jonah 3:3. Hebrew, like English, uses such terms without prepositions for duration of time; the implied thought is *for three days and three nights.*" The OT uses the number three slightly more often than the number seven. An act is repeated three times to enhance it or bring it to consummation. For example, Elijah stretches himself out three times upon a child to bring him back to life (1 Ki 17:21), and Daniel prays three times a day (Dan 6:11).

From a literary standpoint, the exact same Hebrew words are used elsewhere only in 1 Sam 30:12: an Egyptian servant abandoned in the desert "had not eaten bread or drunk water for three days and three nights" (שְׁלֹשָׁה יָמִים וּשְׁלֹשָׁה לֵילוֹת). H. B. Bauer concludes from his study of the temporal implications of this and other passages that include "three days" or "the third day" that the phrase can imply either a longer[a] or shorter[b] time span, depending on the particular circumstances in the context.[17] In some contexts, the phrase can refer to the period of a journey (Gen 22:4; Ex 3:18; Num 33:8; Jonah 3:3).

None of the contexts where either "three days" or "the third day" occurs clearly describes an experience where death directly threatens and from which it might be inferred a deliverance is possible only within this limited period, with Hos 6:2 being the only exception. In each case, the time period is specified, not to imply the still present possibility of deliverance, but to emphasize the comparative duration of the affliction under the circumstances given. The "do or die" meaning of the phrase in Hos 6:2 appears to be how we should understand it in Jonah 2:1 (ET 1:17).

(a) Josh 2:16; 1 Sam 20:5, 19; Jonah 3:3; 2 Chr 20:25

(b) Josh 1:11; 2 Sam 20:4; 2 Ki 20:8; Hos 6:2; Ezra 8:32; Neh 2:11

---

[16] Ugaritic Texts 51:VIII:1–12; 67:II:1–12 (Gordon, *Ugaritic Textbook*, 173, 178).

[17] Bauer, "Drei Tage."

2:2 וַיִּתְפַּלֵּל יוֹנָה—The Hithpael of the verb פָּלַל (here third masculine singular imperfect with *waw* consecutive) means "to pray" and is also used in 4:2. The vast majority of its eighty-four occurrences in the OT are in the Hithpael stem. Only four instances are in another conjugation, the Piel. The verb belongs to the general semantic field "pray"[18] and does not refer to any specific kind of petition. The verb is not bound to any particular context. It can be used, for example, for expressing lament (Is 38:2–5), making vows (1 Sam 1:10–11), interceding for others (Job 42:10), or confessing sin (Dan 9:4–21; Ezra 10:1). Individuals may pray (פָּלַל) as they appear before God (1 Sam 1:9–10; 2 Ki 19:14–15). Other times, a leader will pray on behalf of the congregation, especially in the case of a sin against Yahweh (Num 11:2; 21:7; cf. Gen 20:7, 17).

Miles away from Jerusalem, Jonah will still direct his prayer to Yahweh at the temple (2:5, 8 [ET 2:4, 7]) and that connects his cry for mercy to the context of Israel's corporate worship.

אֶל־יְהוָה אֱלֹהָיו—That "Yahweh" is called "his God" agrees with Jonah's faith expressed in the psalm (2:3–10 [ET 2:2–9]) and with his prior confession of faith in Yahweh in 1:9.

מִמְּעֵי הַדָּגָה:—See the second textual note on 2:1, which had the similar phrase בִּמְעֵי הַדָּג. Here the preposition on מְעֵי is מִן (rather than בְּ), and the form of the noun is feminine (הַדָּגָה).

2:3–10 The distinction between the prose of 2:1–2, 11 (ET 1:17; 2:1, 10) and the poetry of 2:3–10 (ET 2:2–9) is supported by the frequency of the prose particles. It is generally recognized that the direct object marker אֵת, the relative pronoun אֲשֶׁר, and the definite article (written with ה) occur infrequently in texts considered to be poetic.[19] Of the 81 words in Jonah's psalm (2:3–10 [ET 2:2–9]), only 3 are prose particles (3.7%), well within the normal range for poetry. Of the 608 words in the rest of the narrative (1:1–2:2 [ET 1:1–17] and 2:11–4:11 [ET 2:10–4:11]), there are 93 such particles, or 15.3%, well within the normal range for prose. These linguistic differences confirm that Jonah consists of a narrative framework (1:1–2:2 [ET 1:1–17] and 2:11–4:11 [ET 2:10–4:11]) with a poetic interlude (2:3–10 [ET 2:2–9]).

Other criteria for detecting Hebrew poetry are features visible in 2:3–10 (ET 2:2–9), including the use of imagery, the dominance of parallelism,[20] the freedom of syntax, the high number of wordplays (paronomasia), and a semblance of meter. The

---

[18] E. Gerstenberger, "פלל," *TDOT* 11:569.

[19] For discussions, see Andersen and Freedman, *Hosea*, 60–66; Freedman, "Prose Particles in the Poetry of the Primary History"; Andersen and Forbes, " 'Prose Particle' Counts of the Hebrew Bible." Raabe, *Obadiah*, 6, writes:

> In standard prose the particle frequency is 15 percent or more, whereas in poetry the frequency is 5 percent or less. That is to say, for a text generally recognized to be poetic on other grounds (i.e., the dominance of parallelism and terse lines), if it has one hundred words, then *'et, 'ăšer* and words having the definite article written with *h* will comprise five or fewer of the words. For practical purposes, a "word" can be identified as the ink marks written between the white spaces.

[20] For discussions of parallelism, see Berlin, *The Dynamics of Biblical Parallelism*, and Petersen and Richards, *Interpreting Hebrew Poetry*.

cadence of Jonah's psalm resembles the *qinah* meter.[21] See the second and third textual notes on 2:3 (ET 2:2).

Another poetic feature is a timeless quality of verbal aspects. It is best not to slavishly translate perfect forms as past tense and imperfect forms as future tense because in poetry "the perfect tense often conveys information without significant attachment to time as long as the poet is establishing a solid context or point of view"[22] Therefore, it would be wrong to cite the perfect verbs to sustain the argument that Jonah composed his psalm only after he was vomited by the fish (2:11 [ET 2:10]). Rather, Jonah's psalm is concurrent with his time in the great fish.

2:3 וַיֹּאמֶר—After this word, the book shifts from prose to poetry. The translation is arranged to reflect this shift.

קָרָאתִי מִצָּרָה לִי אֶל־יְהוָה וַיַּעֲנֵנִי—This line displays the *qinah* (3:2) meter. The first line has three Hebrew words, each with its own accent: literally, "I called [קָרָאתִי] from distress [מִצָּרָה, the noun צָרָה with the preposition מִן [מִן] to me [לִי]," yielding, "I called out in my distress." The second line also has three Hebrew words: "to [אֶל] Yahweh [יְהוָה], and he answered me [וַיַּעֲנֵנִי]." However, the construct phrase has a single accent (אֶל־יְהוָה), so the second line has only two stressed units. The final verb, וַיַּעֲנֵנִי, is the Qal third masculine singular imperfect of עָנָה, "to answer," with *waw* consecutive and first common singular suffix.

The sequence here of a perfect verb (קָרָאתִי) followed by an imperfect with *waw* consecutive (וַיַּעֲנֵנִי) is a good example of the typical use of the *waw* consecutive for successive action: "I called … and (*then*) he answered me." See Joüon, §§ 118 a, c; 119 y.

מִבֶּטֶן שְׁאוֹל שִׁוַּעְתִּי שָׁמַעְתָּ קוֹלִי:—This couplet too has a 3:2 pattern (three accented words followed by two accented words). The phrase מִבֶּטֶן שְׁאוֹל ("from the belly of Sheol") is only used here in the OT and "conveys despair of the darkest hue."[23] The corresponding words in the prose part of the book that bridge to the poetry here are מֵעִים (Jonah is in the fish's "internal organs," 2:1–2 [ET 1:17; 2:1]) and יַרְכְּתֵי (Jonah descends to the ship's "innermost recesses" [1:5]).

The verb שָׁוַע occurs only in the Piel (here first common singular perfect) and specifically means "cry out for help" (BDB). Its form (שִׁוַּעְתִּי) is unusual because וּ is not the *shureq* vowel. Instead, it is the doubled middle root consonant, *waw*, which then takes the vowel *patach* (-ַו-).

---

[21] In general, Hebrew poetry lacks the kinds of regular meter commonly found in classical Greek and Latin poetry. However, Hebrew poetry often has a kind of rhythm or cadence. Moreover, the Hebrew lament called a *qinah* (קִינָה, e.g., 2 Sam 1:17; Ezek 19:1; 27:2; 32:2; Amos 5:1) has a fairly regular, though inconsistent, meter. This is a cluster of five-stress sequences (five words, counting construct phrases as one word) that comprise two poetic lines separated by a caesura. The first line has three stresses (words or construct phrases), and the second has two stresses. The content of a poem marked as a *qinah* usually is a dirge or elegy. See Watson, *Classical Hebrew Poetry*, 87–113, especially p. 98.

[22] Sasson, *Jonah*, 163. Sasson also writes: "Thus, prophets and poets may use the perfect when in fact they are alluding to an event that either is taking place as they speak or is meant to occur in the future."

[23] Sasson, *Jonah*, 172.

2:4 וַתַּשְׁלִיכֵנִי מְצוּלָה בִּלְבַב יַמִּים—The verb שָׁלַךְ occurs only in the Hiphil and Hophal. This form is the Hiphil second masculine singular imperfect with *waw* consecutive and first common singular suffix: "you cast me." "Yahweh" in 2:3 (ET 2:2) is the implied subject.[24] Although the verb "hurl" (Hiphil of טוּל) was used four times in chapter 1 (1:4, 5, 12, 15), the verb שָׁלַךְ, "throw, cast," is more appropriate here in poetry, for it is used by the psalmists to refer to being cast away from God's presence (Pss 51:13 [ET 51:11]; 71:9) or to being thrown down by him in anger (Ps 102:11 [ET 102:10]; cf. Is 14:19; 34:34), and טוּל is never used in that way.

In prose שָׁלַךְ often takes the preposition אֶל or עַל, "cast *to, into*," but poetry frequently omits prepositions when they can be understood from the context. The translation supplies "*toward* the depth." In the OT, the noun מְצוּלָה often refers literally to the watery "depth, deep" (BDB [under the root צוּל]) of the sea, but often is metaphorical for profound distress and despair. It can even be personified as something that "swallows up" (בָּלַע) a person (Ps 69:16 [ET 69:15]). Yahweh can keep sinners mired in מְצוּלָה (Ps 88:7 [ET 88:6]), as well as rescue them from such calamity (Ps 68:23 [ET 68:22]).

Some commentators want to omit בִּלְבַב (the preposition בְּ and לֵבָב in construct: "in the heart of") as a gloss on מְצוּלָה. That omission would reduce this line from four to three stressed words (followed by two in the next: וְנָהָר יְסֹבְבֵנִי) in order to preserve the 3:2 *qinah* metrical pattern visible elsewhere in the psalm.[25] Others prefer to retain בִּלְבַב but omit מְצוּלָה as a gloss.[26] However, it is conceivable that through this staccato-like meter, the psalm purposely introduces a quickened four-beat tempo for dramatic effect. Hebrew authors use discontinuity in meter to focus attention upon what is significant.[27] Here the fact that Jonah is not only in the watery "depth" but also "in the heart of the seas" indicates that he is in a predicament from which he cannot possibly escape, apart from Yahweh's aid. Other poetic passages speak of mountains being cast "into the heart of the seas" (בְּלֵב יַמִּים) as an ultimate catastrophe, but which believers need not fear (Ps 46:3; see also Mt 21:21). Yahweh was able to redeem his people through the Red Sea by causing the waters to congeal "in the heart of the sea" (בְּלֶב־יָם, Ex 15:8).

וְנָהָר יְסֹבְבֵנִי—Usually in prose נָהָר refers to a "river" on land. In some poetic contexts, especially those that also speak of the "sea," Mitchell Dahood understands נָהָר as "ocean current." He believes נָהָר is best understood in this way in Pss 24:2; 46:5 (ET 46:4); 89:26 (ET 89:25); Is 44:27 as well as here in Jonah 2:4 (ET 2:3).[28] The verb יְסֹבְבֵנִי is the Poel third masculine singular imperfect of סָבַב with first common singular suffix, "surrounded me." In this poetic context, the imperfect (with-

---

[24] Morphologically, it is possible that the verb could be the third feminine singular Hiphil imperfect with *waw* consecutive, in which case the feminine noun מְצוּלָה, "depth," would be the subject. However, "the depth cast me into the heart of the seas" makes no sense. Normally שָׁלַךְ ("to throw") takes as a personal subject (Yahweh or people).

[25] See, for example, Landes, "The Kerygma of the Book of Jonah," 6, n. 13.

[26] See, for example, Rowley, *Studies in Old Testament Prophecy*, 84, n. 9.

[27] Cf. Lessing, *Interpreting Discontinuity*, 212–72.

[28] Dahood, *Psalms I*, 151.

out *waw* consecutive) refers to past time. The imperfect can be used in that same way in Ugaritic.[29] The identical form recurs in 2:6 (ET 2:5) with תְהוֹם as subject. The Poel of סָבַב is used in other threatening situations (e.g., Ps 59:7, 15 [ET 59:6, 14]). It can also be used for God surrounding his people in a protective manner (Deut 32:10; Ps 32:7, 10).[30]

כָּל־מִשְׁבָּרֶיךָ וְגַלֶּיךָ עָלַי עָבָרוּ—The nouns מִשְׁבָּר and גַּל (here both are plural with second masculine singular suffix) are synonyms denoting ocean waves. Since מִשְׁבָּר is from the root שָׁבַר, "to break," it is traditionally rendered "breaker." More common in the OT is גַּל, usually rendered "wave." A number of OT passages use עָבַר, "pass over, go over," with the preposition עַל (here with first common singular suffix: עָלַי) to say that waves "go over" someone's head figuratively, implying deep despair (BDB, s.v. עָבַר, 1 f, citing Pss 42:8 [ET 42:7]; 88:17 [ET 88:16]; 124:4–5). Here Jonah's words are literally true: "all your breakers and waves over me pass over."

2:5 וַאֲנִי אָמַרְתִּי נִגְרַשְׁתִּי מִנֶּגֶד עֵינֶיךָ—The pronoun אֲנִי is redundant and emphatic because the inflection of the first common singular perfect verb אָמַרְתִּי already shows the person ("Then *I myself* said …").

The verb גָּרַשׁ is used most often in the Piel, meaning "to drive out, chase away" and implying the severance of an existing relationship.[31] For example, Yahweh "drove out" Adam and Eve from paradise (Gen 3:24). They were excluded from their original communion with God. Cain said to Yahweh, "You have driven me away" from the cultivated land (Gen 4:14). Sarah urged Abraham to expel Hagar and her son Ishmael (Gen 21:10). Zebul drove Gaal and his brothers out of Shechem (Judg 9:41), and Abimelech drove out David (probably out of Gath) when he feigned madness (Ps 34:1 [ET: superscription]; cf. 1 Sam 21:10–15). The form here, נִגְרַשְׁתִּי, is the Niphal first common singular perfect, which has the corresponding passive meaning: "I am driven away."

The combination of the prepositions מִן ("from") and נֶגֶד ("before"), מִנֶּגֶד, with עֵינֶיךָ ("your eyes") is a synonym of the phrase used for Jonah fleeing: מִלִּפְנֵי יְהוָה ("away from the presence of Yahweh") in 1:3 (twice), 10. Thus Jonah now is sorry that he sought to escape from Yahweh.

אַךְ אוֹסִיף לְהַבִּיט—This clause presents the only major textual issue in Jonah. The MT has the particle אַךְ, which can function in at least three different ways:[32] (1) temporally ("just as, no sooner"); (2) emphatically ("indeed, truly"); or (3) adversatively ("but, nevertheless"). For it here, translators choose a meaning that accords with their interpretation of Jonah's circumstances.

The LXX has ἆρα, which functions interrogatively at the beginning of a clause, resulting in "*How* shall I again gaze upon your holy temple?" Similarly, Theodotion translated with πῶς, "how?" On the basis of the LXX and Theodotion, many transla-

---

[29] See Gordon, *Ugaritic Textbook*, 68.

[30] Cf. Sasson, *Jonah*, 176.

[31] H. Ringgren, "גָּרַשׁ," *TDOT* 3:68.

[32] Cf. Muraoka, *Emphatic Words and Structures in Biblical Hebrew*, 129–30.

tions and interpreters emend אַךְ to אֵיךְ, "how?"[33] Thus Jonah despairs of ever seeing Yahweh's temple again.

However, that emendation is untenable when we observe that the LXX changes other assertions in Jonah's psalm into questions or wishes. Two examples are as follows: First, in 2:7c (ET 2:6c) the MT reads: "Then you brought up my life from destruction/the pit, O Yahweh my God." The LXX reads: "the corruption of my life" (φθορὰ ζωῆς μου) and makes this phrase the subject of the clause. The verb is rendered in a third person imperative, which casts the phrase as a wish: "Let the corruption of my life ascend, O Lord my God." As a second example, in 2:8b–c (ET 2:7b–c), the verb is rendered as a Greek optative (ἔλθοι), which changes the MT's "My prayer came to you, to your holy temple" to "May my prayer come to you."[34]

To be sure, if the reading were אֵיךְ, it would continue Jonah's mood of despair. But it is also possible that the prophet's shift in mood from despair to hope begins here. Sasson summarizes the history of these two translations, and his conclusion is persuasive:

> Emending the Hebrew of Jonah because of a variant reading located in an ancient translation is not a useful approach, especially because we have repeatedly observed how translators adapt whenever it suits their (or their audience's) theology.[35]

Now that we have settled on following the Hebrew reading אַךְ, which signals the reversal of Jonah's thoughts from despair to hope, two views are possible. It may function as either an asseverative ("surely") or an adversative ("but"). The former could signify a humble yet confident faith; the latter, a defiant stance. Given Jonah's desperate situation, the asseverative reading makes the most sense. However, given his recalcitrant demeanor throughout chapters 1 and 4, we may also argue for an adversative understanding. Perhaps Jonah is engaging Yahweh on both levels.

The Hiphil of יָסַף (first common singular imperfect: אוֹסִיף) followed by an infinitive usually means "to do something again" (see BDB, s.v. יָסַף, Hiphil, 2 a).

Here it is followed by the Hiphil infinitive construct of נָבַט, "to gaze," with the preposition לְ (לְהַבִּיט), hence, "Surely, I will again gaze." In the OT נָבַט almost always is Hiphil, meaning "look in a specific direction, watch, look at,"[36] or "gaze." It can refer to human beings trying to gaze and stare at Yahweh (Ex 3:6), at his form (Num 12:8), at manifestations of divine grace (Num 21:9), or, as here, toward "his holy temple." To "gaze" upon Yahweh is to be radiant with joy (Ps 34:6 [ET 34:5]). The direction in which the subject of the verb looks is often introduced by אֶל, as here (see the next textual note).

---

[33] This reading is recommended in the *BHS* apparatus and was adopted by the RSV, JB, and Simon, *Jonah*, 21. See also the authors cited in Allen, *Joel, Obadiah, Jonah and Micah*, 216, n. 17.

[34] Perkins, "The Septuagint of Jonah," 48–49.

[35] Sasson, *Jonah*, 179–80.

[36] H. Ringgren, "נבט," *TDOT* 9:126.

אֶל־הֵיכַל קָדְשֶׁךָ:—This phrase ("upon/to your holy temple") will be repeated in 2:8 (ET 2:7). In the construct phrase הֵיכַל קָדְשֶׁךָ ("temple of your holiness"), the noun קֹדֶשׁ (with second masculine singular suffix) is an attributive genitive that functions as a modifier and so is translated by an adjective ("holy temple"). See Waltke-O'Connor, § 9.5.3b, including examples 7 and 20.

The noun הֵיכָל can have three meanings: the king's "palace," Yahweh's "temple," or more specifically, "the 'middle area' in the temple of Solomon, also called the 'holy place.' "[37] The distinction between these meanings is relatively minor. Yahweh reigns as King over his people, and he exercises that reign in part through Israel's king. The temple is Yahweh's dwelling place, his royal palace. Although Yahweh is so great that "heavens and the highest heavens" can not contain him (1 Ki 8:27), he takes up residence in Zion (Is 8:18; Ps 132:13). The presence of Yahweh in the temple is manifested by his "glory" (כָּבוֹד, Ps 63:3 [ET 63:2]), the "cloud" of his "glory" (1 Ki 8:10–11; 2 Chr 5:13–14), and his "name," which dwells there (e.g., Deut 12:5). In biblical theology, a "name" represents the person who bears it; hence where Yahweh's name is, there he himself is present (Pss 99:6; 116:4–6). It is therefore Yahweh's presence that makes the temple holy. Yahweh's holy temple is both located on earth in Jerusalem (Ps 79:1) and in heaven (Ps 11:4; Micah 1:2).

2:6 אֲפָפוּנִי מַיִם עַד־נֶפֶשׁ—The verb אָפַף, "to surround, encompass" (here Qal third common plural perfect with first common singular suffix), is always used to convey distressing situations. It occurs only in Qal and elsewhere in 2 Sam 22:5 ‖ Ps 18:5 (ET 18:4); Pss 40:13 (ET 40:12); 116:3.

The noun נֶפֶשׁ can mean "throat" (Sheol's in Is 5:14) or "neck" (here and Pss 69:2 [ET 69:1]; 105:18).[38] Thus מַיִם עַד־נֶפֶשׁ (the phrase is also in Ps 69:2 [ET 69:1]) means "water up to the neck." Compare עַד־צַוָּאר in Is 8:8 and Waltke-O'Connor, § 11.2.12, footnote 103.

תְּהוֹם יְסֹבְבֵנִי—"The deep surrounded me" is parallel to "an ocean current surrounded me" (2:4 [ET 2:3]) and uses the identical verb form (see the second textual note on 2:4 [ET 2:3]). The noun תְּהוֹם ("the deep") serves as a poetic term for the primordial body of water. Usually (as here) the LXX translates it as ἄβυσσος, "abyss." Following Hermann Gunkel, older scholarship derived תְּהוֹם from the Akkadian Ti'âmat, the name of the primordial goddess in the *Enuma Elish*, whose carcass was divided to create the world.[39] However, this derivation is less likely than it initially appears, since the Hebrew term should then have a middle consonant *aleph* (not a *he*) and a feminine ending. "Most scholars now accept that the Hebrew does not derive directly from the Akkadian, but that both words derive independently from a common proto-Semitic root *tiham*."[40]

The noun תְּהוֹם occurs thirty-six times in the OT and is generally associated with vast water, but it has much deeper and varied connotations than typical words for

---

[37] M. Ottosson, "הֵיכָל," *TDOT* 3:383.

[38] See Sasson, *Jonah*, 184.

[39] Gunkel, *Schöpfung und Chaos in Urzeit und Endzeit*, 112, 115.

[40] Johnston, *Shades of Sheol*, 119–20.

"flood" and "ocean." Most notably, תְּהוֹם refers to the primeval ocean/flood that existed near the beginning of creation (Gen 1:2; Ps 104:6). It sometimes refers explicitly to the depths of the sea or ocean (Ps 135:6; Prov 8:28). Often it connotes death and destruction (Gen 7:11; Ex 15:5; Ezek 31:15). Other times, the idea of an extreme or distant place is the primary emphasis (Job 38:16). It can be paired with another extreme in order to form a merism that communicates vastness, such as "the heavens (above) … the deep lying down below" (Gen 49:25; Deut 33:13).

One possible interpretation of תְּהוֹם here is that it expresses the state of the earth prior to Yahweh's speaking, life-giving acts of creation (Gen 1:2). Jonah's condition is accordingly presented as a reversal of creation, that is, death.

סוּף חָבוּשׁ לְרֹאשִׁי—The noun סוּף usually refers to some sort of "cane" or "rush" that grows on the banks of Egyptian waters (Ex 2:3, 5; Is 19:6). Since those marsh plants rarely grow in seawater, and Jonah is in the ocean depths, translations usually render it here as "seaweed/kelp was bound to my head." חָבוּשׁ is the Qal passive participle of חָבַשׁ, "to bind," which can be used for wearing head coverings (Ex 29:9; Lev 8:13; Ezek 24:17). לְרֹאשִׁי is the noun רֹאשׁ, "head," with the preposition לְ and first common singular suffix.

2:7 לְקִצְבֵי הָרִים יָרַדְתִּי—The noun קֶצֶב derives from the verb קָצַב, "to cut." The noun occurs elsewhere only in 1 Ki 6:25 and 7:37 in reference to the "cut" or "shape" (BDB, 1, and *HALOT*, 1) of the cherubim and the moveable bronze basins in the temple. Probably in this context, where the plural of קֶצֶב is in construct with הָרִים ("mountains"), it refers to the "extremities" or "bases" (see BDB, 2, and *HALOT*, 2) and is translated "roots." The phrase קִצְבֵי הָרִים ("roots of mountains") recurs in Sirach 16:19 in parallel with "the foundations of the earth."[41] With the verb יָרַד ("descend"; here Qal first common singular perfect) the preposition לְ on לְקִצְבֵי means *to the roots*. Thus Jonah descends to the lowest depths of the sea.

הָאָרֶץ בְּרִחֶיהָ בַעֲדִי לְעוֹלָם—This is a nominal (verbless) clause that requires supplying an English verb ("were"), literally, "the land—her bars [were] behind me forever." It begins with הָאָרֶץ as a *casus pendens* (GKC, § 143 a, c) or nominative absolute (Waltke-O'Connor, § 4.7b). Here and in some other OT passages, אֶרֶץ is a synonym of Sheol and שַׁחַת ("the pit/destruction") and refers to the realm of the dead beneath the ground. Hence הָאָרֶץ may be translated as "the underworld" (see *HALOT*, 5; cf. BDB, 2 g).[42] This meaning has been advocated for אֶרֶץ in Jer 17:13; Pss 46:3 (ET 46:2); 141:7; Job 10:21–22. It is now well-attested with cognate examples in Akkadian, Ugaritic, and Aramaic. The Ugaritic cognate for אֶרֶץ can describe the realm of the god Mot ("death"). A relevant OT example is Ex 15:12, where the clause אֶרֶץ

---

[41] The emendation of לְקִצְבֵי to לְקְצְוֵי ("to the ends") by *BHS* is unnecessary and unwarranted. From the context קִצְבֵי הָרִים refers to the bases of the mountains, which extend down to the very bottom of the sea. Support for this interpretation comes from the use of the same phrase in Sirach 16:19 (cited above). Following the LXX, RSV and JB both avoid the problem of translating the term קְצְבֵי in Sirach 16:19 by omitting it completely.

[42] Gunkel first called attention to this (*Schöpfung und Chaos in Urzeit und Endzeit*, 18, n. 1). See also Tromp's examples in *Primitive Conceptions of Death and the Nether World in the Old Testament*, 23–46.

תִּבְלָעֵמוֹ, "the earth/the underworld swallowed him [Egypt]," speaks of the demise of the Egyptian troops in the waters of the Red Sea. In Num 16:32, "the earth [הָאָרֶץ] opened its mouth and swallowed" the followers of Korah. Similarly, "Sheol" is credited with widening its throat and eating voluminously in Is 5:14. These uses are "consistent with the Ugaritic metaphor of Mot's devouring appetite."[43]

The noun בְּרִיחַ can refer to the large "bar" that bolted shut the doors of a city's gate (e.g., Judg 16:3; 1 Sam 23:7). Here it is plural with a third feminine singular suffix (בְּרִחֶיהָ) referring to הָאָרֶץ ("the earth"), which is a feminine noun. "Her gate-bars" refers to the motif of death as a city in the underworld; see "the gates of Sheol" in Is 38:10 and "the gates of death" in Job 38:17. Ps 9:14–15 (ET 9:13–14) captures the movement here in Jonah:

> Have mercy on me, Yahweh, …
>> who lifts me up from the gates of death [מִשַּׁעֲרֵי מָוֶת]
>> that I may declare all your praises.
> In the gates of the Daughter of Zion [בְּשַׁעֲרֵי בַת־צִיּוֹן]
>> I will rejoice in your salvation.

Jonah says that the gate-bars were "around/behind me" (בַעֲדִי, the preposition בַּעַד with first common singular suffix), meaning that he was inside the underworld, within its closed doors. לְעוֹלָם ("forever") means that without Yahweh's aid, he would have remained in perdition for eternity, with no hope for escape.

וַתַּעַל מִשַּׁחַת חַיַּי יְהוָה אֱלֹהָי׃—The verb is the Hiphil second masculine singular imperfect of עָלָה, "to bring up," with *waw* consecutive. Its direct object is חַיַּי ("my life"), the abstract plural noun חַיִּים with first common singular suffix.

The noun שַׁחַת can refer to an ordinary "pit" used as a trap (e.g., Ezek 19:4, 8; Pss 7:16 [ET 7:15]; 35:7) or as a metaphor for death or the grave (e.g., Ps 55:24 [ET 55:23]; 103:4). Since it is a place of decay, often it is best rendered "destruction" (e.g., Ps 16:10), a meaning supported by the common verb שָׁחַת, "to destroy." Here it has the preposition מִן, indicating a deliverance "*from* destruction," as also in Is 38:17; Ps 103:4; and Job 33:18, 30 (cf. 33:24), where Elihu rebukes Job by declaring that Yahweh can work through suffering in order to redeem life. Darkness and death are found in the depths of the pit. But light, liberation, and life are found when Yahweh redeems his people out of the pit. Since Jonah descended into the depths, farther and farther away from life, it is fitting that he now describes his rescue from the pit. Death is downward, while life and salvation are upward.

2:8 This verse recapitulates the entire psalm up to this point.

בְּהִתְעַטֵּף עָלַי נַפְשִׁי—The verb עָטַף, "be feeble, weak," is used in the Hithpael only six times in the OT, usually with either נֶפֶשׁ (one's "life," as here) or רוּחַ (one's "spirit") as subject and often with the preposition עַל in a reflexive sense ("to/upon oneself") that is hard to render in good English. Here the Hithpael infinitive construct with בְּ forms a temporal clause: "When my life ebbed/pined away for me." ESV is a

---

[43] Kaltner and McKenzie, *Beyond Babel*, 236. See further the rest of their discussion on the relevance of Ugaritic for understanding אֶרֶץ.

typical translation: "When my life was fainting away," but clearly this is not a temporary loss of consciousness. This "fainting" is closer to a near-death experience than it is feeling woozy on a hot day. Jonah's near-death fainting fits in well with the preceding part of chapter 2, where the prophet goes down into "Sheol" (2:3 [ET 2:2]), into the "deep" (תְּהוֹם, 2:6 [ET 2:5]), and into "destruction/the pit" (שַׁחַת, 2:7 [ET 2:6]). All three words are associated with death.

Here נֶפֶשׁ means "life" (as opposed to "neck" in 2:6 [ET 2:5]). Jonah's life was at a very low ebb, almost to the point of being extinguished (cf. Ps 107:5). He was much closer to death than to true life. But Yahweh answers his prayer, and he is delivered.

אֶת־יְהוָה זָכָרְתִּי—Using the technique of anastrophe, the direct object—the proper name יְהוָה ("Yahweh")—is placed first for emphasis, before the verb, "I remembered." The first common singular Qal perfect of זָכַר is in pause, hence -כָ- instead of -כַ-. Often זָכַר merges the idea of "remembering" and "orally invoking," especially when a name is its object (and its Hiphil with יהוה can mean "to invoke Yahweh" [Is 62:6]). It is not merely recalling benign facts or events. זָכַר is parallel to שִׂים or עָלָה with עַל־לֵב ("place or come up upon a heart," Is 47:7; 57:11; 65:17), where the heart (לֵב) indicates not only the mind but the entire person. The verb זָכַר is also parallel to verbs of action in Num 15:40.

Taken together, זָכַר denotes a remembering in faith that leads to a change in spiritual condition and to action. Thus people are called to "remember" the works of God in order to learn a theological lesson or repent.[c] They are also called to remember what God has said in the past in order to know what to expect in the future (Ps 77:12 [ET 77:11]). When Jonah in 2:8 (ET 2:7) remembers Yahweh, this does not mean that he had forgotten the God he confessed in 1:9. Rather, the word and the next colon of the verse indicate that Jonah's remembering leads to action: a prayer toward Yahweh's holy temple.

(c) Deut 5:15; 7:18; 8:2; 15:15; Is 44:21–22; Ezek 6:9

When Yahweh remembers, this always involves people or his promises to them. He remembers the covenant he made with humanity (Gen 9:15–16), his covenant with the patriarchs (Lev 26:42, 45), as well as his covenant with Israel (Ezek 16:60). But Yahweh does not always remember with favor. He may remember iniquities and punish them (Is 64:8 [ET 64:9]; Jer 14:10; Hos 9:9).

וַתָּבוֹא אֵלֶיךָ תְּפִלָּתִי—The verb is feminine (third feminine singular Qal imperfect of בּוֹא with waw consecutive: "came") because the subject, תְּפִלָּה, is feminine. The noun תְּפִלָּה (with first common singular suffix: תְּפִלָּתִי, "my prayer") is from the same root as the verb וַיִּתְפַּלֵּל ("prayed") in 2:2 (ET 2:1).

אֶל־הֵיכַל קָדְשֶׁךָ:—This phrase is repeated from 2:5 (ET 2:4); see the third textual note on 2:5. This phrase is in apposition to אֵלֶיךָ in the preceding clause: "to you" is the same as "to your holy temple."

2:9 מְשַׁמְּרִים הַבְלֵי־שָׁוְא חַסְדָּם יַעֲזֹבוּ:—In the OT, the common verb שָׁמַר, "to keep, watch, observe, hold to," is normally Qal, except for this one Piel form (masculine plural participle), thirty-seven Niphal forms, and the Hithpael forms in 2 Sam 22:24; Micah 6:16; Ps 18:24 (ET 18:23). The Piel can denote "repeated, intensive action," so the plural participle, used as a noun, means "adherents" or "followers" of idols (see

HALOT, Piel). RSV is representative of many English translations: "Those who pay regard to vain idols forsake their true loyalty." Ps 31:7 (ET 31:6) contains the identical phrase but with the Qal participle; the psalmist declares that he hates "those who worship/hold to vain idols" (הַשֹּׁמְרִים הַבְלֵי־שָׁוְא).

Michael Barré argues that the Piel participle should be emended to the Qal participle with the preposition מִן, hence מִשֹּׁמְרִים, meaning that Jonah's prayer arose "from (among) those who hold" to idols. He notes that a participle followed by a finite verb (here יַעֲזֹבוּ) has a relative force ("those who hold to … forsake") and that the verbs שָׁמַר ("hold to") and עָזַב ("forsake") often occur in opposition to each other. Barré's reading casts the entire verse as a prepositional phrase codifying the last clause of 2:8 (ET 2:7). Then 2:8b–9 (ET 2:7b–8) reads:

> And my prayer came to you,
>> to your holy temple,
> from (among) those who hold to faithless practices,
>> who abandon/disregard their covenant fidelity.[44]

Even without emending the text, much of Barré's analysis is persuasive. The Piel participle can refer to those idol worshipers from whose company Jonah's prayer arose, and so 2:9 (ET 2:8) explains the circumstances of 2:8b–c (ET 2:7b–c). This commentary's translation of 2:8b–9a (ET 2:7b–8a) agrees with Barré's except that it translates הַבְלֵי־שָׁוְא concretely as "utterly worthless idols" instead of Barré's "faithless practices."

The formerly pagan sailors (1:5) actually were converted by Jonah's confession (1:9) to saving faith in Yahweh (1:14, 16). Jonah here seems to ignore their conversion and refer to them as heathen when he says that it was "from (among)" them that his prayer arose to Yahweh. But that attitude of disdain for Gentiles, even after their conversion to true faith, characterizes Jonah throughout chapter 4 (after the Ninevites are converted), so it is not surprising that Jonah here seems to continue to regard the converted sailors as pagans. Jonah must have heard their prayer to Yahweh in 1:14, though he may not have known about their worship of Yahweh (1:16) after they hurled him overboard (1:15).

The noun הֶבֶל usually refers to idols and literally denotes something worthless, vain, or useless. Here in 2:9 (ET 2:8) its plural is in construct with שָׁוְא, which can refer abstractly to "emptiness, nothingness," and is used for idols in Jer 18:15. The construct chain with these two synonyms expresses a kind of superlative ("vanities of nothingness"), which could be rendered "utterly worthless idols." See Joüon, § 141 m, and Waltke-O'Connor, § 14.5b, including example 8.

Many English translations interpret חֶסֶד in חַסְדָּם יַעֲזֹבוּ as a reference to human loyalty, which the idolaters lack; they "forsake their true loyalty" (RSV; similar is KJV). However, most often in the OT the noun חֶסֶד describes a dominant characteristic of Yahweh, usually translated "steadfast love," "loyal mercy," or the like. Therefore, more on target are translations that interpret חַסְדָּם as a reference to Yahweh's

---

[44] Barré, "Jonah 2,9 and the Structure of Jonah's Prayer," 238–41, 243.

love or mercy toward people, even idolaters, who nevertheless reject it; they "forsake their own Mercy" (NKJV; similar are NIV and ESV). Thus when Israel had forsaken Yahweh and was at her lowest point after the Babylonian sack of Jerusalem in 587 BC, she appealed to Yahweh's חֶסֶד (e.g., Ps 89:2 [ET 89:1]; Lam 3:22). After David sinned grievously, he too appealed to God's חֶסֶד (Ps 51:3 [ET 51:1]) as the basis for his plea for forgiveness and new life. No wonder David sings, "For your loyal love [חֶסֶד] is better than life" (Ps 63:4 [ET 63:3]).

Here the noun takes the third masculine plural suffix in an objective sense: חַסְדָּם refers to the "steadfast love" of Yahweh "to/for them." Yet in Jonah 2:9 (ET 2:8) the antithetical parallelism of "those who hold to utterly worthless idols" versus those "who abandon חַסְדָּם" suggests the personal rather than the abstract understanding of the word (as in Ps 144:2), hence חַסְדָּם is translated "the One who loves them."[45]

In Jonah 4:2 the prophet will state his reason for his flight from Yahweh's presence. It is precisely because God is too full of חֶסֶד! Jonah will protest that Yahweh's forgiving grace is inappropriate in this world that is based upon sin receiving its proper sentence: judgment.

The verb עָזַב (Qal third masculine plural imperfect in pause: יַעֲזֹבוּ) is an antonym of שָׁמַר and is used for such unnatural separations as a doe "forsaking" her fawn (Jer 14:5), parents "forsaking" a child (Ps 27:10), and a wife leaving her husband (Prov 2:17). The word is frequently used for apostasy from Yahweh and his covenant (e.g., Deut 29:25). The theme of Israel forsaking Yahweh is central to the book of Jeremiah:

Be appalled, O heavens, over this;
    be horrified, be utterly desolate, declares Yahweh,
for two evils have my people committed:
they have forsaken me [אֹתִי עָזְבוּ],
    the spring of living waters,
to hew out for themselves cisterns,
    broken cisterns that cannot hold water. (Jer 2:12–13)

2:10 וַאֲנִי בְּקוֹל תּוֹדָה אֶזְבְּחָה־לָּךְ—As at the start of 2:5 (ET 2:4), the redundant personal pronoun אֲנִי with ו emphasizes Jonah himself: "but I …" Here the *waw* is disjunctive, separating Jonah from the idolaters (2:9 [ET 2:8]). The construct phrase תּוֹדָה בְּקוֹל ("with a voice/sound of thanksgiving") means "thanksgiving in songs of liturgical worship" (BDB, s.v. תּוֹדָה, 2, under the root ידה). It occurs also in Ps 26:7 (cf. Ps 42:5 [ET 42:4]).

---

45 Landes, "The Kerygma of the Book of Jonah, 7, including n. 18. Some argue that the *mem* on חַסְדָּם is the enclitic *mem*, an archaic feature that, as Kaltner and McKenzie assert, "can be attached to virtually any part of speech." The argument is that the enclitic *mem* occasionally appears in Hebrew poetry, but because the particle itself and its meaning were lost in the course of transmitting the OT, the Masoretic vocalization often treats it as another morpheme formed with *mem* such as the ending found on masculine plural words (ים-) or the masculine plural pronominal suffix (ם-). "Its precise meaning remains debated, though in certain contexts it appears to denote emphasis" (Kaltner and McKenzie, *Beyond Babel*, 230–31; cf. Hummel, "Enclitic *Mem* in Early Northwest Semitic, Especially Hebrew," especially p. 106).

The form of אֶזְבְּחָה is the Qal first common singular cohortative (hence הָ-) of זָבַח, "to offer a sacrifice." It is rendered as "*I will indeed sacrifice* to you."[46] לָּךְ is the preposition לְ with second *masculine* suffix in pause (לְךָ when not in pause). The phrase אֶזְבְּחָה־לָּךְ is also in Ps 54:8 (ET 54:6), and in reverse order with the imperfect rather than the cohorative in Ps 116:17. In comparison to both Ps 54:8 (ET 54:6) and Ps 116:17, Jonah's wording places more emphasis on himself and less on Yahweh. This is because Jonah begins with וַאֲנִי, "but I ... ," which is absent in Ps 54:8 (ET 54:6), and because the word order in Ps 116:17 refers to Yahweh first: לְךָ־אֶזְבַּח, "*to you* I will sacrifice." Although these comparisons may remain speculative, Jonah emphasizes himself in other verses in his psalm (e.g., 2:5 [ET 2:4]), with the exception of the dramatic change in 2:8 (ET 2:7; אֶת־יְהוָה זָכָרְתִּי, "Yahweh I remembered").

אֲשֶׁר נָדַרְתִּי אֲשַׁלֵּמָה—The relative clause אֲשֶׁר נָדַרְתִּי, "what I have vowed" (with first common singular Qal perfect of נָדַר, "to vow," used also in 1:16), is the direct object of the verb אֲשַׁלֵּמָה, which is the Piel first common singular cohortative (hence הָ-) in pause (hence -לֵּ- instead of -לְ-) of שָׁלֵם, whose Piel can mean "complete, finish" (BDB, 1), or, as here, "pay vows" (see BDB, 4). This whole line, "what I have vowed I will indeed repay,"[47] is probably epexegetical: the sacrifices to be offered are the ones Jonah vowed in the first clause of the verse: "But I, with a voice of thanksgiving, I will indeed sacrifice to you."

יְשׁוּעָתָה לַיהוָה:—The feminine noun יְשׁוּעָתָה is יְשׁוּעָה ("salvation," from the verb יָשַׁע, "to save, deliver") with the addition of the archaic, unaccented ending הָ- which causes the preceding ה (in the feminine ending הָ-) to revert to its original ת (hence עָתָה-). Such feminine noun forms are common in poetry (see GKC, § 90 g; Joüon, § 93 j). The preposition לְ on לַיהוָה denotes possession: "Salvation *belongs to* Yahweh" (see BDB, s.v. לְ, 5 a–b). Almost the same clause, but in reverse order, is in Ps 3:9 (ET 3:8): לַיהוָה הַיְשׁוּעָה, "to Yahweh belongs the salvation" (cf. Is 12:2).

Throughout the OT, יְשׁוּעָה in the singular is associated with or attributed to Yahweh (see *HALOT*, A 1 a), especially in reference to his saving work of deliverance at the Red Sea (see it in Ex 14:13; 15:2). The prophets attribute salvation to Yahweh alone.[d] There are many examples of Yahweh's salvation being correlated to a particular place or event (Is 46:13; 52:10) or an enduring circumstance (Is 49:8; 60:18). Whether individual or corporate, Yahweh's salvation delivers people in distress. Jonah's confession is certainly in line with the rest of the OT proclamation of salvation by Yahweh alone, which is in harmony with the NT proclamation of salvation in Christ alone (e.g., Jn 14:6; Acts 4:12). Here Jonah is acknowledging Yahweh's salvation through his provision of the great fish.

(d) Is 33:2; 37:20; 43:11; 45:20; Jer 2:26–27

---

[46] This translation understands the cohortative singular as a "pseudo-cohortative" (Waltke-O'Connor, § 34.5.3b). Occurring at least ninety times in the OT, this verbal form carries with it a sense of urgency and determination. Another pseudo-cohortative form in this verse is אֲשַׁלֵּמָה (see the second textual note on 2:10 [ET 2:9]).

[47] The cohortative is rendered "I will *indeed* repay," matching the cohortative אֶזְבְּחָה, "I will indeed sacrifice," in the first line of the verse. See Waltke-O'Connor, § 34.5.3b.

2:11 וַיֹּאמֶר יְהוָה לַדָּג—The Qal of אָמַר with לְ (as here) or אֶל can mean to "command" (BDB, 4), as rendered by the LXX (προσετάγη). "Yahweh said to the fish" thus means "Yahweh commanded the fish."

וַיָּקֵא אֶת־יוֹנָה אֶל־הַיַּבָּשָׁה:—The verb וַיָּקֵא could be either the Qal or the Hiphil third masculine singular imperfect with *waw* consecutive of קִיא, which means "to vomit, regurgitate" in both the Qal and the Hiphil.[48] Of the nine OT occurrences of this verb, only one is unambiguously Qal (in Lev 18:28) and only one clearly is Hiphil (in Prov 25:16). The other seven could be either. In all nine occurrences, the verb has the same meaning.[49] Here the implied subject of the verb is the last-mentioned noun, "the fish" at the end of the preceding clause (לַדָּג). The direct object is Jonah (אֶת־יוֹנָה).

The identical prepositional phrase אֶל־הַיַּבָּשָׁה was in 1:13, the sailors' vain attempt to return the ship "to the dry land." The same noun with article (הַיַּבָּשָׁה) was also in Jonah's confession of faith in Yahweh, "who made the sea and the dry land" (1:9).[50]

Commentary

2:1 (ET 1:17) As far as the sailors are concerned, Jonah has drowned and is forever lost (1:14–16). However, it is the drowned man who remains the chief interest of the narrator. So the mariners are left in worship—not of their old gods like Yamm ("sea"), which had proved helpless (1:5), but of Yahweh, the God of the prophet Jonah (1:16). Jonah's confession of Yahweh (1:9) had brought them to faith in the one true God, who now has saved them. In 2:1 (ET 1:17), the attention turns back to Jonah.

The early Latin poem "Carmen de Iona et Niniue" ("A Poem about Jonah and Nineveh") says the fish "sucked with slimy jaws a living feast" and speculates how Jonah must have lived among "half-eaten fleets" and "digested corpses, dissolved and putrid."[51] However, just exactly what is going on the innards of the fish and what Jonah's living accommodations are like are not the concern of the narrator. All we are told is that Jonah is swallowed and consequently is in the inner parts of the great fish for three days and three nights (2:1 [ET 1:17]).

The sailors have rejoiced in Yahweh's power to save even Gentiles like themselves and responded with proper worship (1:16), but Jonah has not done either. More importantly, he still has not complied with the divine command to go preach to Gentile Nineveh. And although Jonah apparently believes that he will be able to escape Yahweh's commission by his own death, Yahweh

---

[48] BDB cites Jonah 2:11 (ET 2:10) under both conjugations. *HALOT* presumes that it is Hiphil here.

[49] Sasson, *Jonah*, 220, suggests that the form here could be Hiphil with Yahweh as subject and the fish as the first, implied direct object, with only the second direct object (Jonah) stated in the text. The meaning would be that Yahweh "caused [the fish] to vomit Jonah," which could be rendered in the passive as Yahweh "made Jonah be vomited [by the fish]."

[50] See the third textual note on 1:9 and the excursus "Yahweh, the Creator God."

[51] The poem, once ascribed to Tertullian, is in CSEL 23:221–26.

makes it clear that there will be no escape from his call. Rather than kill Jonah or let him die, Yahweh saves him by means of the great fish. In doing so, Yahweh further demonstrates that there is nowhere in the world, even death, where Jonah can escape his presence (cf. Amos 9:2–3).

Jonah Was in the Fish "Three Days and Three Nights" (2:1 [ET 1:17])

The Sumerian myth entitled "The Descent of Inanna to the Netherworld" aids in the interpretation of Jonah's "three days and three nights" (2:1 [ET 1:17]).[52] In this myth, Inanna departs to sojourn in the underworld. But before she goes, she instructs her divine messenger, Ninshubur, to set up an elaborate lament for her if she does not return in order to enlist the divine aid of Enlil, Nanna, and Enki to affect her return. Following the lament is an account of Inanna's departure and reception into the lower realm, culminating in her death at the hands of the goddess Ereshkigal. At this point, the text reads: "After three days and three nights had passed, her messenger Ninshubur, her messenger of favorable words, her carrier of true words, fills the heaven with complaints for her."[53] Close study of the entire context of this myth shows that the "three days and three nights" are not meant to cover the time Inanna spends in the underworld. The phrase's complete separation from the account of Inanna's revival and ascent back to the upper world does not suggest that the goddess is raised from the dead after three days and three nights. Rather, when comparing the text of Inanna's instructions to Ninshubur with the account of his execution of her commands, it seems clear that Ninshubur's delay is to allow sufficient time for Inanna to arrive within the netherworld. The "three days and three nights" are intended to cover the time of travel to the chthonic depths.

This is not to suggest that the narrator of Jonah was familiar with the Sumerian story. But it does suggest that in the ancient Near East there was a common understanding that in some contexts "three days and three nights" could refer to the time of travel to what we would term "hell."

In the OT too, "three days (and three nights)" can be the length of a journey. Sometimes the journey is more mundane (e.g., Gen 30:36), but in other passages, including the narrative of Israel's exodus redemption, the goal of a journey of three days is the worship of Yahweh, the true God.[e] If this interpretation is correct, the "three days and three nights" in Jonah 2:1 (ET 1:17) *is the period of time it takes the great fish to bring Jonah back from Sheol and the brink of death* (2:3, 7 [ET 2:2, 6]) *to life and the worship of Yahweh* (2:8–10 [ET 2:7–9]). During this time, Jonah does not just descend into the nether re-

(e) Gen 22:4; Ex 3:18; 5:3; 8:27; cf. Ex 15:22; 19:11; Num 10:33; 33:8; Josh 9:17; Lk 13:32

---

[52] For the text of this myth, see *ANET*, 52–57. Landes, "The 'Three Days and Three Nights' Motif in Jonah 2:1," interprets Jonah by exploring the mythical background of the motif in the story of Inanna's descent.

[53] *ANET*, 55 (lines 169–73).

gion, as in the pagan myth of Inanna; rather, in this span, the great fish returns its passenger from Sheol to "the dry land" (2:11 [ET 2:10]).

The placement of the temporal motif of "three days and three nights" in 2:1 (ET 1:17), before Jonah's descent (2:3, 7 [ET 2:2, 6]) rather than after it (i.e., if it were in 2:11 [ET 2:10]), stresses the distance and separation of Jonah in the nether realm from Yahweh and those alive in the upper realm. Whether this refers to a span of seventy-two hours or only to parts of "three days and three nights" is an issue of greater concern for modern commentators than it was for the ancient narrator. The motif emphasizes the great gulf between death and life and the difficulties Yahweh overcomes in rescuing Jonah from certain death in Sheol. Understood in this way, Jonah journeys from death to resurrection life with Yahweh.

This same literary device, where a time period denotes more than simply the duration of a certain event, is used when John says that Jesus went to Bethany and found that Lazarus had been in the tomb for "four days" (Jn 11:17, 39). The mention of "four days" underscores the fact that Lazarus truly was dead—until Jesus raised him to life.

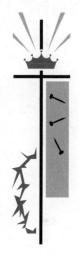

A similar point is made by Luke in the narrative of the conversation of the disciples on the road to Emmaus: since this was on "the third day" since Jesus had been crucified, their hope that he would redeem Israel had been dashed (Lk 24:21)—until their eyes were opened to the reality of his bodily resurrection (Lk 24:31; contrast Lk 24:16). Jesus had accomplished the redemption of the world on Good Friday, but they did not realize this until Easter.

In Jonah's psalm, his descent toward death and Sheol (2:3, 7 [ET 2:2, 6]) fits with him sinking into the ocean depths under God's judgment, and during this descent he uttered his first prayer (2:3, 8 [ET 2:2, 7]). After he is swallowed by the great fish, he realizes that he has been rescued by Yahweh, and that the fish is not a vehicle of punitive judgment. When Jonah prays from the belly of the fish, Yahweh's deliverance has already come to him through Yahweh's appointment of the fish (2:1 [ET 1:17]), not just later, when the fish vomits Jonah onto dry ground (2:11 [ET 2:10]) and his deliverance and return to the land of the living is complete. The psalm then fits into its context of Jonah thanking Yahweh that he has been delivered from death and Sheol by the great fish.

Yahweh Provided the Great Fish (2:1a [ET 1:17a])

Adding to this interpretation is that it is "*Yahweh*" who provides the great fish (2:1 [ET 1:17]). Similarly, in 4:6 it is "Yahweh God/Elohim" who "provided" a qiqayon plant "to save [Jonah] from his evil." In the narrative, whenever this verb, "to provide" (Piel of מָנָה), has "Yahweh" (either alone or with "God/Elohim") as its subject, it refers to an act of salvation. Whenever "God/Elohim" (without also "Yahweh") is its subject, it refers to an act of judgment. We may sketch all the uses of "to provide" (Piel of מָנָה) in Jonah, each of which has a different divine name as subject:

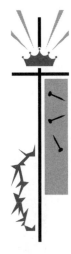

- 2:1 (ET 1:17): "Yahweh" provides a great fish.
- 4:6: "Yahweh God/Elohim" provides a qiqayon plant.
- 4:7: "God/Ha-Elohim" provides a worm.
- 4:8: "God/Elohim" provides a scorching east wind.

The fish, then, is provided by Yahweh as a "means of grace"[54] to save Jonah from Sheol and return him to life, communion with Yahweh in worship (2:5, 8–10 [ET 2:4, 7–9]), and the place ("dry land," 2:11 [ET 2:10]) where he can reassume the commission he had previously abandoned.[55]

So the belly of the great fish appears to be a knife but is really a scalpel. This is the theology of the cross.[56] Jonah's torture is also his treatment, his imprisonment is also his care, his pain is part of his corrective reeducation program. So the great fish is not an instrument of Yahweh's punishment, but rather a vehicle of deliverance that will enable him to continue his ministry and also save the Ninevites. Jonah is already delivered while in his watery grave, for there, in the place of certain death, Yahweh meets him with life (cf. 1 Sam 2:6; 2 Ki 5:7). The Lord of the sea in Jonah 1 is also the Lord of its creatures (cf. Ps 104:26), and he uses both to communicate his will and salvation to Jonah.

The contrast between the obedience of animals (the great fish) and the disobedience of people (fleeing Jonah) is a theme in other OT texts. In Is 1:3, for example, the prophet contrasts the domestic animals, who know their owner, with Israel, who fails to know anything:

The ox knows its owner,
    and the ass its master's trough.
But Israel does not know;
    my people do not understand.

Jer 8:7 states:

Even the stork in the heavens knows her seasons;
    turtledove, swallow, and crane keep the time of their coming.
But my people do not know the justice of Yahweh.

In other narratives, an ass recognizes and obeys Yahweh's Word when the prophet Balaam did not (Num 22:22–31), birds serve as messengers of God (Gen 8:8–12; 1 Ki 17:6), and lions shut their mouths at the bidding of the heav-

---

[54] In Christian theology "means of grace" refers to God's Word and the Sacraments of Baptism and Holy Communion, which are the means through which God bestows his forgiveness, life, and salvation in Jesus Christ. In the OT era, God used a great variety of ways to communicate his salvation (cf. Heb 1:1), and so in this context "means of grace" is used in a broader sense.

[55] This interpretation was already recognized by Jerome, *Commentariorum in Ionam*, commentary on 2:1 (ET 1:17; CCSL 76:394).

[56] See, for example, Walther von Loewenich, *Luther's Theology of the Cross* (trans. Herbert J. A. Bouman; Minneapolis: Augsburg, 1976); Alister E. McGrath, *Luther's Theology of the Cross: Martin Luther's Theological Breakthrough* (Oxford; Blackwell, 1985); Gerhard O. Forde, *On Being a Theologian of the Cross: Reflections on Luther's Heidelberg Disputation, 1518* (Grand Rapids: Eerdmans, 1997).

enly Messenger (Daniel 6). In Jonah, Yahweh provides a great fish (2:1 [ET 1:17]) and a worm (4:7) that both are faithful to their God-given tasks, in contrast to the prophet, who is less willing to say, "Here am I; send me!" (Is 6:8).

To be sure, the figure of a marine creature acting in Jonah 2:1 (ET 1:17) to deliver a human being from danger is unique in the OT. Denizens of the deep occasionally are depicted as distant and thus neutral in their relations with people (e.g., Ps 104:26). More often, the OT depicts Yahweh's mastery and defeat of them as hostile enemies (e.g., Is 27:1; 51:9; Job 40–41).[57] Perhaps because the narrator intends to avoid all hostile connotations, he selects the generic word "fish" (דָּג) rather than a term for a great sea creature or monster, such as "Leviathan" (לִוְיָתָן), "Rahab" (רַהַב), or "dragon" (תַּנִּין).[58] Jeremiah is an example of a Hebrew writer who attributes negative connotations to a sea creature. In Jer 51:34, defeated Judah laments:

> Nebuchadnezzar king of Babylon devoured me and humiliated me;
>> he set me aside like an empty dish.
> Like a sea monster [כַּתַּנִּין] he gulped me down.
> He filled his stomach with my dainty flesh,
>> then spewed me forth.

However, it would be wrong to read into Jonah the imagery in Jeremiah and use this passage to support the allegorical interpretation that Jonah's ingestion by the fish (Jonah 2:1 [ET 1:17]) is merely a symbol for Israel being swallowed by Babylon in the exile.

In the Hebrew of Jonah 2:1 (ET 1:17), the order of characters is Yahweh first, then the fish, and Jonah last (וַיְמַן יְהוָה דָּג גָּדוֹל לִבְלֹעַ אֶת־יוֹנָה). This syntactic placement matches the function of the words as the great fish mediates divine action while keeping Jonah and Yahweh apart—for now. In chapter 4 their dialogue will pick up again. As the tool of Yahweh, the fish saves Jonah from Sheol and then brings him back to life in 2:11 (ET 2:10). In one sense, the great fish experiences the polarities of death (Sheol) and life (Jonah). No wonder it vomited![59]

Jonah's Three Days and Three Nights in the Fish (2:1b [ET 1:17b]) as a Type of Christ's Resurrection on the Third Day

Many NT passages refer or allude to Christ's resurrection on the third day.[f] In some of these, it is stated that Jesus "must" (δεῖ) be crucified and raised on the third day (e.g., Mt 16:21; Mk 8:31; Lk 9:22; 24:7). "Must" implies that the necessity is to fulfill OT Scripture. In addition, both Lk 24:46 and 1 Cor 15:4

(f) E.g., Mt 12:40; 16:21; 17:23; 20:19; 27:63; Mk 8:31; 9:31; 10:34; Lk 9:22; 13:32; 18:33; 24:7, 21, 46; Acts 10:40; 1 Cor 15:4

---

[57] Compare Amos 9:3, where a sea serpent is commanded by Yahweh to bite those who would attempt to hide themselves in the sea from God.

[58] See, for example, "Leviathan" (לִוְיָתָן) in Is 27:1; Ps 74:14; Job 40:25 (ET 41:1); "Rahab" (רַהַב) in Is 51:9; Ps 89:11 (ET 89:10); Job 9:13; and "great sea creature; dragon" (תַּנִּין) in Gen 1:21; Is 27:1; 51:9; Ezek 32:2; Job 7:12.

[59] Cf. Trible, *Rhetorical Criticism*, 159.

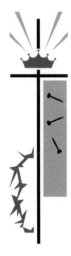

emphasize that Christ's resurrection on the third day is in fulfillment of OT prophecy. So what OT passages prophesy Christ's resurrection on the third day?

The clear candidates are Jonah 2:1 (ET 1:17) and Hos 6:2–3. In Hosea it is the nation of Israel that is smitten by Yahweh and then raised up on the third day so as to live before him. Jonah is the only other OT text that serves as an explicit prophecy of Christ's resurrection on the third day.

This means that Jonah's three-day and three-night excursion in the belly of the great fish is a type of our Lord's resurrection. Jesus uses the hermeneutic of typology when he refers to himself in Mt 12:41: "One greater [πλεῖον] than Jonah is here." In the next verse, he says the same thing about Solomon, who also serves as a type of Christ in that the queen of the South came to hear Solomon's wisdom and came to believe in his God and so be saved. Jesus refers to himself again, saying, "One greater [πλεῖον] than Solomon is here" (Mt 12:42). It is only Matthew who records Jesus' explanation of "the sign of Jonah" (Mt 12:39) in terms of Jonah's experience in the fish's belly (Mt 12:40).

These comparisons, in which Christ is "greater," involve the so-called *Steigerung* or "escalation" aspect of typology: the antitype or fulfillment in Christ is similar to but is always greater than the OT type.[60] Horace Hummel writes of typology: "It is never mere analogy or illustration, but denotes an inner continuity between the anticipation (prophecy) and the climax (fulfillment)."[61] See further the excursus "The Sign of Jonah."

Jonah Prayed to Yahweh (2:2 [ET 2:1])

2:2 (ET 2:1)   The furious action of chapter 1—with its storms and waves and lot casting and panic and fear and finally a man thrown overboard—now ceases in order to allow Jonah time to pray. St. Paul writes: "I will that people pray in every place" (1 Tim 2:8), which in this case is the belly of a great fish!

Throughout the narrative, when Jonah confronts a distressing situation, he prays. Only in Jonah 4:2 does he reveal that he had prayed in the beginning when he received Yahweh's commission to go to Nineveh (1:2). He prays in Nineveh itself after he has witnessed the deliverance of its inhabitants (4:2–3) and here in chapter 2. Not until the end of the narrative, when he prays to himself (4:8), can it be said that Jonah deliberately avoids conversation with Yahweh.

There are seven references to prayer in the four chapters of Jonah. On three occasions, distinct actions of praying are reported, but the body of the prayer is left unrecorded: (1) the sailors' prayers in 1:5; (2) Jonah's references in 2:3, 8 (ET 2:2, 7) to his prior prayer;[62] and (3) the Ninevites' praying to God in 3:8.

---

[60]   See Davidson, *Typology in Scripture*, 416–17 and passim.

[61]   Hummel, *The Word Becoming Flesh*, 325.

[62]   Jonah 2 involves two prayers by Jonah. The psalm that comprises 2:3–10 (ET 2:2–9) is his second prayer. Within this prayer, he refers in 2:3, 8 (ET 2:2, 7) to an earlier prayer. Jonah does not give the content of his first prayer, but simply refers to it. His earlier prayer was uttered in distress, from which Yahweh then saved him, eliciting his second prayer. See fur-

There is one unheeded request for prayer: the captain asks Jonah to call on his God (1:6). Three verbal formulations of prayer are recorded after they are introduced in different ways (1:14; 2:3–10 [ET 2:2–9]; and 4:2–3).

Jonah finds himself beginning his prayer "from the inner parts of the fish" (2:2 [ET 2:1]), essentially the same position he was in in 1:5: "the innermost recesses of the ship." This is the narrator's way of indicating that Jonah repeatedly is in a state of isolation. The prophet will appear alone again, on the east side of Nineveh in 4:5. Jonah's lack of connection to Yahweh (he ignores his God twice, in 1:3 and 4:5, and ends up talking with himself in 4:8) and to people stands in direct contradiction with the divine plan of relationship. See the excursus "The Trinitarian Basis of Old Testament Solidarity."

Jonah's Psalm (2:3–10 [ET 2:2–9])

2:3 (ET 2:2) This verse stands as the introduction to the whole song. It presents the drama of distress, entreaty, and salvation of which the entire psalm is an artful elaboration.

All of the sloshing around makes Jonah's psalm the most concentratedly aquatic one in the OT. Indeed, a tributary of water images flow from the Psalter into Jonah 2. As Jonah finds himself in the watery deep, he joins that company of Israelites who have experienced the threat and terror of an untimely death and cried out to Yahweh for deliverance. Like them, Jonah views death as evil and is unwilling to submit to its life-destroying power. What follows, then, is not a prayer in the normal sense of a plea for help, but a song of thanksgiving for salvation from death. Yahweh has already granted him deliverance by means of the great fish.

The OT saints composing lament psalms typically position themselves in the depths, in pitch darkness, deep down in Sheol or destruction/the pit (e.g., Psalms 88; 130:1–2; Lam 3:55). Normally in these texts, terms like "sea," "river," "breakers," and "waves" are used in a spiritual, metaphorical sense (e.g., Pss 42:8 [ET 42:7]; 69:2 [ET 69:1]; 88:8 [ET 88:7]). In Jonah's psalm, however, this language is both spiritual and literal (see Ex 15:5–10 and Ps 107:25–32 for similar language used both literally and spiritually). In Jonah, the metaphors have flesh: "the belly of Sheol" (2:3 [ET 2:2]) comes with matching blubber and fins!

That Jonah prays is not remarkable; people commonly pray when in desperate circumstances. But there is something remarkable about the way Jonah prays. It is not a spontaneous original prayer of self-expression. Rather, it is a prayer that is derivative from the book of Psalms. God's Word is always first. Just as he spoke creation into existence (Genesis 1), so also his Word creates our faith in him and saves us through that gift of faith. He bespeaks us righteous, and we answer because we have been spoken to.

---

ther the second positive reason (the second reason for *including* the psalm) under "The Place of the Psalm in the Book of Jonah" in "Introduction to Jonah 2."

Thus prayers of faith echo God's Word. This fundamental truth of prayer is demonstrated by the following connections between the Psalter, including the psalms of David (tenth century BC), and the Song of Jonah (eighth century BC).[63]

- "In my distress" (מִצָּרָה לִי, Jonah 2:3 [ET 2:2]; see, e.g., Pss 18:7 [ET 18:6]; 66:14; 81:8 [ET 81:7]; 120:1)

- "Sheol" (שְׁאוֹל, Jonah 2:3 [ET 2:2]; see, e.g., Pss 16:10; 18:6 [ET 18:5]; 30:4 [ET 30:3])

- "I cried out (for help)" (שִׁוַּעְתִּי, Jonah 2:3 [ET 2:2]; see, e.g., Pss 30:3 [ET 30:2]; 88:14 [ET 88:13])

- "The depth" (מְצוּלָה, Jonah 2:4 [ET 2:3]; cf. Pss 69:3, 16 [ET 69:2, 15]; 88:7 [ET 88:6])

- "The heart of the seas" (בִּלְבַב יַמִּים, Jonah 2:4 (ET 2:3); see Ps 46:3 [ET 46:2])

- "All your breakers and your waves crossed over me" (כָּל־מִשְׁבָּרֶיךָ וְגַלֶּיךָ עָלַי עָבָרוּ, Jonah 2:4 [ET 2:3]; Ps 42:8 [ET 42:7])

- "From before your eyes" (מִנֶּגֶד עֵינֶיךָ, Jonah 2:5 [ET 2:4]; Ps 31:23 [ET 31:22]; cf. Ps 139:7)

- "Upon/to your holy temple" (אֶל־הֵיכַל קָדְשֶׁךָ, Jonah 2:5, 8 [ET 2:7]; Pss 5:8 [ET 5:7]; 138:2)

- "Waters ... up to my neck" (מַיִם עַד־נָפֶשׁ, Jonah 2:6 [ET 2:5]; Ps 69:2 [ET 69:1])

- "Seaweed" (סוּף, Jonah 2:6 [ET 2:5]; the same Hebrew term is in "Red Sea," יַם־סוּף, Pss 106:7, 9, 22; 136:13, 15)

- "Gate-bars" (בְּרִחִים, Jonah 2:7 [ET 2:6]; see Pss 107:16; 147:13)

- "You brought up" (וַתַּעַל, Jonah 2:7 [ET 2:6]; see Pss 30:4 [ET 30:3]; 71:20)

- "From destruction/the pit" (מִשַּׁחַת, Jonah 2:7 [ET 2:6]; Ps 103:4; cf. Ps 16:10)

- "My life ebbed away for me" (בְּהִתְעַטֵּף עָלַי נַפְשִׁי, Jonah 2:8 [ET 2:7]; see Ps 107:5; cf. Ps 142:4)

- "Utterly worthless idols" (הַבְלֵי־שָׁוְא, Jonah 2:9 [ET 2:8]; Ps 31:7 [ET 31:6])

- "With a voice of thanksgiving" (בְּקוֹל תּוֹדָה, Jonah 2:10 [ET 2:9]; Ps 26:7; cf. Ps 42:5 [ET 42:4])

- "I will indeed sacrifice to you" (אֶזְבְּחָה־לָּךְ, Jonah 2:10 [ET 2:9]; Pss 54:8 [ET 54:6]; 116:17; cf. Ps 27:6)

- "What I vowed I will indeed repay" (אֲשֶׁר נָדַרְתִּי אֲשַׁלֵּמָה, Jonah 2:10 [ET 2:9]; cf., e.g., Pss 22:26 [ET 22:25]; 50:14; 56:13 [ET 56:12] 66:13; 76:12 [ET 76:11]; 116:14, 18)

- "Salvation belongs to Yahweh" (יְשׁוּעָתָה לַיהוָה, Jonah 2:10 [ET 2:9]; see Ps 3:9 [ET 3:8]; cf. Pss 68:20 [ET 68:19]; 98:2–3; 118:14)

The value of liturgical prayer such as Jonah's is that frequent repetition fills our memory with God's own words, phrases, and images, which then become a rich treasury from which to draw on in times of distress. When we are in great need, familiar and treasured passages of Scripture, liturgy, and hymnody become

---

[63] Sasson, *Jonah*, 208, writes: "Because of their floating nature, the expressions and imagery of Jonah's poem ... may be available at all periods of Israel's literary history."

freshly meaningful. Familiar words recreate images that reawaken faith or mend a broken heart.

Jonah 2:3–10 (ET 2:2–9) is far more than an elaborate patchwork of quotations, motifs, and segments drawn from widely divergent areas of the Psalter and representative of the repertoire of biblical poets. Like other examples of biblical poetry,[g] Jonah's poem reveals a sequence of need, prayer, salvation, and praise:

1. He speaks of trouble and distress in terms of encircling, raging water.
2. He calls to Yahweh out of such distress and is rescued.
3. He understands his rescue as nothing less than a return from Sheol.
4. He acknowledges that the only proper response after such an ordeal is fervent gratitude and renewed piety.

(g) E.g. Pss 18:2–20 (ET 18:1–19); 31:2–25 (ET 31:1–24); 50:14–15, 23; 66:13–14, 17, 19–20; 116:1–19

Far from being a careless collection of quotations from other psalms, Jonah's psalm is consciously and artistically arranged as a chiasm, with a worshipful conclusion:

A   Invocation and answer (2:3 [ET 2:2])

    B   Yahweh acts to allow suffering (2:4a [ET 2:3a])

        C   Description of the psalmist's distress (2:4b–7b [ET 2:3b–6b])

    B'   Yahweh acts to save the psalmist (2:7c [ET 2:6c])

A'   Invocation and answer (2:8 [ET 2:7])

Conclusion: Declaration of faith and worship (2:9–10 [ET 2:8–9])

The longest exact verbal correlation between Jonah and the Psalter is this: "All your breakers and your waves crossed over me" (Jonah 2:4 [ET 2:3] ‖ Ps 42:8 [ET 42:7]). The other verbal parallels are shorter or are not exact. Based on this evidence, about a hundred years ago Julius Bewer held that Jonah's psalm is not so much the result of direct borrowing from the Psalter, but rather demonstrates the common religious language of Jonah's day.[64] Bewer's work prompts us take a closer look at Jonah's connections with the Psalter.

The first two lines in Jonah 2:3 (ET 2:2) hint that the speaker, Jonah himself, will be the major character throughout the prayer:

קָרָאתִי מִצָּרָה לִי אֶל־יְהוָה וַיַּעֲנֵנִי

I called out in my distress
    to Yahweh, and he answered me.

Compare the word order in Ps 120:1:

אֶל־יְהוָה בַּצָּרָתָה לִי קָרָאתִי וַיַּעֲנֵנִי׃

To Yahweh in my distress I called out,
    and he answered me.

The inverted word order in Ps 120:1 places the emphasis on Yahweh, but Jonah's natural word order places the emphasis upon himself. Jonah literally begins with himself and his distress before he invokes the name of Yahweh. The subtle syntactical signal continues as Jonah is central throughout his psalm,

---

[64] Bewer, *Jonah*, 24.

while Yahweh, the inaugurator of events, is given a secondary place. It is as though Jonah refuses to live in the spirit of John the Baptist, who said of Jesus Christ, "He must increase, but I must decrease" (Jn 3:30).

The first word in Jonah's psalm is קָרָ֫אתִי, "I called out." This is the same verb that Yahweh (1:2), the captain (1:6), and the sailors (1:14) used in seeking help to alleviate life-threatening danger. In chapter 1 Jonah was unwilling to "call" (preach) to Nineveh to save it from divine judgment or to "call" upon Yahweh to save the foundering ship. But now, Jonah is finally calling to Yahweh, fulfilling Yahweh's command that he "call" (וּקְרָא, 1:2). Yet ironically, the prophet is only calling out for his own sake! Jonah 2:3 (ET 2:2) sharply emphasizes the first person singular nature of the prophet's prayer by ending each of the four cola of the verse with the appropriate first person singular ending. The call has come to Yahweh, but it is not for the sake of the sailors or the Ninevites; it is only for Jonah himself. Jonah only calls when *his* life is on the line.

The second Hebrew word, מִצָּרָה, "from/in distress," anticipates a lament. However, despite beginning "I called out in distress," Jonah delivers a thanksgiving song that describes a devout worshipper who is saved from certain death, prays toward the temple, vows to offer a sacrifice, and acknowledges that all salvation comes from Yahweh alone.

In 2:3 (ET 2:2), Jonah refers to Yahweh in both the third person ("to Yahweh … he") and the second person ("you heard"). Such alternation is a feature of thanksgiving psalms, relating to the singer's twofold task: (1) to praise Yahweh (second person) and (2) to testify to the congregation of Yahweh's saving help (third person). Another example of this phenomenon is in Ps 27:13–14 after the prayer of 27:11–12.

In Jonah 2:4–5 (ET 2:3–4), the prophet addresses Yahweh with second person pronominal suffixes and verbal forms. Then, as the downward movement continues in the psalm and the prophet reaches the very bottom in 2:6–7b (ET 2:5–6b), he makes no reference to Yahweh. But in 2:7c (ET 2:6c), the name of Yahweh reappears. The next three verses in the psalm each contain the name of Yahweh (2:8a, 10c [ET 2:7a, 9c]), an allusive title (חַסְדָּם, "the One who loves them," 2:9 [ET 2:8]), and/or a pronominal suffix ("I will indeed sacrifice *to you*," 2:10a [ET 2:9a]). This use of Yahweh's name signals the motif of his presence or absence throughout Jonah's experience in the sea. It is Yahweh who "kills [by his absence] and makes alive [by his presence]; he brings [a person] down to Sheol and brings [him] up" (1 Sam 2:6).

Jonah's experience on the verge of death is similar to that in chapter 4. There as well, death appears to be winning the battle. Yet ironically, in chapter 4 it is the giving of life to Nineveh that results in the deterioration of life in Jonah. See the excursus "Sheol."

2:4 (ET 2:3) Jonah's song unleashes a veritable flood of water imagery in 2:4, 6 (ET 2:3, 5). This motif is also concentrated in Psalm 69 (69:2–3, 15–16 [ET 69:1–2, 14–15]) and Psalm 88 (88:7–8, 18 [ET 88:6–7, 17]), which, like

Jonah 2, intertwine it with imagery of Sheol and death (Ps 69:16 [ET 69:15]; 88:4–8, 11–13 [ET 88:3–7, 10–12]). Whereas the water imagery probably is purely metaphorical for those psalmists, it is literally accurate for Jonah.

This verse names Yahweh as responsible for throwing Jonah into the sea. It is not a contradiction of Jonah 1:15, where the sailors, at Jonah's request (1:12), lifted him up and hurled him overboard. The storm account in chapter 1 ascribes the tempest to Yahweh (1:4), and the only action that can ease the storm is the sailors' offering of Jonah (1:12). Their prayer to Yahweh underscores that he is in control of all that is occurring (1:14).[65] Accordingly, in Jonah 2:4 (ET 2:3), the prophet does not wrongly blame God for his predicament, but acknowledges the reality of the situation: Yahweh cast him into the depths, and only Yahweh can get him out.

This means that the sailors are the human instruments that performed the divine will. In 1:14 they pray that the action they are about to undertake against Jonah may coincide with Yahweh's will. The sailors do not perish for disposing of the prophet, nor are they punished for taking "innocent blood" (1:14). Rather, the calming of the sea shows that they were the agents of Yahweh's will. The sailors not only survive, but worship Yahweh (1:16) as his loyal subjects.

That is what Jonah affirms in 2:4 (ET 2:3), albeit from a different perspective. Luther concurs with this understanding when he writes:

> "Thou didst cast me into the deep," he [Jonah] says. For that is the way it feels in our conscience, that every misfortune that befalls us reflects God's wrath. Every creature seems like God and God's anger, even though it be but a rustling leaf.[66]

Confirming Yahweh's agency is the fact that the subject of the verb וַתַּשְׁלִיכֵנִי, "and you cast me" (2:4 [ET 2:3]), must be Yahweh.[67] Jonah's distress is ultimately not due to the storm, the sea, or the sailors. Rather, it is a direct result of Yahweh's call (1:2), which Jonah attempted to evade, precipitating Yahweh's action of hurling the storm (1:4). Jonah requested to be thrown overboard (1:12), perhaps as his last, desperate attempt to evade Yahweh's call, or perhaps because he knew this would placate Yahweh (see the commentary on 1:12).

However, a different line of interpretation of 2:4 (ET 2:3) believes that Jonah is blaming Yahweh for a predicament of the prophet's own choosing. It is then understood that *O mea culpa* becomes in Jonah's perception *O sua culpa*! In the midst of a very traditional and pious-sounding thanksgiving psalm, Jonah may be shirking personal responsibility for his actions as he refers

---

[65] Various other thematic contacts between 1:1–16 and 2:3–10 (ET 2:2–9) are noted by Allen, *Joel, Obadiah, Jonah and Micah*, 219.

[66] AE 19:75.

[67] See the first textual note on 2:4.

to the breakers and the waves as belonging to Yahweh ("all *your* breakers and *your* waves," 2:4 [ET 2:3]). Jonah asserts that Yahweh placed him in the threatening situation, but admits nothing about his own actions that led to this turn of events.

Either way, whether Jonah in 2:4 (ET 2:3) attributes his plight to Yahweh's direction or plays the "blame game," the prophet comes to the realization that his perilous brush with death is not simply the result of his own rebellion or of the cooperative assistance of the sailors; it is also a consequence of Yahweh's actions.

2:5 (ET 2:4)   This verse contains the first of two references in the psalm to Yahweh's holy temple (Jonah 2:5, 8 [ET 2:4, 7]). The precise expression "gaze upon your holy temple" is used only in this verse, but the prepositional phrase "to/upon your holy temple" (אֶל־הֵיכַל קָדְשֶׁךָ), is also in 2:8 (ET 2:7) and Pss 5:8 (ET 5:7); 138:2. For a similar situational parallel, see Ps 18:5–7 (ET 18:4–6).

The dual references to "your holy temple" (Jonah 2:5, 8 [ET 2:4, 7]) are an especially powerful theological testimony because they are uttered by a Northern Kingdom prophet in the eighth century BC. Jeroboam son of Nebat in about 933 BC had erected shrines in Dan and Bethel, housing golden calves as idolatrous representations of the God who had redeemed Israel from Egypt (1 Ki 12:28–30). These northern shrines were false substitutes for the true temple in Jerusalem. Jeroboam and the northern kings who succeeded him were all condemned for perpetuating these cultic sites that caused Israel to sin (e.g., 1 Ki 13:1–5; 14:1–16; 15:34; 16:25–27). When Jonah refers to Yahweh's one "holy temple," he thereby dismisses the northern shrines and affirms that the Jerusalem temple in the Southern Kingdom of Judah is the true dwelling place of Yahweh among his people. Trusting in the promises in Solomon's temple prayer in 1 Ki 8:29–30, Jonah turns his prayer toward the house in Jerusalem, where Yahweh promised to reside in grace, to hear prayer, and to answer it.

This method of praying is classically demonstrated by Daniel, who, like Jonah, disregarded a royal decree mandating idolatry:

> Now Daniel, when he learned that the decree had been published, went to his house. The windows in his upstairs room were opened toward Jerusalem. Three times a day he knelt on his knees and prayed, giving thanks before his God, just as he had been doing before. (Dan 6:11 [ET 6:10])

Israel is commanded to pray nowhere else but toward Yahweh's dwelling place, which he has chosen and designated. In Ex 20:24 Yahweh puts it this way: "In every place where I cause my name to be remembered, I will come to you and bless you."

In the fullness of time, God became incarnate in the person of Jesus Christ in fulfillment of all his promises (2 Cor 1:20). As God's dwelling place with us ("Immanuel," Is 7:14; Mt 1:23), Christ is the new temple (Jn 2:21), and through him we have access to the throne of grace (Rom 5:2; Eph 2:18; Heb 10:19–20). Indeed, all prayers are to be directed to God the Father through his

Son, Jesus Christ, because no one can come to the Father except through the Son (Jn 14:6). Noting the incarnational aspects of the OT temple, Luther, commenting on Jonah 2:8 (ET 2:7), writes that God's holy temple is where he "at the time dwelt bodily." Luther continues:

> Therefore all who lived in the land or outside the land were obliged to address their prayers and fix their hearts to the place where God sojourned bodily through His Word, to assure that they would worship no other God than Him who sat enthroned over the cherubim on the mercy seat. All prayers had to be directed thither, just as today in the New Testament our petitions must be addressed to Christ, who is our mercy seat.[68]

Despite Jonah's determination to flee "away from the presence of Yahweh" in 1:3 (that is, to flee Yahweh's Word that called him and also to flee the land wherein Yahweh dwelt in his temple), he does not seek a complete severance of all his relations with God. He has not resolved to live the rest of his life devoid of all further divine contact. On the contrary, Jonah takes pleasure in God's action when it is for his benefit or when it aims at judging unbelievers. Jonah still seeks the continued assurance that Yahweh is still available to hear his prayers (even if they are nothing more than plaintive laments, as in 4:2–3). And so in 2:5 (ET 2:4), Jonah appears to be echoing the words of another psalmist: "How beloved is your dwelling place, Yahweh of hosts. My soul longs and also pines for the courts of Yahweh. My heart and my flesh sing for joy to the living God" (Ps 84:2–3 [ET 84:1–2]).

On the other hand, for all we know about Jonah's prayer to this point, we still have questions. Is it not strange that Jonah expresses his eagerness to return to the temple (here and again in 2:8 [ET 2:7]), especially when there is no mention of his repentance or willingness to go to Nineveh? Where is the fear and worship of Yahweh that he confessed in 1:9? Why doesn't Jonah ever come clean and confess his sin? Does he perceive his decent into Sheol as sufficient divine punishment? Is he counting on divine steadfast love to overlook his disobedience and cancel his commission to preach to Nineveh? Is not the piety reflected here just a bit too cozy? To what extent does his psalm align the temple with the ship's hold and the fish's belly—as yet another deathlike shelter that he hopes will protect him from fulfilling his divine commission (cf. Jer 7:11)?

2:6 (ET 2:5)   Here the second stanza of the psalm begins by dwelling again on the greatness of the past peril in order to enhance the magnitude of Jonah's present salvation. The prophet goes back to the moment when he was thrown overboard and his head sank beneath the waves. He was entangled among the marine growth at the bottom of the ocean, down at the very roots of the mountains (2:7 [ET 2:6]).

---

[68] AE 19:79–80. By "mercy seat" Luther alludes to Rom 3:25, which applies ἱλαστήριον to Christ. That is the term for the lid of the ark of the covenant in the LXX (e.g., Ex 25:17–22; Lev 16:13–15) and in Heb 9:5.

It appears that the first colon of this verse comes from Ps 69:2:

Save me, O God, for waters have come up to [my] neck.

הוֹשִׁיעֵנִי אֱלֹהִים כִּי בָאוּ מַיִם עַד־נָפֶשׁ:

Jonah had found himself at death's door. The gates of hell had prevailed against him, clanging shut with a terrible finality! He had reached "the belly of Sheol" (2:3 [ET 2:2]), the land of no return. What awaited him but inescapable death? But just as Yahweh had been the one who, as David says, "lifts me up from the gates of death" (Ps 9:14 [ET 9:13]), so this same God had come to save Jonah by means of a great fish (2:1 [ET 1:17]). Thus Jonah anticipates Paul's thanksgiving:

> For we do not want you not to know, brothers, the affliction we experienced in Asia. For we were so utterly burdened beyond our strength that we despaired even of living. Indeed, we felt that we had received the sentence of death. But that was to make us rely not on ourselves but on God, who raises the dead. He delivered us from such a death, and he will deliver us. In him we hope, that he will deliver us again. (2 Cor 1:8–10)

2:7 (ET 2:6) As Jonah sinks deeper and deeper, it is as though he is overwhelmed with feelings of claustrophobia. Utter helplessness grows and closes in upon him. At the moment of greatest darkness and despair, when no human action can release him, Yahweh broke through all his suffocating layers and drew his life out to safety, using the great fish (2:1 [ET 1:17]).

There are several allusions in the prose narrative that suggest that from the beginning of the narrative Jonah's conscious flight from Yahweh's presence has been simultaneously an unconscious pursuit of death. Thus his offer in 1:12 may not be a sacrificial act for innocent bystanders but a further stage in the pursuit of death, which he had unconsciously initiated in 1:3, which has the first two instances of the verb יָרַד, "he went down … he boarded." It is in 2:3 (ET 2:2) and 2:7 (ET 2:6) that Jonah is at his lowest: in "Sheol" (2:3 [ET 2:2]) and down to the very "roots of the mountains" (2:7 [ET 2:6]).

In this verse, the words normally understood as "the land" (הָאָרֶץ) and "destruction/the pit" (שַׁחַת) both refer to Sheol.[69] Jonah speaks of Sheol as a city with gates, which were shut and locked behind him with bars: "The land/underworld—her gate-bars [were] behind me forever." A similar image is in Job 17:16, where despondent Job asks:

Will they [Job's hopes] go down within the bars of Sheol?
    Will we descend together into the dust?

בַּדֵּי שְׁאֹל תֵּרַדְנָה
אִם־יַחַד עַל־עָפָר נָחַת:

Both "the roots" (קִצְבֵי) or deepest extremities of the mountains and "the gate-bars" of the underworld (Jonah 2:7 [ET 2:6]) are expressions of OT and ancient Near Eastern imagery that point to the power of death to imprison its

---

[69] Cf. Tromp, *Primitive Conceptions of Death and the Nether World in the Old Testament*, 23–46.

captives (cf. e.g., Ps 18:5–6 [ET 18:4–5]). Isaiah the prophet says: "On that day Yahweh will punish the host of heaven on high and the kings of earth on earth. They will be gathered together like a prisoner in a pit; they will be shut up in a prison" (Is 24:21–22). This prison—the same as Jonah's—finds its way into the NT by means of 1 Pet 3:19–20; 2 Pet 2:4; and Jude 6. Sheol's prison bars are the background to the words of Jesus in Mt 16:18: "You are Peter, and on this rock I will establish my church, and the gates of hell shall not prevail against her."

Jonah 2:7 (ET 2:6) is the climax of the prophet's experience in the first two chapters because this verse juxtaposes two contrasting verbs: "to go down" (יָרַד), which was used in 1:3 (twice) and 1:5 to detail Jonah's descent since turning a deaf ear to Yahweh, and its opposite, "to go up" (עָלָה), here used in the Hiphil, "to bring up." Throughout the book, Yahweh is the inaugurator of events, and here he "resurrects" Jonah. This is thematically consistent with the doctrine of God emphasized in the rest of the narrative. Yahweh has the first (1:2) and the last (4:10–11) word. He is graciously in command to save the mariners, the Ninevites, and Jonah. Commenting on this verse, Luther writes: "The rope breaks when it is at its tightest. Therefore God is called a Helper in need, because He lends His aid when our position is desperate and impossible."[70]

In a play on the metaphor of Sheol having an insatiable appetite and "swallowing" its prey (Ps 141:7; Prov 1:12), Isaiah reverses the curse of the grave as he sees Yahweh swallowing up death forever (בִּלַּע הַמָּוֶת לָנֶצַח, Is 25:8). The swallower will be swallowed.

This same reversal takes place in Jonah 2:7c (ET 2:6c). Jonah was swallowed (2:1 [ET 1:17]) and was in the depths of Sheol (2:3, 7 [ET 2:2, 6]), but Yahweh brings him up 2:7c (ET 2:6c). By using the verb בָּלַע, "to swallow" (2:1 [ET 1:17]) and by telling us that the prophet descended into Sheol (2:3 [ET 2:2]), the narrator suggests that Jonah descended into the very place of the dead under Yahweh's judgment. But just there he is restored to life (cf. Amos 9:2; Hosea 13:14). Yahweh, who gives life, is the only one who can also revive it (Deut 32:39; 1 Sam 2:6; 2 Ki 5:7). That Yahweh can resurrect the dead is declared in 1 Sam 2:6; Is 26:19; Ezek 37:1–14; Hos 6:2; Dan 12:2–3. Here Jonah's descent is halted, his flight from the presence of Yahweh ended. The prophet's statement "Then you brought up my life from destruction/the pit" appears to come from Ps 103:4.

In Jonah's case, the prodigal returns: "He was dead, but is alive again" (Lk 15:24, 32). Unlike his descent, whose report spans over four verses (2:3–7b [ET 2:2–6b]), Jonah's ascent (2:7c [ET 2:6c]) happens quickly. The five Hebrew words in the last colon of this verse (2:7c [ET 2:6c]) bring swift deliverance. The fish that swallowed Jonah in 2:1 (ET 1:17) is now the means by which Yahweh saves his life. Yahweh may have "hurled" the storm (1:4) in his wrath

[70] AE 19:79.

and then, through the sailors, "hurled" Jonah into the sea (1:15), but now his wrath (Law) has changed to life-giving mercy (Gospel). This is a foretaste of what will happen to the Ninevites in chapter 3 when they repent, believe in God, and are saved.

As the "one greater than Jonah" (Mt 12:41), Jesus experienced victory in a most decisive manner. He bore the entirety of God's wrath at humanity's sin and suffered the judgment of being forsaken by his Father; in that way, he experienced hell while on the cross. By his atoning death, he destroyed the power of death, and he neutralized its sting by his resurrection victory. On the first Easter evening, Jesus gave the keys of the kingdom of heaven to his church (Jn 20:23). The church is now empowered to share in the work of the Savior, who is recreating mankind in his image by unlocking the gates of Sheol's deepest prison house.

2:8 (ET 2:7) In terms of verses, this is the halfway mark in the book,[71] and it is also the place where Jonah and Yahweh appear to be the closest. By placing this account of his prayer while in Sheol after 2:7c (ET 2:6c) ("Then you brought up my life from destruction, O Yahweh my God"), Jonah presents the divine intervention as independent of his prayer. Yahweh's salvation is by grace alone, unconditioned and unprompted. In his helplessness, Jonah experiences the divine act of deliverance first and foremost as gratuitous, as an interruption into his desperate straits. He has prayed (2:8 [ET 2:7]) and, on reflection, can even refer to Yahweh's salvation by means of the great fish (2:1 [ET 1:17]) as the means by which Yahweh "answered" him (2:3 [ET 2:2]). But his immediate experience was of God's absence, now shattered by his presence—of salvation emerging out of hopelessness, of grace, unmerited and free. In this way, this verse recapitulates 2:3 (ET 2:2) and Jonah's experience of Yahweh's judgment giving way to Yahweh's deliverance.

To communicate the pathos of a person who is ready to give up all hope, Hebrew can use either of the nouns נֶפֶשׁ ("life") or רוּחַ ("spirit") with a verb such as עָטַף, "expire, grow faint, lose consciousness," as Jonah does here: "When *my life* [נַפְשִׁי] ebbed away." The only other places where the Hithpael of this verb is used with one of those nouns as its subject are in the Psalter. In all but one of those verses, the subject is the psalmist's "spirit," רוּחַ (Pss 77:4 [ET 77:3]; 142:4; 143:4; cf. also the Qal of עָטַף with the subject לֵב, the psalmist's "heart," in Ps 61:3 [ET 61:2]). The rareness of עָטַף in the Hithpael suggests that Jonah is directly quoting from those verses. The significant change is that in those psalms the psalmist uses רוּחִי, "*my spirit* faints," whereas Jonah uses נַפְשִׁי, "*my life* ebbed away." נֶפֶשׁ is also used in 2:6 (ET 2:5; where it was translated "throat") and throughout the narrative ("life" in 1:14; 4:3, 8). Here, Jonah is thankful that his נֶפֶשׁ, "life," has been delivered. The irony is that in chapter 4 Jonah twice asks for his נֶפֶשׁ, "life," to die (4:3, 8). The prophet

---

[71] The book consists of forty-eight verses. Therefore, its midpoint is between 2:8 and 2:9 (ET 2:7 and 2:8).

is "pro life" when all is well and it is his life—but "pro death" when Yahweh's ways are not his ways (cf. Is 55:8–9) and it is the life of the Ninevites that is spared.

Some might say that Jonah has a fox-hole religion, or perhaps a deep sea or fish-belly religion: he remembers Yahweh only when his life faints and he faces death. Why did he only remember Yahweh when his "life ebbed away" (2:8 [ET 2:7])? Why did he not remember when Yahweh called him in chapter 1?

Like all OT and NT believers, Jonah is *simul iustus et peccator*, "saint and sinner at the same time," in all four chapters of the narrative.[72] Sometimes his faith is weak or not evident at all; at other times it shines forth. Throughout chapter 1 he is fleeing from Yahweh, but in 1:9 he utters a powerful confession of faith in Yahweh that converts the sailors. Jonah's psalm in chapter 2 is a model prayer that can be spoken by any believer. Yet when Jonah prays next (4:2), he clearly lacks evangelistic fervor. So Jonah, like every believer, is inconsistent, yet saved by the Lord who alone is always steadfast.

2:9 (ET 2:8)   This verse may be the most difficult Hebrew in the book to interpret (see the textual notes). Its reference to idolatry differentiates it from the rest of the psalm. But this very difference focuses attention on Yahweh as "the One who loves them" (חַסְדָּם)—who loves all people, even idolaters and Gentiles like the sailors and the Ninevites. The sailors were idolaters (1:5) before Jonah's confession (1:9) converted them to saving faith in Yahweh (1:14, 16). So too were the Ninevites until they were converted through Jonah's preaching (chapter 3). The same noun translated verbally here ("loves") is listed as one of Yahweh's key attributes in Jonah 4:2: "abounding in *loyal love*."

The polarity of adhering (מְשַׁמְּרִים) to idols versus abandoning (יַעֲזֹבוּ) Yahweh characterizes the idolaters' attitudes. Since (literally) "vanities/emptinesses of nothingness" (הַבְלֵי־שָׁוְא) is recognized as a standard reference to idols (see the textual note on 2:9 [ET 2:8]), it seems likely that the antithesis (חַסְדָּם) is not just abstract ("love, mercy"), but a personified reference to Yahweh, the faithful covenant God who fulfills all his good promises, and who can also accomplish his threats of judgment (e.g., Josh 23:14–16). In contrast, the emptiness of the idols is the worthlessness of their promises and their impotence to act and save their worshipers.

Jonah appears to contrast himself with these idol worshipers (cf. Ps 31:7 [ET 31:6]) when he suggests that he is different from those who rely on idols. The clause "who hold to utterly worthless idols" sends us back to the pagan sailors in chapter 1 and forward to the godless Ninevites in chapter 3. But Yahweh is merciful (4:2) and is "the One who loves them" (2:9 [ET 2:8]). They receive his love and mercy when they repent and believe in him. In the Apology

---

[72] All believers are "saints" since they are justified through faith alone. They have begun to lead a new life, yet at the same time, throughout this life they struggle against their old sinful nature, which often manifests itself in rebellion against God. See, for example, Romans 6–7. See further "Jonah as Sinner and Saint" in the commentary on 1:2.

of the Augsburg Confession, Melanchthon comments on Jonah 2:9 (ET 2:8): "Every confidence is futile except a confidence in mercy. Mercy preserves us; our own merits and our own efforts do not preserve us."[73] Apart from this mercy, both sets of Gentiles would be lost, as also would be Jonah.

Yet ironically, the sailors and the Ninevites are not the only ones in the narrative who are clinging to worthless idols. In his unwillingness to help the sailors in 1:4–8 and his disregard for the salvation of the citizens of Nineveh, Jonah has his own idol: himself! The "Jonah sindrome" (misspelling and pun intended) manifests itself when we are unwilling to share Yahweh's salvation with others.

More irony is in store for us at the end of the narrative. Just as the sailors were converted (1:14, 16), Ninevites will finally embrace Yahweh's "loyal love" (חֶסֶד in 4:2) and turn away from their worthless idols (3:5). But in the last chapter, Jonah resents and even risks abandoning Yahweh's love when he asks, in effect, "Yahweh how could you be gracious and merciful to Nineveh?" (see 4:2). Who is it then who "adhere[s] to utterly worthless idols"? By chapter 4, Jonah is skewered on his earlier words here in 2:9 (ET 2:8)!

2:10 (ET 2:9) Jonah further distances himself from the idolaters he describes in 2:9 (ET 2:8) with his statement here in this verse. The prophet accents the difference between him and "them" (2:9 [ET 2:8]) by placing the first person independent pronoun at the beginning of 2:10 (ET 2:9) with disjunctive *waw*, וַאֲנִי, "But I ..."

If in fact Jonah believes that he is going to fulfill his vow of sacrifice to Yahweh, then it would only be logical that he plans to go to the temple in Jerusalem to do this. But Yahweh must remind him in 3:1–2 to do "first things first." After being vomited upon dry ground (2:11 [ET 2:10]), Jonah's first mission will not be to go to Jerusalem, but rather to Nineveh.

"Salvation belongs to Yahweh" (יְשׁוּעָתָה לַיהוָה, 2:10 [ET 2:9]) expresses the fundamental theme of each chapter in Jonah. In chapter 1, Yahweh saves the sailors by bringing them to faith (1:14, 16) through the testimony of his reluctant prophet (1:9). In chapter 2, Jonah is saved; he is both rescued from Sheol and brought to repentance and renewed faith in Yahweh. In chapter 3, the Ninevites are saved through repentance and faith in response to Jonah's preaching (3:4). In 4:6 Yahweh seeks "to save" Jonah "from his evil" (לְהַצִּיל לוֹ מֵרָעָתוֹ).

The closest parallel to "Salvation belongs to Yahweh" is in Ps 3:9 (ET 3:8): "To Yahweh belongs salvation; upon your people [is] your blessing." In Jonah's psalm, the word order is inverted, making the name of "Yahweh" the final word. Ironically—again—at the end of the narrative Yahweh has the last word, with Jonah.[74]

---

[73] Ap IV, between § 179 and § 183 in the octavo edition.

[74] Yahweh speaks the first words (1:1–2) and the last words in the book (4:10–11). Chapter 2 also ends with him speaking to (commanding) the fish (2:11 [ET 2:10]).

The importance of this clause—"Salvation belongs to Yahweh"—is emphasized in its placement as both the conclusion of the psalm's climax (2:9–10 [ET 2:8–9]) and as Jonah's final remark before Yahweh releases him from the great fish (2:11 [ET 2:10]). Jonah's confession that salvation comes only through Yahweh, then, functions as both a summary of the song's theme and a reiteration of Jonah 1. It is hardly an accident that the confessions of both the sailors (1:14) and Jonah (2:10 [ET 2:9]) come as their final words before experiencing Yahweh's complete deliverance.

Both chapters 1 and 2 end with the theme of sacrifice and vows, thus drawing a parallel between Jonah's experience and that of the seamen. This is a proper response of faith for any believer, as expressed in this nineteenth-century hymn:

> Savior, Thy dying love Thou gavest me;
> Nor should I aught withhold, Dear Lord, from Thee.
> In love my soul would bow, My heart fulfil its vow,
> Some off'ring bring Thee now, Something for Thee.[75]

Both Jonah and the sailors faced a similar crisis: peril from the sea. Both cried to Yahweh, and both were saved from the sea. Ironically, Jonah is brought to the same point as the Gentile sailors. In chapter 1, Jonah failed to pray, leaving it to the pagan sailors, but he now catches up to them. Now the Israelite follows the example of the pagan sailors, who "worshiped Yahweh with great worship, sacrificed a sacrifice to Yahweh, and vowed vows" (1:16). Jonah says, "I will indeed sacrifice to you. What I have vowed I will indeed repay" (2:10), although the narrative never states that he did so.

The ironic knife has a very sharp edge here. Jonah, the prophet of Yahweh, must learn from the example of the converted pagans! This is still one more way the narrator places Jonah (and by implication, all Israelites) in the same category as the Gentiles.[76] We can almost hear Paul saying this:

> You are all sons of God through faith in Christ Jesus. For as many of you as have been baptized into Christ have been clothed with Christ. There is neither Jew nor Greek, there is neither slave nor free, there is neither male nor female; you all are one in Christ Jesus. And if you are Christ's, then you are Abraham's seed and heirs according to the promise. (Gal 3:26–29)

Like the sailors, Jonah's only hope is to state the painfully obvious fact that Yahweh alone has the power to cast whomever he wills away from his presence (cf. Pss 51:13 [ET 51:11]; 71:9) and to bring that person back again. Like the sailors, once Jonah admits that he is bound and has no control, then he is given freedom.

---

[75] *TLH* 403:1.

[76] Landes, "The Kerygma of the Book of Jonah," 26, writes:

> One of the important things the writer would have us see is that when faced with similar perils, there is no significant difference between the pagans and Jonah with respect to their supplicating Yahweh, the deliverance they receive from him, and the type of response they make to the source of their salvation.

In Jonah 3, the narrator will again restate this idea when he describes how Yahweh changes his verdict when he sees the repentance of the Ninevites (3:10). In chapter 4, Yahweh's discussion with Jonah will stress the important fact that while people are saved through confession, repentance, and faith, salvation is not based on the response or lack of response of people. Rather, salvation is grounded in God's character as a gracious and merciful God who desires to have pity (4:2, 10–11).

"Salvation belongs to Yahweh" (2:10 [ET 2:9]) is striking in terms of the larger context of the narrative. The emphasis that salvation belongs to Yahweh, not to Jonah, is ironic in that by chapter 4 Jonah would like salvation to belong to him *alone*! But it is Yahweh's to give or withhold—not Jonah's. When Jonah is delivered, both here and in 4:6, he reacts with thanks and praise. This stands in sharp contrast to his reaction in 4:1 to the deliverance of Nineveh. In chapter 2, Yahweh's salvation comes to Jonah even without the prophet expressing remorse for his prior disobedience; nowhere in chapter 2 does he explicitly confess his sin of fleeing from Yahweh in chapter 1. Ironically, Jonah will resent Yahweh bestowing this same salvation upon the Ninevites after they openly repent (3:5–9)!

This contrast may strike at the heart of the narrative. Jonah believes Yahweh's mercy should be for Israelites only, not the sailors or the Ninevites. His confession "Salvation belongs to Yahweh" (2:10 [ET 2:9]) is a true and pious affirmation, much like 1:9 before it and 4:2 after it. But as with those other orthodox confessions of true faith in Yahweh, Jonah's behavior in the context falls far short of living up to it. In chapter 2 (also 1:9; 4:2), Jonah speaks as a saint, but throughout most of chapters 1, 3, and 4, he acts as a resentful sinner. In this larger context, his affirmations sound hollow. It is no wonder that the fish can't stomach him and immediately vomits him out!

The psalm ends with an inclusio. In the first verse of the psalm (2:3 [ET 2:2]), Jonah recounts how he cried out in distress, and "Yahweh" (יהוה) heard his "voice" (קוֹל). Now in the last verse, Jonah's prayer has become the liturgical cry of celebration: he pledges sacrifice "with a voice [קוֹל] of thanksgiving" to the source of salvation, "Yahweh" (יהוה). The divine name "Yahweh" in 2:3 (ET 2:2) is matched by the final word in the psalm. Jonah may have the first Hebrew word in the psalm ("I called out," 2:3 [ET 2:2]), but "Yahweh" is the last word, literally, and he will have the last word in 4:10–11.

The Fish Vomited Jonah onto the Dry Land (2:11 [ET 2:10])

2:11 (ET 2:10) Cetus ("whale") and Columba ("dove," the meaning of "Jonah") are two constellations in the Southern Hemisphere that are locked within the same quadrangle. However, in this verse Jonah and the fish are finally distanced from each other as poetry gives way to prose, even as the great fish yields to the will of Yahweh by vomiting Jonah upon dry ground.

Jonah's deliverance is not complete. He cannot survive in a fish forever, so Yahweh speaks, and Jonah is launched forth. Jonah has been swallowed, chomped, slurped, gargled, and claustrophobically closeted, but now he is vomited out at the command of Yahweh's Word. From the beginning (1:2) to the end (4:10–11), Yahweh directs the events in the narrative by means of his Word (cf. Gen 1:3; Ps 33:9; Jn 1:1–3).

The verb "vomit" (קִיא) is dramatic. We might imagine the prophet being thrown out of the fish's mouth or even walking out. The narrator does not say that the fish spat Jonah out or even coughed him up. Undoubtedly, the fish spews Jonah out in obedience to the Word of Yahweh, but the word "vomit" suggests the fish's repugnance towards Jonah.

The great fish that swallowed (בָּלַע) Jonah (2:1 [ET 1:17]) now vomits (קִיא) him out. The same verbs can be applied to nations. Israel was victorious when the sea swallowed her enemies, the pursuing Egyptians (Ex 15:12). Conversely, when the nation is unfaithful, it will be swallowed up like a fig (Is 28:4) or like a useless vessel (Hos 8:7–8). When they indulge in the same kinds of idolatry and sexual immorality as the Canaanites, the land will vomit them out, just as it did the Canaanites (Lev 18:25–28; 20:22). Yahweh will allow Babylon, like a sea monster, to swallow up his unfaithful people (Jer 51:34); indeed, it is Yahweh who swallowed them up (Lam 2:2, 5).

There is a side of OT satire that is focused on indelicacies like vomiting and excretion. For example, in the book of Judges, Ehud's attack on Eglon is placed in a setting where the king's attendants think that he is relieving himself (Judg 3:24). Elijah's jest is that Baal does not answer his worshipers' prayers because he has gone aside to defecate (1 Ki 18:27). Just so, here Jonah's salvation by regurgitation is a conscious attempt to shame him for his nationalistic pride that would withhold salvation from other peoples. It is as though three days of undigested Jonah is enough for the fish!

The text does not say where exactly Jonah is ejected, only that it is "the dry land" (הַיַּבָּשָׁה). Ironically, Jonah had confessed Yahweh to have created "the dry land" (1:9), and the sailors had vainly attempted to row the boat "to the dry land" (1:13). These references to יַבָּשָׁה pick up an underlying motif of redemption as a new creation, for "the dry land" emerged from the deep in Gen 1:9.[77] Having been delivered from the sea and Sheol, Jonah experiences his own type of new creation (cf. 2 Cor 5:17). See the excursus "Death and Resurrection Motifs in Luther's Baptismal Theology."

Summary of Scene 3

First person singular Hebrew forms ("I," "me," etc., as subject, object, or possessive) occur twenty-four times in Jonah's psalm, indicating that he is on center stage. In contrast, references to Yahweh appear sixteen times. If the psalm evokes traditional terminology, Jonah subverts it in significant ways to place himself in the spotlight. Yet, try as Jonah might, Yahweh still has the first

---

[77] See further the textual note and commentary on "the dry land" in 1:9.

and last words. It is his name that brackets the psalm (2:3 [ET 2:2] and 2:10 [ET 2:9]) and the entire chapter (2:1 [ET 1:17] and 2:11 [ET 2:10]). He is still in charge.

But Jonah would rather not admit this—at least not completely. The prophet's deception peaks when he contrasts himself favorably with those who heed empty idols and forsake Yahweh's loyal love (2:9 [ET 2:8]). No doubt Jonah has in mind people like the sailors in chapter 1 and the Ninevites in chapter 3, but in the end they, unlike Jonah, become models of true faith and piety. Thus Jonah's judgment on idolaters becomes a judgment against himself. The closing line of the psalm, "Salvation belongs to Yahweh" (2:10 [ET 2:9]), further elevates the satire, since Jonah resents the fact that the converted pagans are saved. Though these words might be the essence of the entire narrative, when spoken by Jonah they have a nauseous effect—as demonstrated by the fish. More irony occurs when the fish, who delivered Jonah, is then delivered from him.

This interpretation of Jonah's psalm gains more credence when it is read within the context of the entire narrative. Based upon the prophet's confessions of Yahweh in 1:9 and 4:2, it would seem that when Jonah affirms Israelite traditional theology, his true words are ironic in their context. In 1:9 Jonah describes Yahweh as "the God of the heavens, … who made the sea and the dry land," while Jonah is fleeing from the land to the sea to escape this God! In 4:2 Jonah cites Yahweh's magnificent Gospel attributes—"a gracious and merciful God, slow to anger, abounding in loyal love and changing your verdict about evil"—while Jonah is raging because Yahweh is just that! Just so, the same irony is wrapped up in this psalm. Where does Jonah confess his sins? Where does he vow to fulfill his mission to Nineveh? Nowhere! This disconnect correlates with the fish vomiting out Jonah at the point where he says, "Salvation belongs to Yahweh." Enough of this! The fish vomits out Jonah precisely so he can take Yahweh's salvation to the Ninevites, which he was loathe to do.

Jonah's psalm reflects the language and motifs of the Psalms. While it, like 1:9 and 4:2, expresses the truth about Yahweh, this truth conflicts with Jonah's inappropriate, hypocritical, and self-righteous behavior in the larger context of the book. The negative character portrayal of Jonah in chapter 1 is therefore sharpened in chapter 2. The prophet becomes farther separated from those around him by his appalling disregard for the salvation of others. This time it is the fish that separates him. He will go to Nineveh in chapter 3, but then the separation reappears at the narrative's end, where Jonah is physically separated from everyone and talking only to himself (4:8).

But if Jonah is separated from sailors and the fish, he is not cut off from Yahweh, who says in another context, "Never will I leave you; never will I forsake you" (Heb 13:5, quoting Josh 1:5; cf. Deut 31:6, 8). In the Hebrew of Jonah, two similarly constructed lines highlight this promise of Yahweh and bracket the versification the chapter. Yahweh provides a great fish to swallow Jonah (2:1 [ET 1:17]). Yahweh speaks to the fish, and it vomits up Jonah (2:11

[ET 2:10]). Indeed, it is Yahweh who provides the answer to Jonah (2:3 [ET 2:2]), who casts Jonah into the sea (2:4 [ET 2:3]), whose breakers and waves crash over the prophet (2:4 [ET 2:3]), who delivers Jonah from death by drowning (2:7 [ET 2:6]). Jonah's prayer is directed to him (2:5, 8 [ET 2:4, 7]), as are his sacrifice and vows (2:10 [ET 2:9]). The evidence is overwhelming: Yahweh still binds himself to Jonah, and God continues to deal with him not according to strict justice, but rather in ways that are full of grace.

Jonah's determination to flee from the presence of Yahweh (1:3) was a flight to death. By God's mercy, the great fish swallows him and saves the prophet from Sheol. While sinking down toward "the belly of Sheol" (2:3 [ET 2:2]), and when rescued in the fish's belly, Jonah is met by the God who not only killed him ("you cast me," 2:4 [ET 2:3]) but raises him up and gives him new life ("you brought up my life from destruction," 2:7 [ET 2:6]; see also 1 Sam 2:6).

Figure 1

Jonah Points to Christ

Stichting Fonds Goudse Glazen

This sixteenth-century window in St. John's Church, Gouda,
Netherlands, shows Jonah purposefully walking out of the mouth
of the great fish. Jonah is pointing to a Latin banner containing Jesus'
statement "One greater than Jonah is here" (Mt 12:41 ‖ Lk 11:32).
Jonah prefigures Jesus, the "one greater than Jonah."

Figure 2

Jesus, the "One Greater than Jonah"

Stichting Fonds Goudse Glazen

This sixteenth-century window also in St. John's Church, Gouda, Netherlands, shows Jesus, the "one greater than Jonah," emerging victorious from the tomb, having conquered death for us.

Excursus

The Sign of Jonah

Jonah in the Early Church

> He who brought Jonah alive and unharmed out of the belly of the whale after three days, the three youths out of the furnace of Babylon, and Daniel out of the mouths of the lions, does not lack power to raise us up as well.[1]

This anonymous statement from a fourth-century manual of church order combines three episodes from the OT that were dear to the early Christians because they saw in them a foreshadowing of God's power to raise them from the dead. Jonah and the fish; Shadrach, Meshach, and Abednego in the fiery furnace; and Daniel in the lions' den are among the most popular motifs of early Christian funerary art. But on early Christian sarcophagi, Jonah features as the ultimate icon of death's defeat, appearing far more often than other heroes such as Daniel or Shadrach, Meshach, and Abednego.[2] Commenting on Jonah's popularity in early Christian art, Graydon Snyder observes: "There can be no doubt that the primary artistic representation of early Christianity was the Jonah cycle."[3] Of all known pre-Constantinian Christian frescoes, mosaics, sarcophagi, and sarcophagi fragments, Jonah at rest appears forty-two times, Jonah cast into the sea thirty-eight times, and Jonah vomited from the fish twenty-eight times. By way of contrast, the next most frequent figure is that of Noah, who appears in eight instances. The most frequent NT scene is the Baptism of Jesus, with six occurrences. After the Constantinian peace, which greatly reduced the frequency of Christian martyrdom in the Roman world, this artistic popularity of the Jonah cycle wanes and disappears.[4]

The book of Jonah was far and away the most popular biblical narrative before and even some years after Constantine. For example, Peifer notes that "when St. Jerome changed the Latin translation [of Jonah 4:6] from the traditional 'gourd plant' (*cucurbita*) to 'ivy plant' (*hedera*), near riots broke out in North Africa, and Jerome complained that he was accused of sacrilege at Rome."[5]

---

[1]   *Apostolic Constitutions*, 5.7, quoted in Peifer, "Jonah and Jesus," 377 (cf. *ANF* 7:440).

[2]   See Réau, *Iconographie de la Bible: Ancien Testament*, 410–19.

[3]   Snyder, *Ante Pacem*, 45.

[4]   See Snyder, *Ante Pacem*, 49.

[5]   Peifer, "Jonah and Jesus," 378. The story about the near riots is recounted in a letter from Augustine to Jerome (letters of Augustine, 71.5 [*NPNF*[1] 1:327]). See also Jerome's response (letters of Augustine, 75.22 [*NPNF*[1] 1:342]). In his commentary on 4:6, Jerome mentions the accusation in Rome and defends his translation (*Commentariorum in Ionam* [CCSL 76:414–16]).

The chief reason for Jonah's popularity is that he stands out as the clearest OT prefiguration of the death and resurrection of Christ. Jesus himself authoritatively interprets Jonah's experience to show that the deepest significance of this prophet is to point to the Savior's resurrection (Mt 12:40). Jonah is the only OT prophet with whom Jesus directly compares himself. This is striking when this prophet is considered alongside the towering figures of Elijah, Isaiah, Jeremiah, Amos, and others.

According to 2 Ki 14:25, Jonah is from Gath-hepher, a town identified with a site about three miles northeast of Nazareth.[6] That both Jonah and Jesus were prophets from Galilee is suggestive, but does not explain the significance of Jonah for Jesus. No, the real connection comes through "the sign of Jonah."[7]

"The Sign of Jonah" in the Gospels

"The sign of Jonah" is mentioned three times in the Gospels: twice in Matthew (12:39; 16:4) and once in Luke (11:29; see also Lk 11:30).[8] Far too often interpreters focus on this sign as his deliverance *from* the fish (Jonah 2:11 [ET 2:10]).[9] But when Jonah is swallowed by the fish (2:1 [ET 1:17]) and prays his psalm there, he has already descended toward death and Sheol (2:3, 7 [ET 2:2, 6]) under God's judgment, and now he has been rescued by means of the fish (see especially 2:7c [ET 2:6c]). Paradoxically, when he is in the fish, he has been under Yahweh's judgment and now has been given Yahweh's salvation.

It is the thrust of this excursus that when Jesus refers to "the sign of Jonah," he is stating the paradox that he will soon experience death under his Father's judgment and then will be "brought up … from destruction" (2:7c [ET 2:6c]) by his Father and glorified as the source of everlasting salvation. Jonah's experience in the fish within the narrative of Jonah and "the sign of Jonah" in the NT both signify the authorization of the divine messenger by his deliverance from death. The relationship between Jonah and Jesus lies in the sending of a preacher of repentance whose mission is attested by a miraculous act of deliverance from God's judgment into God's salvation. Thus Jonah concludes his psalm by declaring, "Salvation belongs to Yahweh" (2:10 [ET 2:9]).

---

6   See G. W. van Beek, "Gath-Hepher," *IDB* 2:356; Josh 19:13; and Gray, *I and II Kings*, 615–16.

7   Helping to frame the ensuing discussion is Edwards, *The Sign of Jonah in the Theology of the Evangelists and Q*.

8   Although Mark does not record this phrase, he reports Jesus' refusal to perform a sign (Mk 8:11–13), which is part of the context of "the sign of Jonah" in Matthew and Luke (Mt 16:1, 4 is parallel to Mk 8:11–13). J. Jeremias, "Ἰωνᾶς," *TDNT* 3:410, sees no discrepancy between Mark on the one hand and Matthew and Luke on the other. He says: "Both statements make it clear that God will not give any sign that is abstracted from the person of Jesus and that does not give offence." All of the NT references to Jonah (Mt 12:39–41; 16:4; Lk 11:29–30, 32) are in the immediate contexts of "the sign of Jonah."

9   See, for example, Jeremias, *TDNT* 3:409, who sees this as part of Jonah being a "sign" to the people of Nineveh in Lk 11:30.

"The Sign of Jonah" and Jesus' Stilling of the Storm

The three references to "the sign of Jonah" are not the only NT passages that support this analysis. The stilling of the storm by Jesus (Mt 8:23–27; Mk 4:35–41; Lk 8:22–25) is an important episode reported in all three of the Synoptic Gospels that contains strong allusions to the first chapter of Jonah.[10] After comparing the narrative in Jonah 1 with the synoptic accounts, also taking into consideration "the sign of Jonah" passages where Jesus points toward his atoning death and resurrection (Mt 12:39–40; 16:4; Lk 11:29–30), we can arrive at the understanding that *both Jonah and Jesus are God's sacrifices when they come under his judgment, both are raised to new life, and both provide deliverance for others.*

Both in Jonah 1 and the Synoptics, there is a great storm at sea that is so violent that even experienced seamen panic. The leading character sleeps until awakened by the terrified crew. They ask the awakened leader for help. The leader speaks what should be done, then miraculously the sea is calm. The crew responds with great fear and faith.

Moreover, in each of the three Gospel accounts, the context involves a movement from Jewish to Gentile territory. That is also an important element in Jonah 1 as the prophet left Israelite turf to board the ship he hires in Joppa, which is traditionally under Philistine domain.[11] The sea itself in both Jonah (the Mediterranean) and the Gospels (the Sea of Galilee) is outside the jurisdiction of any people; over its chaos only God has dominion (Pss 65:8 [ET 65:7]; 89:10 [ET 89:9]; 107:23–32).[12]

These strong general similarities are sharpened by many points of detail that are highlighted by comparing the LXX of Jonah 1 to the Gospels.

1. Jonah 1:4: καὶ ἐγένετο κλύδων μέγας ἐν τῇ θαλάσσῃ καὶ τὸ πλοῖον ("and there happened a great wave in the sea, and the boat ...")

   Mt 8:24: καὶ ἰδοὺ σεισμὸς μέγας ἐγένετο ἐν τῇ θαλάσσῃ, ὥστε τὸ πλοῖον ("and behold, a great shaking happened in the sea so that the boat ..."; cf. Mk 4:37; Lk 8:23)

   Identical vocabulary: ἐγένετο ("happened"), μέγας ("great"), ἐν τῇ θαλάσσῃ ("in the sea"), τὸ πλοῖον ("the boat")

2. Jonah 1:5: Ιωνας δὲ ... ἐκάθευδεν ("but Jonah was sleeping")

   Mt 8:24: αὐτὸς δὲ ἐκάθευδεν ("but he was sleeping"; cf. Mk 4:38; Lk 8:23)

   Identical vocabulary: δέ ("but"), ἐκάθευδεν ("was sleeping")

---

[10] The rest of this excursus is dependent, in part, on Woodhouse, "Jesus and Jonah," although some of its conclusions differ from those of Woodhouse.

[11] D. F. Payne, "Joppa," *The Illustrated Bible Dictionary* (Wheaton, Ill.: Tyndale, 1980) 2:809.

[12] In addition to those passages, Lane, *Mark*, 176, n. 94, cites extrabiblical passages that affirm that only God can control the wind and the waves: 2 Macc 9:8; Babylonian Talmud, *Baba Meẓiʿa*, 59b; Jerusalem Talmud, *Berakoth*, 9, 13b.

3. Jonah 1:6: ὅπως διασώσῃ ὁ θεὸς ἡμᾶς καὶ μὴ ἀπολώμεθα ("so God will save us and we will not perish")

   Mt 8:25: κύριε, σῶσον, ἀπολλύμεθα ("Lord, save; we are perishing"; cf. Mk 4:38; Lk 8:24)

   Identical vocabulary: forms of the verb σῴζω ("save") with God/the Lord as subject and the verb ἀπόλλυμι ("perish")

4. Jonah 1:15: καὶ ἔστη ἡ θάλασσα ἐκ τοῦ σάλου αὐτῆς ("and the sea stood from its surging")

   Mt 8:26: καὶ ἐγένετο γαλήνη μεγάλη ("and a great calm ensued"; cf. Mk 4:39; Lk 8:24)

5. Jonah 1:16: καὶ ἐφοβήθησαν οἱ ἄνδρες φόβῳ μεγάλῳ ("and the men feared a great fear")

   Mk 4:41: καὶ ἐφοβήθησαν φόβον μέγαν ("and they feared a great fear"; cf. Mt 8:27; Lk 8:25)

   Identical vocabulary: the verb φοβέω ("to fear") with the cognate noun φόβος ("fear") and the adjective μέγας ("great")

This evidence does not prove that the Septuagint of Jonah 1 influenced the Synoptic Gospels in their accounts of the stilling of the storm, but the specific similarities are many.[13]

Some interpreters probably have gone overboard in expounding these similarities to the extent of allegorizing. For example, Jerome in his comments on Jonah views Jonah 1 as a proto-passion narrative. Jonah is like Christ, who fled the heavens to come to Tarshish, that is, "the sea of this world." Jonah in flight is a sign of the incarnate Christ, who abandons his Father's house and country and becomes flesh.[14] However, Jerome's exposition of Matthew 8 points out legitimate biblical parallels. He compares Jesus asleep on the storm-tossed lake to Jonah sleeping in the hold of the ship (thus Jonah 1:5 relates to Mt 8:24; Mk 4:38; and Lk 8:23). While the other passengers in the ship are being tested, Jesus, like Jonah, is carefree. Each is then awakened, and by his command he saves those who woke him up (Jonah 1:12, 15; Mt 8:26).[15]

On the other end of the spectrum is the argument that the correspondences between Jonah 1 and the synoptic accounts are merely coincidental, and are "dictated by the circumstances of describing a severe storm, the fear it imposes, and the presence of one who sleeps undisturbed."[16]

This commentary navigates between the extremes of skepticism and allegory. The important question may be framed this way: Could the inspired

---

[13] Goppelt is among those interpreters who believe Mark clearly had Jonah's story in mind (*Typos*, 72–73).

[14] Jerome, *Commentariorum in Ionam*, commentary on 1:3 (CCSL 76:382).

[15] Jerome, *Commentariorum in Mattheum*, commentary on 8:24–25 (CCSL 77:52).

[16] So says Lane, *Mark*, 176, n. 91. Lane cites Ps 107:23–32 as another biblical passage with parallels to Jesus' stilling of the storm. However, Lane also notes that the only NT reference to Jesus sleeping is in the accounts of the stilling of the storm. And there is no reference to sleeping in Ps 107:23–32.

Gospel writers have written their narratives of the stilling of the storm in a way that prepares us for this assertion by Jesus later in Matthew and Luke: "Behold, one greater that Jonah is here" (Mt 12:41; Lk 11:32)? Since Jesus himself invokes the name of Jonah in Matthew and Luke, it seems reasonable to posit a connection between Jonah's self-sacrifice, which saved the sailors from the storm, and our Lord's greater sacrifice, which provides salvation for all. Thus "Salvation belongs to Yahweh" (Jonah 2:10 [ET 2:9]) finds its fulfillment in the suffering, death, and resurrection of Jesus Christ.

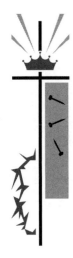

If we bear in mind the connections between Jonah 1 and the stilling of the storm, then we are in a better position to see that "the sign of Jonah" involves more than Jonah's three-day sojourn in the fish (Jonah 2:1 [ET 1:17]) as a type of our Lord's resurrection on the third day. It also involves sacrificial death. Jonah offered himself (Jonah 1:12) and descended to "the belly of Sheol" (2:3 [ET 2:2]), where his "life ebbed away" (2:8 [ET 2:7]) in a kind of death that saved others, who believed and worshiped (Jonah 1:15–16). All the more does the sacrificial death of the Son of Man atone for the sins of all humanity, and this salvation is received by all who believe in him!

Many ancient and modern hymns express this theology. A contemporary example is this Easter hymn:

> All the earth with joy is sounding: Christ has risen from the dead!
> He, the greater Jonah, bounding From the grave, his three-day bed,
> Wins the prize: Death's demise—Songs of triumph fill the skies.[17]

Jesus Gives "the Sign of Jonah" to His Opponents

Confirming that a primary emphasis of "the sign of Jonah" is Jesus' public, sacrificial, vicarious death, which was witnessed by disciples and opponents alike (whereas on Easter only disciples saw the risen Christ), is that all three references to the phrase in the Synoptics occur in contexts where Jesus is responding to opponents who ask him for a "sign." The inquirers are called "the scribes and Pharisees" in Mt 12:38 and "the Pharisees and Sadducees" in Mt 16:1. These designations establish their status as opponents of Jesus. In Mt 12:38, "the scribes and Pharisees" say, "We want to see from you a sign" (θέλομεν ἀπὸ σοῦ σημεῖον ἰδεῖν). In Mt 16:1 (‖ Mk 8:11), the opposition of the questioners is indicated by the circumstantial participle πειράζοντες, "*Testing*, they asked him [Jesus] to show them a sign from heaven." That hostile participle could also be rendered as "*challenging* [Jesus]." Lk 11:16, using the same participle, says: "But others, testing [πειράζοντες], kept seeking from him a sign from heaven." In Lk 11:29, Jesus calls those who seek such a miraculous sign "an evil generation" (similar are Mt 12:39 and 16:4). In Matthew and Luke, Jesus says that "the sign of Jonah" will be the only "sign" he will furnish to such antagonistic interrogators (Mt 12:39; 16:4; Lk 11:29).

---

[17] *LSB* 462:1. Text © 1995 Stephen P. Starke, administered by Concordia Publishing House. All rights reserved.

Jesus' response is even harsher in Mark, where Jesus categorically announces, "Truly I say to you, a sign shall certainly not be given to this generation" (ἀμὴν λέγω ὑμῖν, εἰ δοθήσεται τῇ γενεᾷ ταύτῃ σημεῖον, Mk 8:12).[18] Mark's Gospel does not include Jesus' promise of "the sign of Jonah." James Swetnam argues that Mark deliberately omits it: "What Mark seems to be saying by his silence about Jonah is that the sign of the risen Jesus will not be used in his gospel as a witness to who Jesus is. … The risen Jesus is never portrayed." Instead of the resurrection, Swetnam argues that in Mark, Jesus' own testimony about himself before the Sanhedrin is the definitive witness to the truth of who Jesus is (Mk 14:61–62).[19] While Swetnam overstates his argument, it is true that the other Gospels have much more extensive accounts of the appearances of the risen Christ than does Mark, whose original ending likely was the brief resurrection account in Mk 16:1–8. Mark shows that Jesus is the Son of God in a unique sense. As God incarnate, he alone is on par with God the Father. Therefore no other person, not even such a one as Jonah, is on par with Jesus.

Since "the sign of Jonah" is absent from Mark, a closer study of Luke and especially Matthew is needed to better understand it. We begin with Luke.

"The Sign of Jonah" in Luke

Lk 11:30 says that "Jonah became a sign [σημεῖον] to the Ninevites." Thus "the sign of Jonah" (τὸ σημεῖον Ἰωνᾶ) in Lk 11:29 can be understood as an epexegetical genitive construction with the same meaning. In the context of Luke and Acts, the sign is not difficult to identify: it is the crucified and risen Christ. This is clear from, for example, Peter's remarks in Acts 2:22–24 and 10:36–43 as well as Paul's in Acts 13:26–39 and 17:31.

In Lk 11:29, Jesus' response to his opponents' request indicates that the only sign "this … evil generation" will receive will be one denoting judgment. Jesus is indicating that just as Jonah's mission leads to the conversion and salvation of Gentiles (the sailors in Jonah 1 and the Ninevites in Jonah 3) and also to the destruction of the unfaithful Northern Kingdom of Israel in 722/721 BC, so too Jesus' own ministry will lead to the salvation of Gentiles and the destruction of Jerusalem, which rejected him, in AD 70 (cf. Lk 19:42–44; Rom 11:11–15).

In Lk 11:29–32, "the sign of Jonah" has a different emphasis than in Matthew. In Luke there is no reference to the sea creature (Jonah 2:1, 11 [ET 1:17; 2:10]) or the three days and three nights (Jonah 2:1 [ET 1:17]). Instead, "the sign of Jonah" is that Jonah himself was a sign to the Ninevites, and they repented at his preaching and so were saved. On the Last Day, they will be raised to eternal life and condemn those who rejected Jesus (Lk 11:32). Thus applied to Christ, "the sign of Jonah" is that Christ's preaching brings many to

---

[18] The syntax here, which reflects Hebrew idiom, amounts to an absolute refusal. See BDF, § 454.5.

[19] Swetnam, "No Sign of Jonah"; the quote is on page 127.

repentance and salvation, especially Gentiles—whereas most Jews rejected him, leading to their eternal condemnation. Christ's first sermon in Nazareth confirms both aspects of this "sign": Jesus' mission will extend to Gentiles, just as he alludes to Elijah's mission to Sidon and Elisha's healing of Naaman the Syrian (Lk 4:25–27), yet most of his own people rejected him (Lk 4:28–29).

Therefore, "the sign of Jonah" in Luke 11 is the power of the preached Word of Christ to move all kinds of people (especially outcasts and the lost; see Lk 1:51–55; 2:31–32; 19:10) to repentance and to grant them salvation. This can be explained more fully by passages that expound the theology of preaching and the power of the Word, for example, Is 55:10–11; Rom 10:8–17; 1 Cor 1:18–25; 2:1–5.

"The Sign of Jonah" in Matthew

The context of "the sign of Jonah" in Matthew is similar to that in Luke.[20] However, the emphasis is different. Although Matthew may allow for the sign to be Jonah himself (as in Luke), it is more likely that in Mt 12:39 "the sign of Jonah the prophet" (τὸ σημεῖον Ἰωνᾶ τοῦ προφήτου) is a possessive genitive construction. It refers to Jonah's experience of being cast by Yahweh into the heart of the sea and descending to Sheol, the depths of the earth, and the eternal grave (2:3–7b [ET 2:2–6b]), where his "life ebbed away" (2:8 [ET 2:7]); of being in the fish for three days and three nights (2:1 [ET 1:17]); and of being rescued and restored to full life in God's presence (2:7c, 10–11 [ET 2:6c, 9–10]). Even so, Jesus was forsaken by God the Father (Ps 22:2–3 [ET 22:1–2]) while on the cross; he died and was buried in the earth, but he was not abandoned in Sheol. On the third day, he was raised gloriously to life in God's presence forevermore (cf. Ps 16:10–11; Acts 2:25–28).

In the context of Matthew 12, as Jesus speaks about the repenting Ninevites in the same context as Solomon and the queen of the South (Mt 12:41–42), there is no indication that he or his opponents regard Jonah's experience in the fish for three days and three nights (Mt 12:38–41) as anything less than literally and historically true. Against those who contend that Jesus is only arguing analogically—for which a fable or parable would serve just as well as a historical account of a real person and real events—a key part of the context is his reference to the "men of Nineveh" (ἄνδρες Νινευῖται). Jesus not only regards them as historical figures, but as people who "will arise at the judgment with this generation and condemn it" (Mt 12:41). The passage makes no distinction

---

[20] Mt 12:41–42 presents the same material (the men of Nineveh; the queen of the South) but in reverse order compared to Lk 11:31–32 (the queen of the South, then the men of Nineveh). Mt 16:1–4 includes a saying about "the signs of the times" (Mt 16:2–3) before Jesus' declaration "A sign will not be given to it ['an evil and adulterous generation'] except the sign of Jonah" (Mt 16:4, repeating Mt 12:39). For a study of how form and redaction critics have interpreted the relationships between Matthew, Mark, and Luke, see Edwards, *The Sign of Jonah in the Theology of the Evangelists and Q*.

between the historicity of Jonah and the fish, of the Ninevites, and of Jesus' own death and resurrection, which shall be "the sign of Jonah" (Mt 12:39). To deny one is to undermine the others. The point is this: as a type of Christ, Jonah and his experiences are historical.[21] In light of this, it is noteworthy that in Matthew, Jesus says that no sign will be given "except the sign of Jonah the *prophet*" (Mt 12:39), since the prophets were historical persons.

Jesus continues, "The men of Nineveh will arise at the judgment against this generation" and judge it because the Ninevites repented at the preaching of Jonah, "and behold, one greater than Jonah is here" (Mt 12:41). This is followed by the "queen of the South," who will rise on Judgment Day and condemn "this generation." She came from "the ends of the earth" to hear the wisdom of Solomon and came to believe in the true God of Israel, whereas the present generation largely rejected Jesus, even though "one greater than Solomon is here" (Mt 12:42). In Jonah the city is saved (Nineveh in Jonah 3), whereas in Matthew, the city is destroyed (Jerusalem, Mt 22:7; 23:37–24:28). Thus the sign of Jonah in Matthew is of a greater piece with Matthew's purpose of linking the destruction of Jerusalem and its temple with the failure of the Jews to accept Jesus' call to repentance (cf. Mt 21:41–46; 22:1–7).

The Matthean context of "the sign of Jonah" saying raises a serious question about the common interpretation that "the sign of Jonah" refers primarily or exclusively to Jesus' resurrection. Since Jesus is, in fact, refusing to give any other sign to "this evil and adulterous generation" (Mt 12:39), is it likely that this sign is his resurrection? Are we to understand that Jesus simply says, "No sign will be given to this generation except a resurrection from the dead like Jonah's"? That would be to accede to their demand for a sign that would convince even the most unrepentant skeptics—as if salvation would come through rational proof, rather than through faith (cf. Jn 20:29). After Jesus rose from the dead, he could have appeared publicly to his opponents to prove his identity to them, but this he did not do. Instead, his resurrection appearances were to those who already were his disciples, with the exception of Saul/Paul.[22]

In Mt 12:39, Jesus uses the word σημεῖον ("sign"), which often refers to "an event that is an indication or confirmation of intervention by transcendent powers, *miracle, portent*" (BDAG, 2). But this does not answer the question of the precise meaning of the phrase "the sign of Jonah." The context in Matthew (and the synoptic parallels) is polemical, and Jesus has taken the term σημεῖον ("sign") from his opponents. We would not expect the concessive clause "except the sign of Jonah" to overthrow completely Jesus' fundamental

---

[21] See further "Jonah: Fact or Fiction?" in the introduction.

[22] See, for example, Mt 28:8–10, 16–20; Lk 24:13–53; Jn 20:10–21:25; Acts 1:1–11; 9:1–19; 1 Cor 15:5–8. Unbelieving Thomas might be considered another exception. Perhaps it is in part because Saul/Paul was at the time an unbeliever that he states that the risen Christ appeared to him "last of all as to one untimely born" (ὡσπερεὶ τῷ ἐκτρώματι, 1 Cor 15:8).

refusal in Mt 12:39 to perform a spectacular public miracle that would convince even those who had chosen to reject him (see also Mk 8:12).

Nevertheless, many interpreters understand "the sign of Jonah" in Mt 12:39 to be the resurrection of Jesus on the third day. Certainly for some Jews in Jesus' audience "the sign of Jonah" would have recalled the miracle of Jonah's deliverance (2:11 [ET 2:10]) from the belly of the great fish after "three days and three nights" (Jonah 2:1 [ET 1:17]).[23] However, in the next verse Jesus will point toward his *death and burial*, and this seems to be the primary emphasis of "the sign of Jonah" in Matthew: "For just as Jonah was in the belly of the creature three days and three nights, so shall the son of Man be in the heart of the earth three days and three nights" (Mt 12:40). Yet this emphasis on Jesus' death and burial does not exclude Jesus' resurrection; it anticipates his resurrection. The term κοιλία ("belly") in Mt 12:40 is the same term the LXX uses for Jonah being in the "belly" of the creature (Jonah 2:1–2 [ET 1:17; 2:1]) and also for Jonah's statement that the Lord heard his prayer for deliverance "from the belly of Hades (Sheol)" (ἐκ κοιλίας ᾅδου, Jonah 2:3 [ET 2:2]). In a greater way, God the Father will hear and answer Jesus too (cf. Heb 5:7) by delivering him from death through his resurrection.

Early Jewish sources attest reflection on the significance of Jonah's death (or better, near death). The interpretations of Jonah in the Babylonian Talmud (*Sanhedrin*, 89a–b) and *Pirqe Rabbi Eliezer*, 10, consider God's judgment to have fallen upon Jonah during his three days and three nights in the fish. 3 Macc 6:8 (first century BC) agrees with rabbinic evidence in interpreting the fish as a threat to Jonah, who was under God's judgment for the duration of his interment.[24] Other rabbis considered Jonah to have offered himself (see Jonah 1:12) as a sacrifice to appease God's judgment, which he endured when he was cast into the sea and swallowed by the fish:

> R. Jonathan (*c.* 140 A.D.) said: The only purpose of Jonah was to bring judgment on himself in the sea, for it is written: "And he said to them, Take me and cast me into the sea" (Jon. 1:12). Similarly, you find that many patriarchs and prophets sacrificed themselves for Israel.[25]

Desmond Alexander comments: "In the light of this understanding of Jonah, Jesus could also be alluding to the fact that his own death will take the form of a substitutionary sacrifice" (e.g., Mt 20:28).[26]

Certainly the phrase "three days and three nights" in both Jonah 2:1 (ET 1:17) and Mt 12:40 (but absent from Lk 11:29–32) implies that these prophets' subterranean experiences came to an end. Therefore, this phrase points to

---

[23] The commentary on Jonah 2:1 (ET 1:17) affirms that it is the primary OT text that Jesus has in mind when he repeatedly affirms in the Gospels that he must go to Jerusalem, be crucified, and rise on the third day.

[24] Str-B 1:644–49.

[25] Cited by Jeremias, *TDNT* 3:407, from *Mekilta* (a Tannaitic midrash on Exodus) 12:1.

[26] Alexander, *Jonah*, 94.

Jonah's deliverance as a type of Jesus' resurrection on the third day.[27] But neither the broader context in Matthew nor the content of Mt 12:39–40 points exclusively to the resurrection; rather, they point to the entire *Triduum* ("three days"), the evening of Holy Thursday to the evening of Easter Sunday. This is consistent with the many other Gospel passages where Jesus predicts his resurrection "on the third day" not as an isolated event, but as the finale of the sequence of events beginning with his rejection, suffering, and death.[a]

In the first half of Mt 12:40, ἦν Ιωνᾶς ἐν τῇ κοιλίᾳ τοῦ κήτους τρεῖς ἡμέρας καὶ τρεῖς νύκτας ("Jonah was in the belly of the creature three days and three nights") corresponds exactly to the LXX of Jonah 2:1 (ET 1:17), which at this point is a word-for-word rendering of the Hebrew. The second half of Mt 12:40 locates Jesus' corresponding experience "in the heart of the earth" (ἐν τῇ καρδίᾳ τῆς γῆς). Some have considered the phrase to mean the grave,[28] and certainly Jesus' body did lie in the grave after his death and burial (Mt 27:59–66). However, in addition to the interment of Jesus' body, that phrase also refers to Jesus entering the realm of the dead.[29] The parallel to Jonah's experience; the fact that the term καρδία ("heart") occurs in the LXX in Jonah 2:4 (ET 2:3; ἀπέρριψάς με εἰς βάθη καρδίας θαλάσσης, "You threw me into the depths of the heart of the sea"), which is associated with Sheol (ἐκ κοιλίας ᾅδου, "from the belly of Hades/hell," 2:3 [ET 2:2]); and Jonah's description of his descent to the underworld as κατέβην εἰς γῆν ("I went down into the earth," 2:7 [ET 2:6]) all support the view that "the heart of the earth" (Mt 12:40) is the realm of the dead.[30] This is also supported by the frequent NT proclamation that Jesus then rose "from the dead."[31] (Regarding Christ's descent into hell, see below.)

The primary meaning of "the sign of Jonah" in Mt 12:39–40, then, is the correspondence between Jonah's descent into Sheol and our Lord's experience of forsakenness and death on the cross. Jesus experienced this publicly—in the sight of Jews and Romans, disciples and opponents alike—so this was the "sign" he gave to the "evil and adulterous generation" that rejected him (Mt 12:39; 16:4). As Jonah declared, "'I am driven away from before your eyes" (2:5 [ET 2:4]), so also, when God the Father abandoned his Son, he cried out,

(a) See, e.g., Mt 16:21; 17:22–23; 20:18–19; cf. Mt 26:61; 27:40, 63

---

[27] Within the book of Jonah, there are various possible ways of interpreting the significance of "three days and three nights" in Jonah 2:1 (ET 1:17). See the commentary on 2:1. See also, for example, Landes, "The 'Three Days and Three Nights' Motif in Jonah 2:1." See also the rejoinder to Landes' conclusions in Ackerman, "Satire and Symbolism in the Song of Jonah," 221, n. 11.

[28] For example, Hill, *Matthew*, 220.

[29] Of course, Jesus would not remain there. That is why in Luke the angels ask, "Why do you seek the living one among the dead?" (τί ζητεῖτε τὸν ζῶντα μετὰ τῶν νεκρῶν, Lk 24:5).

[30] See J. Jeremias, "ᾅδης," *TDNT* 1:148; Hanson, "The Scriptural Background to the Doctrine of the '*Descensus ad Inferos*' in the New Testament," 148.

[31] See ἐκ νεκρῶν, "from the dead," in, for example, Mt 17:9; Lk 24:46; Jn 2:22; 21:14; and ἀπὸ τῶν νεκρῶν, "from the dead," in Mt 27:64; 28:7.

"My God, my God, why have you forsaken me?"(Mt 27:46, quoting Ps 22:2 [ET 22:1]). Supporting this interpretation is that the verb "to swallow" (בָּלַע, Jonah 2:1 [ET 1:17]) almost always has negative connotations in the OT.[32] This accords with Mt 12:38–42, where the motif of divine judgment is prominent. The comparison of Jonah and Jesus therefore may also be constructed in terms that denote their experiences under divine judgment: rebellious Jonah deserved to perish in the sea, but far greater was God's judgment against the sin of all humanity, which the sinless Christ bore vicariously (e.g., Mt 20:28; 26:28).

This, then, is "the sign of Jonah": as Jonah was cast into "the belly of Sheol" (2:3 [ET 2:2]), into "the depth" (2:4 [ET 2:3]), out of God's presence, down into "the land/underworld" (2:7 [ET 2:6], synonymous with "Sheol" in 2:3 [ET 2:2]), so it was for the Son of Man when he hung upon the cross for six hours. There God "made him who did not know sin to be sin for us, that in him we might become the righteousness of God" (2 Cor 5:21).

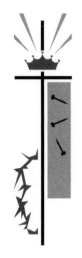

But this is not all, for the references to Jonah's plight are imbedded in a song of praise for deliverance from judgment (Jonah 2:3–10 [ET 2:2–9]) that concludes triumphantly, "Salvation belongs to Yahweh!" (2:10 [ET 2:9]). "The sign of Jonah" in Mt 12:39–40 therefore also implies the resurrection, not, however, simply as a miraculous wonder (as the scribes and Pharisees meant when they used the word "sign"), but as deliverance from divine judgment and as the attestation that Christ had completed the work of redeeming humanity (Rom 4:25). Jesus is the "one greater than Jonah" (Mt 12:41), and as Yahweh heard Jonah's prayer "from the belly of Sheol" (Jonah 2:3 [ET 2:2]; cf. 2:8 [ET 2:7]), all the more will God the Father hear and answer the prayer of Jesus (Heb 5:7), whose life will be brought up from "destruction/the pit" (Jonah 2:7 [ET 2:6]; see Ps 16:10–11; Acts 2:27, 31) through his glorious resurrection, which portends ours (1 Cor 15:42–57).

Jesus goes on to say that the men of Nineveh "will arise" at the time of the judgment and condemn the generation that did not believe Jesus' preaching (Mt 12:41). The verb used in this verse is ἀναστήσονται, which indicates resurrection. Therefore, the context supports the idea that in Matthew 12 "the sign of Jonah" includes Christ's resurrection, which points to and empowers the resurrection of all believers in Christ. That also implies that the Ninevites who repented were believers (Jonah 3:5), ultimately in Christ, and this then confirms the teaching that OT believers share in the same promise of resurrection in Christ as do NT believers (Heb 11:39–40).

A. T. Hanson concludes the portion of his study on the influence of Jonah on the doctrine of Christ's descent into hell as follows: "We may thus confidently claim that the Book of Jonah as a whole is a major scriptural source for

---

[32] Ackerman, "Satire and Symbolism in the Song of Jonah," 220, writes: "When YHWH ordains the great fish to swallow Jonah, the context does not lead us to expect that he will survive." Other interpreters who regard the fish as an instrument of divine judgment include Good, *Irony in the Old Testament*, 46–57; Ellul, *The Judgment of Jonah*, 48; Abramson, "The Book of Jonah as a Literary and Dramatic Work," 40.

the doctrine of the *descensus* in the NT."[33] Jonah descended to "Sheol" and "the roots of the mountains ... the underworld" (2:3, 7 [ET 2:2, 6]). Based on 1 Pet 3:19, the Apostles' Creed affirms that after Jesus' death, "he descended into hell." Jesus' suffering and state of humiliation ended with his death (Jn 19:30), so during his descent, Jesus was no longer vicariously under God's judgment against the sin of humanity. He did not descend to hell to suffer or atone. Rather, as 1 Pet 3:19 states, Jesus "preached" (ἐκήρυξεν) the victory he had accomplished on the cross to the defeated "spirits in prison" in hell.

Conclusion

To summarize, the fundamental difficulty involved in trying to understand "the sign of Jonah" in both Matthew and Luke is the instinctive tendency to look upon Jonah as a sign because of his striking deliverance from the great fish. The fundamental thrust of this discussion, however, is to highlight that the sign involves more: giving oneself as a sacrificial offering for the deliverance of others (see Jonah 1:12, 15; Mt 20:28; 26:28), bearing the divine judgment, descent to the realm of the dead, interment, and then bodily resurrection. As the prophet par excellence, Jesus vicariously bears the entirety of divine judgment against humanity's sin; he is forsaken on the cross, dies, is buried, then rises from the dead on the third day. He thus conquers death and procures for all people an eternal salvation that far transcends the deliverance of Jonah from Sheol through the fish or the respite from the storm for the sailors (Jonah 1:15).

Jonah and Jesus went through judgment, condemnation, and descent (near death for Jonah; actual death for Jesus) before they were raised to new life. The same sequence of events is applied to all baptized believers in Christ: "Therefore we were buried with him through Baptism into death, so that just as Christ was raised from the dead by the glory of the Father, thus we too may walk in newness of life" (Rom 6:4). (See further the excursus "Death and Resurrection Motifs in Luther's Baptismal Theology.") Reflecting on this, Luther writes: "In this way death has become the door to life for us; disgrace has become the elevation to glory; condemnation and hell, the door to salvation."[34]

---

[33] Hanson, "The Scriptural Background to the Doctrine of the '*Descensus ad Inferos*' in the New Testament, " 150.

[34] AE 19:31.

The Trinitarian Basis
of Old Testament Solidarity

Throughout the narrative, the prophet Jonah is withdrawn and isolated. Solitude appears to be one of Jonah's desires. Walled in and cut off from others, he is disconnected from people. In many scenes he appears alienated from everyone, including and especially Yahweh, his God.

Called to go to the great city of Nineveh, Jonah flees from Yahweh by ship (1:2–3). While the crew is awake and praying, Jonah is curled up and sleeping by himself in "the innermost recesses of the ship" (1:5). He asks the sailors to hurl him overboard (1:12), and once separated from them, he finds himself in "the inner parts of the fish" (2:1–2 [ET 1:17; 2:1]), his only companion for three days and three nights. Later he goes to Nineveh, but after the inhabitants are converted to faith in the one true God, Jonah does not remain in their fellowship; rather, angry at God, he seeks death (4:3) and leaves the city (4:5). The epitome of his isolationism comes in his last words, which are a kind of prayer for death, spoken only to himself (4:8).

In the Bible, a full and robust life is not achieved individualistically, as for example, through personal adventure or professional achievement. Instead, it comes through incorporation into the redeemed people of God, by being embedded in the procession of the generations to participate harmoniously in the worshiping community, the body of believers, whose head is Christ. This is life with a promise and an unending future!

Historically, the fascination with self that we see in Jonah began in the West with René Descartes, who proposed a method by which the human self establishes the existence of itself and of reality by its own process of thinking: *cogito ergo sum* ("I think, therefore I am").[1] This Cartesian method isolates the self from the world beyond the self and presupposes that the self can be a self by itself, apart from a relationship with God or anyone else. Following Descartes, John Locke defined a person in terms of self-consciousness, and Gottfried Leibniz thought of personhood as an enduring self-awareness that is present to itself. Immanuel Kant completed these definitions with the note of morality.[2] A person is a self-conscious moral subject.

The writings of American Romantic thinkers like Ralph Waldo Emerson, Henry David Thoreau, and Walt Whitman express this Enlightenment preoccupation with individualism. Note their words:

---

[1] This statement, originally written in French, comes from Descartes' *Discourse on Method* (1637).

[2] Davis, "Our Modern Identity," 159 writes: "The modern age was inaugurated by Kant, with his Copernican revolution or turn to the subject."

Emerson:

- "The Individual is the world."
- "Every man for himself."[3]

Thoreau:

- "If a man does not keep pace with his companions, perhaps it is because he hears a different drummer."[4]

Whitman:

- "I celebrate myself, and sing myself."
- "And nothing, not God, is greater to one than one's self is."
- "I need no assurances. I am a man who is pre-occupied of his own soul."[5]

It is not hard to recognize the words of Emerson, Whitman, and Thoreau in this portion of a contemporary poem titled "I Am Myself" by Mark Mikal.

> Do not try to mold me to suit your needs or standards,
> Nor try to impress your feelings and opinions upon me.
> Do not condemn me, or degrade me,
>   For not matching up to your design.
> To do so would mean the loss of my identity.
> And I would no longer be me. …
>
> I know who I am,
>   I like who I am,
>   I am at peace with myself,
>   And I am happy.
> Simply,
>   I am myself, a person, a being, an individual.
>   I am myself![6]

Emerson, Thoreau, and Whitman melded Enlightenment thought with the American spirit to create a *Zeitgeist* that places emphasis upon the individual, not the group; upon rights, not responsibilities; upon self-expression, not service. Charles Davis writes:

> Modernity may be identified with the affirmation of an autonomous, self-legislating, self-related subject and the insistence upon a doctrine of immanence that refuses submission to anything that attempts to impose itself heteronomously from without as knowledge or value.[7]

---

3   Ralph Waldo Emerson, "Historic Notes of Life and Letters in New England" and "Self-Reliance," in *The Complete Writings of Ralph Waldo Emerson* (New York: William Wise, 1929), quoted by Henderson, *Culture Shift*, 100.

4   Henry David Thoreau, *Walden*, in *The American Tradition in Literature* (ed. George Perkins; 6th ed.; New York: Random House, 1985), quoted by Henderson, *Culture Shift*, 100.

5   Walt Whitman, "Song of Myself," §§ 1, 48, and "Assurances," in *Leaves of Grass* (Boston: Small, Maynard, and Co., 1897), quoted by Henderson, *Culture Shift*, 100.

6   As quoted by Henderson, *Culture Shift*, 101, who says that the original source is unknown (n. 5 on p. 232).

7   Davis, "Our Modern Identity," 159. Postmodern thinking is not fundamentally different from this line of thinking. For example, Michel Foucault, one of the leading figures in the postmodern debate, writes: "The kind of relationship you ought to have with yourself, *rapport à soi* … is one which determines how the individual is supposed to constitute himself as a

Many expositions have explored this understanding of personal identity, and several excellent studies chart the emergence of our notion of self.[8] Of these, Charles Taylor's *Sources of the Self* has enjoyed particular prominence.[9] His thesis is that our pronounced individualism is grounded in modernity's location of the self in the inner depths of one's own interiority, rather than in one's social and public relations. A slogan on a T-shirt sums up where we are: "Galileo was wrong. The universe *does* revolve around me."

On the other hand, communal solidarity is the bedrock, bricks, and cement of OT life.[10] This idea of solidarity is not collectivism, a mere combination of all the individuals. The individual in Israel is not sacrificed for social ends or goals in which he or she has no consciousness of being an individual (as in Hinduism and Eastern religions, in which the goal is for the individual to lose personal identity in the process of becoming one with the transcendent). Rather, participation in the corporate people of God heightens the individual's sense of purpose and meaning as part of a larger whole. In 1935 H. Wheeler Robinson labeled this idea of solidarity "corporate personality."[11] Johannes Pedersen also emphasized Israel's understanding of a strong sense of corporate solidarity and mutual obligations to others.[12] The slogan "all for one, and one for all" from the novel *The Three Musketeers* by Alexandre Dumas gets at this idea.

Israelites see their ultimate existence in relationship with others; this conviction is based upon the nature of their God, Yahweh. A canonical hermeneutic of Holy Scripture understands that the God of Israel who reveals himself in the OT is *one God in three persons*. He is one and the same God who reveals himself in the NT as Father, Son, and Holy Spirit (e.g., Mt 3:16–17; 28:19; 2 Cor 13:14; Gal 4:6). All three persons of the Trinity are involved in the entirety of God's work, from creation and redemption (e.g., Mt 3:16–17) through the end of the age (see Mt 28:19–20). The three persons of the Godhead coex-

---

moral subject of his own actions" ("Afterword: The Subject and Power," in Dreyfus and Rabinow, *Michel Foucault: Beyond Structuralism and Hermeneutics*, 238).

[8] Among others, see *The Category of the Person*, 1–45; 83–140; 217–301; Heller, Sosna, and Wellbery, *Reconstructing Individualism*.

[9] Taylor, *Sources of the Self: The Making of the Modern Identity* (Cambridge, Mass.: Harvard University Press, 1989). Essentially, the development that Taylor charts extends from Augustine through Descartes, Locke, and Kant on into the Romantics, culminating in the affirmation of the human subject as autonomous, disengaged, and self-sufficient.

[10] The connection between individual Israelites and Israel as a united people is demonstrated by passages in which the nouns, verbs, and pronouns alternate between singular and plural. Often this alternation is erased in English translations, since, for example, "you" is used for both singular and plural Hebrew forms. Also, some passages clearly refer to collective responsibility or to an individual as the representative of a group. See, for example, Gen 44:4–9; Ex 34:15; Num 20:14–21; Deut 7:25; 8:19; 14:21. Even the whole people can be called either "the sons of Israel" or (singular) "Israel."

[11] Robinson, "The Hebrew Conception of Corporate Personality." There has arisen a large body of literature critiquing Robinson, including Porter, "The Legal Aspects of the Concept of 'Corporate Personality' in the Old Testament," and Joyce, "Individual Responsibility in Ezekiel 18?"

[12] Pedersen, *Israel: Its Life and Culture*, 1–2:263–310.

ist in loving communion. In love, God has redeemed his fallen creatures, and through incorporation into Christ and his church, God brings us into communion with himself, that we, together with all the saints, may participate in the relationship of divine love between the Father and the Son in the Spirit.[13]

There are Trinitarian texts and themes throughout the OT.[14] In a recent study, R. W. L. Moberly makes the case for a Christian approach to the OT that ultimately sees Father, Son, and Spirit working together in Israel's history. Indeed, such a Trinitarian hermeneutic is a necessity for the proper interpretation of the OT:

> If an Old Testament theology does not make clear that the witness of the Old Testament entails a transformative engagement with God that is as demanding as it is gracious, as corporate as it is individual, as strange as it is familiar, and that receives its deepest realization in the life, death, and resurrection of Jesus, it will be failing in its task.[15]

In keeping with a Trinitarian view, the preexistent, preincarnate Christ appears in various ways in the OT. These forms can include the divine "glory" (כָּבוֹד, e.g., Ex 16:7, 10; 40:34; 1 Ki 8:11),[16] "presence" (פָּנִים, as in Jonah 1:3), and "name" (שֵׁם, e.g., Deut 12:5), all of which at times are used as terms for the preincarnate Son. "Wisdom" is another classic example, especially in Prov 8:22–31 (see also Prov 8:12), a text that has been cited often, beginning with Athanasius (who used it refute Arianism), to demonstrate the preexistence of the Son. However, the most noteworthy example may be "the Angel of Yahweh" (מַלְאַךְ יְהוָה). He speaks as a representative of Yahweh, but at times he shares attributes of Yahweh himself at the same time that he clothes himself in human form (e.g., Gen 16:7–13; 22:11–18; see also "the Angel of God" in Gen 31:11–13). On at least one occasion, he is even worshiped (Judg 13:3–23; cf. Josh 5:13–15).[17] As Francis Pieper notes, the Angel of Yahweh is not just a mes-

---

[13] See, for example, Mt 11:27; Jn 3:31–36; 17:1–26; 1 Jn 1:1–3; 2:24; 2 Jn 3. In Revelation (4:4, 10; 5:8; 11:16; 19:4), the twenty-four elders around God's throne in heaven represent the universal church of both Testaments: the OT believers (the twelve tribes of Israel) plus the NT believers (beginning with the twelve apostles).

[14] Classic Lutheran studies are by Johann Gerhard, "De sanctissimo trinitatis mysterio" (originally published in 1610), *Loci Theologici*, 1:371–446, and Ernst W. Hengstenberg, *Christology of the Old Testament* (originally published in 1828–1835). Christological and Trinitarian hermeneutics are also discussed by Hummel, *The Word Becoming Flesh*, 16–18.

[15] Moberly, "Theology of the Old Testament," 478.

[16] In particular, Jn 1:14 (cf. Jn 2:11; 17:5) identifies the divine "glory" as the incarnate Christ, and Jesus in Jn 12:41 declares that Isaiah "saw his glory" (see Isaiah 6) "and spoke concerning him." Since the Glory of Yahweh appears to Ezekiel in chapter 1 and speaks to him throughout his book, Horace Hummel writes: "It is legitimate, now using NT language and thought, to interpret *Christ as the divine speaker throughout the book* and the one in whose name and by whose authority the prophet gives his messages" (*Ezekiel 1–20*, 1; see also p. 11). Therefore, in a red-letter edition of the English Bible, in which the words of Christ are printed in red, most of the book of Ezekiel should be red!

[17] Harstad, *Joshua*, 249–58, citing Origen, Luther, and Gerhard, interprets the "man" (אִישׁ) who turns out to be "the Commander of the host of the Yahweh" (שַׂר־צְבָא יְהוָה) in Josh 5:13–15 as the preincarnate Christ. Other appearances of "the Angel of Yahweh" include Ex

senger for God, but must truly be God himself, or else God would have recalled him at once as an imposter.[18] Pieper also understands the Angel of Yahweh as the preincarnate second person of the Trinity.[19]

The earliest source dealing with the מַלְאַךְ יְהוָה is Justin Martyr, especially in his *Dialogue with Trypho*. Justin saw Christ throughout the OT and stood ready to defend this Christological understanding of the OT against Trypho and all opponents. Justin writes:

> The Scripture, in announcing that the Angel of the Lord appeared to Moses, and in afterwards declaring him to be Lord and God, speaks of the same One, whom it declares by the many testimonies already quoted to be minister to God, who is above the world, above whom there is no other [God].[20]

Justin was not the only early church father to comment on this figure in the OT. Irenaeus comments about the Angel of Yahweh in passing in *Against Heresies*. He writes regarding those who held to Moses' teaching (e.g., Ex 3:1–14) yet who did not recognize that Moses was speaking about Christ:

> The Son of God is implanted everywhere throughout his [Moses'] writings: … and again, when He becomes visible, and directs Jacob on his journey, and speaks with Moses from the bush.[21]

Eusebius also writes in his conclusion regarding, among other OT examples, the Commander in Josh 5:13–15 and the Angel of Yahweh who spoke to Moses: "That the divine Word, therefore, pre-existed, and appeared to some, if not to all, has thus been briefly shown by us."[22]

These early church fathers had no doubt who the Angel of Yahweh was, and they were confident in saying that this Angel is the same divine Word, the second person of the Trinity, who in the fullness of time (Gal 4:4) took on human flesh (Jn 1:14), was conceived and born of the Virgin Mary, lived and ministered in Israel, was crucified, died, rose on the third day, ascended into heaven, and is seated at the right hand of the Father.

This Christological interpretation helps explain the leading role of "the Angel of Yahweh" in the redemption of Israel. Thus it is "the Angel of Yahweh" who stays Abraham's knife and provides a substitute sacrifice in place of Isaac (Gen 22:11–15). "The Angel of Yahweh" appears in the burning bush to call Moses to bring Israel out from bondage (Ex 3:2, 7–10), and this Angel is then

---

14:19–20; Num 22:22–35; 1 Ki 19:5–8; Is 37:36; Ps 34:8 (ET 34:7). From such passages "it is evident that the *mal'ak YHWH* is closely associated with Yahweh in name, authority, and message, and that he represents Yahweh in the human realm" (D. N. Freedman and B. E. Willoughby, "מַלְאַךְ," *TDOT* 8:321).

[18] Pieper, *Christian Dogmatics*, 1:396.

[19] Pieper, *Christian Dogmatics*, 1:395–97.

[20] Justin Martyr, *Dialogue with Trypho*, 60 (*ANF* 1:227).

[21] Irenaeus, *Against Heresies*, 4.10.1 (*ANF* 1:473).

[22] Eusebius, *Church History*, 1.2.16 (*NPNF*[2] 1:84); see also 1.2.11–13 (*NPNF*[2] 1:83).

a manifestation of "Yahweh" himself (Ex 3:4), with the threefold title "the God of Abraham, the God of Isaac, and the God of Jacob" (Ex 3:6). And it is "the Angel of God" who leads the people of Israel in the exodus redemption (Ex 14:19; see also Ex 23:20, 23; 32:34; Judg 2:1).

Not absent from the OT too is the third person of the Trinity, the Holy Spirit, who was active in creation (Gen 1:2) and also in Israel's redemption and governance, principally through the people's leaders (see רוּחַ, "Spirit," in, e.g., Ex 31:3; 35:31; Num 11:17–29; Deut 34:9; Judg 3:10; 6:34; 11:29; 14:6).

A Trinitarian understanding of Israel's God and an understanding of the role of the preincarnate Christ in Israel's redemption are the foundation for, and best exemplar of, how the nation understands solidarity. Catherine LaCugna writes:

> In short, *all theological reflection*, whether conducted under the rubric of ethics, sacramental theology, ecclesiology, or spirituality, is potentially a mode of trinitarian theology. …

> Indeed, the ultimate theological error, the ultimate nonorthodoxy or heresy or untruth about God, would be to think of God as living in an altogether separate household, living entirely for Godself, by Godself, within Godself.[23]

Yahweh, the God of Israel, does not live in a household by himself. Rather, God's "household" includes his Son (manifested, as, e.g., "the Angel of Yahweh," מַלְאַךְ יְהוָה) and his Spirit (e.g., Gen 1:2; Ps 51:13 [ET 51:11]). This is at the root of Israel's existence and spills over into her understanding of human relationships.

Further Trinitarian reflection clarifies this connection between the nature of Yahweh and solidarity among his people. As LaCugna notes, the eighth-century Greek theologian John of Damascus used the term *perichōrēsis* to highlight the dynamic and vital character of each divine person, as well as the immanence of each in the other two.[24] LaCugna writes:

> Effective as a defense both against tritheism and Arian subordinationism, *perichōrēsis* expressed the idea that the three divine persons mutually inhere in one another, draw life from one another, "are" what they are by relation to one another.[25]

Perichōrēsis means no person in the Trinity exists by himself. At the root of the created universe is a relationship between three eternal persons: Father, Son, and Holy Spirit. *Perichōrēsis* is therefore another way to speak of solidarity. It is the very nature of Yahweh that forms the basis of Israel's understanding of solidarity. Based upon Yahweh's nature, as manifested in creation and especially in his redemption, Israel is fundamentally a people only in re-

---

[23] LaCugna, *God for Us*, 380, 383.

[24] LaCugna, *God for Us*, 270, citing John of Damascus, *De fide orthodoxa*, 8 (PG 94:807–34).

[25] LaCugna, *God for Us*, 270–71. LaCugna continues: "The model of *perichōrēsis* avoids the pitfalls of locating the divine unity either in the divine substance (Latin) or exclusively in the person of the Father (Greek), and locates unity instead in diversity, in a true *communion* of persons."

lation to their God, and their complete dependence on their God makes them mutually interdependent on each other. The cardinal sin—the sin that lay at the root of all sin—is the attempt to be independent from God (cf. Gen 3:6–8, 23–24), to live apart from God and to separate from his people (cf. Gen 4:13–16). Causes of this sin include whatever binds Israelites to impersonal or antipersonal existence. This sin is manifest in the denial that people are created, redeemed, and sanctified by God in Christ to be in relationship with him and others. Thus it is a grave sin for Jonah in chapter 1 to refuse to undertake his mission to Nineveh, for God's people are called always to be in mission in order to bring others into this saving relationship with the triune God.[26]

The confession made by the farmer in Deut 26:5–10 encapsulates the biblical view of solidarity: later generations of God's people recall the history of the patriarchs, Israel in Egypt, the exodus redemption, and inheritance of the promised land as "our" history; God did all that for "us." The confession changes from first person singular to first person plural and back again to first person singular, thus demonstrating that the history of the individual coincides with the history of Israel. Already in the patriarchal narratives, the covenant promises include Abraham's seed, the descendants (Gen 15:13–16, 18–21; 17:7–14, 19–21). The confession of OT salvation history as "our" history continues for Christians today, since the NT affirms that baptized believers in Christ are Abraham's children and heirs of God's OT promises (e.g., Gal 3:26–29). This idea of solidarity is the same as when we confess in the Nicene Creed that Christ became incarnate "for *us* men (people) and for *our* salvation" and that he "was crucified also *for us* under Pontius Pilate."

Another example of this solidarity in Israel is demonstrated by uses of the word עַם, "people."[27] In the OT, both its singular and its plural can refer to the one people of Israel, thus reinforcing the idea that this group of individuals could be understood as "one man" (cf. Judg 20:8). The harshest judgment executed against gross violators of Yahweh's covenant with Israel is that the transgressor "will be cut off" from God's people; this judgment can be expressed with either the singular of עַם, "from the midst of his people" (e.g., Lev 17:4; 20:3, 6), or the plural of עַם, which then usually is translated "from his kinsmen/relatives" (e.g., Gen 17:14; Ex 30:33; Lev 7:20–21). Conversely, a formula for death and burial is that the deceased "was gathered to his kinsmen" (plural of עַם; e.g., Gen 25:8, 17; 35:29; 49:33; Deut 32:50). This implies ongoing life after death in the company of God and fellow believers.

A negative example of Israel's understanding of solidarity is demonstrated in the expressions of an Israelite who is set apart or isolated. The idea that separation from the community is unnatural, uncertain, and indeed dangerous, goes back to Israel's earliest existence. Hans-Jürgen Zobel writes:

---

[26] See the excursus "Mission in the Old Testament."
[27] See E. Lipinski and W. von Soden, "עַם," *TDOT* 11:163–77.

For in a nomadic or seminomadic environment, a separation from the tribe or from the family meant the renunciation of all social and economic security, and if worse came to worst even the repudiation of one's life. Thus every form of isolation has a negative ring about it. "The Hebrew has no love of isolation."[28]

Indeed, to be alone means that something unusual and possibly threatening is happening. Ps 25:15–16[29] states:

My eyes are always toward Yahweh,
> for he is the one bringing my feet out of the net.
Turn to me, and be gracious to me,
> for I am lonely [יָחִיד] and afflicted.

The word "lonely" (יָחִיד) means here the affliction of isolation. Being alone as a longed-for benefit that gives pleasure is alien to the OT. The sense of identity and self-awareness of the individual living in a network of social relationships is therefore significantly different from the sense of identity and self-awareness of the typical privatized individual of Western post-industrial, urban society.

To be alone involves dangers, as was the case for David. Pursued by Saul, Ahimelech the priest at Nob asks David, "Why are you alone, and no man is with you?" (1 Sam 21:2). "Alone" (בַּד) in this verse implies that a separated person is easily overcome (cf. Eccl 4:7–12). Even before the fall into sin, Yahweh said about Adam, "It is not good for the man to be alone" (לְבַדּוֹ, Gen 2:18). To remedy the problem of aloneness, God "causes lonely people [יְחִידִים] to dwell in a household" (Ps 68:7 [ET 68:6]).

Much has been written about a supposed turn in the OT from corporate to individualistic thinking and ethics in Jeremiah and Ezekiel.[30] Yet there is no biblical case that can be built for a gradual emerging of individualism that replaces or obscures the emphasis of the corporate body of believers.[31] Jeremiah and Ezekiel are not responsible for the start of individualism, for there always had been a case for both the individual and one's identity in the group throughout the OT. Walter Kaiser writes of Ezekiel 18:

---

[28] H.-J. Zobel, "בָּדָד," *TDOT* 1:479, quoting Ludwig Köhler, *Hebrew Man* (trans. Peter R. Ackroyd; London: SCM, 1956), 137.

[29] Other psalms also speak of the misery of loneliness. For example, in Psalm 102 a man who is near death (102:24 [ET 102:23]) and mocked by his enemies (102:9 [ET 102:8]) prays (102:7 [ET 102:6]): "I am like a pelican of the wilderness, like an owl in ruined places."

[30] See Mendenhall, "The Relation of the Individual to Political Society in Ancient Israel." Halpern also argues that individual responsibility emerges in Israel as a result of the monarchy's undermining of the solidarity of the traditional kinship groups of households, clans, and tribes ("Jerusalem and the Lineages in the Seventh Century BCE: Kinship and the Rise of Individual Moral Liability").

[31] The debate is summarized in Matties, *Ezekiel 18 and the Rhetoric of Moral Discourse*, 115–25. My contention that solidarity continued during and after the exile finds support in Matties' study.

This chapter, however, sets forth no new doctrine, but combats a fatalistic view of life engendered by self-pity and a one-sided emphasis of moral collectivism or corporate solidarity.[32]

Against any cultural mantra that sings with Frank Sinatra, "I did it my way," the OT refuses to glorify people who display self-service and self-absorption. The advancement of "egocentrism" and the self of the isolated individual find no validation in the OT.

If our postmodern society locates authenticity in the rejection of every form of heteronomy,[33] then the OT authors promote it. They hold that personal existence is constituted by relationships with other people. If Descartes' dictum was "turn to self," then the OT's is "turn toward God and others." *I* am constituted as a person only in reference to *you*. This is a decisive break from the extreme individualism of the Cartesian framework as egocentrism is replaced by heterocentrism. The focus is the other, not the self. According to the OT (and NT), a person is called to be a heterocentric, relational agent.[34] Others are not a means to an end; love for God and neighbor *is* the end (cf. Mt 22:36–40). The OT faith was that communion with God and his people would continue even after the end of this earthly life, when a person was "gathered to his people/kinsmen/fathers" (e.g., Gen 49:33; Num 20:24; cf. Judg 2:10; 2 Ki 22:20). For this faith included the hope of solidarity continuing through the resurrection to everlasting life with God in the company of all the redeemed,[35] which indeed the NT affirms (e.g., Mt 17:3–4; Lk 13:28; 16:23–31; 20:37).

When Jonah is alone in the ship (1:5), when he worships alone ("Yahweh … *I* worship," 1:9), when he is alone in the inner parts of the great fish (2:1–2 [ET 1:17; 2:1]), and when he is alone east of Nineveh (4:5), he stands in direct contrast to Yahweh's plan for all people. Galileo was right. The universe does *not* revolve around me. It revolves around Yahweh and the people he places into my life, both now and for eternity. Thus the Scriptures end with a vision of the church triumphant, not as a collection of isolated individuals, but rather as an innumerable multitude united in corporate worship (Rev 7:9; 19:1, 6)—indeed, as one structure, a unified body, a single person: "I saw the holy city, the new Jerusalem … the bride, the wife of the Lamb" (Rev 21:2, 9).

---

[32] Kaiser, *Toward Old Testament Ethics*, 70.

[33] See Davis, "Our Modern Identity," especially p. 159.

[34] This has implications for sexual ethics. There likely is a connection between modern Western society's focus on self and its increasing acceptance of homosexuality. The unanimous biblical witness is that homosexuality is intrinsically sinful because it is contrary to God's design (one may see the excursus "Homosexuality" in Lockwood, *1 Corinthians*, 204–9). It is centered on another of the same gender. Thus it cannot fulfill God's design for marriage, which is that one man and one woman unite in love directed at the other, who is a fellow human being, yet who is in a fundamental way different than oneself. For the view that Christian marriage reflects the mutual love between Christ and his church, see Mitchell, *Song of Songs*, 40–97. Faithful, lifelong, heterosexual marriage is one expression of the solidarity God desires and gives to his people.

[35] See the excursus "Sheol" and also, for example, Gen 5:24; 2 Kings 2; Is 25:6–9; 26:19; Pss 23:6; 27:10; 73:24; Job 19:25–27; Dan 12:1–3.

Sheol

Sheol in Jonah

The Israelites, who received "the Word of Yahweh" (Jonah 1:1; 3:1) through their prophets, had developed ideas on death that were quite different from the underworld concepts in Mesopotamian, Egyptian, and Canaanite cultures. In contrast to these neighboring beliefs, the Israelites believed that although death marks the end of life on this earth, it is not extinction. Rather, death is a transition to another kind of existence in another realm. After death, all people are subject to physical decay. Upon death the souls of unbelievers enter a gloomy realm in which they await further divine judgment. Believers too may be described as having a moribund experience, but upon death their souls enter the glorious presence of Yahweh and await the bodily resurrection to eternal life.[1]

Some passages refer to Sheol as the realm into which the dead descend. As Jonah recalls his time in the sea, he likens his experience to death and resurrection.[2] He refers to this realm of the dead: in his distress he prayed to his God "from the belly of Sheol" (שְׁאוֹל, 2:3 [ET 2:2]). He has this same place in mind when he declares (2:7 [ET 2:6]):

> To the roots of the mountains [לְקִצְבֵי הָרִים] I went down.
>   The underworld [הָאָרֶץ]—her gate-bars [were] behind me forever.
> Then you brought up my life from destruction/the pit [שַׁחַת], O Yahweh
>   my God.

Etymology, Synonyms, and Distribution in the Bible

"Sheol" (שְׁאוֹל) is a proper name designating the underworld, where the departed descend. The word is not found in other Semitic languages, although an equivalent in Akkadian is *Arallû*, or "the land of no return."[3] The etymology of "Sheol" is uncertain, but it may be related to the Hebrew verb שָׁאַל, "to ask," because of the Canaanite practice of consulting the spirits of the dead

---

[1] See, for example, Is 25:6–9; 26:16–19; Ezek 37:1–14; Pss 16:10–11; 21:5 [ET 21:4]; 23:6; 73:24; 133:3; Job 19:25–27; Dan 12:1–3. As one would expect, the OT revelation is fragmentary and incomplete when compared to the NT revelation, which fills out the picture. However, even the NT offers little information on the blessed state of believers after death and before the resurrection (e.g., Lazarus in Lk 16:19–31; Phil 1:21–23; Rev 6:9–11). The ultimate goal of the biblical faith is not simply this "intermediate state," but rather the bodily resurrection to eternal life in the new heavens and new earth (Isaiah 11; 65:17–25; 66:15–24). The NT reveals that the resurrection will take place only after the risen Christ returns in glory (1 Corinthians 15; Rev 20:11–15; chapters 21–22).

[2] See the commentary on 2:1, 7 (ET 1:17; 2:6); the excursus "The Sign of Jonah"; and the excursus "Death and Resurrection Motifs in Luther's Baptismal Theology.")

[3] Bottéro, *Religion in Ancient Mesopotamia*, 204.

(prohibited in, e.g., Lev 19:31; 20:6, 27). That etymology may be supported by Deut 18:11, which prohibits various pagan worship practices, including "asking [שָׁאַל] a medium or spiritist, or seeking the dead." See also 1 Chr 10:13, which attributes the death of "Saul" (שָׁאוּל) to his "asking a medium" (לִשְׁאוֹל בָּאוֹב), thus creating wordplay between "Saul" (שָׁאוּל) and "asking" (לִשְׁאוֹל). The infinitive שְׁאוֹל, "asking," is spelled identically to "Sheol." Compare also Jonah 4:8, which has a finite form of the same verb: the prophet "asked his life to die" (וַיִּשְׁאַל אֶת־נַפְשׁוֹ לָמוּת).

Sheol (שְׁאוֹל) occurs sixty-six times in the OT[4] and always means the realm of the dead located deep in the earth. Often the descriptions of Sheol relate to what happens to the body after death, namely, burial in the ground and decomposition, which is experienced by believers and unbelievers alike. In twenty-six verses it is accompanied by the verb יָרַד, "to go down" to Sheol (the verb used in Jonah 2:7 [ET 2:6]). Far more common than "Sheol" are the verb "to die" (מוּת) and the noun "death" (מָוֶת), which together occur almost a thousand times. Synonyms of "Sheol" include אֲבַדּוֹן, "place of destruction" (e.g., Job 26:6); קֶבֶר, "the grave" (e.g., Job 3:22); שַׁחַת, "the pit/destruction" (as in Jonah 2:7 [ET 2:6]); בּוֹר, "pit" (e.g., Ps 28:1); and the common noun אֶרֶץ, "earth," when it has the sense of "underworld" (as in Jonah 2:7 [ET 2:6]).

The term "Sheol" in biblical literature is distributed as follows: it occurs in the Psalms and the poetic verses Deut 32:22; 1 Sam 2:6; 2 Sam 22:6 nineteen times; in reflective Wisdom literature (Job, Proverbs, Ecclesiastes, Song) nineteen times; in the Prophets twenty times, including Jonah 2:3 (ET 2:2); and in narrative eight times. This pattern of occurrence prompts several observations. First, the word occurs mostly in psalmodic, reflective, and prophetic literature, where authors are expressing themselves personally. By contrast, Sheol appears only rarely in descriptive narrative, and then almost entirely in direct speech. The word is also rare in narrative accounts of death, whether of patriarchs, kings, prophets, priests, or ordinary people—whether Israelite or foreigner, righteous or wicked. "Sheol" is also entirely absent from Israel's legal material, including the many laws that prescribe capital punishment or prohibit necromancy.

We may infer from this data that Sheol is a term of personal engagement and not a concept to be mentioned dispassionately in historical reports or general legislation. Rather, the word connotes a personal emotional involvement, an apprehension of one's own death or an anticipation of the fate of Yahweh's enemies.

Sheol as Judgment and Separation from Yahweh

The kind of existence a person experiences in Sheol is drawn only sketchily in the OT. Just two prophetic oracles give a lengthy portrayal and describe any

---

4 This includes Is 7:11 where most scholars and versions—ancient and modern—emend the MT to read "Sheol."

form of activity there. Both of these are judgment oracles describing the fate of unbelievers who, in life, were enemies of Yahweh and his people Israel. In Is 14:9–21 the denizens of Sheol are roused to greet a newcomer—the king of Babylon (Is 14:4)—and they describe themselves as weak and infested with worms and maggots. The other text, Ezek 32:18–32, is a lament for slain Egyptians, who are sent down into Sheol, where they join other uncircumcised peoples slain by the sword, including Assyrians, Elamites, Edomites, and others. "They have come down, they lie still" (Ezek 32:21). Their impotence, inactivity, and shame in Sheol contrasts with their mighty feats and glory while alive and with the terror they spread throughout the nations by their fierce warfare.

Sheol in its essence represents separation from Yahweh, which in itself is the most deplorable destiny.[5] In Israelite belief, the essence of life is the ability to worship Yahweh in his presence. For the dead in Sheol, this is impossible because they have no contact with his divine presence. In the words of repentant King Hezekiah after he recovered from illness: "For Sheol cannot thank you, death cannot praise you; those who go down to destruction/the pit cannot hope for your faithfulness" (Is 38:18; see also Pss 88:5, 10–12 [ET 88:4, 9–11]; 115:17).

The KJV frequently translates Sheol as "hell" because it is portrayed so often as the destination of the wicked.[6] Theologically, Sheol is the opposite of Yahweh's presence. It is the lowest point (Deut 32:22; Is 7:11), the cosmological opposite of the highest heavens (Amos 9:2; Ps 139:8).[7] "Sheol" (Ps 88:4 [ET 88:3]) is characteristically "the land of forgetfulness" (Ps 88:13 [ET 88:12]), where people are cut off from Yahweh and forgotten (Ps 88:6 [ET 88:5]). Sheol is a fitting place for the wicked, who in life forgot God (Ps 9:18 [ET 9:17]; see also Pss 31:18 [ET 31:17]; 55:16 [ET 55:15]). It is a place of captivity with gates (Is 38:10) and bars (Jonah 2:7 [ET 2:6]; see also 2:3 [ET 2:2]). Sheol is a tyrant like an evil shepherd (Ps 49:15 [ET 49:14]). It has a gaping mouth and insatiable appetite (Is 5:14; Prov 30:16). The earth opens its mouth and rebels descend to Sheol (Num 16:30, 33). It is a place of worms, maggots, and dust (Is 14:11; Job 17:16). It is a realm of silence (Ps 31:18–19 [ET 31:17–18]) and darkness (Ps 88:4, 13 [ET 88:3, 12]; cf. Lam 3:6). No won-

---

5   For separation from Yahweh and his people as the great evil, see the excursus "The Trinitarian Basis of Old Testament Solidarity."

6   The KJV does this in thirty-one passages. Sometimes it makes good sense, for example, "The wicked shall be turned into hell, and all the nations that forget God" (Ps 9:17 KJV [MT 9:18]). However, in passages that speak of Yahweh bringing believers out from Sheol, this translation is infelicitous, because it implies that believers spend at least some time in hell, for example, Ps 16:10 (KJV): "For thou wilt not leave my soul in hell." ESV and NASB prefer to transliterate "Sheol." NIV renders it "the grave."

7   In context, Amos 9:2 states that the wicked cannot escape Yahweh's judgment, even if they should attempt to hide in the highest heavens or deepest Sheol. Conversely, Ps 139:8 is an affirmation that Yahweh remains present with his believers if they ascend to the highest heavens and even if they should descend to Sheol.

der oil lamps are among the most common items found in Iron Age Israelite tombs.

Those headed for Sheol are the ungodly. They are often described in general terms: as wicked (Ps 9:18 [ET Ps 9:17]), sinners (Job 24:19), the foolish (Ps 49:14–15 [ET 49:13–14]), scoffers (Is 28:15, 18), and the immoral (Prov 5:5; 7:27). A few are specifically named: Korah and his company (Num 16:30, 33) and Joab and Shimei (1 Ki 2:5–6, 8–9). They might also be national enemies of Israel: the Babylonian king (Is 14:9, 11, 15), the Egyptians (Ezek 31:15–17), and many other peoples who warred against Israel (Ezek 32:18–32).

Yahweh Saves Believers from Sheol

In Israelite thought, life and death, and also health and sickness, are never understood purely in medical terms. Rather, any form of sickness or misery is viewed as death intruding into God's good gift of life. Since only God can save from death, he alone also has the power to heal (e.g., 2 Ki 5:7; Is 38:16). Death is usually pictured more as a process than a one-time event. The greater the distress, the greater the experience of death. Thus Jacob's grief over his lost son would bring him down to Sheol (Gen 42:38; 44:29, 31), and Saul's attempts to kill David entangled the son of Jesse with "the cords of Sheol … the snares of death" (2 Sam 22:6 ‖ Ps 18:6 [ET 18:5]). On the other hand, God's blessing of life is more than simply breathing. It is characterized by a fullness, vitality, and total well-being in all aspects of life (cf. Deut 30:19–20; Prov 19:23). Thus when God miraculously provided water, thirsty Samson's "spirit returned to him, and he lived/revived" (וַתָּשָׁב רוּחוֹ וַיֶּחִי, Judg 15:19), and when Jacob heard the good news that his son Joseph was alive, "the spirit of Jacob lived/revived" (וַתְּחִי רוּחַ יַעֲקֹב, Gen 45:26–27).

It is widely accepted that the very name "Yahweh" comes from the verb הָיָה, "to be," even if there remain differences about the precise form and meaning of the Tetragrammaton.[8] Whether its etymology is based on the Qal ("He is") or the Hiphil ("He causes things to be, brings into existence"), the Hebrew text relates the name to that verb, notably in the account of its revelation to Moses: "I am who I am" (Ex 3:14). Yahweh is the only God who exists and who is the Creator of all that exists.[9] Thus Yahweh is the source of all life, and indeed he *is* life. This is repeatedly stressed throughout the OT: for example, "Now choose life … for he [Yahweh] is your life" (Deut 30:19–20); "For with you is the fountain of life; in your light we see light" (Ps 36:10 [ET 36:9]). After Yahweh granted Hannah, formerly a barren woman, new life in the form of a son, she sang, "Yahweh kills and makes alive; he brings down to Sheol and raises up" (1 Sam 2:6). Death only takes place with his permission, and even after death he will raise up his faithful people to a glorious new life.

---

8   See the excursus "The Lord (יהוה)" in Harstad, *Joshua*, 47–51.

9   See the excursus "Yahweh, the Creator God" in the commentary on Jonah 1.

Yet in the OT, some individuals, who are otherwise presumed to be righteous, envisage descent to Sheol, specifically Jacob (Gen 37:35; 42:38; 44:29, 31), Hezekiah (Is 38:10), Job (17:13–16), Heman the psalmist (Ps 88:4 [ET 88:3]), and, of course, Jonah (Jonah 2:3 [ET 2:2]). They all speak in the context of extreme trial, whether loss, illness, affliction, abandonment, or a life-threatening situation. In each case, mention of Sheol is conspicuously absent after God has delivered these OT saints from their afflictions. *We may conclude, then, that the righteous only envisage Sheol when they face a calamity that they interpret as divine punishment, such as tragedy, suffering, or untimely death.* By contrast, when OT believers face the end of a full and blessed life, or where this kind of death is narrated, there is no mention of Sheol (e.g., Gen 25:8; 35:29; 49:33; Job 42:17; 1 Chr 29:28).

Seemingly at variance with this view are two texts that some interpret as saying that Sheol is the destination of all who die. In the context of Yahweh's fiery wrath and the brevity of all human life (Ps 89:46–48 [ET 89:45–7]), Ethan the psalmist asks in Ps 89:49 (ET 89:48):

> What mortal can live and not see death
> and deliver his soul from the hand of Sheol?

Then follows a lament of how unfaithful Israel is now persecuted and no longer receives the steadfast love Yahweh once swore to and showed King David. Therefore, based on the larger context, we may conclude that the psalmist refers to death and Sheol as the divine judgment that all sinners (that is, all people) deserve, including the Israelites, and no person can deliver himself from this judgment. However, the psalmist leaves open the possibility that Yahweh—and he alone—can and does deliver his faithful people from death and Sheol, as other OT passages affirm.

The second, more challenging text is Eccl 9:7–10, where Solomon is speaking to believers, who already receive God's favor upon their lives (Eccl 9:7). He instructs his readers to enjoy their food and drink, wife, and toil "under the sun" (Eccl 9:7–9). He then concludes, "All which your hand finds to do, do it with your strength, for there is no work or thought or knowledge or wisdom in Sheol, which you are going there" (בִּשְׁאוֹל אֲשֶׁר אַתָּה הֹלֵךְ שָׁמָּה, Eccl 9:10). Milton Horne believes Qoheleth "is in the midst of a crisis of meaning; things in his world do not measure up to his traditional beliefs. He therefore comes across as one who, like Job, subverts the views of his community of faith." Horne also thinks that Qoheleth does not present a systematic theology.[10] Solomon is debating with himself, sometimes expressing skepticism and doubt from a human perspective based on what we can and cannot see ("under the sun," e.g., Eccl 1:3), but other times voicing faith and God's perspective (which could be called "above the sun"), which transcends the visible world. In doing this, Solomon does not articulate a consistent, systematic presentation of nor-

---

[10] Horne, *Proverbs–Ecclesiastes*, 375.

mative OT doctrine. He observes that all people without distinction die, believer and unbeliever alike (Eccl 8:8; 9:5), and so all may *appear* to go to Sheol. This is part of Qoheleth's reflection on the absurdity of observable life. In the clearer revelation of Yahweh elsewhere in the OT, Sheol is only the destiny of those who perish without Yahweh's grace.

We may conclude that Sheol rarely appears to be a Hebrew term for the underworld that awaits all mortals. In most passages, it clearly refers to the realm of the dead who are under divine judgment, who perish without faith in Yahweh.[11]

As for Jonah's use of "Sheol" in 2:3 (ET 2:2), in light of the Israelite continuum between life and death, he is describing his movement toward death and indicating that he was under Yahweh's judgment for his flight, which was stated in 1:3 and which Jonah himself confessed to the sailors (1:10). His request to be hurled overboard (1:12) may have been his own admission that he deserved the punishment of death. His words "I am driven away from before your eyes" (2:5 [ET 2:4]) indicate a fundamental truth in Israel's conception of death and Sheol as a radical separation from God, a sense of being bereft of Yahweh's saving presence.

Jonah realizes that Sheol would have been his permanent address if Yahweh had not intervened to save him, in answer to his prayer (2:3, 7–8 [ET 2:2, 6–7]). In the rest of Jonah's psalm, the prophet describes Sheol in terms of a watery chaos (2:4, 6 [ET 2:3, 5]), the underworld with prison bars (2:7 [ET 2:6]), and loss of life (2:8 [ET 2:7]). As Sheol is the lowest point in the universe, Jonah's descent that began in 1:3 and continued in 1:5 reaches its maximum depth in 2:3, 7 (ET 2:2, 6).[12] This is consistent with other OT passages where Sheol is described as a realm to which people can only go down. No person has the ability to arise or return from it (Job 7:9–10; cf. Job 10:21):

Thus he who descends [יוֹרֵד] to Sheol does not come up [לֹא יַעֲלֶה].
He does not return again [לֹא־יָשׁוּב עוֹד] to his house.

(a) E.g., 1 Sam 2:6; Pss 16:10–11; 30:4; 49:15–16 (ET 49:14–15); 86:13; Job 14:13–14

Yet miracle of miracles, Yahweh "brought up" Jonah (2:7 [ET 2:6]) from "the belly of Sheol" (2:3 [ET 2:2])! Yahweh comes to Jonah's rescue and does what no mortal could do. That Yahweh saves Jonah from Sheol is consistent with many other OT texts that express similar resurrection themes: Yahweh alone has the ability to save and redeem his people from Sheol and raise them up to new life.[a]

Just as Jonah's deliverance from Sheol portends the resurrection of Jesus Christ,[13] so also these other passages are fulfilled by Christ's resurrection (thus

---

[11] As we would expect, the NT reveals more clearly and fully the eschatological fate of unbelievers. Christ shall come again in glory, and his parousia is followed by the universal judgment. All unbelievers shall be raised bodily and thrown into the lake of fire, where they shall be tormented forever (Rev 20:11–15).

[12] The Hebrew verb יָרַד, "to go down," occurs in 1:3, 5; 2:7 (ET 2:6). See especially the textual notes and commentary on 1:3. It is the antonym of Yahweh's call for Jonah to "arise" (1:2).

[13] See the excursus "The Sign of Jonah."

Acts 2:25–28 cites Ps 16:10–11 and Acts 13:35 cites Ps 16:10). Yahweh's power over Sheol is climactically displayed in Jesus Christ, "who has destroyed death and has brought life and immortality to light through the Gospel" (2 Tim 1:10). Jonah's "resurrection" points to our Lord's (Mt 12:40), which is the guarantee that on the Last Day all we who believe shall be raised with glorified bodies like our Lord's (Rom 8:29–30; 1 Corinthians 15). Sheol, where is your power? Thanks be to God, he gives us the victory over this enemy through Jesus Christ, our Lord (1 Cor 15:55–57).

Christian hymnody often expresses Christ's triumph over Sheol using imagery from Jonah, such as the second stanza of the recent composition "When Time Was Full," which refers to Jesus:

> This holy Jonah undecayed Lay still within the whale;
> This Lord of Life on death then preyed, Hell's titan to impale:
> From gaping jaws came forth this King, With death the casualty!
> Colossal foe, where now your sting? Where, grave, your victory?[14]

Death and Resurrection Motifs in Luther's Baptismal Theology

In the sea, Jonah experiences both Yahweh's judgment and his salvation. Jonah in effect dies in the water and is raised to new life so that he can live by faith. The prophet who was guilty of fleeing from Yahweh (1:3, 10) was hurled into the sea, where both he and the sailors expected him to perish because of Yahweh's judgment (1:12–15). "But Yahweh provided a great fish to swallow Jonah" (2:1 [ET 1:17]). Paradoxically, the verb בָּלַע, "to swallow," is used almost exclusively in the OT to denote judgment, while the verb מָנָה, "to provide," indicates that Yahweh provided the great fish to save Jonah from a permanent residence in Sheol (2:3 [ET 2:2]).[1] Jonah then responds with a psalm of praise (2:3–10 [ET 2:2–9]), which is his most glorious expression of faith in the entire book. Then his faithful obedience follows in 3:3–4.[2]

These events provide important baptismal connections, in much the same way as the OT narrative about the universal flood, through which Noah and his family were saved, and the salvation of Israel through the Red Sea during the exodus, leading to the psalm of praise in Exodus 15, also relate to Baptism and the resurrection. In 1 Pet 3:18–22, the apostle expounds upon the flood as a type of Baptism, which now saves us. Paul explains in 1 Cor 10:1–2 that during the exodus the Israelites "were baptized" into Moses in the cloud and in the sea.[3] These connections find expression in many traditional hymns, such as these stanzas from the eighth-century Easter hymn by John of Damascus:

> Come, you faithful, raise the strain Of triumphant gladness!
> God has brought His Israel Into joy from sadness,
> Loosed from Pharaoh's bitter yoke Jacob's sons and daughters,
> Led them with unmoistened foot Through the Red Sea waters.
>
> 'Tis the spring of souls today: Christ has burst His prison
> And from three days' sleep in death As a sun has risen;
> All the winter of our sins, Long and dark, is flying
> From His light, to whom is giv'n Laud and praise undying.[4]

---

[1] For these two verbs, see the textual notes and commentary on 2:1 (ET 1:17). For the resurrection motif of Yahweh saving Jonah from Sheol, see the excursus "Sheol."

[2] Jonah only expresses his faith verbally in 1:9; 2:3–10 (ET 2:2–9) and by his obedient actions in 3:3–4. In the rest of the book, the prophet is rebellious (chapter 1) or begrudges the grace Yahweh shows to others (chapter 4).

[3] For the significance of 1 Cor 10:1–5 for the theology and practice of Holy Baptism and the Lord's Supper, one may see Lockwood, *1 Corinthians*, 323–27.

[4] *LSB* 487:1–2.

When Martin Luther discusses the second chapter of Jonah, he makes it clear that the prophet was certain of his judgment; Jonah is painfully certain of his own demise (see 2:3b–8a [ET 2:2b–7a]). This despair Luther distinguishes in two regards: physical and spiritual. Jonah's despair over his physical life is the more obvious of the two:

> Jonah's heart may have told him that he had to die. He may have despaired of ever returning to land alive again and of moving about before God among his people in the land of Israel, from which he had fled [1:3, 10]. As we heard earlier, Jonah's "to flee from the presence of the Lord" [1:3] meant to flee from the land of Israel, where God had His abode and where He was worshiped. Similarly, we often read in the Second Book of Kings that God removed Israel from His sight and that He threatened to do the same with Judah, that is, to banish the people from the country where His Word and worship prevailed (2 Kings 17:18; 24:20). This interpretation is supported by the subsequent statement of Jonah that he would not again be able to look upon God's holy temple [2:5, 8 (ET 2:4, 7)], that is, the temple in Jerusalem.[5] That proves that he was in the throes of death, that he was convinced he was about to die. Here his faith was assailed by great distress and anxiety. There was little room for crying to God; this was despair of life. And this is not surprising; for who could entertain much hope for life when engulfed in the depth of the ocean and, in addition, when swallowed by a whale?[6]

Estranged from his homeland, his inheritance, and even the presence of Yahweh itself (2:5a [2:4a]), Jonah is at the outermost extremes of alienation. Luther also writes:

> Jonah may have felt that he, by reason of his disobedience, was eternally cast out from God like one of the damned. ... All kinds of instances of God's anger and of His punishment of sinners must have come to his mind, for example, Adam and Eve, Cain, the Deluge, Sodom and Gomorrah. This is one of the types of the real pain of hell that will overtake the ungodly after this life.[7]

Although being cast into the raging sea and being swallowed by the great fish seemed like certain death, Yahweh provided the great fish to deliver Jonah's life. We might even consider the fish to be a type of Christ, just as the early church used the fish as a symbol for Christ, as well as the anagram ΙΧΘΥΣ, "Jesus Christ, of God the Son, (is) Savior." This is the great reversal for Jonah. What is death is also life; both death and new life come at the same time, through one and the same means of salvation. Luther writes:

> Now the former order of things is reversed: What a moment ago served the purpose of death must now serve to further life. The fish who was but recent-

---

5   Luther's statement is based on his translation of 2:5 (ET 2:4) as *Denn ich gedacht, ... Ich würde dehnen heyligen tempel nicht mehr sehen*, "Then I thought, ... 'I would see your holy temple no more' " (WA 19.227). This commentary follows the MT of 2:5, which expresses confident hope: "Surely I will again gaze upon your holy temple." See the second textual note on 2:5.

6   AE 19:77.

7   AE 19:77.

ly the tool of death must now be life's implement; it must be a gateway to life, though just a short time before it held Jonah captive and consigned him to death. The ocean, too, must make way for Jonah and give its guest free access to the land. The roots of the mountains [2:7 (ET 2:6)] no longer hold him; earth's bars [2:7 (ET 2:6)] are pushed aside; the weeds [2:6 (ET 2:5)] cover him no more, etc. All of this is a source of comfort and confidence for us. It teaches us to rely on God, with whom life and death are alike. They are both trivial to Him, playthings as it were, as He bestows the one and takes the other, or exchanges one for the other. But for us these are momentous and impossible things, which God employs to display His power and skill to us.[8]

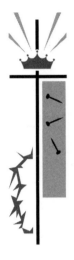

These words are very similar to the reversal Luther, following St. Paul, describes in Baptism: the drowning that means death and burial with Christ is also the means through which God provides resurrection to new life in Christ (Rom 6:1–11; Col 2:11–13). Whereas the old sinful nature is put to death, the new man of faith is raised to life and lives in Christlike righteousness (Rom 6:6–11; Eph 4:22–24; Col 3:9–10). Again Luther writes of Jonah's fish: "*It vomited out Jonah upon the dry land* [2:11 (ET 2:10)]. In this way, death and sin are an opportunity for life and righteousness for the saints; shame becomes an opportunity for glory."[9] Thus God's means of grace involves death, but brings about everlasting life. As Hannah sang, "Yahweh kills and makes alive; he brings down to Sheol and brings up" (1 Sam 2:6).

From early in his ministry until late in his life, Luther spoke of Baptism in the same way. For example, in *The Babylonian Captivity of the Church* (1520), he writes that Baptism is "actual death and resurrection."[10] To be sure, Luther employs a variety of images to denote what Baptism effects and accomplishes, including the images of regeneration and new birth (Jn 3:5; Titus 3:5), washing and cleansing (Eph 5:26–27; Titus 3:5), as well as dying and rising (Rom 6:1–11; Col 2:11–13).[11] These images functioned as equivalents in describing the work of God in Baptism. The unity of these three images is most clearly seen in Luther's Small Catechism, where he explains the benefits of Baptism:

It works forgiveness of sins, rescues from death and the devil, and gives eternal salvation to all who believe this, as the words and promises of God declare [Mk 16:16]. ... Certainly not just water, but the word of God in and with the water does these things, along with the faith which trusts this word of God in the water. For without God's word the water is plain water and no Baptism. But with the word of God it is a Baptism, that is, a life-giving water, rich in grace, and a washing of the new birth in the Holy Spirit [Titus 3:5–8]. ... It indicates that the Old Adam in us should by daily contrition and repentance be drowned and die with all sins and evil desires, and that a new man

---

[8] AE 19:82.

[9] AE 19:21.

[10] AE 36:68.

[11] See Trigg, *Baptism in the Theology of Martin Luther*, 75–81, 92–94, for examples of the profundity of ways in which Luther speaks of the benefits, gifts, and effects of Baptism.

should daily emerge and arise to live before God in righteousness and purity forever.[12]

Luther repeatedly employs the images of dying and rising within this broader framework of expressing Baptism as the monergistic, regenerative work of God. "The power, effect, benefit, fruit, and purpose of baptism is that it saves."[13]

Even if the early Luther was still influenced by his theology of humility as shaped by German mysticism, especially that of Johann Tauler, Luther's early writings refer to the baptismal dying and rising as a spiritually experienced reality:

> "Baptism" (*baptismus*), "dipping" (*mersio*), "to baptize" (*baptiso*), and "to dip" (*mergo*) all mean that [Rom 6:4] *We were buried therefore together* ... , that is, spiritually. The Greek has "we are buried." ... For it is a logical consequence, *with Him by Baptism into death*, namely, a spiritual death, that is, to the world and to sin, *so that as Christ*, after His death, *was raised*, bodily, *from the dead by the glory of the Father*, by the power of His brilliance, *we too*, after this spiritual death, *might walk*, progress, *in newness*, which comes through the grace of Baptism.[14]

The biblical identification of Baptism as death and resurrection is well expressed by Luther in his 1519 sermon "On the Holy and Blessed Sacrament of Baptism":

> The significance of baptism is a blessed dying unto sin and a resurrection in the grace of God, so that the old man, conceived and born in sin, is there drowned, and a new man, born in grace, comes forth and rises. ...

> Therefore this whole life is nothing else than a spiritual baptism which does not cease until death, and he who is baptized is condemned to die. ... There is no help for the sinful nature unless it dies and is destroyed with all its sin. Therefore the life of a Christian, from baptism to the grave, is nothing else than the beginning of a blessed death. For at the Last Day God will make him altogether new.[15]

In this sermon, Luther does not cite Romans 6, where death and resurrection language is most explicitly used for Christian Baptism. Instead, he cites Titus 3, John 3, and Ephesians 2 and states:

> Thus, St. Paul, in Titus 3[:5], calls baptism a "washing of regeneration," since in this washing a person is born again and made new. As Christ also says, in John 3[:3, 5], "Unless you are born again of water and the Spirit (of grace), you may not enter into the kingdom of heaven." For just as a child is drawn

---

[12] SC IV 10, 12 (*Luther's Small Catechism with Explanation* [St. Louis: Concordia, 1986, 1991], 22–23).

[13] LC IV 24. See Trigg, *Baptism in the Theology of Martin Luther*, 32–34, 75. See also Kolb, "What Benefit Does the Soul Receive from a Handful of Water?" 353. Kolb indicates that Luther referred to Baptism as "God's bath."

[14] 1515–1516 Romans lectures (AE 25:51).

[15] AE 35:30–31.

out of his mother's womb and is born, and through this fleshly birth is a sinful person and a child of wrath [Eph. 2:3], so one is drawn out of baptism and is born spiritually. Through this spiritual birth he is a child of grace and a justified person. Therefore sins are drowned in baptism, and in place of sin, righteousness comes forth.[16]

In his 1519 sermon on Baptism Luther explicitly refers to Noah's flood as foreshadowing this Sacrament, as did St. Peter (1 Pet 3:18–22):

> Baptism was foreshown of old in Noah's flood, when the whole world was drowned, except for Noah with his three sons and their wives, eight souls, who were saved in the ark. That the people of the world were drowned signifies that in baptism sins are drowned. But that the eight in the ark, with animals of every sort, were preserved, signifies—as St. Peter explains in his second epistle [2 Pet 2:5]—that through baptism man is saved. Now baptism is by far a greater flood than was that of Noah. For that flood drowned men during no more than one year, but baptism drowns all sorts of men throughout the world, from the birth of Christ even till the day of judgment.[17]

The reformer's death and resurrection imagery comes out in his 1520 treatise *The Babylonian Captivity of the Church.* He writes:

> When the minister immerses the child in the water it signifies death, and when he draws it forth again it signifies life. … This death and resurrection we call the new creation, regeneration, and spiritual birth. *This should not be understood only allegorically as the death of sin and the life of grace, as many understand it, but as actual death and resurrection.*[18]

Luther had no difficulty speaking of a washing that kills. When he writes about the death of the old Adam, the sinful nature with which each person is conceived and born (Ps 51:7 [ET 51:5]), Luther is using no metaphor. "To be born anew, one must consequently first die."[19]

Death and resurrection continued to be a primary motif in Baptism for Luther throughout his theological corpus.[20] While the motif is less explicit in the Large Catechism, Luther does say that Baptism saves and that "to be saved, as everyone well knows, is nothing else than to be delivered from sin, death, and the devil, to enter into Christ's kingdom, and to live with him forever."[21] Later in the Large Catechism he admonishes believers to spend a lifetime learn-

---

[16] AE 35:30.

[17] AE 35:31–32.

[18] AE 36:67–68; emphasis added.

[19] *The Heidelberg Disputation*, 1518 (AE 31:55).

[20] For English translations of other writings in which Luther speaks of Baptism as death and resurrection, see his commentary on Ps 2:8, 1532 (AE 12:59); his commentary on 1 Cor 15:29–30, 1532–1533 (AE 28:149–50); Third Sermon for Epiphany, 1534 (on Jesus' Baptism; Mt 3:13–17), *Sermons of Martin Luther: The House Postils* (ed. Eugene F. A. Klug; Grand Rapids: Baker, 1996), 1:221–22; his sermon on Jn 14:6, 1537 (AE 24:51); his lectures on Gen 3:15, 1536 (AE 1:196) and on Gen 48:20, 1545 (AE 8:182).

[21] LC IV 25.

ing about God's promises in Baptism and how it brings "victory over death and the devil, forgiveness of sin, God's grace, the entire Christ, and the Holy Spirit with his gifts."[22] Throughout the Christian's life, Baptism retains its significance as God's means for the Christian to die and rise, as is clear in this comment: "Now, here in baptism there is brought, free of charge, to every person's door just such a treasure and medicine that swallows up death and keeps all people alive."[23]

Following the catechisms, Luther continued to speak of the Christian life as a death beginning at Baptism and leading to resurrection. One example is from his commentary on 1 Corinthians 15 from the years 1532–1533:

> For his life on earth is nothing other than death; as soon as a Christian is baptized, he is thrust into death, as St. Paul declares in Rom. 6:4. And all who accept Christ are already sacrificed and sentenced to death. They are like people who have already died and are awaiting their resurrection.[24]

Luther persisted in speaking of Baptism in this way until the end of his life. In his Genesis commentaries, which were the basis for the academic lectures during the last ten years of his life (1536–1546), he engaged in a lengthy discussion about death and resurrection, which occur in and through Baptism:

> In his letter to the Corinthians (1 Cor. 10:2) Paul declares that the Israelites were baptized under Moses in the cloud and in the sea. If in this passage you look merely at conduct and words, then Pharaoh, too, was baptized, but in such a way that he perished with his men, while Israel passed through safe and unharmed. Similarly, Noah and his sons are preserved in the baptism of the Flood, while the entire remaining world outside the ark perishes because of this baptism of the Flood.
>
> These are fitting and learned statements, for Baptism and death are interchangeable terms in the Scripture. ...
>
> In accordance with this meaning, the Red Sea is truly a baptism, that is, death and the wrath of God, as is manifest in the case of Pharaoh. Nevertheless, Israel, which is baptized with such a baptism, passes through unharmed. Similarly, the Flood is truly death and the wrath of God; nevertheless, the believers are saved in the midst of the Flood.[25]

What unites the images of death and resurrection with washing and cleansing is not only the theme of drowning in the water of Baptism, but also biblical passages that ascribe cleansing power to the shed blood of Jesus Christ, who was crucified, died, and was buried, then rose from the dead.[26] In this way

---

[22] LC IV 41.

[23] LC IV 43.

[24] AE 28:132.

[25] AE 2:152–53.

[26] Jesus uses baptismal language to speak of his passion in Lk 12:50 (see also Mk 10:38–39 and the fuller text in Mt 20:22–23). Passages that speak of cleansing by the shed blood of Christ include Hebrews 9; 1 Pet 1:2; Rev 7:14.

Luther connects both of the Sacraments, Baptism and the Lord's Supper, with the redemptive blood of Jesus Christ. In 1527, Luther, commenting on 1 Jn 5:6, 8, said this (see also 1 Jn 1:7):

> He comes through water joined with the blood, that is, through Baptism, which is colored with the blood … Yet he also came by blood, for the water of Baptism is sanctified through the blood of Christ. Therefore it is not plain water; it is water stained with blood because of this blood of Christ which is given to us through the Word, which brings with it the blood of Christ. …
>
> If you are baptized with water, the blood of Christ is sprinkled through the Word. … For although we have been immersed only once, yet Baptism endures every day. … Thus we have been cleansed through the blood, the water, and the Word of the Spirit; and thus we are saved.[27]

Thus when Luther here speaks of Baptism as cleansing, this involves a washing in the death-defeating blood of Christ.[28]

Jonah's decent to Sheol (2:3 [ET 2:2]) and the underworld (2:7 [ET 2:6]) while in the midst of so much water ("the depth in the heart of the seas … ocean current … all your breakers and your waves … the deep," 2:4–6 [ET 2:3–5]) is a washing that kills, for by it Jonah's old man is drowned; he cries out, "Waters surrounded me up to my neck" (2:6 [ET 2:5]). Yet in 2:7c (ET 2:6c), the prophet is "resurrected" to a new life of faith (the Hiphil of עָלָה, "you *brought up* my life from destruction"). Jonah's faith resounds throughout his psalm of praise to Yahweh in chapter 2, in stark contrast to chapter 1, where he said nothing at all to Yahweh. Following Jonah's watery death and resurrection, at Yahweh's command, the fish vomits him onto the dry land (2:11 [ET 2:10]). The second time the Word of Yahweh comes to him (3:1), Jonah, as a "new man" (Eph 4:24; Col 3:10), walks "in newness of life" (Rom 6:4). He travels to Nineveh (Jonah 3:3) and preaches God's Word (3:4).

This reversal from death to life is not only for Jonah and all the baptized. It is manifest supremely in the death and resurrection of Christ himself. Luther points to "the sign of Jonah" (Mt 12:39–40) as the point at which this connection is made. He writes:

> He says that no other sign will be given this evil generation "except the sign of the prophet Jonah. For as Jonah was three days and three nights in the belly of the whale, so will the Son of man be three days and three nights in the heart of the earth" [Mt 12:39–40]. The answer is the same here; only the words and the figure of speech are different. He says: "This shall be your sign: 'Destroy this temple, and in three days I will raise it up'" [Jn 2:19]. That is: "I shall be the

---

[27] AE 30:314, 316.

[28] Old, *The Shaping of the Reformed Baptismal Rite*, 278–80, notes that people in the OT were sprinkled with blood for purification and cleansing. Isaiah prophesied that the Suffering Servant "will sprinkle many nations" (Is 52:15), which alludes to such OT rites, as also do NT passages including Heb 9:13–14, 19–22; 10:22; 12:24; 1 Pet 1:1–2 (see Mitchell, *Our Suffering Savior*, 100–108). Luther is relying upon such biblical passages. Since baptismal washing cleanses us from sin, that washing must be connected to the blood of Christ, since it is "the blood of Jesus, his [God's] Son," that "cleanses us from all sin" (1 Jn 1:7).

Jonah whom you will cast into the ocean and into the jaws of the whale, whom you will crucify and kill; and on the third day I shall rise again."[29]

Jonah's descent into the ocean and subsequent ingestion ("swallow" in 2:1 [ET 1:17]) by the fish are correlated to Christ's death. Likewise, Jonah's regurgitation on the third day ("vomited" in 2:11 [ET 2:10]) is parallel to Christ's resurrection. This connection has double significance. First, it provides an explicit Christological interpretation of Jonah. The language of Jonah being consumed and then delivered alive corresponds to Christ's experience of death and burial, then resurrection. Second, it provides hope for the baptized in that just as Jonah was alive on the dry ground after descending "to the roots of the mountains … the underworld" (2:7 [ET 2:6]) and then spending three days and three nights in the belly of the fish (2:1 [ET 1:17]), so too did the risen Christ prove himself alive to the frightened apostles on Easter, and likewise all baptized believers in Christ, though they suffer death and burial, shall undergo a glorious resurrection on the Last Day. Luther writes:

> Christ says: "If you believe in Me, death shall not devour you either. Even if death should hold you for three days or so, as he detained Me for three days in the earth and Jonah for three days in the belly of the whale, he shall nonetheless spew you out again."[30]

So Jonah, Jesus, and the baptized are connected. Jonah's experience is a type of the death and resurrection of Christ, who sets the pattern for his church. The motif of cleansing and washing is very closely tied to that of dying and rising. Luther pulls the two together in a 1540 sermon on Baptism:

> Yesterday we began to speak about the baptism of Christ and said that he accepted it from John for the reason that he was entering our stead, indeed, our person, that is, becoming a sinner for us, taking upon himself the sins which he had not committed, and wiping them out and drowning them in his holy baptism. …
>
> But he takes them and drowns and smothers them in baptism and the Cross. …
>
> [Jesus says, "]The purpose of my baptism is to wash away and drown the sins of all the world, that through it all righteousness and salvation may be accomplished.["] …
>
> Baptism is such a glorious and powerful thing that it washes away sin, drowns and destroys death, and heals and cleanses all disease.[31]

Luther affirms the NT connection between Baptism and the life of faith; the ongoing reality of regeneration can be called the "present tense" of Baptism.[32] Baptism is a daily and ever-present reality in the life of the Christian. This understanding is continuously expressed throughout Luther's writings.[33]

---

[29] AE 22:242.

[30] AE 22:359.

[31] AE 51:315, 317, 318, 327.

[32] So Trigg, *Baptism in the Theology of Martin Luther*, 146 (see also p. 79).

[33] Trigg, *Baptism in the Theology of Martin Luther*, 146, argues for this continuity: "Many

Following that understanding, Jonah's sinful old Adam perishes in chapter 2, but manages to revive itself again in chapter 4, where the prophet will sulk and rebel against Yahweh. In this way, Jonah is just like every baptized believer in Christ; like us, he is *simul iustus et peccator*, "simultaneously a justified saint and a sinner." Jonah in chapter 4 needs to remember his "baptism" in the sea, repent, die to sin, and rise again to a new life of faith—the same faith he joyfully expressed in chapter 2. This daily need for repentance, renewed faith, and a renewed life by God's grace continues throughout the earthly life of every child of God. See St. Paul's autobiographical description in Romans 7 of his ongoing struggle as a baptized Christian. The American poet Hart Crane reflects this in the second stanza of his poem "After Jonah":

> We have his [Jonah's] travels in the snare so widely
> ruminated,—of how he stuck there, was reformed,
> forgiven, also—
> and belched back like a word to grace us all.[34]

Many ancient and modern hymns draw on the motifs in Jonah as they allude to Holy Baptism with water imagery and refer to Christ's resurrection as the guarantee of our everlasting life. A recent example is by the Lutheran composer Herbert Brokering:

> Water, water, prophet on the run, Running, running to the setting sun.
> Yahweh calling, prophet sailing; Waves come crashing, prophet wailing.
> Prophet sailing, prophet wailing, Wind and water, storm assailing.
>
> Hiding, hiding, prophet on the run, Praying, praying, running, running
> done;
> All alone, all done with living, Disconnected, unforgiving.
> Silent, silent, kneeling, kneeling, Surely, surely healing, healing.
>
> Prophet, prophet called upon to run, Running, running to the rising sun.
> East wind, sackcloth, cattle bawling, Nineveh, your God is calling.
> Mercy, mercy, God forgiving; Wellspring, water, wellspring living.
>
> Dead and risen, risen. It is I, Jesus, Jesus, risen to the sky.
> Amen, amen, cross and glory, Written in a water story.
> Life and light and love unceasing, Living well of hope increasing.[35]

---

important themes within Luther's baptismal theology proper show almost complete continuity between the years 1519–20 and the later period from 1527 onwards." He states that Luther's understanding of the benefits of Baptism and his emphasis upon its significance as death and resurrection show no appreciable change from *The Babylonian Captivity of the Church* (1520) to the end of his life. "In particular, Luther's stress upon the 'present tense' of baptism is as strong in the *De Captivitate* as it is in the later period."

[34] Hart Crane, "After Jonah," in *The Poems of Hart Crane* (ed. Marc Simon; New York: Liveright, 1986), 176.

[35] © 2005 Herbert Brokering. Used by permission.

Jonah 3:1–10

Yahweh's Second Call to Jonah and the Ninevites' Conversion

Introduction to Jonah 3

In chapter 2, Yahweh provides a great fish to swallow Jonah (2:1 [ET 1:17]) and bring him back from the depths of Sheol (2:3 [ET 2:2]). Jonah praises Yahweh for his deliverance (2:10 [ET 2:9]), and then Yahweh commands the fish to vomit the prophet onto dry ground (2:11 [ET 2:10]). But the prophet's commission to go to Nineveh (1:1–2) still stands. There is work to do. Now is not the time for Jonah to rest or sleep (cf. 1:5).

The first two chapters of the narrative are a rehearsal for the second two. Chapters 1 and 2 provide preliminary scenes that introduce specific theological themes that climax in chapters 3 and 4. And so with Jonah's efficient, yet graceless, exit from the fish (2:11 [ET 2:10]), the narrative progresses to the place the prophet has been so desperately trying to avoid: Nineveh. This time Yahweh gives the prophet a specific message (3:2), and surprise of surprises, Jonah responds faithfully! But just as the morning dew is short-lived (Hos 6:4), so too is Jonah's response to Yahweh's salvation (2:10 [ET 2:9]) and command (1:2; 3:2).

The first two verses in chapter 3 are almost identical to the first two of chapter 1. Yahweh gives Jonah the same command a second time, showing that he is indeed "gracious and merciful … slow to anger" (4:2)!

As chapter 3 unfolds, it is also remarkably similar to chapter 1 in another way. After the response by the group as a whole (the mariners in 1:5; the Ninevites in 3:5), the leader (the captain in 1:6; the king in 3:6) emerges and takes measures to avert disaster. The divine Word spoken by the prophet (Jonah's confession in 1:9; his sermon in 3:4) brings both groups of pagan non-Israelites to repentance and saving faith in the God of Israel. Both chapters end with Yahweh granting salvation to the Gentiles.

Further structural similarities are evident when we compare chapter 3 with chapter 4. This is shown in the following chart.[1]

Chapter 3	Chapter 4
Focus on the Ninevites	Focus on Jonah
1. Crucial situation: threatened destruction of Nineveh (3:4)	1. Crucial situation: Nineveh is saved from destruction (presupposed in 4:1)
2. Response of the Ninevites: faith in God, acts of repentance, turning from evil (3:5–8)	2. Response of Jonah: evil, anger, complaint to God, request for death (4:1–3)
3. Response of Yahweh to the Ninevites: he graciously changes his prior verdict to destroy the city (3:10)	3. Response of Yahweh to Jonah: through word and action he graciously coaxes Jonah to change his prior desire for Yahweh to destroy the city (4:4, 6–11)

---

[1] This chart is adapted from the one in Landes, "The Kerygma of the Book of Jonah," 26.

As George Landes has pointed out,[2] this comparison between chapters 3 and 4 reveals an important development in the second half of the narrative. In the first half there is correspondence both in theme and general content between chapters 1 and 2. However, in the second half the conformity extends only to the thematic elements common to chapters 3 and 4 (each has a crucial event, human response, and divine response). The content of chapter 3 is significantly different from the content of chapter 4 (e.g., the human response in chapter 3 is faith, while the human response in chapter 4 is anger).

As Landes notes, "the conformity of content in Chapters 1 and 2 thus serves to heighten and emphasize the lack of such conformity in Chapters 3 and 4."[3] In chapters 1 and 2, Jonah is on the same level as the Gentile sailors. They are brought to repentance and faith in chapter 1, and he is brought to repentance and renewed faith in chapter 2. Both chapters end with worship of Yahweh through vows and sacrifice—by the mariners in 1:16 and by Jonah in 2:10 (ET 2:9). However, in chapters 3 and 4, Jonah's behavior is the opposite of the Ninevites' response. They repent and believe in God (3:5–9), but Jonah refuses to repent or change his desire for the destruction of Nineveh (4:1–3). His attitude is in striking contrast to that of the Ninevites as well as that of Yahweh (3:10; 4:2).

Another introductory observation about Jonah 3 is that it is closely related to Jeremiah 36. Yahweh expresses this hope in Jer 36:3:

> Perhaps the house of Judah will listen to the whole evil that I am planning to do to them, so that they will turn, each from his evil way [וְיָשֻׁבוּ אִישׁ מִדַּרְכּוֹ הָרָעָה], and I will forgive their iniquity and their sin.

That expression of hope uses vocabulary also employed in Jonah 3:8 (see below) and in Jonah 3:10: "Then God saw their works, that they turned from their evil way, and God changed his verdict about the evil that he threatened to do to them." Jonah 3:10 shares this vocabulary with Jer 36:3: רָעָה, "evil," both as divine punishment and as human activity; the verb שׁוּב, "to turn"; דֶּרֶךְ, "way"; and עָשָׂה, "to do," with God as subject. Again using three of those four words, Jeremiah expresses hope that it is not too late (Jer 36:7):

> Perhaps their plea for mercy will fall before Yahweh and they will turn, each from his evil way [וְיָשֻׁבוּ אִישׁ מִדַּרְכּוֹ הָרָעָה], for great is the anger and the wrath that Yahweh spoke against this people.

Similar vocabulary is in Jonah 3:8, where the Ninevite king issues a decree for his fellow citizens: "They must turn, each from his evil way" (וְיָשֻׁבוּ אִישׁ מִדַּרְכּוֹ הָרָעָה). Another parallel between Jonah 3 and Jeremiah 36 is that the citizens of both cities, Nineveh and Jerusalem, "called for a fast" (וַיִּקְרְאוּ־צוֹם, Jonah 3:5; קִרְאוּ צוֹם, Jer 36:9) before the judgment message reached the king.

But there the similarities between the two chapters end. The king of Nineveh responds to the message of Jonah by proclaiming a more austere repen-

---

[2] The analysis in this paragraph and the next follows and illustrates that in Landes, "The Kerygma of the Book of Jonah," 27.

[3] Landes, "The Kerygma of the Book of Jonah," 27.

tance than any recorded in Israel, either before or since. In contrast, King Jehoiakim does not react the way Yahweh and Jeremiah had hoped in Jeremiah 36. The Judean king orders the scroll with Yahweh's words to be cut up and thrown into the fire (Jer 36:23). Jerusalem then falls to Babylon in 587 BC, while in the eighth century, Nineveh is saved.

In that way Jerusalem and Nineveh are antitheses in a surprising manner. In Jonah 3:3 Nineveh is described as "a great city belonging to God," a title we least expect for a city of pagan Gentiles famous for their violence (Jonah 3:8; cf. Nahum 3:1).[4] On the other hand, Jerusalem had been "beautiful in loftiness, the joy of the whole earth … the city of the great King" (Ps 48:3 [ET 48:2]), but "because of you [Israel's corrupt leaders] Zion will be plowed as a field, and Jerusalem will become ruins, and the temple mount will become as the high places of the forest" (Micah 3:12). Yahweh opposes the proud Israelites but gives grace to the humbled Ninevites (cf. James 4:6).

A prophet confronting a wayward people and its king is a familiar OT scene: as Jeremiah confronted Jehoiakim (Jeremiah 36), so too did Moses oppose Pharaoh and the Egyptians (Exodus 1–15); Samuel deposed Saul (1 Samuel 15); Elijah challenged Ahab and his prophets of Baal (1 Kings 18); Micaiah predicted the death of Ahab and the defeat of his troops (1 Kings 22); and Amos prophesied the death of Jeroboam II and exile of the Northern Kingdom (Amos 7:10–17). To those OT examples can be added John the Baptist's rebuke of adulterous Herod (Mt 14:1–12), Christ himself before Pilate and Herod (Lk 23:1–25), and Paul before Felix, Festus, and Agrippa (Acts 23–26). In many of these incidents, the message of the prophet is lengthy and impassioned, and he himself is completely ignored or angrily rejected.

A surprising reversal of that common scene takes place in Jonah 3. There are some other passages where a king and his people are persuaded by a prophet's call for repentance,[5] but the prophet's own behavior makes Jonah 3 doubly surprising. Jonah the prophet is neither eloquent nor impassioned. He speaks only one sentence (3:4) and addresses it to no one in particular. He does not mention the crimes of the city or its king, nor does he describe the imminent punishment in any detail. We might expect Jonah to begin with the call "Repent!" (cf. Ezek 14:6; 18:30; Mt 3:2; 4:17), but in fact he does not issue an imperative of any sort. And yet Jonah is far from being ignored or rejected; the king and his constituents respond in customary acts of repentance, extended in an unheard-of way even to their animals. The only one angry at the end is, ironically, the prophet Jonah! This magnifies the irony with the intent that the reading audience may repent of Jonah-like arrogance and join the penitent Ninevites in sincere faith.[6]

---

[4]   For Nineveh, see also "Jonah: Fact or Fiction?" in the introduction and the commentary on Jonah 1:2.

[5]   For example, King David repented when he was rebuked by Nathan (2 Samuel 12); Hezekiah wept before God after Isaiah prophesied his imminent death (2 Kings 20); and Josiah led the kingdom of Judah in repentance after the rediscovery of the Torah (2 Kings 22–23).

[6]   See "The Purpose of Satire in This True and Didactic Story" in "Jonah as Satire with Irony" the introduction.

269

Jonah 3:1–3a

Scene 4: Jonah's Second Call

Translation

3 **¹Then the Word of Yahweh came to Jonah a second time, saying, ²"Arise, go to Nineveh, the great city, and call out to it the call that I am about to speak to you." ³ªSo Jonah arose and went to Nineveh according to the Word of Yahweh.**

Textual Notes

3:1 וַיְהִ֧י דְבַר־יְהוָ֛ה אֶל־יוֹנָ֖ה שֵׁנִ֥ית לֵאמֹֽר׃—This verse is identical to 1:1 except that בֶּן־אֲמִתַּי ("the son of Amittai") in 1:1 is replaced by שֵׁנִית here. This is the feminine form of the ordinal numerical adjective שֵׁנִי, "second." Here and often elsewhere, the feminine form is used as an adverb, "a second time, again" (see BDB, s.v. שֵׁנִי, under the root שׁנה III). For the prophetic "Word of Yahweh" as portending Jesus, the incarnate Word, and for the construction וַיְהִי ... אֶל־ ("was/came to"), see the first textual note on 1:1.

3:2 ק֚וּם לֵ֣ךְ אֶל־נִֽינְוֵ֔ה הָעִ֖יר הַגְּדוֹלָ֑ה—This first part of Yahweh's second call to Jonah is identical to the first part of his original call ("Arise, go to Nineveh, the great city"). See the first two textual notes on 1:2.

וּקְרָ֤א אֵלֶ֙יהָ֙—In Leningradensis (hence *BHS*), the conjunction is pointed anomalously as the vowel letter *shureq* (וּ) with the *hireq* vowel (וּ). Normally the conjunction is pointed as *shureq* when the initial consonant has *shewa*, so the expected form is וּקְרָא as in 1:2.

The Qal masculine singular imperative of קְרָא is repeated from 1:2 (וּקְרָ֣א עָלֶ֔יהָ), but here it takes the preposition אֶל instead of עַל (both with third feminine singular suffix, referring to נִינְוֵה since cities are feminine in Hebrew). These two prepositions often seem to be used interchangeably, especially in Jeremiah and later OT books. The LXX translates both 1:2 and 3:2 identically and neutrally: καὶ κήρυξον ἐν αὐτῇ, "and preach *in* her/it." However, אֶל more commonly means "to," whereas "against" is more often a meaning of עַל. The combination קְרָא עַל can refer to announcing judgment, as in Jonah 1:2, "call out *against*" Nineveh (see the third textual note on 1:2 and BDB, s.v. קְרָא, 3 a and d). The content of what Jonah was to preach was not given in 1:2, but the construction made clear that it was to be a message of judgment. Sasson argues that the change here to אֶל is significant and that Yahweh here gives Jonah a more neutral directive: "The idiom קְרָא אֶל (better perhaps the verb קְרָא with the אֶל here used merely to introduce the indirect object) controls the delivery of *some* message which Jonah is to convey to the Ninevites."[1] It is plausible that the shift from עַל in 1:2 to אֶל in 3:2 involves a change in Yahweh's assignment to his prophet. Whereas in 1:2 Yahweh instructed Jonah to preach "against" the city,

---

[1] Sasson, "On Jonah's Two Missions," 26–27.

now in 3:2 Yahweh commands Jonah to announce "to" it an as-yet unspecified message.[2] The message itself is not revealed to Jonah until he enters the city, and we, the audience, hear it only when Jonah preaches it in 3:4. These different nuances for עַל versus אֶל further signal a change in Jonah's prophetic status. Whereas 1:2 might suggest that Jonah was given a measure of freedom in how to word his judgment oracle, the rest of 3:2 specifies that Jonah is to be completely dependent on Yahweh for the wording of his prophetic statement. It will not even be given to him until it is time to preach it. This subtle change in the wording of Jonah's second call is perhaps intended to prepare us for the unexpected consequences of his mission (3:5–10).

אֶת־הַקְּרִיאָה אֲשֶׁר אָנֹכִי דֹּבֵר אֵלֶיךָ:—These words emphasize the divine origin of Jonah's proclamation. The message he is to communicate is not his own; it comes from God.[3]

The preceding imperative קְרָא, "to proclaim, call," takes the cognate direct object noun קְרִיאָה, "proclamation" (BDB), with the article. The cognate accusative construction can be rendered "proclaim the proclamation" or "call the call." This noun occurs only here in the OT. It is a neutral term in that it does not indicate whether the content of the message is judgment or salvation. If a judgment oracle were intended here, we might have expected a term such as מַשָּׂא, "oracle," which is often used to introduce judgment oracles against Gentile nations (see, e.g., Is 13:1; 15:1; 17:1; 19:1; 21:1), including an oracle against Nineveh (Nah 1:1). Therefore, like the change from עַל to אֶל (see the preceding textual note), the use of this term too may subtly prepare us for the unexpected salvation of Nineveh.

The LXX translates קְרִיאָה as κήρυγμα, which occurs elsewhere in the LXX only in 2 Chr 30:5, where it renders קוֹל, referring to Hezekiah's "decree" for Israel to celebrate the Passover, and in Prov 9:3 and 1 Esdras 9:3. In the NT, κήρυγμα is the term used in Mt 12:41 and Lk 11:32, where Jesus refers to "the preaching of Jonah" (see the excursus "The Sign of Jonah"). It also is the term used in one of the alternate endings of Mark; Rom 16:25; 1 Cor 1:21; 2:4; 15:14; 2 Tim 4:17; Titus 1:3 that refers to the "preaching" of the Gospel of Jesus Christ, resulting in the salvation of all who believe. Compare Jonah 3:5: "Then the men of Nineveh believed in God."

The relative clause אֲשֶׁר אָנֹכִי דֹּבֵר אֵלֶיךָ modifying קְרִיאָה uses the Qal participle (דֹּבֵר) of the verb דָּבַר. In the Qal, the only forms of דָּבַר that occur in the OT are

---

2   The literary technique of repetition is a common feature of OT narrative. Often there is some minor but significant change in the repeated version, reflecting a different standpoint or interpretation of events between the first and second texts. For example, compare Gen 24:1–22 with Gen 24:34–49 (especially 24:3–4 with 24:41). Also compare the three versions of the interaction between Potiphar's wife and Joseph in Genesis 39 (especially 39:12–13 and 39:17–18). Significant also is the repetition of a sentence *without* a change in language despite an intervening event, such as the dialogue between Yahweh and Elijah in 1 Ki 19:9–18, where Elijah's failure to change his response leads Yahweh to redirect him for a further mission.

3   The OT prophets constantly draw attention to the fact that their messages come directly from God. For an impressive list of phrases that illustrate this, all drawn from the book of Isaiah, see Young, *My Servants the Prophets*, 171–75. Similar lists could be constructed for other prophetic books.

the infinitive construct (once in the OT), the active participle (thirty-nine occurrences), and the passive participle (one occurrence). The active Qal forms mean "speak" (BDB) and thus are synonymous with the far more common Piel forms.

In general, the temporal force of a participle must be determined from the context. However, participles are often used for actions that will take place in the near future, in which case "a future action, mainly an approaching action, is represented as being already in progress" (Joüon, § 121 e). Therefore, it is likely that by using דֹּבֵר here Yahweh refers to "the call that I *am about to speak* to you." Similarly, Jonah's sermon in 3:4 also uses a participle: "Yet in forty days Nineveh *is about to be changed* [נֶהְפָּכֶת]," and as soon as Jonah preaches his sermon, the change starts (3:5–9).

The Syriac Peshitta translates the Hebrew here in 3:2 literally with a participle and pronoun, ܘܐܡܪ ܐܢܐ, "that I am speaking." The Vulgate translates with the present tense, *quam ego loquor ad te*, as do most English translations, for example, "the message that I tell you" (ESV). The LXX translates with an aorist, ὃ ἐγὼ ἐλάλησα πρὸς σέ, and some English translations likewise use the past tense, for example, "as I told you to" (JB). However, for the past tense, a perfect verb could have been used (e.g., אֲשֶׁר דִּבַּרְתִּי אֵלֶיךָ).

3:3 וַיָּקָם יוֹנָה וַיֵּלֶךְ אֶל־נִינְוֶה כִּדְבַר יְהוָה—This verse begins with the same two words as 1:3, וַיָּקָם יוֹנָה, "Jonah arose" (see the first textual note on 1:3). There Jonah only appeared to arise in obedience to obey Yahweh's command in 1:2, קוּם, "Arise," because he proceeded to flee toward Tarshish. But here in 3:3, the two verbs וַיָּקָם ... וַיֵּלֶךְ (the Qal third masculine singular imperfects of קוּם and הָלַךְ with *waw* consecutive) indicate that Jonah "arose and went," faithfully fulfilling Yahweh's command in 3:2, which uses the same two verbs: קוּם לֵךְ, "Arise, go" (the masculine singular Qal imperatives of קוּם and הָלַךְ).

Regarding נִינְוֶה, see the discussion of "Nineveh" in the textual notes on 1:2.

Explicitly confirming Jonah's obedience here is the construct phrase כִּדְבַר יְהוָה, "according to the Word of Yahweh." The noun דָּבָר, "word," is in construct with the Tetragrammaton and has the preposition כְּ "expressing conformity to a standard or rule" (BDB, s.v. כְּ, 1 c (1)). This phrase occurs only here in Jonah, but twenty-five times elsewhere in the OT, many noting how believers faithfully carry out a divine mandate (e.g., Josh 8:27; 1 Ki 12:24; 17:5; Jer 13:2; 2 Chr 35:6).

Commentary

3:1 Jonah is the only biblical prophet who must be given his assignment a second time because of his prior disobedience.[4] In calling Jonah again, Yahweh graciously makes no reference to the prophet's previous failure (1:3–2:1 [ET 1:3–17]). Jonah 3:1 repeats 1:1 except that the grace-filled שֵׁנִית ("a sec-

---

[4] Moses twice is given the assignment to ascend Mount Sinai and receive the Ten Commandments (Ex 19:20; 34:1–2), but that was necessitated by Israel's disobedience (Exodus 32), not by any failure on the part of Moses. Compare Acts 10:13–16, where Peter resists the command given him thrice in a vision.

ond time") replaces "the son of Amittai," naming Jonah's father.[5] Due to Jonah's "baptism" in the sea (Jonah 2), Yahweh has no word of condemnation for his "flighty dove" (cf. Micah 7:19; Rom 8:1).[6]

At this point in the narrative, Jonah has been to hell and back. He has experienced Yahweh's gracious deliverance from "Sheol" (2:3 [ET 2:2]) and "the underworld" (2:7 [ET 2:6]).[7] He is not the same person. The "salvation" that "belongs to Yahweh" (2:10 [ET 2:9]) has given Jonah a new start, and its fruits are brought forth in 3:3 when he leaves his old life and arises as a new man, "created to be like God in true righteousness and holiness" (Eph 4:24 NIV). After Peter denied Christ, he too received a second chance from this same God (Jn 21:15–19). His experience taught him to call God "the God of all grace" (1 Pet 5:10).

Not only does Yahweh forget Jonah's sin (cf. Jer 31:34), neither does he now prompt Jonah to fulfill the prophet's earlier promise, "What I have vowed, I will indeed repay" (2:10 [ET 2:9]).[8] Yahweh's words carry no rebuke for Jonah and no warning of what would happen if he once again failed to obey. So in this merciful manner, the plot rewinds and begins anew. The bedraggled, seaweed-draped, vomit-stained, and traumatized prophet likely was a bit more receptive to the Word of Yahweh this time!

3:2–3a Jonah's overall movement in chapter 1 and into chapter 2 was characterized by the verb "to go down," away from Yahweh (who told him to "arise," 1:2) and from other people, down toward death (see יָרַד in 1:3, 5; 2:7 [ET 2:6]; see also his movement in 1:15; 2:3–6 [ET 2:2–5]). In chapter 3, Jonah's action is characterized by קוּם, "arise" (3:2–3), הָלַךְ, "to go, walk" (3:2–3), and "call" (קָרָא, 3:2, 4; see also the noun קְרִיאָה, "proclamation, call," in 3:2).

From the first two chapters, we are familiar with the narrator's fondness of repetition. His repetition of key verbs in 3:2–4 invites us to compare and contrast Jonah with the pagan Gentiles who are converted to saving faith in the one true God. Yahweh first commanded Jonah to "arise, go, ... call out" to Nineveh (קוּם, הָלַךְ, and קָרָא, 1:2). The captain of the ship called on Jonah to "arise" and "call" on his God (קוּם, קָרָא, 1:6). In chapter 1, Jonah spurned those calls by Yahweh and the captain, but now in 3:2–4, those verbs describe how Jonah

---

5   Compare שֵׁנִית, "a second time," in Gen 22:15, where it introduces Gen 22:15–18, the second of two gracious divine words spoken by the Angel of Yahweh to Abraham. The first divine word was the command not to slay his son Isaac (Gen 22:11–12).

6   For Jonah's "baptism" and the motifs of dying to sin and rising to new life, see the excursus "Death and Resurrection Motifs in Luther's Baptismal Theology." For the meaning of "Jonah" as a "dove" connoting unfaithfulness, see the commentary on 1:1.

7   See the excursus "Sheol."

8   The commentary on 2:10 (ET 2:9) opined that after Jonah was vomited onto the dry land (2:11 [ET 2:10]), he promptly received his second call to go to Nineveh, which he obeyed. The prophet would have to wait until after his mission to Nineveh before he could fulfill his promise to offer sacrifice at the Jerusalem temple and fulfill any other vows. The book ends without revealing whether or not Jonah did so.

faithfully carries out Yahweh's repeated call. The people and king of Nineveh will display a faithful response to Yahweh's Word by means of these same verbs. The Ninevites "call" for a fast (קָרָא, 3:5). The king "arises" from his throne (קוּם, 3:6) to don sackcloth and issue his decree that all his people should sincerely "call" to God (קָרָא, 3:8).

Supporting the view that the repetition of these three verbs is deliberate and significant is the fact that none of the three occur again in the book after 3:8.

Thus קוּם, "arise," echoes throughout chapter 3 as a "resurrection" reminder of Jonah's renewed call, which he now carries out, in contrast to his disobedience in chapter 1, which led to his descent and near death in Sheol (2:3, 7 [ET 2:2, 6]).

Yahweh's original command for Jonah to "go" (הָלַךְ, 1:2) is repeated in 3:2, and then Jonah "went" (הָלַךְ, 3:3), showing Jonah's slow but finally willing response to Yahweh's command. This verb is often used to describe a person's life of faith in response to God's Word; in such passages, it is usually translated as "walk."[9] This suggests that הָלַךְ in 3:3 ("Jonah … went/walked") does not simply refer to Jonah's mode of transportation. Rather, it describes his mode of life in response to Yahweh's grace. He is now walking in the ways of Yahweh, "according to the Word of Yahweh" (3:3). In the NT, Paul uses περιπατέω, "to walk," to convey a similar meaning (e.g., Rom 6:4; Gal 5:16; Eph 4:1; Col 1:10; 1 Thess 2:12).

The repetition of Yahweh's call to Jonah using the same verbs in 1:2 and 3:2 accents an ongoing theme in the book. What Yahweh commands, says, and does will eventually accomplish his will. Even if Yahweh's Word is not heeded or fulfilled immediately, as it is not in chapters 1–2, it will be fulfilled in time, as it is in chapter 3. He will not be thwarted. After all, he is the God of the heavens, who made the sea and the dry land (1:9).

The repetition of the same verbs in reference to the pagan Gentiles who are converted to faith (the sailors in chapter 1; the Ninevites in chapter 3) accents both the omnipotence and the free grace of Yahweh, over against the powerlessness and futility of people like Jonah who resist his Word. Although his chosen prophet or people may refuse to believe (for a time or permanently), Yahweh can and will raise up other believers whom he saves through faith.[10]

To highlight that Yahweh's powerful grace operates through his Word, the author has worded the chain of events in chapter 3 in such a way that the verb קָרָא, "to call," functions much like טוּל, "to hurl," did in chapter 1. There Yahweh "hurled" the great wind (1:4) that set in motion more hurling (1:5) that finally ends up with the hurling of Jonah into the sea (1:12, 15). Similarly, the imperative of קָרָא, "call out," in 3:2 sets in motion a series of callings. Jonah "called out" to the Ninevites in 3:4, and the people "called" for a fast in 3:5,

---

[9] See the many passages cited in BDB, s.v. הָלַךְ, Qal, II 3 a and c. In other passages, the Hithpael of the verb refers to "walking" with God (e.g., Gen 5:22, 24; 6:9; 17:1; 24:40).

[10] See the excursus "Mission in the Old Testament."

with the king of Nineveh issuing a decree that commands every Ninevite sincerely to "call" to God (3:8).

The grammar expounds the theology. Yahweh's call accomplishes his salvific purpose (cf. Is 55:10–11). Paul puts in this way in 1 Thess 5:24: "The one who calls you (ὁ καλῶν) is faithful, and he will do it."

Commenting on Jonah's call into the office of prophet, Luther refers, by extension, to the pastoral office:

> Thus both the office and the Word employed in the office must be comprehended in the divine command. If that is done, the work will prosper and bear fruit. But when men run without God's command or proclaim other messages than God's Word, they work nothing but harm. Jeremiah, too, drives both these facts home, saying (Jer. 23:21): "I did not send the prophets, yet they ran; I did not speak to them, yet they prophesied." You who are to preach, impress these two points on your minds![11]

Both the Word and the office are divine and are commanded by God. And so Yahweh (re)calls Jonah into the office, and he promises to give him the very words he is to say.

The change from עַל ("call out *against*" Nineveh) in 1:2 to אֶל ("call out *to* it") in 3:2 subtly suggests that Yahweh may already have in mind the change in his verdict from the destruction of Nineveh to its salvation (3:10). This beginning of divine reprieve—hinted at in the change of prepositions—will be further intimated in the ambiguity of Jonah's announcement in 3:4. In the sermon Yahweh gives Jonah, he uses the Niphal participle of הָפַךְ to say that Nineveh "is about to be changed." The Niphal of that verb can refer to the destruction of a city, but it can also refer to another kind of change. What is conveyed to us by these subtle hints is an indication of things to come.[12] The slight change in prepositions from 1:2 to 3:2 foreshadows the change in the Ninevites—pagans who are brought to repentance and faith by the preached Word—and the complete change in Yahweh's disposition toward them, expressed in 3:10.

Two of the imperatives from 3:2, "Arise, go" (קוּם לֵךְ), become indicatives in 3:3: "Jonah arose and went" (וַיָּקָם יוֹנָה וַיֵּלֶךְ). Yet the third imperative in 3:2,

---

[11] AE 19:83.

[12] In other texts, Hebrew narrative cleverly uses these kinds of indirect changes to communicate important truths. For example, when Manoah's wife (Judg 13:3–5) is told by the Angel of Yahweh that she will conceive and bear a son, she repeats to her husband the terms of the divine promise almost word for word, but she significantly changes the final clause of the annunciation. The Angel says, "The child will be a Nazirite to God from the womb, and he will begin to save Israel from the hand of the Philistines" (Judg 13:5). But in her repetition she concludes, "The child will be a Nazirite to God from the womb until the day of his death" (Judg 13:7). It is telling that the divine promise that ended with liberation (13:5) now concludes with death (13:7). The woman's silence on the explicit promise of salvation and her counterpoising it with the phrase "until the day of his death" are hints of what kind of future lies before Samson. This dissonance subtly sets the scene for a powerful but spiritually dubious judge of Israel. Samson ends up sowing much destruction during his life, and the greatest salvation he brings will be through his death (Judg 16:30). Cf. Rom 5:8–9; Phil 2:8.

"call out" (וְיִקְרָא), has no corresponding indicative in 3:3 ("he called out" does not come until 3:4). That absence leaves Jonah's response as yet incomplete. The first time around, Jonah obeyed only one of the two imperatives ("arise, go") in 1:2; he "arose" (1:3). Now he obeys two of the three imperatives in 3:2. In comparison to 1:2–3, his obedience now is more complete, but it is not yet total or assured. Suspense lingers. This time will the prophet call out Yahweh's Word?

Summary of Scene 4

Jonah 3:1–3a does not explicitly state that Jonah has repented, that the experience with the sea and the great fish have humbled him, that Yahweh's salvation (2:10 [ET 2:9]) prompts his obedience, or that he now plans to change his theology to accommodate God's desire to save all people, even pagan Gentiles like the Ninevites (Jonah resents that in 4:1–2).

So why does Jonah go to Nineveh this time? After all, this was a demanding journey of about five hundred miles from the Mediterranean coast across desert routes. The approximate travel time in antiquity from Jerusalem to Nineveh is estimated to have been between a month and forty-five days, based on caravan speed.[13] So why go?

One answer might be that Jonah realizes he cannot escape Yahweh. This God has pursued him from Israel, across the sea, into the ocean depths, even to "the belly of Sheol" and "the underworld" (2:3–7b [2:2–6b]), then out onto the land again (2:11 [ET 2:10]). At this point, Jonah may simply be giving in, passively but not joyfully acquiescing to what Yahweh wants.

Another answer as to why Jonah goes to Nineveh this time might be that he hopes or anticipates that the Ninevites will not respond, in which case they would be destroyed. Nothing would be sweeter for him than this (cf. 4:2)! Jonah knows all about Yahweh's mercy (4:2), but he also knows that destruction and death can occur if repentance and faith are not forthcoming. His near-death experience (1:15–2:8a [ET 1:15–2:7a]) after his own rebellion (1:3) would have reinforced that. If Jonah is given any freedom in crafting his sermon in 3:4, we might surmise that he even may be attempting to steer the Ninevites to destruction by delivering a sermon that is only five words long, contains no call for the Ninevites to repent, and says nothing about escape or salvation. It is as though Jonah marches off to Nineveh with an explosive briefcase tucked under his arm, presumably packed with pounds of prophetic rhetorical explosives!

Or perhaps Jonah goes to the great city because of his renewed faith. After all, Yahweh had saved him from the death he surely knew he deserved.[14] Despite his rebellion, Yahweh had provided a great fish for his deliverance (2:1

---

[13] Burrows, "The Literary Category of the Book of Jonah," 93, estimates the travel time as "about a month." Isserlin, *The Israelites*, 26, asserts that the journey "could have taken him a month and a half." Isserlin estimates camel caravan speeds to have been between fifteen and thirty-seven miles per day (p. 25).

[14] His command that the sailors should hurl him into the sea (1:12) can be interpreted as an admission that he deserved that punishment.

[ET 1:17]), not abandoned him in Sheol (2:3 [ET 2:2]; cf. Ps 16:10), raised him up to new life (Jonah 2:7c, 10–11 [ET 2:6c, 9–10]), and reinstalled him into the prophetic office (3:1–2; cf. Jn 21:15–19). Yahweh has come "to seek and to save what was lost" (Lk 19:10). Just as Paul urges the baptized members of the congregation in Rome to present themselves to God as people who once were dead but now are alive (Rom 6:1–18), so also Jonah has been through his own "baptismal" drowning of the old man and resurrection of the new man of faith.[15] He is now empowered to follow Yahweh's command, just as Yahweh's other servants have done: the wind and the sea (1:4–15) and the great fish (2:1, 11 [ET 1:17; 2:10]).

But if this is true, it will become apparent in chapter 4 that Jonah is still *simul iustus et peccator*, "saint and sinner at the same time,"[16] and this to the very end of the narrative.

---

[15] See the excursuses "Sheol" and "Death and Resurrection Motifs in Luther's Baptismal Theology."

[16] See "Jonah as Sinner and Saint" in the commentary on 1:2. See also "The Place of the Psalm in the Book of Jonah" in "Introduction to Jonah 2"; the commentary on 2:8 (ET 2:7); and the excursus "Death and Resurrection Motifs in Luther's Baptismal Theology."

Scene 5: Jonah's Preaching Converts Nineveh and Yahweh Changes His Verdict

Translation

3 ³ᵇNow Nineveh was a great city belonging to God, a walk of three days. ⁴Jonah began to enter the city a walk of one day. He called out and said, "Yet in forty days Nineveh is about to be changed."

⁵Then the men of Nineveh believed in God and called for a fast and put on sackcloths, from the greatest of them to the least of them. ⁶When this word reached the king of Nineveh, he arose from his throne and removed his royal robe from upon himself. He covered [himself with] sackcloth and sat upon the ash heap. ⁷Then he issued an edict and proclaimed in Nineveh, "From the decree of the king and his nobles: People and animals—both herd and flock—must not taste anything and must not feed, and water they must not drink. ⁸They must cover [themselves with] sackcloths—both people and animals—and they must call to God fervently, and they must turn, each from his evil way and from the violence that is in their hands. ⁹Who knows whether God may turn and change his verdict and turn away from the fierceness of his anger so we will not perish?"

¹⁰Then God saw their works, that they turned from their evil way, and God changed his verdict about the evil that he threatened to do to them, and he did not do [it].

Textual Notes

3:3b Halfway through 3:3 the narrator interrupts the action to describe Nineveh with two statements about the city, each posing exegetical problems.

וְנִינְוֵה הָיְתָה עִיר־גְּדוֹלָה לֵאלֹהִים—The unusual word order, with the subject (וְנִינְוֵה) preceding the verb (הָיְתָה), signals a parenthetical digression about the city (3:3b). See Joüon, § 159 f. For other examples of this construction in Jonah, see the first textual note on 1:4. הָיְתָה is the third feminine singular Qal perfect of הָיָה. It is feminine because its subject, נִינְוֵה, is feminine, as are all Hebrew names of cities.

This first statement about Nineveh presents two exegetical challenges. The first is the force of the perfect verb הָיְתָה. Does "Now Nineveh *was* a great city" mean that the book of Jonah was written after Nineveh's destruction in 612 BC? Not at all. The perfect verb is best understood as meaning that when Jonah arrived in the city, it had been and still was a great city. See further "The Date of Writing" in the introduction.

The second exegetical challenge is the prepositional phrase that describes the city. Here the phrase "great city" occurs without the article: עִיר־גְּדוֹלָה. Elsewhere in Jonah, the phrase occurs with the article: "Nineveh, the great city" (נִינְוֵה הָעִיר הַגְּדוֹלָה, 1:2; 3:2; 4:11). But only here is the city described with the additional prepositional phrase

לֵאלֹהִים (the preposition לְ with אֱלֹהִים), "to God." Many commentators and translators understand this phrase not as a reference to God, but as expressing a kind of superlative, for example, "an *exceedingly* great city" (ESV, NKJV; emphasis added). However, Hebrew has several other customary ways of expressing a superlative.[1] This is not a common way, nor do all grammarians agree that the phrase here should be regarded as a superlative.

D. Winton Thomas, in an article about the various ways in which Hebrew can express a superlative, discusses eight passages in which either אֱלֹהִים or אֵל allegedly is used to form a superlative.[2] Thomas states: "In all these examples it may be conceded that the divine names have a superlative force so long as we understand that the superlative force is imparted, not by the addition of the divine names as intensifying epithets, but by the fact that a person or thing is brought into a relationship with God." Thomas argues that Jonah 3:3 means that "Nineveh was 'great to God,' that is, even to God, who has a different standard of greatness from men."[3] In seven of the eight passages considered by Thomas, a noun is in construct with a term for "God." Jonah 3:3 is the only one of the eight passages in which a superlative allegedly is formed by "God" in a prepositional phrase. Indeed, Jack Sasson notes that there are no other OT examples of a prepositional phrase serving as a superlative and that the ancient versions did not translate this phrase in Jonah 3:3 as a superlative. Sasson argues against interpreting it as superlative. He suggests that it might mean that Nineveh was "a large city to the gods," meaning that it was "important to the many gods of the Assyrian empire" or that it "contains many shrines." But most likely, according to Sasson, the preposition לְ is a circumlocution for a genitive, and so " 'the large city' is said to 'belong' to God." This "explains why the Ninevites readily follow Jonah's directives and why Nineveh is made the object of God's grace."[4] Even other scholars who advocate interpreting the phrase as a superlative admit that "probably the idea was that God *originated* the thing … or that it belonged to Him."[5]

Often in the OT the preposition לְ is a circumlocution for a genitive and denotes possession, in which case it means "belonging to" (BDB, s.v. לְ, 5 a and b; see also Waltke-O'Connor, § 11.2.10c). The affirmation here that Nineveh is a great city "belonging to God" fits with Jonah's confession in 1:9 that Yahweh is the God "who made

---

[1] See, for example, GKC, § 133 g; Waltke-O'Connor, §§ 14.3.3b; 14.5; Joüon, § 141 j.

[2] Thomas, "A Consideration of Some Unusual Ways of Expressing the Superlative in Hebrew." The passages cited by Thomas that have a noun in construct with אֱלֹהִים or אֵל are Gen 23:6; 30:8; Ex 9:28; 1 Sam 14:15; Pss 36:7 (ET 36:6); 80:11 (ET 80:10); Job 1:16.

[3] Thomas, "A Consideration of Some Unusual Ways of Expressing the Superlative in Hebrew," 216.

[4] Sasson, *Jonah*, 228–29. Similar is the position of Rofé, who reads the phrase genitivally, "His [God's] great city" (*The Prophetical Stories*, 165, including n. 76).

[5] A. B. Davidson, quoted in Waltke-O'Connor, § 14.5b. For Jonah 3:3, Waltke-O'Connor advocates the translation "an *exceedingly great* city" (§ 14.5b, example 19). However, Sasson's critique of Thomas also applies to Waltke-O'Connor, since the other examples it cites as allegedly comparable (examples 15–18) are all construct chains; there is no comparable example of a prepositional phrase.

the sea and the dry land," since all creation belongs to him. It also is consistent with what Yahweh himself will say about the city in 4:10–11. In light of Yahweh's comparison of Nineveh to the qiqayon plant and his use of "labor" and "raise/make grow" for the plant in 4:10, Yahweh is implying in 4:11 that he himself cultivated the city, just as he did the plant.

The Hebrew construction here is similar to David's declaration with the preposition לְ in Ps 24:1: "Belonging to Yahweh is the earth and its fullness" (לַיהוָה הָאָרֶץ וּמְלוֹאָהּ). Since the whole earth is Yahweh's, certainly Nineveh belongs to him as well. The promise that Yahweh would claim formerly hostile non-Israelites (Gentiles) as his people is expressed in Is 19:24–25:

> On that day Israel will be a third [people] in relation to Egypt and Assyria, a source of blessing in the midst of the world, whom Yahweh of hosts will have blessed, saying, "Blessed is my people Egypt, the word of my hands Assyria, and my inheritance Israel."[6]

Luther, citing the repentance of the Ninevites in 3:5–9, interprets לֵאלֹהִים as indicating "that none but saints inhabited the city and that Jonah rightly called it 'a city of God.'"[7]

The interpretation of the phrase as a reference to Nineveh's importance to God[8] is also plausible based on Jonah 4:11.

Some less likely views may be mentioned briefly. One is that the phrase affirms Nineveh's status as a potential divine residence: "great for-God."[9] Another is that if the noun אֱלֹהִים is taken as a true plural ("gods"), the phrase could mean that many "gods" were worshiped in the city or that it had a large number of temples.[10]

Even if we did not fully know how to interpret עִיר־גְּדוֹלָה לֵאלֹהִים here in 3:3, by the time we read 4:10–11, its meaning becomes clear. The concept of words and phrases that grow in meaning confirms this interpretation.[11] The author of Jonah repeats key words and phrases, which take on added significance with each new repetition, until the climactic one reveals the full import. In this way the narrative progresses toward its goal.[12] The progressive descriptions of Nineveh are as follows:

1. "Arise, go to Nineveh, the great city" (1:2).
2. "Arise, go to Nineveh, the great city" (3:2).

---

[6] This promise anticipates the large-scale conversions of Gentiles to faith in Jesus Christ during the church era. Such Gentile conversions took place on a smaller scale already during the OT era. See the excursus "Mission in the Old Testament."

[7] AE 19:85.

[8] Stuart, *Hosea–Jonah*, 437. Compare the NIV, which omits "God" and translates: "Nineveh was a very important city."

[9] Trible, *Rhetorical Criticism*, 178.

[10] Wiseman, "Jonah's Nineveh," 36.

[11] Magonet, *Form and Meaning*, 31–33, discusses this concept of a "growing phrase" and applies it to עִיר־גְּדוֹלָה לֵאלֹהִים. The following analysis is dependent on his.

[12] A prime example is יָרֵא, "to fear, worship," used in 1:5, 9, 10, 16, culminating in the conversion of the sailors and their worship of Yahweh (1:16). See the first textual note on 1:5 and the first textual note on 1:16 as well as the commentary on those verses.

3. "Now Nineveh was a great city belonging to God" (3:3).

4. "Shall I myself not have pity upon Nineveh, the great city, in which there are more than twelve myriads of people who do not know [the difference] between their right and their left, and many animals?" (4:11).

Thus the fourth, climactic description of Nineveh confirms the interpretation that 3:3 declares that Nineveh is great and that it belongs to God, even though the full extent of Yahweh's compassion for the city is not revealed until 4:11.

מַהֲלַךְ שְׁלֹשֶׁת יָמִים:—This second piece of information about the city, that it was "a walk of three days," also poses a challenge. See the commentary below on 3:3b, "A Walk of Three Days," and also under "Jonah: Fact or Fiction?" in the introduction.

Hebrew often forms nouns by prefixing מ to a verbal root (Joüon, § 88L d). The noun מַהֲלַךְ is from the verb הָלַךְ, "go, walk" (as in 3:2–3). Here it is in construct (hence ־לַךְ). The noun recurs in 3:4 and occurs elsewhere in the OT only in Ezek 42:4; Zech 3:7; Neh 2:6. It literally means a "walk, journey, going" (BDB). That it does not refer to a fixed linear distance is evident when King Artaxerxes asks Nehemiah, "How long will your journey [מַהֲלָכְךָ] be, and when do you return?" (Neh 2:6). His twofold question only seeks to ascertain when Nehemiah expects to return to his job, not the exact distance he will travel. Whereas Nehemiah embarked on a journey of hundreds of miles, in Ezek 42:4 the noun is an architectural term referring to a "passageway" in the eschatological temple that is only about a hundred and fifty feet long and fifteen feet wide. In Zech 3:7 the plural has an abstract meaning: Yahweh promises the high priest Joshua that if he is faithful, he will receive "access" to join others who stand before Yahweh.

Jonah was inside the great fish for "three days" (שְׁלֹשָׁה יָמִים, 2:1 [ET 1:17]; see the fourth textual note on 2:1). This exact phrase also occurs in 1 Sam 30:12; 1 Ki 12:5; 2 Ki 2:17. However, usually the numeral is in construct, as here: שְׁלֹשֶׁת יָמִים. That construct phrase occurs over thirty times in the OT.

3:4 וַיָּחֶל יוֹנָה לָבוֹא בָעִיר מַהֲלַךְ יוֹם אֶחָד—The first verb is the Hiphil third masculine singular imperfect with *waw* consecutive of חָלַל, to "begin" (BDB, s.v. חָלַל III, Hiphil, 2; *HALOT*, s.v. חלל I, Hiphil, 2). This verb frequently takes an infinitive construct with the preposition לְ, "begin to" do something. לָבוֹא is formed with the Qal infinitive construct of בּוֹא, "to enter." בּוֹא often is followed by the preposition בְּ, "into," so בָעִיר is, literally, "enter into the city." The phrase מַהֲלַךְ יוֹם אֶחָד ("a journey of one day") repeats the noun מַהֲלַךְ from 3:3; see the last textual note on 3:3. This clause does not just refer to the moment he entered the city. Rather, it refers to his entire first day of walking about in the city. This was just the beginning because it would take three days for him to walk everywhere throughout the huge city.

וַיִּקְרָא וַיֹּאמַר—These two verbs ("He called out and said") refer to action contemporaneous with the preceding clause: throughout Jonah's first day of walking about in the city, he is continually heralding his message. These verbs should not be taken as sequential, as if Jonah waited until he had walked about in Nineveh for one day before he began to preach.

עוֹד אַרְבָּעִים יוֹם וְנִינְוֵה נֶהְפָּכֶת:—These five Hebrew words comprise Jonah's sermon. The adverb עוֹד can mean "yet" and refer to the future (BDB, 1 a (*b*)). Here the time in the future is set by אַרְבָּעִים יוֹם. Hebrew customarily uses the plural of a numeral for a corresponding multiple of ten, so the plural of אַרְבַּע, "four," is אַרְבָּעִים, "forty." Numbers greater than ten normally take the singular יוֹם ("day"), though English requires the plural, "days." English also requires a preposition: "yet *in* forty days."

The LXX has ἔτι τρεῖς ἡμέραι and the Vulgate *adhuc quadraginta dies*. Both constructions indicate an interval of time ("yet, still, more") before a future event. Note that the LXX reads "three days" instead of the "forty days" in the MT, Vulgate, and Syriac Peshitta. Nearly every early church father before Jerome follows the LXX.

The Niphal participle (נֶהְפָּכֶת) of הָפַךְ is feminine singular (and in pause, hence -פָ֫- instead of -פֶּ-) because its subject, נִינְוֵה, is feminine. The Qal can mean "to turn," "to change," or "to destroy," and the Niphal can have the corresponding passive meanings, to "be turned, changed" into something else (BDB, s.v. הָפַךְ, Niphal, 2 c; see also *HALOT*, Niphal, 3) or "be demolished, overthrown" (*HALOT*, Niphal, 2; see also BDB, Niphal, 2 d).

The temporal force of a participle must be determined from its context. Participles are often used for imminent actions that will take place soon, so they can be described "as being already in progress" (Joüon, § 121 e). See the third textual note on 3:2 (אֲשֶׁר אָנֹכִי דֹּבֵר אֵלֶיךָ, "that I am about to speak to you"). Since the change in Nineveh starts to take place (see 3:5–10) as soon as the words leave Jonah's lips, the best translation is "Nineveh is about to be changed." Jonah may well have hoped or expected that no change would take place in Nineveh until it would be destroyed forty days hence. However, Yahweh could foresee that the change in Nineveh (repentance) would begin immediately by the power of his preached Word, and Yahweh had instructed Jonah to use these exact words in his sermon (see 3:2).

Two additional points must be made about the meaning of הָפַךְ. First, passages in which this verb refers to the destruction of a city are indissolubly linked in the OT with the destruction of Sodom and Gomorrah. By using הָפַךְ, Jonah is echoing this earlier, devastating judgment of Yahweh upon non-Israelite cities. It then aids in characterizing Nineveh as an exceedingly wicked city, thereby making its repentance all the more remarkable. The Qal of הָפַךְ is used in Gen 19:25, 29 to refer to Yahweh destroying Sodom and Gomorrah (and in Gen 19:21, where he promises not to destroy Zoar, whence Lot flees). In those contexts, it is a synonym of שָׁחַת, "destroy" (Gen 19:13–14, 29). Sodom became the archetype of wickedness because of the abomination of homosexuality (Gen 19:4–11).[13] God's destruction of Sodom and Gomorrah became a type of the eschatological judgment for all unbelievers, especially the depraved.[a]

(a) See, e.g., Deut 29:22 (ET 29:23); Is 1:7–10; Jer 49:18; 50:40; Ezek 16:46–56; Amos 4:11; Mt 10:15; 11:23–24; Lk 17:29; 2 Pet 2:6; Jude 7; Rev 11:8

Second, הָפַךְ could be understood in different ways. Jonah likely would have understood his message to be one of impending doom of the sort that befell Sodom, and the Ninevites clearly took it as a warning that they would perish (see Jonah 3:9).[14]

---

[13] Hummel, *Ezekiel 1–20*, 485–86, demonstrates that the description of Sodom's sin in Ezek 16:48–50 is consistent with that in Genesis 19.

[14] Wiseman ("Jonah's Nineveh," 49), followed by Stuart (*Hosea–Jonah*, 489), notes that the Assyrian hearers might interpret Jonah's prophecy in an ambivalent way if it were rendered

However, this verb also can refer to a radical reversal from one extreme to another, including a change of heart. For example, Moses states that "Yahweh your God turned [וַיַּהֲפֹךְ, Qal imperfect] for you the curse [of Balaam] into a blessing, because Yahweh your God loves you" (Deut 23:6 [ET 23:5]; similar is Neh 13:2). It refers to a radical change of heart in Saul (the Qal in 1 Sam 10:9). It is used for a radical turning from sorrow to joy (Qal in Jer 31:13; Niphal in Esther 9:22) or evil speech to holy invocation (Qal in Zeph 3:9). The Niphal, which is in Jonah 3:4, refers to a radical change in God's own heart, from anger to compassion for his people in Hos 11:8.[15]

Thus the wording of the sermon Yahweh spoke to Jonah (3:2), recorded by the author of the book (3:4), can be understood by us, the reading audience, in one of two ways. Probably this is part of the irony intended by the author.[16] "Yet in forty days Nineveh is about to be changed" could refer to its destruction like Sodom and Gomorrah or to its change from impenitent wickedness to repentance and faith. In this context, הָפַךְ is a double entendre promoting either Law and judgment, or Law and Gospel. Either way, Nineveh will be changed! This gives Jonah's oracle a tautological nature: whether the city disregards the warning and is destroyed or repents and is spared, his oracle will come true.

Pseudo-Philo acknowledges this double entendre when he writes about the conversion of the Ninevites: "The city has truly been overturned, as it was proclaimed, but in its hearts and not its walls. It is no longer the same city."[17] The two possible meanings of the verb allow for the fact that Yahweh seeks a change in the people's hearts (see 3:9–10), while Jonah longs for their destruction (see 4:1, 5). Jonah's distress in chapter 4 is partly because he does not realize that his sermon came true in the sense Yahweh intended. How ironic!

3:5   וַיַּאֲמִינוּ אַנְשֵׁי נִינְוֵה בֵּאלֹהִים—The verb is the Hiphil (third masculine plural imperfect with *waw* consecutive) of אָמַן, which here takes the preposition בְּ attached to the object (בֵּאלֹהִים), the men of Nineveh "believed in God" (NASB). This combination, the Hiphil of אָמַן with בְּ, occurs fairly often meaning "to have trust in, to believe in" God (*HALOT*, s.v. אמן I, Hiphil, 3; see also BDB, s.v. אָמַן, Hiphil, 2 c). It could also be rendered "have faith in." The OT uses this construction for the faith of Abram, through which Yahweh reckoned to him "righteousness" (Gen 15:6), and for the faith of the people of Israel after their salvation through the Red Sea (Ex 14:31).[b]

As with Abram and the people of Israel, the faith of the Ninevites here is far more than simply believing that Jonah's prediction would come true. Neither is Nineveh's belief in God simply an assent to the existence of Israel's God or that he is the only

(b) See also Num 14:11; 20:12; Deut 1:32; 2 Ki 17:14; Ps 78:22; 2 Chr 20:20

---

with the Akkadian word *abāku*, which was used both for "to overthrow, bring to judgment, take away (of men and animals)" and "to turn upside down."

[15] But the Niphal refers to Pharaoh's heart changing from remorse to evil intent in Ex 14:5.

[16] Good, *Irony in the Old Testament*, 48–49, writes: "The verb (*hāphak*) can also mean 'to be changed' in a positive sense, from something bad to something good. The latter is certainly not in the prophet's mind, but, given the response of the populace, may we not say that it is in the author's mind?"

[17] Pseudo-Philo, *De Jona*, §§ 48–49, quoted in Bolin, *Freedom beyond Forgiveness*, 125–26, including n. 19, who cites Duval, *Le livre de Jonas*, 1:81.

God. As James says, "You believe that God is one. … Even the demons believe [that] and shudder" (James 2:19). Rather, "the call" from Yahweh (3:2) that Jonah preached (3:4) brought the Ninevites to saving faith in Yahweh, just as Jonah's confession of Yahweh in 1:9 did for the sailors (see 1:16).

When the Hiphil of אָמַן refers to trusting or believing in humans, it almost always has a negative connotation. To "believe" in the words of people is to be gullible and foolish (Prov 14:15; 26:25). Nor does God "believe" or put absolute trust in his servants (Job 4:18; 15:15). Such statements of *mis*trust are reminiscent of Jesus' statement that he needs no witness from people because he knows what is in a person (Jn 2:25).

However, when people "believe" in God, as here, the Hiphil of אָמַן with בְּ "denotes saying yea and amen to God's Word as it was revealed to them by the prophet."[18] To be sure, this indicates that the Ninevites believe God's warning through the prophet Jonah. Yet as Desmond Alexander states, it goes farther: it "denotes more, however, than just believing what someone has said; it expresses the idea of trusting a person."[19] Mere intellectual assent does not get at the real meaning. As Gerhard Ebeling notes, it involves declaring that God's promise is true and valid.[20]

It is amazing that the narrator of Jonah uses this expression to describe the response to God by the Gentile Ninevites, who had been pagan enemies of Israel and her God. Now they do not merely assent to God's existence, but take Jonah's message to heart and believe God's Word that within forty days they would be changed— either by being destroyed, or through repentance, faith, and being saved by God, which is the hope they express in 3:9. The very response of faith that Israel could not give without signs and wonders (Ex 4:9) or even refused to give despite miracles (Isaiah 7), the evil people of Nineveh give after the sermon of a reluctant preacher!

The English phrase "believed in" has idiomatic value, particularly in Christian theology, as a comprehensive statement of faith. However, in some passages, the Hiphil of אָמַן with בְּ has a less comprehensive meaning. For example, after Moses struck the rock, Yahweh informed him and Aaron that they would not bring Israel into the promised land, "because you did not believe/trust in me" (יַעַן לֹא־הֶאֱמַנְתֶּם בִּי, Num 20:12; cf. Deut 32:50–51). As in the case of Nineveh, Moses' response demonstrated the extent to which he did or did not believe what God had said and did trust (or did not trust) God to fulfill his Word. Belief or lack of it is demonstrated by the ensuing response. Scripture subsequently makes clear that Moses in particular did not permanently lose all faith in God, but died as a believer (Deut 34:5–12) and entered everlasting glory (Mt 17:3).

Therefore, we should be cautious in interpreting Jonah 3:5 as referring to a comprehensive faith involving extensive knowledge of Yahweh, the covenant God of Is-

---

[18] Laetsch, *The Minor Prophets*, 235.

[19] Alexander, *Jonah*, 121; see also Wolff, *Obadiah and Jonah*, 150.

[20] Ebeling, *Word and Faith*, 209, writes: "The Hiph[il] form הֶאֱמִין has, in the causative or declarative sense, the meaning: to let something be נֶאֱמָן or declare it to be נֶאֱמָן, that is, to let it be valid or adjudge that it corresponds to what it promises."

rael. While in some passages the Hiphil of אָמַן with בְּ is a more comprehensive statement of faith, that nuance comes from the context and is not a lexical requirement.[21] Restraint is in order also because the Ninevites are said to believe "in God" (בֵאלֹהִים) rather than "in Yahweh" (בַּיהוה). Nevertheless, that they truly did believe in God with saving faith is supported by the rest of the narrative of Jonah as well as by the words of Christ himself, who affirms that these Ninevites shall rise on the Last Day (Mt 12:41).[22]

וַיִּקְרְאוּ־צוֹם—Here קָרָא, "to call," has the sense "to call for, proclaim." The object is the noun צוֹם, a "fast, period of fasting" (*HALOT*). The people voluntarily fast before the king mandates it in 3:7. This shows the genuineness of their repentance.

וַיִּלְבְּשׁוּ שַׂקִּים—Here too the people of Nineveh perform a ritual of repentance even before the king commands it in 3:8. The verb is the Qal third masculine singular imperfect with *waw* consecutive of לָבֵשׁ, to "put on" (BDB, Qal, 1 a; *HALOT*, Qal, 1 a) or "clothe oneself." Here and often elsewhere it takes as its accusative object the garment or material that one puts on. The indefinite object שַׂקִּים is the plural of the noun שַׂק, "sackcloth," which recurs in the singular in 3:6 and the plural in 3:8. This generally refers to a rough cloth that was coarsely woven, usually from goat hair, and then dyed. This cloth was used for various articles, including sacks, so שַׂק can also refer to a "sack," such as those used by Joseph's brothers to take their grain home from Egypt (Gen 42:25, 27, 35). The term is transliterated in the NT as σάκκος (Mt 11:21; Lk 10:13; Rev 6:12; 11:3).

Most of the biblical references to sackcloth are as garments worn by persons in a state of grief or mourning. For example, after Abner's death, David instructs all the people to put on sackcloth and mourn (2 Sam 3:31). At the preaching of Ezra, all Israel puts on sackcloth and repents for the nation's sins (Neh 9:1).[c] As an article of clothing it denotes humiliation, mourning, and repentance—so much so that its removal is equated with joy: "You have turned my mourning into dancing for me; you have loosened my sackcloth and girded me in joy" (פִּתַּחְתָּ שַׂקִּי וַתְּאַזְּרֵנִי שִׂמְחָה), Ps 30:12 [ET 30:11]). The donning of sackcloth is often accompanied by sitting in ashes, as the king will do in Jonah 3:6, and/or fasting, as the people and animals do in 3:5, 7–8.[d]

Nineveh's repentance manifests itself in a form that rivals even the most pious Israelite times of repentance. Not only the king, but all the people and even the livestock put on sackcloth and fast (Jonah 3:5–8). Jonah 3:8 is worded to suggest that just like the people, the livestock too covered themselves with sackcloth! In that way, the Ninevites' penitence exceeds any recorded for Israel.

מִגְּדוֹלָם וְעַד־קְטַנָּם:—The two adjectives גָּדוֹל ("great") and קָטָן ("small") each have the third masculine plural pronominal suffix (ـָם). Each forms a comparative superlative, that is, a superlative in comparison to others in the group (the Ninevites): "the greatest of them" and "the least of them" (see Waltke-O'Connor, § 14.5c, in-

(c) See also Gen 37:34; 1 Ki 21:27; 2 Ki 19:1–2; Jer 6:26; 48:37; Esth 4:1–4; Dan 9:3; Mt 11:21; Lk 10:13

(d) See also, e.g., 1 Ki 21:27; Is 58:5; Jer 6:26; Esth 4:3; Dan 9:3; Neh 9:1

---

[21] For a full lexical treatment, see A. Jepson, "אָמַן" in *TDOT* 1:298–309.

[22] See further the excursus "The Sign of Jonah."

cluding example 32; GKC, § 133 g; Joüon, § 141 j). This phrase with the prepositions מִן ... וְעַד (literally, "from ... and until") is also a merism: naming the two extremes ("greatest ... least") includes everyone in between as well. "From small(est) [קָטָן or קָטֹן] to great(est) [וְגָדֹול]" or vice versa (as here) occurs often in the OT (see BDB, s.v. גָּדֹול, 7).

3:6 וַיִּגַּע הַדָּבָר֙ אֶל־מֶלֶךְ נִינְוֵה—The verb is the Qal third masculine singular imperfect with *waw* consecutive of נָגַע, which can mean "to reach as far as" (*HALOT*, 3) or "extend to" (BDB, 4). However, נָגַע most often means "to strike, harm" (see BDB, 2 and 3; *HALOT*, 2) and can connote divine judgment, as in, for example, 1 Sam 6:9 and Jer 51:9.

The subject, דָּבָר, can mean "word," "message," or even "event." הַדָּבָר֙ could refer to either "the divine Word," that is, the prophecy spoken through Jonah (3:4), or the people's reaction to it (3:5). Probably both reached the king, and perhaps we are to understand both. Leningradensis (and so *BHS*) lacks a *shewa* with the *kaph* in מֶלֶךְ, but that likely is a scribal error; other manuscripts have ךְ-.

וַיָּקָם֙ מִכִּסְאֹו—This clause, with the verb קוּם (Qal third masculine singular imperfect with *waw* consecutive) and noun כִּסֵּא (with מִן and third masculine singular suffix), "he arose from his throne," is antonymous to the last clause of the verse: "He sat upon the ash heap."

וַיַּעֲבֵר אַדַּרְתֹּו מֵעָלָיו—The Hiphil of עָבַר (third masculine singular imperfect with *waw* consecutive) can mean "take away, remove" (see *HALOT*, 8), especially when accompanied by the preposition מִן, "from" (מֵעָלָיו, "from upon himself"). The object, אַדֶּרֶת (with third masculine singular pronominal suffix), can have the abstract meaning "splendor, majesty" or, as here, the concrete meaning "a robe of state" (*HALOT*, 2) or "royal robe." Achan stole a costly אַדֶּרֶת from Mesopotamia (Josh 7:21, 24). But most often אַדֶּרֶת refers to a "mantle" or covering made of skin, as worn by Elijah (2 Ki 2:8, 13–14).

וַיְכַס שַׂק—The Piel of כָּסָה, "to cover," can be used for clothing, in which case it normally takes two accusative objects: the person who is covered/clothed and the material or article of clothing (e.g., Ezek 16:10; 18:7, 16; see *HALOT*, s.v. כָּסָה, Piel, 2 a). When verbs take two accusatives, the second commonly is an accusative of material (Waltke-O'Connor, § 10.2.3c). This clause is unusual because the verb takes only one object, the article of clothing (שַׂק, "sackcloth"). The translation supplies "himself," which must be the implied first object: "he covered [himself with] sackcloth." Compare the second textual note on 3:8, which uses the Hithpael of כָּסָה with a single object.

וַיֵּשֶׁב עַל־הָאֵפֶר׃—The verb is the Qal third masculine singular imperfect with *waw* consecutive of יָשַׁב, "to sit down." The noun אֵפֶר can refer to the "ashes" (BDB) of a sacrificed and burnt animal (e.g., Num 19:9–10). However, this does not necessarily mean that the king of Nineveh performed any kind of sacrifice similar to the sailors' promise in Jonah 1:16. Sitting in ashes was a customary sign of grief and mourning (e.g., Jer 6:26; Job 2:8; 42:6; Esth 4:1, 3); here the term may refer to "the waste heaps in front of the village" (*HALOT*, 1 a). Another mourning custom was to toss "ashes" upon one's head (2 Sam 13:19; Is 61:3). In some passages, אֵפֶר, together with עָפָר, "dust" (see Gen 2:7), refer to the substances out of which God created man (Gen 18:27; cf. Job 30:19). The term that the LXX uses here, σποδός, has the same range of meanings as אֵפֶר.

3:7 וַיַּזְעֵק וַיֹּאמֶר בְּנִינְוֵה—The first verb is the Hiphil third masculine singular imperfect with *waw* consecutive of זָעַק, which in Qal can mean "to cry out" for help. The Hiphil here means "to make a proclamation" (*HALOT*, 3) or "to cause an edict to be proclaimed, issue an edict." וַיֹּאמֶר בְּנִינְוֵה ("And he said/proclaimed in Nineveh") then describes the place in which the king's edict was proclaimed.

מִטַּעַם הַמֶּלֶךְ וּגְדֹלָיו לֵאמֹר—The king's edict is quoted through 3:9. However, it is not clear whether this phrase is the first part of the quote or whether it precedes the quote. In 1:14; 2:3 (ET 2:2); 4:2, the quotes of direct discourse begin immediately after finite forms of אָמַר, and וַיֹּאמֶר was in the first part of 3:7. Therefore, most English translations understand this phrase as part of the quote, stating the authority by which the edict has been issued: "By the decree of the king and his nobles: Let …" (ESV).

The noun טַעַם usually means, "taste, judgment" (BDB), and the verb טָעַם in the next clause means "to taste, eat." Only here in the OT does the noun טַעַם mean "order, decree" (*HALOT*, 3), and it likely is a loan word from the Akkadian *ṭēmu* (*HALOT*).[23] The preposition מִן on it here indicates cause: "according to" or "by" the king's decree (BDB, s.v. מִן, 2 g). וּגְדֹלָיו is the plural of גָּדוֹל ("great" in, e.g., 2:1 [ET 1:17]; 3:2) used as a substantive, "a noble, royal official," with third masculine singular pronominal suffix: "his nobles" (*HALOT*, s.v. גָּדוֹל, 9). Compare מִגְּדוֹלָם ("from the greatest of them") in 3:5.

Three prohibitions now follow in 3:7. The negative particle אַל with an imperfect verb forms a negative imperative or prohibition, translated with "must not."

הָאָדָם וְהַבְּהֵמָה הַבָּקָר וְהַצֹּאן אַל־יִטְעֲמוּ מְאוּמָה—The syntax is unusual because the long compound subject, consisting of two pairs of nouns, precedes the verb. This syntax emphasizes the comprehensive application of the decree. The definite articles are generic, and English requires the nouns to be translated indefinitely. The first pair consists of "man/people [הָאָדָם] and beast/animals [וְהַבְּהֵמָה]." The second pair expands upon the "animals" to include both הַבָּקָר, large domesticated herding animals, such as cattle and oxen, and הַצֹּאן, small domesticated animals in flocks, such as sheep and goats.

The first prohibition uses the verb טָעַם (Qal third masculine plural imperfect: יִטְעֲמוּ), which usually means to "taste," so this prohibits even "eating in small quantity" (BDB, 1). The comprehensiveness of this prohibition is reinforced by this verb's object, מְאוּמָה, "anything."

אַל־יִרְעוּ—The second prohibition ("must not feed") uses the Qal (third masculine plural) imperfect of רָעָה, which usually refers to animals that "feed, graze" (*HALOT*, A 1 a) unless it refers to people metaphorically (*HALOT*, A 1 b). Only here

---

[23] Trible, *Rhetorical Criticism*, 185, translates the noun and verb in the same way so as to create a pun: "The taste (judgment) of the king and his great ones is that the people not taste."

in the OT does the verb refer to both animals and humans literally (*HALOT*, A 1 c). This groups animals and humans together and prepares for Yahweh expressing his compassion for both the people and animals of Nineveh in 4:11.

וּמַ֫יִם אַל־יִשְׁתּֽוּ׃—This third and final prohibition, "And water they must not drink," uses the Qal third masculine plural imperfect of שָׁתָה, which usually refers to people drinking (water, wine, etc.; e.g., Gen 9:21; Ex 17:1, 2, 6), but sometimes refers to animals drinking (Gen 24:19, 22; 30:38). Here and in Num 20:19, both people and animals are the subject (so BDB, s.v. שָׁתָה, Qal, 1 d).

3:8 The three prohibitions in 3:7 are now followed by three positive commands in 3:8. Each uses a verb that could be either a jussive (Joüon, § 114 h) or an imperfect with the modal nuance "must" (Joüon, § 113 m). Whether a jussive or a modal imperfect, the proper translation for each is "they *must* …"

וְיִתְכַּסּוּ֙ שַׂקִּ֔ים הָֽאָדָ֖ם וְהַבְּהֵמָ֑ה—This first command is just as comprehensive as the previous prohibitions (see the third textual note on 3:7), since it too applies to "man/people [הָֽאָדָ֖ם] and beast/animals [וְהַבְּהֵמָ֑ה]." The verb is the Hithpael (third masculine plural imperfect with conjunctive *waw*) of כָּסָה, "to cover," in the sense of "clothe" (see the fourth textual note on 3:6, which had the Piel). Usually the kind of covering is introduced with בְּ (see *HALOT*, s.v. כָּסָה, Hithpael), but here the clothing is the object, שַׂקִּ֔ים, "sackcloths" (see the third textual note on 3:5) as an accusative of material. The Hithpael has a reflexive or middle meaning, "cover, clothe oneself" (BDB), which is appropriate for the human subjects. This wording suggests that the animals too "must cover [themselves with] sackcloths" in repentance, even though in actuality the Ninevites would have covered their animals. That the animals participated means this repentance exceeds any in Israel. This penitence of the animals relates to Yahweh's concluding words in 4:11 that reveal his compassion for not only the people, but also the animals of Nineveh.

וְיִקְרְא֖וּ אֶל־אֱלֹהִ֑ים בְּחָזְקָ֑ה—The Ninevites are to couple their outward acts of repentance (fasting and sackcloth) with an inward response of vigorous prayer. This clause gives no subject for the verb (Qal third masculine plural imperfect or jussive of קָרָא with conjunctive *waw*). The subject of the preceding clause was "people and animals." Therefore, grammatically the implied subject here could include both, meaning that both people and animals "must call to God fervently." Again, the wording suggests that the animals participated in Nineveh's repentance, preparing for 4:11, even though in reality the people alone would have prayed.

The noun חָזְקָה (*hozqah*, with *qamets chatuph* under the *chet*: חָ-), "strength," is a synonym of חָזְקָה and other words from the common verb חָזַק, "be or grow firm, strong" (BDB). In the OT, חָזְקָה always has the preposition בְּ and an adverbial meaning. It occurs elsewhere only in Judg 4:3, where it refers to foreigners oppressing Israelites "forcibly, violently" (BDB, 1), and in Judg 8:1; 1 Sam 2:16; and Ezek 34:4, where Israelites treat other Israelites "severely, abusively" or threaten violence. Hence it is surprising for the narrator of Jonah to use it to describe how the Ninevites are to pray. Most English translations render it "mightily" (e.g., KJV, ESV), but NIV gives "urgently." It is perhaps best understood as the opposite of weakly and insincerely. The Ninevites are urged to call to Yahweh "fervently" in bold ardor and sincere faith (cf. Heb 4:16). It points to the inner conviction of faith that accompanies the outward display of repentance.

Joel 2:13 stresses repentance by such inward action over outward demonstrations: "Rend your heart and not your garments," since Yahweh is gracious (the rest of Joel 2:13 resembles Jonah 4:2). The priority of inward penitence is classically stated in Ps 51:18–19 (ET 51:16–17):

> You do not desire sacrifice, or I would give it;
>> burnt offering you do not favor.
> The sacrifices of God are a broken spirit;
>> a broken and contrite heart, O God, you will not despise.

וְיָשֻׁבוּ אִישׁ מִדַּרְכּוֹ הָרָעָה וּמִן־הֶחָמָס אֲשֶׁר בְּכַפֵּיהֶם:—In form וְיָשֻׁבוּ is the Qal third masculine plural of שׁוּב, either imperfect or jussive, with conjunctive *waw*, meaning "they must turn" (see the first textual note on 3:8). The Qal of שׁוּב occurs four times in Jonah 3:8–10 and nowhere else in the book. In these verses it means "turn from one course of action to a different one." In 3:8, 10 it refers to the Ninevites' repentance. The Qal is common elsewhere in the OT, occurring close to seven hundred times with a broad variety of meanings. Generally it indicates that someone who was going one direction turns and goes in the opposite direction. Often it refers to a physical turning and return to the place of origin (e.g., Gen 18:33; Ruth 1:6, 22; see BDB, s.v. Qal, 2 and 3). In many other passages, שׁוּב refers to a spiritual turn from impenitent unbelief to contrition and saving faith in Yahweh (e.g., Deut 4:30; Hos 6:1), in which case it can mean "*turn back* to God" (BDB, Qal, 6 c; *HALOT*, Qal, 2) or "repent" (BDB, Qal, 6 d).[24]

Here its meaning of repentance and faith overlaps with that of "*turn back* from evil" (BDB, Qal, 6 e). שׁוּב often takes the preposition מִן in the sense of withdrawing, turning, or repenting "from" previous activities and spiritual obduracy. This construction emphasizes desisting and abandoning the prior way of life. Here שׁוּב takes two prepositional phrases, each beginning with מִן: "They must turn, each *from* his evil way [מִדַּרְכּוֹ is דֶּרֶךְ with מִן and the third masculine singular suffix] and *from* [וּמִן] the violence that is in their hands."

This language relates to the "two ways" theme that is common in the OT especially in Wisdom literature (e.g., Psalm 1; Proverbs). The image is that the Ninevites had been traveling an "evil way, path" that was contrary to the way of Yahweh. In the OT, דֶּרֶךְ frequently refers to such an evil mode of life characterized by unbelief and wicked actions (see BDB, 6 d). The implication is that the Ninevites abandon that road and instead begin to walk on Yahweh's דֶּרֶךְ (see BDB, 6 a, b, c). It is essentially a denouncement of their former way of life and an acceptance of Yahweh's true path of faith, which yields good works.

---

[24] In Ruth 1:6–22 שׁוּב occurs twelve times (eleven Qal, one Hiphil), and these two meanings overlap: Naomi physically returns from Moab to Bethlehem, and this return will lead to a rejuvenation of her faith in Yahweh. It also involves the conversion of Ruth to saving faith in Yahweh (Ruth 1:16–17). Even though Ruth the Moabitess had never been to Israel before, she too is said to return there (הַשָּׁבָה in Ruth 1:22) because of her conversion and allegiance to Naomi. See Wilch, *Ruth*, 131–32, 148–50, 182.

Because דֶּרֶךְ can be construed as either a masculine or a feminine noun, it can take adjectives of either gender. Here it takes the feminine adjective הָרָעָה, which has the article because the pronominal suffix on מִדַּרְכּוֹ makes the noun definite. The identical phrase (מִדַּרְכּוֹ הָרָעָה) is in 1 Ki 13:33; Jer 18:11; 25:5; 26:3; 35:15; 36:3, 7. But the comparable phrase with the masculine adjective also occurs (מִדַּרְכּוֹ הָרָע, Ezek 13:22; מִדַּרְכֶּם הָרָע, Jer 23:22; see also דֶּרֶךְ רָע, "evil way," in Prov 2:12; 8:13; 28:10), referring to faithlessness and evil deeds.

The noun חָמָס, "violence" (BDB), occurs only here in Jonah. That it is "in their hands" (בְּכַפֵּיהֶם, the plural of כַּף with בְּ and the third masculine plural suffix) reinforces that it refers to physical brutality. It encompasses a broad range of sins, as evidenced by the great number of words that are parallel with it in poetic texts, including, for example, שֹׁד, "destruction" (e.g., Hab 1:3); תֹּךְ, "oppression" (Ps 72:14); and רִיב, "strife" (Ps 55:10 [ET 55:9]). In his holiness and righteousness, Yahweh cannot ignore the חָמָס of Israel and therefore punishes her (Ezek 12:19; Amos 6:3–7; Micah 6:12–15; Zeph 1:9). The word is never used for the execution of justice through corporal or capital punishment. Rather, it denotes the "rude wickedness of men, their noisy, wild, ruthlessness" (BDB), cruel crimes against fellow human beings that are an affront to the God who created all people, originally in his own image (Gen 1:26–27; James 3:9).

Here when ascribed to the Ninevites, their "violence" (3:8, 10) is a synonym of "their evil" (רָעָתָם, 1:2) and "evil way" (3:8, 10). It is an assault upon the very nature of Yahweh, provoking his judgment. Therefore, they must to turn aside from it if they hope for the outside chance that Yahweh will have mercy upon them.

3:9 מִי־יוֹדֵעַ—The interrogative pronoun מִי, "who?" with the Qal masculine singular participle of יָדַע, "to know," means, "Who knows?" This expression occurs ten times in the OT.[25] In four cases, the larger context holds hope that God may act graciously rather than in judgment so that people may be saved (2 Sam 12:22; Joel 2:14; Jonah 3:9; Esth 4:14). The others express the limitation of human knowledge (Eccl 2:19; 6:12; 8:1), uncertainty about the future (Eccl 3:21), or trepidation at God's anger (Ps 90:11; Prov 24:22).

Illustrating the hopeful passages is 2 Sam 12:22, where David explains why he fasted and wept while his child who was conceived by royal lust was still alive: "Who knows? Yahweh may have mercy on me, and the child may live." David's מִי יוֹדֵעַ functions in the same way as the king of Nineveh's edict here (Jonah 3:9). It is similar to the hope expressed by the prophet Amos with אוּלַי, "perhaps Yahweh, the God of hosts, will have mercy on the remnant of Joseph" (Amos 5:15) and to the use of אוּלַי ("perhaps") in comparable passages.[26] The emphasis is that Yahweh alone will decide what happens, but human beings still dare to hope that he will act in compassion rather than executing the judgment they deserve. The speaker acknowledges that Yahweh would be justified if he carried out judgment, but hopes that his mercy will prevail. Therefore, it is an expression of repentance and faith.

---

[25] Cf. Crenshaw, "The Expression *Mî Yôdēaʿ* in the Hebrew Bible."

[26] See אוּלַי in Jonah 1:6 and also in Ex 32:30; Zeph 2:3; Lam 3:29.

The use of מִי יוֹדֵעַ in Joel 2:14 intersects with that of Jonah 3:9. In Joel 2:1–11 it appears that a prophetic oracle of judgment has shut the door against any future hope, but a call to repentance is nevertheless introduced in Joel 2:12–14. This tiny ray of hope arises from two realities: Yahweh's nature and the possibility of genuine repentance. Joel 2:14 is preceded by the declaration about Yahweh's character: "He is gracious and compassionate, slow to anger and abounding in loyal love, and changing his verdict about evil" (Joel 2:13). These words are based on the Torah (Num 14:18; Deut 4:31) and are almost identical to the formulation in Jonah 4:2 (see the textual notes and commentary there).

Yahweh is free to dispense justice in his own anger, yet throughout Israel's history—and preeminently in Christ—he shows himself to be gracious and compassionate toward the undeserving. That is the foundation of the hopeful passages with the expression מִי יוֹדֵעַ. A divine prophecy of doom may not necessarily be executed upon those who repent and trust in Yahweh's mercy, for—who knows?—they may be spared. Those who cry out מִי יוֹדֵעַ appeal to Yahweh's proper work of the Gospel. They believe that his "anger lasts for a moment, his favor a lifetime" (כִּי רֶגַע ׀ בְּאַפּוֹ חַיִּים בִּרְצוֹנוֹ, Ps 30:6). See also Ezek 18:23, 32; 33:11. God does not desire "any to perish, but all to come to repentance" (2 Pet 3:9). In essence, the cry amounts to "Thy will be done" (Mt 6:10).

יָשׁוּב וְנִחַם הָאֱלֹהִים—Here הָאֱלֹהִים is the subject of both verbs. With God as subject, שׁוּב, "turn," often means "*return* (to shew favour)" (BDB, Qal, 6 g; cf. *HALOT*, Qal, 2 b). He may "relent" (NIV) from wrath and "return" to his characteristic disposition of being gracious and merciful (Jonah 4:2). Similar is the meaning of שׁוּב in the next clause (see the next textual note). The imperfect verb יָשׁוּב (Qal third masculine singular) in this context has a hypothetical yet hopeful nuance, "God *may* turn." Such an imperfect "of possibility" indicates "the possibility that the subject may perform an action" (Waltke-O'Connor, § 31.4e).

The verb וְנִחַם is the Niphal third masculine singular perfect of נָחַם with *waw* consecutive. Such a perfect with *waw* consecutive usually takes on the same sense as the preceding imperfect (Waltke-O'Connor, § 32.2.1d). Like יָשׁוּב, it has a tentative yet hopeful nuance of possibility, "*may* … change his verdict." The Niphal of נָחַם recurs in 3:10 and 4:2. For the lexical meaning and theology, see further the excursus "When Yahweh Changes a Prior Verdict." See also the discussion of the fifth allusion from Genesis 6–10 in "Jonah and Noah" in the introduction as well as the commentary on 3:9–10.

The lexicons give a variety of meanings for the Niphal of נָחַם in this and similar passages, including "be sorry, moved to pity, have compassion … rue, suffer grief, repent" (BDB, 1 and 2), "regret" (*HALOT*, 1), "become remorseful" (*HALOT*, 1 a). In some cases with God as subject, it is best rendered "regret": God "regretted" that he had created mankind (Gen 6:6–7) and so sent the universal flood; he also "regretted" that he had made Saul king (1 Sam 15:11, 35) and so deposed him. Sometimes God prophesies judgment but then carries out only part of the punishment before he "relented" (2 Sam 24:16), sparing some. God for a long time held back the well-deserved judgment against the nation of Judah, but finally he grew "weary of relenting" and executed it (Jer 15:6). God may promise not to "relent" (Ezek 24:14, shortly before the destruction of Jerusalem).

Sometimes God declares judgment but also promises to "relent" (not carry it out) if the people repent (Jer 18:8). In other passages, God decrees only judgment, with no contingency for the people's repentance, but then God never executes the punishment. This is the case in Jonah (3:9–10; 4:2). In these contexts, the Niphal of נָחַם is best translated as God "changed his verdict." This is appropriate legal language for God as Judge, and it relates to the Pauline language for justification in the NT (see the commentary). Regarding the Ninevites, Yahweh "changed his verdict" and so "he did not do [it]" (3:10). This change from Law to Gospel is described with the same verb elsewhere in the OT, where God pronounces judgment upon Israel but then does not execute it (Ex 32:12, 14; Joel 2:12–27). Surprisingly here, Yahweh changes his verdict for Gentile Ninevites. This is in stark contrast to the Gentile cities of Sodom and Gomorrah, which God destroyed and "did not relent" (Jer 20:16).

וְשָׁב מֵחֲרוֹן אַפּוֹ—With God as subject, here שׁוּב means "*turn back* from (מִן) judgment" (BDB, Qal, 6 h). וְשָׁב (Qal third masculine singular perfect with waw consecutive) has the same hypothetical, hopeful force as the two verbs in the preceding part of the verse: "*may … turn away from the burning/fierceness of his anger*." This idiom (שׁוּב מֵחֲרוֹן אַפּ-) is used elsewhere in the OT to express prayers or hopes, as here, that Yahweh might "turn from the burning of (his) anger" (Ex 32:12; Deut 13:18 [ET 13:17]) and statements that he did (or did not) do so (Josh 7:26; 2 Ki 23:26; Ps 85:4 [ET 85:3]; cf. Hos 11:9). Similar are statements with "the burning of (Yahweh's) anger" as the subject of שׁוּב (Num 25:4; Jer 4:8; 30:24; Ezra 10:14; 2 Chr 29:10; 30:8; cf. 2 Chr 28:11).

The phrase מֵחֲרוֹן אַפּוֹ has the noun חָרוֹן with the preposition מִן in construct with the noun אַף with third masculine singular suffix. חָרוֹן means "burning (of anger)" (BDB) and is from the verb חָרָה, "to burn, be kindled," which usually refers metaphorically to anger. אַף (from אָנַף) often means "nose" (BDB, 1) but frequently is metaphorical for "anger" (BDB, 3). Thus חֲרוֹן אַפּוֹ literalistically means "the burning of his nose."

Like the king's description of his fellow Ninevites, which ends with the admission "and from the violence that is in their hands" (3:8), this phrase consists of a prepositional phrase whose object is body language for destructive action.[27] Even though the king hopes that Yahweh may "turn away from the burning/fierceness of his anger," he acknowledges that Yahweh's anger is fully justified and may be executed. This would be according to the biblical doctrine of *lex talionis*: those who live by violence will die by violence.[28] This correspondence is frequently displayed in prophetic judgment scenes: destroyers will be destroyed (Is 33:1); devourers will be devoured (Jer 30:16); reproachers will be reproached (Ezek 36:6–7); and plunderers will be plundered (Hab 2:8).

---

[27] See Gruber, *Aspects of Nonverbal Communication in the Ancient Near East*, 491–502.

[28] See Miller, *Sin and Judgment in the Prophets: A Stylistic and Theological Analysis*.

Jonah 3:10 will describe the judgment Yahweh threatened as "the evil" (הָרָעָה), which corresponds to the "evil" (רָעָה) done by the Ninevites (Jonah 1:2; 3:8). The *lex talionis* reveals the juridical character of Yahweh's judgment. Paul Raabe writes:

> The correspondence pattern serves to depict the just nature of the punishment, not some strange fate coming "out of the blue" but a rational and appropriate punishment, one that fits the particular crime committed by the guilty party. According to Ezek 18:25–30 and 33:17–20, Yahweh's judgment is "fair" because he judges people "according to their ways."[29]

וְלֹא נֹאבֵד:—This clause ends the decree of the king proclaimed in Nineveh. The *waw* on לֹא followed by the imperfect (Qal first common plural of אָבַד) forms a purpose clause: "so we will not perish." The identical clause was spoken by the ship's captain (see the fifth textual note on 1:6). There too the Gentile leader acknowledged the justice of the punishment inflicted by Israel's God, but hoped for a reprieve: "Perhaps [אוּלַי] that God of yours will show compassion toward us so we will not perish."

3:10 וַיַּרְא הָאֱלֹהִים אֶת־מַעֲשֵׂיהֶם כִּי־שָׁבוּ מִדַּרְכָּם הָרָעָה—This verse returns to the narrative description of what happened. The statement that God "saw" (third masculine singular Qal imperfect of רָאָה with *waw* consecutive) refers to more than physical observance (cf. BDB, s.v. רָאָה, Qal, 6 b). It connotes compassion, as in Ex 2:25, where God "saw" (וַיַּרְא) the afflicted children of Israel and then redeemed them from Egypt. The direct object here is מַעֲשֵׂיהֶם, the plural of מַעֲשֶׂה (from עָשָׂה, "to do") with third masculine plural suffix. "Their works" were visible evidence of their repentance.

Often after the verb רָאָה and its object, a כִּי clause explains the object that was seen (Joüon, § 157 d; *HALOT*, s.v. רָאָה, Qal, 5 a). "That they turned from their evil way" explains "their works" that Yahweh "saw." This could be paraphrased as "Yahweh saw by their works that they had turned from their evil way."

The כִּי clause uses שׁוּב (שָׁבוּ, Qal third common plural perfect) with the same meaning it had in 3:8, namely, "*turn back* from evil" (BDB, Qal, 6 e), overlapping with "*turn back* to God" (BDB, Qal, 6 c), "repent" (BDB, Qal, 6 d). The prepositional phrase מִדַּרְכָּם הָרָעָה ("from their evil way") shows that they fulfilled the king's command that they should turn, "each from his evil way," אִישׁ מִדַּרְכּוֹ הָרָעָה (3:8). See the fourth textual note on 3:8.

וַיִּנָּחֶם הָאֱלֹהִים עַל־הָרָעָה—The Niphal of נָחַם (third masculine singular imperfect with *waw* consecutive), "And God changed his verdict," fulfills the king's tentative hope, expressed with the same verb (וְנִחַם הָאֱלֹהִים, "God may … change his verdict," 3:9). The preposition עַל can mean "concerning" (BDB, II 1 f (*g*); *HALOT*, 3) or "about." הָרָעָה describes the judgment Yahweh had declared as "the evil." Since "evil" had been perpetrated by the Ninevites (רָעָה, 1:2; 3:8), their punishment is described by the corresponding term according to *lex talionis* (see the third textual note on 3:9). Even though God himself never is the author of evil (1 Cor 14:33; James 1:13), his punishment can be described from the human viewpoint as an "evil," though in such passages רָעָה is usually translated "calamity, disaster" (*HALOT*, 5 a).

---

[29] Raabe, *Obadiah*, 201.

אֲשֶׁר־דִּבֶּר לַעֲשׂוֹת־לָהֶם וְלֹא עָשָׂה׃—This relative clause modifies הָרָעָה at the end of the preceding clause, the prophesied "evil" that Yahweh, literally, "spoke [דִּבֶּר] to do to them [לַעֲשׂוֹת־לָהֶם]." In prophetic contexts, דִּבֶּר, "speak," can be rendered "promise" or (as here) "threaten" depending on whether the prophecy is of weal or woe (BDB, s.v. דָּבַר, Piel, 6, which lists other passages where it is followed by לַעֲשׂוֹת).

The clause "he threatened to do to them" highlights that Jonah's short sermon in 3:4 was Yahweh speaking, since Yahweh spoke the words Jonah uttered (see 3:2). When the preacher proclaims God's Word, God himself is preaching.

The dramatic change from Law (judgment) to Gospel (salvation) is accentuated by the juxtaposition of two forms of the same verb, עָשָׂה, "to do." Yahweh "spoke/threatened" that he was going "to do" (לַעֲשׂוֹת, Qal infinitive construct with לְ) the evil, but then "he did not do" (וְלֹא עָשָׂה). Most translations supply a direct object of the last verb, "do [it]," but the terse Hebrew ends the chapter with the verb, leaving the emphasis on Yahweh's compassionate action.

Commentary
"A Walk of Three Days" (3:3b)

3:3b The narrative of Jonah's recommission to preach to Nineveh (3:1–3a) is interrupted by two parenthetical statements about the city itself: "Now Nineveh was a great city belonging to God, a walk of three days" (3:3b). That even this pagan, bellicose city belonged "to God" hints at the eventual outcome, namely, its salvation through faith in God (see the first textual note on 3:3b).

There is considerable debate about "a walk of three days." Does the phrase mean that Nineveh required a three-day walk to traverse its diameter or to navigate its circumference (which would be over three times longer than its diameter) or that Jonah needed three days to walk throughout the city in order to preach to everyone? Luther commented: "Such a walk does not imply a beeline course, but a walk hither and yon, here and there."[30] That is one of several possible solutions, each of which has advantages and disadvantages.

Excavations have revealed that at the height of Nineveh's size and influence as capital of the Assyrian Empire during the seventh century, it occupied an area of some 1,850 acres. The width of its broadest part was approximately three miles, and its walls measured approximately 7.75 miles or 12.5 kilometers in circumference. That, of course, would not require a three-day journey, unless one stopped frequently to browse or chat.

According to Herodotus, in antiquity a day's march for an army was 150 stadia,[31] about 17 miles, which would make a three-days journey about 50 miles. That approximates the figure of Diodorus Siculus, who reported the circumference of Nineveh as 480 stadia,[32] a little over 50 miles. Yet Diodorus

---

[30] AE 19:84.

[31] Herodotus, *Histories*, 5.53.

[32] Diodorus Siculus, *Library*, 2.3.

lived five centuries after Nineveh had ceased to exist and was not accurate. Another interpretation is needed.

It is possible that the phrase describes not just Nineveh proper, but also her surrounding suburbs and outlying fields. Accordingly, the conception in this verse of a city of much greater size is due to Nineveh's vast administrative complex, a triangle stretching from Khorsabad in the north to Nimrud in the south and Nineveh in the west.[33] That the city required "a walk of three days" might be a reference to a metropolitan district comprising Nineveh itself, Assur, Calah (Nimrud), and even Dur Sharrukin (Khorsabad), all cities within one to three days' walk of each other. This is an attractive explanation.

The narrative contains one other element that favors the suggestion that the term Nineveh covers a broader region than just the city itself. This is the phrase "the great city" (הָעִיר הַגְּדוֹלָה, 1:2; 3:2; 4:11). Significantly, this very same expression occurs in connection with Nineveh in Gen 10:11–12: "From that land he [Nimrod] went to Assyria, where he built Nineveh, Rehoboth Ir, Calah, and Resen between Nineveh and Calah; it is the great city [הָעִיר הַגְּדֹלָה]." In that passage, "the great city" apparently refers to the entire metropolitan area composed of Nineveh and the other cities. C. F. Keil remarks:

> It follows that the four places formed a large composite city, a large range of towns, to which the name of the (well-known) great city of *Nineveh* was applied, in distinction from Nineveh in the more restricted sense, with which Nimrod probably connected the other three places so as to form one great capital, possibly also the chief fortress of his kingdom on the Tigris.[34]

If Keil's interpretation of Gen 10:11–12 is accurate, then the expression "Nineveh, the great city" may well designate not only the walled city of Nineveh, but also the surrounding region. Indeed, the phrase may even have been understood in a semi-technical sense, meaning "Greater Nineveh."

Although this approach resolves the problem of the "walk of three days," the text of Jonah describes Nineveh as a "city," and Jonah is portrayed as going and sitting down outside of it (4:5). Moreover, the city's population is stated in 4:11. So the "Greater Nineveh" theory also presents us with problems.

Another solution, as Donald Wiseman suggests, is that the "walk of three days" refers to a diplomatic process: The first day is for arrival in the city, followed by one customary day of visiting, business, and rest; then the third day is for departure. "This suggestion would accord with the ancient oriental practice of hospitality whereby the first day is for arrival, the second for the primary purpose of the visit and the third for return."[35] This is a possible solution.

---

[33] Allen, *Joel, Obadiah, Jonah and Micah*, 221–22, including n. 10, summarizing Parrot, *Nineveh and the Old Testament*, 85–86, who lists this as a possibility.

[34] Keil, *The First Book of Moses*, 167; see also Aalders, *Genesis*, 1:227. The description "great city" is used of Nineveh only in Genesis and Jonah.

[35] Wiseman, "Jonah's Nineveh," 38 (see also pp. 42–44).

Another understanding of the phrase is advocated by Johannes Bauer, who concludes that throughout the OT, the time span of "three days" can be an imprecise expression for an appreciable passage of time or a large distance (cf. Gen 30:36; Ex 3:18).[36] Its use in this verse could simply be a standard way of saying that Nineveh was a very large city. There would be no need to determine whether it refers to the city's circumference or to a journey throughout its streets, to Nineveh proper or also to the surrounding area. "A walk of three days" together with "belonging to God" conveys the enormity of the city.[37] However, militating against Bauer's view is the fact that the "three days and three nights" during which Jonah was in the great fish (Jonah 2:1 [ET 1:17]) and "yet in forty days" in Jonah's sermon (3:4) are both accurate, literal references to periods of time, not just figurative expressions for any long passage of time.

Jonah's Efficacious Ministry in Nineveh (3:4–10)

3:4 Prophets could cross cultural and ethnic boundaries and still be recognized. For example, Balaam steps over cultural boundaries and is still recognized by Israel as a prophetic figure (Numbers 22–24). Later the Babylonian king Nebuchadnezzar employs the Israelite Daniel to serve in his court (e.g., Dan 2:16). Of course, the messages of true prophets of the one true God differed radically from those of false Israelite prophets and their pagan counterparts. Nevertheless, the social functions, roles, and to a degree even the forms of prophetic speech were similar in antiquity throughout the Fertile Crescent.[38] This helps us understand how the Ninevites promptly realize that a prophet is in their midst.

Beginning here and through the rest of the chapter, the events follow a common OT pattern: Yahweh threatens disaster and sometimes the disaster happens, the people respond with acts of repentance, and subsequently Yahweh delivers them. Parallels occur throughout the book of Judges as well as in, for example, 1 Sam 7:2–13; Jer 18:7–11; Joel 2:11–19. Except for Jeremiah, these parallels deal only with Israel. In Jer 18:7–11, the prophet states that this threefold pattern is applicable not only to Israel, but to all people. Both Israel and the nations are treated in the same way. God does not show favoritism (Rom 2:11; Eph 6:9; Col 3:25).

In this verse Jonah only goes one day's journey into the city and then offers one of the most ambiguous and mysterious sermons of all time. Luther reasons that since a five-Hebrew-word sermon is far too short, the taciturn "Yet

---

[36] Bauer, "Drei Tage."

[37] Wolff, *Obadiah and Jonah*, 148, claims: "The reader is not supposed to do arithmetic. He is supposed to be lost in astonishment."

[38] The discovery of the Mari texts has greatly increased our understanding of pagan prophecy outside Israel. See Nissinen, *Prophecy in Its Ancient Near Eastern Context*, 47–114. One of the most startling discoveries is the Akkadian cognate of the Hebrew word for "prophet" (נָבִיא). See Witherington, *Jesus the Seer*, 14–15.

in forty days Nineveh is about to be changed" must be a sermon summary, indicating that "he [Jonah] preached on sin."[39] Though this is possible, Yahweh's mandate in 3:2 ("call out to it the call that I am about to speak to you") makes it more likely that the quotation in 3:4 is the full sermonette.

In keeping with the character of Jonah in chapter 1, we might suppose that he is a half-hearted preacher, dragging his feet all the way, asking, "How can I do this so that the Ninevites will not repent and be delivered?" Jonah 4:2 makes it clear that throughout the narrative the prophet harbors frustration with his God who is so ready to forgive when judgment is merited. In getting upset with the results of his preaching (4:1), Jonah demonstrates that his motives in preaching were not the best, and perhaps the worst. And yet because the verbal repetition in 3:2–3 (" 'Arise, go to Nineveh. …' So Jonah arose and went to Nineveh") implies that Jonah is now complying with Yahweh's commands, and because he will later complain to God for canceling the judgment he had pronounced, we can reasonably assume that "yet in forty days …" is indeed what Yahweh commanded him to call out.

Does Jonah speak his sermon in the Ninevites' native Akkadian, a Semitic language like Hebrew that nevertheless to the Israelites was "a stammering jargon and an alien tongue" (Is 28:11)? Or do the Ninevites understand Hebrew? Jack Sasson writes:

> Hebrew narrative art hardly ever pauses to recognize language distinctions, and it does so only when it is important to the plot, for example, when Joseph is said to speak through interpreters so that his brothers cannot identify Hebrew as his native tongue [Gen 42:23]; or when Sennacherib's chamberlain, who otherwise speaks Hebrew, is urged toward Aramaic, lest the Judeans understand what he says (Isa 36:4–11).[40]

Nineveh was a religious city. In it were great ziggurats, stair-stepped temples reaching to the skies; the tower of Babel (Genesis 11) may have been such a ziggurat. A priestly bureaucracy organized life so that it would have order and security. In this environment, Jonah doesn't accuse the Ninevites of "their evil" (1:2). He doesn't denounce their sin and wickedness. He calls into question their future. He introduces eschatology into their present security.[41] This is the same strategy Paul uses in a similar situation in Athens. To the Epicure-

---

[39] AE 19:85.

[40] Sasson, *Jonah*, 232.

[41] For a critique of our culture's denial of eschatological truths, see Gibbs, "Regaining Biblical Hope." Bottéro, *Religion in Ancient Mesopotamia*, 95, writes of Mesopotamian eschatological beliefs: "As for the end of the world, the documents we possess do not tell us much about whether the old sages of Mesopotamia ever thought much about it." Rather than conceiving of an absolute beginning and an absolute end, their religious system was cyclical: the Mesopotamians reenacted Marduk's defeat over Tiamat every new year, and this celebration sought to guarantee the present state of existence. Bottéro writes: "During the festival the gods were exalted in order to renew not only time, with the entrance into a new annual cycle, but the universe itself, as if the gods were re-creating the universe in order to launch it once again into continuing duration" (p. 158).

ans and Stoic philosophers in Acts 17:31, the apostle says that God "has set a day in which he is about to judge the world with justice by the man whom he has appointed, providing proof of this to all by raising him from the dead."

For the Ninevites, Jonah is the man who has been "raised from the dead,"[42] and the set day is forty days hence. "Forty" is a stock biblical number that couples testing and hope. Forty days in Noah's ark is a purgation (Gen 7:12), cleansing centuries of moral pollution, washing away generations of unreflective gratification—followed by a new start. Israel's forty years in the wilderness is a training to live by the promises of Yahweh, to live by faith in the risky high-promise land of blessing (Num 14:33–34; Deut 8:2–3). The forty days of Elijah "on the run" brings him out of the dangerous threats emanating from Jezebel's court to the place of revelation (1 Ki 19:8). The forty days of Jesus' temptations are a probing of motive and intent, a clarification of the ways in which God works salvation—in contrast to the ways in which religious idolatry seduces people away from God, away from faith (Mt 4:2; Lk 4:2). The apostles spend the forty days of the "joyful Eastertide"[43] with the risen Christ before his ascension (Acts 1:3) and then are given the gift of the promised Holy Spirit on Pentecost (Acts 2).

In each of these cases, the number forty works eschatologically: the fortieth is the last day, when the goal arrives, which shapes the content of the preceding thirty-nine days (or years). Under the pressure of the last day, the preceding days become pregnant with a new beginning, and life begins in a new way. In Nineveh the prophecy "Yet in forty days Nineveh is about to be changed" (Jonah 3:4) does its work. Nineveh is indeed changed: the people hear the message not just as a prediction of doom, but as a proclamation that gives them reason to believe in God (3:5) and to hope (3:9).

The use of the verb "be changed, overthrown" (see the third textual note on 3:4), which was used for the destruction of Sodom and Gomorrah in Genesis 19 (19:25, 29), dresses Jonah in the garb of the angelic messengers of Gen 19:1, 13 and makes Nineveh into another Sodom, an unhallowed haunt of wickedness meriting destruction. But the difference is also striking. Lot's family had only a few hours' notice, but the Ninevites are allowed forty days.

At the very least, the king understands the number as one of hope: "Who knows?" Nineveh may be saved (3:9). In light of 4:2, it seems Jonah anticipated that the change would be from judgment to salvation. On the other hand, the Ninevites understood it as a warning that the change would be from life to death. Their quick and fervent action (3:5) is indicative of their belief that Yahweh was about to lower the boom on them.

Thus the word given to Jonah to preach, "be changed," is a hinged word. Nineveh will be changed, either to further hardening in unbelief, leading to destruction, or to repentance and new life. The prophetic announcement is not a

---

[42] See Jonah 2 and the excursus "The Sign of Jonah."

[43] Cf. "This Joyful Eastertide" (*LSB* 482).

forewarning of an inflexibly determined fate, for history lies open to the freedom of Yahweh, the Judge who also is the Savior.[44] In the subsequent course of events, Jonah's sermon is a curse that turns into a blessing (cf. Gen 3:15, the curse with the first Gospel promise). The Word of Yahweh effects judgment-to-salvation since it is a Law-and-Gospel Word, a from-death-to-life Word.[45] It booms: "Nineveh will be destroyed and restored, razed and then raised." This verb, then, prefigures the Niphal of נחם later in the chapter: the Ninevites base their appeal on the hope that God may "change his verdict," and he did (3:9–10).

The irony of Jonah's sermon is illustrated by the punch line of a cartoon from *Judaism for Beginners*: "A good prophet is one who is wrong."[46] That is to say, a good prophet first preaches Law, which drives people to repentance, so they can rightly trust in the Gospel of God's salvation in Jesus Christ, which the prophet preaches next and which averts the judgment announced in the Law.

3:5 The section of 3:5–9 falls into three parts: the people's response to Jonah's preaching (3:5), the king's personal response (3:6), and his royal decree reinforcing the people's response (3:7–9). "Sackcloth" is a key term in all three parts (3:5, 6, 8). The first and third parts are parallel, since both include fasting, sackcloth, and total involvement ("from the greatest of them to the least of them," 3:5; "people and animals," 3:7–8). The third part not only repeats, but expands the first part because repentance extends even to the animals.

That "the gifts and *calling* [κλῆσις] of God are irrevocable" (Rom 11:29; cf. καλέω, "to call," in Rom 8:30; 9:24–26) is shown by the repetition of Yahweh's efficacious call and the human responses to it. Twice Yahweh calls Jonah to carry out his prophetic office, instructing him to "call out" to Nineveh (1:2; 3:2). On the second occasion, he even commands his prophet to "call out … the call that I am about to speak to you." The captain had urged Jonah to "call" to his God (1:6). In the psalm, Jonah recounts how he himself "called out" to Yahweh (2:3 [ET 2:2]). And now in 3:4, he "called out" his five indeterminate Hebrew words. In response, the Ninevites "called for" a fast (3:5).

In 3:5, like a dry haystack into which a pine-knot torch is thrown, Nineveh explodes into repentance. Luther observes that Yahweh could have uttered what Jesus exclaimed when he saw the faith of another Gentile (a Roman): "In no one in Israel have I found such faith!" (Mt 8:10). Luther writes: "If Jerusalem had done this [repented like Nineveh], as it did in the days of David, Solomon, Ezekiel, and Josiah, it would not have been so miraculous, since it had the Law, many prophets, many God-fearing kings, princes, priests, and other excellent people who daily preached and admonished."[47]

---

[44] See further the excursus "When Yahweh Changes a Prior Verdict."

[45] For the biblical motif that God kills in order to make alive, see the excursuses "Sheol" and "Death and Resurrection Motifs in Luther's Baptismal Theology."

[46] "The Dilemmas of Prophecy" in *Judaism for Beginners* (New York: Writers and Readers, 1990), quoted in Sherwood, *A Biblical Text and Its Afterlife*, 120 (the cartoon is reproduced as Sherwood's figure 6, between pp. 148 and 149).

[47] AE 19:85.

What is shocking here is that it only takes one five-word sermon for Nineveh to repent. The whole community responds, "from the greatest of them to the least of them" (Jonah 3:5)—a merism that refers to the entire population. Nineveh's response cannot be more opposite to Jonah's initial reaction to Yahweh's call (1:3). The contrast is as stark as it is satirical: in response to Yahweh's Word, the Israelite fled, but the Gentiles repent.

There is more satire on the way.[48] The verb "believe, trust" (the Hiphil of אָמַן), which is the root that forms the name of Jonah's own father, "Amittai" (אֲמִתַּי; see the second textual note on 1:1), now appears for the first and only time in the book.[49] Ironically, its subject is not Jonah, but the Ninevites, who "*believed* in God" (3:5)! The OT has more passages that attest that people "believed in Yahweh" than passages that state that people "believed in God." Aside from the present passage, the words "in God" occur with the Hiphil of אָמַן, "believe, trust," only one other time, in Ps 78:22:

Indeed, they did not believe in God [כִּי לֹא הֶאֱמִינוּ בֵּאלֹהִים];
neither did they trust in his salvation.

Since some may argue that "in God" (rather than "in Yahweh") in Jonah 3:5 indicates that the pagan people of the city merely acknowledged some form of divine power consistent with their own religious perspectives, it is important to note that the parallelism in Ps 78:22 indicates that "believe in God" is equal to "trust in his salvation." Therefore, Jonah 3:5 indicates that the Ninevites indeed were brought to saving faith in the one true God.

Moreover, the narrative flow of the book indicates that the converted Ninevites' belief "in God" is akin to that saving faith demonstrated by the Gentile sailors on the ship in Jonah 1, who first "became afraid/feared" (1:5, 10) and then, converted by the power of Jonah's confession in 1:9, eventually "worshiped Yahweh with great worship" (1:16).[50] Furthermore, the Ninevites, upon hearing Jonah's proclamation, immediately declare a fast and put on sackcloth as their "fruits of repentance" (Lk 3:8). Both customs are signs of mourning, sorrow, and repentance. For fasting, see, for example, 1 Sam 7:6; Jer 36:6; Ezra 8:21; for sackcloth, see, for example, Gen 37:34; 1 Ki 20:31; 2 Ki 19:1–2.

The Ninevites are moved wholeheartedly to trust in Yahweh. Christ's words in Mt 12:41 confirm the sincerity of their response. Jesus declares that "the men of Nineveh will arise" on Judgment Day and "will condemn" those who do not believe him. This statement by our Lord only makes sense if the

---

[48] See "The Purpose of Satire in This True and Didactic Story" in "Jonah as Satire with Irony" in the introduction.

[49] In chapter 1, the verb used for the Gentile sailors, who were converted to saving faith through Jonah's confession of Yahweh (1:9), was not the Hiphil of אָמַן, "to believe, trust," but rather יָרֵא, "to fear, worship" (1:16; it is also in 1:5, 9, 10), and the cognate noun יִרְאָה, "worship" (1:16). However, the Hiphil of אָמַן, "to believe, trust," would have been appropriate in 1:16 to express the sailors' faith in Yahweh.

[50] See the commentary on 1:9 and the first textual note and commentary on 1:16.

Ninevites became true believers in the triune God, believers who are justified by grace alone and through faith alone. It also implies that believing in God and worshiping Yahweh, who is God over all (Jonah 1:9), is essentially the same faith as believing in Jesus Christ, "who is God over all, blessed forever. Amen" (Rom 9:5).

Although Nineveh finally will be destroyed by a coalition of the Medes, Babylonians, and Scythians in 612 BC, the repentance of those who inhabited the city in Jonah's day (over a century earlier) is held up by Jesus as standing in stark contrast to the continuing obduracy of his own contemporaries, most of whom refused to acknowledge that he is the Savior.

The Ninevites exhibit what the Lutheran Confessions call "the entire scope of repentance," which consists of "contrition, faith, good fruits." The reformers maintained that this repentance with saving faith and good works can bring about "a lessening of public and private punishments and calamities" (Ap XII 164). Affirming the Ninevites' saving faith, Melanchthon writes in Article XII of the Apology:

> Moreover, it is worth teaching that our common maladies are lightened through our repentance and through the true fruits of repentance, through good works done from faith and not, as they imagine, by works done in mortal sin. The example of the Ninevites is a case in point. By their repentance— we mean the entire scope of repentance—they were reconciled to God and prevented the destruction of the city. (Ap XII 165–66)

The impact of the Ninevites' faith on their behavior is similar to that of the sailors in chapter 1. In 1:5 the seamen "became afraid," "called out," and "hurled" their possessions overboard. In 3:5 the Ninevites "believed," "called for a fast," and "put on sackcloths," thus depriving themselves of their possessions (food and clothing). Although these verses use some different vocabulary, the actions match in number, order, and kind. They move from inward response ("became afraid" in 1:5 renders the same Hebrew verb that means "worship" in 1:16, which is a synonym of "believe" in 3:5) to verbal response ("called" translates the same Hebrew verb in 1:5 and 3:5) to outward action ("hurled" and "put on"). In this way, the narrator paints a favorable portrait of each group as it appeals to Yahweh.

When Jesus' mother and brothers were "outside" seeking him (Mk 3:31), Jesus put it this way to those who were inside with him, listening to his words:

> "Who are my mother and my brothers?" And looking around at those sitting around him, he said, "Behold my mother and my brothers. Whoever does the will of God, this one is my brother and sister and mother." (Mk 3:33–35)

Thus Jesus' relatives, who were familial "insiders," became "outsiders," and the familial "outsiders," who were not members of his natural family, became "insiders" through their relationship to him through faith. Similarly, the Ninevites, who were not Israelites but Assyrians, became "insiders" through faith in the God of Israel. But ironically, the Israelite prophet Jonah is on the outside of the boat (1:15) when the mariners worship, vow, and sacrifice to

Yahweh (1:16), and he will be outside the great city of Nineveh in 4:5 while the city revels in the grace of the God who shows no partiality (Job 34:19; Acts 10:34; Gal 2:6; Eph 6:9).

The Ninevites' belief in God (Jonah 3:5) is more than mere assent to God's existence or even an affirmation of the truthfulness of Jonah's prophecy (3:4). But while the Ninevites "believed in God" (3:5), at the same time they are uncertain of their future and how God would deal with them. The king's question, "Who knows?" (3:9), confirms that the Ninevites did not know the outcome of their situation, yet believed that there was still hope that God would be gracious toward them.

The early church apologist Justin Martyr, in his *Dialogue with Trypho, a Jew*, cites the Ninevites' repentance as incriminating the Jews of his day. Even these pagans repented and believed, whereas the Jews who had rejected Jesus did not believe in this same God. Justin assumes that the Ninevites had a high degree of confidence in Yahweh's mercy:

> [The Ninevites] proclaimed a fast of all creatures, men and beasts, with sackcloth, and with earnest lamentation, with true repentance from the heart, and turning away from unrighteousness, in the belief that God is merciful and kind to all who turn from wickedness; so that the king of that city himself, with his nobles also, put on sackcloth and remained fasting and praying, and obtained their request that the city should not be overthrown.[51]

Justin rightly accounts for the Ninevites' trust in God, but seems to assume that the Ninevites had the same understanding of God's impartial mercy as Jonah expresses in 4:2. However, the text of chapter 3 does not articulate the precise content of the Ninevites' belief, except to say that they "believed in God," performed works of penance, were exhorted to pray fervently and cease doing evil (3:5–8). Finally, the Ninevites left their future in God's hands, unsure what would happen. The narrative of Jonah does not indicate that the Ninevites confidently knew God would be merciful toward them. On the contrary, Yahweh's change of verdict (3:10) is the great surprise of the narrative. The Ninevites hoped for this change ("Who knows?" 3:9), but did not presume it. Justin does not capture their uncertainty, but erases the tension between their present belief and their hope for the future. The eschatological tension between "now" and "not yet," between present experience and future hope, characterizes the lives of all believers.[e]

(e) See, e.g., Pss 9:19 (ET 9:18); 42:6 (ET 42:5); 69:7 (ET 69:6); Rom 4:18; 5:2–5; 8:24–25; 1 Jn 3:1–3

Chrysostom, in contrast, describes the tension between the trust and the humility of the Ninevites quite well. He captures the sense of "Who knows?" (3:9) and notes that Yahweh had not issued a conditional sentence that promised deliverance upon repentance:

> Let us imitate the spiritual wisdom of the barbarians. They repented even on uncertain grounds! For the sentence had no such clause, "If ye turn and

---

[51] Justin Martyr, *Dialogue with Trypho*, 107 (*ANF* 1:252).

repent, I will set up the city;" but simply, "Yet three days,[52] and Nineveh shall be overthrown." What then said they? "Who knoweth whether God will repent of the evil He said He would do unto us?" Who knoweth? They know not the end of the event, and yet they do not neglect repentance! They are unacquainted with God's method of shewing mercy, and yet they change upon the strength of uncertainties![53]

Chrysostom believes Nineveh had no presumptuous conception of God's grace and mercy when they repented. Their repentance in the face of uncertainty with no promise of Yahweh changing his verdict is a powerful demonstration of the genuineness of their faith. Chrysostom preserves the remarkable nature of their repentance without certainty of deliverance.

Augustine too properly understands the force of "Who knows?" as he posits that the Ninevites were uncertain about their future. They implore God for mercy, but have no certainty that they will receive it. He writes:

> They said to themselves, Mercy must be implored; they said in this sort reasoning among themselves, "Who knoweth whether God may turn for the better His sentence, and have pity?" It was "uncertain," when it is said, "Who knoweth?" On an uncertainty they did repent, certain mercy they earned:[54] they prostrated them in tears, in fastings, in sackcloth and ashes they prostrated them, groaned, wept, God spared.

Augustine compares God's action of overthrowing Nineveh through repentance and rebuilding it in faith to the conversion of the apostle Paul, to Jer 1:10, and to the work of a physician, who cuts in order to heal.[55] This is what God seeks to do for all people.

The only time in the OT when a fast is proclaimed in Jerusalem is in Jeremiah 36, not long before the destruction of the city in 587 BC. The two words that invite a comparison with Jonah 3:5 are צוֹם, "fast," and קָרָא, "to call" (Jer 36:9). The sequence of events in Jeremiah is not exactly the same as in Jonah. In Jeremiah 36, the fast had already been proclaimed before Baruch read from the scroll, whereas in Jonah the people call for a fast when they hear the prophetic call. After Baruch's words, Jehoiakim, the king of Judah in Jerusalem, burns the scribe's scroll, but after the king of Nineveh hears of Jonah's words, he repents and declares a fast (Jonah 3:6–7), mandating what the people have already undertaken voluntarily (3:5).

This contrast articulates one of the main themes in Jonah: at Yahweh's Word, foreigners are converted and respond in faith, whereas Israelites respond in disobedience (Jonah) and unbelief (Jehoiakim). The response of the

---

[52] Chrysostom, like other early church fathers before Jerome, follows the LXX, which reads "three days" instead of "forty days" (MT, Vulgate, Peshitta).

[53] Chrysostom, *Homilies on the Statues*, 5.17 (*NPNF*[1] 9:377).

[54] In this context, the verb Augustine uses, *meruerunt*, could be translated "they obtained [mercy]."

[55] Augustine, *Enarrations on the Psalms*, on Ps 51:8 (ET 51:6; Vulgate 50:8; *NPNF*[1] 8:193; PL 36:592–93).

Ninevites corresponds to what Yahweh expects from his own chosen people (cf. Ex 14:31; 2 Chr 20:20), but throughout the OT God frequently does not receive this response from Israel.[f]

Besides Jonah's five-word sermonette (3:4), could there be other factors that led Nineveh to repent? One possibility is Yahweh's provision of the great fish (2:1, 11 [ET 1:17; 2:10]). Perhaps the Ninevites heard about this man who spent three days and three nights in the belly of a fish. He had opposed Yahweh's Word (1:3) and as a result nearly perished (2:3–8 [ET 2:2–7]), but was "resurrected" (2:7c [ET 2:6c]) and now was in town preaching Yahweh's Word! Who wouldn't pay attention? Just as Yahweh had spared his disobedient prophet and raised him to new life, perhaps this God would spare the Ninevites if they called to him, as had Jonah (2:3, 8 [ET 2:2, 7]).

Donald Wiseman argues for the possibility that a cosmic sign could have facilitated Nineveh's repentance. He notes the occurrence of a total solar eclipse on June 15, 763 BC, during the reign of the Assyrian king Assur-dan III (772–755 BC),[56] a contemporary of the Israelite king Jeroboam II (ca. 786–746 BC), to whom Jonah ministered (2 Ki 14:25). Wiseman cites Ninevite versions of omen texts from the series *Enuma Anu Enlil* that predict the calamities that might happen following such an eclipse: "The king will die, rain from heaven will flood the land. There will be famine." And, "A deity will strike the king and fire consume the land." Wiseman notes that "a total eclipse is to be a time of solemn fasting when the king hands over the throne to a substitute king (of Nineveh) until the danger passes."[57]

In Assyrian religion, solar eclipses and also earthquakes were taken as signs of divine anger. Wiseman notes a record of an earthquake occurring during the reign of Assur-dan, although it is unclear whether this is the same Assur-dan as the one referred to above.[58]

In addition, Wiseman points out that there are several references to famine in Assyrian records from the reign of Assur-dan III. Based on these facts, Wiseman writes:

> All this gave rise to rebellions in various cities until 758 B.C. when the king went to Guzana (Gozan) and thereafter stayed for two years quietly in his land. It may be that the "calamity and violence" of Jonah 3:8 could refer to such a time, for his initial call had been to "Go to Nineveh and make a proclamation about it, for their calamity has come to my notice" (1:2).[59]

The accumulation of evidence that Assur-dan was a weak ruler, that cosmic happenings would have been understood by the Ninevites as signs as divine wrath, that defeat in battle and loss of territory would have created internal

---

[56] These are the dates advocated by Lemanski, "Jonah's Nineveh," 42. Hallo, *The Ancient Near East*, 131, gives the dates 773–755.

[57] Wiseman, "Jonah's Nineveh," 45–47.

[58] Wiseman, "Jonah's Nineveh," 48.

[59] Wiseman, "Jonah's Nineveh," 50.

hardship and unrest all points to this being a desperate time in Nineveh's history.[60] Wiseman cites a message from an unnamed Assyrian king to Mannu-ki-Assur, the governor of Guzana from 793 BC, that might prove analogous to the events in Jonah: "Decree of the king. You and all the people, your land, your meadows will mourn and pray for three days before the god Adad and repent. You will perform the purification rites so that there may be rest."[61]

However, extant Assyrian documents from this period make no unambiguous references to the specific events recorded in Jonah 3:4–10. No documentation yet discovered tells of Jonah's prophecy or a sweeping mass conversion of Nineveh to belief in Israel's God. Later generations might not have considered an event of this kind to be suitable for inclusion in the royal annals.

Whereas the sailors faced imminent death from the storm at sea (Jonah 1:4–13), the Ninevites were given "forty days" (3:4), which would allow some time to hesitate or procrastinate. They could have responded like Pharaoh did to Moses in Exodus 8. That prophet offered Pharaoh, "Glorify yourself over me by [telling me] the time I should pray for you and your officials and your people, to get rid of the frogs from you and from your houses" (Ex 8:5 [ET 8:9]). Instead of asking for immediate relief, Pharaoh responded with the shocking word "tomorrow" (Ex 8:6 [ET 8:10]). Or, like Felix at the preaching of St. Paul, the Ninevites could have said, "That's enough for now. Go! When I find a good time, I will call you again" (Acts 24:25). In contrast to Pharaoh and Felix, the Ninevites understand the prophetic and apostolic message, *now* is "the time of [God's] favor," and *today* is "the day of salvation" (Is 49:8, quoted in 2 Cor 6:2; see also Ps 95:7–11, quoted in Heb 3:7–4:7).

Also unlike the sailors, who heard Jonah's magnificent confession of faith, "Yahweh, the God of the heavens, I worship, who made the sea and the dry land" (1:9), the Ninevites apparently hear from Jonah only the prophet's announcement, "Yet in forty days Nineveh is about to be changed" (3:4), which does not even mention "Yahweh" or "God." Jonah neither gives them his credentials nor explains his words. In spite of all this, they respond immediately with faith.

Why? Ultimately it is a mystery why some who hear the divine Word believe and are saved, while others who may hear the same Word disbelieve and perish eternally. This is the mystery of election.[62] What is certain is that it is God who moves people to repentance and faith, and he does this through his Holy Spirit, who works through his Word. Jonah's preaching caused the Ninevites to believe in God. However rudimentary their faith may have been, they were saved through faith by the power of the Gospel in its OT form.

[60] See also Hallo, *The Ancient Near East*, 132.

[61] Wiseman, "Jonah's Nineveh," 51, citing E. F. Weidner, *The Inscriptions from Tell Halaf* (Archiv für Orientforschung 6; 1940), 13–14, no. 5.

[62] See FC Ep and SD XI, "Concerning the Eternal Predestination and Election of God."

Still, it is remarkable that the narrative says no more about the process or means of their conversion. Relevant here is Meir Sternberg's discussion of three types of omissions in OT narratives. First, "blanks" are omissions of irrelevant information. Second, temporary gaps signify information that is delayed. Third are permanent gaps of information never supplied.[63] Jonah contains all three types. Blanks occur in 1:1 (where and when did the Word of Yahweh come to Jonah?) and 2:11 (ET 2:10)–3:3 (where was Jonah deposited, and how did he get to Nineveh?). A temporary gap occurs in 1:3, which gives no reason for Jonah's flight away from Yahweh, but this information is supplied in 4:2, where Jonah fills the gap. A permanent gap occurs here in 3:5 if we ask why it is that the Ninevites—all of them—believed and acted in repentance, whereas Israel so often did not repent nor believe despite prophetic preaching.[64]

It comes as no surprise that this permanent gap in information has led commentators to speculate.[65] However, within the narrative world of the book, this gap proleptically prepares us for the biggest gap in the book: Jonah's "non answer" after 4:11. There, when Jonah is angry with Yahweh about the Ninevites' salvation, the only explanation he receives is a rhetorical question that emphasizes Yahweh's compassion (4:10–11). Here perhaps we are to be content with that same explanation as the underlying reason for such a radical change in the city of Nineveh: Yahweh's compassion.

We can ask a similar question about the NT. Why is it Saul of Tarsus who is changed, converted, and given the office of apostle to the Gentiles? Paul supplies at least part of an answer in these words:

> Faithful is this word and worthy of all acceptance: Christ Jesus came into the world to save sinners, of whom I myself am foremost. But for this very reason I was shown mercy: so that in me foremost Christ Jesus might display his unlimited patience as a pattern for those who would believe on him unto eternal life. (1 Tim 1:15–16)

So Yahweh's unlimited patience and mercy also change the Ninevites. Commenting on this Luther writes: "Let us, rather, observe what a fine faith dwelt in these people, who did not only believe Jonah's announcement that the city would perish but also sought comfort in God's mercy."[66] And commenting on the sermon of Jonah (3:4), Luther writes about the repentance of the Ninevites:

> In view of this, I am tempted to say that no apostle or prophet, not even Christ Himself, performed and accomplished with a single sermon the great things

---

[63] Sternberg, *The Poetics of Biblical Narrative*, especially pages 235–63.

[64] Nineveh therefore also stands in contrast to the heathen nations addressed in the prophetic oracles against the nations, since we have no evidence that those nations repented in response to the oracles. See "Prophecies Both *against* and *for* the Nations" in the excursus "Mission in the Old Testament."

[65] For an overview of various views, see Sasson, *Jonah*, 244.

[66] AE 19:88–89.

Jonah did. His conversion of the city of Nineveh with one sermon is surely as great a miracle as his rescue from the belly of the whale, if not an even greater one.[67]

When St. Paul describes his own preaching in 1 Cor 2:1–5, he emphasizes that his sole message is Christ crucified, and this kind of Christian preaching demonstrates the power of the Spirit, in contrast to preaching that relies on lofty speech or human wisdom. Neither the apostle's description nor the example of Jonah's brief sermon need drive a wedge between the efficacy of the Word and the faithful use of biblical rhetoric,[68] but the radical success of both preachers shows that it is God's Word, not eloquence or loquaciousness, that has the power to change lives and lead hearers to eternal life.

3:6 This verse describes the king's personal reaction. As the head and representative of his people, his penitence dramatizes that of the entire populace. Generally in the OT, most kings are not fond of prophets: Pharaoh disdains Moses (Exodus 5–11); Ahab rebuffs Micaiah (1 Kings 22); Zedekiah rejects Jeremiah (Jeremiah 37–39); and Manasseh probably has Isaiah sawn in two (cf. Heb 11:37). But Jonah encounters a ready audience in the temporal authority in Nineveh. In fact, it seems that the unnamed king is driven to repent merely by hearing a secondhand report of Jonah's sermon ("When this word reached the king," Jonah 3:6). Thus some time elapsed after Yahweh had spoken through Jonah before the king responded with repentance and his call for prayer, and the earlier sermon had already hinted that Nineveh could "be changed" through repentance unto salvation (3:4). Therefore, Yahweh's action might be summarized as follows: "Before they call, I will answer; even as they speak, I will hear" (Is 65:24). Paul puts it this way:

> The Gentiles, who did not pursue righteousness, have obtained righteousness—the righteousness that is by faith. (Rom 9:30)

The OT records the repentance of other foreign leaders. For example, Pharaoh learns not to take Sarai for a wife (Gen 12:10–20), as does Abimelech of Gerar (Gen 20:1–18). When the Philistines are smitten in judgment for capturing the ark, "the town's cry for help went up to heaven" (1 Sam 5:12). The king of Nineveh joins the "cloud of witnesses" of OT saints (Heb 12:1) as he humbles himself before Yahweh.

Just as the captain of the ship in chapter 1 emerges to lead the crew into repentance and worship (Jonah 1:6, 16), so now the king emerges from the Ninevites. Faced with destruction, the sailors "cried out" (וַיִּזְעֲקוּ, 1:5), each to his own god. That Hebrew verb recurs in the book only once more, when the king, faced with destruction, "issued an edict" (וַיַּזְעֵק, 3:7). Since both 1:1 and 3:1 emphasize "the Word of Yahweh" (דְּבַר־יְהוָה), it is appropriate that the king of Nineveh responds to the divine Word: "When this word [הַדָּבָר] reached the

---

[67] AE 19:37.

[68] See Lessing, "Preaching Like the Prophets."

king of Nineveh, he arose from his throne" (3:6). The use of דְּבָר here, even without reference to Yahweh, is by now in the narrative understood to be Yahweh's "Word." Just as the captain echoes Yahweh's words back to Jonah in 1:6 (the captain's imperatives to Jonah, "Arise, call," repeat Yahweh's imperatives to Jonah, "Arise … call" in 1:2), so here the king echoes Yahweh's words throughout Nineveh. Luther writes:

> Although this king had not heard Jonah preach in his presence, nevertheless, after he had been informed about Jonah's preaching, he also preached and converted one-third of his own city by his own preaching.[69]

The irony then is that both Gentile leaders function as "prophets" to and for the Israelite prophet Jonah!

Assur-dan III was king of Assyria from about 772 until 755, and Assur-nirari V ruled from about 754 until 745.[70] At this time, Assyria was controlled by weak kings surrounded by powerful provincial governors. During this period of decline, events such as internal dissension and defeat in war and a total solar eclipse in 763 BC, followed by flooding and famine, could well have been interpreted by the Ninevites as divine judgment.

According to Donald Wiseman, during a time of extreme crisis (e.g., a solar eclipse or an earthquake), it was not unknown for an Assyrian king to descend from his throne and be replaced by a substitute king in what is known as a *šar puhi* ritual. The substitute king would reign until the time of danger had passed. The actions of the king here in 3:6—possibly Assur-dan III—might reflect such a *šar puhi* ritual, and this might also account for the king and his nobles being associated in the issuing of the decree ("from the decree of the king and his nobles," 3:7).[71]

Alternatively, Paul Lawrence believes that the issuing of the decree in 3:7–9 is a consequence of the political situation, with the weak king finding it necessary to issue a decree in conjunction with his powerful officials.[72]

The king here is called "the king of Nineveh" (3:6) and not "the king of Assyria." Two alleged problems arise with this title. First, cuneiform documents never use this phrase to designate the reigning Assyrian monarch. Second, the OT never uses this title elsewhere, but instead refers to "the king of Assyria" (e.g., Is 36:13). Most modern commentators believe that "the king of Nineveh" is historically inaccurate and a sign that the narrator of Jonah is not recounting a true historical event. However, as Jack Sasson points out, that judgment "demands too much historical precision." Sasson goes on to note that the OT can use royal titles in ways that do not correspond exactly to historical conventions. For example, in contexts that clearly are historical, the OT

---

[69] AE 19:24.

[70] Jeroboam II, to whom Jonah prophesied (2 Ki 14:25), ruled from about 786 until 746 BC.

[71] Wiseman, "Jonah's Nineveh," 47, 51.

[72] Lawrence, "Assyrian Nobles and the Book of Jonah."

uses "Pharaoh" as a substitute for the royal name or as a title attached to a specific name (i.e., Pharaoh Neco, 2 Ki 23:29), even though Egyptian literature does not use the title in those ways. Another example is the OT's use of the title "the king of Samaria" (1 Ki 21:1; 2 Ki 1:3), where it would be more accurate to use the term "the king of Israel." Mesopotamian literature also refers to foreign leaders using less than precise technical terms.[73]

In response to Jonah's message that Nineveh would "be changed" (3:4), the king is changed in dwelling, dress, and dignity. The king's action begins with him rising from his throne and ends with him sitting in ashes. The chiastic symmetry of his actions is deliberately portrayed:

A   He arose from his throne,
  B   removed his royal robe,
  B'   covered himself with sackcloth,
A' and sat upon the ash heap.

Between his two resting places the king changes his clothing. Not even David's repentance, after he hears the words of Nathan the prophet, is so lucidly portrayed. Yet David likely had performed those same actions, because later "David arose from the earth, washed, anointed himself, and changed his clothes" (2 Sam 12:20). But the more common response of kings to prophetic warnings is apathy or enmity, as exemplified by Jehoiakim, king in Jerusalem. On hearing the words of Jeremiah read to him, "the king would cut them off with a scribe's knife and throw them into the fire in the brazier until the whole scroll was consumed in the fire in the brazier. Yet they did not fear nor rend their garments—neither the king nor any of his servants who heard all these words" (Jer 36:23–24).

The reaction of the Ninevite king is all the more remarkable in that elsewhere in the OT Assyrian kings are portrayed as an arrogant, boasting monarchs who not only defy Yahweh and threaten Jerusalem, but also argue that their power is greater than Yahweh's because they have been able to defeat the God of Israel/Judah just as they defeated the gods of other nations (Is 10:5–34; chapters 36–37 ‖ 2 Kings 18–19; Nahum 2–3). Representative are these words from Is 10:8–11:

> "Are not my commanders all kings?" he says. "Is not Calno like Carchemish, or Hamath like Arpad, or Samaria like Damascus? Just as my hand reached out to kingdoms of idols, with more images than Jerusalem and Samaria, just as I did to Samaria and her idols, shall I not do to Jerusalem and to her graven images?"

In contrast, the king in Jonah 3:6 rises from his throne, removes his robe, puts on sackcloth, sits in ashes, and proclaims a fast. For similar actions see Job 2:8; Dan 9:3; and Esth 4:1, 3. Sackcloth and fasting, as well as torn clothes

---

[73] Sasson, *Jonah*, 248. As an example from Mesopotamian literature, Sasson notes that "the Mari records speak of 'kings' of the Benyaminites, when referring to tribal leaders who, strictly speaking, are not holders of crowns."

and ashes or dust on the head, are expressions of mourning and self-negation. For example, in Gen 37:34–35, Jacob tears his garments and wears sackcloth, saying he will follow his (supposedly) dead son Joseph down into Sheol. The repentant actions in Jonah 3:5–8 indicate that the king, the citizens, and the animals are "dying," just like Jonah in chapter 2 (especially 2:3, 7–8 [ET 2:2, 6–7]). But just as the prophet found out, so also the Ninevites find here: "Yahweh puts to death and gives life; he casts down to Sheol and raises up again" (1 Sam 2:6). Through repentance and death comes new life.[74]

The "throne" (כִּסֵּא, Jonah 3:6) is a symbol of sovereignty and even divinity according to ancient Near Eastern conception, so the king abdicates it to show his humility before God. The Hebrew term for the "royal robe" (אַדֶּרֶת) that he removes can also mean "glory, magnificence" (BDB, 1), and it represents the king's invested power. This same noun also refers to the "mantle" worn by Elijah, which fell to Elisha (1 Ki 19:13, 19; 2 Ki 2:8, 13, 14). Therefore, it might—albeit very subtly—suggest ironically that the repentant king of Nineveh here has greater "prophetic" insight than does resentful Jonah (especially in chapters 1 and 4).

So the king and Jonah are antitypes. Jonah's response to Yahweh's "Word" (דְּבַר) and command to "arise" (קוּם) was to flee in the other direction (1:2–3). But when "the word" (דְּבָר, 3:6) came to the king, he responded faithfully: he "arose" (קוּם, 3:6) and commanded that the people "call" to God in fervent prayer (קָרָא, 3:8). These two actions are precisely what the ship's captain unsuccessfully attempted to persuade Jonah to do in 1:6: "Arise [קוּם], call [קְרָא] to your God." This is a theme expressed throughout the narrative: the Israelite prophet Jonah rebels, but pagan Gentiles (the sailors in chapter 1; the Ninevites in chapter 3) repent, believe in Yahweh, and are saved. This theme anticipates what will happen throughout the world in the NT era: many Jewish people will reject the Messiah sent by Israel's God, but many Gentiles—and a faithful remnant of Jewish people—will repent, believe in him, and so be saved.

3:7 The focus now shifts from the king's personal reaction (3:6) back to the city's communal response to the crisis via a royal edict that regularizes the spontaneous reaction of the populace (their faith, fasting, and sackcloth in 3:5). Officialdom the world over is accustomed to governing by means of such decrees. "The king and his nobles" issue a joint decree to both "people and animals" (3:7). These phrases encompass all life in the city, from the monarch and his court down to the common populace and even their livestock, making this the most comprehensive repentance recorded anywhere in the OT or NT.[75]

---

[74] See the excursuses "Sheol" and "Death and Resurrection Motifs in Luther's Baptismal Theology."

[75] The closest biblical parallel to repentance and salvation of people extending to the deliverance also of animals is the narrative of Noah and the animals in the ark saved from the flood. See "Jonah and Noah" in the introduction.

The word translated "nobles" is the plural of the adjective גָּדוֹל, "great one" (as in "the greatest of them" in 3:5). It denotes the highest echelon of power around the king. (Regarding the possible historical circumstances surrounding the joint decree, see the commentary on 3:6.) Some interpreters argue on two grounds that 3:7 does not reflect Assyrian practice in the eighth century BC, but later Persian practice (perhaps fifth or fourth century BC). They base their argument on the lack of documentary evidence from Assyria of a king issuing a decree in conjunction with his nobles or of animals being clothed in sackcloth and on evidence that both of these practices occurred in the Persian period. However, on linguistic and other historical grounds, such a late date of composition is unlikely. An argument from silence is the weakest form of argument; the absence of evidence is not the evidence of absence. We today possess only a tiny fraction of all the written documents that existed in antiquity, and many historical events would have gone unrecorded by the ancients. What is more, the first half of the eighth century is one of the most poorly documented periods in Assyrian history, and the two practices in 3:7 likely were rare, in which case they emphasize further the unusual nature of the Ninevite response.

The phrase "people and animals" in 3:7–8 is a merism, an expression of two opposites that also includes everything in between (like "from the greatest of them to the least of them" in 3:5), so the edict applies to all living creatures. The next phrase too is a merism. It encompasses all domesticated animals, from large cattle (הַבָּקָר, "herd") to small sheep and goats (הַצֹּאן, "flock").

In chapter 2, Yahweh assigned a fish a great responsibility (2:1, 11 [ET 1:17; 2:10]). Now more animals join in the narrative. The decree in 3:7–8 is not some kind of hyperbole, but to be carried out literally. The conversion of the people is so complete that they even want their animals to participate in the acts of repentance. This reflects that Yahweh's care embraces not only people, but even animals (4:10–11). Clothing animals in the garb of mourning and penitence is attested in the Persian and Roman periods.[76] It can be compared with the modern practice of placing catafalques upon horses with the same color worn by those bereaved.

Yahweh's concern even for animals takes us back to his creation of them in Genesis 1–2 and to his provision for their preservation from the flood by means of the ark, as well as the Noahic covenant in Gen 9:8–17.[77] Yahweh's compassion for animals also finds expression in the Torah of Moses. Deut 22:6–7 is one example:

---

[76] For example, in Judith 4:10 animals join an entire population in wearing sackcloth to demonstrate mass repentance: "They and their wives and their children and their cattle and every resident alien and hired laborer and purchased slave—they all girded themselves with sackcloth" (RSV).

[77] See "Jonah and Noah" in the introduction.

If a bird's nest happens to be before you beside the road, in any tree or on the ground, with young birds or eggs, and the mother is sitting on the young or on the eggs, you shall not take the mother with the children. You certainly must let the mother go, although the children you may take, so that it may go well with you and you may have a long life.

The prohibition of muzzling an ox when it treads the grain (Deut 25:4) is applied by St. Paul to ministers in the church (1 Cor 9:9–12; cf. 1 Tim 5:17–18). Prov 12:10 declares: "A righteous man has regard for the life of his beast, but the mercies of the wicked are cruel." The eschatological visions of the restored creation include animals in Is 11:6–8; 65:25. Paul echoes this when he states that the whole creation, now subject to futility, groans as it awaits the final consummation and revelation of the sons of God (Rom 8:19–22).

The last words of the book of Jonah underscore Yahweh's compassion for animals; it ends with "and many animals" (וּבְהֵמָה רַבָּה, 4:11). Ironically, throughout the book the animals are more responsive to Yahweh than the Israelite prophet Jonah (cf. Is 1:3).

Addressing Jonah, the captain uttered short sentences (1:6). Addressing the Ninevites, the king issues a lengthy decree (3:7–9). Though the two speeches differ in length, addressees, and formality, their conclusions correspond in theme, vocabulary, and syntax. They open with parallel rhetorical expressions that hope for, but do not presume salvation. "Perhaps" (אוּלַי), says the captain (1:6), "Who knows?" (מִי־יוֹדֵעַ), asks the king (3:9). Next come clauses with the identical subject (הָאֱלֹהִים, literally, "the God"): "Perhaps that God of yours will show compassion toward us," said the captain. "Who knows whether God may turn and change his verdict?" asks the king. The identical purpose clause formed by same two Hebrew words (וְלֹא נֹאבֵד) concludes both speeches: "so we will not perish" is the goal of both the captain and the king. Both foreign leaders proclaim a theology of hope that rests entirely on God's compassion toward all—even Gentile foreigners—who repent and trust in him.

In contrast, Jonah's deep sleep in 1:5–6 indicated that he had little hope for the ship. Jonah's anger over Nineveh's repentance and salvation through faith (4:1) and his subsequent pouting (4:5) indicate that he resents the hope that God gave the city. His desire to be thrown overboard (1:12; cf. 1:15) and to die (4:3, 8–9) indicates that he has little hope for his own future.

3:8 Jonah 3:5–7 builds up the totality of Nineveh's repentance by mentioning the greatest and least, king and commoner, man and beast. The preceding verse (3:7) prohibited eating or drinking in even the smallest amount. Now, by means of a series of jussive verbs in 3:8, the edict turns to commands that call for positive acts. The first prescribes the wearing of "sackcloths," which the people and king donned voluntarily in 3:5–6.

The second command, "And they must call to God fervently," uses the verb קָרָא, "to call," for the last time in the book. Yahweh first commissioned Jonah to "call out" against Nineveh (1:2), then the captain exhorted Jonah to "call" to his God (1:6), and the sailors "called out" to Yahweh in supplication (1:14).

"Resurrected" Jonah was commissioned again by Yahweh to "call out" his sermon in Nineveh, as he did (3:2, 4). In 3:5 the people of Nineveh "called" for a fast. Here in 3:8, more converted pagans (like the sailors in 1:14) are to "call" in prayer to the one true God, even as the Israelite Jonah "called out" to Yahweh in 2:3 (ET 2:2).

The third command extends to the end of 3:8: "They must turn, each from his evil way and from the violence that is in their hands." The verb שׁוּב, "to turn," will recur twice in 3:9, expressing the corresponding hope that just as the people "turn" from their evil (3:8), so God may "turn" from his anger. Hence this verb interacts with "be changed" (the Niphal of הָפַךְ) in 3:4. While "be changed" in 3:4 could refer to the city's destruction by the wrath of Yahweh, instead the city is "changed" as the people "turn" from their wickedness, and Yahweh then "turn[s]" from his anger.

The king of Nineveh knows that fasting, sackcloth, and prayer would be hypocritical if the people persisted in evil and violence; from this they must turn. This will be what Yahweh notices. Jonah 3:10 does not say, "God saw their sackcloth and fasting and heard their prayer," but rather, "God saw their works, that they turned from their evil way." Their outward works attested to the genuineness of their inner change. Their repentance expressed itself through both faith and good works. Faith can be seen by God alone, but both God and people can see good works.

The theme of both outward and inner change is addressed by Yahweh through Isaiah:

> Is not this the fasting I have chosen: to loose the chains of wickedness and unfasten the cords of the yoke, to set the crushed free and tear off every yoke? Is it not to divide your food with the hungry and to bring poor wanderers into your house—when you see the naked, you clothe him, and you do not hide yourself from those who are your own flesh? (Is 58:6–7)

Yahweh's efficacious Word accomplishes an inner change that results not only in outward rites of repentance but also in righteousness and justice among God's people. That Yahweh "saw" the results of this change in Nineveh mandated by the king (Jonah 3:10) is consistent with Jesus' description of the universal judgment. He echoes Is 58:6–7 as he describes how, as the enthroned King, he has seen the acts of Christian love performed for even "the least of these my brothers" and regards them as having been done "for me" (Mt 25:31–40).

Texts such as Jer 7:22–23; Hos 6:6; and Joel 2:12–13 and many others like them are examples of this "both/and" call of the prophets.[78] God calls and em-

---

[78] Some of these passages, including Is 58:6–7, imply or state that God does *not* desire acts of piety such as sacrifice, fasting, and rending one's clothing. However, these passages employ the rhetorical technique of dialectical negation. See Bartelt, "Dialectical Negation." One example from the NT illustrates the linguistic idea in a representative manner. Peter states that as the prophets were "searching for what person or time the Sprit of Christ within them was revealing as he witnessed beforehand the sufferings of Christ and the glories afterward,

powers his people to manifest their inner faith through outward signs and fruit (cf. John 15). But while Israel often is like an unfruitful vine (Is 5:1–7), the Ninevites respond with authentic faith.

While "to fear/worship" is the word in chapter 1 that progressively describes the change of the sailors from fear to faith and worship (יָרֵא in 1:5, 10, 16; also of Jonah in 1:9), "turn/repent" is the word that describes the conversion of the Ninevites in chapter 3 (שׁוּב in 3:8, 10; also of God twice in 3:9). The Qal form of this verb is used four times in 3:8–10, and only here in the book,[79] just as "fear/worship" occurs in Jonah only in the account of the sailors' conversion (1:5, 9, 10, 16). The Ninevites are called to "turn" from their wicked way (3:8) in the hope that Yahweh may "turn" from his anger (3:9). When he sees that the city has "turned" in repentance, Yahweh changes his verdict[80] about the city from judgment to justification through faith (3:10; cf. Gen 15:6; Rom 3:21–22, 28; 4:6).

Clauses similar to "They must turn, each from his evil way" (3:8) are used repeatedly in Jeremiah.[g] Here the clause is spoken not by an Israelite prophet, but rather by a recently pagan king, and one from Assyria at that! That this king speaks the same words Yahweh utters through his prophet Jeremiah recalls the similar situation in Jonah 1, where the pagan captain used commands spoken earlier by Yahweh: "Arise, call" (1:6) repeats Yahweh's earlier commands to Jonah, "Arise, … call" (1:2). When the captain and king quote Yahweh, the satire is evident: the Israelite Jonah is unfaithful to Yahweh's Word, but the pagan Gentiles are converted to faith in accord with Yahweh's Word. It is bad enough that Jonah in chapters 1 and 4 functions poorly as a prophet. It is even worse that the prophet from Israel is "out propheted" by Gentile converts from paganism!

"Violence" (חָמָס) is another word spoken by the king in 3:8.[81] It refers to brutality that comes from wicked design and practice, especially in connection with cities, including those in Israel (e.g., Jer 6:7; Ezek 7:23; Amos 3:10; Micah 6:12). Assyrian warfare was exceptionally violent. Perhaps within the very lifetime of Jonah himself (or a few decades later), the Northern Kingdom was devastated in

(g) Jer 18:11; 23:14, 22; 25:5; 26:3; 35:15; 36:3, 7

it was revealed to them that it was *not themselves, but you* they were serving" (1 Pet 1:11–12). A simplistic reading of these verses could easily give the impression that the OT prophets did not minister at all to their OT audiences, nor did the prophetic Word minister to the prophets themselves; instead, the OT prophets ministered exclusively to the NT church. However, instead of being "either/or," the text should be understood as affirming "both/and." Bartelt writes: "If one translates what Peter says in verse 12 as dialectical negation, the integrity of the prophets as preachers to their own time is persevered: 'It was revealed to them that they were not (just) serving themselves, but you" (pp. 62–63).

[79] The only other form in Jonah is the Hiphil in 1:13, where the sailors vainly tried to "return" the ship to dry land.

[80] See the second textual note on 3:9 and the commentary on 3:9–10.

[81] Some commentators argue that since the narrative of Jonah does not stress the role of the Ninevites as "arch-enemies and oppressors of Israel," Nineveh must have a neutral significance in the book (e.g., Clements, "The Purpose of the Book of Jonah," 18). However, the brutality of Assyria would have been simply taken for granted by Israelites, and חָמָס here evokes the "violence" typical of the Assyrians.

722/721 BC by the Assyrians, who exiled much of its surviving population (see 2 Kings 17). One particularly gruesome form of violence by the Assyrians is illustrated in their carved reliefs depicting their military conquests: the practice of impaling defeated foes on large poles planted in the ground. This form of execution, which they also inflicted in Judah, was one of the earliest precursors to the Roman practice of crucifixion—the form of violence suffered by God's Son, the one man who embodied the nation of Israel (Mt 2:15).[82]

3:9 The syntactical position of "Who knows?" (מִי־יוֹדֵעַ) corresponds with its theological function. It comes after the turning of the Ninevites away from sin and toward God in faith (3:5–8) and before their hope that God would turn away from his wrath and deal with them graciously (the rest of 3:9). Since this clause expressing human uncertainty leaves it to God to decide how he will act, it undercuts the idea that human repentance automatically manipulates God into dispensing salvation. The turning of the Ninevites and their animals does not in itself guarantee the turning of God, since he had issued no promise of grace for them (cf. 3:4). Who knows? Only God does![83]

This means that the Ninevites are not repenting in order to force God to call off the catastrophe. Their belief is not in magic. Rather, the Assyrian king remains uncertain as to what will happen next. He knows that Yahweh is not obligated to turn away from his righteous judgment. Yet he is hopeful that the God of Israel will respond in grace. There is no mechanical relationship between human acts of piety or worship and God's saving action.[84] This prevents any simple *quid pro quo* or *opus operatum* understanding of the relationship between human and divine change.[85]

Since God had issued no guarantee that any actions by the Ninevites would allow them to be spared, God is their only hope. In this way, grace remains grace. The forgiveness of sins is not grounded in human repentance, but rather in God's attributes of mercy and compassion (Jonah 4:2), which are ultimately rooted in the atonement of Jesus Christ: "He himself will save his people from their sins" (Mt 1:21). Christ is the source of the grace shown to OT believers just as surely as he is the fount of grace for NT believers. Paul puts it this way: "For while we were yet sinners, Christ died for us" (Rom 5:8). The Augsburg Confession in Article V, "Concerning the Office of Preaching," states this same theology:

---

[82] Hengel, *Crucifixion*, 23, n. 4, cites the illustrations in *ANEP*, §§ 362, 368, 373; the last one depicts the practice after the Assyrian defeat of Lachish during Sennacherib's invasion of Judah in 701 BC (see 2 Ki 18:13–19:37). On Mt 2:15, one may see "Jesus, God's Son, as the Nation, God's Son" in Gibbs, *Matthew 1:1–11:1*, 139–45.

[83] In this way, the situation of the Ninevites (and of the sailors in chapter 1) differs from that of Israel or of Christians today, who do have God's certain promise that all who repent and believe in him shall be saved (e.g., Joel 3:5 [ET 2:32]; Acts 2:21; Rom 10:13).

[84] Allen, *Joel, Obadiah, Jonah and Micah*, 193, writes: "The author guards carefully against the charge of making God the automatic reactor to human activity, as if man could be the arbiter of his own fate."

[85] See, for example, Ap IV 203–8; XII 11–12; XXIV 11–12.

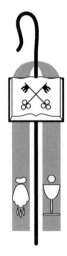

Through these [the Gospel and Sacraments], as through means, he [God] gives the Holy Spirit who produces faith, *where and when he wills*, in those who hear the gospel. It teaches that we have a gracious God, not through our merit but through Christ's merit.[86]

The Israelite prophet Jonah preaches the sermons (God's Word) that convert the sailors (1:9) and the Ninevites (3:4). Ironically, however, it is the non-Israelites in the narrative who express the theology of grace by despairing of their own works and merits and by trusting in God alone, hoping that he will be gracious to them (the captain in 1:6; the sailors in 1:14b; and the king of Nineveh in 3:9). It is they, rather than Jonah, who have such extraordinary insight into the ways of Yahweh. The Gentiles articulate and rejoice that Yahweh acts mercifully as he so pleases, whereas the Israelite prophet Jonah resents (4:1) and even tries to prevent (4:2, referring to 1:3) Yahweh from doing so. Nevertheless, throughout the book of Jonah, Yahweh's pleasure is for his *opus proprium* to be his final word.[87] Thus each chapter concludes with the Gospel (1:16; 2:10–11 [ET 2:9–10]; 3:10; 4:10–11).

The first four Hebrew words of Jonah 3:9 are identical to the first four of Joel 2:14: "Who knows whether he [God] may turn and change his verdict?" (מִי יוֹדֵעַ יָשׁוּב וְנִחָם). The expression has the same meaning in Jonah as in Joel, but there is one significant difference in the surrounding context. In Joel, Yahweh's change of verdict, from judgment to blessing, would be *for Israel* (see also similar wording regarding Israel in Ex 32:14). In Jonah, it is *for Gentiles*, even violent, rotten, wicked Ninevites! In that way, Jonah 3:9 relates to similar wording in Jer 18:7–8, where Yahweh extends a promise of changing his verdict for any nation that turns from its evil.

Even more shocking is another intertextual comparison. The mighty King David once approached Yahweh with a humble "Who knows?" when he petitioned for the life of the child he conceived in adultery with Bathsheba: "Who knows whether Yahweh may be gracious and the child may live?" (2 Sam 12:22). Yet the prayer of the king of Israel failed to evoke a favorable response. But now the king of Nineveh, a new convert from paganism, offers the same prayer, and it is answered favorably by Israel's God, much to the chagrin of Jonah (4:1)!

This turn of events illustrates this saying of Jesus Christ: "The last will be first, and the first last" (Mt 20:16; cf. Mt 19:30). When a Roman expressed faith in Israel's Messiah (Mt 8:5–9), Christ made the point this way:

> Many from east and west will come and recline at table with Abraham, Isaac, and Jacob in the kingdom of heaven, but the sons of the kingdom [Israelites who reject Jesus] will be thrown out into the outer darkness. (Mt 8:11–12)

---

[86] AC V 2–3; emphasis added.

[87] God's *opus proprium*, "proper work," is the justification of the sinner through faith, by the merits of Christ. See, for example, AE 13:78–79; 14:335; 16:233–34; 51:18–19.

3:10 No fire and brimstone falls on this latter-day Sodom after all! The wording of this verse, "God saw their works" (וַיַּרְא הָאֱלֹהִים אֶת־מַעֲשֵׂיהֶם), echoes this statement about Yahweh and his creation: "God saw everything that he had worked[88] [וַיַּרְא אֱלֹהִים אֶת־כָּל־אֲשֶׁר עָשָׂה], and behold it was very good" (Gen 1:31). Yahweh's action in forgiving the Ninevites is similar to his observation of the goodness of his original creation, only now the good works of the Ninevites are the result of God working in them a new creation (2 Cor 5:17; Gal 6:15). God could have said, "I will make all new things; the old won't do." Instead he says, "I am making all things new" (Rev 21:5).

Just as the sailors are delivered from the fatal effect of the storm (1:15–16) and Jonah is saved from death and Sheol (2:3, 7–8 [ET 2:2, 6–7]), now the Ninevites are delivered from certain doom to life everlasting. Jonah was the object of divine anger expressed by the fury of the storm (1:15). He was conscious of his guilt that merited the sentence of death (1:12). He was saved from Sheol by Yahweh's means of grace, a fish (2:1 [ET 1:17]).[89] Nineveh was converted to faith in God by means of his Word, preached by Jonah (3:4). Now the salvation of the city is effected since Yahweh "did *not* do" (3:10) judgment. Leslie Allen writes: "Divine inactivity is here the counterpart to the divine activity in rescuing Jonah at 2:1 [ET 1:17]. The parallelism of the narrative creates a logical presupposition that Jonah would hail with joy this new demonstration of divine goodness."[90] But don't hold your breath for that response by the prophet!

On another level, the "turn" by the Ninevites (3:8, 10) and by Yahweh (3:9) eradicates the "evil" (רָעָה) formerly performed by Nineveh (3:8, 10) and the "evil" threatened by Yahweh but averted (3:10). This turns us back to chapter 1. There Yahweh speaks of Nineveh's "evil" in 1:2, and the sailors speak twice of "evil" (1:7–8) in reference to the storm hurled by Yahweh (1:4). By the end of 3:10, everyone has their "evil" removed. Even Yahweh changes his verdict of destruction for Nineveh (3:10). Everyone is free from evil—except Jonah. He perceives the salvation of the city as "a great evil" (4:1). Yahweh will try to remove the prophet's "evil" by means of the qiqayon plant, which he provides "to save him from his evil" (לְהַצִּיל לוֹ מֵרָעָתוֹ, 4:6). Will this succeed? The book ends without telling us.

Jonah 3:10 should not be taken to mean that God was the author of "evil," even if he had not averted it.[91] Marcion, however, cited "evil" in this passage

---

88 The noun translated "their works" (מַעֲשֵׂיהֶם) in Jonah 3:10 is formed from the verb עָשָׂה, which is used in Gen 1:31, where it is usually translated "that he *had made*" (e.g., ESV, NIV).

89 See the commentary on 2:1 (ET 1:17). Hence one could relate the fish as a means of salvation for Jonah to the fish as an early church symbol for Christ and the anagram (ΙΧΘΥΣ) for "Jesus Christ, Son of God, (is) Savior." See the fourth argument for the integrity of the psalm in "Introduction to Jonah 2," and the excursus "Death and Resurrection Motifs in Luther's Baptismal Theology."

90 Allen, *Joel, Obadiah, Jonah and Micah*, 227.

91 See the fourth textual note on 1:2, which has רָעָה, "evil."

to support his argument that the God revealed in the OT was a divinity inferior to the wholly good God revealed by Jesus. Tertullian first summarizes Marcion's argument: "Look here then, say you: I discover a self-incriminating case in the matter of the Ninevites, when the book of Jonah declares, 'And God repented of the evil that He had said that He would do unto them; and He did it not.' "[92] Then Tertullian refutes Marcion by explaining God's role as judge:

> We say, in short, that evil in the present case means, not what may be attributed to the Creator's nature as an evil being, but what may be attributed to His power as a judge. In accordance with which He declared, "I create evil" [Is 45:7], and, "I frame evil against you" [Jer 18:11]; meaning not to sinful evils, but avenging ones. What sort of stigma pertains to these, congruous as they are with God's judicial character, we have sufficiently explained.[93] Now, although these are called "evils," they are yet not reprehensible in a judge; nor because of this their name do they show that the judge is evil: so in like manner will this particular evil be understood to be one of this class of judiciary evils, and along with them to be compatible with (God as) a judge.[94]

In Jonah 3:10, "evil" does not denote wrongdoing, but divine justice, which is destructive to sinful humans, just as the sailors called the storm sent by Yahweh an "evil" (רָעָה, 1:7–8). Tertullian continues: "What therefore He had justly decreed, having no evil purpose in His decree, He decreed from the principle of justice, not from malevolence. Yet He gave it the name of 'evil,' because of the evil and desert involved in the very suffering itself."[95]

The noun in the clause "God saw their *works*" (מַעֲשֶׂה occurs only here in Jonah) comes from the verb עָשָׂה, "do, act, make." This provides another opportunity to compare and contrast the scenes in chapters 1 and 3. In 1:11 the sailors use the verb when they ask in desperation, "What shall we *do*?" They heed Jonah's answer (1:12, 15) and are saved, prompting their "great worship" of Yahweh (1:16). Similarly, in chapter 3, the Ninevites heed Jonah's sermon and reveal their faith by their "works" (3:10), including the king's self-abasement from high on his throne to low in the ashes. Indeed, there is wholesale repentance in Nineveh from king to cow. Thus the sailors and Ninevites are both people of action. These Gentiles know what to *do*.

In contrast, when the verb עָשָׂה is used of the Israelite Jonah, it shows the futility of his misdirected actions. The exasperated sailors ask him, "What is this you have *done*?" because they knew he was fleeing from Yahweh (1:10). The only other time Jonah is the subject is in 4:5, where he, still seething from the city's salvation, "made" a hut in which to sulk while waiting to see what would happen to the city.

[92] Tertullian, *Against Marcion*, 2.24 (*ANF* 3:315).
[93] See Tertullian, *Against Marcion*, 2.14 (*ANF* 3:308–9).
[94] Tertullian, *Against Marcion*, 2.24 (*ANF* 3:316).
[95] Tertullian, *Against Marcion*, 2.24 (*ANF* 3:316).

Yahweh, however, also is the subject of the verb עָשָׂה. Yahweh is the Creator who "made" the sea and the dry land (1:9). The sailors confess in their prayer to him, "Just as you please, you do" (1:14). As he had in 1:15–16, now again Yahweh reveals that his good pleasure is that all people repent, believe, and so be saved (1 Tim 2:4). After seeing the good "works" of the converted Ninevites, God canceled his verdict that he threatened "to do to them, and he did not do [it]" (Jonah 3:10). Elsewhere in the book of Jonah, infinitive constructs that depict actions done by Yahweh always reach fruition, whereas infinitive constructs that describe the actions of people denote actions done in vain. The single exception to this usage is precisely here, when God does *not* carry out the evil he threatened "to do [לַעֲשׂוֹת] to them." The exception here highlights the exceptional grace of God in not executing judgment.[96]

Finally, that "God changed his verdict about the evil that he threatened to do to them" (3:10) calls for comment.[97] In sequence and language, this account of God's change parallels the events in Exodus 32. After Israel's golden-calf apostasy, Yahweh threatened to destroy the people, but then Moses interceded, and "Yahweh changed his verdict about the evil that he threatened to do to his people" (Ex 32:14). Later in Israel's history, this same phraseology occurs in Jer 26:3, 13, 19. There Yahweh first expresses this hope: "Perhaps they will listen and turn, each from his evil way, and I will change my verdict about the evil [וְנִחַמְתִּי אֶל־הָרָעָה] that I am intending to do to them because of the evil of their actions" (Jer 26:3). Then Jeremiah preached to the people: "Improve your ways and your actions, and listen to the voice of Yahweh your God. Then Yahweh will change his verdict about the evil that he threatened against you" (וְיִנָּחֵם יְהוָה אֶל־הָרָעָה אֲשֶׁר דִּבֶּר עֲלֵיכֶם, Jer 26:13). Lastly, the change is stated as a historical recollection from the time of Hezekiah, who feared Yahweh and prayed to him: "And Yahweh changed his verdict about the evil he threatened against them" (וַיִּנָּחֶם יְהוָה אֶל־הָרָעָה אֲשֶׁר־דִּבֶּר עֲלֵיהֶם, Jer 26:19). Jeremiah is referring to Micah 3:12, where that prophet warned:

> Therefore, because of you, Zion shall be plowed as a field,
> > and Jerusalem shall be ruins,
> > and the temple mount be forested hills.

Jer 26:19 reports that King Hezekiah responded to that prophecy and prayed for Yahweh to change his verdict about the announced disaster. The chapter goes on to indicate the efficacy of Hezekiah's prayer. The prophecy did not come to pass in Hezekiah's lifetime because Yahweh changed his verdict.[98]

These passages in Exodus and Jeremiah refer specifically to Israel. All the other passages where God changes his verdict about the evil that he intended

---

[96] See further the first textual note on 1:3.

[97] See further the excursus "When Yahweh Changes a Prior Verdict."

[98] For a similar narrative about Hezekiah and the prophet Isaiah, see 2 Ki 20:1–11 ǁ Is 38:1–8.

to do also refer to Israel alone (2 Sam 24:16; Jer 42:10; 1 Chr 21:15; the same idea underlies Judg 2:18; Amos 7:3, 6). The same reprieve that Yahweh granted Israel through Moses at the golden-calf apostasy and that he gave to Judah at the time of Hezekiah is now shown by Yahweh to the Gentile Ninevites. In fact, the only two OT passages that combine the elements of Yahweh "turning away from the fierceness of anger" (שׁוּב מֵחֲרוֹן אַפּ-) and "changing his verdict about evil" are Ex 32:12, where Moses pleads, "Turn away from the fierceness of your anger," and Jonah 3:9.

Shocking, indeed! The grace Yahweh elsewhere only shows to his chosen people Israel is now expanded to embrace the pagan world and their animals. Holy cow(s)! This anticipates the ever-widening scope of God's grace in the NT era, when the Gospel of his plenary forgiveness in Jesus Christ shall be heralded throughout the world to all peoples, even to the ends of the earth and to the close of the age.

Chrysostom calls upon Jeremiah 18 to explain Yahweh's mercy here:

> For God even preferred that His own prediction should fall to the ground, so that the city should not fall. Or rather, the prophecy did not even so fall to the ground. For if indeed while the men continued in the same wickedness, the sentence had not taken effect, some one perhaps might have brought a charge against what was uttered. But if when they had changed, and desisted from their iniquity, God also desisted from His wrath, who shall be able any longer to find fault with the prophecy, or to convict the things spoken of falsehood? The same law indeed which God had laid down from the beginning, publishing it to all men by the prophet [Jeremiah], was on that occasion strictly observed. What then is this law? "I shall speak a sentence," saith He, "concerning a nation or a kingdom, to pluck up, and to pull down, and to destroy it; and it shall be, that if they repent of their evil, I will also repent of the wrath which I said I would do unto them" [Jer 18:7–8]. Guarding then this law, he saved those who were converted and released from His wrath those who desisted from their wickedness.[99]

Yahweh is perfectly consistent with his promise in Jeremiah 18 when he applies it to Nineveh, maintains Chrysostom:

> The threatening effected the deliverance from the peril. The sentence of overthrow[100] put a stop to the overthrow. O strange and astonishing event! the sentence threatening death, brought forth life! The sentence after it was published [Jonah 3:4] became cancelled; the very opposite to that which takes place among temporal judges! for in their case the proclamation of the sentence causes it to become valid, is fully to ratify it; but on the contrary, with God, the publication of the sentence, caused it to be cancelled. For if it had not been published, the offenders would not have heard; and if they had not heard, they would not have repented, and if they had not repented, they would not have warded off the punishment, nor would they have obtained

---

[99] Chrysostom, *Homilies on the Statues*, 5.16 (*NPNF*[1] 9:376–77).

[100] Many translations render the substance of Jonah's sermon in 3:4 as "Nineveh shall be overthrown" (e.g., RSV, ESV, KJV, NKJV; similar are NASB and NIV).

that astonishing deliverance. For how is it less than astonishing, when the judge declares sentence, and the condemned discharge the sentence by their repentance![101]

In order to bring repentance and salvation, Yahweh declared a sentence of judgment against Nineveh (Jonah 3:4). When human judges issue their verdict, it is for the purpose of implementing the verdict. How remarkable, says Chrysostom, that Yahweh published his judgment for the purpose of sparing the guilty! The sentence was commuted, and those deserving death instead received everlasting life.

Origen makes a similar argument for mercy as Yahweh's ultimate purpose. He posits that the purpose of Jonah's prophecy against Nineveh is that the city would repent:

> God did not wish to sentence without saying anything, but *giving them the opportunity for repentance* [Wis Sol 12:10] and conversion, he sent a Hebrew prophet, so that, when he said, *still in three days*[102] *and Nineveh will be overthrown* [Jonah 3:4], those sentenced might not be sentenced, but would obtain the mercy of God by repenting.[103]

Origen argues that God's purpose all along was the repentance and salvation of Nineveh. Thus the account of the Ninevites in chapter 3 makes the same point as the psalm of Jonah in chapter 2, where he concludes, "Salvation belongs to Yahweh" (2:10 [ET 2:9]).

The remarkable turn of divine justice recorded with judicial language in Jonah 3:9–10 is displayed fully in Jesus Christ, the only sinless, righteous man, who nevertheless suffered the divine judgment deserved by the world of sinners. Yet the purpose of God's execution of that death sentence was to forgive and justify all who believe in him. By the death and resurrection of Jesus Christ, our sentence of death is canceled, and God's wrath is averted. God's verdict for us who believe is justification and everlasting life (e.g., Rom 5:12–21). The Ninevites' hope was realized: "God may turn and change his verdict and turn away from the fierceness of his anger so we will not perish" (Jonah 3:9). So too shall our hope be realized: "Therefore, since we have now been justified by his [Christ's] blood, how much more shall we be saved by him from the wrath [of God]" (Rom 5:9).

Summary of Scene 5

Little effort, poor skills, a short sermon—and total success! Even with crooked human writers, Yahweh writes straight. Jonah's message in 3:4 is concise and blunt. Jonah apparently hoped that the outcome would be the destruction of his hearers (see 4:1). His sermon says nothing explicit about

---

[101] Chrysostom, *Homilies on the Statues*, 5.16 (*NPNF*[1] 9:377).

[102] The LXX reads ἔτι τρεῖς ἡμέραι.

[103] Origen, *Homilies on Jeremiah*, 1.1.2, on Jer 1:1–10 (trans. John Clark Smith; The Fathers of the Church [Washington, D.C.: Catholic University of America Press, 1998] 97:3).

salvation and states no contingencies or qualifications depending on how the Ninevites respond. At face value, the prophecy seems to assume the people will ignore it. Yet in the next verse (3:5), the pagan Gentiles believe in ways that are simply amazing! The astonishing salvation of Gentiles through faith, by the power of the preached Word, will recur on a far larger scale throughout the NT era, and in subsequent world history, as countless Gentiles are grafted into the true Israel of God through faith in Jesus Christ (Rom 10:10–17; Gal 6:16).

Because of the double entendre of "be changed" (see the third textual note on 3:4), Jonah's prediction will be fulfilled whether Nineveh crumbles or repents. The verb "contains the irony of reversal."[104] Through repentance Nineveh is overturned, but in the way gracious Yahweh intends (4:2), not as Jonah wanted (4:1). From the Ninevites' perspective, the prophecy offered at least a glimmer of hope, a delay of "forty days" (3:4) during which time they could repent and see what would happen ("Who knows?" 3:9). From God's perspective, their repentance is an opportunity for him to change his verdict from judgment to salvation. But from Jonah's perspective, Nineveh's salvation overturns his prophecy and discredits him. Only able to see his own limited, self-serving perspective, Jonah becomes angry and confronts God with his feelings in chapter 4.

As Thomas Bolin notes: "The verbal and thematic links between Jer. 18.7–10 and Jon. 3.5–10 have been noticed for centuries."[105] Some scholars argue that the text from Jeremiah is the background for the scene in Jonah,[106] reasoning that the Ninevites function as a concrete narrative illustration of Jeremiah's abstract ideas. However, this is a weak reason to argue for dependence; one could just as easily propose that God caused the concrete events to happen first and provided the abstract explanation of the underlying theology later.[107] Moreover, this opinion overlooks the context of Jeremiah 18, where Yahweh's statement arises out of a narrative illustration, namely, Jeremiah's visit to the potter's house. Both Jonah 3 and Jeremiah 18 indicate that Yahweh is free to change his verdict from threatened destruction to salvation if the sinful people repent and return to him in faith.

In the design of the book of Jonah, the episode of the converted sailors in chapter 1 balances the episode of the converted Ninevites in chapter 3. Both plots follow the pattern of divine judgment upon unbelievers, the speaking of a word about or from Yahweh (1:9; 3:4), which causes repentance with sincere efforts to avoid calamity, and the people's change from unbelief to faith (1:16;

---

[104] Trible, *Rhetorical Criticism*, 190. What follows in the rest of this paragraph is, in large part, her analysis.

[105] Bolin, *Freedom beyond Forgiveness*, 141. In large part, the discussion in this paragraph follows Bolin (pp. 141–42).

[106] See, for example, Allen, *Joel, Obadiah, Jonah and Micah*, 193; Fretheim, *The Message of Jonah*, 105–6; Wolff, *Obadiah and Jonah*, 154.

[107] Jonah dates to the eighth century and Jeremiah to the late seventh and early sixth centuries BC.

3:5) correlates with the change from Yahweh's judgment to his salvation. For the seamen, the storm ceases (1:15); for the Ninevites God changes his verdict (3:10). Yet the move from ignorance to faith happens differently. For the sailors, recognition of Yahweh comes in stages and a number of events transpire between the word about Yahweh (1:9) and their worship of him (1:16). For the Ninevites, their recognition of Yahweh comes much more quickly, immediately after the preaching of Yahweh's Word (3:4–5).

The captain and the king share similar sentiments and vocabulary, tentative expressions of hope ("perhaps" in 1:6; "Who knows?" in 3:9), reference to the Deity as "God" (אֱלֹהִים, 1:6; 3:8–9), and the purpose clause "so we will not perish" (1:6; 3:9). Both Gentile commanders lead their people in repentance and faith. In worshiping, the sailors offer a sacrifice and make vows (1:16); in repenting, the Ninevites call a fast and put on sackcloth (3:5–8). Both Gentile responses are typical of Israelite piety.

The earliest rabbinical reference concerning the reception of Jonah's message in 3:8–10 is in the Mishnah, where the repentance of the Ninevites appears as the major example for repentance in general, and the Gentile Ninevites are portrayed as shining examples for all who would repent.[108] Yet there is no suggestion in Jonah 3 that later generations of Ninevites will be immune from judgment if they relapse into violence and evil. The prophecy of Nineveh's destruction by Nahum about 130 years later makes this abundantly clear.

But *these* Ninevites are spared. The conflict between Yahweh and these former idolaters is resolved. But as soon as chapter 4 begins, we discover that this closure regarding the converted Gentiles is only masquerading as a resolution to the book. The festering problem is not Nineveh, but the Israelite Jonah.

---

[108] Mishnah, *Ta'anith* 2:1 (Danby, *The Mishnah*, 195).

Excursus

When Yahweh Changes a Prior Verdict

The king of Nineveh decreed citywide acts of repentance in the hope ("Who knows?") that "God may turn and change his verdict and turn away from the fierceness of his anger so we will not perish" (3:9). That hope was realized when "God saw their works, that they turned from their evil way, and God changed his verdict about the evil that he threatened to do to them, and he did not do [it]" (3:10). Thus God changed his prior decision to destroy the city[1] and instead saved the inhabitants, who shall rise on the Last Day to everlasting life (Mt 12:41).[2]

The record of God's turn and change in Jonah 3:9–10 (see also 4:2) offers an opportunity to consider two different ways of looking at God: open theism and classical theism.[3] Since one major difference between these two theologies is how they understand OT texts depicting Yahweh's change of disposition or a prior decision, the bulk of this excursus will analyze these passages.[4] The amount of time and space devoted to these verses is necessary because the open theist believes they are to be taken so literally that they depict God as being limited in his ability to know the future. Traditional theism, however, has generally understood these texts as describing God in human language that is not to be taken as entirely literal, but at least partly as metaphorical. They are anthropomorphisms, that is, descriptions of God as having a human form and human characteristics.[5] More precisely, they are anthropopathisms, that is,

---

[1]   A key verb is the Niphal of נָחַם, translated as God may and did "change his verdict." It occurs in Jonah 3:9–10 and 4:2 as well as other OT passages. For its translation, see the second textual note on 3:9. Other common translations of it are that God may and did "repent" (Jonah 3:9 KJV) or "relent" (Jonah 3:9 ESV, NASB, NKJV). The following excursus does not depend on the exact translation choice, nor even on this verb alone. Other verbs and expressions in the context convey the same theological point, namely, the change in God's intent from executing judgment to bestowing salvation. These other verbs and expressions include that God "may turn [שׁוּב] … and turn away from [שׁוּב מִן] the fierceness of his anger" (3:9); that God "did not do" what he had threatened to do (3:10); and the OT creedal formula that Yahweh averts his wrath because he is "a gracious and merciful God, slow to anger and abounding in loyal love" (4:2).

[2]   See further the excursus "The Sign of Jonah."

[3]   In Lutheran circles the debate has been analyzed most recently by Maier, "Does God 'Repent' or Change His Mind?"

[4]   Much of this excursus is an adaptation of Reed Lessing, "Pastor, Does God Really Respond to My Prayers?" *Concordia Journal* 32 (2006): 256–73. Used by permission of *Concordia Journal*.

[5]   John Calvin, a traditional theist, posits what he believes Scripture means when it says that God changes his mind:

>   Surely its meaning is like that of all other modes of speaking that describe God for us in human terms. For because our weakness does not attain to his exalted state, the description of him that is given to us must be accommodated to our capacity so that we may

portrayals of God as if he had human emotions and thoughts; thus they do not negate the doctrine of the immutability of God and his will.[6] The biblical doctrine of God's immutability underlies the certainty and reliability of God's inerrant, efficacious Word. Both his warnings of judgment for unbelievers and his promises of forgiveness and mercy for repentant believers in Christ are trustworthy and true.

This excursus will draw on selected writings of Luther and offer insights that will indicate that open theists are wrong to deny God's omniscience and immutability. Yet also some classical theists build their discussions upon misguided categories. Some who overemphasize the sovereignty of God espouse double predestination—the view that God has determined the eternal fate of all people by electing some to salvation (as Scripture affirms) but also by electing or predestinating others to damnation (contrary to Scripture). Such overemphasis can also lead to the view that prayer is ineffectual.

Essential for the interpretation of biblical passages in which God changes his verdict are the categories of Law and Gospel, with a focus on Christ. God's purpose is for his Law work of judgment to prepare for his Gospel work of salvation. His warnings of condemnation for sinners stand firm. Yet for sinners who repent and believe in Christ, God's verdict changes from judgment to salvation. Jesus Christ is the reason why God can express toward repentant sinners his character as "a gracious and merciful God, slow to anger and abounding in loyal love" (Jonah 4:2). On the cross Jesus suffered the entirety of God's judgment against humanity's sin, and thus God's wrath is averted from all believers, including the Ninevites who "believed in God" (Jonah 3:5). For all in Christ, God has "change[d] his verdict … so we will not perish" (Jonah 3:9). It is not God himself, his nature, his attributes, or his will that changes. Rather, God's *disposition* toward us changes so that we are no longer objects of his wrath but recipients of his love in Christ. This love is also the basis for our confidence that prayer is effective: God hears our prayers and answers them according to his will, in harmony with his gracious promises in Christ.

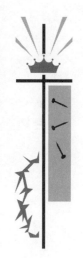

understand it. Now the mode of accommodation is for him to represent himself to us not as he is in himself, but as he seems to us. (Institutes of the Christian Religion, 1.17.13)

6   So Gerhard, "De Natura Dei," § 155, *Loci Theologici,* 1:314–15; Pieper, *Christian Dogmatics,* 1:440–41. See also FC SD III 57; IV 16, 32; V 17; VI 3, 15, 17.

Hunter, *The God Who Hears*, 52, writes: "My conviction is that references to God's 'repenting,' 'relenting' or 'changing his mind' in Scripture are figures of speech; technically speaking, they are anthropopathisms—expressions which explain God in terms usually used to describe human emotions."

Classical and Open Theism

In recent years "open theism" has sparked a considerable debate concerning the doctrine of God's immutability.[7] Those who advocate the "open" position have likened it to a new reformation, the uncovering of a biblical truth that has long been obscured. According to open theists, God has decided and determined some future matters, and these are settled, but other matters he has left for people to decide. These are not settled. Open theists deny God's omniscience and immutability, but they assert that this does not indicate a lack in God. God knows everything that can be known. The difference between their view and classical theism, they declare, is not the nature of God, but the nature of the future. The future is not something that has any reality; therefore, there is nothing there to be known.[8]

Richard Rice describes the "two basic convictions" of open theism: (1) love is the most important attribute of God, and (2) in addition to "care and commitment," love means "being sensitive and responsive." In his responsive love, God flexibly interacts with his creatures to accomplish his objectives so that "history is the combined result of what God and his creatures decide to do."[9] According to open theists, this dependence of God on his creation does not detract from his greatness. Rather, it enhances his greatness, since it takes an even greater God to be able to risk and to grow along with his creatures in a genuine relationship. A frozen, unchangeable God is inferior to the "God of the possible."[10]

Open theists contend that the reason the church has clung to classical theism is that in its infancy, Christian theology came under the influence of Greek

---

[7] Several of the standard works of open theists are Pinnock, Rice, Sanders, Hasker, and Basinger, *The Openness of God: A Biblical Challenge to the Traditional Understanding of God*; Boyd, *God of the Possible: A Biblical Introduction to the Open View of God*; and Pinnock, *Most Moved Mover: A Theology of God's Openness.* For an overview of the issues involved, see Erickson, *What Does God Know and When Does He Know It? The Current Controversy over Divine Foreknowledge.* Erickson weighs the arguments by considering hermeneutical issues, the historical development of the doctrine of divine knowledge, the philosophical suppositions of both open and classical theism, and the practical implications of the two competing views. In doing so, the book covers much more than just God's knowledge. It discusses his immutability, impassibility, and relationship to time.

[8] Open theism differs from process theology in at least two important ways. The first is that process theology believes God is dependent on the world, whereas open theism does not. The second is that according to process theology, God never acts unilaterally, whereas in open theism, God can and does sometimes intervene in the world, even overriding the will of people. Regarding these issues, Hasker ("A Philosophical Perspective," in Pinnock et al., *The Openness of God*, 134–54, especially p. 134) helpfully distinguishes between five theories about God's foreknowledge and action in the world: (1) theological determinism (Calvinism); (2) middle knowledge (Molinism), which "attributes libertarian (indeterministic) freedom to human beings and yet retains a strong doctrine of divine providential control"; (3) simple foreknowledge, in which God has complete knowledge of the future but not the knowledge of all possibilities of the future; (4) open theism; (5) process theology.

[9] Rice, "Biblical Support for a New Perspective," in Pinnock et al., *The Openness of God*, 15–16.

[10] See Boyd, *God of the Possible*, 126–28.

philosophy. Because many of the early church fathers lived in an intellectual atmosphere dominated by Greek philosophy, especially middle Platonism, they read the Scriptures in light of God as a perfect being who is timeless, transcendent, immutable, and impassible. Among other things, this leads to equating God's faithfulness with the doctrine of his immutability. (It is true that in classical theism, God's unswerving faithfulness is linked to the immutability of his will.)

Open theism teaches that people have the ability to assert their own will in such a way as to change God and modify the course of history. Gregory Boyd writes: "In the open view, God has sovereignly ordained that prayer be one of our central means of influencing what transpires in history."[11] He also says: "The open view is able to declare, without qualification or inconsistency, that some of the future *genuinely depends on prayer*."[12]

According to classical theists, however, the omniscient God knows the future in its entirety. The Scriptures certainly affirm this (e.g., Is 41:22–23; 46:9–10; Jn 21:17; 1 Jn 3:20). God hears and answers prayer according to his will, but this does not change God's immutable will, nor does it undermine the permanency of his Word, which endures forever.[a]

(a) Is 40:8; 54:10; Pss 102:26–28 (ET 102:25–27); 119:89, 160; Prov 19:21; Mk 9:44; Jn 3:36; 1 Pet 1:25

As a corollary, some classical theists also infer that all things (including evil ones) have been predetermined from eternity and that God is unpersuadable, for what God foreknows must happen. However, that corollary is not biblical. Scripture asserts that God desires all to be saved (1 Tim 2:4), has elected some to salvation (Rom 8:29–30; Eph 1:3–12), and responds to prayer (Mt 7:7, 11; Jn 14:13–14; 15:7). But God is not the author of evil, nor has he predestined anyone to damnation; no Scripture passages support those ideas.

Open theists read texts where Yahweh changes his disposition or a previous decision in a literal way and make this their paradigm for understanding the nature of God.

Classical theists understand these same texts as at least partly figurative or metaphorical. Biblical texts attributing change to God describe how he *appears* to us; they do not depict God as he really is in himself. To us it *looks* like God changes, but he really does not.[13] A key text is Mal 3:6: "I, Yahweh, do not change" (see also James 1:17, and see below on Num 23:19; 1 Sam 15:29). Prayer is indeed heard and answered by God according to his will and his promises in Scripture, but prayer is not a way to manipulate God into doing

---

[11] Boyd, *God of the Possible*, 97.

[12] Boyd, *God of the Possible*, 95.

[13] This appears to be Maier's answer to the question that is the title of his article, "Does God 'Repent' or Change His Mind?" For example, Maier comments in this way on Exodus 32: "God is fully in control of the situation. He is acting and speaking according to a preconceived purpose and goal, and having his will accomplished, as was foreordained" (p. 143). Maier's answer to the question appears to be no. He believes that texts portraying God's change are best understood as being "anthropomorphic and anthropopathic" (p. 143).

what we want him to do nor a way for us to shape history according to our own desires (cf. Lk 22:42).

Yahweh May or May Not Change a Prior Verdict

An analysis of the texts that speak of Yahweh changing or not changing his disposition or one of his previous decisions gets to the heart of the debate, yet in-depth study of the language of such texts is one of the most neglected areas of biblical scholarship. Within the last two hundred years, only one monograph and several articles have been devoted to the Niphal of נחם, a key verb in passages where God "changes his verdict, repents, relents."[14] OT theologies treat the subject only in passing, if at all.[15] Even commentaries on those biblical books that contain some of the nearly forty explicit references to a divine change of disposition or decision tend to skip past this term with little or no comment. A major exception is the excursus entitled "When God Repents" in the commentary on Amos by Francis Andersen and David Noel Freedman.[16]

This neglect of the Niphal of נחם is not a recent development. As early as the Septuagint and the Targumim, there is evidence that translators had difficulty coming to terms with this language. Through the centuries, Jewish and Christian interpretations that have upheld the doctrine of God's immutability have sometimes struggled with passages where he reverses a previous decision and changes his disposition toward people. These passages pose a challenge for those who go beyond Scripture by assuming that God determines every situation (even evil) and is unresponsive to human repentance and prayer. Similar factors may account at least in part for the contemporary neglect of verses with this verb.

The KJV, followed by the RSV, usually translates the Niphal of נחם with "repent." More recent translations have sought other words; the most common is "relent," but others include "regret" (e.g., 1 Sam 15:11 ESV), "be sorry" (e.g., Gen 6:6 ESV), "be grieved" (e.g., 1 Sam 15:11 NIV), "show compassion" (Jer 15:6 NIV), "think better of" (e.g., 2 Sam 24:16 JB), "change one's mind" (e.g., 1 Sam 15:29 NIV), and "go back on one's word" (e.g., 1 Sam 15:29 JB). The essence of the verb seems to be the reversal of a decision or verdict as well as a change in disposition toward people. Hans Walter Wolff suggests that "to repent concerning" (the Niphal of נחם with עַל) "designates a change of mind prompted

[14] Jeremias, *Die Reue Gottes: Aspekte alttestamentlicher Gottesvorstellung*; Van Dyke Parunak, "A Semantic Survey of *NḤM*"; H. J. Stoebe, "נחם," *TLOT* 2:734–39; Fretheim, "The Repentance of God."

[15] See, for example, Rowley, *The Faith of Israel*, 67, and Jacob, *Theology of the Old Testament*, 291. Von Rad, *Old Testament Theology*, 2:198–99, deals with the subject only in passing in his comments on Jeremiah 18. Schultz, *Old Testament Theology*, 2:109–10, briefly comments: "The repentance of God ... grows into the assured conviction that human development is not for Him an empty, indifferent spectacle, that it is just this inner immutability of His being which excludes that dull, dead unchangeableness which remains outwardly the same, however much circumstances may change."

[16] Andersen and Freedman, *Amos*, 638–79.

by the emotions, a turning away from an earlier decision on the part of someone deeply moved."[17] Thus, the word includes not only a change of attitude, but a reversal in action toward people who themselves have changed.

The verb נָחַם appears fifty-one times in the OT in Piel forms ("to comfort, console") and twice in Pual forms ("be comforted"). In Piel texts, Yahweh or people are variously presented as providing (or not providing) comfort to others in the face of death, misfortune, or divine anger.[b] Some passages use the Piel of נָחַם in parallel with נוּד, "to nod (the head); lament (the dead); show sympathy."[18] This parallelism seems to indicate that the comfort involves a deeply emotional quality. As H. van Dyke Parunak points out, "sympathetic pain, or 'compassion,' lies at the heart of the biblical concept of comfort."[19]

Of primary interest here, however, are the occurrences of נָחַם in the Niphal and the Hithpael, since these are the forms of the verb used to refer to Yahweh changing (or not changing) his disposition or a prior decision. The Niphal occurs forty-eight times in the OT, and the Hithpael seven times. Of this total of fifty-five occurrences, thirty-five (thirty-four Niphal occurrences and one Hithpael) are used in reference to God changing his disposition or verdict.[20]

The expression that Yahweh does or does not change his previous disposition or decision operates within numerous OT time periods and a wide variety of OT genres.[21] It appears at some of the key junctures in the OT canon: the flood story (Gen 6:6–7), the Sinai revelation (Ex 32:12, 14), and the institution of the monarchy (1 Sam 15:11, 29, 35). Its appearance in psalmody and creedal statements seals its pivotal status in Yahweh's revelation of himself (see, e.g., Jer 18:7–10; Joel 2:13; Jonah 4:2; Ps 106:45).

Approaching this idiom as an anthropomorphism or anthropopathism involves metaphor. Because of the enormous gulf between God and us, his fallen creatures, James Voelz writes: "Metaphor is the essential means by which we are able to make statements about God."[22] For God to condescend to speak to us in the Scriptures about himself in language we can understand requires at least some use of metaphor. An extended discussion on metaphor is not possi-

(b) See, e.g., Is 52:9; Job 42:11; Ps 23:4; Ruth 2:13; Lam 1:17; 2:13; 1 Chr 7:22

---

[17] Wolff, *Joel and Amos*, 298. Efforts to discover the meaning of the word through its etymology have not been successful. The most reliable method for determining word meaning is a careful examination of contextual usage (see, e.g., Barr, *The Semantics of Biblical Language*, 116–17). The interpreter should rely on etymology only if the context indicates that the speaker or writer used the word with an awareness of its etymology or if a word is rare and attested in only a few contexts that may not be clear or helpful.

[18] This parallelism occurs in Is 51:19; Nah 3:7; Ps 69:21 (ET 69:20); Job 2:11, 42:11.

[19] Van Dyke Parunak, "A Semantic Survey of *NHM*," 517.

[20] With God as subject, the Hithpael can mean "have compassion" (Deut 32:36; Ps 135:14) or "take vengeance" (Ezek 5:13). Only in Num 23:19 does the Hithpael pertain to a change of verdict by Yahweh, so that is the only Hithpael passage included in this total and considered below. Also, because the Niphal in Is 1:24 means "take vengeance," that passage is excluded from the total and the discussion.

[21] This insight into approaching נָחַם by means of metaphor, as well as the discussion of its usages in the OT follows, to some extent, Fretheim, "The Repentance of God," 53–59.

[22] Voelz, *What Does This Mean?* 170.

ble here,[23] yet for the purposes of this discussion a literary metaphor is defined as a figure of speech that draws a comparison between two things. Prime examples are the parabolic sayings of Jesus: "The kingdom of heaven is like …" (e.g., Mt 13:24). Metaphorical language for God himself says, in effect, "God is like …"

All metaphors inherently have continuity with the subject depicted, as well as discontinuity. That is, every metaphor speaks both a "yes" and a "no"—an "is" and an "is not." When Jesus says, "The kingdom of heaven is like … ," in some respects the comparison is literally true, but in other aspects the comparison breaks down and must not be taken literally.[24] Interpreters must seek to discern the extent to which the correspondence is literal and how it is merely figurative. There is danger on either side. The interpreter must not go too far in either direction: interpreting the metaphor literally in every respect or denying that there is any essential correspondence between the language and the reality it describes.

When Yahweh Does Not Change His Verdict

Most of the thirty-five OT passages in which the Niphal or the Hithpael of נָחַם is used in reference to Yahweh changing his disposition or a prior decision affirm that he does change in this way. However, the statement that he does *not* change his disposition or a previous decision appears in seven texts.[c] Of these, three describe Yahweh's refusal to change his decision concerning the destruction of Jerusalem in 587 BC (Jer 4:28; Ezek 24:14; Zech 8:14). Jer 20:16 speaks of Yahweh not changing his prior decision to destroy Sodom and Gomorrah. These texts speak the "no" of the metaphor. Yahweh carried out his threats to destroy those cities. Ps 110:4 speaks of his unwillingness to change Christ the Lord's eternal priesthood according to the order of Melchizedek (cf. Hebrews 5–7). His promises in Christ also stand firm.

The remaining two verses in which Yahweh refuses to change his disposition or a decision are Num 23:19 and 1 Sam 15:29. They appear to place Yah-

(c) Num 23:19; 1 Sam 15:29; Jer 4:28; 20:16; Ezek 24:14; Zech 8:14; Ps 110:4

---

[23] Recent movements in linguistic philosophy and literary criticism have engendered a lively discussion on the subject and definition of metaphor. For overviews, see Miall, *Metaphor: Problems and Perspectives*, and Levin, *The Semantics of Metaphor*. There are two aspects of metaphor: the "tenor" (idea or object described) and the "vehicle" (image used to depict it). The interaction of these two aspects provides meaning for the metaphor. This is the terminology of Richards, *The Philosophy of Rhetoric*, 96–97. Soskice, *Metaphor and Religious Language*, 24, groups metaphor theories under three headings: "those that see metaphor as a decorative way of saying what could be said literally [substitution theories]; those that see metaphor as original not in what it says but in the affective impact it has [emotive theories]; and those that see metaphor as a unique cognitive vehicle enabling one to say things that can be said in no other way [incremental theories]" (see her further description of those theories on pp. 24–32). She writes: "Metaphor should be treated as fully cognitive and capable of saying that which may be said in no other way" (p. 44).

[24] For example, it would be wrong to interpret the parable of the Sower (Mt 13:3–9, 18–23) to mean that Jesus calls pastors to cast literal seed into the pews when they preach or that parishioners must beware of literal birds that might deprive them of the Gospel.

weh's unwillingness to change within a statement of a standard principle: "God is not a man … that he would change his will" (Num 23:19; 1 Sam 15:29 is similar). That principle understands "a man" as sinful and unreliable since the fall (Genesis 3), so it does not negate the fact that God the Son became incarnate as a sinless and perfect man in the person of Jesus Christ. Because some interpreters cite these two passages to refute the idea that Yahweh can ever change his verdict, a closer examination of each text is warranted.

Num 23:19 is set within the larger context of the Balaam narrative located in Numbers 22–24. Balaam, having been hired by Balak, the king of Moab, to curse the Israelites, instead pronounces a series of four oracles of blessing upon them. The text under consideration is within the second of these oracles. In his defiance of Balak, Balaam defends his action:

> God is not a man that he should lie
>   or a son of man that he would change his will [וְיִתְנֶחָם].
> When he has said something, will he not do it?
>   When he has spoken, will he not fulfill it?
> Behold, I have received [a command] to bless.
>   He has blessed, and I cannot turn it back. (Num 23:19–20)

The four lines in Num 23:19 emphasize an important difference between Yahweh and people. The first statement, "God is not a man that he should lie," is reinforced by the second, parallel statement, "or a son of man [a human being] that he would change his will [יִתְנֶחָם]." Similarly, the first rhetorical question, "When he has said something, will he not do it?" is reinforced by the second question, "When he has spoken, will he not fulfill it?" Unlike sinful humans, Yahweh is not capricious in distributing or revoking blessings and curses. Since he has promised to bless Abraham's descendents (Gen 12:2–3), he will not change this decision and remove his blessing. Here again we see the "no" of the metaphor. Yahweh has made an unconditional promise of grace for Abraham and his offspring, and he will never revoke it, but will fulfill it in Jesus Christ, the "Son of Abraham" (Mt 1:1; cf. Num 24:17). This promise now stands fulfilled, for all baptized believers in Christ are blessed children of Abraham (Gal 3:26–29).

1 Sam 15:29 is primarily focused upon the events surrounding Yahweh's final rejection of Saul in response to the king's unfaithfulness concerning the Amalekites. After Saul defies Yahweh's instructions, Yahweh informs Samuel that he regrets making Saul king and will give the kingdom to another. 1 Sam 15:29 reads: "And also the Glory of Israel will not lie or change his decision [וְלֹא יִנָּחֵם], for he is not a man that he should change his decision [לְהִנָּחֵם]." 1 Samuel 15 is unique in this discussion because 1 Sam 15:29 uses the Niphal of נָחַם and appears to deny Yahweh's willingness to rescind any previous decision, but this verse falls between two other verses with the Niphal of נָחַם that each state that Yahweh "regretted" making Saul king (1 Sam 15:11, 35). Thus, as with Num 23:19, so also 1 Sam 15:29 must be interpreted as a specific refusal by Yahweh to change one particular decision—in this case, his choice of

David as Israel's new king. Of course, the line of this new king will eventuate in the Messiah, the Son of David, the eternal King.

In both Num 23:19 and 1 Sam 15:29, the expression that God is not a man that he should change his decision is used as a response by a prophet to someone seeking to persuade Yahweh to reverse a specific previous decision that involved his election of Israel, leading to the Savior of all peoples, Jesus Christ. In both cases, the prophet responds in a way that affirms Yahweh's unswerving commitment to his previous decision. When we consider the significance of these two divine choices for Israel—the promise to Abraham of blessing and the election of David as king—it is not difficult to understand why God declared the inviolability of these decisions and the impossibility of a change of his will concerning them.

The covenant Yahweh established with Abraham is foundational to the promise he makes to David, since his covenant with Abraham included the promise of a future king. In Gen 17:6, Yahweh says to the patriarch, "And kings will go forth from you." Following Yahweh's promise to David of an everlasting dynasty (2 Sam 7:4–17; see also 1 Chr 17:3–15), 2 Sam 7:18–19 states: "Then King David went in and sat before Yahweh, and he said: 'Who am I, O Lord Yahweh, and what is my house, that you have brought me this far? And as if this were too little in your sight, O Lord Yahweh, you have also spoken about the house of your servant in the distant future. Is this your usual way of dealing with man, O Lord Yahweh?' " The phrase translated "your usual way of dealing with man" is תּוֹרַת הָאָדָם. Here "Torah" is best understood as the "decree" that Yahweh has established for all people in Christ.[25]

Reinforcing the connection between the divine promises to Abraham and David is the use of "Lord Yahweh" (אֲדֹנָי יְהוִה) seven times in 2 Sam 7:18–20, 22, 28–29. This compound of the divine name was also used in the pivotal covenant of Yahweh with Abram in Gen 15:2, 8. It occurs only seven other times in other historical books, but nowhere else in Genesis or 1 and 2 Samuel. Its repeated use in both the promise to Abram in Genesis 15 and in the Davidic covenant of promise in 2 Samuel 7 is too striking to be accidental and without special reason: the two covenants are thereby drawn into a closer relationship. The plan of Yahweh that began with Abraham continues with David and eventuates in Jesus Christ.

Thus Num 23:19 and 1 Sam 15:29 express the "no" aspect of the metaphor. Yahweh is not a sinful, fickle human. He does not change his will and decision to grant blessing for all humanity through the Savior to be born from the line of Abraham and David. Yahweh is not capricious, leaving people in a perpetual state of anxiety regarding the course of his actions. His unconditional promises to Abraham and David are the foundation of the NT kerygma of Jesus, the Christ (see, e.g., Lk 1:54–55; 2:4; Gal 3:29).

---

[25] See Kaiser, "The Blessing of David: A Charter for Humanity."

When Yahweh Does Change His Verdict

The "yes" of the metaphor is located in Yahweh's response to human disobedience, human repentance, or intercessory prayer. God can change his disposition and his actions in the world. Texts in Genesis, Exodus, Jeremiah, Joel, and Jonah will inform this discussion and provide important insights into the "yes" aspect of the metaphor.

The first reference in the OT to Yahweh's change of disposition or of a previous decision occurs in Genesis 6–9. The spread of sin introduced in Genesis 3 reaches a climax as Gen 6:5 states that every thought of the human heart is continuously evil. This statement provides a clear theological reason for Yahweh sending the flood. Gen 6:6 then states: "Yahweh regretted [וַיִּנָּחֶם] that he had made mankind on the earth, and he was deeply saddened in his heart [וַיִּתְעַצֵּב אֶל־לִבּוֹ]." This divine sorrow that accompanied the recollection of his previous action is expressed by the Hithpael of עָצַב, "have pain, be grieved, be deeply saddened."[26] The phrase "in his heart" further emphasizes this divine grief.[27] The continuous evil emanating from the hearts of all people, according to Gen 6:5, is thus contrasted in Gen 6:6 with what Franz Delitzsch calls Yahweh's "heart-piercing sorrow."[28] It is only with this sense of deep grief that Yahweh decides to destroy all people and animals, with the exception of Noah and his family and the animals in the ark.[29] By thus revealing Yahweh's sorrow over the situation, Gen 6:6 demonstrates that Yahweh does not delight in condemning sinners, but rather seeks their repentance and salvation (Ezek 18:23, 32). He grieves that he must judge. The "yes" of the metaphor is located in the human and divine pathos that often accompanies a decision that ends a relationship. Yahweh's mercy may give way to judgment because of human sin. This is in accord with his unchanging will, expressed in his Law.

Yet Yahweh may also change from judgment to grace—even despite the ever-present sin of people. This is in accord with his unchanging will, expressed in his Gospel. In Ex 32:7–10, he informs Moses of Israel's idolatry with the golden calf. Yahweh's anger is evident as he disowns Israel by telling Moses that they are "*your* people, whom *you* brought up from the land of Egypt" (Ex 32:7). Yahweh then announces his intention to annihilate the nation (Ex 32:10). However, Moses intercedes for the people and offers a series of reasons why

---

[26] This is the only time that נָחַם and עָצַב occur together in the OT. Wenham points out that the root עצב is most often "used to express the most intense form of human emotion, a mixture of rage and bitter anguish" (*Genesis 1–15*, 144).

[27] The word לֵב, "heart," does not primarily mean the seat of emotions; rather, it points to one's decision, will, attitude, or inner life. See H.-J. Fabry, "לֵב," *TDOT* 7:399–437.

[28] Delitzsch, *A New Commentary on Genesis*, 1:233.

[29] Wenham, *Story as Torah*, 34, notes:

> The flood is presented as a great act of decreation, destroying human and animal life, covering the plants and mountains, so that the earth returns to the watery chaos that existed before the second day of creation. Noah, the survivor of this chaos, becomes as it were another Adam, the forefather of the human race after the flood.

Yahweh should reconsider (Ex 32:11–13). Here Moses uses a Niphal imperative of נחם with the clause "turn from the fierceness of your anger" in a call for
Yahweh to relent and reconsider.[30] Yahweh does change his verdict and spares
Israel. Yahweh's willingness to change in response to the intercessory prayer
of Moses is responsible for the continued existence of Israel, leading to the
eventual birth of Jesus (Rom 9:5), the great High Priest, whose intercession
saves all who believe in him (Hebrews 5–7). The "yes" of the metaphor is located in Yahweh's decision to respond to human prayer for Christ's sake, so
that his grace overrides his righteous judgment of human sin (cf. Rom 5:20).

No other book in the OT contains as many references to Yahweh's changes
of previous decisions as does Jeremiah.[31] Perhaps the most significant passage
dealing with Yahweh's willingness to change his verdict is in Jeremiah 18. This
chapter does not speak of Yahweh's sovereignty as his complete control over
passive "clay" as if he fashions some people for the purpose of destroying them.
Rather, it describes his freedom and ability to recreate out of corrupted material a new vessel according to his good will and pleasure. William Holladay
compares the force of the spinning clay to human obstinacy: "Because of the
centrifugal force developed on the wheel the clay presses against the hands of
the potter. … Though he [God] is sovereign, the people have a will of their own
which they exert against him."[32] Yet despite the corrupted human will, Yahweh
uses the Niphal of נחם to say that if a people responds to his Word by repenting of its evil, he will change his verdict about its threatened destruction (Jer
18:8). Conversely, if he promises to build up a people, but that nation refuses
to listen to his voice, he will change his decision about the good he had promised
to do to it (Jer 18:10). The "yes" of the metaphor is located in God's revealed
will that he takes into consideration the human response to his Word (either repentance or unbelief) when he shapes his future actions for or against people.

The Niphal of נחם is also used in Joel 2:1–17 in an oracle against Judah
that has two sections. Joel 2:1–11 contains a description of the invasion and
destruction of Judah that will accompany the coming of "the Day of Yahweh"
(Joel 2:1, 11). The graphic tone of these verses emphasizes the certainty and
finality of the coming destruction. Yet even as Joel envisions the final phase of

---

[30] The only other verse in the OT with a Niphal imperative of נחם is Ps 90:13, in a psalm by
Moses (Ps 90:1 [ET superscription]).

[31] For example, in Jer 22:1–5 Yahweh's future action is shaped by the response of human
beings to his Word. He reviews some of the typical commands in the Torah and says, "For if
you indeed carry out this Word, then kings who sit on David's throne will come through the
gates of this palace, riding in chariots and on horses. … But if you do not listen to these
words, I swear by myself, declares Yahweh, that this palace will become a ruin" (Jer 22:4–5).
So one possible future action is judgment, but this has not been predetermined from eternity; rather, this judgment upon Judah has arisen because of the nation's infidelity. At the same
time, Yahweh's constant, unconditional Gospel promise is always at work through his Word,
seeking to lead hearers to repentance and faith. Even in such times calling for judgment, his
proper work is to forgive and save repentant sinners.

[32] Holladay, *Jeremiah 1*, 515.

the invasion, he recognizes the possibility that Yahweh might change his decision if Israel will repent. In order to convey the reason why Yahweh may yet change, Joel uses a well-known confessional formula. Thomas Dozeman states that Joel's "confession of Yahweh's gracious character is a hinge in the prophet's speech between the finality of the divine judgment that was reflected in the description of the Day of Yahweh in Joel 2:1–11 and hope in Joel 2:14."[33]

Joel's confessional saying (2:13) has the same five affirmations describing Yahweh that Jonah uses in 4:2. The first is the adjective חַנּוּן, usually translated "gracious."[34] Next, Joel describes Yahweh as רַחוּם, normally translated "merciful," but since the cognate verb (the Piel of רָחַם) means "have compassion," the adjective may be translated "compassionate."[35] Yahweh is then described as "slow to anger."[36] Then Yahweh is described as possessing great חֶסֶד, one of the most significant words in the OT. While there is some debate concerning the precise meaning of the term, it is frequently used to describe, directly or indirectly, Yahweh's "faithfulness" and "loyal love" according to his covenant with Abraham. Finally, Yahweh is described as "changing his verdict about evil." By placing the last phrase with the Niphal of נָחַם alongside Yahweh's other attributes, Joel is stating that Yahweh is so great in grace, mercy, patience, and loyal love that he is willing to forgive a break in the relationship. Yahweh, in response to human repentance, changes a prior decision of judgment (Joel 2:1–11) and instead has mercy on his people and blesses them (Joel 2:18–27). The fact that he did this in the book of Joel is as sure as the fact that he is gracious, compassionate, slow to anger, and great in loyal, steadfast loving-kindness. The "yes" of this metaphor in Joel is located in Yahweh's characteristic graciousness and mercy, which leads him to withhold judgment even when it is well-deserved and instead to forgive and love his repentant people.

Following that fivefold confession of Yahweh's characteristics (Joel 2:13), the prophet Joel again uses the Niphal of נָחַם (2:14) to express the possibility that Yahweh may change his previous decision. Preceding it in 2:14 he asks, מִי יוֹדֵעַ, "Who knows?"[37] A comparable use of this expression is in Jonah 3:9, where the king of Nineveh commands his people to pray fervently in the hope that Yahweh may change his previous decision announced by Jonah in 3:4. The king employs the Niphal of נָחַם as a way to seek Yahweh's grace (Jonah 3:9),

---

[33] Dozeman, "Inner-Biblical Interpretation of Yahweh's Gracious and Compassionate Character," 212.

[34] With the exception of Ps 112:4, the adjective only describes Yahweh. In these contexts, חַנּוּן is used to denote an active interest in the well-being of his people.

[35] Of the thirteen uses of this adjective in the OT, twelve refer to Yahweh. Since the adjective and verb are related to the noun רֶחֶם, "womb," they may connote motherly compassion as well as fatherly mercy.

[36] This phrase is anthropomorphic in that the word translated "anger" (אַף) may also denote "nose." The picture is of Yahweh slowly drawing a deep breath as he calms his wrath.

[37] A brief look at this expression indicates that often in the OT people used this term to indicate their humility when they asked Yahweh to change his course of action. See the first textual note and the commentary on Jonah 3:9.

just as Joel does in 2:14. Those who pray this way are asking Yahweh to change from Law to Gospel. They believe his "anger lasts for a moment, his favor a lifetime" (Ps 30:6) and that Yahweh does not "take pleasure in the death of anyone," but desires people to repent and live (Ezek 18:32; cf. 2 Pet 3:9).[38]

These texts from Genesis, Exodus, Numbers, 1 Samuel, Jeremiah, Joel, and Jonah affirm two complementary aspects in the OT understanding of Yahweh. First, the unchangeable nature of Yahweh and the immutability of his will assure us that his gracious promises are trustworthy and certain, as confirmed by their fulfillment in Jesus Christ. These promises to Abraham and David form the backbone of the OT narrative, "an everlasting covenant" (Gen 17:7). No one and nothing will separate Yahweh's people from his love (cf. Rom 8:31–39). This is the "no" of the metaphor: Yahweh's faithfulness to his promises and to his ultimate purposes in Christ knows no change. He is God, not an unreliable man.

The "yes" of the metaphor indicates that the God of Israel was not an unfeeling, indifferent Deity. Yahweh enters into a real relationship with his chosen nation in which his love compels him to be responsive. He must punish those who do not believe, yet he is a compassionate God who in order to demonstrate his abounding love is willing to change prior decisions of judgment when people repent. This is particularly clear in texts where Yahweh's change is rooted in his attributes of deep compassion and mercy. The "yes" is that God is a gracious and relational God, as manifested supremely in the incarnation and earthly ministry of Jesus Christ among us.

The OT is not ashamed to say that Yahweh can reverse prior decisions depending on how Israel may respond to his Word. He is responsive to what is happening and can adjust his actions. *This means Yahweh is not an impersonal or deterministic force; rather, he relates to people.* This is at least one reason for Israel's aniconic perspective, since idols do not change (cf. Jer 10:3–5; Ps 115:4–7). Understood this way, the prohibition of images is concerned with protecting Yahweh's relatedness and not just his transcendence. One of the characteristics of the gods of the nations is that they cannot be moved or affected by anything (cf. 1 Ki 18:27–29).[39]

---

[38] See the first textual note and the commentary on Jonah 3:9.

[39] Andersen and Freedman, *Amos*, 642, 644, reflecting on the use of םחנ, write:

> Just as there is an important and unbridgeable distance between Yahweh and the gods of Canaan, or those of Mesopotamia or Egypt or Greece or Rome, so there is at least an equal or greater distance from an Aristotelian unmoved mover, or even a Platonic Idea (or Ideal). The biblical God is always and uncompromisingly personal.

Andersen and Freedman also opine that an "essential feature of biblical theology" is "the biblical interpretation of the divine status and involvement in human affairs" (p. 641). Also helpful is the discussion by Bolin in *Freedom beyond Forgiveness*, 141–45. Roberts, "A Christian Perspective on Prophetic Prediction," 243, comments: "The biblical God, unlike the static, eternally unchanging god of Greek philosophy, can change his mind. He repents of proposed plans of action, he reacts to the changing attitudes of his human subjects, and this may result in a divinely inspired prediction failing to materialize."

The confession that Yahweh can and does change his disposition toward people as he works through Law and Gospel highlights the priority of his grace (Joel 2:13; Jonah 4:2). His willingness to avert judgment when people repent and believe in him and his constant availability for answering prayers uttered in faith stand in the service of his unchanging divine intention to bless all the families of the earth through Abraham (Gen 12:3) and his Seed (Galatians 3). The Niphal of נחם therefore reflects the extent to which Yahweh will go in order to fulfill his constant salvific purpose.

Conclusion

Yahweh is constant. God will not fail to carry out his Law's threats of eternal damnation for unbelievers. Yet his promises too are certain. Nothing can deter him from fulfilling his gracious promises to Abraham and David. This is the Gospel, and thus the NT affirms, "Jesus Christ is the same yesterday and today and forever" (Heb 13:8). God is eternally resolute with respect to his grace.

If God's people apostatize, his favor turns to wrath. Yet when people repent, he changes his disposition toward them from anger to mercy. He responds to prayer and can change his actions on earth (Jonah 3:5–10).

The issues raised in this excursus are far from being merely academic. Important matters of faith and practice are involved, especially regarding conversion and prayer. Does God desire all people to repent and believe in Christ? The answer is a resounding yes! God works through his Word to grant repentance, faith, and life everlasting. Can God change his actions, even the course of earthly history? Again, Scripture answers in the affirmative.

As Christians, we may ask, "Does God really respond to our prayers?" Any answer must wrestle with the biblical doctrine of the immutability of God and his will. Is he unchanging in such a way that prayers are boomerangs that fly back only to form and shape his people? Or is God authentically open to changing a previous decision? Bruce Ware acknowledges this tension in Christian prayer: "Open theists are certainly right to seek to ground and embrace the *real relationship* between God and his human creatures, particularly his own people. Classical theism is vulnerable at this point and is in need of some correctives."[40] At the same time, Ware correctly argues that we must not discard the whole of classical theism.[41] We must retain the doctrines of God's immutability and omniscience. His will remains constant, and his Word is trustworthy and true.

---

[40] Ware, *God's Lesser Glory*, 164.

[41] Ware, "An Evangelical Reformulation of the Doctrine of the Immutability of God," 439. Ware anchors this argument in an observation of Anselm, whom he paraphrases as saying, "one's essence need not change as a result of changing relationships with others" (see Anselm, *Monologion*, chap. 25, in *Anselm of Canterbury* [trans. and ed. Jasper Hopkins and Herbert Richardson; London: SCM Press, 1974], 1:40–41).

The open theist extrapolates from the "yes" of the metaphor to suppose that the future is unknown even to God. However, that reduces the infinite God to the level of his finite and fallible creatures. The classical theist emphasizes the "no" of the metaphor, yet also must take into consideration biblical passages with the "yes." To be faithful to the whole of Scripture, we must assent to all that it reveals about God, holding both the "no" and the "yes" of the metaphor in tension, without resolving the paradox in a way that violates Scripture.

Constancy is an apt description for our God. His immutability should not be interpreted to imply that he is aloof and unbending; it must be tempered with the biblical portrait of God as gracious and responsive to those who believe in him. This was Luther's position.[42] Luther's view grew out of his pastoral concerns as demonstrated in his Small Catechism. Here he seeks to teach the unlearned laity in a form they could understand.[43] He points those being catechized to the goodness of God and to his revealed promises as the grounds for confidence that God does hear and answer prayer. In his Large Catechism, Luther writes:

> You can hold such promises[44] up to him and say, "Here I come, dear Father, and pray not of my own accord nor because of my own worthiness, but at your commandment and promise, which cannot fail or deceive me."[45]

Luther affirmed that "the prayer of a righteous man has great strength as it works" (James 5:16). This is what the Scriptures teach at the same time that they also teach the doctrines of God's complete foreknowledge and unchanging will.

Luther put this theology of prayer into practice in his own life. At one point when Philip Melanchthon was gravely ill, Luther prayed that God would restore Melanchthon to health and prolong his life. Luther is reported to have said:

> There our Lord God had to give in to me; for I threw down the sack before His door and rubbed into His ears all His promises that He would hear prayer which I could enumerate from Scripture, saying that He would have to hear me if I were to trust His promises.[46]

God answered Luther's prayer by sparing Melanchthon's life. Had he not, God's promises still would have remained true. Nevertheless, Luther interpreted Melanchthon's recovery as a sign of God's good will and of his responsiveness to prayer.

---

[42] For many of the insights in this section, I am indebted to Roser, "Can God Be Persuaded? A Discussion of the Immutability of God in Luther's Catechesis on Prayer."

[43] *SC*, Preface, 1.

[44] In the previous paragraph, LC III 19, Luther quotes Ps 50:15 and Mt 7:7–8.

[45] LC III 21.

[46] As noted by Pieper, *Christian Dogmatics*, 3:82–83.

Luther taught this doctrine of prayer in accord with his understanding of *Deus absconditus*, "the hidden God," and *Deus revelatus*, "the revealed God."[47] With these categories of the hidden and revealed God, Luther attributed to God a will that is immutable, eternal, and infallible while at the same time affirming that he responds to prayer. That is to say, Luther teaches that God has a complete and certain foreknowledge of the future and his will is absolutely immutable. However, about God's will and future actions, we can know only what God has revealed in Christ and in the Scriptures. The rest must be placed in the category of "the hidden God." If we seek God apart from his self-revelation, we find that God is beyond dealing with; he is hidden in his majesty from us mortal sinners, who deserve nothing but wrath and damnation. But in grace and mercy, this same God comes to us as "the revealed God" through Scripture and, climactically, in the person of God the Son, Jesus Christ. It is from this perspective that we see him changing prior decisions, such as sparing the Ninevites who repented (Jonah 3:5–10) despite his earlier decree that they would be destroyed (Jonah 3:4). This paradox between the hidden and the revealed God enables the baptized to embrace the substance of classical theism while also listening to the concerns of open theism.[48]

Luther's distinction between the hidden and the revealed God is a biblical one. Moses may have said it best: "The hidden things belong to Yahweh our God, but the revealed things belong to us and to our children forever, that we may do all the words of this Torah" (Deut 29:28). The hidden things are known to God alone. The revealed things are ours through his Word and Sacraments, with all his gracious promises, including those that depict God as responding to our prayers, such as "Ask, and it will be given to you; seek, and you will find; knock, and it will be opened to you" (Mt 7:7).

The debate between classical and open theism is often framed in the categories of divine foreknowledge versus human freedom. However, the discussion would be better served by utilizing the categories of Law and Gospel. In Scripture, and for Luther, it is for Christ's sake (*propter Christum*) that God is moved from anger and judgment to mercy and clemency. God's shift between

---

[47] Luther discusses the differences between *Deus absconditus* and *Deus revelatus* in *The Bondage of the Will* (AE 33:138–40, 145–46). In *God Hidden and Revealed*, Dillenberger offers a thorough and valuable summary of various interpretations of Luther's *Deus absconditus*. Elert, *The Structure of Lutheranism*, 117–26, also discusses the *Deus absconditus* and its place in the doctrine of God. The phrase *Deus absconditus* comes from the Vulgate translation of Is 45:15. For discussions of the theme in the OT, see Balentine, *The Hidden God: The Hiding of the Face of God in the Old Testament*, and Saebo, "Yahweh as *Deus absconditus*: Some Remarks on a Dictum by Gerhard von Rad."

[48] McGrath notes this in his critique of open theism: "A quick read of this volume [Pinnock et al., *The Openness of God*], however, showed that the contributors seem not to realize that Luther has been down their road long before them. This alarmed me" ("Whatever Happened to Luther?" 34). Open theists have addressed Luther's view of God's immutability, but only by virtue of a passing reference to one of the reformer's chief works: *De servo arbitrio* (*The Bondage of the Will*). See Sanders, *The God Who Risks*, 153–55.

his *opus alienum* (his "alien work" of judging sinners according to his Law) and his *opus proprium* (his "proper work" of justifying repentant sinners through faith in Christ alone) is all part of his one unchanging will.

Put another way, the triune God is living and active and continually operates through the power of his Word. In his Word, he shows himself as changeless in his attributes and purposes, but his attitude toward people and his relationship with them can—and do—change from judgment to grace as he moves them to repentance and faith in Christ. Thus divine immutability does not imply that God is unconcerned, inactive, or unrelated to his creatures. Therefore, when speaking about how God reveals himself, we can use terms in biblical creeds such as Jonah 4:2,[49] including that God changes his verdict, implying that God's attributes remain constant even as he changes his actions in the world.

Peter Toon offers a summary that is a fitting conclusion for this excursus when he writes this: "God as perfect Deity does not change in his essential nature; but because he is in relationship with people who do change, he himself changes his relation and attitude from wrath to mercy and from blessing to judgment, as the occasion requires."[50] God has chosen to interact with his human creatures by entering into a personal relationship with humanity, first in his covenant with Abraham, Israel, and David, and ultimately through Jesus Christ, who has reconciled us to God through his incarnation, perfect life, atoning death, resurrection on the third day, and ascension to the right hand of the Father. The triune God is constantly at work to fulfill his ultimate and changeless purposes. God accomplishes them through his Law and his Gospel, and this involves changes in his disposition toward people and even in his actions for or against them as people respond in obduracy or in repentance and prayer.

NT passages such as Rom 9:6; 11:29; Titus 1:2; and Heb 6:17–18; 7:21 do not refer to the unchangeableness of God in a general way, but to two specific unchangeable characteristics: (1) his righteous judgment and (2) his loyalty in carrying out his redemptive purpose in Christ. The more general reference in James 1:17 refers to God as being totally reliable: he is the giver of every good and perfect gift, and he never tempts his children with evil (James 1:13). Corresponding to the OT passages that refer to Yahweh changing his prior verdict are NT passages that refer to God responding to prayer and his forbearance and self-restraint in judgment, so that people may repent, believe in Christ, and so be saved.[d]

(d) E.g., Lk 11:1–13; 13:6–9; 18:7–8; Rom 2:4; 3:25; 9:22; 1 Pet 3:20–21; 2 Pet 3:9, 15

And so Israel's God is revealed as a relational God, living and dynamic, whose ways of relating to the world can be captured in the language of personality and activity. It is ironic that some Christian theologies have difficulty with this language, for in Jesus Christ, God has revealed himself in a most per-

---

[49] For the creedal language of Jonah 4:2, see the textual notes and commentary on it.

[50] P. Toon, "Repentance," *The New International Dictionary of the Bible* (ed. J. D. Douglas; Grand Rapids: Zondervan, 1987), 853.

sonal way. The Athanasian Creed probes the biblical mystery of the triune God: each of the three persons is uncreated, infinite, and eternal, yet God the Son became a man who "suffered for our salvation, … rose again the third day from the dead, ascended into heaven, … will come to judge the living and the dead."[51]

The people of Nineveh were thankful for this God who was willing and able to change his verdict from judgment to salvation. Finally, it is only under a God who is "gracious and merciful" and "slow to anger" (Jonah 4:2) that anyone can possibly live. If he were not patient, the ancient Ninevites (and Israelites and Jonahs!) as well as all peoples of the world would have been consigned to destruction long ago. Without his change from judgment to grace, no one ever would have been saved. God works through his Law and his Gospel to enable us to live by faith (cf. Hab 2:4). For all who, like the Ninevites (Jonah 3:5), believe in this God, he turns aside his wrath and instead bestows life everlasting in communion with him.[52]

---

[51] *LSB* 320.

[52] That the Ninevites shall rise to everlasting life is affirmed by Jesus in Mt 12:41. See the commentary on Jonah 3:5 and the excursus "The Sign of Jonah."

Jonah 4:1–11

Yahweh's Attempt to Rescue Jonah from the Prophet's Great Evil

Introduction to Jonah 4

Characterization in the OT is sometimes achieved by the narrator's direct statements. For example, at the end of the account of David and Bathsheba, the narrator concludes the scene by implicating David: "But the thing that David had done was evil in the eyes of Yahweh" (2 Sam 11:27). In Jonah 4, however, the narrator assumes a secondary role. In contrast to the first three chapters, this chapter features a large amount of dialogue, which is intended to reveal climactically the character of both Jonah and Yahweh through their words. In this chapter, Jonah and Yahweh converse in direct speech, revealing their true thoughts. "As elsewhere in biblical narrative, the revelation of character is effected with striking artistic economy,"[1] and dialogue carries most of the character presentation.

The strategy of the divinely inspired narrator is calculated and deliberate. He does not show his hand in the first three chapters because he has composed the book to culminate in this final chapter. The direct speech of Jonah and Yahweh in chapter 4 stands out so drastically because the master narrator has provided few clues in chapters 1–3 for this drastic turn of events that takes place in this scene outside Nineveh.[2] By the end of this chapter, we see that the sailors and the Ninevites—and even animals, a plant, and the weather[3]—have served as foils to Jonah wielded by Yahweh to fulfill his salvific purposes.

It appears as though the structure of chapter 4 is ordered in a similar way to the chiasm of chapter 1:[4]

---

[1] Alter, *The Art of Biblical Narrative*, 37. Though Alter is speaking about the narrative in 1 Samuel 24, his description also applies to Jonah 4. Alter gives several examples of this narrative style in the OT (pp. 37–41).

[2] For example, only in Jonah 4:2 does the narrator reveal, by quoting Jonah's own words, why the prophet fled from Yahweh at the beginning of the book (1:3). During the first three chapters, the reader is left to wonder about Jonah's motivation until discovering it in chapter 4. Ruth is another superbly narrated book with similar literary devices that enhance suspense until the resolution in the fourth and final chapter (see Wilch, *Ruth*, 47–52).

[3] This includes the storm in chapter 1; the great fish in chapter 2 (ET 1:17–2:10); the animals included in the Ninevites' repentance in chapter 3; and the qiqayon plant, worm, sun, and scorching east wind in chapter 4.

[4] This outline of chapter 4 is based on the analysis of Fretheim, *The Message of Jonah*, 117. For the chiastic structure of Jonah 1:4–16, see "Introduction to Jonah 1."

A   Report of Jonah's anger and a question (4:1–2).
  1   Report of Jonah's anger (4:1).
  2   Jonah's question (4:2).
    B   Jonah requests death, and God questions Jonah (4:3–4).
      1   Jonah requests death (4:3).
      2   God questions Jonah (4:4).
        C   Jonah responds, and God provides (4:5–6a).
          1   Jonah builds a hut (4:5).
          2   God provides a plant to save Jonah (4:6a).
        C'   Jonah responds, and God provides (4:6b–8a).
          1   Jonah rejoices with great joy (4:6b).
          2   God provides a worm to kill the plant and a scorching wind to afflict Jonah (4:7–8a).
    B'   Jonah requests death, and God questions Jonah (4:8b–9a).
      1   Jonah requests death (4:8b).
      2   God questions Jonah (4:9a).
A'   Report of Jonah's anger and a question (4:9b–11).
  1   Report of Jonah's anger (4:9b).
  2   Yahweh's question (4:10–11).

The first three chapters can be juxtaposed with chapter 4 in the overall design of the narrative. Chapters 1 through 3 contain many of the same themes that we see in chapter 4, but there are several counterpoints. Each of the first three chapters has only half of a conversation: in chapters 1 and 3, "the Word of Yahweh" comes to the prophet (1:1–2; 3:1–2), but Jonah does not verbally reply to Yahweh. In chapter 2, Jonah prays to Yahweh, but Yahweh does not reply verbally. Only in chapter 4 is there a mutual conversation between Yahweh and his prophet.

Another counterpoint is that the prayer in chapter 2 gives an ambiguous but predominately positive picture of Jonah,[5] while the prayer in chapter 4 (4:2–3) gives a forthrightly negative picture of the prophet. In chapter 2, a brief narrative (2:1–2, 11 [ET 1:17–2:1, 10]) surrounding the prayer (2:3–10 [ET 2:2–9]) does not explore the character of Jonah; in chapter 4 an extended narrative (4:1, 4–11) surrounding the prayer probes deeply into his character. In chapters 1 and 2, Yahweh overpowers Jonah, first by hurling the storm (1:4) and then by providing the fish that swallows him (2:1 [ET 1:17]), thus saving him from the raging sea. But in chapter 4, Yahweh uses much less powerful aspects of his creation (a worm, a plant, and a wind) as he seeks to persuade Jonah.

Further differences between the first and third chapters and the last chapter revolve around the use of questions.[6] In chapter 1, the captain and the sailors ask Jonah questions (1:6, 8, 10–11), and in chapter 3, the king asks a rhetori-

---

[5]   Jonah's faith in and gratitude to Yahweh ring out in chapter 2, but some details of the language still reflect a degree of self-centeredness. See the first textual note on 2:5 (ET 2:4); the first textual note on 2:10 (ET 2:9); and the commentary on 2:3 (ET 2:2).

[6]   The questions are in 1:6, 8b (four inquiries), 10–11; 3:9; 4:2, 4, 9, 11. It is also possible that 1:8a could be a question. The common emendation of 2:5b creates another question, but this commentary rejects that emendation. See the discussion of questions in Sasson, *Jonah*, 113–15 and 179–82.

cal question (3:9). The questions in chapter 4 are different from those previously asked in the narrative. Both Jonah and Yahweh ask questions of each other. Jonah questions Yahweh's character in 4:2. Then Yahweh's rhetorical questions to Jonah seek to persuade Jonah to accept the justice of Yahweh's character as a gracious and merciful God who justifies sinners through faith (cf. Rom 4:5; 5:6).

In the first and third chapters, Yahweh only issues commands (both 1:2 and 3:2 have the same three imperatives), but in chapter 4 God only asks questions and makes statements. Thus in the earlier chapters of the narrative, Yahweh attempts to direct Jonah by issuing nothing but commands, but in the final chapter he consistently tries to persuade and convince the prophet by compelling inquiries:

- "Is it right that you are inflamed?" (4:4)
- "Is it right that you are inflamed over the qiqayon plant?" (4:9a)
- "Shall I myself not have pity upon Nineveh, the great city?" (4:11)

Jonah's question in 4:2 expresses his core conviction that it is unfair for Yahweh to show mercy to those who deserve punishment as the consequence of their sin. Yahweh's final question to Jonah points out that if Jonah claims the right to feel sorrow over the demise of a qiqayon plant that he did not create or cultivate, surely Yahweh has a right to be merciful toward his own creatures without being subject to the charge of injustice.

In chapter 4, Jonah's words and Yahweh's words are split with mathematical precision.[7] They get absolutely equal "air time" since each utters a total of forty-seven Hebrew words. Even the lengths of their statements correspond exactly. This symmetry of words is too precise to be accidental:

A   Jonah speaks thirty-nine Hebrew words to Yahweh in 4:2–3.
  B   Yahweh speaks three Hebrew words in 4:4.
  B' Jonah speaks three Hebrew words in 4:8.
    C   God speaks five Hebrew words in 4:9a.
    C' Jonah speaks five Hebrew words in 4:9b.
A' Yahweh speaks thirty-nine Hebrew words in 4:10–11.[8]

The narrative begins with Yahweh's commission to Jonah (1:1–2) and ends with two statements and a lengthy question to Jonah that highlight his compassion (4:10–11). Thus Yahweh gets the first word and the last. In this way, Yahweh demonstrates that he is in charge ("you are Yahweh; just as you please, you do," 1:14) and Jonah is not. Jonah's attempted but aborted escape to Tarshish was narrated in chapter 1, and the flashback via Jonah's question in 4:2 supplies his motivation for responding in that way to the first words of

---

[7]   Compare examples of biblical books that use precise numbers of verses. The book of Ecclesiastes breaks neatly into two halves of 111 verses each at 6:9. The collection of proverbs in Prov 10:1–22:16 contains 375 sayings, and 375 is the numerical value of the letters in שלמה, "Solomon," who is the author of these proverbs (see 10:1) and of most of Proverbs (see 1:1; 25:1). See Murphy, *The Tree of Life*, 21, 52.

[8]   Sasson, *Jonah*, 317.

Yahweh. We are never told how he responds to Yahweh's statements and question in 4:10–11.

Chapter 4 builds, to some degree, upon earlier prophetic appeals to die. The misgivings of Moses and his prayer for death (Num 11:10–15) and Elijah's prayer that Yahweh would take his life (1 Ki 19:4) provide the general background of Jonah's desire to die. Jonah in 4:3, 8 uses similar vocabulary to that of Elijah in 1 Ki 19:4. Yet there is a major difference between Jonah and these earlier prophets. Moses made his request because of the crushing burden of bearing the sinful people of Israel, and Elijah uttered his request when fleeing from Jezebel's death threat. Ironically, Jonah utters his death wish after Nineveh is saved through his efficacious prophetic ministry.

In this chapter, the interchange between "Yahweh" (יהוה) and "God/Elohim" (אֱלֹהִים) has theological significance. Jonah's theological confession in 1:9 named "Yahweh, the God of the heavens, … who made the sea and the dry land," thus identifying "Yahweh," the covenant name of the God who redeemed Israel (see "Yahweh" in Ex 3:2–18), as the supreme God who created the universe (see "Yahweh God/Elohim" in Gen 2:4). That identification helps explain the names used throughout the first three chapters by Jonah, the sailors and their captain, and the Ninevites and their king.[9] In 4:2 Jonah makes another theological confession, in which he adds the attributes that "Yahweh" is a "God/El"[10] who is "gracious and merciful," patient and compassionate. It is within the context of this new confession of God's attributes that we must consider the interchange of Yahweh and Elohim in chapter 4.

In chapter 4, the initial question is posed by Jonah, who (as he always does) addresses God by his covenant name, "Yahweh" (4:2–3). This is appropriate because Jonah's question affirms Yahweh's attributes of grace and mercy. When God graciously provides the qiqayon plant to furnish shade for Jonah, he is called "Yahweh God/Elohim" (יְהוָה־אֱלֹהִים, 4:6). But then when God acts destructively by providing a worm to strike the qiqayon plant, he is called "(the) God/Ha Elohim," (הָאֱלֹהִים, 4:7). Similarly, when he provides the scorching wind that afflicts the prophet, he is called "God/Elohim" (אֱלֹהִים, 4:8). Finally, the concluding statements and question that end the book, which contrast Jonah's selfishness with God's compassion, are posed by "Yahweh" (יְהוָה, 4:10–11).

Thus, at the beginning of chapter 4, Jonah uses "Yahweh" in his confession of God's grace and forbearance. Then "God" is used when Jonah is

---

[9] Jonah always calls the God "Yahweh" (Jonah 1:9; 2:3, 7, 8, 10 [ET 2:2, 6, 7, 9]; 4:2, 3). The sailors first prayed to their "gods/elohim" (1:5), and their captain exhorted Jonah to call on "your God/Elohim" (1:6). Then after they are converted to saving faith through Jonah's confession or sermonette (1:9), the mariners pray to and worship "Yahweh" (1:14, 16). Through Jonah's second sermonette (3:4), the Ninevites come to believe in "God/Elohim" (3:5) and are exhorted to pray to "God/Elohim" (3:8), since "God/Elohim" (3:9) might have mercy on them.

[10] This term for "God," אֵל, occurs in Jonah only in 4:2.

disciplined by means of the creation. Finally, "Yahweh" returns at the conclusion, which expresses his compassion. God as Yahweh is gracious (4:2) and cares for his prophet through his creation (4:6). God as Elohim brings painful discipline (4:7–8), but paradoxically that discipline is designed to lead Jonah to an understanding of him as Yahweh, the compassionate God (4:10–11)!

Theologically speaking, the Law (*opus alienum*) is meted out by Elohim, and the Gospel (*opus proprium*) is given by Yahweh.[11]

---

[11] God's *opus alienum*, "alien work," is his judgment according to his Law (see Is 28:21), and his *opus proprium*, "proper work," is that of justifying the sinner by grace for Christ's sake.

Scene 6: Jonah's Response to Yahweh's Change of Verdict to Save Nineveh

Translation

4 **¹However, it was evil to Jonah—a great evil—so it inflamed him. ²He prayed to Yahweh and said, "Ah, Yahweh! Was not this my word while I was still upon my ground? For this reason I previously fled toward Tarshish because I knew that you are a gracious and merciful God, slow to anger and abounding in loyal love, and changing your verdict about evil. ³And now, Yahweh, take my life from me, for my death would be better than my life!"**

Textual Notes

4:1 וַיֵּרַע אֶל־יוֹנָה רָעָה גְדוֹלָה—The *waw* here has a disjunctive meaning ("however") because Jonah's negative reaction in this verse contrasts with the preceding events of salvation in chapter 3. וַיֵּרַע is the Qal third masculine singular imperfect with *waw* consecutive of רָעַע, "to be evil" (*HALOT*, 2; BDB, 3 and 4). That the verb means "be evil" is supported by the following cognate noun רָעָה in the phrase גְדוֹלָה רָעָה, "a great evil." That noun refers to Nineveh's moral and ethical "evil" in 1:2 and 3:8, 10 (see further the commentary). Syntactically, רָעָה גְדוֹלָה is a cognate accusative that functions adverbially; it modifies and intensifies the verb וַיֵּרַע, "it was evil," by adding that the evil involved in the verb was "a great evil." Some grammarians call this kind of construction an "accusative of the internal object" because the accusative noun (here רָעָה) is from the same root as the verb (see Joüon, § 125 q–r, and GKC, § 117 p–q). Similar was this cognate accusative phrase in 1:16 that functioned adverbially:

וַיִּירְאוּ הָאֲנָשִׁים יִרְאָה גְדוֹלָה אֶת־יְהוָה
The men worshiped Yahweh *with great worship.*

Weaker meanings for the verb are advocated by lexicons that suggest that here it could mean "be displeasing" (BDB, 1) or "brought a great despondency" (*HALOT*, 2 b). The LXX renders Jonah's reaction as καὶ ἐλυπήθη Ιωνας λύπην μεγάλην, "And Jonah was grieved with a great grief." The Vulgate translates, *Et adflictus est Iona adflictione magna*, "And Jonah was despondent with great despondency." Most English translations say, "It displeased Jonah exceedingly" (KJV, NKJV, RSV, ESV; NASB is similar; cf. NIV: "Jonah was greatly displeased"). Wolff argues that Jonah is not merely displeased, but that he has fallen into an evil inclination (*Bosheit*).[1] The translation above agrees with Wolff in rendering the Hebrew in its strongest sense, which is supported by the context, especially the following phrase רָעָה גְדוֹלָה.

---

[1]   Wolff, *Studien zum Jonabuch*, 38–39.

What is the subject of the verb? There is no stated subject in 4:1. The implied subject must be one or more of the persons or events in chapter 3. The subject cannot be Jonah because he is the indirect object in the prepositional phrase אֶל־יוֹנָה, "to Jonah." Neither can the subject be רָעָה גְדוֹלָה, "a great evil" (4:1), because this noun and adjective are feminine, while the verb וַיֵּרַע is masculine. It is fairly common for the Qal of רָעַע to be used impersonally, without an explicit subject.[2] (The same is true of the following verb, וַיִּחַר; see the next textual note.) See the similar impersonal phrase וַיֵּרַע לְ in Neh 2:10; 13:8. In such cases a literal translation must supply a subject, usually the pronoun "it," hence this commentary's translation is "It was evil to Jonah."

To what does this refer? What was so evil to Jonah? It is possible that this includes all that happened in 3:5–10: the Ninevites' believing in God, performing acts of repentance, and turning from their evil, as well as God changing his verdict. Most likely, however, it is the specific fact that God changed his verdict from destruction to the salvation of the Ninevites (3:10) that Jonah perceives as "a great evil" (4:1). This view finds support in 4:6, where God provides the qiqayon plant "to save him [Jonah] from his evil," since Yahweh will use the plant in his attempt to persuade Jonah that he was justified in saving Nineveh out of his pity (4:10–11).

וַיִּחַר לוֹ:—This is a result clause: "So it inflamed him." Because the salvation of Nineveh was perceived by Jonah as "a great evil" (4:1a), it infuriated him. This sets the tone for the entire chapter since Jonah's anger is the problem Yahweh seeks to remedy through his words and actions in 4:4–11. Moreover, the entire book of Jonah is designed to cure in us readers any Jonah-like anger at the salvation of those unlike ourselves.[3]

The idiom here uses the Qal (third masculine singular imperfect with *waw* consecutive) of חָרָה, "burn, be kindled, be hot," impersonally (with no stated subject), followed by the preposition לְ (with third masculine singular suffix), literally, "It was hot for him," referring to the heat of anger. This idiom portrays "the emotion as coming to the undergoer from outside" (Waltke-O'Connor, § 22.7b; see example 3). This common idiom is used for both people and God becoming inflamed with anger (BDB, s.v. חָרָה, Qal 1 b and 2 b, respectively). Twice in the chapter (4:3, 8–9) Jonah is ready to die; his emotional state is anger to the point of extreme depression. The Vulgate renders, *Et iratus est*, "And he was irate."[4] Less accurate is the LXX, which translates, καὶ συνεχύθη (from συγχέω), "and he was confused, bewildered." Elsewhere in the OT, another common use of חָרָה is with the noun אַף, "nose; anger" as its subject: literally, "His nose became hot" means "He [God or a person] became enraged" (see BDB, s.v. חָרָה, 1 a and 2 a).

The verb חָרָה frequently indicates anger toward people or circumstances (e.g., Num 24:10), sometimes out of jealousy, as in the case of Saul's anger toward David

---

[2] See Davies, "The Uses of *R*ᶜ Qal and the Meaning of Jonah IV 1," 107.

[3] See "The Purpose of Satire in This True and Didactic Story" in "Jonah as Satire with Irony" in the introduction.

[4] Wycliffe, Tyndale, KJV, RSV, JB, NEB, and NASB also render Jonah's response as that of anger.

(1 Sam 20:7; see also 20:30). Often Yahweh is the subject for the verb. He becomes angry when a person is uncooperative (Ex 4:14), disobedient (Josh 7:1), unfaithful (Ex 32:10), or ungrateful (Num 11:4–10). His anger goes hand-in-hand with his own self-proclaimed jealousy, "I, Yahweh your God, am a jealous God" (Ex 20:5; see also Deut 4:24; Ezek 36:6; Nahum 1:2).

People can reflect this righteous divine anger. Moses becomes angry at the Israelites for making their idolatrous golden calf (Ex 32:19), and the "Spirit of God" rushes upon Saul so that he becomes angry over the injustice that the Ammonites were threatening to do to the Israelites of Jabesh-gilead (1 Sam 11:6).

However, Jonah's anger is unrighteous. He is inflamed because Yahweh is *not* inflamed and does not destroy Nineveh, but instead saves the Ninevites by converting them to faith (3:5) made evident in their acts of repentance (3:5–9).

4:2 וַיִּתְפַּלֵּל אֶל־יְהוָה וַיֹּאמַר—These same Hebrew words, "He prayed to Yahweh and said," were used (with the addition of "Jonah" and spread over 2:2–3a [ET 2:1–2a]) to introduce Jonah's psalm. See the first textual note on 2:2 (ET 2:1). There Jonah uttered a beautiful prayer of thanksgiving for Yahweh saving him from death and Sheol (2:3–10 [ET 2:2–9]). Ironically, here, however, his prayer is an angry complaint because Yahweh has saved Nineveh.

אָנָּה יְהוָה—Jonah's complaint begins with the same two Hebrew words as the sailors' prayer in 1:14, where they were rendered "We pray, O Yahweh." This implies that the Gentiles and the Israelite have equal standing before God and equal access to him through prayer. For the interjection אָנָּה, see the second textual note on 1:14. Here, spoken by Jonah alone, the two words are rendered "Ah, Yahweh!"

הֲלוֹא־זֶה דְבָרִי עַד־הֱיוֹתִי עַל־אַדְמָתִי—"Was not this my word while I was still upon my ground?" is very similar to the complaint of the grumbling Israelites in the wilderness (Ex 14:12):

הֲלֹא־זֶה הַדָּבָר אֲשֶׁר דִּבַּרְנוּ אֵלֶיךָ בְמִצְרַיִם
Was not this the word that we spoke to you in Egypt?

The complaining Israelites wished they had remained in slavery in Egypt instead of being called to leave and (they think) to die in the wilderness. Jonah wishes Yahweh had not called him to leave Israel and preach to Nineveh, and he prays for death (4:3, 8).

Grumbling Jonah begins his prayer by questioning God. The first clause begins with the interrogative *he* (-הֲ) and the negative particle spelled *plene*, לוֹא.[5] Since Jonah is referring to the past, it is rendered, "*Was* not this my word?" דָּבָר (with first common singular suffix, דְבָרִי) often has a broader meaning than a single "word," as in 3:6, where it refers to Jonah's sermonette (3:4). Here Jonah's "word" is his following thought or belief about Yahweh's gracious character (4:2e).

The temporal clause עַד־הֱיוֹתִי uses the preposition עַד in the sense of "while" with the infinitive construct of הָיָה with first common singular suffix (הֱיוֹתִי), "while

---

[5] Sasson argues that הֲלוֹא is not interrogative, but adverbial: "Please, Lord, this certainly was my opinion" (*Jonah*, 270; see also p. 277).

I was." See similar constructions with עַד and an infinitive construct in Ex 33:22 and Judg 3:26. עַל־אַדְמָתִי uses the preposition עַל in the sense of "upon" with the noun אֲדָמָה with first common singular suffix, literally, "upon my ground," meaning "in my land, Israel." Jonah obviously considers Nineveh to be foreign territory; it is not his, nor does he think it should be Yahweh's.

עַל־כֵּן—The combination עַל־כֵּן ("for this reason") uses the preposition עַל to indicate "the cause or reason" (BDB, s.v. עַל, II 1 f (b)) with the adverb כֵּן, "so, thus" (see BDB, s.v. כֵּן II, 3 f).

קִדַּמְתִּי לִבְרֹחַ תַּרְשִׁישָׁה—The Piel of קָדַם (here first common singular perfect: קִדַּמְתִּי) can mean "go before, in front" in either a spatial sense (BDB, 2; *HALOT*, 3) or in a temporal sense, as here (BDB, 3; *HALOT*, 4), "to do something earlier, beforehand, previously." What Jonah previously did is then denoted by the Qal infinitive construct of בָּרַח, "to flee," with the preposition לְ. The same form of the same verb (לִבְרֹחַ) was used in 1:3 in the purpose clause stating that Jonah arose "to flee" to Tarshish. The Qal participle בֹּרֵחַ was used in 1:10 to describe Jonah as "fleeing." תַּרְשִׁישׁ, "Tarshish," occurred in 1:3 three times, twice (as here) with directional ending (ָה-), "*to* Tarshish." Thus Jonah's terminology here precisely matches the description of his behavior in chapter 1.

Often when a finite Hebrew verb (here קִדַּמְתִּי) with an adverbial meaning (denoting time, manner, etc.) is followed by an infinitive construct (here לִבְרֹחַ), the finite verb functions as a subordinate auxiliary and is best translated adverbially, while the infinitive conveys the most important action and is best translated as a finite verb. See Waltke-O'Connor, § 36.2.1d, including examples 13–15; GKC, § 114 m, especially footnote 2 (cf. Joüon, § 124 n). Therefore, קִדַּמְתִּי לִבְרֹחַ probably means, literally, "I did beforehand to flee," hence, "I previously fled" (similar are KJV, NKJV). Alternatively, it could mean "I quickly fled" (similar are RSV, ESV, NIV) or perhaps "in order to forestall this I fled" (NASB). The LXX translates, προέφθασα τοῦ φυγεῖν, which probably means "I anticipated this and so fled," since προφθάνω can mean "*to act with foresight* or *in anticipation*" (LEH).

כִּי יָדַעְתִּי—This conjunction כִּי is causal ("because"), introducing the reason why Jonah fled. The verb יָדַע (here Qal first common singular perfect), "to know," frequently involves far more than mere knowledge of facts. Often יָדַע takes as its object a כִּי clause about God and means "*know by faith/believe* that [כִּי] God ... ," for example, "I believe that [כִּי] Yahweh saves his anointed" (Ps 20:7 [ET 20:6]).[a] Here the following כִּי clause is such an object clause about God.

כִּי אַתָּה אֵל־חַנּוּן—See BDB, s.v. כִּי, 1 a, for the function of this כִּי, which introduces a long clause that is the object of the verb יָדַעְתִּי in the preceding clause. The descriptive object clause about God has five parts and extends through the end of 4:2.

The first divine attribute that Jonah says he knows by faith is "that [כִּי] you [אַתָּה] are a gracious [חַנּוּן] God [אֵל]." This is the only occurrence of אֵל in Jonah.[6] The adjective חַנּוּן, "gracious" (BDB), is derived from the verb חָנַן, "be gracious, show fa-

(a) See also, e.g., Deut 4:39; 7:9; Is 43:10; 49:26; 60:16; Pss 135:5; 140:13 (ET 140:12)

---

6   For the interchange in chapter 4 between the two other terms for God, "Yahweh" (יהוה) and "Elohim/God" (אֱלֹהִים), see "Introduction to Jonah 4."

vor." In the OT, the verb can have God or people as its subject, but the adjective is almost exclusively applied to God (the sole exception is Ps 112:4, where it describes a righteous man). A telling illustration of its meaning is provided by a similar clause in Ex 22:25–26 (ET 22:26–27):

> If you take the garment of your neighbor as a pledge, return it to him by sunset because his garment is the only covering he has for his body. In what will he sleep? When he cries out to me, I will hear, for I am gracious [כִּי־חַנּוּן אָנִי].

Yahweh hears the cry of the person who is cold. Here is a God who is moved by simple human need.

וְרַחוּם—This adjective is the second of the five divine attributes cited by Jonah. In the OT, the adjective רַחוּם, "compassionate, merciful," almost exclusively modifies God (as with חַנּוּן, the sole exception is Ps 112:4). It expresses the preserving love and compassion that is unique to the God of Israel. It is frequently paired with חַנּוּן in some form of the well-known formula derived from Ex 34:6, where Yahweh himself declares that he is "a God who is merciful [אֵל רַחוּם] and gracious [וְחַנּוּן], slow to anger and abounding in loyal love and truth." Similar are Joel 2:13; Pss 86:15; 103:8; 111:4; 145:8; Neh 9:17, 31; 2 Chr 30:9.

The adjective רַחוּם is related to the noun רֶחֶם, "womb," and so likely contains echoes of the love "of a mother towards her children" (*HALOT*, s.v. רַחוּם), especially as it is related to the helpless child in her uterus. The adjective רַחוּם is often used for God as "merciful" in the face of Israel's disobedience. Whereas Israel has been unfaithful, Yahweh remains merciful, and on account of his mercy, he has not destroyed his people; if they return to him, he will not turn his face away from them (e.g., Ps 78:38; 2 Chr 30:9). With respect to Nineveh's sin against Yahweh, it is in the same position as Israel, who stood guilty before the righteous God. Yet God now shows himself "merciful" toward Nineveh, just as he is toward Israel. Jonah 4:2 is the only time in the OT that Yahweh has revealed himself as רַחוּם, "merciful," by how he has treated a nation other than Israel. Nineveh is receiving from Yahweh the same mercy that previously he had shown only to Israel and that Jonah thinks should be shown *only* to Israel.

אֶרֶךְ אַפַּיִם—The third attribute is that Yahweh is literally and anthropomorphically "long of two nostrils," meaning "slow to anger." אֶרֶךְ is the construct of the adjective אָרֵךְ, "long, slow," which occurs most often in this phrase. This is an example of an adjective in construct to express limitation (Joüon, § 129 i). אַפַּיִם is the dual of אַף, "nose; anger," which was the term for God's wrath in 3:9.

This phrase reveals several characteristics of Yahweh. First, he is affected and moved by what people do.[7] Second, while human sin provokes his anger (Rom 1:18), his initial reaction usually is not to mete out judgment immediately; it takes some time for him finally to express himself in this way (see, e.g., Gen 15:16; Rom 2:5, 8). Third, even when his patience expires, he manifests his anger quickly, and then his people

---

[7] This is relevant for the debate between classical and open theism. See the excursus "When Yahweh Changes a Prior Verdict."

can expect him to return to being gracious: "His anger lasts for a moment, but his favor is for a lifetime" (Ps 30:6 [ET 30:5]).

Yahweh's anger falls under the category of his alien work (Is 28:21). His anger is contingent: if there were no sin, then there would be no divine anger. His anger is taken away by the sinless Messiah, who atones for humanity's guilt (Isaiah 53; 1 Thess 1:10). On the basis of the Gospel, Yahweh is not angry at those who believe in him (Rom 5:9). Thus anger is not integral to his identity: the Bible affirms that "God is love" (1 Jn 4:16), but never says, "God is anger."

וְרַב־חֶסֶד—This fourth divine characteristic is expressed with the adjective רַב, "much, great," which often is used in construct to mean "abounding in" (BDB, 1 d). The noun חֶסֶד frequently denotes an attribute of God, centering on his fidelity to his covenant promises, loyalty, grace, kindness, and mercy. Here it is rendered "loyal love" although no translation captures its full meaning. It is not merely an abstract quality of Yahweh's nature, but an attribute that he reveals by his dealings with his people and a quality he instills in them.[8] Believers can display this quality in their relationships among humans and with Yahweh. Among believers, חֶסֶד usually expresses the idea of mutual undeserved kindness. When one person receives חֶסֶד, he or she will, in faith, practice חֶסֶד toward others (see, e.g., Josh 2:12–14; 1 Sam 20:8).

Frequently חֶסֶד is the object of the verb עָשָׂה used with a preposition to say that God "does" חֶסֶד "with" or "for" someone.[b] Yahweh may also impart חֶסֶד by giving (Micah 7:20), sending (Ps 57:4 [ET 57:3]), remembering (Ps 25:6), and many other verbs of delivery. His חֶסֶד is manifest in many ways, such as the gift of a wife for Isaac (Gen 24:12, 14, 27) and the establishment of the dynasty of David (2 Sam 7:15), both of which continue the line of Abraham leading to the Christ.

(b) E.g., Gen 19:19; Deut 5:10; 2 Sam 2:6; Job 10:12; Ps 18:51 (ET 18:50)

Yahweh's חֶסֶד is a signpost at nearly every stop in the tour of Israelite history. Perhaps most significant for the narrative of Jonah is the connection between Yahweh's חֶסֶד and his change of verdict from destruction to salvation (3:10). Yahweh forgives and changes his verdict about the children of Israel on the grounds of his חֶסֶד (Num 14:19; Ps 106:45).

Here Jonah implies that when he was called to go to Nineveh in chapter 1 he already knew that Yahweh's חֶסֶד might result in Nineveh's salvation, and that salvation is what angers him now. Just as elsewhere in the OT Yahweh often changes his verdict about dispensing judgment against Israel on account of his חֶסֶד, so also he changes his verdict about leveling Nineveh (Jonah 3:4) also according to his חֶסֶד. Once again, Yahweh demonstrates his same characteristics in dealing with the Ninevites as he does when dealing with the Israelites. But in the mind of Jonah, Yahweh's gifts "belong" to Israel alone, not to the Gentile nations and especially not to the converted Ninevites!

וְנִחָם עַל־הָרָעָה:—The fifth and last divine attribute that Jonah says he "knew" uses the Niphal masculine singular participle of נָחַם. The participle implies that Yahweh characteristically and frequently "changes his verdict" from judgment to salva-

---

[8]   See Wilch, *Ruth*, 30–37, 87–88, who builds his comments on חֶסֶד in Ruth 1:8; 2:20; 3:10.

tion. For this meaning of the Niphal of נָחַם, see the second textual note on 3:9 and the excursus "When Yahweh Changes a Prior Verdict." It is followed by עַל in the sense of "about, concerning" (cf. BDB, II 1 f (*h*)) and the noun רָעָה, "evil," referring to a divine verdict of judgment, as in 3:10. Compare also the storm as an "evil" sent by Yahweh in 1:7–8.

4:3 וְעַתָּה יְהוָה קַח־נָא אֶת־נַפְשִׁי מִמֶּנִּי—The conjunction and adverb וְעַתָּה, "and now," is a typical introduction to the main point of a speech, prayer, or letter. It often comes after the preliminaries, as in Gen 44:33; 1 Sam 25:7; Is 5:3, 5.[9] Here it is followed by the vocative address יְהוָה, "Yahweh."

Jonah's petition uses the masculine singular imperative (קַח) of לָקַח, "to take." The particle of entreaty נָא indicates that the speech is a plea or prayer, but it cannot be translated. נָא was used by the sailors twice: in their plea to Jonah in 1:8 (לְנוּ הַגִּידָה־נָּא) and in their prayer to Yahweh in 1:14 (אַל־נָא נֹאבְדָה). The definite direct object of the imperative is נַפְשִׁי, "my life." נֶפֶשׁ referred to Jonah's "life" also in 1:14; 2:8 (ET 2:7); 4:8 (and possibly 2:6 [ET 2:5]). מִמֶּנִּי is the preposition מִן with first common singular suffix ("from me").

Jonah's petition is quite similar to that of Elijah in 1 Ki 19:4. See the commentary.

Jonah's petition here also has verbal parallels to the sailors' plea in Jonah 1:14. Both are prayers addressed to "Yahweh" (יהוה) using נָא that speak of the loss of Jonah's "life" (נֶפֶשׁ), and both end with a subordinate clause introduced by כִּי.[10] These linguistic similarities indicate that Jonah and the seamen are on the same level before Yahweh. This subtlety expresses what Peter heralds at the home of Cornelius: "I now realize how true it is that God does not show favoritism; rather, in every people, a person who fears him and does righteousness is accepted by him" (Acts 10:34–35). But there is one striking difference between the prayers. The mariners' prayer continues in faithful submission to Yahweh's will in 1:14b. Jonah's prayer is the opposite: he would rather die than submit to Yahweh (4:3, 8–9). Another striking difference is that the mariners placed a high value on the sanctity of Jonah's life; they hurled him overboard only after he commanded them to do so and they had exhausted all other means for saving the ship (1:12–13). Here Jonah has little regard for the value of his life.

כִּי טוֹב מוֹתִי מֵחַיָּי׃—The conjunction כִּי is causal ("for"), introducing the reason for Jonah's preceding prayer that Yahweh take his life. טוֹב could be the Qal third masculine singular perfect of the stative verb טוֹב, "to be good." If so, מוֹתִי is its subject. As the lexicons note, it is often difficult to decide whether טוֹב is the verb or the homographic adjective (*DCH*, BDB, and *HALOT*, s.v. טוב, Qal; cf. Joüon, § 80 q). If not the verb, then טוֹב is a predicate adjective, "good." In either case, with the preposition מִן, "than" (attached to מֵחַיָּי׃ חַיִּים), it forms a comparative construction: "better than." Since Jonah is speaking about a future fulfillment of his prayer, the translation requires the optative "would be better than."

---

[9] See Brongers, "Bemerkungen zum Gebrauch des adverbialen *we'attāh* im Alten Testament," 296–99.

[10] Cf. Fretheim, *The Message of Jonah*, 90.

In form מוֹתִי could be the Qal infinitive construct of מוּת with subjective first common singular suffix, "my dying, for me to die," but it is more likely that it is the noun מָוֶת with first common singular suffix, "my death." Elsewhere in the OT, the Qal infinitive construct with that suffix occurs twice. Its form in 1 Ki 13:31 (בְּמוֹתִי) agrees with the form here. However, in 2 Sam 19:1 (ET 18:33), its stem vowel is *shureq* (מוּתִי). Also in Jonah 4:8, where the infinitive has the preposition and no suffix, its stem vowel is *shureq* (לָמוּת). Since the author of Jonah uses לָמוּת in 4:8, he probably would have used מוּתִי here for the infinitive construct with suffix. Another reason why מוֹתִי more likely is the noun (with suffix) is that here in 4:3 Jonah compares it to another noun: מֵחַיָּי ("than my life"), which is חַיִּים with the preposition מִן and first common singular suffix in pause (hence -ָ- instead of -ַ-). Jonah clearly uses the noun מָוֶת at the end of 4:9.

The noun חַיִּים ("life") is an abstract plural. In Jonah it is used only by the prophet and for his own life: here; 2:7 (ET 2:6; חַיָּי); and again in 4:8 (מֵחַיַּי). Since it, and probably also מוֹתִי, are nouns, they are so rendered in the translation above: "my death … my life." Nevertheless, most English translations render them by verbs: "It is better for me to die than to live" (KJV, NIV, ESV).

Commentary

Jonah's Evil and Anger at Nineveh's Salvation (4:1)

4:1 The end of chapter 3 presents a joyful conclusion. The repentance and salvation of Nineveh in the third chapter resolves the conflict that began when Nineveh's "evil" provoked Yahweh (1:2). "God saw … that they turned from their evil way, and God changed his verdict about the evil" (3:10). At that point in the narrative, no clues were present to indicate that the story would continue. It appears as though all the loose ends are tied up. After 3:10 we might have been tempted to conclude the narrative with these words: "The Ninevites—along with the sailors, Jonah, and Yahweh—all lived in harmony forevermore."

But not so fast! In chapter 4, Jonah's anger seemingly comes out of nowhere! Jonah 4:1 is really only the beginning of the second central conflict taking center stage in the narrative. This conflict is between Yahweh and Jonah. It began in 1:1–3, when Jonah anticipated that gracious Yahweh might save Nineveh according to the Gospel and that is why the prophet fled from Yahweh's presence (see 4:2). This conflict is caused by Jonah's unwillingness to have Nineveh receive the same Gospel that saved his own life (chapter 2). Throughout chapter 1, the prophet maintained icy silence toward Yahweh, but with the first verse of chapter 4, this conflict erupts in Jonah's open hostility toward Yahweh, bringing confusion and surprise upon us readers.

Herman Gunkel observed that the OT seldom probes the psychology of its characters.[11] Robert Alter extended Gunkel's discussion by extracting from the OT a scale for how much it reveals about its characters. At the lower end come

---

[11] Gunkel, *The Legends of Genesis*, 53–67.

descriptions of actions or of physical appearance. In the middle comes speech, either by or about the characters. At the upper end comes "the reliable narrator's explicit statement of what the characters feel, intend, desire."[12]

The fact that the narrator supplies Jonah's inward feelings moves us as close as possible to a full definition of this prophet's character. Reading up to 3:10, we have been led to conclude that all is well regarding the Ninevites—and that is true about their relationship to God. But now Jonah's anger over the salvation of the Ninevites calls for us to reevaluate Jonah. Meir Sternberg writes:

> So reading a character becomes a process of discovery, attended by all the biblical hallmarks: progressive reconstruction, tentative closure of discontinuities, frequent and sometimes painful reshaping in face of the unexpected, and intractable pockets of darkness to the very end.[13]

Jonah's first recorded prayer was from the belly of the great fish (2:2–10 [ET 2:1–9]).[14] His second is from the depths of his burning anger (4:2–3). Neither place is comfortable. In both instances, he has been swallowed up—first by the great fish and now by his great anger. It is significant that both prayers have similar vocabulary, with "He prayed [וַיִּתְפַּלֵּל] to Yahweh [אֶל־יְהוָה] and said [וַיֹּאמֶר/וַיֹּאמַר]" appearing in both 2:2–3 (ET 2:1–2) and 4:2. This verbal connection places Jonah's complaint in 4:1–3 in stark contrast to his song of praise in 2:3–10 (ET 2:2–9). The cessation of Yahweh's anger over Nineveh (see 3:9–10) is the signal for Jonah's anger to start. How ironic![15]

In Lk 15:7 Jesus states that there is much joy in heaven over one sinner who repents. But the repentance of the entire population of Nineveh—and even its animals[16]—brings no joy to Jonah, only intense anger. The prophet's anger is not just a matter of theological disagreement. Jonah is totally opposed to the gracious and merciful character of his God when God's mercy results in the salvation of Gentiles. The contrast between Jonah's response to Yahweh's salvation of Nineveh and the mariners' response to their salvation is startling. When the storm on the sea was stilled, "the men worshiped Yahweh with great

---

[12] Alter, *The Art of Biblical Narrative*, 116–17. Bar-Efrat renders a similar judgment (*Narrative Art in the Bible*, 47–92).

[13] Sternberg, *The Poetics of Biblical Narrative*, 323–24.

[14] Jonah apparently uttered a first prayer for deliverance after he was hurled into the sea. He refers to that first prayer in 2:3, 8 (ET 2:2, 7). However, the content of that first prayer is not recorded in the book. Then after Jonah was saved from Sheol by being swallowed by the great fish, he uttered a second prayer: the psalm of thanksgiving that is recorded in 2:3–10 (ET 2:2–9). Therefore 4:2–3 constitutes his third prayer mentioned in the book, but it is only the second recorded prayer. See the second reason *for including* the psalm in its present location under "The Place of the Psalm in the Book of Jonah" in "Introduction to Jonah 2."

[15] See "The Purpose of Satire in This True and Didactic Story" in "Jonah as Satire with Irony" in the introduction.

[16] The acts of repentance in 3:7–8 include the animals, even though they were not among "the men of Nineveh" who "believed in God" (3:5) and were saved through faith.

worship" (1:16). But when the storm of God's anger toward Nineveh is stilled and Yahweh changes his verdict, Jonah boils over with rage.

Jonah's feelings at Yahweh sparing Nineveh are described by means of both the verb רָעַע, "to be evil," and its cognate noun, רָעָה, in "a great evil" (4:1). The irony is that the Ninevites turn away from their "evil" (רָעָה in 3:8, 10a), which in turn prompts Yahweh to change his verdict about the "evil" (destruction) he had threatened (רָעָה in 3:10b), whereupon double "evil" (both the verb and the noun) immediately comes upon Jonah! In the Hebrew word order, this "evil" literally encloses the prophet: his name, "Jonah," is sandwiched between the preceding verb and the following noun (וַיֵּרַע אֶל־יוֹנָה רָעָה). What Nineveh and God have turned from in 3:8–10 now inflames Jonah, and in his anger he surrounds himself with "evil."

Jonah 4:1 is the only verse in the book with the verb רָעַע, "to be evil," and also the only instance where the noun "evil" is modified by the adjective גָּדוֹל, "great." The cognate accusative construction with the verb and the noun emphasizes the "evil" (see the first textual note on 4:1). The other cognate accusative constructions in the book are in 1:10, 16 (three constructions); 3:2; and 4:6. The vocabulary chosen for these emphatic statements rehearses some of the major themes of the narrative: "fear" (1:10), "worship," "sacrifice," and "vows" (1:16), the divine message ("call" in 3:2), "evil" (4:1), and "joy" (4:6).[17]

The noun or adjective רָעָה, "evil," is employed nine times throughout the narrative of Jonah.[c] It is used in two closely related ways. On the one hand, it refers to the wickedness of the Ninevites (1:2; 3:8, 10a) and of Jonah (4:1, 6). On the other hand, it refers to the divine punishment that Yahweh threatens and sometimes carries out (1:7–8; 3:10b; 4:2).

(c) Jonah 1:2, 7–8; 3:8, 10 (twice); 4:1–2, 6

"Evil" frames the entire narrative. The book begins with the "evil" perpetrated by the Ninevites (1:2). "Evil" afflicts the sailors in the form of the storm sent by Yahweh (1:7–8). Then the focus returns to the Ninevites as they repent and turn from their "evil way" (3:10a). Thereupon God changes his verdict and does not carry out the "evil" destruction of the city (3:10b); Yahweh characteristically changes his verdict about "evil" (4:2). Finally, "great evil" comes to Jonah (4:1), from which God seeks to save him (4:6).

In the narrative, "great" applies to the "great city" (1:2; 3:2–3; 4:11; cf. 3:5, 7), the storm (twice in 1:4; also 1:12), "great fear/worship" (1:10, 16), the "great fish" (2:1 [ET 1:17]), and "great joy" (4:6), but "great evil" (רָעָה גְדוֹלָה) only applies to Jonah (4:1).

It is an unforgiving heart that asks, "Lord, how many times … shall I forgive my brother?" (Mt 18:21). Yahweh forgives the sailors in chapter 1 and the Ninevites in chapter 3 and takes away all the "evil"—except in the reference

---

[17] See the literal translations of those verses, which reproduce the cognate accusative constructions in English.

to Jonah! Yahweh will attempt "to save him [Jonah] from his evil" (4:6), but the book ends without revealing whether that availed.

In Jonah, human "evil" sets into motion the reaction of Yahweh in judgment, unless he changes his verdict. "Evil" spreads contagiously from person to person: Nineveh's "evil" prompts the call of Jonah (1:2), whose subsequent flight (1:3) brings the "evil" storm that threatens the sailors (1:7–8), even though they are never called perpetrators of "evil." Yahweh alone can choose to break into this continuum of human evil and prevent the "evil" (judgment) from taking place (3:10b; 4:2). This is what he does for the converted Gentiles—the sailors (1:15) and the Ninevites (3:10b)—and what he attempts to do so for the Israelite prophet Jonah (4:6).

Here in 4:1 Jonah places Yahweh's change of verdict from judgment to salvation under his own human judgment! Yahweh saving Gentiles is, according to Jonah, the great evil! Indeed, the final use of "evil" (רָעָה) in the book depicts Yahweh trying "to save" Jonah "from his evil" (4:6) just as he had already saved the formerly unbelieving Ninevites from their "evil" (1:2; 3:8, 10a). Jonah is where Nineveh was: in need of deliverance from his all-consuming evil! This is ironic satire at its best.[18]

The greatest evil in the book is ... Jonah! As Luther writes about Jonah, "he, a servant of the true God and a member of the holiest land and nation, should turn out to be the worst and most grievous sinner, worse than the idolatrous heathen."[19] The shocking irony is that Jonah himself is alive only because of this very same grace active on his behalf. In chapter 2 he himself had just been graciously delivered from the depths of the sea, from Sheol itself, and quite undeservedly at that! Now he wants to place a limitation on who should receive that very same grace. In his psalm (2:3–10 [ET 2:2–9]), Jonah praises God for being gracious to him, but to extend the same benefits to the evil Ninevites elicits the prophet's ire. Jonah is angry because he cannot control the spread of the Gospel. But as he readily admitted after personally benefiting from it, the Gospel does not belong to him. "Salvation belongs to Yahweh" (2:10), and Yahweh alone decides who shall receive it (cf. Acts 1:8; 13:47).

While flight and descent are characteristic of Jonah's responses to Yahweh in chapters 1 and 2,[20] anger characterizes his responses in chapter 4. The verb חָרָה, "be hot; be infuriated," occurs four times in the book, all in this chapter in reference to Jonah (4:1, 4, 9 [twice]). Ironically, Jonah's anger is a response to Yahweh being "slow to anger" (אֶרֶךְ אַפַּיִם), as Jonah describes him in 4:2. Jonah indicates that Yahweh is not angry when he should be angry. This makes Jonah, well, angry!

---

[18] See "The Purpose of Satire in This True and Didactic Story" in "Jonah as Satire with Irony" in the introduction.

[19] AE 19:64.

[20] See בָּרַח, "flee," in 1:3, 10 (also 4:2), and יָרַד, "go down, descend," in 1:3 (twice), 5; 2:7 (ET 2:6; cf. also 2:3 [ET 2:2]). "Go down" is an antonym of Yahweh's command that Jonah should "arise" and go to Nineveh (1:2).

In 4:9 Jonah becomes angry again, this time not because Yahweh turns away his anger (as he did from the Ninevites), but because he exercises his judgment or anger upon Jonah by sending a worm to destroy the qiqayon plant. When Yahweh removes the pouting prophet's shade, Jonah challenges this action by Yahweh too. Nineveh Yahweh rescues; Jonah Yahweh judges! In light of such unfairness it would be better to die, says Jonah (4:3, 8–9).

He does have a point. Should guilty people escape responsibility, especially if they have perpetrated evil and brought calamities upon others?[21] Should repentance, even if genuine, remove the punishment demanded by their atrocities? Where is the justice in letting the guilty escape the recompense due them? Who wants to live in a world devoid of justice, one in which evildoers can sin with impunity?

Justice stands in tension with mercy, and when the two come into conflict, Yahweh's mercy prevails. Ultimately, it is the intercession of Jesus Christ, who suffered the divine judgment for the sin of all humanity, that fully satisfies God's justice and is the source of his superabounding mercy. However, Jonah considers it intolerable that Israel's experience in Exodus 32, where Moses' intercession after Israel's golden-calf apostasy led to Yahweh's change of verdict (Ex 32:11–14), should be mirrored in Nineveh, which is converted after Jonah's own prophetic intervention (Jonah 3:4).[22] He cannot stomach Yahweh cheapening his mercy by offering it to Ninevites!

Not only does Jonah announce God's Word, which brings mercy to people who in no way deserve it (3:4), he then goes on to prove that he as well is not worthy of that same mercy! This is exactly the point of chapter 4, and indeed the entire book: *grace is not earned or deserved, but Yahweh lavishes it on the undeserving, who receive it through repentance and faith* (Jonah 1:15–16; 3:5–10; cf. Rom 4:5)!

We simply stand under God's overflowing grace like rain, allowing its cool refreshment to fill our dry cracks. Then we pick up the bucket and dump it on someone else. Grace flows from Yahweh not on those who attempt to earn it, but on those who confess their need for it. The Spirit-empowered response is then to share it. But Jonah is like the angry older brother in the parable of the Prodigal Son (Lk 15:28–30): he views God's lavish welcome for undeserving sinners who repent as an insult to his "deserving" self. The prophet has yet to embrace the Law and Gospel character of God expressed in James 2:13: "For judgment is without mercy to one who has not shown mercy. Mercy triumphs over judgment."

Yahweh's word of judgment is not thereby reduced to a threat with no teeth in it. Sinful behavior can lead to temporal punishment and will lead to the eter-

---

[21] For Nineveh's well-deserved reputation as a violent aggressor, see the commentary on 1:2.

[22] Ex 32:14 uses the Niphal of נחם to say that Yahweh "changed his verdict," and this is the same verb used in Jonah 3:9–10; 4:2. See further the excursus "When Yahweh Changes a Prior Verdict."

nal judgment of sinners (Gal 6:7–8), but that is not Yahweh's goal for *any* of his creatures. His actions serve his overarching goal to bring the gift of life and salvation for all people, as indeed he has done in Jesus Christ. His threats and punitive actions aim to bring people to repentance, to prepare them to receive in faith his gift of life everlasting through his Word of mercy. This salvific goal is vividly illustrated by the sailors and the Ninevites. The sailors were brought to repentance by the storm and converted to saving faith in Yahweh (1:16) through Jonah's testimony about him (1:9). The Ninevites, who heeded the preached Word and were changed through repentance and saving faith, now await the resurrection, when they shall arise with all believers and condemn those who failed to believe (Mt 12:41; Lk 11:32).[23]

Jonah Explains Why He Fled (4:2a–c)

4:2a–c   The narrator records Jonah's commentary explaining his actions in 1:3. Only now do we learn Jonah's rationale for his earlier flight. The narrator deliberately had omitted any explanation for why Jonah responded to Yahweh's Word in 1:2 by heading for Tarshish in 1:3, and so readers are left to wonder about the reason until this final chapter.

Meir Sternberg states that the absence of an explanation between Jonah 1:2 and 1:3 is "the only biblical instance where a surprise gap controls the reader's progress over a whole book."[24] Besides "a surprise gap," various other terms have been used to label this kind of literary feature, including the "synoptic/resumptive technique" (the repetition of an earlier episode in which the second account is longer, but dependent on the first),[25] a vacancy, a lacuna, a hiatus, and a blank.[26] But it is most frequently referred to as a "gap," a "lack of information about the world. It is an event, motive, causal link, character trait, plot structure or law of probability contrived by a temporal displacement."[27] Some gaps in narratives are only temporary: they are "open[ed] at some point upon the continuum of the text only to [be filled in] explicitly and satisfactorily … at a subsequent stage,"[28] as in Jonah 4:2. Other types of gaps are permanent because they produce "questions or sets of questions to which no single, fully ex-

---

[23]   See further the excursus "The Sign of Jonah."

[24]   Sternberg, *The Poetics of Biblical Narrative*, 318.

[25]   Brichto, *Toward a Grammar of Biblical Poetics*, 13–14.

[26]   See Craig, *A Poetics of Jonah*, 74.

[27]   Steinberg, *The Poetics of Biblical Narrative*, 235. He gives this definition of the technique (p. 186):

> From the viewpoint of what is directly given in the language, the literary work consists of bits and fragments to be linked and pieced together in the process of reading: it establishes a system of gaps that must be filled in. This gap-filling ranges from simple linkage of elements, which the reader performs automatically, to intricate networks that are figured out consciously, laboriously, hesitantly, and with constant modifications in the light of the additional information disclosed in later stages of reading. Even genres considered far from sophisticated literary technique demand such gap-filling.

[28]   Sternberg, *Expositional Modes and Temporal Ordering in Fiction*, 51.

plicit and authoritative answer is made by the text."[29] Jonah ends with such a permanent gap because we are never told how Jonah responds to Yahweh's final question (4:11).

Why does the narrator withhold Jonah's reason for fleeing until now? In this integrated and highly sophisticated narrative, nowhere in the first three chapters are we told why Jonah flees. Once we arrive at 4:2, we understand that the narrator has done his utmost to provoke our search for a rationale. Jonah registers his protest in the first chapter by fleeing (1:3) and such actions as descending to the inmost parts of the ship, sleeping (1:5), and offering to be thrown overboard (1:12). The narrator records these but never explains the reason for them, heightening our curiosity. Even Jonah's lengthy psalm (2:3–10 [ET 2:2–9]) provides no decisive means to close the gap. Attempts to fill it remain unsuccessful until the prophet finally answers our question, "Jonah, why did you run?"

In contrast to the call narratives of Moses (Ex 4:1, 10, 13), Isaiah (Is 6:5), and Jeremiah (Jer 1:6), where those prophets quickly resolve the gap by explaining why they initially were unwilling to preach, the question about Jonah's initial unwillingness extends over the length of three chapters. There are many ways we could have answered it. For example, until 4:2, we might have believed that Jonah was afraid to go to Nineveh because it was a city full of blood (Nahum 3:1) or that he was too tenderhearted to carry a message of doom to a great city. It is even possible that we might have correctly inferred that Jonah fled toward Tarshish precisely because of his mean spirit toward Nineveh: he did not want to preach to it because he did not want it to be saved. But we could not be absolutely sure that was the reason until Jonah speaks his mind in 4:2.

So the narrator keeps us guessing almost to the end of the book. The reversal in 3:10–4:3 (when Nineveh is spared, Jonah changes from the prophet who faithfully spoke Yahweh's Word in 3:2–4 to an angry antagonist who opposes Yahweh in 4:2–3) shatters any benign view of Jonah and changes our entire view of the narrative. Ironically, the same kind of change or overturning that was promised in 3:4 also happens in us as we read the narrative! By means of this gap that is now filled, we become more intimately involved.

First, we are forced by our own questions about Jonah's motivation in 1:2–3 to seek explanations for our own motivations for why we fail to proclaim the Gospel to the "Ninevites" in our life. Second, when Jonah finally does fill the gap, we are appalled. How can Jonah be so upset that Nineveh has turned from its evil and now is saved? Where is the prophet's forgiving spirit? And how dare he accuse and condemn Yahweh for being … Yahweh! Jonah 4:2 reveals that the prophet is far more vengeful than we suspected. His reason for fleeing the command (1:3), then, is Yahweh's loving attitude toward people who are not Israelites (he even has compassion for their animals [4:11])!

---

[29] Sternberg, *Expositional Modes and Temporal Ordering in Fiction*, 50.

As Jonah's prayer fills the gap, it shifts the focus of the entire narrative. It brackets all that has happened in between 1:3 and 4:2, from Yahweh hurling the great storm (1:4) through his deliverance of Nineveh (3:10), and brings us back to the beginning. Jonah's reference to "my word" in 4:2 opposes the Word of Yahweh that started it all (1:1–2). In this way, the noun "word" (דָּבָר, 1:1; 4:2) frames the entire narrative. The divine Word comes to Jonah in the opening verse of the book, "The Word of Yahweh came to Jonah" (1:1), and again in 3:1, "The Word of Yahweh came to Jonah a second time." The divine Word is emphasized again in 3:2: "And call out to it [Nineveh] the call that I am about to speak to you." In 3:3 Jonah arises and goes to Nineveh "according to the Word of Yahweh." The "word" which the prophet delivers on behalf of Yahweh reaches the king in 3:6: "When this word reached the king of Nineveh …" Then 3:10 uses the verb דָּבַר, "to speak, threaten," which is cognate to דָּבָר, "word": when Yahweh "saw their works," he "changed his verdict about the evil that he threatened [דִּבֶּר] to do to them, and he did not do [it]."

With the conclusion of the narrative about Yahweh's efficacious Word, which brought the Ninevites to repentance and salvation in chapter 3, the prophet now expresses his thoughts in terms of his own "word" by saying, "Was this not my word [דְבָרִי]?" (4:2). Jonah appoints himself as a religious advisor to Yahweh and rails against his God, emphasizing the irreconcilable difference between the divine "Word" and his human "word." Apparently Jonah has not read the words of another eighth-century prophet: "All flesh is grass. … The grass withers, the flower fades, but the Word of our God stands forever" (Is 40:6, 8).

Jonah's prayer to Yahweh in Jonah 4:2–3 takes us back not only to 1:3, but also to the prophet's prayer in chapter 2. The first textual note on 4:2 points out the verbal correspondences between the beginnings of both prayers (2:2–3 [ET 2:1–2] and 4:2). Earlier, Jonah was in a quandary in the belly of the great fish (2:1–2 [ET 1:17; 2:1]). Now he is in a quandary because he announced a prophetic message that Yahweh would change Nineveh, and in Jonah's opinion, the change went in the wrong direction. These connections suggest that structurally 4:2–3 is the counterpart to 2:3–10 (ET 2:2–9). In important ways, these two prayers are opposites. This includes a difference in genre: 2:3–10 (ET 2:2–9) is a poetic psalm, whereas 4:2–3 is a prose speech. The content is also opposite. Whereas Jonah praised the mercy of Yahweh in chapter 2, he now turns around and deplores it in chapter 4. In the psalm, Jonah praised Yahweh for the salvation that came to him through the provision of the great fish. Now in his speech, his tone is dramatically different: he castigates Yahweh for giving his grace to the Ninevites.

From a purely quantitative standpoint, the psalm obviously has a greater length compared to its parallel in 4:2–3. However, this imbalance is intentional; the narrator has intentionally created other imbalances at several points in the narrative. Most obvious are those verses that have no parallels in the corresponding section. In general, chapters 1 and 3 are parallel, and chapters 2 and

4 are parallel.[30] However, 1:9–15b and 1:16 have no counterpart in chapter 3, and 4:5 and 4:8–11 are unmatched by any material in chapter 2. Only in some parts of the book does the narrator maintain perfect symmetry.[31]

Despite the lack of exact correspondence between these prayers, the narrator has included several similarities. For example, the prayers share the key words: חֶסֶד, "loyal love," in both "the One who loves them" (2:9 [ET 2:8]) and "abounding in loyal love" (4:2); חַיַּי, "my life," in both 2:7 (ET 2:6) and 4:3; נַפְשִׁי, "my life," in both 2:8 (ET 2:7) and 4:3.[32] Both prayers refer back to an earlier distress Jonah experienced. In chapter 2, he recalls his descent to Sheol and the underworld (2:3, 7 [ET 2:2, 6]), and in chapter 4 he recalls why he tried to flee to Tarshish (4:2). Both prayers are responses by Jonah to Yahweh's action of deliverance: saving Jonah himself in chapter 2 and saving Nineveh in chapter 3. And both prayers by this eighth-century prophet use older material: the psalm employs words and themes from the book of Psalms, including some by David (tenth century BC),[33] and the prayer in Jonah 4:2 employs Israel's ancient creedal formula from Ex 34:6–7 (by Moses in the fifteenth century BC).

Crucial for the contextual interpretation of Jonah's current prayer (4:2–3) is the need for some satisfactory explanation for the discrepancy between the spiritual condition of Jonah in his psalm (2:3–10 [ET 2:2–9]) and his disposition toward Yahweh in chapters 1, 3, and 4. It almost appears as though we meet two entirely different "Jonahs" in our reading of the narrative. The "Jonah" of the historical prose often appears callous and prideful, whereas the "Jonah" of the psalm mostly is thankful and humble.[34]

But before we jump too quickly in this direction we must note that the portrayal of Jonah in the prose narrative is not absolutely negative. In 4:6 he rejoices over the qiqayon plant, and the context implies that his joy is in response to a divine act of deliverance (from the searing sun; cf. 4:8). Yahweh God "provided" the qiqayon plant "to save him [Jonah] from his evil" (4:6). Although he does not burst forth in a new psalm of praise to Yahweh, his delight is essentially the same as in his psalm, where he rejoiced that Yahweh "provided a great fish" (2:1 [ET 1:17]) to save him from Sheol.[35] Additionally, Jonah's re-

---

[30] See "Introduction to Jonah 1" and "Introduction to Jonah 2."

[31] For a good example of perfect symmetry, see "Introduction to Jonah 4," which explains that the lengths of the speeches of Jonah and Yahweh match perfectly in terms of the number of Hebrew words. Another example is the identical purpose clause, "so we will not perish," spoken by both Gentile leaders: the captain in 1:6 and the king of Nineveh in 3:9.

[32] These similarities are noted by Allen, *Joel, Obadiah, Jonah and Micah*, 198–99, including n. 108.

[33] See the first textual note on 2:10 (ET 2:9) and the commentary on 2:3 (ET 2:2).

[34] The wording in parts of the psalm, however, reveals a certain self-centeredness; see, for example, the first textual note on 2:5 (ET 2:4). This is especially true when Jonah's language is compared to that of the Psalms (see the first textual note on 2:10 [ET 2:9] and the commentary on 2:3 [ET 2:2]).

[35] See the excursus "Sheol."

bellious reaction to Yahweh's Word at the beginning of the narrative (1:3) should not be construed to mean the prophet lacks any faith in Yahweh or does not joyfully trust in God as the Savior of Israelites. His displeasure is with Yahweh's will and ways as they relate to non-Israelites. There is no good reason to suppose that his confession of faith in Yahweh in 1:9 is completely insincere or hypocritical. All this is to say that the Jonah of chapters 1, 3, and 4 is the same Jonah as in chapter 2.

The differences are best explained by who Jonah really is: "simultaneously a saint and a sinner" (*simul iustus et peccator*).[36] In 4:2 Jonah's sinful, nationalistic old Adam speaks and declares that Yahweh is a God who is soft on sin and weak on justice. Even though the prophet has been hurled overboard (1:15), swallowed (2:1 [ET 1:17]), vomited onto dry ground (2:11 [ET 2:10]), and used as the agent to bring Yahweh's forgiveness to Israel's (and Jonah's) enemies (3:4, 10), he still has yet to learn the lesson that "Yahweh is good to all, and his mercies are upon all of his creatures" (Ps 145:9).

Jonah's issue here is not simply that Yahweh changes his verdict from judgment to salvation, but *for whom* he has changed it on this occasion. The prophet is aware that Israel's very existence depends upon Yahweh's willingness to change his verdict and be merciful to his people despite their ongoing sin.[37] At another time in Jonah's ministry, Yahweh was compassionate to Israel (2 Ki 14:25), refusing to blot out her name (2 Ki 14:27), in spite of her persistent sinfulness, epitomized by her king (2 Ki 14:23–24). If Yahweh had dealt with Israel as the nation deserved, she would have perished long ago.

Jonah's real problem is the indiscriminate extension of Yahweh's mercy to another people. He complains about Yahweh's leniency toward the guilty Gentiles. The elect nation of Israel should reap the blessings of God's grace, but the unbelieving nations should be made to reap the harvest of destruction, not be converted and saved. That's only fair! After all, this same Jonah announced the greatness of Israel's future (2 Ki 14:25). Now he is called upon to offer a future to Nineveh, in the heart of the very country (Assyria) that will put an end to the glorious vision for Israel (2 Ki 17:5–6). The Northern Kingdom of Israel, the larger part of Yahweh's covenant nation, will fall to Assyria in 722/721 BC, and the future executioner is now offered a new life. This is not a just way for Yahweh to proceed! By delivering Nineveh during the reign of Jeroboam II in the early to mid eighth century, Yahweh prepares for Israel's destruction later in the same century.

So the basic issue, then, between Yahweh and Jonah is that of Yahweh's justice, of Yahweh not treating the Ninevites according to what they deserve. Yahweh is much too free with his mercy. It is good that he is merciful to Israel,

---

[36] See further "Jonah as Sinner and Saint" in the commentary on 1:2; "The Place of the Psalm in the Book of Jonah" in "Introduction to Jonah 2"; the commentary on 2:8 (ET 2:7); and the excursus "Death and Resurrection Motifs in Luther's Baptismal Theology."

[37] See Ex 32:9–14, where all Israel (save Moses) was almost destroyed. See further the excursus "When Yahweh Changes a Prior Verdict."

but for the other peoples he needs to be more strict in applying the rules of the very moral order he himself ordained in the first place.

Why does Yahweh do this? This question offers a comparison between Jonah and Job. Job is deeply wounded and perplexed in the face of Yahweh's ways with him. Like Jonah, Job experiences a great upheaval in his life. Both men are angry at Yahweh's behavior towards them, and both demand some kind of explanation from him. Yet whereas Job finally accepts that Yahweh's ways are not his ways (Job 42:1–6), Jonah's resistance remains unresolved—an open question at the bitter end (Jonah 4:10–11).

To a certain extent, the narrative of Jonah, like the book of Job, is a theodicy.[38] Why does God allow evil to afflict his own people and also leave the wicked unpunished—at least for a time? Why should God forgive Nineveh and thus allow the Assyrians to destroy Israel in 722/721 BC? To be sure, later generations of Ninevites will revert to the city's earlier pagan ways. More than a century after its conversion through Jonah, Nineveh and Assyria will be destroyed by the Babylonians and Medes in 612 BC (see Nahum). Why does God not destroy the city now?

In 4:2 Jonah indicates that he had anticipated that Yahweh would act in a way that would reveal his "gracious and merciful" character. What is ironic is that earlier in the narrative, the prophet is surprisingly slow in understanding what is happening aboard the ship in the storm. In every event in chapter 1, the sailors are one step ahead of Jonah. They immediately recognize the need for prayer and urge Jonah to join them (1:5–6). They are aware that someone is responsible for the storm and throw lots to discern who is to blame (1:7). When the sailors, who know Jonah had fled from Yahweh (1:10), try to row back to the dry land (1:13), they are anticipating what should have been Jonah's instruction: "Take me back to shore so that I may go to Nineveh." The irony is that the one time in the book that Jonah anticipates what Yahweh will do, it brings him great grief!

More irony is involved in the use of יָדַע, "to know." The king confesses that he does not know how Yahweh will respond: in humility he says, "Who knows whether God may turn and change his verdict and turn away from the fierceness of his anger so we will not perish?" (3:9). In contrast, Jonah here confesses, "I knew that you are a gracious and merciful God" (4:2), but in the context of Jonah's anger and pride. The prophet who "knew" the ways of Yahweh in fact does not know! He ends up calling "evil good and good evil" (Is 5:20). "Woe to those who are wise in their own eyes!" (Is 5:21).

Jonah's Creedal Confession of Gracious Yahweh (4:2d–e)

4:2d–e   The book of Jonah has two creedal statements about Yahweh, both uttered by Jonah. The first was in 1:9. The second is here in 4:2: Yahweh is "a gracious and merciful God, slow to anger and abounding in loyal love,

---

[38]   See Fretheim, "Jonah and Theodicy."

and changing [his] verdict about evil." The foundation of this confession is Ex 34:6–7,[39] where Moses records Yahweh's self-description:

> [6]Yahweh, Yahweh, a God who is merciful and gracious, slow to anger and abounding in loyal love and truth, [7]keeping loyal love for thousands, forgiving iniquity and rebellion and sin; yet surely he will not hold guiltless, visiting the iniquity of fathers upon children and upon children's children, up to the third and fourth generations.

Jonah revises these verses from Exodus in several ways, some of which emphasize the grace of Yahweh. Jonah places "gracious" prior to "merciful," but then has the same "slow to anger and abounding in loyal love." In place of Moses' reference to Yahweh's "truth," Jonah has "changing your verdict about evil" (using terminology from Jonah 3:8–10), which can be compared to Moses' later phrase in Ex 34:7, "forgiving iniquity and rebellion and sin." But Jonah entirely omits the second half of Ex 34:7. Altogether, Jonah's changes emphasize "gracious" (which he puts first) and "changing your verdict about evil" (a phrase Jonah adds) while eliminating "truth" and punishment ("yet surely he will not hold guiltless, visiting the iniquity …").

Strengthening the assumption that Jonah is deliberately adapting the Exodus passage is the fact that other Jonah verses borrow from the language of Exodus. The narrator's wording in Jonah 3:9 of the decree of the king of Nineveh also alludes to the book of Exodus, specifically Ex 32:12b, where Moses implores Yahweh, "Turn [שׁוּב] from your fierce anger, and change your verdict [Niphal of נָחַם] about this evil against your people." Moreover, Jonah 3:10 is almost an exact quote of Ex 32:14: "Yahweh changed his verdict about the evil that he threatened to do to his people."

When Jonah 3:9–10 and 4:2 are placed along side of Ex 32:12–14 and Ex 34:6–7, it is clear that the same grace and mercy Yahweh showed to Israel he now gives to the Ninevites. Grace has universal implications! Jonah's response is similar to the miserly complaint of the workers who labored all day in the vineyard in Mt 20:12, who complain about the workers who were hired most recently: "These last men worked only one hour, and you have made them equal to us who have borne the burden of the day and the heat." "Made them equal to us" is the key phrase that could also express the cause of Jonah's anger. While Jonah knows that Yahweh is "gracious and merciful" (Jonah 4:2), he believes Yahweh should display these characteristics exclusively with Israel (cf. Joel 2:13), and certainly not with Nineveh. Jonah cannot fathom that Yahweh relates to a Gentile nation in the same way that he relates to his chosen people Israel. This implies that the chosen people are no better than the others; by God's grace, they are equal!

There are sixteen other OT passages that use the same language of at least some of the major parts of Jonah's confession in 4:2.[d] Of them, the vocabulary

(d) Ex 34:6–7; Num 14:8; Deut 4:31; Pss 78:38; 86:5, 15; 103:8; 111:4; 112:4; 116:5; 145:8; Joel 2:13; Hab 1:3; Neh 9:17, 31; 2 Chr 30:9

---

[39] See Dentan, "The Literary Affinities of Exodus XXXIV 6f." See also Limburg, who analyzes Jonah 4:2 and ten OT texts that are similar to it (*Jonah*, 89–92).

in Jonah 4:2 correlates most closely with Joel 2:13. Thomas Dozeman compares these two passages. They have striking similarities. Both include "changing his/your verdict about evil" (absent from Ex 34:6–7). Both of their contexts include the hopeful expression that perhaps God will not bring about a threatened destruction (Joel 2:14a; Jonah 3:9a); both have a repetition of the motif of mercy (חוּס, "to have pity," in Joel 2:17 and Jonah 4:10–11). Moreover, both prophets were to announce a threatening word from Yahweh. Joel was to announce the judgment in store for Judah on the Day of Yahweh (Joel 2:1, 11), whereas Jonah was to proclaim that Nineveh soon will be "changed," perhaps by destruction (Jonah 3:1–4; cf. 1:2; 3:9). Both Judah and Nineveh are called to repent; this involves traditional rites such as fasting, weeping, and sackcloth (Joel 2:12; Jonah 3:5–8), and is "also expanded in each context to include a change in character: thus, just as the people of Judah must rend their hearts in addition to their garments" (Joel 2:13), "so also must the Ninevites turn from their evil and violent ways" (Jonah 3:8). At the end of each account is an appeal that shows concern for the relationship between other nations and Israel's God (Joel 2:17; Jonah 4:10–11).[40]

Ps 145:8–9 is another text that shares similar vocabulary with Jonah 4:2:

> Gracious and merciful is Yahweh, slow to anger and great in loyal love. Yahweh is good to all, and his mercies are upon all of his creatures.

This passage cites Israel's creedal language in relation not simply to Israel, but to "all of his creatures." The formulas rooted in Yahweh's covenant with Israel (Ex 34:6–7) have broader implications involving the providential goodness of Yahweh, which extends to all that he has made. In this way, the God of the covenant never ceases to be the God of all creation. Other nations are objects of Yahweh's care, as is stated in the Noahic covenant (Gen 9:9–16) and reaffirmed in places like Amos 9:7.

Yet ironically, the "loyal love" of Yahweh, which brought forth Jonah's praises in his psalm (חֶסֶד, 2:9 [ET 2:8]) when Yahweh displayed it toward him, is now one of the characteristics that cause Jonah grief when Yahweh displays it toward another people (4:2). The irony is that apart from the characteristics of Yahweh Jonah now names, the prophet would not be alive to complain about them!

Jonah's response to Yahweh's essential Gospel characteristics, which he names in this verse, prompts some commentators to label him a monster.[41] Mon-

---

[40] Dozeman, "Inner-Biblical Interpretation of Yahweh's Gracious and Compassionate Character," 207–10 (the quotes are on p. 210). Schultz, "The Ties That Bind," 37, notes: "The use of Exod 34:6–7 within the Minor Prophets has received extensive treatment, focusing on the context and modifications of the individual occurrences." See the works listed by Schultz in note 33 (pp. 37–38). In addition to the connections between Jonah 4:2 and Joel 2:13, both passages are also connected to Micah 7:18 and Nahum 1:2–3.

[41] Allen rhetorically asks this about Jonah: "What religious monster is this?" (*Joel, Obadiah, Jonah and Micah*, 229) and (in n. 11) says that von Rad, *Der Prophet Jona*, 11, calls Jonah a *religionspsychologisches Monstrum*.

sters (the Latin *monstrum*, "monster," originally meaning "divine omen," comes from the Latin *monere*, "to show, warn, reveal") reveal issues that led to the matrix of social and religious relations that generated them. What makes Jonah such a monster is that he is denying the very grace to Nineveh that Yahweh has already extended to him. God's grace is not the possession of the elect. It is not at our disposal to dispense as we see fit. It is something that we, simply through faith in Christ, are continually *given* without any merit on our part. And if that grace is not embraced and lived out in our relations with others, we evolve into religious monsters!

Jonah 4:2 is just the second time in the narrative where the prophet at least partially confesses his sin of evading Yahweh and his call to preach to Nineveh. However, both times he avoids a full acknowledgement of the extent of his transgression against his God. Three times in chapter 1 his flight was characterized as being "away from the presence of Yahweh" (twice in 1:3; once in 1:10), but in 4:2 he merely admits, "I previously fled toward Tarshish." His only previous admission was in 1:12. Twice the sailors seek to find out who was responsible for "this evil"—the storm that came upon them (1:7–8), but Jonah in reply to their inquiry did not acknowledge responsibility for "evil"; he only conceded, "I know that it is on my account that *this great storm* is against you" (1:12). In the psalm of chapter 2, Jonah made no mention of running away from the presence of Yahweh. Thus throughout the book, Jonah exhibits the habit of confessing his sin only partially; he never fully lays his guilt before his God. In 4:2 as he draws on Ex 34:6–7, he scrupulously avoids the explicit language of Moses, "forgiving iniquity and rebellion and sin" (Ex 34:7).

Jonah 4:2 is the third time that the prophet, when presented with a crisis, offers a theological statement. The first time was in 1:9, where he declared that he was a worshiper of Yahweh (the confession of faith that led to the conversion of the sailors), and the second was the psalm he uttered in chapter 2 after being swallowed by the great fish. Both 1:9 and his psalm (2:3–10 [ET 2:2–9]) draw on older biblical texts,[42] as also does 4:2 (see the commentary above).

Jonah's First Wish for Death (4:3)

4:3 This verse is Jonah's first wish for death. It comes in the form of a prayer to Yahweh. His second death wish will be in 4:8 and is not overtly addressed to God; it seems more like a prayer to himself.

Yahweh alone creates and sustains all life.[43] He desires all people to be saved and live so as to glorify him (e.g., Pss 50:15; 86:9; 1 Cor 10:31; 2 Cor 4:15). Therefore, any wish for death is self-centered; it disregards the Lord of

---

[42] For OT antecedents of Jonah 1:9, see the commentary on 1:9 and the excursus "Yahweh, the Creator God." For the dependence of Jonah's psalm on other biblical psalms, see the first textual note on 2:10 (ET 2:9) and the commentary on 2:3 (ET 2:2).

[43] See the excursus "Yahweh, the Creator God."

life. Even though Jonah confesses the gracious characteristics of Yahweh in 4:2, he surrounds it with nine references to himself in 4:2–3. Preceding his confession, he says, "Was not this *my* word while *I* was still upon *my* ground? … *I* previously fled … because *I* knew," and following it, he says, "Take *my* life from *me* for *my* death would be better than *my* life!" Jonah's affirmations about himself undermine his affirmations about Yahweh. Colossal egocentrism ensnares true faith. The human context betrays the divine text. "I" and "my" prevail unto death, almost literally! As the narrative continues, finally the divine text will prevail over the human context: gracious and merciful Yahweh will continue to reach out to Jonah despite the prophet's obsession with himself. Gracious Yahweh seeks to subvert egocentric and angry Jonah.

Although Jonah's prophecy of Yahweh's words (Jonah 3:4) converted and saved the city, he feels that he can no longer live with that result. "Over my dead body" is his vehement reaction to Yahweh's grace. Himself forgiven, he cannot accept that non-Israelites should be forgiven as well. That Yahweh's grace is available to all people through repentance and faith is an intolerable threat to Jonah's worldview. As Yahweh shows compassion to Nineveh, Jonah's entire world collapses. His extreme anger is an indication of the depth of commitment he has to his own fundamental beliefs, which now lie shattered at his feet.

Jonah's plea in this verse is not identical to[44] but is reminiscent of his earlier instruction to the mariners, "Lift me up and hurl me into the sea" (1:12). When pressed by uncomfortable circumstances, Jonah's reaction is to seek death as an escape, to throw in the towel. He is consumed by a four-letter word from the pit of hell: *quit*! If Yahweh is going to forgive non-Israelites, then Jonah prefers death rather than life!

With this response, Jonah indicates that his problem with Yahweh is not simply at an esoteric or intellectual level. Rather, Jonah's struggle is fundamentally theological in character, and it has a direct relationship to life as it actually is lived. It is a conflict over the Gospel—and who owns it, provides it, manages it, and delivers it. The prophet cannot bear that he is not in charge of the Gospel, not able to keep it for himself and his own people! Luther writes:

> He [Jonah] would rather not preach, yes, he prefers to be dead rather than to
> see the grace of God, which he regards the exclusive possession of the children of Israel, imparted also to the Gentiles, who have neither the Word of

---

[44] The two situations are distinguished by some differences. In chapter 1, neither Jonah nor anyone else uses the noun "death" or the verb "to die," but the captain and the sailors do use "perish" (1:6, 14). Jonah's confession of Yahweh in 1:9 converts the sailors, who then are saved (1:15–16), but Jonah expresses no anguish over their salvation. He has already been hurled into the sea before the storm stops and the sailors worship Yahweh (1:15–16). Jonah in 1:12 has not reached the depth of despair that overwhelms him in 4:3, 8 and moves him to request death. In chapter 4, Jonah is angry, depressed, and despairing since he has witnessed the Ninevites' faith in God and acts of repentance (3:5–9), culminating in Yahweh's decision not to destroy the city (3:10). Adding insult to injury, he—Jonah—had been the instrument of it all!

God nor the law of Moses nor divine worship nor the prophets nor anything else but who even contend against God and His Word and His people.[45]

Without the ability to limit Yahweh's gift of the Gospel, Jonah seeks death. "Die" and "death" (the verb מוּת and noun מָוֶת) together occur four times in this chapter (מוּת in 4:8 and מָוֶת in 4:3, 8–9). Death was also a prominent theme in chapter 2, but was expressed with different vocabulary as Jonah went down to Sheol and the underworld (2:3, 7 [ET 2:2, 6]), and his life pined away (2:8 [ET 2:7]). The captain (1:6), the sailors (1:14), and the king of Nineveh (3:9) all prayed not to "perish"; in the face of death, they sought life. Ironically, however, when the Ninevites are spared from death, Jonah wishes to die (4:3). Again selfishly, when Jonah's qiqayon plant is not spared (4:7; see also 4:10), he expresses his second wish to die (4:8).

Throughout the narrative, the issue is life versus death. Jonah and Yahweh never agree about who should live and who should die. After the unbelieving sailors and the Ninevites are converted to saving faith and are given new life, Jonah concludes, "Death is much to be preferred to life with a God such as this."[46]

Suicide is anathema to Yahweh. It shows scorn not only for the sanctity of life (cf. Ex 20:13) but also for the God who gives and preserves all life. There are a few biblical examples of someone committing suicide, notably Judas, who hung himself after realizing he had betrayed innocent blood (Mt 27:3–5; cf. Acts 1:18). Samson's last act against the Philistines kills him as well as thousands of his enemies (Judg 16:29–30). The wounded Saul kills himself to avoid the shame of being killed by the Philistines (1 Sam 31:1–6). Ahithophel, David's advisor who has deserted to Absalom, hangs himself when his advice is trumped by Hushai (2 Sam 17:23). And the rebellious Zimri burns himself to death when his coup d'état fails (1 Ki 16:18).

David Daube analyzes every instance of an act of suicide or a wish for death in the OT. Of interest here is that he designates the requests made by Moses, Elijah, Jeremiah, and Jonah as the tradition of "the weary prophet."[47] But Jeremiah's so-called request for death is in reality a wistful (and futile) yearning that he should never have been born (Jer 20:14–18) and not a desire that his life come to an end. Consequently, it should be categorized with Job 3:2–7 as a curse on life. This leaves the requests of Moses, Elijah, and Jonah in a group for consideration.[48]

Moses in exasperation prays for death, burdened by the constant complaining of the Israelites, in Numbers 11. He places the responsibility for his frustration on the people, but also upon Yahweh, who had called him to bear the burden of the prophetic office. Moses becomes displeased after he hears

---

[45] AE 19:51.

[46] Fretheim, *The Message of Jonah*, 49.

[47] Daube, "Death as a Release in the Bible," especially 96–98.

[48] Sasson also deems Moses and Elijah to be the examples closest to Jonah (*Jonah*, 284–85).

the weeping of the people and knows that the anger of Yahweh against them has been kindled (Num 11:10). Moses complains that his predicament is due to Yahweh's less-than-compassionate dealings with him (Num 11:11) and the continuance of his misery is in part due to Yahweh's actions (Num 11:15). Put this way, it is clear that Moses is not only brought to despair by the murmuring of the Israelites, but he is also frustrated at Yahweh for calling him to attempt to lead this people, who continually provoke Yahweh to unleash his anger and vengeance against them (e.g., Num 11:1). Yahweh's response is to anoint seventy assistants for Moses to ease the burden of dealing with the people (Num 11:16–17).

In 1 Kings 19, in flight from Jezebel, Elijah begs Yahweh to take his life (1 Ki 19:4). Queen Jezebel has sworn to kill him (1 Ki 19:2) because of his triumph over the prophets of Baal on Mount Carmel (1 Kings 18). It also appears that Elijah feels that he is a failure as a prophet ("I am no better than my fathers," 1 Ki 19:4), and he thinks he is the only true follower of Yahweh left. However, Elijah overlooks Obadiah and the hundred prophets of Yahweh still in hiding (1 Ki 18:3–4). In response, Yahweh commissions Elijah to anoint Elisha as his successor (1 Ki 19:16) and declares that he will preserve seven thousand people in Israel who have not worshiped Baal (1 Ki 19:18).

Jonah strikes a noble pose by echoing a prayer of Elijah. The first six Hebrew words of Jonah's plea in 4:3 include the same four terms that comprised Elijah's plea in 1 Ki 19:4:

עַתָּה יְהוָה֙ קַח נַפְשִׁי

Now, Yahweh, take my life.

This is just one of the ways in which the book of Jonah compares and contrasts this prophet with Elijah.[49]

Elijah had continued, "For I am no better than my fathers." Elijah, wearied by his endless struggle with Baalism, was convinced that he would not succeed in saving Israel from idolatry, just as his fathers had not succeeded. However, Jonah's lame explanation for his plea is "for my death would be better than my life!" (4:3). Through Jonah's preaching (3:4), Nineveh has been converted from idolatry to saving faith in the one true God, but Jonah is disappointed with the very success of his mission! He would rather join his forefathers in death than face a life in fellowship with Gentiles who believe in his same God!

This is biting satire of Jonah.[50] He is not worthy of the mantle of Elijah, who willingly ministered outside Israel (1 Ki 17:9–24). Jonah apes Elijah's

---

[49] See further "Jonah and Elijah" in the introduction. Elijah sat under a broom tree when he prayed to die (1 Ki 19:4), and later Jonah will utter another wish for death while under a qiqayon plant (Jonah 4:8). As Elijah then experienced a revelation of Yahweh on Mount Horeb (1 Ki 19:9–18), Jonah will receive a revelation in Jonah 4:10–11.

[50] See "The Purpose of Satire in This True and Didactic Story" in "Jonah as Satire with Irony" in the introduction.

words but shows himself to be far inferior to his predecessor. He seems to have Elijah's depression without Elijah's excuse. Yahweh does not grant Jonah's request to die, but instead seeks to teach him the truth expressed by Jesus. When the master treats all the workers in his vineyard equally (picturing how God regards all believers in Christ as equal members of his kingdom), those (like Jonah) who have "borne the burden of the day and the heat" (Mt 20:12) complain to him, but he replies, "Do not I have the right to do what I want with what is my own? Or are you envious because I am good?" (Mt 20:15).

The most significant shared feature is that Yahweh denies the entreaties for death by all three of these prophets, Moses, Elijah, and Jonah. Normally a prophet's prayer would be powerful and efficacious; see James 5:13–18, which even names Elijah. When Yahweh denies a prophet's petition, he lessens the standing of that prophet, both in relation to himself and in the eyes of the people. Moreover, the immediate divine response to the requests for death by Moses and Elijah was a diminishment in their prophetic authority. A portion of Moses' authority was divided among the seventy elders (Num 11:16–17). Elijah anointed Elisha to share the authority of his prophetic office and to succeed him (1 Ki 19:19–21; 2 Ki 2:1–14). Yahweh's denial of Jonah's two requests for death (Jonah 4:3, 8) therefore hints at an imminent reduction in Jonah's authority and status as a prophet of Yahweh.

So Jonah finally has carried out his mission (3:1–4), but what has it gained him? Nothing, not even the delight of seeing Nineveh destroyed! It just isn't fair that Nineveh receives the same salvation as Jonah himself (2:10 [ET 2:9]). St. Paul's comments in Rom 9:30–32 apply to the Ninevites who were saved through faith, as well as to the legalistic Jonah:

> What then shall we say? That the Gentiles, who did not pursue righteousness, have obtained righteousness—a righteousness by faith. But Israel, who pursued a law of righteousness, has not attained that law. Why? Because they did not pursue it by faith, but as if it were by works.

Summary of Scene 6

When the Israelites stand on the shore of the Red Sea and see Pharaoh's chariots approaching, they complain to Moses: "Was not this the word that we spoke to you in Egypt, saying, 'Leave us alone that we may serve Egypt'? For it was better for us to serve Egypt than that we should die in the wilderness" (Ex 14:12). Supporting the view that Jonah in 4:2 alludes to Ex 14:12 is the correspondence between Jonah 3:5 and Ex 14:31. Another connection between Jonah and Exodus 14 is the noun "dry land" (יַבָּשָׁה) in Ex 14:16, 22, 29 and also Jonah 1:9, 13; 2:11 (ET 2:10).[51]

Connecting the question "Was not this my word while I was still upon my ground?" in Jonah 4:2 with the similar words used in Ex 14:12 yields the fol-

---

[51] In both Jonah and Exodus 14, "dry land" denotes a place of safety and security, Yahweh's provision in the midst of threatening peril.

lowing insights.[52] Both texts demonstrate the unwillingness of people to leave a previous place of security (Egypt or "my ground," Jonah's position in Israel) at Yahweh's command to face a new locale. Both prefer negative past experiences over moving into the future planned by God. Israel preferred slavery in Egypt instead of what looked like coming death; Jonah prefers death rather than life under the grace of God that welcomes even converted Gentiles. The effect of these comparisons sets up Jonah as the disobedient Israel in his day.

Jonah is self-centered, self-righteous, and self-willed. He assumes that he can choose his own mission and message. Nevertheless, the sailors were changed and converted to saving faith (1:16) by Jonah's confession of faith (1:9), and Nineveh has been converted to saving faith (3:5–9) through Jonah's prophecy (3:4). Even Yahweh has changed his verdict from judgment to salvation (3:9–10). The only figure in the book who remains unchanged is Jonah.

Or does he? That is the question in the final section (4:4–11).

---

[52] The comparison of these two texts is based on the discussion in Magonet, *Form and Meaning*, 74–76.

Scene 7: Yahweh's Provisions and Jonah's Responses

Translation

4 ⁴Then Yahweh said, "Is it right that you are inflamed?"

⁵But Jonah went out from the city and sat down east of the city. He made for himself there a shelter. Then he sat underneath it in the shade until he would see what would happen in the city.

⁶Yahweh God provided a qiqayon plant to grow up over Jonah to be shade over his head [and] to save him from his evil. Jonah rejoiced over the qiqayon plant with a great joy. ⁷But (the) God provided a worm when the dawn arose on the next day, and it struck the qiqayon plant so that it withered. ⁸Also when the sun dawned, God provided a scorching east wind. The sun struck on the head of Jonah so that he became faint. He asked his life to die, and he said, "My death would be better than my life!"

⁹Then God said to Jonah, "Is it right that you are inflamed over the qiqayon plant?"

He replied, "It is right for me to be inflamed to the point of death!"

¹⁰So Yahweh said, "You yourself had pity upon the qiqayon plant for which you did not labor and that you did not raise, which came to exist in a night, and in a night it perished. ¹¹Shall I myself not have pity upon Nineveh, the great city, in which there are more than twelve myriads of people who do not know [the difference] between their right and their left, and many animals?"

Textual Notes

4:4 וַיֹּאמֶר יְהוָה הַהֵיטֵב חָרָה לָךְ:—Here and again in 4:9a, Yahweh asks Jonah, "Is it right that you are inflamed?" Yahweh seeks to change Jonah's spiritual disposition by asking him to ponder whether his attitude is consistent with the character of his God, who is "gracious and merciful," as Jonah himself confessed in 4:2. Yahweh's rhetorical questions and actions in 4:4–11 aim to turn Jonah from his anger (4:4) and "save him from his evil" (4:6), namely, his resentment at Yahweh saving Gentiles through faith (see 4:1).

The verb הַהֵיטֵב is the Hiphil infinitive absolute of יָטַב with the interrogative particle -הַ prefixed, forming a question.[1] The same Hiphil infinitive absolute recurs twice

---

[1] Joüon, § 161 b, argues that the particle -הַ in 4:4 is not interrogative, but exclamatory: "You are really angry!" However, such an exclamation would serve no purpose. There is no reason why Yahweh should point out to Jonah that the prophet is angry; he already knows that! In 4:9a, where Yahweh uses הַהֵיטֵב again, it is clear that Yahweh uses it to ask a question, since Jonah replies in 4:9b.

in 4:9, once with ־הָ and once without. The Hiphil of יָטַב can mean to "do [something] well, right" in an ethical or theological sense (BDB, 5), and that is its meaning in 4:4, 9. An infinitive can be used in place of a finite verb at the beginning of a sentence (Joüon, § 123 u), notably in direct speech (Waltke-O'Connor, § 35.5.2a). Probably this infinitive absolute functions as a finite verb and predicate (cf. GKC, § 113 c). Its subject is the following verbal clause, חָרָה לְךָ, "You are inflamed." Another way to explain the syntax is that the infinitive could be adverbial (so GKC, § 113 k, citing Jonah 4:9; see also Waltke-O'Connor, § 35.4). The question then would mean "Rightly are you inflamed?"

All three times in 4:4, 9, the Hiphil infinitive absolute of יָטַב is followed by a Qal form of חָרָה used impersonally with the preposition לְ, literally, "it was hot to" Jonah, meaning that Jonah is "inflamed." For this idiom, see the second textual note on 4:1. Here the Qal third masculine singular perfect (חָרָה) is followed by לָךְ, "it is hot to you," meaning "you are inflamed." לָךְ is the preposition לְ with second *masculine* suffix, which normally forms לְךָ, but here it is in pause and so it is identical in form to לְ with the second feminine singular suffix (לָךְ).

4:5 וַיֵּצֵא יוֹנָה מִן־הָעִיר—"Jonah went out from the city." The verb is the Qal third masculine singular imperfect of יָצָא with *waw* consecutive.

וַיֵּשֶׁב מִקֶּדֶם לָעִיר—Literally, this says that Jonah "sat from the east to the city." The verb (repeated later in the verse) is the Qal third masculine singular imperfect of יָשַׁב with *waw* consecutive. The combination of the prepositions מִן (on מִקֶּדֶם) and לְ (on לָעִיר) is used with geographical directions (here קֶדֶם, "east") to mean "on the east side of, to the east of." See BDB, s.v. מִן, 1 c.

While the noun קֶדֶם often has the spatial meaning "east" (see BDB, 1 b), it can also have the temporal meaning "ancient time, the past" (see BDB, 2). As a double entendre, the word may indicate that Jonah is to the east of the city while he is also looking at Nineveh from the viewpoint of its past history. He refuses to "remember their sin no more" (Jer 31:34) and allow grace to be grace (cf. Rom 5:20).

Since Jonah locates himself to the east of the city, he will be the first to feel the "scorching east wind" (רוּחַ קָדִים חֲרִישִׁית) sent by Yahweh in 4:8.

וַיַּעַשׂ לוֹ שָׁם סֻכָּה—The verb is the Qal third masculine singular imperfect of עָשָׂה, "to make," with *waw* consecutive. The preposition with third masculine singular suffix (לוֹ) has the force of a dative of advantage: "for himself, for his benefit" (see BDB, s.v. לְ, 5 h (α)). שָׁם is the adverb "there."

The noun סֻכָּה refers to a small "shelter, hut, booth" constructed of natural materials such as branches in order to provide protection from the elements (e.g., Gen 33:17; 1 Ki 20:12). This is the noun used for the shelters constructed for the Feast of Booths (Lev 23:34, 42–43; Deut 16:13; Neh 8:14–17; Zech 14:16, 18–19). This festival was to remind the Israelites of their semi-nomadic wanderings in the desert before entering the promised land, so the "booths" were merely temporary shelters. That they were flimsy is implied by Is 1:8, which warns that because of Israel's sins, "the daughter of Zion will be left like a shelter [כְּסֻכָּה] in a vineyard, like a shed in a cucumber patch," that is, a forlorn and fleeting abode. Job 27:18 uses the term to epitomize endeavors that quickly pass away.

וַיֵּשֶׁב תַּחְתֶּיהָ בַּצֵּל—As earlier in the verse, the verb is the Qal third masculine singular imperfect of יָשַׁב, "to sit," with *waw* consecutive. When the preposition תַּחַת, "under," has a suffix, it usually takes the form of suffix appropriate for a plural noun, hence תַּחְתֶּיהָ. Its suffix is third feminine singular, referring to the feminine noun סֻכָּה ("shelter") in the preceding clause. בַּצֵּל is the noun צֵל, "shade," with the definite article and the preposition בְּ in a spatial sense: "in the shade." The noun צֵל will recur in 4:6.

עַד אֲשֶׁר יִרְאֶה מַה־יִּהְיֶה בָּעִיר:—The conjunction עַד ("until"), the relative pronoun אֲשֶׁר ("which"), and imperfect verb יִרְאֶה (Qal third masculine singular of רָאָה, "to see") form a temporal clause looking toward the future, literally, "until which [time] he would see what would happen in the city." See BDB, s.v. עַד, II 1 a (b). Joüon, § 113 k, notes that the imperfect has the nuance of purpose: Jonah sat there in order to see what would happen. The interrogative מָה, "what?" can be used with רָאָה to express an indirect question: "to see what …" (BDB, s.v. מָה, 1 b). Here הָיָה (Qal third masculine singular imperfect, יִּהְיֶה) means "to happen, occur, take place" (BDB, Qal, I 1 a and b). בָּעִיר is, literally, "what would happen *in the city*" (NASB), but many English translations have "what would become of the city" (KJV, RSV, ESV).

4:6   וַיְמַן יְהוָה־אֱלֹהִים קִיקָיוֹן—The verb is the Piel third masculine singular imperfect with *waw* consecutive of מָנָה, "to provide." The Piel of מָנָה occurs four times in Jonah, always with God as the subject (2:1 [ET 1:17]; 4:6–8). However, each time God is designated by different epithet, and each clause involves paronomasia. See the first textual note on 2:1 and the end of "Introduction to Jonah 4." Here the subject is the double designation יְהוָה־אֱלֹהִים, "Yahweh God," which in Jonah occurs only here. Compare הַשָּׁמַיִם אֱלֹהֵי יְהוָה in 1:9; יְהוָה אֱלֹהָיו in 2:2 (ET 2:1); and יְהוָה אֱלֹהָי in 2:7 (ET 2:6).

The direct object is the noun קִיקָיוֹן. The context indicates that it refers to some kind of leafy plant that would furnish good shade. How it is to be categorized botanically continues to perplex commentators. The options fall into four categories:[2]

- Some ancient translations merely transliterate the term, including Targum Jonathan and the Greek versions of Aquila and Theodotion (κικεών).
- "Gourd" is supported by the mainstream LXX (κολόκυνθα), Augustine,[3] the Old Latin (*cucurbita*), and the Syriac Peshitta, ܩܰܪܐܐ ܙܥܽܘܪܐ, "a young gourd-plant."[4] Bernard Robinson suggests the possibility that קִיקָיוֹן is an Assyrian loan word. He opts for the translation "gourd," although after extensive study, he is unable to make a definitive choice.[5]
- "Vine" or "ivy" is supported by the Greek version of Symmachus (κισσός) and Jerome's Vulgate (*hedera*).

---

[2] See Robinson, "Jonah's Qiqayon Plant," 103, and Bolin, *Freedom beyond Forgiveness*, 154.

[3] Augustine, letter 82.35 (to Jerome) and letter 102.30, 35 (*NPNF*[1] 1:361, 423–24).

[4] Payne Smith, s.v. ܩܰܪܐܐ.

[5] Robinson, "Jonah's Qiqayon Plant."

- Most modern commentators identify the plant with the ricinus, the castor-oil tree, on the basis of the Egyptian *kiki* and the classical Greek κίκι. This is supported by the Babylonian Talmud, *Shabbath*, 21a.[6]

Luther writes: "Nothing is gained by fighting over a matter of no importance, since the Hebrew word means neither 'ivy' nor 'gourd,' but it is the name of a tree unknown to us but indigenous to that region."[7] The identity of the plant is not crucial. As with the "gourds" (the Hebrew term is of uncertain meaning) in 2 Ki 4:39, what is crucial is the effect and function of the plant in the context of the narrative. The same is true about the "great fish" (whale?) in Jonah 2:1 (ET 1:17; see the first textual note and commentary on 2:1). Therefore this commentary opts for transliteration and renders קִיקָיוֹן as "qiqayon plant."

וַיַּעַל ׀ מֵעַל לְיוֹנָה—The verb is the Qal third masculine singular imperfect with *waw* consecutive of עָלָה. With a plant as subject, the Qal of עָלָה can mean to "spring up, grow" (BDB, 4). The combination of prepositions מֵעַל (מִן plus עַל) followed by לְ can simply mean "over" (BDB, s.v. עַל, IV 2 e). This clause literally states that the plant "grew over Jonah." However, God has provided the plant for this purpose, and וַיַּעַל is parallel to the two infinitive constructs that begin the next two clauses, each of which clearly forms a purpose clause. Therefore וַיַּעַל too is translated as a purpose clause: "Yahweh God provided a qiqayon plant *to grow up* over Jonah to be shade ... [and] to save ..."

לִהְיוֹת צֵל עַל־רֹאשׁוֹ—An infinitive construct with the preposition לְ commonly forms a purpose clause (Joüon, § 124 l; GKC, § 114 g; Waltke-O'Connor, § 36.2.3d). The verb is the Qal infinitive construct of הָיָה with לְ. The noun צֵל, "shade," is repeated from 4:5. Since the implied subject of this clause is the plant itself, a precise translation is that God caused the plant to grow "to be (a source of) shade over his head." The other passages that refer to Jonah's "head" (רֹאשׁ) stress his vulnerability: he laments in 2:6 (ET 2:5), "Seaweed was bound to my head," and in 4:8 the sun will strike his "head."

לְהַצִּיל לוֹ מֵרָעָתוֹ—Again an infinitive construct with לְ forms a purpose clause (see the preceding textual note). This is the most important purpose clause because it expresses the ultimate goal of God's dealings with Jonah in these verses: "to save him from his evil." הַצִּיל is the Hiphil infinitive construct of נָצַל, whose Hiphil means "to save, rescue, deliver." The Hiphil of נָצַל almost always takes a direct object to refer to the one who is saved. However, its object is introduced by the preposition לְ in Dan 8:7 and here: לוֹ, "(to) him," refers to Jonah. The object has לְ perhaps also in 4QapPs[b] 44:3.

Frequently the Hiphil of נָצַל takes the preposition מִן prefixed to the threat "from" which a person is saved. That construction is used here, with מִן on מֵרָעָתוֹ, "from his evil." The noun רָעָה (here with third masculine singular suffix) is the same noun used for the "evil" experienced by Jonah in 4:1 when Nineveh was saved. Here it refers to

---

[6] See Jastrow, s.v. קִיקָיוֹן.

[7] AE 19:29.

that prior "evil." It also is the same noun that referred to the "evil" perpetrated by Nineveh (1:2; 3:8, 10a), the storm sent by Yahweh that the sailors regarded as an "evil" (1:7–8), and the "evil" threat of destruction averted by Yahweh (3:10b; 4:2).

Elsewhere in the OT, the Hiphil of נָצַל plus מִן often refers to Yahweh rescuing people "from" mortal dangers. "Many are the evils [רָעוֹת] of [suffered by] a righteous man, but from them all Yahweh saves him" (Ps 34:20 [ET 34:19]). He saves a person from death itself (Pss 33:19; 56:14 [ET 56:13]), Sheol (Ps 86:13), personal enemies (Ps 18:1 [ET superscription]), the sword (Ex 18:4; Ps 22:21 [ET 22:20]), and all fears (Ps 34:5 [ET 34:4]). Since this verb and preposition are typically used for Yahweh saving people from deadly peril or extreme anguish, the construction indicates the seriousness of Jonah's spiritual evil. By means of the qiqayon plant, Yahweh seeks to deliver Jonah by changing his anger into grateful faith and joy that Yahweh's compassion extends even to repentant Gentiles and their animals (4:10–11).

וַיִּשְׂמַח יוֹנָה עַל־הַקִּיקָיוֹן שִׂמְחָה גְדוֹלָה:—The verb שָׂמַח (Qal third masculine singular imperfect with *waw* consecutive), "to rejoice, have joy," here takes an accusative phrase with the cognate noun שִׂמְחָה, "joy": "Jonah rejoiced over the qiqayon plant with a great joy." For the syntax, see Joüon, § 125 q–r; GKC, § 117 p–q; and the first textual notes on 1:16 and 4:1, which have similar cognate accusatives. The preposition עַל has the nuance of rejoicing "on account of, because of" (BDB, II 1 f (b)), or in idiomatic English, "over" the qiqayon.

The verb שָׂמַח often appears in a liturgical setting describing joyful worship before God (e.g., Lev 23:40; Deut 12:12, 18; 27:7). In the Psalms, the noun שִׂמְחָה can refer to "joy" at Yahweh's salvation and in his presence (e.g., Pss 16:11; 21:7 [ET 21:6]; 68:4 [ET 68:3]). However, the verb can also be used for enemies rejoicing over the demise of the righteous.[a]

(a) E.g., Micah 7:8; Obad 12; Pss 35:15, 19, 24; 38:17 (ET 38:16); Job 31:29

There is nothing wrong with Jonah rejoicing over the plant Yahweh provided to protect him from the searing sun. However, Jonah should have rejoiced far more greatly over the repentance and salvation of the people of Nineveh. Instead, this prophet rejoices only when Yahweh saves him personally (chapter 2) and when Yahweh provides for his own personal comfort (4:6). This reveals Jonah's self-centeredness.

4:7 וַיְמַן הָאֱלֹהִים תּוֹלַעַת—The verb וַיְמַן, "provided," is repeated from 2:1 (ET 1:17) and 4:6 (see the first textual note on 4:6). It will recur in 4:8. Only here is its subject הָאֱלֹהִים, literally, "the God." For the sake of good English, the definite article is not reflected in translations.

The verb's indefinite direct object, תּוֹלַעַת, can also be spelled תּוֹלֵעָה, and probably is from the root תלע. This feminine noun is a general term for any crawling invertebrate. It may refer to a "*worm, grub*, vine-weevil" (BDB, 1; cf. *HALOT*) or perhaps "larva, maggot, beetle." Here, as in some other OT passages, it is an agent of Yahweh's judgment. In Ex 16:20 those Israelites who defied Yahweh's command and collected more than a daily amount of manna find that the next day the excess manna stinks and is infested with these creatures, probably meaning "worms." In Deut 28:39, Yahweh threatens to send this creature, as the "fruit-grub" (*HALOT*, 1 a β), to destroy unfaithful Israel's vineyards. In Is 14:11 and 66:24, the word probably means "maggot" or "worm" as the vicious agent that will consume the corpses of unbelievers throughout eternity: "Their worm will not die, and their fire will not be extinguished, and they will be an abhorrence to all flesh" (Is 66:24). Some of Jesus' most severe teaching invokes the power of this worm and quotes Is 66:24: "And if your eye causes you to sin, pluck it out; it is better for you one-eyed to enter the kingdom of God than having two eyes to be thrown into Gehenna, where 'their worm [ὁ σκώληξ] does not die, and the fire is not extinguished' " (Mk 9:47–48).[8]

In some passages תּוֹלַעַת is used metaphorically for people as a term of humility and shame. Thus the lowly people of Israel are the "worm Jacob" (Is 41:14). In Psalm 22, from which Jesus will quote while on the cross (Ps 22:2 [ET 22:1]; Mt 27:46), David declares (Ps 22:7 [ET 22:6]):

I am a worm and not a man,
the reproach of humanity and despised by the people.

Therefore the תּוֹלַעַת is a tiny, inconspicuous creature, which is given power by Yahweh to carry out his judgment against sin. It represents decay and death, both temporal and eternal.

בַּעֲלוֹת הַשַּׁחַר לַמָּחֳרָת—This temporal clause modifies the preceding clause ("God provided a worm"). God did that "when the dawn arose on the next day" after he had provided the qiqayon plant (4:6). בַּעֲלוֹת is the Qal infinitive construct of עָלָה, "to arise," with the preposition בְּ. Hebrew commonly uses an infinitive construct with בְּ (or with כְּ, as in 4:8) to form a temporal clause (GKC, § 164 g; Joüon, § 166 l). The noun שַׁחַר (here with the article) refers to the "dawn" (BDB) or sunrise and often is the subject of the verb עָלָה. The noun מָחֳרָת is from the same root as the common adverb מָחָר, "tomorrow." It means "the morrow" (BDB) or "the next day." Here it takes the preposition לְ in a temporal sense (BDB, s.v. לְ, 6 a), "on."

וַתַּךְ אֶת־הַקִּיקָיוֹן וַיִּיבָשׁ:—The verb וַתַּךְ is the Hiphil third feminine singular imperfect with waw consecutive of נָכָה. It is feminine because its subject is the feminine noun תּוֹלַעַת ("worm") in the first clause of the verse. The Hiphil of נָכָה, "to strike, smite," is commonly used for God executing judgment (BDB, 4). It occurs in Jonah only in 4:7 and 4:8, where the identical form is repeated. Frequently it means "smite fatally" (BDB, 2). Here it refers to the "worm gnawing or boring so as to kill [the] plant" (BDB, 2 b). Its definite direct object is אֶת־הַקִּיקָיוֹן, and the definite article ("the qiqayon") anaphorically refers back to the same qiqayon introduced into the narrative in 4:6.

In this context, the verb וַיִּיבָשׁ should be taken as a result clause: "so that it withered." It is the Qal third masculine singular imperfect with waw consecutive of יָבֵשׁ, "to be dry, dried up," or "of grass, herbage … wither" (BDB, 1 d). It is masculine because its subject is the preceding masculine noun, הַקִּיקָיוֹן.

---

[8] BDAG explains that σκώληξ, the term in, for example, LXX Ex 16:20, 24; Deut 28:39; Is 14:11; 66:24; Jonah 4:7; Ps 21:7 (MT 22:7; ET 22:6); and also in Mk 9:48 is a "symbol of insignificance and wretchedness. … Acc[ording] to Is 66:24 a never-dying worm shall torment the damned."

4:8 וַיְהִי ׀ כִּזְרֹחַ הַשֶּׁמֶשׁ—This temporal clause gives the context ("when …") for the next clause, where God provides. It is basically synonymous with the temporal clause in 4:7 (בַּעֲלוֹת הַשַּׁחַר לַמָּחֳרָת). However, in 4:7 the first clause stated that God provided, and the temporal clause came second. כִּזְרֹחַ is the Qal infinitive construct of זָרַח with the preposition כְּ. Hebrew commonly uses an infinitive with כְּ (or with בְּ, as in 4:7) for a temporal clause (GKC, § 164 g; Joüon, § 166 m). זָרַח, to "rise," here and often elsewhere has the "sun" (שֶׁמֶשׁ) as its subject (BDB, s.v. זָרַח, Qal, 1 a; *HALOT*, 1), in which case it can be rendered "dawned."

וַיְמַן אֱלֹהִים רוּחַ קָדִים חֲרִישִׁית—For the verb וַיְמַן, see the first textual note on 4:6. Only here in Jonah is its subject אֱלֹהִים ("God") without the article. Its indefinite direct object is the construct phrase רוּחַ קָדִים, literally, "wind of the East," a common phrase meaning "east wind," which often is "violent and scorching" (BDB, s.v. קָדִים, 1). The feminine noun רוּחַ is modified by the adjective חֲרִישִׁית, which is the feminine form of חֲרִישִׁי. For it, the LXX (συγκαίοντι), Vulgate (*urenti*), and Peshitta (ܡܚܒ) support the meaning "scorching" (*HALOT*). This adjective is one of five Hebrew words in the OT that occur only in the narrative of Jonah. The others are סְפִינָה, "ship" (1:5), the verb עָשַׁת in the Hithpael, "to regard, show compassion" (1:6),[9] קְרִיאָה, "call, message" (3:2), and קִיקָיוֹן, "qiqayon plant" (4:6, 7, 9, 10).

In other OT passages, Yahweh uses an "east wind" (רוּחַ קָדִים) to judge, annihilate, and destroy. This clearly implies that Jonah is now under Yahweh's judgment. Yahweh caused an east wind to blow locusts that devoured the crops of Egypt (Ex 10:13). A "fierce east wind" parted the Red Sea (Ex 14:21), through which Israel was saved but in which the Egyptians perished. By means of an "east wind," Yahweh shatters Tarshish ships (Ps 48:8 [ET 48:7]) and the ships of Tyre (Ezek 27:26) and desiccates vegetation so that it dies (Ezek 17:10; 19:12; cf. Hos 13:15).

The kind of east wind that brings judgment to Jonah is well-known in the Near East as the *sirocco*, *Hamsin*, or *Sharav*. Like the Santa Ana winds of southern California, it is a dry wind from the desert that dissipates any moisture and the will to act by humans and animals. It is the arid furnace-like blast of heat that parches the body by evaporating its perspiration. When this wind blows today in the Near East, it is not unusual for the temperatures to reach 110 degrees Fahrenheit and the humidity to get as low as two percent. The wind is capable of blocking out the sun with the dust that it raises. The force of the wind alone can frequently become destructive. It blows every fall and spring during the transitions between the rainy and dry seasons.

וַתַּךְ הַשֶּׁמֶשׁ עַל־רֹאשׁ יוֹנָה וַיִּתְעַלָּף—The verb וַתַּךְ is the Hiphil third feminine singular imperfect with *waw* consecutive of נָכָה, "strike, smite." The identical form was in 4:7 (see the third textual note on 4:7). It is feminine because its subject, הַשֶּׁמֶשׁ ("the sun"), is a feminine noun (usually). The Hiphil of נָכָה often takes the preposition עַל introducing the object that is struck. Contrast עַל־רֹאשׁ יוֹנָה ("on the head of Jonah") here with עַל־רֹאשׁוֹ in 4:6, but there Yahweh provided the plant "over his head" that produced shade for him.

---

[9] The Aramaic Peal of עֲשַׁת occurs in Dan 6:4, and a different, homographic Hebrew verb occurs in Jer 5:28. See the fourth textual note on Jonah 1:6.

The verb וַיִּתְעַלָּף is the Hithpael third masculine singular imperfect of עָלַף with *waw* consecutive and in pause (hence -לָּ- instead of -לַּ-). Here and in Amos 8:13, the Hithpael means "swoon away" (BDB) or "become faint" (*HALOT*, 2), whereas in Gen 38:14 (the only other OT occurrence of the Hithpael), it means "wrap, cover oneself." In its context here, after the clause about the sun striking Jonah's head, the verb forms a result clause: "*so that* he became faint."

וַיִּשְׁאַל אֶת־נַפְשׁוֹ לָמוּת—The first verb is the Qal third masculine singular imperfect of שָׁאַל, "to ask," with *waw* consecutive. Its direct object is אֶת־נַפְשׁוֹ ("his life"). לָמוּת is the Qal infinitive construct of מוּת with the preposition לְ. Literally, this clause is "He asked his life to die."

The verb שָׁאַל can be used for "asking" God in prayer. This identical clause is so used in 1 Ki 19:4, which first states that Elijah "asked [for] his life to die" (וַיִּשְׁאַל אֶת־נַפְשׁוֹ לָמוּת), then quotes his prayer: "Now, Yahweh, take my life" (עַתָּה יְהוָה קַח נַפְשִׁי). However, Jonah in 4:8 says nothing to God; he speaks the next clause, but does not address it to anyone. Therefore this death wish here contrasts with that in 4:3, which comes at the end of a clear prayer to Yahweh. This wish may be compared to 1:12, where Jonah instructs the sailors to hurl him into the sea, since throughout chapter 1 Jonah never addresses God. Here, in the absence of a prayer to God, Jonah's death wish may be a kind of prayer to himself.

The clause here may also be compared to three passages where שָׁאַל takes נֶפֶשׁ as its object in the sense of "seek [someone's] life," that is, seek to kill someone. If so, Jonah "sought [for] his life to die." However, in the other passages, the clause is negated in some way: Solomon did *not* seek the life of his enemies (1 Ki 3:11 ‖ 2 Chr 1:11), nor did Job (Job 31:30).

וַיֹּאמֶר טוֹב מוֹתִי מֵחַיָּי:—Probably מוֹתִי is the noun מָוֶת with first common singular suffix ("my death") rather than the Qal infinitive construct of מוּת with subjective first common singular suffix ("for me to die"). Probably טוֹב is not the Qal verb, but the predicate adjective "good." In either case, it forms a comparative ("better") with the preposition מִן prefixed to the abstract plural noun חַיִּים, "life," with first common singular suffix (מֵחַיָּי, "than my life"). Since this is a wish, the translation uses the optative: "My death *would be* better than my life!" See the second textual note on 4:3, which has the identical expression טוֹב מוֹתִי מֵחַיָּי.

4:9 וַיֹּאמֶר אֱלֹהִים אֶל־יוֹנָה—Even though Jonah avoids speaking to Yahweh in 4:8, "God" (אֱלֹהִים) now speaks "to Jonah" (אֶל־יוֹנָה). This reveals his continuing concern for his prophet.

הַהֵיטֵב חָרָה־לְךָ עַל־הַקִּיקָיוֹן—The Hiphil infinitive absolute of יָטַב occurs twice in 4:9. Here it (הַהֵיטֵב) has the interrogative -הַ, "Is it right that … ?" as also in 4:4. See the textual note on 4:4. The idiom חָרָה־לְךָ, literally, "it is hot to you," means "you are inflamed," as in 4:4. See the second textual note on 4:1. The preposition עַל has the nuance "on account of, because of" (BDB, II 1 f (*b*); see also *HALOT*, 2) or "over" the qiqayon.

וַיֹּאמֶר הֵיטֵב חָרָה־לִי עַד־מָוֶת:—Jonah's reply uses the same Hiphil infinitive absolute of יָטַב (but without interrogative -הַ), "It is right," and the idiom חָרָה לְ (but with לִי, "*I* am inflamed") as Yahweh's question. See the preceding textual note. Is it right … ?" is also in 4:4. See the textual note on 4:4.

The prepositional phrase עַד־מָוֶת, "until/to the point of death," occurs only here in the OT.[10] The context shows that Jonah means his anger is so extreme that he prefers death over life (4:3, 8). The LXX translates it literally: ἕως θανάτου.

Jesus uses that same Greek phrase in the Garden of Gethsemane (Mt 26:38 ‖ Mk 14:34): "My soul is deeply sorrowful, even to death" (περίλυπός ἐστιν ἡ ψυχή μου ἕως θανάτου). Then he implores his disciples, "Remain here and stay awake." However, the contextual meaning of the phrase is the opposite. The sinless Christ is in agony over his impending passion, which will accomplish salvation for the whole world. His sorrow "even to death" anticipates that he will indeed die on the cross in accord with the Father's will. In contrast, angry Jonah begrudges the salvation of Nineveh, which God accomplished only after calling the unfaithful prophet a second time (Jonah 3:1–4). Yahweh's will is not that Jonah die, but that he repent of his anger and live; this is Yahweh's goal in his dealings with his wayward prophet in 4:4–11.

The OT does have some phrases similar to עַד־מָוֶת but with מָוֶת in construct. Yahweh established the cities of refuge with the stipulation that an accidental killer must reside in one of them (הַגָּדוֹל) עַד־מוֹת הַכֹּהֵן, "until the death of the (high) priest" (Num 35:25, 28, 32; Josh 20:6; cf. 1 Ki 11:40), after which the killer would be free to return to his normal life. Thus the death of the high priest had the effect of atoning for the sin of manslaughter. That foreshadowed the ministry of the great High Priest, Jesus Christ (cf. John 17; Hebrews 3–9), whose death atoned for all sin.

4:10 וַיֹּאמֶר יְהוָה אַתָּה חַסְתָּ עַל־הַקִּיקָיוֹן—Yahweh now addresses Jonah in the second person. The second masculine singular pronoun אַתָּה is redundant with the second masculine singular verb חַסְתָּ (Qal perfect of חוּס), and so together they are rendered as "You *yourself* had pity." The emphasis on Jonah here sets up a contrast to the emphasis on Yahweh in 4:11, who will describe himself as the subject of the same verb.

In the OT, חוּס, to "pity, look upon with compassion" (BDB), describes the actions of the messianic King (Ps 72:13) and David when he spared King Saul (1 Sam 24:11 [ET 24:10]). Yahweh spared his people when they fell into idolatry in the wilderness (Ezek 20:17). But most of the time, this verb is negated: Yahweh commands the Israelites *not* to spare the pagan Canaanites (Deut 7:16) or wicked Israelites (Deut 13:9 [ET 13:8]; 19:13, 21; 25:12). The Israelites are to destroy the heathen and administer justice according to the Torah. When Israel becomes apostate, Yahweh will allow foreign kings and armies to devastate them, and they will show no pity (Is 13:18; Jer 21:7). Indeed, Yahweh himself will show no pity when he judges his apostate people.[b] "Clearly implicit throughout the usage of this term is the right of the sovereign (or his representative) to have pity or not have pity as he sees fit in specific circumstances of life."[11]

(b) Jer 13:14; Ezek 5:11; 7:4, 9; 8:18; 9:10; 24:14

---

[10] Waltke-O'Connor, § 14.5b, example 22 (see also footnote 28), weakens its force by deeming it a superlative: "I couldn't be more angry." However, that ignores Jonah's two wishes in the context (4:3, 8) for actual death.

[11] Fretheim, *The Message of Jonah*, 49.

Jonah is not sovereign over the qiqayon plant. As Yahweh pointedly reminds him in the rest of the verse, Jonah did not create or nurture the plant. It was not his to begin with! Jonah should realize that Yahweh alone has the right to spare (or not spare) his own creatures.

In Jonah 4:10–11, the LXX translates חוּס with φείδομαι, "to spare … have pity on" (LEH). In the NT, φείδομαι is used to state that God "did *not spare* his own Son, but gave him up for us all" (Rom 8:32). Neither did God "spare" (φείδομαι) the angels who sinned (2 Pet 2:4), the wicked world in the days of Noah (2 Pet 2:5), or the natural olive branches (Jewish people who rejected Jesus, the Christ [Rom 11:21]).

אֲשֶׁר לֹא־עָמַלְתָּ בּוֹ—This relative clause describes the qiqayon plant, literally, "which you did not labor for it." עָמַלְתָּ is the Qal second masculine singular perfect of עָמַל, "to toil, labor," which is used for constructing a building (Ps 127:1) and for manual labor that makes one hungry (Prov 16:26). Its nine other OT occurrences are all in Ecclesiastes, where it usually connotes strenuous, wearisome work (1:3; 2:11, 19–21; 5:15, 17 [ET 5:16, 18]; 8:17). Here (בּוֹ, "for it") and in Eccl 2:21b, עָמַל takes the preposition בְּ attached to what one works "for."

But the clause here is negated (לֹא). Jonah did *not* suffer the hardships or sorrow of earthly toil in order to receive the benefits of the qiqayon plant. He "rejoiced … with a great joy" over something he received for free—something "Yahweh God provided" for him (4:6). Should not Jonah also rejoice over the salvation of the Ninevites, who received Yahweh's grace as a free gift (cf. Rom 6:23)?

וְלֹא גִדַּלְתּוֹ—The negated (וְלֹא) verb is the Piel second masculine singular perfect of גָּדַל with third masculine singular suffix, referring to the qiqayon: literally, "And you did not raise it." The Qal of גָּדַל often means to "grow up" (BDB, 1). The Piel usually has a causative meaning, "to cause to grow," with plants as the object (Is 44:14; Ezek 31:4), or referring to parents who "raise" children (e.g., Is 23:4; 49:21; 51:18; Hos 9:12), including God, who "raised" the Israelites as his sons (Is 1:2). The use of the verb גָּדַל here may connect the qiqayon plant with Nineveh, since in the next verse Yahweh uses the cognate adjective גָּדוֹל to call it "the great city" (4:11; also in 1:2; 3:2; and without the article in 3:3). It may also relate to 2:7 (ET 2:6), where Yahweh "brought up" Jonah's "life from destruction." Throughout the narrative, Yahweh intends to preserve life (cf. 1:2; 1:15; 3:2, 10; 4:2).

שֶׁבִּן־לַיְלָה הָיָה וּבִן־לַיְלָה אָבָד׃—The combination שֶׁבִּן is the relative particle שֶׁ, "which," prefixed to בֶּן, "son," in construct. Previously in Jonah, שֶׁ occurred in two combinations that meant "on whose/my account" (בְּשֶׁלְּמִי in 1:7 and בְּשֶׁלִּי in 1:12). The usual construct form of בֵּן is בֶּן־. However, the construct form here, בִּן־, is regularly used when followed by the name of Nun, Joshua's father (e.g., Ex 33:11; Josh 1:1). It is also used before Yakeh, Agur's father (Prov 30:1), and once before an infinitive (Deut 25:2). Both שֶׁ and בִּן־ may indicate that Jonah was composed in an old, northern dialect of Hebrew.[12]

---

[12] See further "The Date of Writing" in the introduction. Critical scholars used to explain such features as evidence of a late date of composition, but that view has been discredited. Landes

The phrase בֶּן־לַיְלָה occurs twice in this verse but nowhere else in the OT. It is an example of an attributive genitive. Hebrew commonly uses "combinations of the construct states אִישׁ *a man*, בַּעַל *master, possessor*, בֶּן־ *son*, … with some appellative noun, in order to represent a person (poetically even a thing) as possessing some object or quality, or being in some condition" (GKC, § 128 s). The exact way in which the noun applies must be determined from the context. "A man of words" is an eloquent man (Ex 4:10); "a son of a hundred years" is a centenarian (Gen 21:5); and "sons of his bow" are arrows (Lam 3:13).

Here לַיְלָה, "night," describes the lifespan of the plant. בֶּן־לַיְלָה הָיָה means that the plant was "grown in a night" (GKC, § 128 v) or "came into being in a night" (ESV). וּבֶן־לַיְלָה אָבָד means that "it perished in a night." אָבָד is the Qal third masculine singular perfect of אָבַד in pause (hence -בָ-). Elsewhere in Jonah אָבַד was used for the prospect that the sailors (1:6, 14) and Ninevites (3:9) might "perish."

4:11 וַאֲנִי לֹא אָחוּס—The questions in Jonah 4:2, 4, 9 were posed using the interrogative *he* (-הֲ). However, a Hebrew question need not begin with an interrogative pronoun or adverb, especially if it expects a simple answer of yes (as here) or no (Waltke-O'Connor, § 40.3b). Without an interrogative, the context or the arrangement or emphasis of the words may indicate a question. See GKC, § 150 a; Joüon, § 161 a. Like the Hebrew, all the ancient versions render 4:11 as a question without using an interrogative: the LXX by ἐγὼ δὲ οὐ φείσομαι, the Vulgate by *Et ego non parcam*, and the Syriac by ܘܐܢܐ ܠܐ ܐܚܘܣ. The fact that Yahweh twice asked Jonah a question in the preceding context ("Is it right … ?" 4:4, 9) makes it more likely that this too is a question by Yahweh to Jonah.

The redundant pronoun וַאֲנִי is emphatic: "Should I *myself* not pity … ?" Yahweh's emphasis on himself here balances his emphasis on Jonah in 4:10, which also was conveyed with a redundant pronoun and the same verb (אַתָּה חַסְתָּ, "You yourself had pity …"). אָחוּס is the Qal first common singular imperfect of חוּס. For its meaning, see the first textual note on 4:10.

עַל־נִינְוֵה הָעִיר הַגְּדוֹלָה—Yahweh's pity "upon" (עַל) Nineveh matches Jonah's pity "upon" the qiqayon (4:10). "Nineveh, the great city" is repeated from 1:2; 3:2 (cf. 3:3). See the second textual note on 1:2.

אֲשֶׁר יֶשׁ־בָּהּ—This relative clause about Nineveh, literally, "which there is in her," has יֵשׁ, which usually occurs in the construct (as here) and "asserts *existenc*e" (BDB, 2) and so is equivalent to the English verb "is, are." The suffix on בְּ is third feminine singular (בָּהּ) because cities are feminine.

---

believes that בֶּן־ is the most archaic vocalization of the term and "could well represent a North Israelite-Ephraimite dialectal feature" ("Linguistic Criteria and the Date of the Book of Jonah," 153). While the present knowledge of Hebrew dialects is limited, the linguistic peculiarities of Jonah may well indicate a north Israelite dialect that differed in various respects from the classical Hebrew of Jerusalem. Other writers too have indicated the possibility that the language of Jonah represents a northern dialect. See, for example, Driver, *An Introduction to the Literature of the Old Testament*, 322, and Eybers, "The Purpose of the Book of Jonah."

הַרְבֵּה מִשְׁתֵּים־עֶשְׂרֵה רִבּוֹ אָדָם—In form הַרְבֵּה is the Hiphil infinitive absolute of רָבָה, "be much, many." It is often used as an adverb. Here it is used as a noun meaning "much, many, a great number." With the following preposition מִן (on מִשְׁתֵּים), it forms a comparative, "more than," as also in 2 Chr 25:9. See BDB, s.v. רָבָה, Hiphil, 1 d (5), and *HALOT*, s.v. הַרְבֵּה, 1 a.

The numeral שְׁתֵּים־עֶשְׂרֵה רִבּוֹ is, literally, "two [and] ten myriad," that is, twelve myriads or 120,000. See Waltke-O'Connor, § 15.2.5c, example 15. For שְׁתֵּים as a construct form of שְׁתַּיִם, a dual form meaning "two," see GKC, § 97 b, footnote 1. For the loss of the *daghesh* in the sibilant with *shewa* (-שְׁ-) in מִשְׁתֵּים, see GKC, § 20 m. The most common term for a "myriad" or "ten thousand" is רְבָבָה (eighteen times in the OT). The synonym רִבּוֹא occurs three times in the singular. This synonym, רִבּוֹ, occurs elsewhere in the OT in the singular only in 1 Chr 29:7 (twice); as the Kethib in Hos 8:12; and in Aramaic in Dan 7:10. While Daniel is exilic and Chronicles is post-exilic, Hosea (like Jonah) is from the eighth century BC, so this form cannot be used to argue for a late date for Jonah.[13] Oswald Loretz cites the Ugaritic *rbt* with the same meaning to support a Canaanite origin of the form.[14] Perhaps רִבּוֹ is chosen because it is from the same root and has a similar spelling as רַבָּה, "many"; see the last textual note on 4:11.

In Jonah 3:7–8, אָדָם served as the antonym to בְּהֵמָה, "animals," so it was rendered generically as "people." Here, it is possible that the count is just of the "men." Some other biblical numbers count only the men, not the women and children (e.g., Ex 12:37; Mt 14:21; 15:38). But בְּהֵמָה later in 4:11 may imply that אָדָם here includes all "people."

אֲשֶׁר לֹא־יָדַע בֵּין־יְמִינוֹ לִשְׂמֹאלוֹ—This relative clause modifies the preceding noun אָדָם, a collective singular meaning "men" or "people," so this clause has a singular verb (יָדַע) and singular pronominal suffixes (וֹ- twice). English requires translating these singulars as plurals: "who do not know … their … their …"

The expression with the verb יָדַע, "to know," and preposition בֵּין, "between," refers to the ability to "distinguish between" different options (see BDB, s.v. יָדַע, Qal, 1 d). This idiom occurs elsewhere in the OT only in 2 Sam 19:36, where eighty-year-old Barzillai protests, "Can I distinguish between good and evil [הַאֵדַע ׀ בֵּין־טוֹב לְרָע]? Can [I], your servant, taste what I eat and what I drink?" The verb יָדַע without the preposition has a similar meaning in Deut 1:39, where Moses refers to the Israelites' young children, "who today do not [yet] know good and evil." Also similar is יָדַע in Is 7:15–16: after the prophecy of Immanuel, to be born to a virgin, comes the warning that Israel shall be desolated "before the child knows to reject the evil and choose the good" (Is 7:16).

In the OT, "the right" and "the left" can refer to literal directions (e.g., Ex 14:22). Geographically, they can refer to the south and north, respectively (e.g., 1 Ki 7:39, 49). Aside from those directional uses, they occur together figuratively in passages

---

[13] See further "The Date of Writing" in the introduction.

[14] Loretz, "Herkunft und Sinn der Jona-Erzählung," 20, n. 15.

that speak of not turning to the right or left of the Torah or divine commands, that is, not deviating from God's Word.[c]

(c) E.g.,
Deut 5:32;
28:14; Josh
1:7; 23:6;
2 Ki 22:2 ‖
2 Chr 34:2;
Prov 4:27

Most likely the phrase in Jonah 4:11 refers to the Ninevites as spiritually imma-ture and relatively ignorant of God's Word. Their belief in God and acts of repentance in 3:5–9 reveal a basic knowledge of right and wrong. However, as Gentiles, they had not learned the Torah of Moses nor benefited from the prophets of Israel, until the brief ministry of Jonah among them. Even then, Jonah's brief prophecy (3:4) hardly provided a thorough education about God's truths.

וּבְהֵמָה רַבָּה—The collective feminine singular noun בְּהֵמָה is repeated from 3:7–8. Here too it includes all the different kinds of domesticated "animals" in Nin-eveh. It is modified by the adjective רַבָּה, the feminine of רַב, "much, many." The He-brew wording in 3:7–8 emphasized that the בְּהֵמָה participated in the same acts of repentance as the human population of Nineveh (see the textual notes on those verses). So it may be that in 4:11, the use of רַבָּה for the animals is intended to associate them closely with the people, who are counted using the similar term from the same root, רִבּוֹ, "myriads."

Commentary

The Place of Jonah 4:4–11 in the Book

Within the narrative of Jonah as a whole, chapter 4 is parallel to chapter 2.[15] In particular, Jonah 4:4–11 is parallel to 2:11 (ET 2:10), since in both of these sections Yahweh replies to a previous prayer of Jonah (his psalm in 2:3–10 [ET 2:2–9]; his angry prayer in 4:2–3) by means of his Word and his use of an-imals and nature. Of course, 2:11 (ET 2:10) and 4:4–11 are ill-matched if length is the only criterion used to connect them. However, in the second and fourth chapters, the greater length of 4:4–11 compared to 2:11 (ET 2:10) is balanced by the greater length of the prior prayer, 2:3–10 (ET 2:2–9), compared to 4:2–3.

Jonah 4:4–11 is the conclusion of the book.[16] It deliberately looks back to earlier material (just as 4:2 recalled 1:3). The triple use of the verb מָנָה to say

---

[15] See the second reason *for* including the psalm in its location under "The Place of the Psalm in the Book of Jonah" in "Introduction to Jonah 2."

[16] This commentary divides chapter 4 into two sections, 4:1–3 and 4:4–11, for two main rea-sons. First, the focus in 4:1–3 is on Jonah (his "great evil" in 4:1 and his resentful prayer in 4:2–3), while in 4:4–11 the focus is on Yahweh, who speaks and acts to attempt "to save" Jonah "from his evil" (4:6). Second, the Hebrew text divides chapter 4 into these two sec-tions. Sasson points out that the oldest extant Hebrew manuscript and the Masoretic Text have a major division between 4:3 and 4:4 and so consider 4:4–11 to be the final section of the book (*Jonah*, 270–71). Between 4:3 and 4:4, the Masoretic Text has a ס, an abbreviation for סְתוּמָה, "closed," meaning that there is a space between the end of 4:3 and 4:4, which begins on the same line of Hebrew text.

Nevertheless, Sasson (*Jonah*, 271–72) disregards the Hebrew textual tradition and argues for dividing chapter 4 into 4:1–6 and 4:7–11. Yet another way to view the structure is that 4:1–4 constitutes a single incident that reports Jonah's angry reaction to events in Nineveh (4:1), his prayer to Yahweh (4:2–3), and Yahweh's response in the form of a rhetorical question to him (4:4). Parallel clauses using the idiom חָרָה לְ, "to be inflamed, " delimit the incident (4:1, 4). At the opening, Jonah becomes "inflamed" over the salvation of Nineveh. At the

that Yahweh "provided" in 4:6, 7, 8 recalls his former provision of the great fish, described with the same verb in 2:1 (ET 1:17). Jonah 4:10 repeats the verb אָבַד, "perish," from 1:6, 14; 3:9. The final verse (4:11) artistically reuses the phrase "Nineveh, the great city," which opened both halves of the book (1:2; 3:2). In these ways and more, the themes of the narrative are drawn together in a climax, demonstrating (again!) that the narrative is a carefully structured composition.

Within 4:4–11, the purpose of 4:4–5 and 4:9–11 is to function as a framework around the nucleus of 4:6–8, which relates three divine acts. The theme of the surrounding framework is the unreasonableness of Jonah's anger over the salvation of the city of Nineveh. The opening frame (4:4–5) is God's first verbal attempt to dissuade Jonah from his anger. Then the three actions by Yahweh seek to move Jonah to repent (4:6–8). The closing frame (4:9–11) is Yahweh's final verbal plea for Jonah to turn from his anger and share in God's compassion toward all of his creatures.

The Opening Frame: Jonah's Unjustified Anger (4:4–5)

4:4 Jonah 4:4 portrays the marvelous grace of Yahweh in the face of Jonah's judgmental anger. Yahweh does not break off the conversation with the recalcitrant prophet. He refuses to acquiesce when Jonah asks him to take his life (4:3). Even for such a sinner, Yahweh does not want death (cf. Ezek 18:23, 32; 2 Pet 3:9)! Here the Lord of history, who rules the wind and sea and the mighty power of Sheol,[17] who has converted and saved a formerly wicked metropolis, stoops down to hold conversation with a pouting child. What patience! What grace!

Only two other prophets ever explicitly receive Yahweh's Word outside the boundaries of the promised land: Elijah at Mount Horeb (1 Ki 19:8–18) and Ezekiel in Babylon, first by the Kebar Canal (Ezek 1:3).[18] Yet even when Yahweh extends a revelation of his Word to Jonah in this "extraterrestrial" way, the prophet is unmoved by such a radical act of kindness. Jonah hears only Yahweh's judgment that his anger has not been an appropriate response. The rhetorical question "Is it right that you are inflamed?" (4:4) implies that the converse is true: it is good and right that God's grace is not limited either geographically or ethnically only to Israel, but is freely available to all who repent and believe.

4:5 In this verse Jonah exhibits one of his characteristics: he responds to a command or question by remaining silent. This is Jonah's way of rejecting what was spoken to him. It is a passive-aggressive response that betrays hos-

---

end, Yahweh questions whether it is right for him to be "inflamed." This structure is adopted by some English translations, including the ESV, which has 4:1–4 as one paragraph.

[17] See Jonah 2:3 (ET 2:2) and the excursus "Sheol."

[18] In addition, Daniel received divine revelations in Babylon during the exile. However, in the Hebrew canon, Daniel is not included among the Prophets, but among the Writings, reflecting the view that he is a Wisdom figure.

tility toward the speaker. Thus his silence in 1:3 was a rejection of Yahweh's command that he preach, and in 1:5 his silence revealed that he did not care if the sailors perished. Now Jonah's silence shows that he remains convinced that it was wrong for God to forgive the Ninevites. The mute prophet holds on to his convictions: Nineveh should perish!

Jonah's refusal to answer Yahweh's question in 4:4 demonstrates the depths of his rage. Jonah is through with talking, either by preaching to Nineveh or by praying to Yahweh. This is ironic![19] A silent prophet is a contradiction in terms. In his refusal to speak, Jonah abandons his primary function as a prophet. Every true prophet is called to preach repentance and faith so that his hearers may be saved.

"Jonah went out from the city" (4:5) of Nineveh, to which Yahweh had called him twice (1:2; 3:2). This can be seen as a minor act of rebellion, similar to his flight away from Yahweh and away from Nineveh in 1:3. He makes himself a small shelter to sit under for protection from the sun and waits to see what will happen in the city.

Some scholars debate the position of 4:5 in the book almost as vigorously as they debate the origin and location of the psalm in chapter 2. Their questions abound. Didn't Jonah already know that the Ninevites had repented and that Yahweh was not going to destroy them (see 3:10)? Indeed, their salvation was the reason for his anger in 4:1–3. Why should he now go out from the city and watch what happens in it? Jonah 4:5 has also been questioned because of the verses that follow. From 4:6 through the end of the narrative (4:11), nothing more is said about the city or what happens in it. In fact, Yahweh in 4:11 refers to what had happened in Nineveh in chapter 3, not as the place of any subsequent activity following 3:10. Still more questions arise. Why does Yahweh provide a qiqayon plant when Jonah already had constructed his shelter? Why does the narrative make no further mention of the shelter, even after the demise of the plant?[20]

The problems raised by these questions have long been noticed. In medieval times the suggestion was made that the verbs in 4:5 should be understood as having a pluperfect tense: "Jonah *had* gone out from the city. … He *had* made for himself a shelter." This is a view that many support today.[21] The assumption for this is that the verse refers back to the time before Nineveh repented, that is, the period after Jonah's sermon in 3:4 but before the Ninevites believed in God and displayed their repentance in 3:5–9. Some interpreters who

---

[19] See "The Purpose of Satire in This True and Didactic Story" in "Jonah as Satire with Irony" in the introduction.

[20] For answers to these last two questions, see the commentary on 4:6.

[21] See the discussion in Salters, *Jonah and Lamentations*, 34–35. Many have followed the argument revived by Lohfink, "Jona ging zur Stadt hinaus (Jon 4, 5)," that the verbs should be taken as pluperfects. See, for example, Wolff, *Obadiah and Jonah*, 159–60, 163, and Allen, *Joel, Obadiah, Jonah and Micah*, 230–31, including n. 16.

are unconvinced by the pluperfect solution still suggest that 4:5 originally belonged after 3:4. However, they have the daunting task of trying to support the transposition without any manuscript support or any explanation for why the verse allegedly became misplaced.

Jonah 4:5 makes sense in its present location, and not because it should be understood in a pluperfect tense. The verse highlights another theme that extends throughout the narrative: Jonah's misguided search for his own shelter, while Yahweh provides true refuge. The prophet often seeks safe haven in that which is unsafe. He fled away from the presence of Yahweh and sought refuge on a ship heading for Tarshish, but even when he descended into "the innermost recesses of the ship" (1:5), that did not save him from the storm, nor did it enable him to evade his God. Neither did his request to be hurled into the sea (1:12, 15) allow him to escape Yahweh's call. God provided the great fish (2:1 [ET 1:17]) that delivered him from "the belly of Sheol" and the underworld (2:3, 7 [ET 2:2, 6]) and restored him to "the dry land" (2:11 [ET 2:10]), where Yahweh called him a second time (3:1–2). Now here, Jonah builds a shelter to save himself from the heat, but it will not save him from the heat of his anger—nor from the heat of the sun and the scorching east wind (4:7–8). Even there, Yahweh seeks to move Jonah to take refuge in his generous grace and compassion.

As for why Jonah is *still* waiting to witness the destruction of Nineveh, this action is consistent with the prophet's past. Beginning in 1:3 Jonah demonstrates that he has no desire to hear and obey the Word of Yahweh. Just so, in this verse he shows that he is still deaf to the divine Word. He disregards 3:10 and also what he himself confessed about Yahweh being gracious in 4:2. He stubbornly acts as if the sermonette he preached in 3:4 might still be fulfilled by the city's destruction, even though Yahweh has already changed his verdict from judgment to salvation (3:10; cf. 4:2).

Another reason for retaining this verse in its location within the flow of the narrative is the literary device of "forking": at a critical juncture, the narrative leaves the account of the prophet himself and focuses instead on the religious conversion of people into saved believers. Such a fork first occurred in 1:15, where the narrative left Jonah when he was hurled from the ship. Instead of describing Jonah's descent beneath the waves, it described the sailors' worship, sacrifices, and vows (1:16). Then Jonah was picked up—by the narrative and literally by the fish!—in 2:1 (ET 1:17). Another example of forking came at the end of 3:4. The narrative left Jonah when his location was "a walk of one day" into the city. The account turned instead to the repentance of the Ninevites (3:5–9) and the clemency of Yahweh (3:10). Only in 4:1 did the narrative return to the prophet himself. Based on this literary style, 4:5 should remain here and not be inserted after 3:4.

Having established that 4:5 belongs where it is, we are still presented with the riddle of what Jonah is doing "east of the city" of Nineveh (4:5). Jonathan Magonet proposes three solutions:

(1) First, it is possible that Jonah "suspects that the Ninevites' repentance might be short-lived and that during or after the forty days they will revert to their old ways." As a prophet, Jonah may be aware that repentance may dissipate quickly; Israel's often did. He awaits the Ninevites' return to their former state of unbelief, which will then prompt Yahweh to render his judgment of destruction. Jonah is hoping that when the king and people see that they are not going to be destroyed, they will go back to their "evil way" (3:8, 10), and then the judgment he had foretold might still fall on them.

(2) A second possibility is that Jonah may be pitting his will against Yahweh's, as if trying to force God to destroy the city after all. "Such defiance, against all logic, is quite in line with his attempt to flee from God's word in the first place [1:3] and his readiness to die [4:3, 8–9]."

(3) A third option is to understand that Jonah is simply "recording his protest."[22]

All three options are possible, and perhaps we are to understand all three as interrelated.

While Jonah remains silent, his posture expresses his disagreement with God and defiance of his Word. Throughout the book, the skillful narrator makes maximum use of the contrasting verbs "arise" (קוּם) and its antonyms "sit" (יָשַׁב) and "go down" (יָרַד). "Sit" (יָשַׁב) occurs only in 3:6, where the king "sat upon the ash heap," and twice in 4:5, where Jonah "sat down east of the city" and "sat underneath" his shelter.

The contrast begins in 1:2, where Yahweh first commands Jonah to "arise" (קוּם) and go to Nineveh, but he then "arose" (קוּם) to flee from Yahweh and "went down" (יָרַד) to Joppa (1:3; see also "went down" in 1:5). In 1:6, the captain seems to speak for Yahweh as he approaches the prophet and commands him to "arise" (קוּם) and call upon his God, but Jonah refused. In chapter 2, Jonah "went down" (יָרַד, 2:7 [ET 2:6]) even farther—to Sheol (2:3 [ET 2:2]) and the underworld (2:7 [ET 2:6])—but Yahweh "brought up his life" from death (2:7 [ET 2:6]). In 3:3 Jonah finally "arose" (קוּם) and went to Nineveh. In 3:6, after the king learned of the prophet's proclamation, he "arose" (קוּם) from his throne in response to God's Word, then exchanged his royal robe for sackcloth "and sat [יָשַׁב] upon the ash heap," magnifying the depth of his repentance (3:6).

Now in 4:5 Jonah "sat" (יָשַׁב), not in repentance upon ashes, but in defiant judgment, after becoming inflamed that Yahweh had extended his grace to the Gentiles who were converted through Jonah's own preaching of the divine Word (3:4). Similarly in chapter 1, the Gentile sailors were converted by the prophet's confession about Yahweh (1:9), even though it seems Jonah did not intend for them to be converted and saved through his ministry; at his own request, he had been hurled overboard to descend into the sea (1:15) before they

---

responded in worship (1:16). Both conversion narratives therefore highlight the power of the divine Word to bring salvation, regardless of the failings of the preacher.

By using קוּם and יָשַׁב, the narrator focuses attention on the contrasting actions of faith or disobedience: Jonah's initial rebellion against Yahweh's command, the king's repentant response to the prophet's prediction, and now Jonah's resentment. The contrast between the king arising and sitting in ashes and Jonah sitting as if he is judge over Nineveh underscores the disparity in their attitude toward God. The king arose from his throne and sat in humility because he was concerned for the Ninevites, and he decreed that the whole city must call to God (3:8). Jonah sits, maintaining silence toward God, hoping the city will yet be destroyed.

Why does the narrator tell us where Jonah sits? Nineveh was flanked on the west by the Tigris River and on the north the Khoser River. There were a few hills on the town's eastern and southern sides.[23] Jonah in all likelihood perches himself on one of the eastern hills to witness the city's immanent judgment. Jonah's location demonstrates the biblical theme stated in Lk 14:11: "For everyone who is exalting himself will be humbled and the one humbling himself will be exalted" (cf. James 4:10; 1 Pet 5:6). The king left his throne to sit in the ashes penitently; Jonah takes his seat high and at rest in his self-made shade. The converted pagan is humble; the native Israelite is proud.

The Virgin Mary puts the theology of the cross this way:

> He has brought down the powerful from thrones,
>   and exalted the lowly.
> The hungry he has filled with good things,
>   but the rich he has sent away empty. (Lk 1:52–53)

Because of his pride, Jonah is an empty, hollow excuse for a prophet.

Another way in which the narrator contrasts proud Jonah with the others in the narrative who repent is through the use of רָאָה, "to see," which occurs only in 3:10 and 4:5. In 3:10 God "saw" (רָאָה) the Ninevites' deeds of repentance and changed his verdict from judgment to mercy. But Jonah looks at Nineveh to "see" (רָאָה) what would happen in the city, probably seeking its judgment. Jonah is then the opposite of Yahweh! The prophet has eyes but cannot see (Is 6:10).

The three references to "the city" in 4:5 focus upon Nineveh. Inside the city walls, the king sits in ashes. He and the entire populace, including the animals, are in great discomfort as they abstain from any food and drink and wear sackcloth (3:5–9). The king speaks on behalf of all as he expresses the hope ("Who knows?") that God will be merciful "so we will not perish" (3:9). Jonah, meanwhile, sits outside the city, longing for strict justice that will lead to the city's demise.

---

[23] See the topographical map in Parrot, *The Arts of Assyria*, 2.

Jonah looks over the great city of Nineveh and is silent. In contrast, the "one greater than Jonah" (Mt 12:41 ‖ Lk 11:32), Jesus Christ, looks over the great city of Jerusalem from the Mount of Olives and weeps over it (Lk 19:41). "Look at the world," pleads the narrator. "See it through God's eyes, and let his vision of mercy overcome your natural inclination toward revenge." Every person you see is someone Christ died to save (cf. Rom 5:6, 8; 14:15).

Yahweh Provides Three Things to Try to Move Jonah to Pity (4:6–8)

4:6 The last events in the narrative are in 4:6–8. Three incidents unfold, each beginning with Yahweh's action of providing something. Cumulatively, they eventually lead Jonah to talk, at least to himself (4:8b). This enables the brief conversation between Yahweh and Jonah in 4:9, which is followed by the concluding question posed by Yahweh to Jonah in 4:10–11. Throughout these verses, Yahweh's goal is redemptive, "to save him [Jonah] from his evil" (4:6).

Yahweh's response to Jonah's silent action is silent action in return. Rather than attempt to speak to Jonah further, which is clearly useless at this point, Yahweh furnishes the second of his four provisions in the book, each of which is described using the Piel of מָנָה, "to provide." Yahweh is the God who created the entire universe (1:9), and in these four Jonah passages, he uses animals, plants, and the elements of nature to help accomplish his good purposes.[24] First, Yahweh "provided" the great fish (2:1 [ET 1:17]) to save Jonah from death in Sheol (2:3 [ET 2:2]), causing Jonah to rejoice via his psalm (2:3–10 [ET 2:2–9]; "with a voice of thanksgiving," 2:10 [ET 2:9]). Similarly here, Yahweh "provided" the qiqayon plant (4:6), and Jonah responds with "great joy" (שִׂמְחָה גְדוֹלָה).

Because the adjective גָּדוֹל, "great," had been used a few verses earlier for Jonah's "great evil" (רָעָה גְדוֹלָה, 4:1), we are invited to compare that with his "great joy" in 4:6. In 4:1 Jonah was surrounded by a great "evil" because of the salvation Yahweh conferred on Nineveh.[25] In 4:6 Jonah has "great joy" because of his own personal comfort. The prophet feels bad when events do not go his way. He feels good when they do. Could narcissism be painted in any sharper colors?

In the greater context of the narrative, however, 4:6 is puzzling. It defies the narrative's logic. Why does Jonah need a qiqayon plant to shade him if he has built a shelter or hut for himself (4:5)? What happens to the shelter? Probably the best way to understand the qiqayon plant is that it is an extra bonus provided by God for the occasion. A shelter by itself would not have furnished

---

[24] See the excursus "Yahweh, the Creator God."

[25] The commentary on 4:1 points out that in the Hebrew clause וַיֵּרַע אֶל־יוֹנָה רָעָה ("It was evil to Jonah—a great evil"), "Jonah" is preceded by the verb "to be evil" and followed by the noun "evil."

complete comfort. The qiqayon plant that grew above or on the shelter (depending on whether the plant was more like a tree or ivy) was an extra gift provided by God for the occasion. Anyone who has sat in a tent for a day in the Near East understands that additional shade is welcome! After the demise of the plant, God "provided" the "scorching east wind" (4:8), which may well have blown away the shelter, so it could not protect Jonah.

Besides the verb "provided," which evokes 2:1 (ET 1:17), three more words in this verse (4:6) evoke past events: "shade" (צֵל), "head" (רֹאשׁ), and "evil" (רָעָה). The "shade" afforded by the qiqayon plant follows immediately upon the "shade" from the shelter (4:5). Built by opposing characters (Yahweh and Jonah), these shelters give Jonah double protection from opposite perspectives. Opposite prepositions are used: Jonah was "underneath" his own shelter (4:5), but Yahweh provided the qiqayon plant to grow "over" Jonah, to be shade "over his head" (4:6).[26]

Earlier in the belly of the fish, Jonah lamented that "seaweed was bound to my head" (2:6 [ET 2:5]) in his entombment under the waves. Now Yahweh's redemptive purpose is for the qiqayon plant to shade "his head" in order "to save him from his evil" (4:6).

As a noun and adjective, "evil" has been associated with various characters throughout the narrative, beginning with the Ninevites (1:2), moving to the sailors (1:7–8), back to the Ninevites, who turn from it (3:8, 10a), so that Yahweh averts his judgment, the "evil" he had threatened (3:10b), as he characteristically does (4:2), though "evil" then surrounds Jonah (4:1). Yahweh has dispelled all the "evil," except for that to which Jonah stubbornly clings. The first and last occurrences of "evil" in the narrative each have a pronominal suffix (רָעָתָם, "their evil," in 1:2 and רָעָתוֹ, "his evil," in 4:6), forming a grammatical inclusion. These two uses of "evil" with a pronominal suffix surround seven instances of it in its absolute form. This subtle use of the word reveals its importance—indeed, a sevenfold absolute and superlative importance—in the narrative.

An impasse between Yahweh and Jonah is evident, not unlike that which occasioned Jonah's flight in the first place (1:2–3). When the prophet refuses to listen to Yahweh's words, Yahweh uses physical elements. The first time he hurled a great storm upon the sea (1:4). Something like that is needed again. However, rather than sending something destructive, this time Yahweh sends something beneficial: a qiqayon plant. Rather than expose Jonah to the elements, he protects the prophet from them.

Yahweh's purpose in sending the qiqayon plant is not simply to protect Jonah from the heat of the sun. His intent is "to save him from his evil" (לְהַצִּיל לוֹ מֵרָעָתוֹ, 4:6). English translations miss one of the key thrusts of the narrative when they variously translate רָעָה in 4:6 as "grief" (KJV), "dis-

---

[26] This is noted by Sasson, *Jonah*, 298.

comfort" (RSV, NIV, ESV), "distress" (NEB), or "misery" (NKJV). "Evil" is what Yahweh is trying to save Jonah from—his "great evil" (4:1) of resenting the salvation of Gentiles, of holding a grudge with an unforgiving heart! Yahweh's purpose is to "save" Jonah from "his evil" (4:6) by convincing the prophet to share his own desire for all people to be saved through repentance and faith (1 Tim 2:3–4). The qiqayon will serve this purpose because it is the object lesson Yahweh will use in his final appeal to Jonah in 4:10–11. Whether or not Yahweh succeeds in getting Jonah to turn from his "evil" is the unanswered question with which the book will end.

There is a subtle change in the use of the divine names at this point. In 4:2–3 Jonah prays to "Yahweh" and "Yahweh" replies in 4:4. But in 4:6 it is "Yahweh Elohim/God" who provides the qiqayon plant, and it is simply "(Ha) Elohim/(the) God" in the object lessons in 4:7–8 and who speaks in 4:9. Then again it is "Yahweh" who speaks in 4:10–11.[27] These changes indicate that with the three provisions in 4:6–8 (the plant, the worm, and the wind), Jonah is moving farther away from Yahweh, the covenant name of Israel's gracious God (see, e.g., Gen 15:18; Ex 3:15–16; Deut 4:31). Up until this point in the narrative, the name "Yahweh" has been used primarily when he deals with Jonah and "Elohim/God" mainly when he deals with the Gentiles.[28] This use of "Elohim/God" in 4:6–9 (until 4:10–11, when "Yahweh" makes his final appeal) places Jonah in the same relationship to "God" as the converted pagans, especially the Ninevites![29]

Just as "God" delivered the Ninevites from their "evil" (3:10), so he must do the same for Jonah. The wordplay in 4:6 between צֵל, "shade," and לְהַצִּיל, "to save," hints at a deeper purpose in Yahweh's ways with Jonah. "Words similar in sound are drawn together in meaning."[30]

The verb עָלָה, "to go/grow up," describes the growth of the qiqayon plant over Jonah in 4:6. The same verb (albeit in the Hiphil) also plays a part in describing Jonah's release from the fish (וַתַּעַל, 2:7 [ET 2:6]). And it launches the story in 1:2, where Yahweh calls Jonah because the Ninevites' "evil has arisen [עָלְתָה] before me." This movement of going up contrasts with the repeated use of יָרַד, "go down, descend," in 1:3, 5; 2:7 (ET 2:6). Yahweh's purpose in raising up Jonah from Sheol and the underworld (2:3, 7 [ET 2:2, 6]) by means of the great fish is parallel to his purpose of saving Jonah from his evil by means of the qiqayon plant.

---

[27] This is noted by Allen, *Joel, Obadiah, Jonah and Micah*, 232.

[28] See Kidner, "The Distribution of Divine Names in Jonah."

[29] This is the argument of Walton, "The Object Lesson of Jonah 4:5–7 and the Purpose of the Book of Jonah." When the Gentile sailors were converted to saving faith, they addressed and worshiped God as "Yahweh" (1:14, 16). However, the Ninevites "believed in God" (3:5) and prayed to "God" (3:8–9); then "God" had mercy on them (3:10).

[30] Roman Jakobson, "Closing Statement: Linguistics and Poetics," in Sebeok, *Style in Language*, 371.

Jonah's connection with Elijah is worth exploring again.[31] Many commentators believe the narrator of Jonah uses Elijah as both a source and a foil.[32] Jonah's flight echoes Elijah's flight in 1 Kings 19, although the reasons are quite different. Both prophets are depressed, and both request death (1 Ki 19:4; Jonah 4:3, 8). Elijah's broom tree is paralleled by Jonah's qiqayon plant (1 Ki 19:4 and Jonah 4:6). In the Elijah account, Yahweh pleads twice with Elijah (1 Ki 19:9, 13). There is similar repetition in Jonah: Yahweh repeats his call of the prophet (1:2; 3:2) and when Jonah becomes inflamed, Yahweh repeats his question, "Is it right that you are inflamed?" (4:4, 9). Elijah travels to Horeb and has a dramatic encounter with Yahweh, who does *not* speak to him through the violent wind (1 Ki 19:11), but does speak to him from the "soft murmuring sound" or "still small voice" (1 Ki 19:12). God will now deal with Jonah by means of the "scorching east wind" (Jonah 4:8). The contrast couldn't be any more striking. Elijah at Horeb, the locale of Yahweh's revelation of the Torah to Israel through Moses, speaks with Yahweh as his faithful emissary, whereas Jonah petulantly bickers with God about his personal discomfort outside of the promised land.

In both 1 Kings 19 and Jonah 4, Yahweh attempts to edify his prophet by means of his creation. In Elijah's case, the prophet finally understands that Yahweh's Gospel work will not be accomplished by wind, earthquake, or fire (1 Ki 19:11–12). Rather, Yahweh will accomplish his redemptive purpose through a "gentle whisper" (1 Ki 19:12), that is to say, through his Word with its Gospel promises for the sake of Jesus Christ. He will mete out judgment through the political and prophetic affairs of Israel and Aram (1 Ki 19:15–18). Elijah responds in faithful obedience (1 Ki 19:19). In Jonah's case, his lack of responsiveness—after everything Yahweh has done to him and for him—is almost overwhelming.

Elijah is the quintessential prophet in the wake of Moses, clearly one major OT fulfillment of Moses' promise that God would raise up "a prophet like me" (Deut 18:15)—a promise ultimately fulfilled in Christ (Mt 17:3–5; Acts 3:22–26; 7:37). The echoes of the Elijah narrative in Jonah invite a comparison of the two. If Elijah is the most daring, courageous, victorious prophet of Yahweh in Israel's history, then Jonah is certainly the antithesis of that mighty hero of old.

Jonah is no Elijah. He tried to defend his earlier flight (4:2, referring to 1:3) on theological grounds: Yahweh is gracious, but Nineveh deserved judgment. Jonah himself had proclaimed the verdict that Nineveh would be "changed" (3:4), then Yahweh "changed his verdict" from judgment to salvation (3:10). Jonah thinks he has every right to be angry at God! But the object lesson of the qiqayon plant shows Jonah that what he thinks is sound theology is nothing

---

[31] See "Jonah and Elijah" in the introduction.

[32] A partial list includes Magonet, *Form and Meaning*, 102; Wolff, *Obadiah and Jonah*, 80–81, 168; Stuart, *Hosea–Jonah*, 435.

more than selfishness.[33] When Jonah benefits from unmerited divine grace, he has "great joy" (4:6). The Israelite Jonah has no right to be angry when Yahweh grants this same grace to others, even repentant Gentiles. So in the end, the issue is not Nineveh's sinfulness, but Yahweh's right to be gracious when and where he pleases. This is the same issue in the NT: Jesus incurs anger when he opens the kingdom of God to all sinners who repent and believe in him (e.g., Mt 9:10–11; Lk 15:1–2; 1 Tim 1:15).

4:7 At this point, the narrative invites us to compare Jonah and Nineveh in the following ways.

(1) Both had an impending "evil" (רָעָה). Nineveh's had arisen before Yahweh (1:2). Jonah's surrounded him (4:1) and consumes him (4:3, 8).

(2) Both receive grace. God spares Nineveh from the threatened "evil" (3:10b). For Jonah he sends a qiqayon plant "to save him from his evil" (4:6).

(3) Both experience a change. Nineveh was changed through repentance and faith (3:5–9), and God "changed his verdict" for the Ninevites from judgment to salvation (3:10). Jonah, however, stubbornly refuses to repent of his evil. Consequently, the divine change for Jonah is in the opposite direction. Rather than allowing his gracious provision in 4:6 to continue to protect Jonah, God removes his protection in 4:7. He provides a worm to devour the qiqayon plant and expose Jonah to judgment. The prophet's own attempt to protect himself—the shelter (4:5)—does him no good, so it has vanished from the narrative.

God does to Jonah what Jonah wishes God had done to Nineveh. By means of the destroying worm, God retracts his grace and leaves Jonah exposed to his own evil. Jonah was angry in 4:2–3 because God's grace worked for repentant Nineveh, but in 4:7–9 he is angry because his own impenitence has removed him from God's grace!

Jonah 4:7 has the third of the four uses of the Piel of מָנָה, "to provide," each with a divine term as subject.[34] Whereas "Yahweh provided" the saving fish in 2:1 (ET 1:17) and then "Yahweh God provided" the plant to save Jonah in 4:6, now it is "God" who "provided" the destructive worm in 4:7. As the narrative progresses, Jonah's obduracy causes him to get farther and farther away from Yahweh, the gracious covenant God who had called him (1:2; 3:2; see especially "Yahweh" in 4:2).[35] In 4:10–11, however, where the emphasis is on divine grace and mercy, the more personal name "Yahweh" reappears.

In 2:1 (ET 1:17) and 4:6, infinitive constructs were used to indicate that Yahweh "provided" an animal or plant for a redemptive purpose: the great fish "to swallow" (לִבְלֹעַ, 2:1 [ET 1:17]) Jonah and save him from Sheol, and the qiqayon plant "to save" (לְהַצִּיל) Jonah "from his evil" (4:6). In contrast, no in-

---

[33] Wolff, *Obadiah and Jonah*, 172.

[34] See the textual notes and commentary on 2:1 (ET 1:17); 4:6.

[35] Cf. Kidner, "The Distribution of Divine Names in Jonah."

finitive constructs follow "provided" in 4:7 or 4:8. Instead, each of these two verses describing judgment has a clause with the verb וַתַּךְ, "struck." In the OT, the Hiphil of נָכָה, "strike, smite," is frequently used in the context of military battles (e.g., Deut 1:4; Josh 7:3). The worm does not bite or eat the qiqayon plant; like a divine warrior, he "struck" it. Then in 4:8 the same verb is used to state that "the sun struck [וַתַּךְ] on the head of Jonah."

Theodore Laetsch writes: "It is God's providence that sends both weal and woe to His children, as He in His loving wisdom sees fit."[36] In his wisdom, God properly uses Law and Gospel, seeking to shape Jonah into a more faithful prophet. The worm begins its work "when the dawn arose on the next day" (4:7). Alas, there is no early bird to catch this worm! If the prophet was sleeping, until the sun and scorching wind awakened him, this event is connected to 1:5–6, when the prophet was in a deep sleep on board the storm-tossed boat, until the captain awakened him and implored him to call upon his God. This too is a wake-up call for Jonah. However, just as he refused to pray in chapter 1, neither does he pray to God in 4:8 (though he replies defiantly to God's question in 4:9).

In another context, Job puts it this way:

Yahweh has given and Yahweh has taken away;
may the name of Yahweh be blessed. (Job 1:21)

Here, Yahweh gives the qiqayon plant and then Yahweh takes it away. But whereas Job praised Yahweh, Jonah pouts. From delight in 4:6 to his death wish in 4:8, Jonah reacts according to how events affect *him*.

4:8 Poor Jonah! There he sits as the sun fries his head. The progression of the divine names that are the subject of מָנָה, "to provide," comes to an end in this verse. The subjects were "Yahweh" (2:1 [ET 1:17]), "Yahweh God" (4:6), and "(the) God" (4:7), but here it is simply "God." This movement is from the most to the least personal of the Deity's names. The first two miracles, which use the name "Yahweh," benefited Jonah, while the last two, which use "God" (אֱלֹהִים), are acts of judgment. As Jonah continues in his prophetic ministry, his relationship with Yahweh, the gracious God (4:2), deteriorates more and more. By 4:11 we are left wondering what, if anything, remains of this relationship.

Ironically, Jonah hoped that judgment would fall on Nineveh, but instead it is he who suffers its ravages, and no reference is made to Nineveh being affected. Since Jonah selected a vantage point east of the city (4:5), perhaps on one of the hills there, he has no protection from the "scorching east wind" (4:8). Douglas Stuart comments: "In some Moslem countries, the punishment for a crime committed while the sirocco is blowing may be reduced ... so strongly does the prolonged hot wind affect thinking and actions."[37] The same image of

---

[36] Laetsch, *The Minor Prophets*, 241.

[37] Stuart, *Hosea–Jonah*, 505–6.

the "east wind" is used in Hos 13:15 to describe the terrible devastation that Yahweh brings on callous and unbelieving Israel:

> Even though he thrives among his brothers, an east wind [קָדִים]—a wind of Yahweh [רוּחַ יְהֹוָה]—will come, coming up from the desert. His spring will be ashamed, and his well will dry up. It will plunder his treasury of all desirable vessels.

Hosea is comparing the Northern Kingdom of Israel with a plant that dies. The sirocco rising up from the wilderness will dry up its water supply. Deprived of its true Source of life, the land and its people will finally be deprived of everything.

The prophet Ezekiel too makes use of this same vivid imagery (Ezek 17:10; 19:12). So also does Jeremiah in 4:11–12:

> At that time this people and Jerusalem will be told, "A glowing wind from the barren heights in the desert [רוּחַ צַח שְׁפָיִם בַּמִּדְבָּר] is on the way to the daughter of my people, but not to winnow or cleanse; a wind too full for these will come for me." Now I myself pronounce judgments against them.

Jonah 4:8 is the second time in the narrative that Jonah is at the mercy of the wind. The first was in 1:4, when "Yahweh hurled a great wind upon the sea" that whipped up a gigantic storm. Now the second wind stirs up the blistering heat of the desert. Both render Jonah's life intolerable. In the face of both winds, Jonah seeks death (1:12; 4:3, 8).

This wind probably sweeps away the crude shelter that Jonah built in 4:5. Now the sun beats directly upon his head. How can a person function with a God like this, who converts and is gracious toward Israel's enemies, but who, as soon as he has given one little thought to his servant's comfort, promptly makes his life miserable again?

When Jonah "became faint" (וַיִּתְעַלָּף), he again experienced death within life. The same verb was used in 2:8 (ET 2:7; בְּהִתְעַטֵּף, translated "my life *ebbed away* for me"), when Jonah recalled his time in "the belly of Sheol" (2:3 [ET 2:2]) and the underworld (2:7 [ET 2:6]), before Yahweh raised him to new life. Will Jonah now experience another resurrection in faith and life?[38] That essentially is the unanswered question at the end of the book (4:10–11).

Drowning Jonah had prayed to Yahweh (2:3, 8 [ET 2:2, 7]).[39] But now, angry Jonah under the withered qiqayon plant faints and asks that his life be taken from him! Why the dramatic change in Jonah? What has happened after the "great fish" (2:1 [ET 1:17]) and before the "great evil" (4:1) and "great joy" (4:6) over the qiqayon plant? The conversion of the Ninevites (3:5–10)! Yah-

---

[38] Cf. the excursus "Death and Resurrection Motifs in Luther's Baptismal Theology."

[39] Jonah uttered the prayer consisting of 2:3–10 (ET 2:2–9) when he was in the belly of the fish (see 2:2 [ET 2:1]). But in 2:3, 8 (ET 2:2, 7), he refers to an earlier prayer that he uttered before being swallowed by the great fish—a prayer that Yahweh answered by providing the fish that saved him from Sheol. See the second reason *for* including the psalm in its present location in "The Place of the Psalm in the Book of Jonah" in "Introduction to Jonah 2."

weh hopes Jonah will draw this conclusion: "If this is what it is like to experience God's judgment, I do not want the Ninevites to suffer it either." Jonah's response, however, is not that at all. Rather than turning to Yahweh in repentance, he reverts to his former state of anger. Once again he cries for death (4:8, echoing 4:3).

Why does Jonah decide there is no longer any reason to live? The answer seems to lie in a new conviction he has reached concerning the meaning of the creedal formula he quoted in 4:2. He knows it is Yahweh's nature to be "gracious and merciful," and, consequently, to change his verdict from executing a threatened judgment to bestowing salvation through faith (see 3:5–10). Jonah therefore suspects that the prophecy of a change through judgment that he proclaimed in Nineveh (3:4) may result in their everlasting salvation, which he wants neither to see nor to have any responsibility for. This, of course, is the way the events turn out!

Jonah's theology appears to be this: Yahweh's wrathful desire to judge those outside Israel should outweigh his merciful desire to save them. Jonah does not object to divine compassion and salvation when it is received by himself (e.g., 2:10 [ET 2:9]) or fellow Israelites, but when it is also bestowed upon outsiders, he cannot stomach it any more than the great fish could stomach him (2:11 [ET 2:10])! And so the prophet refuses to let Yahweh transform Jonah's anger into love, his pity for plants into pity for people, his conception of what the object of the divine mercy ought to be into what Yahweh has shown him it actually is. That is why he thinks his only option is death.

When Jonah desired death in 4:3, he clearly expressed his wish in the form of a petition to Yahweh: "And now, Yahweh, take my life." But in 4:8 the prophet does not cry to Yahweh for help. Feeling totally helpless and alone, with no external source to grant him the death he so much desires, he directs his last request not to Yahweh but to himself! Jonah literally "asked his life [נֶפֶשׁ, 'life, self'] to die." This plea to himself corresponds to the decrease in his intimacy with his God expressed by the changing divine names used with the verb מָנָה, "to provide" (2:1 [ET 1:17]; 4:6–8). As the narrative progresses toward its conclusion, Jonah moves farther and farther away from his God.

In Hebrew narrative, a report of inward speech gets us as close as possible to the core of a person.[40] Just so, with these direct words of Jonah, we are given an inside look at the prophet's spiritual state. At the root of Jonah's death wish is a longing for a God who is partial like himself. "Over my dead body" is Jonah's cry when he realizes Yahweh is gracious, merciful, and responsive to the cries of all sinners who repent, including the Ninevites (3:5–9). Ironically, Jonah demonstrates in 4:8 his desire for a parochial god, and in doing so, his confession of Yahweh as the God who made heaven and earth, the sea and the dry land (1:9) appears to be fading fast.

---

[40] Alter discusses his character-revelation scale in Hebrew narrative in *The Art of Biblical Narrative*, 116–17.

Yet Yahweh is still seeking to forgive and empower Jonah to make a paradigm shift. The paradigm shift from Ptolemy to Copernicus may illustrate Yahweh's strategy. Ptolemy, a second-century Egyptian astronomer, worked out a systematic presentation of the universe in which the earth was the fixed center, with the sun and all stars revolving around it. Copernicus, a sixteenth-century Polish astronomer, argued to the contrary, namely, that the earth revolves around the sun. This was a complete reversal of the way people thought of the earth and the universe.

Jonah is not at the center of the universe any more than the earth is at the center. Events and circumstances don't revolve around Jonah, nor even around Israel. Instead, they revolve around the One who is at the center: Yahweh, the Creator of the universe.[41] Jonah is Ptolemaic; he has placed himself at the center of his universe. Yahweh seeks to make him Copernican, to live and revolve around the true center: the triune God, who is the Savior of all who believe. This is an ongoing theme of the narrative. There are two truths foundational to human enlightenment: there is one true God, and we are not he.

Jonah—stuck in the pre-Copernican era—seems like such a small, forlorn figure. He is satisfied when the qiqayon plant grows and cools him, then despondent to the point of death when the plant withers and he is parched by the hot sun and wind. How can he be reduced to such puny emotions, such piddling obsessions—such small comfort, such trite discomfort? Here is a man who has been in and out of a great fish's belly (2:1, 11 [ET 1:17; 2:10]), who went down to Sheol and destruction, then was raised back to life (2:3, 7 [ET 2:2, 6]), who traveled to Nineveh (3:3), preached Yahweh's message there (3:4), and saw its fearsome inhabitants repent and believe in God (3:5–9). Yet he takes more comfort in a plant than in their salvation! A mere plant's death makes him wish for death; he finds that more discomforting than the knowledge that all who die without faith in the one true God will perish eternally. He is still so hardhearted!

Throughout chapter 4, these Hebrew words are repeated: טוֹב, "good/better" (4:3, 8) and רָעָה, "evil" (4:1, 2, 6); חַיִּים, "life" (4:3, 8) and מָוֶת or מוּת, "death" or "die" (4:3, 8, 9). These are the same options Yahweh sets before Israel through Moses in Deut 30:15: "life and good, death and evil" (הַחַיִּים ... הַטּוֹב ... הַמָּוֶת ... הָרָע). When faced with this same choice, the Israelite prophet Jonah chooses evil and death, while ironically, the Gentile Ninevites chose good and life by believing in the God of Israel.

The Closing Frame: Yahweh's Last Words Justify His Pity (4:9–11)

4:9 The closing frame (4:9–11) of the final section (4:4–11), like the opening frame (4:4–5), quotes God's dialogue that seeks to turn his prophet from selfish anger and to share God's compassion for his creatures. The Ninevites

---

[41] See the excursus "Yahweh, the Creator God."

would have perished if God had not ministered to them through Jonah himself. God calls all of his people to share the same missionary spirit as the Savior, Jesus Christ, who "came to seek and to save the lost" (Lk 19:10).

God does not give up on Jonah, but persists. His question "Is it right that you are inflamed ... ?" begins in the same way as his question in 4:4, but there "Yahweh" was named as the subject of the same verb ("And/then he said"), whereas here it is "God." This is a further indication that the relationship between Jonah and the God of Israel has deteriorated. Yahweh uses the same Hebrew idiom from 4:1, 4, where Jonah was "inflamed" over the salvation of Nineveh, to refer to the prophet as now "inflamed" merely over the qiqayon plant. Jonah answers by turning the interrogative into a declarative: "It is right for me to be inflamed," then adds, "to the point of death!" The divine pleading does not work. The dogged Jonah remains unrepentant and unbowed.

Yahweh diligently sends his prophets to warn sinners to repent and so avert the doom they would otherwise suffer (e.g., Jer 7:25; 25:4; 35:15). God takes no pleasure in the death of the wicked, but rather, desires that they turn from their wicked way and live (Ezek 18:23; 33:11). Therefore, Jonah's demand for judgment upon the repentant Ninevites is contrary to God's will, which he has revealed through his faithful prophets (e.g., Jeremiah and Ezekiel), whose inspired messages are recorded in the Scriptures. "God our Savior ... desires all people to be saved and to come to the knowledge of the truth" (1 Tim 2:3–4).

4:10 Yahweh finally has Jonah in a position where the prophet, if he is honest, must admit that his own words have revealed his hypocrisy. Earlier Jonah had been willing to die to escape Yahweh, knowing that his self-sacrifice would also save the sailors (1:12, 15). Now Jonah has declared his desire to die because of the demise of the qiqayon plant (4:9b). If the prophet is willing to die for the sake of a meager plant that he had not created or cultivated, how can he fault Yahweh for showing compassion to his own creatures—people for whom God the Son shall willingly die (Rom 5:6–8)?

Could any artist have drawn Jonah's portrait more deftly and satirically?[42] Jonah did not give the plant life or contribute to its growth, and in the end it is merely a senseless object that only lives a short while. In this elaboration in 4:10, Yahweh is not teaching Jonah that he should not bother to care about something in which he has invested nothing and whose existence is fleeting. Rather, everything in God's creation matters. However, God created plants to sustain people and animals (Gen 1:11–12, 29–30) and to benefit people in other ways (e.g., Jonah 4:6). As Luther said: "Of how much less value is such a shrub than a person, to say nothing of such a city?"[43] If Jonah cares so much about a plant, how much more should he care about the people and animals of Nineveh!

---

[42] See "The Purpose of Satire in This True and Didactic Story" in "Jonah as Satire with Irony" in the introduction.

[43] AE 19:94.

This principle of correspondence and intensification is the basis of Yahweh's reasoning in the second half of his final remark (Jonah 4:11). The structure of this argument in 4:10–11 is commonly labeled by either of two Latin phrases: *a minori ad maius*, "from the lesser to the greater," or *a fortiori*, literally, "from the stronger (argument)." This structure is characterized by the analogous application of an argument that obviously is true in one case to a second case that is more significant than the first.[44] The force of the argument derives from the concomitant increase in the applicability of the line of reasoning and in the gravity of each situation. It can therefore be stated this way: "If such reasoning applies in this lesser case, then how much more does it apply in the case of greater importance." An example from the NT is from Lk 11:13, where Jesus says, "Therefore if you, being evil, know to give good gifts to your children, by how much more will your Father from heaven give the Holy Spirit to those asking him?" Crucial to this kind of argument is the establishment of correspondence between the two examples under consideration.

In Jonah 4:10–11, the two cases under consideration in the argument are Jonah's disposition toward the qiqayon plant and Yahweh's disposition toward Nineveh. Jonah's attitude toward the plant and Yahweh's attitude toward the city are both described by the same verb, חוּס, "to pity" (4:10–11; see the first textual note on 4:10). The argument hinges on this verb, which is the only word that occurs in both 4:10 and 4:11 (besides עַל, "upon," and אֲשֶׁר, "which"). Moreover, in Jonah, the verb occurs only in 4:10 and 4:11. Nowhere in the narrative does Jonah "pity" anyone or anything else—and his lack of pity for people is the heart of the problem!

The verb "pity" implies that the object itself has no merit or worthiness. The people or things that are pitied do not deserve special consideration. They have not earned forgiveness, mercy, or exemption from judgment. They cannot appeal to justice or legal requirements that they be pitied. Rather, the reason they are shown pity lies completely in the realm of the Gospel. The Ninevites displayed this awareness in 3:5–9, when they made no claim to deserve clemency, but instead threw themselves entirely upon God's mercy. It is the "gracious and merciful" (4:2), forgiving and compassionate character of God himself—to be reflected also by God's people—that is the cause of this pity. St. Paul expresses this memorably:

> Be kind to one another, compassionate, graciously forgiving each other, just as God in Christ has graciously forgiven you. (Eph 4:32; cf. Mt 18:33)

Yahweh teaches Jonah about the breadth of divine compassion, which far transcends the prophet's narrow and rigid concept of justice. In the process, Yahweh also teaches us about his abounding grace, which is not just for Israel.

---

[44] This type of reasoning is universal and is found in other ancient Near Eastern writings. Sasson cites an example from a Mari letter. He also cites Gen 44:8, where Joseph's brothers are arguing their innocence; 2 Ki 5:13; and Ezek 15:1–6 (*Jonah*, 307–8, including n. 111).

In Christ there is more than enough grace and forgiveness to cover the sins of all people. Therefore, the church's continual cry is *Kyrie, eleison*, "Lord, have mercy!" (Mt 17:15; cf. Mt 20:30–31).

The Niphal of the verb נָחַם was used in 3:10 and 4:2 to speak of God "changing his/your prior verdict" from destruction to salvation.[45] In contrast to that verb, חוּס, "to pity," does not relate to the past; it is concerned only with compassion at the present moment. By using this new verb here, Yahweh invites Jonah to see Nineveh in a new way—indeed, to see as God sees, with pity that forgets past sins. Yet the use of חוּס, "to pity," here in the closing verses of the book relates to 3:10 and 4:2 and confirms that Yahweh's change of verdict stems from his pity. Both verbs highlight characteristics of Yahweh. His superabounding grace (Rom 5:20) is so great it cannot be described adequately by any single phrase. Instead, it takes at least these six phrases in Jonah to begin to describe Yahweh's character: Jonah confessed in 4:2 that Yahweh is "gracious" and "merciful," "slow to anger," "abounding in loyal love," and "changing your verdict about evil" (4:2), and now Yahweh characterizes himself as one who shows "pity" (4:11).

In these last two verses of the narrative, Yahweh says nothing about the faith and repentance of Nineveh nor about his own change of verdict. Instead, he shifts to the idea of pity. This shift leads to a better perspective on chapter 3. The Ninevites' belief in God and works of repentance (3:5–9) were not the true cause for Yahweh's change of verdict; they were not the ultimate reason why the Ninevites were saved. Rather, the ultimate reason was gracious Yahweh's pity upon them. Their faith in God (3:5) was wrought by his preached Word (3:4) and merely was the means through which they received Yahweh's forgiveness. As an expression of their faith, they performed deeds of repentance. However, neither their faith nor their deeds somehow merited their salvation. The same is true of us, and of all who believe. Saving faith, which bears fruit in our lives, is simply the means through which we receive from Christ "grace upon grace" (Jn 1:12–16).

The Hebrew wording in Jonah 4:10–11 sharpens the contrast between Yahweh and the prophet: "*You yourself* had pity upon the qiqayon plant. … Shall *I myself* not have pity upon Nineveh?" This throws the spotlight on the chasm of difference between Jonah and Yahweh.

Prompted by 4:10, if we return to 4:7, we find that its record of the incident of the worm and the qiqayon plant did not include the reaction by Jonah. The narrator deliberately withheld the information that Jonah "had pity" until the closing argument in 4:10–11. The strategy of delayed information (also in 1:10; 4:2) strengthens the power of the punch line through surprise.

With tremendous patience, Yahweh's final speech lays bare the absurdity of Jonah's position. The qiqayon plant meant nothing to Jonah except shade

---

[45] See the excursus "When Yahweh Changes a Prior Verdict."

from the sun. It was sheer luxury. He had neither responsibility for nor governance over it. Jonah has not been true to either of his confessions of Yahweh, who is both Creator and Redeemer: "the God … who made the sea and the dry land" (1:9), "a gracious and merciful God, slow to anger and abounding in loyal love, and changing your verdict concerning evil" (4:2). Jonah is the personification of that arrogant isolationist who thinks he holds the God of heaven and earth in his pocket, and who desires to withhold God's grace from those he deems less worthy than himself. Jesus battles the same kind of error when he says to the chief priests and elders, "The tax collectors and the harlots go into the kingdom of God before you" (Mt 21:31).

Jonah did not care about the qiqayon plant for its own sake, just as he cared nothing for the Ninevites and their animals. He was concerned only about his own comfort, which the plant enhanced. In contrast to Yahweh's compassion for the large masses of Ninevites—both human beings and animals—Jonah's pity was only for a single plant. According to the OT, plants are not considered to have "life" in the same sense that people and animals are alive. The water teems with "living creatures" (נֶפֶשׁ חַיָּה, Gen 1:20) and the land produces "living animals" (נֶפֶשׁ חַיָּה, Gen 1:24). After Yahweh God breathed into Adam the breath of life, "the man became a living being" (וַיְהִי הָאָדָם לְנֶפֶשׁ חַיָּה, Gen 2:7). But the descriptions of plants in Genesis 1 and 2 do not use the terminology of a "living being/creature" (נֶפֶשׁ חַיָּה). Thus in pitying the qiqayon plant, Jonah demonstrates care for an object that has no real "life." Moreover, Jonah himself has no right to make judgments regarding life and death. He is a creature, not the Creator. George Bernard Shaw's words are applicable here to Jonah: "The reasonable man adapts himself to the world: the unreasonable one persists in trying to adapt the world to himself."[46]

The qiqayon "came to exist in a night, and in a night it perished." The verb translated "perish" (אָבַד) is a key word throughout the narrative. In 1:6 the captain exhorts sleeping Jonah to call upon his God "so we will not perish" (וְלֹא נֹאבֵד). In 1:14 the sailors pray to Yahweh before hurling Jonah overboard at his own request: "Do not let us perish [נֹאבְדָה] on account of the life of this man." Similar to the captain in 1:6, the king of Nineveh exhorts the populace to display repentance and pray fervently to God: "Who knows whether God may … turn away from the fierceness of his anger so we will not perish" (וְלֹא נֹאבֵד, 3:9).

Whereas the Gentile captain, sailors, and king are concerned that people not perish, Jonah is only concerned about a qiqayon plant that perished. The great irony is that the prophet who would not arise to call to his God in order to save the ship and its crew from perishing and who at first fled rather than preach the divine Word that could save Nineveh from perishing is the very

---

[46] George Bernard Shaw, "Maxims for Revolutionists," § 124, in the play *Man and Superman* (1903).

prophet who has compassion (חוס) when the qiqayon plant does indeed perish. This is biting satire![47]

4:11 Yahweh in this verse asks the last of the twelve questions in the narrative.[48] Yahweh's three questions to Jonah in chapter 4 gain momentum (4:4, 9, 11). Yahweh's final question in 4:11 is the greatest, both in length (it contains the most Hebrew words) and in theological significance.[49] Yahweh's concluding, gentle question to his rebellious prophet is another expression of his mercy.

The book of Jonah does not say how the prophet answered this question, but that has not stopped some interpreters from appending an answer. Thomas Bolin notes that "the Yom Kippur liturgy gives Jonah a final response, taken from the end of Micah (Mic. 7.18–20), which duly transforms the book into a lesson on repentance and the assurance of final divine pardon."[50] And Bolin cites another ending recorded in *Midrash Jonah*, which emphasizes Jonah's abject submission to Yahweh:

> At that moment he [Jonah] fell upon his face and said, "Conduct your world according to the principle of your mercy, as it is written, 'to the Lord our God are mercy and forgiveness' [Dan 9:9]."[51]

However, these and all attempts to add to the text miss the point of the entire narrative. It is finally not about how Jonah answers, but rather about how *we* answer Yahweh's penetrating question. The Gospel of Mark functions in like manner, ending abruptly, leaving us to ponder how we will respond to the resurrection of our Lord—whether we will keep silent in fear, as did the women (Mk 16:8), or whether we will proclaim the Gospel of our crucified and risen Savior.[52] The book of Acts also ends without the kind of conclusion we would expect; the message Luke sends by this ending is that the history of the church continues to be written in the lives of Christians.

The fact that at the end of Jonah the conflict between Yahweh and his prophet is left unresolved invites us to participate in the conflict.[53] It is as though the narrator says, "Come, choose sides. Who is right in this conflict, Yahweh or Jonah?" So this final question of the book challenges us to place ourselves

---

[47] See "The Purpose of Satire in This True and Didactic Story" in "Jonah as Satire with Irony" in the introduction.

[48] See the commentary on 1:6, which contains the first question. Only some of these questions are marked explicitly in the Hebrew; see the first textual note on 4:11.

[49] It contains thirty-nine Hebrew words, and so matches exactly the length of Jonah's address to Yahweh with a question in 4:2–3. See "Introduction to Jonah 4."

[50] Bolin, *Freedom beyond Forgiveness*, 178, citing the discussion of Micah 7:18–20 in Fishbane, *Biblical Interpretation in Ancient Israel*, 349.

[51] *Midrash Jonah*, as quoted in *Yalkut Shimoni*, cited in Bolin, *Freedom beyond Forgiveness*, who quotes it from Zlotowitz, *Yonah/Jonah*, 144. See also Sasson, *Jonah*, 320.

[52] Cf. Magness, *Sense and Absence: Structure and Suspension in the Ending of Mark's Gospel*, 20–28, 119–25.

[53] For a detailed discussion, see Crouch, "To Question an End, to End a Question: Opening the Closure of the Book of Jonah."

into the shoes of Jonah and confront our own inclination to assume that the Gospel is only for us and others like us—to assume that we have a right to salvation, whereas other people deserve only judgment.

The effect is to lay the foundation for the NT kerygma: "For God so loved the world that he gave his only-begotten Son, so that *whoever* believes in him may not perish, but may have everlasting life" (Jn 3:16). The Gentile sailors and Ninevites were converted to saving faith, and thus their prayer that they not "perish" was fulfilled (Jonah 1:6, 14; 3:9). The Israelite prophet Jonah found it next to impossible to accept that the God of Israel would save non-Israelites simply through faith. Similarly, the first Jewish Christians had a very difficult time accepting that the Gospel of God's salvation in Jesus Christ is for all people alike. In some cases, they came to this realization only after divine revelation, and even then only gradually (e.g., Acts 10–11). Eventually God led St. Paul to ask questions that recall the end of Jonah: "Is he only the God of the Jews? Is he not also [the God] of the Gentiles?" (Rom 3:29).

It is amazing that many commentators call Jonah 4:10–11 an abrupt ending. It is perfect! The narrative of Jonah ends in just the way the narrator intends it to end. There is no answer from Jonah.

David Noel Freedman writes of the prophet: "I think he must have been shocked out of his mind!"[54] This same shock is intended also for us. We demand a finish. Did Jonah spend the rest of his life avoiding this grace-filled God? Does he angrily stomp back to Joppa and try for another ship to Tarshish? Or does he go back into Nineveh, embracing the mercy of Yahweh for all people and recognize his unity in faith with the converted Assyrians? Does he ever return to Jerusalem to offer sacrifice and fulfill his vow in gratitude for Yahweh's salvation, as he had promised to do in 2:10 (ET 2:9)?

The strategy of the narrator is to turn the attention away from Jonah and toward us. Yahweh's penetrating question at the end is aimed not just at Jonah, but also at us.[55] The final question keeps us from the smug appraisal that holds Jonah at a safe distance from ourselves. We are meant to walk away scratching our heads, thinking about how the narrative applies to our own unforgiving attitudes toward outsiders. This means that the judgment deserved by Jonah is also intended for … *me*. A Jonah lurks within every Christian's heart, whimpering his insidious message of smug prejudice, empty creedalism, and exclusive solidarity.[56] The words of the Latin author Horace prick our hearts: "Why

---

[54] Freedman, "Did God Play a Dirty Trick on Jonah at the End?" 31.

[55] Nixon, *The Message of Jonah*, 31, writes: "As a lengthy prophetic oracle addressed to God's people it was intended that they should recognize themselves in the person of Jonah son of Amittai. The final question is addressed to them."

[56] On empty creedalism, see the commentary on 1:9 and 4:2, where Jonah recites OT creedal language about Yahweh at the same time that he shows apathy or even anger about the salvation of non-Israelites (the sailors in chapter 1; the Ninevites in chapter 3). On solidarity, see the excursus "The Trinitarian Basis of Old Testament Solidarity."

laugh? Change but the name, and the tale is told of you."[57] He who has ears to hear, let him hear, and allow the saving love of Yahweh to forgive and refashion his or her heart!

Oh, it would be so much tidier for us who consider ourselves to be "insiders" in the kingdom of God if the "outsiders" remained outside. But the God who is "gracious and merciful" (Jonah 4:2) seeks to bring all people into his church. Several of Jesus' parables make precisely this point (e.g., Lk 10:25–37). The elder brother in the parable of the Prodigal Son in Lk 15:11–32 reflects the same attitude as Jonah, and at the end of the parable, Jesus leaves us wondering how the brother will respond to his father's compassionate generosity, echoing the inconclusive ending of Jonah. Those within the community of believers are continually faced with the challenge of reflecting Yahweh's compassion for those outside.

Jesus' parable of the Workers in the Vineyard hammers home this same truth. The generous owner asks the workers who are growling at grace bestowed on others, literally, "Is your eye evil because I am good?" (Mt 20:15), meaning "Do you resent my generosity?" That concluding question resembles the ending of Jonah.

The unmerciful servant in another parable of Jesus also portrays the heart of Jonah. Having been forgiven a great debt, he did not forgive his servant a lesser debt (Mt 18:23–35). Similarly, in the parable of the Pharisee and Tax Collector at prayer, the Pharisee is acutely aware of his own spiritual stature but is dismissive of the tax collector's humble penitence (Lk 18:9–14).

In all of these parables, there is a tension between the religious "insiders" who believe they are worthy of God's favor and "outsiders" who hardly dare imagine that God is gracious toward them (Lk 18:13; "perhaps" says the captain in Jonah 1:6; "Who knows?" says the king of Nineveh in Jonah 3:9). Yet it is not the self-righteous boaster in the temple, but the humble believer who stands far off who is justified (Lk 18:14). In his attitude toward Nineveh, Jonah is displaying the same attitude as many Pharisees did in Jesus' day. The story of Jonah is the story of the religious "insider"—whether in eighth-century Israel, at the time of Jesus, or in today's church—who cannot bring himself to forgive and welcome "outsiders," even though God already has.

When the narrator of Jonah draws us into his story, he is employing what is commonly labeled "the rhetoric of entrapment." The questioning process that climaxes in 4:11 leaves us with a question that necessitates our own response to the central conflict of the narrative. "Thus the questions provide an excellent means by which the listener can be drawn progressively more deeply into the story and see it finally as a story about himself."[58]

---

[57] Horace, *Satires*, 1.1.69–70 (trans. H. R. Fairclough; LCL [Cambridge, Mass.: Harvard University Press, 1926], 9, 11).

[58] Fretheim, *The Message of Jonah*, 31.

Nathan employs the rhetoric of entrapment when he confronts David after the king's sin with Bathsheba.[59] The prophet crafts a parable for David about a rich man with many flocks who steals a poor man's pet lamb. David immediately recognizes the injustice and pronounces judgment. At this point, Nathan says to David, "You are the man!" (2 Sam 12:7). It is the king who is guilty of gross injustice. David recognizes Yahweh's Word in Nathan's parable and immediately repents. This is also God's goal for us through the inspired narrative of Jonah.

Just as surely as the Pharisees and scribes (Lk 15:2) stand behind the elder brother in Lk 15:11–32, so the function of the final question in Jonah 4:11 is to challenge the attitude of a group of people among the narrator's contemporaries who are just like Jonah. It used to be an axiom of critical orthodoxy to regard Jonah as a postexilic composition and assume that the audience was those who embraced the reforms of Ezra and Nehemiah, but that view rightly has fallen into disfavor. Gerhard von Rad could write even a generation ago: "We have no knowledge of any 'universalistic' opposition to the 'particularist' measures taken by Ezra and Nehemiah, and the Book [of Jonah] itself contains no evidence to support such a theory."[60] Others hold more generally that Jonah is written to warn that even those people who are well-acquainted with the authoritative texts of the OT may still fall.[61] What is clear is that the narrator deliberately gives a sympathetic representation of Gentiles, who are converted to saving faith (the sailors in chapter 1; the Ninevites in chapter 3). This evangelistic theme probably counters an opposite, exclusivistic conviction among some contemporaries of the book's narrator. The narrative calls Israel—and us—back to God's mission to proclaim the Gospel to all nations, including the "Ninevehs" of our day.[62]

Jonah shares with Nahum the common theme of "Nineveh," which repents in Jonah, but is judged in Nahum. These two are the only canonical books to end with questions.[63] The final reference to Nineveh in Jonah 4:11 has a twist:

---

[59] Similarly, the wise woman from Tekoa in 2 Samuel 14 uses a parable to entrap David. Another example of the rhetoric of entrapment in the OT includes Yahweh addressing the people of Judah and Israel by initially focusing on the sins of other nations in Amos 1:3–2:3, then hitting unsuspecting Judah and Israel with judgment against them in Amos 2:4–16. Like Nathan, Isaiah's Song of the Vineyard (Is 5:1–7) uses a parable designed to get listeners to pass judgment upon themselves. In such parables, the narrator crafts his story in such a way as to elicit his listeners' outrage at some hypothetical injustice. These censures are then taken up and reapplied to a real situation involving the audience. See Lessing, "Preaching Like the Prophets."

[60] Von Rad, *Old Testament Theology*, 2:292.

[61] See Ben Zvi, *Signs of Jonah*, 109–10. Ben Zvi pictures a group of people who are being self-critical as responsible for the book.

[62] See the excursus "Mission in the Old Testament."

[63] Cf. Glasson, "The Final Question—In Nahum and Jonah." This shows that repentance and faith are needed by every generation. The Ninevites converted through Jonah were saved, as Jesus affirms in Mt 12:41, but over a century later, Nahum prophesied the judgment of a later

in the three previous references, "Nineveh, (the) great city" (1:2; 3:2–3) stood under judgment, but in 4:11, "Nineveh, the great city" is the object of Yahweh's compassion. Yahweh and the narrator consistently call Nineveh "great" (1:2; 3:2–3; 4:11), whereas Jonah does not (3:4). The "great" size of Nineveh is emphasized by three related Hebrew terms in 4:11: הַרְבֵּה, "more than," רִבּוֹ, "myriads," and רַבָּה, "many [animals]." This also contrasts the city's magnitude with the single shade plant that Jonah pitied (4:10). In the narrative, many things are "great": Nineveh, the storm (1:4, 12), and the fish (2:1 [ET 1:17]). But the only thing "great" about Jonah was his "evil" (4:1) and his "joy" over one qiqayon plant (4:6). Everything in the narrative seems so big, except finally … Jonah, who is systematically and satirically whittled down to size.

The Ninevites "do not know [the difference] between their right and their left," indicating their relative ignorance of God and his self-revelation in the Scriptures.[64] They would have had no knowledge of the one true God if it were not for Jonah's preaching (3:4), which was the means of their conversion, just as Jonah's confession of Yahweh in 1:9 led to the conversion of the sailors. This highlights the importance of the proclaimed Word of God (Rom 10:14–15).

The intimidating, thundering God of the opening chapter here is compassionate and moved at the thought of losing 120,000 Ninevites and many cattle. Jack Sasson's study on the population of Nineveh at the time of its heyday, roughly 620 BC, indicates that about 327,600 people lived in the city. This means that for Jonah's time, in about 760 BC, "more than twelve myriads [120,000] people" (Jonah 4:11) is "not at all implausible."[65] Though this may seem modest compared to the populations of modern cities, it would have been enormous for a resident of Jerusalem, which is thought to have had a population of 6,000–8,000 in the eighth century that expanded to 24,000 around 700 BC.[66]

The vast number of Ninevites, reprehensible for "their evil" in 1:2, nevertheless belonged to God (3:3). Yahweh's compassion for the huge city is enfleshed by Jesus when he reacts to the crowds of people in his ministry (e.g., Mt 9:36; Mk 6:34; 8:2).

The collective paring of "people" and "animals" in Jonah 4:11 picks up on their pairing in the royal edict of 3:7–8, where the animals were made to participate in the human actions of repentance. The city was also populated by an-

---

generation of Ninevites, who had reverted to unbelief and idolatry. Each new generation must seek Yahweh (cf. Judg 2:10).

[64] See the fifth textual note on 4:11. Cf. Freedman, "Did God Play a Dirty Trick on Jonah at the End?" 31.

[65] Sasson, *Jonah*, 311–12. Olmstead, *History of Assyria*, 326, places the population of Nineveh at 300,000 during the time of Sennacherib (around 700 BC). In light of these estimates, Allen (*Joel, Obadiah, Jonah and Micah*, 234) is unjustified in treating 120,000 as only a general number that represents "a teeming population, myriads of creatures for whom God cared, and dumb animals galore."

[66] Broshi, "The Expansion of Jerusalem in the Reigns of Hezekiah and Manasseh," 23–24.

imals that inevitably would be caught up in any destruction that befell the human inhabitants, and on them too Yahweh takes pity. Here Yahweh affirms that his compassion encompasses every one of his living creatures. This recalls the narrative of Noah, through whose ministry Yahweh preserved animals as well as people in the ark to repopulate the new world.[67]

The theology here is affirmed also in a phrase in Ps 36:7 (ET 36:6): literally, "Man and animals Yahweh saves" (אָדָם־וּבְהֵמָה תוֹשִׁיעַ יְהוָה). God's concern extends to all his creatures (see also Pss 136:25; 147:9; Mt 6:26; 10:29; Lk 12:6). To be sure, human beings are the ultimate object of Yahweh's saving work; it is to atone for the sin of all people that Christ died on the cross. Yet that redemption has implications for the entire creation. The salvation accomplished through the death and resurrection of Jesus Christ is cosmic in scope, since it enables the eschatological creation of the new heavens and new earth (Is 11:6–9; 65:17–25; Rom 8:19–23; 2 Pet 3:13; Revelation 21–22). Yahweh tries to point Jonah in this direction by moving him beyond his narrow selfishness to share his divine concern not only for the Ninevites, but also for their animals.[d]

The Ninevites' faith and repentance (3:5–9) did not merit God's grace. Rather, it was Yahweh's own "pity" that moved him to save the city (see the discussion of "pity" in the commentary on 4:10). The fundamental factor that motivates God to act is his "loyal love" (חֶסֶד, 4:2) for Israel and for the world. This concluding message of the book of Jonah is also the central proclamation of the church today:

(d) See also Num 22:21–35; Deut 11:15; 25:4; Pss 104:21; 145:15–16

> God was in Christ, reconciling the world to himself, not counting their trespasses against them, and entrusting to us the word of reconciliation. (2 Cor 5:19)

Summary of Scene 7

Jonah experiences a resurrection from a watery grave and a miraculous ride home in a fish (2:1, 11 [ET 1:17; 2:10]). These gifts are unexpected and undeserved. For his own salvation Jonah gave thanks (2:10 [ET 2:9]). Then he receives Yahweh's sheltering gift of the qiqayon plant, over which he rejoiced (4:6). How much more should he have rejoiced when the myriads of Ninevites believed in God (3:5), were spared from divine judgment (3:9–10), and received everlasting salvation through faith! On the Last Day they shall be raised together with all who believe in Christ and shall stand as witnesses against all who reject the only Savior: "The men of Nineveh will arise in the judgment with this generation and condemn it" (Mt 12:41).

All this love, all of these miracles, and Jonah expresses no gratitude to Yahweh. None! In 4:2–3 Jonah's angry complaint filled a gap in the opening verses of the narrative (1:1–3). In explaining why he arose to flee to Tarshish, his prayer cites the ancient confession of divine attributes: "gracious and merci-

---

[67] See "Jonah and Noah" in the introduction.

ful," "slow to anger and abounding in loyal love." His prayer consisted of thirty-nine Hebrew words.

At the end of the chapter, Yahweh's disputation (4:10–11) also contains thirty-nine Hebrew words. It fills the gap in content and structure from within the chapter itself. Yahweh relates in 4:10 what 4:7 omitted, that Jonah pitied the withered qiqayon plant. Yahweh then argues by analogy (*a fortiori*, all the more) for his own pity for Nineveh (4:11). Balanced in their respective locations, subject matter, use of direct discourse, contrast of speakers, and number of words, 4:2–3 and 4:10–11 counter each other as first angry Jonah berates merciful Yahweh, and then merciful Yahweh seeks to persuade angry Jonah.[68]

Both passages surprise us. The filling of each gap discloses the unexpected in Jonah: first, his hubris in rebuking God for his grace, and second, his pettiness in pitying a mere plant (but not 120,000 people). The symmetry of chapter 4 shows that Jonah and Yahweh go "toe to toe" against each other. However, it is not a contest of equals. Jonah's selfish rage is balanced by Yahweh's patience toward his rebellious prophet as well as by his pity for Nineveh. Jonah begins the argument, but Yahweh has the last word. Because it is a question—and Jonah is given the opportunity to answer, but does not—there is no closure; the narrative thread is left untied.

In doing so, the book suspends the destiny of Jonah, leaving the completion of the prophet's personal story unknown to us. The narrator's strategy is to withhold the prophet's answer to Yahweh's question in order to leave room for us to provide our own answer. How do we regard God's generous grace toward all? This is the narrator's attempt to keep Jonah current for readers of every generation. It finally means that the narrative is about Yahweh and Jonah *and us.* Will we joyfully participate in God's mission to bring his redemptive love to every lost and condemned creature? Or will we selfishly attempt to withhold God's grace from those for whom Christ died, knowing that without faith in Jesus, they will perish eternally?

Shall God have compassion upon all people? Whatever Jonah's answer may have been, in the fullness of time (Gal 4:4), "one greater than Jonah" appeared (Mt 12:41 ‖ Lk 11:32): Jesus the Nazarene. He has spoken the definitive answer with his whole heart, written in his own blood. The life, death, resurrection, ascension, and promised second coming of Jesus are the Father's yes—yes, yes, a thousand times and forever yes! St. Paul says as much. All of God's promises are "yes in [Christ]; so through him the amen [is spoken] by us to the glory of God" (2 Cor 1:20).

---

[68] See "Introduction to Jonah 4" and Sasson, *Jonah*, 317.

Index of Subjects

423

Index of Passages

436

78, 85, 99, 117, 124, 150, 159, 179, 220, 262, 267, 269, 271, 272, 273, 274, 275, 276, 281–83, 284, 286, 294, 296–99, 302, 304, 305, 306, 307, 309, 313, 315, 316, 317, 321, 322, 335, 339, 348, 352, 355, 361, 363, 366, 371, 373, 375, 388, 390, 391, 392, 397, 401, 402, 405, 411

3:4–5, 323
3:4–10, 128, 296–321
3:5, 32, 34, 55, 65, 67, 121, 124, 129, 140, 160, 179, 180, 220, 238, 267, 268, 271, 274, 283–86, 287, 288, 298, 299–307, 310, 311, 313, 322, 323, 325, 341, 348, 352, 358, 359, 374, 396, 405, 412
3:5–6, 312
3:5–7, 312
3:5–8, 267, 285, 302, 310, 315, 323, 369
3:5–9, 22, 24, 25, 48, 56, 84, 222, 268, 272, 280, 299, 352, 371, 375, 388, 390, 391, 393, 398, 401, 404, 405, 412
3:5–10, 24, 57, 271, 282, 322, 337, 339, 351, 361, 400, 401
3:6, 9, 78, 179, 180, 267, 274, 285, 286–87, 288, 299, 307–10, 311, 352, 364, 392
3:6–7, 303
3:6–8, 24
3:6–9, 34
3:7, 10, 15, 67, 99, 180, 285, 287–88, 307, 308, 310–12, 359
3:7–8, 25, 45, 129, 285, 299, 311, 358, 388, 411
3:7–9, 45, 46, 87, 299, 308, 312
3:8, 32, 33, 38, 39, 40, 44, 48, 68, 101, 124, 176, 179, 180, 208, 268, 269, 274, 275,

285, 286, 288–90, 292, 293, 299, 310, 312–15, 317, 350, 359, 360, 369, 380, 392, 393, 395
3:8–9, 323, 396
3:8–10, 289, 314, 323, 359, 368
3:9, 33, 39, 45, 56, 62, 106, 123, 124, 131, 175, 282, 284, 287, 290–93, 298, 302, 312, 313, 314, 315–16, 317, 320, 321, 324, 325, 335, 336, 346, 347, 348, 356, 365, 367, 368, 369, 386, 389, 393, 406, 408, 409
3:9–10, 38, 283, 291, 292, 299, 314, 321, 322, 323, 324, 358, 361, 368, 375, 412
3:10, 24, 25, 33, 34, 35, 39, 40, 44, 45, 55, 67, 68, 69, 70, 78, 84, 85, 88, 131, 137, 176, 222, 267, 268, 275, 289, 290, 291, 292, 293–94, 302, 313, 314, 316, 317–21, 323, 324, 350, 351, 355, 356, 357, 358, 359, 360, 364, 366, 371, 380, 385, 390, 391, 392, 393, 395, 396, 397, 398, 405
3:10–4:1, 24
3:10–4:3, 363
3:10–4:11, 25
4, 2, 14, 24, 31, 43, 45, 51, 56, 66, 83, 117, 126, 128, 181, 212, 267–68, 345–49, 357, 388, 397
4:1, 15, 22, 24, 25, 27, 33, 34, 35, 44, 67, 68, 70, 84, 99, 127, 160, 187, 222, 267, 283, 297, 312, 316, 317, 321, 322, 346, 350–52, 357–62, 376, 377, 383, 388, 391, 394, 395, 396, 398, 400, 402, 403, 411
4:1–2, 110, 276, 346, 359

4:1–3, 30, 33, 35, 84, 97, 153, 267, 268, 350–75, 388, 390
4:1–4, 388
4:1–6, 388
4:1–11, 177
4:2, xiii, 15, 25, 28, 33, 38, 39, 41, 43, 44, 45, 46, 48, 50, 53, 55, 57, 68, 70, 78, 80, 82, 83, 84, 94, 95–96, 108, 113, 121, 124, 173, 177, 178, 181, 191, 201, 208, 219, 220, 222, 224, 267, 268, 276, 287, 289, 291, 292, 298, 302, 315, 316, 322, 324, 325, 329, 335, 337, 340, 341, 345, 346, 347, 348, 349, 352–56, 357, 358, 359, 360, 361, 362–70, 371, 374, 376, 385, 386, 388, 391, 395, 397, 398, 399, 401, 402, 404, 405, 406, 408, 409, 412
4:2–3, 34, 178, 179, 208, 209, 215, 346, 347, 348, 358, 363, 364, 365, 371, 388, 396, 398, 407, 412, 413
4:3, 21, 24, 27, 35, 40, 50, 82, 83, 84, 116, 118, 123, 124, 127, 130–31, 175, 177, 218, 240, 312, 346, 348, 351, 352, 356–57, 361, 365, 370–74, 383, 384, 388, 389, 392, 397, 398, 400, 401, 402
4:3–4, 346
4:4, 26, 35, 124, 267, 346, 347, 376–77, 383, 384, 386, 388, 389, 390, 396, 397, 403, 407
4:4–5, 389–94, 402
4:4–11, 30, 35, 97, 177, 346, 351, 375, 376–413, 388–89
4:5, 73, 92, 137, 153, 209, 240, 248, 283, 295, 302, 312, 318, 346, 365, 377–78,

444